# Managing Employment Re

## Fifth edition

John Gennard and Graham Judge

The Chartered Institute of Personnel and Development is the leading publisher of books and reports for personnel and training professionals, students, and all those concerned with the effective management and development of people at work. For details of all our titles, please contact the publishing department:
*tel:* 020 8612 6204
*email:* publish@cipd.co.uk
The catalogue of all CIPD titles can be viewed on the CIPD website:
www.cipd.co.uk/bookstore

# Contents

| | | |
|---|---|---|
| | *List of Figures* | vi |
| | *List of Tables* | vii |
| | *Walkthrough of textbook features and online resources* | viii |
| | *Acknowledgements* | x |
| Chapter 1 | Introduction | 1 |
| Chapter 2 | Employment Relations – What Is It? – And Theoretical Considerations | 14 |
| Chapter 3 | The Economic and Corporate Environment | 62 |
| Chapter 4 | The Legislative Framework | 99 |
| Chapter 5 | The Importance of the European Union | 133 |
| Chapter 6 | Employment Relations Institutions | 177 |
| Chapter 7 | Employment Relations Strategies and Policies | 216 |
| Chapter 8 | Employee Involvement | 258 |
| Chapter 9 | Employee Engagement | 308 |
| Chapter 10 | Other Employment Relations Processes | 335 |
| Chapter 11 | Negotiation (Including Bargaining) | 373 |
| Chapter 12 | Employee Performance and Behaviour | 414 |
| Chapter 13 | Managing Employee Grievances | 454 |
| Chapter 14 | Managing Redundancies | 491 |
| | *Index* | 531 |

# List of Figures

Figure 1.1    The abilities required of a personnel/HR professional
              practitioner                                                    7
Figure 3.2    The changes in the use of different forms of labour            84
Figure 5.1    The 'Co-operation' procedure (Article 252)                    151
Figure 5.2    The 'Co-decision' procedure (Article 251)                     153
Figure 5.3     The 'Social dialogue' procedure                              154
Figure 7.1    Strategic employment relations management: an overview        227
Figure 8.1    Procedures for establishing information and consultation
              agreements                                                    286
Figure 10.1   The unionised sector                                          340
Figure 10.2   The non-unionised sector                                      341
Figure 11.1   The definition of negotiation                                 375
Figure 11.2   Different types of negotiating situations                     376
Figure 11.3   The reconciliation of differences over time                   409

# List of Tables

Table 2.1   Theoretical approaches to employment relations                42
Table 3.1   Union presence by sector of ownership and management
            attitudes as a percentage of workplaces                       65
Table 3.2   Pay determination methods 1998 and 2004                       66
Table 3.3   The use of temporary agency workers and fixed-term
            contracts, by occupation                                      83
Table 3.4   Use of temporary agency workers and fixed-term contracts,
            by occupation                                                 85
Table 4.1   Claims accepted by employment tribunals                      117
Table 4.2   All unfair dismissal jurisdictions disposed of at a hearing  118
Table 4.3   Representation of claimants at employment tribunals          118
Table 6.1   Trade unions with a membership of 100,000 or more
            in 2008                                                      194
Table 6.2    Individual complaints concerning employment rights
            1985–2009                                                    202
Table 6.3   The use of third-party intervention in industrial disputes
            1979–2009                                                    208
Table 8.1   Direct employer-employee communication, by sector of
            ownership, 2004                                              281
Table 8.2   Issues discussed at team briefings, 2004                     282
Table 8.3   Summary of direct communication arrangements, 2004          283
Table 9.1   Top behaviours of engaging and disengaging managers         329
Table 10.2  The papermaking partnership                                 350
Table 11.1  An aspiration grid                                          395
Table 13.1  Grievances, by industrial distribution, 2005               459
Table 13.2  Types of grievance raised, 1998 and 2004                    460
Table 13.3  Aspiration grid: grid centring on three days' suspension
            without pay                                                  482

# Walkthrough of textbook features and online resources

OVERVIEW

The chapter begins by outlining the process by which UK legislation is approved – parliamentary readings of the Bill followed by Royal Assent as an Act of Parliament – and then goes on to consider the most important and major influences in employment law, namely the *contract of employment,* which defines and regulates the relationship between the employer and the employee. The chapter notes how the state intervenes with this relationship by providing the employee with certain

## OVERVIEW

Each chapter opens with an Overview outlining the purpose and content of the chapter.

LEARNING OUTCOMES

When you have completed this chapter, you should understand and be aware of:

● the importance of the employment contract
● the legislative process
● the principal function of the law
● how the law impacts on relationships at work

## LEARNING OUTCOMES

At the beginning of each chapter a bulleted set of learning outcomes summarises what you can expect to learn from the chapter, helping you to track your progress.

REFLECTIVE ACTIVITY

Explain the key stages in the UK legislative process at which employers can attempt to influence the contents of legislation.

## REFLECTIVE ACTIVITIES

Questions and activities throughout the text encourage you to reflect on what you have learnt and to apply your knowledge and skills in practice.

CASE STUDY

### The European Union

Planet Corporation employs 4,500 workers who produce a wide range of electronic domestic appliances for the European and North American markets. It is a UK-based multi-national company and – apart from the UK, where it employs 1,500 workers – it has establishments in France (1,000 employees), Germany (1,500 employees), Italy (100 employees) and Hungary (400 employees).

The UK workforce feels strongly that their wages are well below what the company can afford. This feeling has grown stronger since the European plants with which they identify most closely (France, Germany and Italy) became part of the euro zone. It is easier now to compare pay and conditions plus living standards with workers in these countries, and it certainly seems to the UK workforce that their colleagues there are getting a much better deal.

## CASE STUDIES

A number of case studies within each chapter, from different sized organisations and different sectors, will help you to place the concepts discussed into a real-life context.

SUMMARY

In this chapter we have tried to identify the relationship between good employment relations and the law. We have stressed that employment relations is as much about 'good practice' as it is about legal compliance, but we have recognised that the employment relations professional cannot afford to be dismissive of the law. This is because the law impacts on almost every activity in the workplace. Furthermore, individual employees are very much aware of their 'rights' at work and do not hesitate to use the mechanisms open to them (employment tribunals) to assert those rights.

## CHAPTER SUMMARIES

Towards the end of each chapter, a chapter summary draws conclusions from the issues raised in the chapter.

THEORY

## THEORY SIGNPOSTS

Marginal signposts are included to highlight different theories and models throughout the text, encouraging you to critically evaluate these ideas.

KEY LEARNING POINTS

- Because all employment relations discussions have the capacity of legal challenge, it is important for managers to operate good employment practice.
- The scale of legal developments is such that employment relations professionals must continue to monitor changes and develop their own skills to do this.
- Employment relations professionals do not need to be lawyers, but they do need to understand the interaction between the law and employment relations.
- The employment relations professional should not view the law as simply a process of compliance. Good employment relations cannot be achieved by waving a legal rulebook and stating what employees and others cannot do. Good employment relations is achieved by the positive action employers take to win the trust and confidence of their workforce. To use the law as a blunt instrument to drive change could never be described as good employment practice.
- Employment relations professionals have to understand the range and importance of individual employee employment rights – but this is not sufficient. They must, for example, in the event of disciplinary cases, be able to manage the

## KEY LEARNING POINTS

Bulleted lists of key learning points at the end of each chapter are designed to consolidate your learning and pull out key points for you to remember.

REVIEW QUESTIONS

1 You are scheduled to give a training session to line managers in your organisation on the topic 'Employment law is nothing more than good employment practice'. Explain what is meant by 'good practice' in this context, and how it can ensure that your own organisation is protected against damaging employment tribunal decisions.

2 You have been asked by your chief executive officer (CEO) to provide the senior management team with a briefing note on how employment relations within the organisation might be affected by the age discrimination regulations. The organisation currently has no policy on retirement and has heard that this might

## REVIEW QUESTIONS

Test your understanding of a chapter or topic and tackle these end-of-chapter review questions.

EXPLORE FURTHER

Bercusson, B. (1996) *European Labour Law*. London: Butterworths.

Deakin, S. and Morris, G. (2005) *Labour Law*. Oxford: Oxford University Press.

Industrial Relations Service (various dates) *Employment Review: Policy, practice and law in the workplace*.

Kahn-Freund, O. (1972) *Labour and the Law*. London: Stevens, for the Hamlyn Trust.

Lewis, D. and Sargeant, M. (2009) *Essentials of Employment Law*, 10th edition. London: Chartered Institute of

Wells, K. (2003) 'The impact of the Framework Employment Directive on UK disability discrimination law', *Industrial Law Journal*, Vol.32, No.4: 253–73.

Weblinks

www.bis.gov.uk is the website of the Department for Business, Innovation and Skills, and will give you access to the main provisions of Acts of Parliament relevant to employment relations.

www.cipd.co.uk for information about the CIPD Employment Law Service.

## EXPLORE FURTHER

Explore further boxes contain suggestions for further reading and useful websites, encouraging you to delve further into areas of particular interest.

## ONLINE RESOURCES FOR STUDENTS

- Annotated weblinks – click through to a wealth of up-to-date information online
- Regular updates – access the very latest in employment relations

Visit www.cipd.co.uk/sss

## ONLINE RESOURCES FOR TUTORS

- Lecturer's Guide – practical advice on teaching the CIPD module using this text
- PowerPoint slides – build and deliver your course around these ready-made lectures, ensuring complete coverage of the CIPD module
- Additional case studies – for you to use with students in seminars or lectures

Visit www.cipd.co.uk/tss

# Acknowledgements

We would like to thank the following individuals for their help and assistance with this, the 5th edition of *Employee Relations*: Kirsty Smy and Robert Williams, who were extremely patient when timetables and deadlines ran a little over what had been agreed; Debbie Campbell, John's secretary, who has, as usual, worked tirelessly to ensure that the various documents we submitted to her were presented in an acceptable and readable format. Graham would also like to thank his colleagues within the Yattendon Investment Trust HR department who, without always realising it, provide him with tremendous support.

Finally, we would like to thank our wives, Anne and Kim. Without their support this book, and the previous editions, would never have been written.

# Managing Employment Relations

The content of this CIPD module is covered as follows:

| Managing Employment Relations learning outcome | *Managing Employment Relations* chapters |
|---|---|
| Understand, analyse and critically evaluate: | |
| 1. Different theories and perspectives on employment relations. | Chapter 2  Employment Relations – What is it? – And Theoretical Considerations |
| 2. The impact of local, national and global contexts shaping employment relations climates. | Chapter 3  The Economic and Corporate Environment<br>Chapter 4  The Legislative Framework<br>Chapter 5  The Importance of the European Union |
| 3. The roles and functions of the different parties to control and manage the employment relationship. | Chapter 6  Employee Relations Institutions |
| 4. The importance of organisational-level employment relations processes that support organisational performance, including the design and implementation of policies and practices in the areas of: employee engagement; diversity management; employee communication, involvement and participation; negotiation and bargaining; conflict resolution; and change management and management control. | Chapter 7  Employment Relations Strategies and Policies<br>Chapter 8  Employee Involvement<br>Chapter 9  Employee Engagement<br>Chapter 10  Other Employee Relations Processes<br>Chapter 11  Negotiation (Including Bargaining) |
| 5. The importance of employment relations procedures that help mitigate organisational risk, including the design and implementation of policies and practices in the areas of discipline, grievance, dismissal and redundancy. | Chapter 12  Employee Performance and Behaviour<br>Chapter 13  Managing Employee Grievances<br>Chapter 14  Managing Redundancies |
| 6. The integration of employment relations processes and how they impact on policy, practice and organisational outcomes such as performance and employee engagement. | Chapter 7  Employment Relations Strategies and Policies<br>Chapter 8  Employee Involvement<br>Chapter 9  Employee Engagement<br>Chapter 12  Employee Performance and Behaviour |

## CHAPTER 1

# Introduction

## KEY THEMES

The key themes associated with this book are:

- the difference in perspective between the CIPD HR Profession Map and an academic qualification
- the relevance of employment relations in non-union environments as well as in unionised ones
- that an employment relations system at any level consists of actors and their institutions, government agencies and economic, legal and technological environmental context
- the impact of changes in the corporate environment on the balance of bargaining power between the employers and employees and on the employment relations policies adopted by an organisation
- the influence of Europe and European institutions on the employment relationship, and the need for practitioners to be aware of, and understand, this influence
- the importance for management to act on the basis of just cause and to behave in a fair, reasonable and consistent manner
- that negotiation is two or more parties coming together to make an agreement by purposeful persuasion and constructive compromise
- the need to evaluate whether new employment practices introduced into one organisation can be successfully transplanted into another
- the day-to-day grind of intra- and inter-management negotiations.

## THE CIPD HR PROFESSION MAP

In the last decade there has been a shift in the focus of HR. It is now charged with improving the performance of the organisation by building sustainable organisational capability – not just delivering on the day-to-day people management role, although that remains important. In the light of this trend, the CIPD decided that rather than just update its existing standards, a radical re-visioning was necessary to equip the profession for the challenge ahead. So in 2008 it commissioned market research in one of the most comprehensive surveys of the HR community ever undertaken. Around 4,500 people answered detailed questions about their job, their professional needs and their aspirations. The results showed that:

- Increasing numbers of HR people go beyond their traditional role and are now required to understand what drives business performance and to bring into focus the employee capabilities their organisations will need in the future.

- Whereas 50% of participants saw themselves as HR generalists, 50% saw themselves as specialists – for example, reward, learning and development and employment relations – but also in roles such as that of 'business partner'. They wanted to go narrower and deeper in their basic and subsequent training.

- 30% had an international dimension to their job.

- 29% were studying. This included recent entrants studying to become CIPD-qualified but also people doing MBAs and other master's degree programmes. The survey demonstrated that the HR community were looking for more structured learning and accreditation as they progressed in their careers.

The key messages from the market survey were:

1 There is a greater need for HR people to know the organisation inside out. You must demonstrate an understanding of business strategy and an ability to apply that understanding working in partnership with senior people to contribute to organisational performance.

2 The profession has become broader in reach, with greater depth in its expertise. A greater number of critical specialisms were identified in HR. Many of the old ones remain important, but there are also new ones and more people pursuing careers based on one or more of these specialisms.

3 HR professionals rely on a combination of technical knowledge (what you need to know), practical application (what you need to do) and behaviours (how you need to do it). The market research showed loud and clear that what defines HR professionals is practical application. A major feature of this book is that it concentrates on the practical application of knowledge to the workplace. The shift in the role of the HR professional is from a primary focus on supporting line managers to manage their people well to a primary focus on ensuring that the organisation has the sustainable capability it needs to deliver its aims both today and in the future.

The HR Map has been informed by an extensive programme of consultation with senior HR professionals and their leaders in business, the public services and management education. The clear message is that in order to deliver 'sustainable capability', HR practitioners need to:

- know their organisation inside out. This means truly understanding the drivers of sustainable business performance and the barriers to achieving it

- know the main ways in which HR expertise can make an impact and contribute beyond the confines of the traditional role

- have the behavioural skills to turn knowledge into effective action.

The CIPD HR Profession Map charts the profession from three main perspectives – functional specialisms, levels of competence and key behaviours. The Map contains 10 different HR specialisms, which are referred to as the *Professional areas*. These are:

- Strategy, insights and solutions
- Leading and managing the function
- Organisation design
- Resourcing and talent planning
- Organisational development
- Learning and talent development
- Performance and reward
- Employment relations
- Employee engagement
- Information and service delivery.

The list of professional specialisms starts with *Strategy, insights and solutions* because this is about HR's awareness of the business context and the wider organisational environment from which everything else needs to flow. *Leading and managing* comes next because, having understood the business challenge, you then need to design an HR function to meet these needs and priorities. The other specialist areas all have more familiar labels.

Each specialist area has four bands of competence moving from what might reasonably be expected of an entry-level person (Band 1) through to what is essential expertise from a board-level HR director (Band 4). Examples of an activity at four levels of competence might be:

- Band 4 (HR director) – Leads processes to identify, articulate and reinforce the organisation's core values and behavioural expectations, and influences leadership at all levels to behave in a manner that is consistent with them.

- Band 3 – Develops ongoing communications and management plans to ensure that employees and other stakeholders understand and respect the organisation's values and behavioural expectations and act in accordance with them.

- Band 2 – Ensures that the values and behavioural expectations permeate through the organisation's processes, policies, intranet and other literature.

- Band 1 (entry-level) – Advises staff and managers about the organisation's values and behavioural expectations.

So to take the specialist area of *Employment relations* as an example, here the employment relations practitioners in their first job are required to develop their understanding of the organisation's goals in employment relations and how activity in this area contributes to delivering them. They are expected to feed ideas and observations to senior colleagues, to look for ways to support line managers more effectively, and to evaluate the impact of their work. Thus entry-level practitioners are gaining experience of how to approach a senior professional even while they make a contribution to 'big picture' thinking in their own right at junior level.

In addition to the 10 professional areas and four levels of professional competence, the HR Profession Map sets out eight behaviours (how you need to do it) corresponding to what HR practitioners need in order to be effective. These behaviours are divided into three clusters:

*Insights and influence*

- Curious
- Decisive thinker
- Skilled influencer

*Operational excellence*

- Driven to deliver
- Collaborative
- Personally credible

*Stewardship*

- Courage to challenge
- Role model.

Let us take the example of 'Courage to challenge'. It says in broad terms first that someone exhibiting this behaviour 'shows courage and confidence to speak up and challenge others, even when confronted with resistance or unfamiliar circumstances'. The behaviour is then broken down into various components, which are called up in different ways depending on the seniority of the role – or in Map terms, the Band. Thus one component of 'Courage to challenge' develops in this way (read from the bottom up):

- Band 4 (HR director) – Acts as a 'mirror' to colleagues challenging actions which are inconsistent with expressed values, beliefs and promises.
- Band 3 – Holds own position determinedly and with courage when it is the right thing to do, even when those in power have divergent views.
- Band 2 – Observes, listens, questions and challenges to ensure full discussion.
- Band 1 (entry-level) – Uses questions to explore and understand others' viewpoints, taking these into account.

By bridging the 10 professional areas, the eight behaviours and the four bands of competence together, the CIPD has created the most comprehensive picture yet of the HR profession.

In short, then, the CIPD HR Profession Map sets out what HR practitioners need to know and do, and how they need to go about doing it at all stages in their career whether they are specialists or generalists working in the UK or internationally. It was created with input from HR practitioners drawn from every size of organisation and across every sector. Its three-dimensional structure allows us to consider the knowledge and activities required to demonstrate competence across 10 professional areas and four different levels within HR careers. The third dimension is the behaviours – how you do what you do. It is designed to be flexible and dynamic enough to set out clearly what is required today while also being capable of adapting to the future requirements of the profession. The Map provides a framework to help navigate your own professional career paths. It underpins the CIPD approach to qualifications and membership levels. The philosophy of the CIPD HR Profession Map is very much that of this book.

The employment relations practitioner thus requires business orientation, application capability, knowledge and understanding of employment relations activities, and persuasion and presentation skills. An individual with the CIPD Associate Membership qualification should be capable of adding value to the business. They cannot do this on their own – they need to collaborate with others both within and outside the organisation in order to make a value-adding organisational contribution. These outcomes are not what an academic would emphasise in a master's degree programme. Here students would be expected to be aware of the plurality of perspectives on employment relations issues and themes, and be able to critically evaluate competing theories and perspectives. Skills development to solve employment relations problems would have much less emphasis.

## THE RELEVANCE OF EMPLOYMENT RELATIONS TO ALL ORGANISATIONS AND ALL SECTORS

It is a misunderstanding to think that employment relations is a relevant management activity only if the organisation recognises and deals with trade unions. In a non-union environment, as in unionised ones, collective relationships exist. In non-union firms there are employee representation bodies (for example, an employee council, a Works Council, joint consultative committees, etc), and just as in unionised environments, employee grievances have to be resolved, disciplinary matters processed, procedures devised, implemented, operated, reviewed and monitored. In addition, in non-union situations, as well as unionised ones, the support and loyalty from one's management colleagues, at all levels of seniority, has to be gained by using *inter alia* negotiating, interviewing and communication skills. Employment relations knowledge, understanding and skills acquisition is just as relevant to non-union environments as to unionised environments.

As we shall explain, an important employment relations concept is the relative balance of bargaining power between the buyers and sellers of labour services, and that important determinants of this relationship are external to the organisation – for example, government economic and legislative policies. One result is that the key employment relations policies and practices can be rendered irrelevant, illegal or more expensive to operate because of legislative intervention – for instance, the changes in representational rights in grievance and disciplinary procedures and the statutory recognition procedures contained in the Employment Relations Act (1999), or the changes in maternity leave, disciplinary procedures, etc, introduced by the Employment Act (2002). The professional employment relations manager has to be capable of offering advice as to how their organisation might deal with such situations that stem from decision-making sources over which companies have no direct control. This book is designed to help in this regard.

Changes in the corporate environment, by influencing the balance of bargaining power, help explain changes over time (for example, the present decade relative to the 1970s) in the employment relations behaviour of employees and employers in terms of processes used, the subject of rules, regulations and agreements, and their authorship. In the 1970s when the corporate environment was very different from today, trade unions grew steadily, strike action was more frequent and higher wage increases were obtained by employees from their employers. In today's corporate environment, trade union membership has fallen, strike action has fallen, employers are able to decide unilaterally on the rules and regulations governing employment, and – courtesy of low inflation – wage increases are much smaller. Employment relations managers/professionals require an understanding of the impact of changes in the corporate environment on management employment relations strategy, policies and agreements in order to predict the impact of possible external changes on the organisation's employment relations and how they might seek to mitigate them.

In conducting their employee relations activities, professional managers should behave in a fair and reasonable manner and seek to persuade their management colleagues to behave in a like manner. This means acting with just cause (for example, having a genuine reason to dismiss a worker or for selecting an employee for redundancy) and behaving in procedural terms via a series of stages in which behaviour is compatible with the standards of natural justice. For instance: a statement of the complaint against the individual is made, a proper investigation is undertaken, the accused is given the opportunity to cross-examine witnesses, there is sufficient time made available for the accused to prepare a defence, an appeals procedure exists, and different individuals are involved at the different stages in the operation of the procedure.

It is important that personnel/HR managers appreciate the underlying principle of employment relations procedures so that they establish standards of behaviour which will pass the tests of reasonableness. However, personnel/HR managers must appreciate not only what constitutes fair and reasonable behaviour but why such good practice is essential to protecting and advancing management's interests – namely, the avoidance of adverse financial consequences through the payment of compensation to individuals wronged by such actions, also damaging the organisation's labour-market image in the eyes of existing and potential employees. As we have already indicated, managers by behaving in a fair and reasonable manner (best practice), help to add value to the business. This is a key theme of the book.

Change and innovation in employment relations policies and practices to gain a competitive advantage or to deliver a service at a higher quality is essential in a modern competitive-based economy. New and developing management practices (for example, performance-related pay, single union–no strike agreements) of the 1980s have been successfully introduced into organisations. However, employment relations practitioners cannot assume that such practices can automatically be transferred successfully to their own organisation, which may be operating in a very different environment. They need to be able to evaluate whether practices successfully introduced in one organisation can be successfully transplanted into their own. Organisations cannot change policies and practices constantly without any reference to organisational needs and existing practices. A further assumption of this book is that 'new initiatives' in management practice have to be evaluated in a rational manner as to whether they can be introduced with equal success into another organisation.

Yet another theme of this book is the importance of personnel/HR professional practitioners understanding why negotiating skills are necessary for the effective solution of people management problems. They need to be able to identify the different negotiating situations (grievance-handling, bargaining, group problem-solving) in which managers may find themselves, appreciate the different stages through which negotiation may proceed, and be familiar with the skills required in different negotiation situations.

## THE INFLUENTIAL MANAGER

If personnel/HR professional practitioners, at any level of seniority, are to be proactive and to have influence in an organisation, they must demonstrate certain abilities (see Figure 1.1). First, they require a successful record of professional competence in the personnel/HRM field which is recognised by their managerial colleagues both within and outside the personnel/HRM

**Figure 1.1  The abilities required of a personnel/HR professional practitioner**

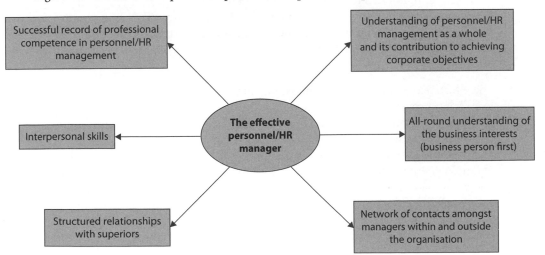

function. Second, they must demonstrate an understanding of the personnel/ HRM function as a whole and how its separate components integrate. Third, they must understand the interests of the business/organisation as a whole and that these take preference over those of any management function as a whole or in their component parts. Fourth, they must develop a network of contacts with managers, both within and outside the personnel/HRM function, in their own organisation and with managers in other organisations, including employers' associations and professional bodies such as the Chartered Institute of Personnel and Development (CIPD) and the British Institute of Management (BIM). Fifth, they also require to build fruitful relationships with their superiors and to possess excellent interpersonal skills, particularly with respect to communications and team-building. Each of these five abilities is a necessary condition for an effective and influential personnel/HRM professional practitioner – and each is an insufficient ability on its own.

All people managers, regardless of their seniority (personnel assistant, officer, manager, executive, etc), need to understand the nature of business of the organisation in which they manage in terms of its mission, objectives, strategies and policies. In the private sector, the effective and influential personnel/HRM professional practitioners will understand the 'bottom line' for the business and be able to contribute constructively at the appropriate level of decision-making (department, section, management team, working party, etc) to discussions on how the business might be developed and expanded. In the public sector, the effective and influential personnel/HR practitioner will understand the objective of efficiency, effectiveness, economy, 'value for money' and the quality of service delivery to the customer or client.

The effective personnel/HRM professional practitioner can explain how the various components of resourcing, development, reward and relations contribute to the achievement of the objectives of the personnel/HR function. This means that he or she must fully understand how the strategies and policies of the components of the personnel/HR function link together to achieve the goals of the function. Such a horizontal integration of the personnel/HRM function will not be new to you because it has been a central theme in your people management and development studies. It is important during your employment relations studies that you understand the vertical and horizontal integration.

The effective personnel/HRM professional practitioner in a management team has a proven competence recognised by their management colleagues in employment relations as well as employee resourcing, training and development and pay and reward. It is essential, therefore, if personnel/HR practitioners are to be effective, that they have an adequate knowledge and understanding of employment relations and have acquired the appropriate skills to apply that knowledge and understanding to solve employment relations problems to enable the organisation to achieve its commercial and/or societal objectives. An implication of this statement is that it is not only existing and prospective personnel/HR professional practitioners who need to acquire employment relations knowledge, understanding and skills but so do *all* managers, regardless of their seniority or specialism.

The personnel/HRM practitioner who lacks professional competence in employment relations will be a less effective manager. The trend in many organisations to devolve their personnel/HRM function across management teams reinforces this view. Devolution often means that the services of a personnel/HR professional practitioner with a specialism will not always be required. However, the activities of the employment relations function (for example, communications policy, handling employee grievances, dealing with disciplinary matters and the adjustment of the size of the workforce) must nevertheless be delivered to the management team. Generalist personnel/HR practitioners with employment relations skills are essential to any management team. Specialist personnel/HR practitioners are less attractive to a management team.

This book therefore aims to provide the generalist personnel/HRM professional practitioner – and any other managers who have to manage people – with the appropriate employment relations knowledge and to provide them with the understanding and skills they require to apply that knowledge and understanding to solving people management problems. In short, this entails the application of knowledge to the workplace to solve problems. This, in turn, will contribute to the organisation's achieving its commercial and/or social objectives. It will have the additional advantage of enhancing the credibility of the personnel/HRM practitioner in the eyes of their managerial colleagues both within and outside the personnel/HRM function.

A central theme of the book is that 'good practice' in the delivery of the personnel/HRM strategy and policies adds value to the business and thereby contributes to the achievement of the corporate/organisational economic and social objectives. It explains not only what constitutes good practice (that is, acting with just cause and behaving fairly and reasonably) but why operating to good practice standards is sound business practice – for example, the avoidance of falling foul of industrial tribunal decisions in terms of having 'bad' practices exposed and thus embarrassing the organisation. The book also aims to help personnel/HR professional practitioners develop and acquire skills, not only to solve people management problems but also to develop and improve their interpersonal skills and thereby the quality of their relationships with superiors.

If HR practitioners are to be effective and influential, they require to be generalist *and* specialist personnel/HR managers. Generalist HR managers require an adequate knowledge, understanding and skills of employment relations. If they neglect this and concentrate exclusively on development, resourcing and reward, they will be less effective managers.

## EMPLOYMENT RELATIONS ACTIVITIES

The purpose of employment relations activity is to determine the 'rules' that will govern the employment relationship at the workplace. These rules represent the reconciliation of employers and employees and in so doing assist the organisation to achieve its business and/or social objectives. This difference of interests revolves around the 'price' (including the quality and quantity) at which labour services will be bought and sold. Although there is this difference of interests, both management and employees have a common interest in reconciling such differences. The alternative is mutual destruction of the organisation. The closure of the enterprise is of no benefit to employers or employees. There is mutual advantage to both employers and employees in making rules to resolve their differences as buyers and sellers of labour market services. These employment rules take the form of agreements and regulations and are made through the use of various employment relations processes – employee involvement, collective bargaining, employee engagement, unilateral imposition by management, joint consultation, arbitration, mediation and conciliation, and parliamentary legislation.

The agreements and regulations express the price at which employees will supply their labour to the employer and are made at different levels (workplace, company, industry) and have different degrees of authorship. Some are written solely (imposed) by the employer with little or no influence from the employees, whereas others – usually as a result of collective bargaining – are jointly authored by the employer and representatives of the employees. Agreements and regulations cover two broad ranges of issues. One is substantive issues (pay, holidays, hours of work, incentive schemes, pensions, sick pay, maternity leave, family-friendly policies, etc) and the other is procedural issues. Employment relations procedures provide fair and reasonable standards of behaviour to resolve in a peaceful manner issues over which employers and employees have differences. Such procedures normally cover issues such as employee complaints against the behaviour of employers (known as grievances), employer complaints about the behaviour of employees (referred to as disciplinary matters), the need to reduce the size of the workforce (redundancy), employee claims that the responsibilities of their jobs have increased (job grading) and employee requests for union representation (union recognition procedures).

The content of agreements and regulations and the employment relations processes used to secure them reflect the relative balance of bargaining power between employers and employees. This balance is heavily influenced by changes in the corporate environment in which an organisation undertakes its employment relations activity. The major factors in shaping the external corporate environment are the economic and legal policies of national governments and the European Union political decision-making institutions. In an attempt to enhance their economic interests, both employers and employees, via representative organisations, spend relatively large sums of money on the political lobbying process to persuade the Government to introduce appropriate economic and legal policies. A further factor in the external environment influencing employment relations is the implementation by employers of technological change.

The balance of bargaining power is a central concept that must be understood by the employment relations professional practitioner. It helps explain the constraints within which managements can exercise their power. Abuse of power to obtain one's aims is not professional behaviour. It will inevitably lead to pressure for legal restraints to be imposed to curb the abuse. Unprofessional behaviour suggesting that 'might is right' will result in employees behaving in that way when the balance of bargaining power shifts away from management towards the employees. Professionalism means tackling matters in a systematic and careful manner. The fact that at a point in time the state of the balance of bargaining power means that management can 'succeed' without behaving in this way is no excuse for managers not to behave in a professional way. Good practice dictates that they behave in a professional manner gaining consent by discussion, consultation, negotiation and involvement, not by the crude exercise of power.

However, personnel/HR professional practitioners require more than just knowledge and understanding of employment relations parties, processes, agreements and regulations and the external environment in which these activities take place if they are to solve people management problems effectively. Employment relations problem-solving also requires the development and application of certain skills, of which the most significant are communication (oral and written), interviewing, listening, negotiating, evaluating and analysis.

This book thus endeavours to widen and develop employment relations knowledge and understanding. It provides sufficient knowledge, understanding and skills for employment relations practitioners and those who manage people in other management functions to operate as professional people managers in a number of different situations, including both unionised and non-union environments. The book also aims to introduce you to how essential it is for employment relations professional practitioners to become effective and influential in the organisation by understanding the concepts of good practice and the balance of bargaining power, and by acquiring and developing the general management skills referred to above.

## THE BOOK, AND THE EMPLOYMENT RELATIONS SPECIALISM

The CIPD employment relations specialism centres on understanding, analysing and critically evaluating:

- different theories and perspectives on employment relations
- the impact of local, national and global contexts shaping employment relations
- the roles and functions of the different parties to control and manage the employment relationship
- the importance of employment relations procedures that mitigate organisational risk, including the design and implementation of policies and practices in the areas of discipline, grievance, dismissal and redundancy
- the importance of organisational-level employment relations processes that support organisational performance
- the integration of employment relations processes and how they impact

on policy, practice and organisational outcomes such as performance and employee management.

In this book, sections that fall within *employment relations management in context* describe the corporate environment in which organisations undertake their internal employment relations activities. A growing and important part of this external environment is the evolution of the 'social' dimension (Social Chapter, Social Charter) of the European Union. Sections also cover the role of the national government as an economic manager and as a law-maker, as well as 'stage agencies' such as the Advisory, Conciliation and Arbitration Service (ACAS), the Central Arbitration Committee, the Certification Officer, the Health and Safety Commission and the employment tribunal system. The management in context is covered by Chapter 2 (*Employment Relations – What is it? – And Theoretical Considerations*), Chapter 3 (*The Economic and Corporate Environment*), Chapter 4 (*The Legislative Framework*) and Chapter 5 (*The Importance of the European Union*).

The sections on *the parties in employment relations* deal with management objectives and styles, employment relations strategies, gaining employee commitment and participation, and managing with or without unions. They also cover the changing role and functions of the employers' associations – such as the Confederation of British Industry (CBI) and the Engineering Employers' Federation – and management associations organised at the level of the European Union. The parties in the employment relations system chapter covers employee organisations (trade unions, professional associations, staff/employee associations, etc) and employer organisations. Chapter 7 looks at management strategy and policies together with issues such as management style and the management of change.

There is a wide range of *employment relations processes* which impact on employment relationships in organisations: joint consultation, employee involvement schemes, third-party intervention (arbitration and conciliation), collective bargaining, industrial sanctions (lock-outs, suspension, collective dismissals) and parliamentary legislation. These are covered in Chapters 7, 8 and 9.

The *employment relations outcomes* covers various dimensions of agreements (both collective and individual), their types (substantive and procedural), their authorship (joint or singly by employer), the levels at which they are concluded, and their scope (subjects covered by agreements, rules and regulations). This is dealt with in Chapter 10.

The *employment relations skills* chapter covers the definition of negotiations, the different types of negotiation situations and the various stages involved in the negotiating processes. It also covers the skills required by managers in preparing for and conducting bargaining, in representing claims/offers and counter-offers, in searching for the common ground, in concluding the negotiations, and in writing up the agreement.

The employment relations specialism module also covers the skills required by an employment relations professional practitioner in handling employee complaints against management behaviour (commonly referred to as grievances), in handling disciplinary proceedings, in managing a redundancy situation and in managing health and safety. It additionally covers the management skills and knowledge and understanding required in devising, reviewing and monitoring procedural arrangements.

Chapter 11 deals with negotiation in general terms (that is, its definition, its different types and its component stages) and bargaining collectively with the workforce. The chapter places great stress on the skills required of management in the preparation stages, in grievance-handling and bargaining, and in particular in identifying any common ground with the other party via the use of techniques such as 'if and then' and the aspiration grid.

Chapter 12 deals with handling employee behaviour and performance issues (including disciplinary proceedings) and stresses the importance of management behaving in a fair and reasonable manner (good practice), whereas Chapter 13 covers grievance-handling. Chapter 14 centres on managing redundancy situations and the devising, reviewing and monitoring of redundancy procedures.

> *We hope you enjoy reading this book. If you can acquire and develop a deep understanding and appreciation of its contents, you have an excellent chance of reaching the CIPD practitioner Professional Standards in Employment Relations.*
>
> **John Gennard**
> **Graham Judge**

## CHAPTER 2

# Employment Relations – What Is It? – And Theoretical Considerations

## OVERVIEW

This chapter is in three parts. Part 1 explains what employment relations is about: it defines the subject. Part 2 examines the main theoretical perspectives that have been developed to explain employment relations behaviour. Part 3 analyses the differences within and between employers and employees and then their common interests.

Employment relations involves actors (employers and their institutions – eg employers' associations), employees and their institutions (eg trade unions, staff associations) and state agencies (eg the Advisory, Conciliation and Arbitration Service and the Central Arbitration Committee) using processes (employee involvement, employee engagement, collective bargaining, etc) to conclude within an internal and external economic, political (legal) and technological environment, rules to govern behaviour at the level of the workplace and the work community. These rules can be singly or jointly authored, can operate at different levels (national, sector, workplace) and can be of different types (procedural, substantive). The major theoretical approaches to employment relations are examined – specifically, one system theory (Dunlop), Marxist approaches (Hyman and Kelly) including the labour process debate (Bravermann) and Fox's frames of reference (pluralism, unitarism and radicalism). The chapter then examines the employers' and employees' interests in the labour market, noting differences between them. It concludes by identifying the common interests between employers and employees.

## LEARNING OUTCOMES

This chapter introduces you to the components and competing theoretical underpinning of any employment relations system at an international, national, company or enterprise level:

- the actors (the participants) in the employment relations game – managers and their organisations (eg companies and employers' associations), workers and their organisations (eg trade unions) and governmental agencies, such as the Advisory, Conciliation and Arbitration Service (ACAS)

- the processes (mechanisms) available to employers and employees whereby they agree rules and regulations to govern the employment relationship and at the same time accommodate their differing interests

- the rules, regulations and agreements made (and by whom) to regulate the employment relationship (the outcome – output – of the employment relations game): these rules establish, for employers and for employees, both rights and obligations

- the external environmental context – The employment relations game is influenced by the economic, technological and legal (political) environment. This determines the relative balance of bargaining power between employers and employees, and in turn influences the mechanisms (processes) used by the actors to establish employment rules, etc, and the content of those rules, regulations and agreements

- competing theoretical approaches to employment relations – systems theory, Marxist approaches, and frames of reference (unitary, radical and pluralist).

## INTRODUCTION

Thirty years ago, the conventional approach to employment relations centred on trade union behaviour, collective bargaining, industrial disputes and UK Government–trade union relationships. Trade unions were regarded as workplace adversaries negotiating with employers and as social partners expressing an 'employee view' on economic and social matters, particularly through the Trades Union Congress, to governments.

Collective relationships were seen as adversarial. The employer–individual employee relationship was perceived as secondary. The context in which the employment relations game took place was one of full employment. If this led to inflation, the UK Government contained it by interfering directly with the collective bargaining process through the imposition of an incomes policy designed to limit the rate of increase in money wages. Although the extent to which this employers-propose/unions-oppose approach squares (or squared) with reality can be questioned, there is no doubt that the perspective is of less relevance to today's employment relationship. The institutions of trade unions, collective bargaining procedures and arrangements, strikes and tripartism have declined steadily over the last 30 years. Indeed, the 2004 *Workplace Employment Relations Survey* reported that 66% of workplaces have no union members at all.

Attitudes to work and relationships at work have changed since the late 1970s. The driving force has been a marked change in the context in which the game of employment relations has been played. The last 30 years have seen increased product and labour market competition, reductions in international trade barriers, the imposition of public sector financial constraints, pressures for better value for money, the implementation of rapidly changing and easily transferable technologies, and increasing demands by customers that products and services are customised to their needs. For an analysis of these changes on UK employment relations, read/consult Millward *et al* (2000) *All Change at Work.* In this changed environment, the focus of employment relations has changed. There is now greater focus on the individual employee than on the employees as a collective body. Current collective relationships are based on relatively more co-operation in which both parties are motivated to add value to the organisation. Such employment relationships are seen as based on:

- the success of the enterprise
- building employee trust, feelings of fairness and greater commitment
- enhancing the satisfaction employees get from their work
- providing all employees with a voice to influence, and be involved in, decisions that are likely to affect their interests (employee voice). The form of this employee voice is no longer solely that of a trade union. There are now others – for example, Works Councils, business enhancement forums and quality circles
- helping the organisation to improve productivity, profitability and efficiency.

These changing approaches to employment relations are reflected in management-led changes in communication methods (for example, team briefing), in work organisation (quality circles, teamworking and single status), in changes in payment systems (performance-related pay), in changes in employees' representative systems (business-focused consultation arrangements), in the recognition of the employees' need for employment security (training and development of employees), in attitudes towards trade union recognition, in patterns of working (part-time, shift work, annualised hours) and in employment status (temporary/agency workers, fixed-term contracts).

Although the context in which employment relations takes place has changed over time giving rise to different behaviour by the parties and different outcomes, the basic purpose of the game remains the same. The purpose of employment relations is to establish rules, regulations and agreements to regulate the employment relationship. The priority given to the individual employment relationship as opposed to the collective employment relationship within companies depends on management's view as to what is in the best interests of the business/organisation employment relations. It is concerned with how to gain, in a number of different situations, employees' commitment to the achievement of an organisation's business goals and objectives. It is also about changing attitudes so that the organisation establishes rules, regulations and agreements which enable an organisation to implement successfully organisational change.

An Institute of Personnel and Development (IPD) Position Paper (1997) advocated an employment relations system in which the regulatory rules, etc, encouraged the achievement of higher skill levels, better skill utilisation, greater co-operation within the workplace and acceptance by the workforce of initiatives to develop higher added value through differentiated goods and services. In this model of employment relations, organisations are seen to succeed by:

- raising the skills of their employees

- providing high-quality services and products

- giving excellent customer service.

These in turn generate high profits, high earnings and a relatively more secure future for employees. In practical terms, the model embraces effective performance, good people management practices based on trust, fairness and delivery of the deal, a knowledge and understanding of employees' aspirations, and attention to the 'employee voice' obtained through a variety of channels (for example, employee involvement and participation and trade union representatives).

A CIPD paper of November 2005 entitled *What Is Employee Relations?* argued that employment relations could be seen primarily as a skills set or a philosophy, rather than as a management function or well-defined area of activity. It contended that the emphasis of employment relations continued to shift from institutions to relationships. For most organisations, the paper said, the key to adopting high-performance work practices was through employee engagement as a combination of commitment and organisational citizenship.

## THE ACTORS

For the authors, however, an employment relations system in any organisation has a number of components – actors, processes, environment context and rules (agreements, statutes, etc). The purpose of the employment relations system is to establish particular rules to govern the workplace and work community. These rules change in response to internal and external pressures affecting the organisation. First we look at the actors.

The principal 'actors' are:

- individual employers and their managers

- individual employees

- employee representative bodies (staff associations, trade unions, Works Councils, etc)

- 'employers' associations

- private companies

- public bodies
- voluntary organisations (for example, Save the Children Fund)
- government agencies.

## EMPLOYERS

Employers seek to maintain and enhance their interests by organising themselves into companies or enterprises of which there are four main types:

- private businesses in which a distinction can be made between:
    - the private company owned and managed by either an individual or family and which has no shareholders – such companies retain control of the decision whether to sell themselves to another company
  and:
    - the private company owned by shareholders but controlled by managers – such a company can be acquired by other companies with the agreement of the shareholders irrespective of the views of the managers. Public companies may also establish productive capacity or service provision in other countries, thereby becoming multinational companies

- public corporations
- central and local government
- voluntary bodies.

Private businesses employ some 18 million people. Although there are large numbers of small incorporated businesses, the most common form of organisation is the registered company. A major feature of the corporate sector is the concentration of output into a small number of very large private limited companies (many of which have production or service capacity in more than one country) alongside a substantial but growing number of much smaller private firms serving local 'niche' markets. This concentration of output into fewer enterprises is the result of corporate mergers within countries and across national boundaries.

There is, in large private sector businesses, a divorce of ownership by individual and institutional shareholders (such as banks and pension fund managers) and management control, which lies with a team of professional managers who are accountable to the owners for the performance of the company. Corporate strategy and its associated policies are normally decided by an executive group selected by the chief executive officer/managing director. This strategy is then taken to the plc board of directors for approval, modification or rejection. Senior, middle and junior managers are appointed to implement the policies in order to achieve the corporate strategy. In private corporations, the authority chain is from the top downwards through management structures.

Public sector organisations can be divided into public corporations, central government and local authorities. Public corporations, which include organisations such as the Royal Mail and NHS trusts, in 2008 employed some 1 million people. In the same year the central government employed just over half a million, of which half worked for the Civil Service. The numbers employed in local authorities in 2008 was around 2.3 million. By 2008, employment in the public sector was still at its lowest level since the post-World War II period, having reached this level in 2004.

Voluntary bodies are usually small not-for-profit organisations with social rather than economic objectives. They do, however, include some large organisations such as Oxfam, the Save the Children Fund, the British Heart Foundation, local housing associations and the Red Cross. The voluntary sector also contains worker or producer co-operatives where the enterprise is owned and controlled by its members. In 2008 it was estimated that some 750,000 were employed in voluntary organisations.

Employers' associations were also used by companies to protect and advance their interests, particularly by lobbying the political decision-making bodies of the UK Government and the European Union (Commission, Council of Ministers and Parliament). The Annual Report of the Certification Officer, 2008/09, reports that in 2009 there were 67 such associations on the Certification Officer's list of trade unions and employers associations. Some of the latter are national bodies covering a whole industry (for example, the Engineering Employers' Federation and the Construction Federation); others are specialised bodies representing a segment of an industry (for example, the Newspaper Society, which represents the interests of provincial newspaper employers in England, Wales and Northern Ireland); and yet others are local associations representing geographically based industrial interests (for example, the Lancashire Textile Manufacturers' Association and the Lancaster, Morecambe and South Lakeland Master Plumbers' Association). Since 1983 the total number of employers' associations has decreased. In 1983 there were 375 employers' associations. The reduction in number is mainly due to mergers: for example, in 2008/09 10 employers' organisations ceased to exist as the result of a single amalgamation to form what is now called EEF Ltd.

Employers' associations major activities fall into the following areas:

- assistance to member firms in the resolution of disputes with their employees
- general help and advice on good practice in employment relations matters
- representation of members' interests to political decision-makers at all levels
- representation of members' interests at employment tribunals
- in some cases, the negotiation of collective agreements with trade unions.

The best-known nationwide employers' organisation in the UK is the Confederation of British Industry (CBI). Its membership includes individual companies and national and regional trade and employers' associations. It does not specifically engage in employment relations activities but its political lobbying activities can, and do, have an impact on issues that affect workplace employment relations. Although it does not engage in negotiations with employee representatives, it does maintain a direct working relationship with the Trades Union Congress (TUC) as well as an indirect one via joint membership of bodies such as ACAS and the Health and Safety Executive.

The ways in which employers' associations can assist the employment relations specialist in their everyday job are discussed in Chapter 6.

## EMPLOYEES

Some employees attempt to strengthen and enhance their interests by presenting a collective face to the employer, notably in relation to minimum conditions on which they are prepared to work for an employer. The most common employee organisations are:

- professional associations
- staff associations
- trade unions.

In enterprises where such organisations do not exist, employers often create a collective employee organisation (sometimes called an employee council, a Works Council, a representative committee, a business involvement group, or similar) so that they can obtain a collective and representative voice from their employees. It is only in very small firms that a truly individual and personal relationship can exist between employer and employee. Once an organisation grows, in employment terms, beyond a critical size, the views of the employees are best collected (in time and efficiency terms) through some representative organisation. It becomes too time-consuming to talk to each separate employee.

### Professional associations

Professional associations are not central employment relations players. They usually control the education and training of new members to a profession by acting as 'qualifying associations'. They also establish, maintain and review professional and ethical standards for their members. In addition, they advance the standing and status of the profession in the wider community. However, some professional associations also protect and improve their members' employment interests in pay bargaining. In the health service, for example, there are groups of professional employees – such as nurses and midwives – who use their professional associations in the dual capacity of a professional and bargaining body. Doctors use the British Medical Association (BMA) in the same capacity, as do lawyers the Law Society.

### Staff associations

Staff associations are in some cases the creation of employers who wish to keep their business non-unionised. The majority, however, are independent of the employer. Despite low membership subscriptions and lack of militancy, staff associations can, and do, provide an acceptable alternative to trade unions for many employees. This is particularly true of certain white-collar groups. Nevertheless, most staff associations are characterised by weak finances and a narrow membership base often confined to a single employer (for example, the Cheshire Building Society Staff Association and the Harrods Staff Union).

Larger staff associations tend to acquire their own staff and premises and rely less on the employer for services and facilities. In 2009 the Certification Officer's list of employee organisations contained some 26 staff associations concentrated mainly in the financial sector of which 15 were recognised to be independent of employer influence and domination. These staff associations are characterised by high membership density often exceeding 75%.

### Trade unions

Trade unions are the best-known form of employee representative organisation. They were formed to protect and advance the interests of their members against employers and members of other trade unions. In the UK, trade unions have different recruitment strategies. Occupation-based unions – for example, BALPA (airline pilots) and ASLEF (train drivers) – focus on recruiting employees who perform certain jobs. Other unions confine their recruitment to all grades of employees employed in a particular industry. These are referred to as industrial unions, although few, if any, such exist at present in the UK. General unions, such as the GMB, organise any workers regardless of skill across the boundaries within and between industries. The largest UK union, Unite – formed in 2007 by the merger between AMICUS and the Transport and General Workers' Union – organises professional, craft and lesser-skilled employees in manufacturing, financial services, the public sector, transport and construction centres.

In the UK, trade union organisation is characterised by a large number of small unions co-existing with a very small number of large trade unions. In 2009, 71% (132) of the total number of trade unions registered with the Certification Officer had memberships of less than 5,000. On the other hand, 8% (14) of the unions had memberships in excess of 100,000. In 2009, the Certification Officer's Report recorded the number of trade union members at 7.7 million, an increase of 28,463 (0.37%) over the figure for 2008. In 2009 the percentage of the workforce in trade unions was 27%, but in the private sector was only 15%. Trade union membership is increasingly becoming a public sector phenomenon. The Trades Union Congress (TUC), established in 1868, acts as the collective voice of the UK trade union movement to government and international trade union bodies (such as ETUC and the International Confederation of Trade Unions) as well as attempting to influence the behaviour of its affiliated unions.

Unions represent different interests in terms of jobs, types of workers, industries, services and public and private sectors of the economy. They also have different interests within them (skilled, unskilled, non-manual workers, professional workers, etc) but these are accommodated through their decision-making procedures, which are based on the principle of representative democracy. Trade unions in the UK are characterised by:

- being job-, not class-centred
- preferring to achieve their objectives by industrial methods (for example,

collective bargaining) rather than by political means (for example, industrial action against government measures they dislike)

- being pragmatic rather than principled.

All the above issues surrounding trade unions are discussed in more detail in Chapter 6.

## GOVERNMENT AGENCIES

There are state agencies that have a statutory role in employment relations, whether that role is in respect of individual or of collective issues. In the UK, there are four major agencies of this kind: the Advisory, Conciliation and Arbitration Service (ACAS), the Central Arbitration Committee (CAC), the Certification Office for Trade Unions and Employers' Associations, and the employment tribunals.

### The Advisory, Conciliation and Arbitration Service (ACAS)

ACAS is independent of direct ministerial intervention, although its sponsoring ministry is the Department for Business, Innovation and Skills (BIS). It is a non-departmental public body governed by an independent council responsible for setting its strategic direction, policies and priorities. It consists of a chairperson and 11 other members drawn from trade unions, employers' bodies, small business organisations, academia and non-TUC unions. Appointments to the Council are made by the Department for Business, Innovation and Skills. ACAS recovers some of its costs through paid-for services that it provides (eg mediation in individual disputes), although many of its services remain free at the point of use and it is a non-profit-making organisation. This enables ACAS to be independent, impartial and confidential.

ACAS seeks to:

- promote good practice through the issuing of Codes of Practice on discipline and grievance procedures, on the disclosure of information to trade unions for collective bargaining purposes, and on time off for trade union duties and activities
- provide information and advice and guidance on a wide range of employment relations matters through its helpline, which can be contacted by anyone and is free, confidential and impartial
- conciliate in complaints to employment tribunals. It has a statutory duty to act as conciliator in a wide range of individual employment rights complaints including alleged unfair dismissal, alleged discrimination and equal pay claims. For individuals and organisations to participate in this conciliation is voluntary. It is impartial, confidential, free of charge and independent of the employment tribunals
- conciliate and mediate in the case of collective disputes
- resolve employment disputes by facilitating arbitration by which the parties to a dispute agree of their own volition that a jointly agreed arbitrator consider the dispute and make a decision to resolve it.

A voluntary conciliation and arbitration service has been available for over 100 years, but ACAS was founded in its present form in 1975. It was during the turbulent times of the 1970s and 1980s that ACAS became a household name, trusted to resolve high-profile industrial unrest. It is still trusted today. A report commissioned by ACAS to test its attributes, published in 2009, found that of those who had heard of ACAS, most identified the organisation as neutral, impartial, reliable and reputable.

### The Central Arbitration Committee (CAC)

The CAC is a permanent independent body with statutory powers whose role is to resolve disputes in England, Scotland and Wales under legislation relating to recognition and de-recognition of trade unions, disclosure of information for collective bargaining, information and consultation of employees, European Works Councils and European Companies and Co-operative Society and cross-border mergers. The CAC's powers to arrange for voluntary arbitration in trade disputes has not been used for some years.

There are four stages to the statutory trade union recognition procedure. First, the CAC accepts the application by deciding that a majority of workers in the bargaining unit would be likely to favour recognition of the union concerned. The second stage requires an agreement, or a decision from the CAC, on the appropriate bargaining unit. The next stage is for the CAC to decide if recognition without a ballot should be declared or if a ballot should be held. The final stage in the process is for the parties to agree, or for the CAC to determine, the method of bargaining. Agreements in this regard overwhelmingly predominate. The involvement of the CAC in its other jurisdiction has, and remains, subdued.

The CAC consists of a chairperson, 11 deputy chairpersons, 28 members experienced as representatives of employers and 26 members as representatives of workers. All members of the Committee are appointed by the Department for Business, Innovation and Skills after consultation with ACAS. CAC decisions are made by panels of three committee members appointed by the chairperson and consisting of either the chairperson or a deputy chairperson, one member whose experience is representative of employers and one member whose experience is representative of workers. The chairperson meets with the deputy chairperson once every six months, and the whole CAC meets annually to discuss policy issues and developments.

### The Certification Officer

The post of Certification Officer was established in 1975 and the post's responsibilities include:

- maintaining a list of trade unions and determining the independence of trade unions from employer influence and domination

- dealing with complaints by members that a trade union has failed to maintain an accurate register of members, failed to keep proper accounting records, failed to have its accounts properly audited, failed to submit annual accounting returns or failed to permit access to its accounting records, or that a trade union's financial affairs should be investigated

- dealing with complaints by members that a trade union failed to hold secret ballots for electing members of its executive committee, its president and general secretary

- ensuring the observance by trade unions of the statutory provisions governing the operation of their political funds

- seeing that the statutory procedures for amalgamations, transfer of engagements and changes of names are complied with, and dealing with complaints by members about the conduct of merger ballots

- maintaining a list of employers' associations and ensuring that the statutory requirements concerning accounting records, financial affairs, political funds and the statutory procedures for amalgamation and transfer of engagements in respect of employers' associations are observed.

All the above issues surrounding agencies are discussed in more detail in Chapter 6.

THEORY EMPLOYMENT RELATIONS PROCESSES

In the game of employment relations, the players use various employment relations processes (mechanisms) to make rules to govern behaviour in the workplace and work community. The most important of these processes are:

- unilateral action

- employee involvement and participation schemes

- employee engagement

- collective bargaining

- third-party intervention

- industrial sanctions.

In addition to these processes, the state can interfere in the rule-making game by establishing minimum terms that the employer must offer to his or her employees. It does this by way of legal regulation. Unlike the processes listed above, management has no direct control over what legal regulation the UK Government and/or the European Union introduces. However, management does try to influence such regulation via their political lobbying activities. For example, in 1998 employers succeeded in persuading the Labour Government to alter its original proposal, contained in its White Paper *Fairness at Work*, that there should be no limit on the amount of compensation that could be awarded to an individual who is unfairly dismissed by his or her employer. As a result of employer pressure, the Government restricted its increase to the limit on such compensation from £12,000 to £50,000.

## UNILATERAL ACTION

Unilateral action is where the employer is the sole author of the rules, agreements and regulations that govern the conditions under which employees work. In deciding employment conditions in this way, the employer may or may not give attention to the views (voice) of the employees. It is a methodology that was formerly associated with non-union companies, but in the last 30 years there has been an increase in the number of employers unilaterally imposing employment conditions (and changes in them) on their employees. They have justified this on the grounds of business efficiency and management's right to manage. However, even in highly unionised organisations (for example, local authorities and the NHS trusts) there have been examples of the unilateral imposition of changes by management on issues such as wage increases, the taking of holidays, overtime opportunities, and changes in job descriptions. At the extreme, managers who unilaterally impose changes to their employees' employment conditions are effectively saying 'Accept these new terms or consider yourself dismissed.' Take it or leave it.

Another area in which employers exercise sole authorship of the workplace rules is the devising of company rules, which are applicable to all employees and set out in the company handbook/rule-book. If employees breach these rules, serious consequences – including dismissal – can arise. Such rules usually include the steps to be followed in the event of an accident, directions on maintaining security, safety and/or hygiene, the dress code, and an obligation on employees to report to the employer a change of address.

It is difficult to find out exactly how many solely management-authored workplace rules are made since there is no regular source of such information. The Workplace Industrial Relations Survey series, however, provide some information with respect to pay determination. The 2004 *Workplace Employment Relations Survey* revealed, over the economy as a whole, that more than 73% of employees had their pay determined by non-collective-bargaining mechanisms and that 70% of employees (compared with 69% in 1998) had their pay determined by workplace management. For a further 22% (19% in 1998) pay was determined by a higher level (than workplace) of management in the organisation. In 2004, in the private manufacturing sector, 39% of employees had their pay determined by collective bargaining. In the public sector in 2004, only 5% of employees had their pay determined by management at the workplace and 8% by a higher level of management in the organisation. The 2004 *Workplace Employment Relations Survey* concluded that in 51% of the workplaces it surveyed, there was an absence of any formal structure for employees to have a voice to their employer.

## EMPLOYEE INVOLVEMENT

THEORY

'Employee involvement' is a broad term that covers a range of processes designed to enable employees to voice their views to the employer and so have an involvement in management decision-making and the feeling of participating in the development of the business. There is, however, no commitment on the part of management to act on the employees' views. In the final analysis, the employer writes the workplace rules but in doing so takes account of the views of the employees. Employee involvement processes include indirect forms of participation such as consultative committees or Works Councils as well as direct communication forms such as regular workforce meetings between senior management and the workforce, problem-solving groups that discuss aspects of performance (for example, quality) and briefing groups, which usually involve regular meetings between junior managers and all the workers for whom they are responsible.

Consultation is different from communication because it invites the participation of staff by seeking views, bringing individuals into the management decision-making process and delegating a measure of autonomy through empowerment. Consultation can take place either directly with staff or through a representative forum (such as a Works Council) or some other form of joint consultation machinery. Employee involvement and participation is analysed in greater detail in Chapter 7.

In joint consultation, management seeks views, feelings and ideas from employees and/or their representatives prior to making a decision. Although joint consultation may involve discussion of mutual problems, it leaves management to make the final decision. There is no commitment to act on the employees' views. At the end of the day the final decision rests with management. Issues dealt with by joint consultation vary from social matters – such as the provision of canteen or sports facilities – to issues such as the scheduling of production.

The *Workplace Employment Relations Survey* (2004) provides information on the extent of joint consultative arrangements in establishments. It revealed that 38% of workplaces had a functioning joint consultative committee at the workplace – while 62% of workplaces had no joint consultative committees. These committees were responsible for discussing a range of topics rather than a single issue, such as health and safety. In the private sector only 31% of workplaces had a JCC compared with 74% in the public sector. Workplace committees are much more frequent amongst large workplaces, and higher-level committees – through which management prefers to consult with employees on a multi-site basis, rather than have a consultative committee for each establishment – are more frequent in larger organisations.

## THEORY    EMPLOYEE ENGAGEMENT

This is a relatively recent employment relations process. Although the rules of the workplace and the work community from this process involve an input from the employees, the final wording of the rules rest with management. There is no one agreed definition of employee engagement. Nonetheless, MacLeod and Clark's report (2009) *Engaging for Success: Enhancing performance through employee engagement* gives three main definitions:

> Engagement is about creating opportunities for employees to connect with their colleagues, managers and the wider organisation. It is also about

creating an environment where employees are motivated to want to connect with their work and really care about doing a good job ... it is a concept that places flexibility, change and continuous improvement at the heart of what it means to be an employee and an employer in a twenty-first-century workplace.

Professor Katie Truss (2006)    **THEORY**

A positive attitude held by the employee towards the organisation and its values. An engaged employee is aware of the business context and works with colleagues to improve performance within the job for the benefit of the organisation. The organisation must work to develop and nurture engagement which requires a two-way relationship between employee and employer.

Institute of Employment Studies (2008)    **THEORY**

A set of positive attitudes and behaviours enabling high job performance of a kind which is in line with the organisation's mission.

Professor John Storey (2008)    **THEORY**

Much of the discussion of employee engagement tends to get confused as to whether it is an attitude, behaviour or an outcome – or indeed, all three. Supporters of employee engagement believe that all three are part of the engagement story. An employee might feel pride and loyalty (attitude) and/or be a great advocate for the company to customers or go the extra mile to finish a piece of work (behaviour). Outcomes may include lower accident rates, higher productivity, more innovation, lower labour turnover and reduced absence rates.

Advocates of engagement argue it is a workplace approach designed to ensure that employees are committed to their organisation's goals and values, are motivated to contribute to organisational success, and are able, at the same time, to enhance their own sense of well-being. Engaged organisations are said to have strong and authentic values with clear evidence of trust and fairness based on mutual respect where two-way promises and commitments – between employers and staff – are understood and are fulfilled. Employee engagement strategies are said to enable people to be the best they can at work, recognising that this can only happen if they feel respected, involved, heard, well-led and valued by those they work for and with. Employee engagement is analysed in more detail in Chapter 9.

## COLLECTIVE BARGAINING

Collective bargaining is not only an employment relations process for determining employment rules which are jointly authored but also a system of industrial governance whereby unions and employers jointly reach decisions concerning the employment relationship. The process involves employees – via their elected representatives and unions – participating in the management of the enterprise. Collective bargaining is a problem-solving mechanism but can only take place if employees are organised and if the employer is prepared to recognise the trade union(s) for collective bargaining purposes.

In practice, the outcome of collective bargaining is not confined to union members. Unionised companies apply collectively bargained terms and conditions of employment to their non-union employees as well as their unionised ones. Companies that do not recognise unions have regard to collectively bargained rates in their industry or in comparator firms when deciding on their own employees' employment conditions if they are to remain competitive in the labour market. Many non-union companies (for example, Marks & Spencer, IBM, Mars) seek to retain union-free workplaces by paying better than the union-negotiated pay rates and other employment conditions for their industry. This means that such companies must have an interest in the outcome of collective bargaining although they are not direct parties to it.

The former Department of Trade and Industry survey of trade union membership in 2006 revealed, over the period autumn 1996 to autumn 2006 inclusive, that collective bargaining as part of the employment relations game declined sharply. In 1996, overall the proportion of employees covered by collective bargaining was 34.5%, and in 2005 33.5%. In the public sector, the coverage of collective bargaining in 1996 was 69%, compared with 71% in 2006. In the private sector, the corresponding figures were 22% and 19.6% respectively. Collective agreements in the public sector had more than three times the proportion of employees covered than in the private sector. By nation and region, Northern Ireland in 2006 had the highest percentage of employees covered by collective agreements (47.8%), while the south-east of England had the lowest coverage at 27%.

## REFLECTIVE ACTIVITY

What are the main processes used to regulate employment conditions in your organisation?

Why are these the main processes, rather than others?

## THIRD-PARTY INTERVENTION

In situations where the actors in the employment relations system are unable to resolve their collective differences over the making of employment rules and/ or over the interpretation and application of existing rules, they may agree voluntarily to seek the assistance of an independent third party. Third-party intervention can take one of three forms:

- conciliation
- mediation
- arbitration.

In the case of disputes between an employer and an individual employee over unfair dismissal, non-payment of a termination of employment payment or commission of sex, race, equal pay and disability discrimination, the law requires the Advisory, Conciliation and Arbitration Service (ACAS) to attempt a conciliated settlement before the claim can proceed to an employment tribunal.

In the *conciliation* of collective disputes, the role of the third party is to keep the two sides talking and assist them to reach their own agreement. The conciliator acts as a link between the disputing parties by passing on information that the parties will not, for whatever reason, pass directly to each other, from one side to the other, until either a basis for agreement is identified or both parties conclude that there is no basis for an agreed voluntary settlement to their problem. Conciliation permits each side to re-assess its situation continually. The conciliator plays a passive role and does not impose any action or decision on the parties.

In the *mediation* of collective disputes, a mediator listens to the argument of the two sides and makes recommendations on how their difference(s) might be resolved. The parties are free to accept or reject these recommendations. On the other hand, the *arbitration* process removes from employers and employees control over the settlement of their differences. The arbitrator hears both sides' case and decides the solution to the parties' differences by making an award. Both parties, having voluntarily agreed to arbitration, are morally bound, but not legally obliged, to accept the arbitrator's award. Pendulum arbitration is a specific form of arbitration which limits the third party to making an award that accepts fully either the final claim of the union or the final offer of the employer. It reduces arbitration to an all-or-nothing win-or-lose outcome for the disputants. By creating an all-or-nothing expectation, pendulum arbitration is said to provide the incentive for bargainers to moderate their final positions and reach a voluntary agreement.

Third-party intervention is facilitated by ACAS, established as Royal Commission in 1974 and put on a statutory basis by the Employment Protection Act (1975). Mediation and arbitration is undertaken by an independent person (or occasionally persons) selected jointly by the parties to the dispute, from a list held by ACAS of competent arbitrators made up of academics, trade union officers and employers. The listed members of this panel are all experienced and knowledgeable in employment relations. There is also the Central Arbitration Committee, which is a standing independent arbitration body. Originally established as the Industrial Court in 1919, it can deal with issues relating to industrial disputes, to a single employer or to a particular employee group. As well as providing voluntary arbitration in trade disputes, it arbitrates on unilateral claims by trade unions over alleged failure of employers to disclose information for collective bargaining purposes, in disputes over the establishment of European Works Councils and in disputes over trade union recognition. These are all areas in which the law permits one party to take the other against its wishes to arbitration. The roles of ACAS and the CAC are discussed more fully in Chapter 6.

Third-party intervention is a little-used option by the players of the employment relations game. The number of completed collective conciliation cases handled by ACAS fell from 2,284 in 1979 to 960 in 2008/9. Mediation is rarely used. In the whole of 2008/9 there were only three mediation hearings arranged by ACAS. In 2008/9 the number of arbitration hearings arranged by ACAS was 26, compared with 190 in 1990 and 63 in 2003/4. The process of third-party intervention in the employment relations game is discussed in more detail in Chapter 6.

Some disputes between individual employees and their employers, or between individual colleagues, or groups of colleagues, do not involve actual or potential claims to an employment tribunal. As a result, the latter period of the first decade of the twenty-first century saw the rise of individual mediation whereby the employer brings in a neutral third party to help individuals or groups resolve their differences. It has been used in a variety of situations ranging from the breakdown of relationships between line mangers to bullying and harassment cases. A mediator first meets with the disputant parties separately to find out how they see the situation and what they hope to achieve from the mediation process. He or she then brings the two parties together and helps them thrust out a protocol of acceptable behaviour, and both parties agree to stick to it. Bringing in a neutral third party does not always have a positive result, but whatever the outcome, the individual mediation process is generally cheaper, quicker and easier on all concerned than going to law. Individual mediation can play a powerful role in settling workplace disputes.

ACAS will provide individual mediation on a fee-charged basis. In 2008/9 its mediators took on 230 new assignments, the great majority of which at the request of the employers concerned, and 195 were completed successfully. This represented a 24% increase in demand over 2007/8. Resolution rates have remained very high at just over 90%; 95% of the people who initiated the requests for mediation were very pleased, or satisfied, with the service provided.

## INDUSTRIAL SANCTIONS

To resort to the imposition of industrial sanctions is costly to both employers and employees. The main sanctions available to the employer are:

- locking out some, or all, of the workforce
- closing the factory
- relocating operations to another site, including overseas (offshoring)
- dismissing employees who participate in industrial action.

The main industrial sanctions that employees can impose on employers are:

- a ban on overtime
- working-to-rule
- imposition of a selective strike
- holding an all-out strike.

The threat of the imposition of industrial sanctions can be important in bringing about a settlement of the differences between the employers and the employees. The threat that one player might impose industrial sanctions, with their ensuing costs, on the other may be as important as if sanctions were imposed. It is the threat effect that can oblige players to adjust their position and negotiate a peaceful settlement. Both parties will be reluctant to go ahead and impose industrial sanctions because of their associated costs. However, their existence means that the employment relations players have to take them into account and adjust their behaviour accordingly.

Employers and employees have to think carefully before imposing or threatening to impose industrial sanctions. There is little to be gained in imposing industrial action if it is unlikely to be successful, especially if economic pressures may quickly mount as the organisation's product market competitors take advantage of its industrial problems to poach its customers. It is pointless to relocate operations to another site unless an alternative competent workforce is available (or can be recruited) at the new site. To impose sanctions that fail to bring further concessions from the other player undermines, at a future date, the credibility of the threat to use them.

### The extent of industrial action

In the UK, official statistics on the use of industrial sanctions relate only to strikes. They measure three dimensions of strike activity: their numbers (how frequent they are), their size (the number of workers involved) and their duration (the number of working days lost). This last measure is often distorted by a few big strikes. For example, in 1979 an engineering industry-wide strike accounted for 55% of the 29.5 million working days lost in that year. In 2007, the number of working days lost in the UK was 1.04 million.

Levels of strike action today are nowhere near the levels of 30 years ago. In 1979, nearly 30 million working days were lost, closely followed by 27 million in the miners' strike of 1984/5. Of the past years, only two have had more than 1 million days lost and there has been no discernible trend. In 2007 there was during the year the equivalent of one afternoon of discontent.

Why have there been fewer strikes? First, there are now simply – particularly in the private sector – fewer unionised workplaces. Second, union tactics have also changed. The all-out indefinite strike is exceedingly rare today. Most strikes are targeted and/or of limited duration. Third, union members' attitudes are different. Put simply, union members want their unions to work with employers to solve problems wherever possible rather than rush into confrontation. Finally, the union agenda today is much wider. While that has led to strikes over issues that hardly figured in the 1970s (such as pensions), negotiations about access to training or a better work–life balance are not generally settled by industrial action.

Although dispute levels have declined in the last 30 years, some significant strikes still occur:

- 2008/9: the Grangemouth oil refinery in Scotland – A dispute over proposed changes to the company's pension scheme caused workers to strike, resulting in potential supply shortages to Scotland and Northern Ireland. Although a strike was not averted, an agreement was brokered over the safe shutdown of the Grangemouth plant, enabling a swift resumption of operations after the stoppage.

- 2009: a four-day strike involving tanker drivers and contractors supplying Shell over pay – It involved more than 10% of all UK petrol stations. By the end of the strike, half of all Shell garages had experienced some shortage, and one in five had closed. Talks took place at a secret location, enabling the parties to resume direct negotiations which finally led to a resolution of the dispute.

- 2008/9: a dispute at the Total oil refinery in Lindsey, Lincolnshire, spilling over into ACAS investigations – ACAS was asked to investigate an unofficial strike which led thousands of contract workers at more than a dozen oil refineries, gas terminals and power stations to stage a series of illegal walk-outs in sympathy. These walk-outs were triggered by Total's refinery subcontractors hiring an Italian firm who brought their own workforce of Italian and Portuguese workers. A return to work agreement was eventually secured through the good offices of ACAS.

- 2009: strike action in the Royal Mail over the manner in which Royal Mail sought to implement a reform in working practices and to improve the competitiveness of the Royal Mail.

## LEGAL INTERVENTION

The processes described above are private means whereby the rules of the workplace and the work community are determined. Employers have considerable choice over which of these private rule-making processes is used. However, on occasions the state interferes in the private relationships between employer and employees and sets minimum employment conditions (work rules) that employers must provide for their employees – for example, the National Minimum Wage. Although employers have no control over what parliamentary legislation is introduced, they try to influence its content by political lobbying to maximise its positive effects and/or minimise its negative impact on their interests.

### UK Parliament regulation

In the UK today, legal intervention into the employment relationship comes from two sources: the UK Government and the European Union. Since 1997, UK governments have introduced new minimum standards (workplace rules) of protection for employees at the workplace. In April 1999 the National Minimum Wage Act (1998) introduced a national minimum wage. The Employment Relations Act (1999) gave individual employees the right to be represented for collective bargaining purposes by a trade union where the majority of the relevant workforce wish it. It also created the right for individuals to be accompanied by a fellow employee or trade union representative during grievance and disciplinary procedures, over serious matters. The Employment Act (2002) provided individual employees with the right to request more flexible working arrangements and imposed on all organisations regardless of size, statutory discipline and grievance procedures. The Work and Families Act (2006) extended maternity and adoption paid leave, extended the right to request flexible working to carers of adults and provided the entitlement to four weeks' paid leave, making it additional to bank (and public) holidays. The Employment Act (2008) replaced the existing statutory disputes resolution procedures in relation to procedural unfairness and dismissal cases.

### The European Union directives

The European Union is committed to establishing a 'level playing-field' of minimum social and employment standards in its Single European Market in which goods, capital, people and services can move freely. In 1997 the UK Government accepted that more social and employment measures could be harmonised between member states by the use of the EU's qualified-majority voting procedure instead of by unanimous agreement. One implication of this has been that an employment relations professional in the UK has experienced increasing legal regulation from the European Union. Chapter 5 examines how the EU has impinged on the work of the employment relations profession in the areas of equal opportunities, employment protection and working conditions, information and consultation rights, and health and safety.

## THE ENVIRONMENTAL CONTEXT                                THEORY

The employment relations game does not take place in a vacuum. It takes place in an organisational setting which in turn operates within constraints imposed by the behaviour of organisations external to that organisation. This internal and external context influences the outcome of work rules achieved and the processes used by the parties to make these rules.

Whether the outcome of the employment relations game results in employment rules that are closer to satisfying the interests of the employers or the employees is influenced heavily by the environmental context in which the game is played. Issues relating to the environmental context are relevant to employers who bargain individually with their employees as well as to those who bargain collectively with their workforce. The environmental context is a key employment relations concept which influences, *inter alia*, the employer's preferred employment relations process, the subject matter of agreements, rules and regulations, and whether workplace and work community rules are jointly authored by employers and employees or solely by one of the parties.

### THE MACRO LEVEL                                          THEORY

The factors in the environmental context external to the organisation that influence the relationship between employers and employees, and therefore the outcome of the employment relations game, are:

- economic

- legal (political)

- technological.

The Government's economic and legal policies have major implications for the outcome of employment relations activities. Economic policies that are directed towards the creation of full employment and the maximising of economic growth weaken the position of the employer relative to that of the employees in the workplace, which will be the outcome of the employment relations game. In an expanding economy the demand for labour services increases, causing the price of those labour services to rise. The content of the rules that result are thus more favourable to employees. On the other hand, if macro-economic policies are directed at restraining economic activity, the demand for labour services falls, resulting perhaps in redundancies and raising unemployment. In such circumstances the content of the rules arising from the employment relations game are likely to be more favourable to the employees. If economic activity leads to severe economic recession – as happened in the UK during 2008/9 – wage increases are likely to be frozen or wage rates cut.

If the Government introduces legislation favourable to employers' interests – for example, by restricting the circumstances in which trade unions may instruct their members to take industrial action without the employer being able to seek redress through the courts (for instance, to seek redress for compensation for a downturn in revenue through sales, etc) – then the environmental context is relatively more favourable to the employer than the employee, and the outcome of the employment relations game in terms of the content of the workplace rules will reflect this. Conservative Governments from 1979 to 1997 inclusive provided an environmental external context relatively more favourable to employers by passing nine pieces of parliamentary legislation which regulated the labour market activities of trade unions progressively more tightly. As a result, strikes fell dramatically and wage increases were reduced relative to other periods.

If a government introduces legislation favourable to the interests of individual employees, the environmental external context becomes more favourable to the employee relative to employers. The Labour Governments (1997 to 2010), via their legislative programme together with that from the EU, enhanced the external environmental context in which the employment relations game was played relatively more favourably to the employees.

The implementation of new technology also impacts on the outcome of the rules agreed, via various employment relations processes governing behaviour at the workplace. Technological developments based on computers, lasers and telecommunications have in some sectors of the economy destroyed jobs – for example, those of compositors (typesetters) in the printing industry – de-skilled jobs, blurred demarcation lines between existing jobs and industries, and created for employers an alternative and lower-paid workforce. These impacts have meant that the rules agreed have been closer to those desired by employers rather than by employees. It is easier in such an external environmental set of circumstances for employers to achieve redundancies (to employ fewer) and to make changes in working practices.

However, in other sectors of the economy, by creating new jobs, new skills and making some industries more capital intensive, the implementation of technological change has produced an external environmental context more favourable to employees relative to the employer. For example, the growth of the telephone bank service has created a new business which in part replaces the jobs lost in traditional banks, and the workplace rules in such businesses will reflect this.

The economic and legal environment surrounding the employment relations system significantly influences the workplace rules that emerge in that system. This is why employer and employee organisations spend large sums of money in lobbying political decision-makers. It is why the actors' institutions find it advantageous to become involved in politics.

## REFLECTIVE ACTIVITY

What factors determine at the national level the environmental context in which the employment relations game is played? Explain, with appropriate examples, how the external environmental context of your organisation – or of another with which you are familiar – influences employer or employee behaviour in employment relations.

## THE MICRO LEVEL

**THEORY**

An analysis of the external environmental context at the organisation level cannot explain why some groups of employees retain a favourable context vis-à-vis the employer despite recession and high unemployment, or why some employers are in a relatively weak context position despite general levels of depressed economic activity. To explain these situations we have to examine the environmental context at the individual organisation level.

At this level the internal environmental context is influenced by some of the following factors:

- whether employees can inflict costs on the organisation (for example, are the employees concerned at a crucial/key point in the production/service provision process?)
- whether there is an alternative workforce available to the employer (ie within the organisation or external to the organisation)
- the product market situation of the organisation (are sales increasing or decreasing?)
- whether the group of employees is aware of its potential power
- whether the group of employees has previously exercised its power

- whether, if the group has exercised its power, the outcome was favourable (did the employees feel they had gained something they would otherwise not have got?). For example, in assessing the internal environmental context in which a group of employees is operating, management has to consider how crucial the group is to the workflow production/service supply process. The more central the group is to workflow, the greater is its potential influence within the organisation. Its staff, for example, are in strategic positions to disrupt workflow.

The external environmental context of a group of employees relative to that of management is strengthened if there is a lack of an appropriate alternative workforce available to undertake the group's work on an individual or a departmental basis. In short, a group of workers who it is difficult to substitute has greater influence relative to the employer than a group whose services are easily replaceable. These relative differences in the external environmental context will be reflected in the rules operated to regulate the employment relationship and the process whereby those rules are made. For example, if the internal environmental context is relatively more favourable to the employees, then they are likely to improve employment conditions to a higher level than the employer would ideally like.

## AGREEMENTS, RULES AND REGULATIONS

The outcome of the employment relations game is the establishment of rules, regulations and agreements by which the employment relationship is governed. The rules establish rights *and* responsibilities for both employers and employees. The function of the employment relations system is to explain why particular rules are established in a specific employment relations system, and how and why they change in response to internal and external environmental contexts. The rules relate to a group of employees or may be the result of bargaining between an employer and an individual employee resulting in a personal contract. The distinguishing characteristic of such contracts is that none of its terms has been bargained collectively. The employee has negotiated as an individual – although in doing so he or she may have received assistance from a third party.

However, in practice, few personal contracts are genuinely individualised. At BT, for example, all terms and conditions for senior managerial staff were standard across all personal contracts. The only difference was that pay was determined 'individually' with no published rates at (and no transparency in the criteria by) which pay increases were given to individuals.

### TYPES OF AGREEMENTS

It is conventional to divide the rules, regulations and agreements stemming from the employment relations game into two broad types. First, there are substantive rules which cover the money aspects of employment conditions (pay, hours of work, paid holidays, shift premiums, etc). An example of a substantive agreement is shown below.

---

**AGREEMENT BETWEEN:**

**UNION OF SHOP, DISTRIBUTIVE AND ALLIED WORKERS (USDAW)**

**and**

**A B C LIMITED**

The following has been agreed between USDAW and ABC Limited, regarding the 2002/3 Pay and Conditions claim.

The following are the rates of pay which now apply and are effective from Monday 5 June 2002.

*Rates of pay*

| | |
|---|---|
| Boners | £170.82 |
| Butchers | £156.47 |
| M/c Op/Prep | £151.23 |
| Gen Worker 'A' | £146.66 |
| Gen Worker 'B' | £146.66 |
| Drivers | £152.57 |

*Nightshift premiums*
Will be increased from their present levels to 18.5% of basic hourly rate.

*Working hours*
With immediate effect to become:

| | | |
|---|---|---|
| Dayshift | Monday to Friday | 6.00 am until 2.30 pm |
| | or | 8.00 am until 4.30 pm |
| Nightshift | Sunday to Thursday | 9.00 pm until 5.18 am |

*Breaks*
During each shift the following breaks will apply:
- 1 × 30-minute lunch break
- 1 × 15-minute tea break
- 2 × 10-minute tea breaks

*Service day holidays*
Qualification periods for 5 days' holiday to be reduced to 13 years.

*Death in service*
Sum assured benefit increased to £10,000.

*Holidays*
5 days of public holiday to become annual holiday commencing 1 April 2003.

---

Second, there are procedural rules (agreements) which set standards of conduct to be met by employers and employees in resolving specific differences. In this sense they provide the 'law and order' for the workplace. They constitute criteria by which reasonable, fair and consistent behaviour by employers can be judged by employees and outside institutions, such as employment tribunals. Procedural 'rules' also send a message to all employees on how they will be treated should the specific issue arise.

In practice, organisations – whether unionised or not – have a wide range of procedural arrangements and agreements that cover such specific rules as:

- disputes
- employee grievances
- discipline
- redundancy
- union recognition
- job grading
- health and safety
- promotion
- staff development and career review.

An example of a procedural agreement (*Appeals against grading*) is shown below. The 2004 *Workplace Employment Relations Survey* reported that in 88% of establishments surveyed there was an individual grievance procedure, whereas 91% had a formal procedure for dealing with disciplinary issues.

---

### CLERICAL STAFF PROCEDURE AGREEMENT
### SECTION FIVE: APPEALS AGAINST GRADING

*1 Individual right to appeal*
Where an employee is dissatisfied with the decision of the University at the annual review concerning an application for regrading on the grounds of increased duties and responsibilities, he/she may apply in writing within three weeks to the Director of Personnel to have his/her case considered by an Appeals Panel constituted as below.

*2 Appeals Panel – membership*
The Appeals Panel shall consist of five members, as follows:
a) two members nominated by the University
b) two members nominated by the Association
c) one member, who shall act as Convenor, acceptable to the University and the Association.

### PROCEDURE FOR APPEALS
*Persons involved in the hearing*
a) the appellant

b) a colleague or trade union representative of the appellant if he/she wishes

c) a Personnel Officer

d) the Head of Department or his/her nominee.

*Prior to the hearing*

a) The Panel shall have available to it all the original documentation.

b) Each party shall make available a statement of case to the Panel.

c) Written statements and supporting documents, if any, should be in the hands of the Personnel Officer eight working days prior to the hearing. These together with copies of all the original documents will be circulated to the members of the Panel four working days prior to the hearing.

*The hearing of the appeal*

a) The appellant or his/her representative may, if they wish, present a short summary of the case to the Panel.

b) The members of the Panel may then ask questions of any of those present.

c) The appellant will withdraw from the hearing.

d) The Personnel Officer will be asked to present the University's case.

e) The Head of Department or his/her nominee will be asked to present the departmental view of the merits of the case, and the members of the Panel may ask questions.

*Consideration of the appeal*

a) The Panel will then consider its decision after all parties have withdrawn.

b) The decision will be by a simple vote of the Panel. The decision of the Panel is binding on all parties.

---

## REFLECTIVE ACTIVITY

Select three procedures which operate in your organisation. Explain how they demonstrate that management behaves fairly and reasonably in operating these procedures.

## THE LEGAL STATUS OF COLLECTIVE AGREEMENTS

Rules that are set out in collective agreements have a unique status in the UK in that they are not legally binding on the parties who have signed them. If either the union or management acts contrarily to the agreement, the other party cannot enforce its rights outlined in the agreement via the courts. Collective agreements are binding in honour only. In almost every other democratic society, collective agreements between unions and employers are legally binding and enforceable through the courts.

A consequential property of non-legally-binding collective agreements is that they are not comprehensive: their wording can be relatively imprecise. This reinforces the requirement for employers to have a disputes procedure to resolve differences with their employees over whether the agreement is being applied properly. The style of UK collective agreements also reflects that they are normally subject to review and renegotiation on an annual basis.

## DIMENSIONS OF AGREEMENT RULES

Employment rules can be analysed by their dimensions. The main dimensions are:

- scope (ie the subjects covered)
- formality (ie whether they are written or unwritten)
- level
- bargaining units (ie the employees covered).

The scope (ie the subjects covered) of employment regulation rules varies widely but normally covers some, or all, of the following:

- pay levels and structure
- overtime and shift payments
- incentive (bonus/performance-related pay) payments
- hours of work and paid holidays
- working arrangements and productivity
- training and re-training opportunities
- the means of resolving disputes, individual grievances, etc.

It is traditional for pay rates and working arrangement rules to be reviewed and amended annually by the signatories to the agreement. Hours of work and paid annual holidays are normally reviewed and changed at less frequent intervals. Procedural arrangements invariably remain unchanged for many years.

Rules and regulations governing employment conditions can also be analysed in terms of their formality. The vast majority of rules regardless of authorship are written out in full, but there are some which do not exist in written form. Such rules are held to remain in force through 'custom and practice'. The employees have operated the working practice for many years. The employers have gone along with this behaviour although they have never formally agreed it with their employees. The practice has become accepted – and if management was to try to change it, the employees are likely to expect something in return.

Employment regulation rules can operate at different levels. Some apply only to the place where those covered by them work; others apply to all workers in the company, as is seen in the Ford Motor Company and ICI. Some rules cover a group of workers in an enterprise whereas others relate to all (or certain grades of) workers in an industry. Over the past 30 years, many employers have withdrawn from operating under national agreements, often supplemented by local bargaining, preferring to bargain collectively (especially over pay) with their employees at a more decentralised level, considering this necessary to recruit, motivate, retain and reward the right calibre of employees if the success of the business is to be secured.

The workplace rules can also be analysed in terms of the number of workers they cover. In the case of collectively bargained agreements, that number is referred to as the size of the bargaining unit. In some unionised organisations, management operates by concluding separate agreements with separate trade unions that represent different groups of employees and that thus have a multiplicity of bargaining units and collective agreements. With the decline in the presence of trade unions at the workplace, such situations are less common than they were 10 years ago.

However, other companies prefer to have a single set of rules and regulations to cover all relevant groups. They have one unit covering significant numbers of employees and possibly a different number of trade unions or employee representative groups. In unionised situations this is referred to as single-table bargaining, in which all recognised trade unions sit at the same table with the employer. Yet other managements may believe their business objectives to be more achievable if they have one employing 'unit' in which all employees are represented by a single representative body – a situation that is known in unionised companies as a single-union agreement situation.

Non-union companies, like unionised ones, have substantive and procedural sets of rules but these will have been authored by the employer and only the most professional of employers will have consulted with their workforce in doing so. In non-union companies, employment rules can also be analysed in terms of their scope (ie issues covered by information and consultation arrangements) and the number of workers to which they apply. Some information and communication systems apply to all workers in the enterprise, whereas others apply only to some groups. Quality circles, on the other hand, are usually confined to small groups from the same work area who carry out similar job tasks and activities. Performance-related pay schemes often will apply to certain occupational groups (eg managers in strategic positions) within an enterprise or workplace. Financial participation schemes again differ as to the workers covered. Some embrace all employees (eg profit-sharing and profit-related pay) whereas others are confined to certain occupational groups (eg share option schemes). Although the practices used in non-union companies may not be directly based on trade union organisation, they often parallel practices in unionised companies.

## WORKFORCE AGREEMENTS

The Working Time Regulations (1998) have given rise to a new form of agreement entitled 'workforce agreements'. The Regulations allow for some of the measures to be adopted through agreements between workers and employers so as to permit flexibility to take account of the specific needs of local working agreements. Employers and workers are expected to come to a consensus on which of three types of agreements – collective agreements, workforce agreements and relevant agreements – is the most appropriate to their circumstances.

Workforce agreements enable employers to fix working time arrangements with workers who do not have any terms or conditions set by a collective agreement. Workforce agreements allow employers to decide for themselves how to use the flexibilities permitted in the implementation of the Regulations. A workforce agreement may apply to the whole of the workforce or to a group within it. Where it is to apply to a group of workers, the group must share a workplace function or organisational unit within a business.

**THEORY**  EMPLOYMENT RELATIONS THEORIES

We now know that the study of employment relations involves actors (employers and their institutions and employees and their institutions, government agencies) using various processes (employee involvement, employee engagement, collective bargaining, etc) to conclude, within an internal and external economic, political (legal) and technological environment, rules to govern behaviour at the level of the workplace and the work community. These rules can be singly or jointly authored, operate at different levels (national, sector, workplace) and be of different types (procedural/substantive). We can now move on to examine the main theoretical perspectives that have been developed to explain employment relations behaviour (see Table 2.1 below), after which we identify which of these approaches correspond to the central theoretical thrust of this book.

Table 2.1 Theoretical approaches to employment relations

| Systems theory | Marxist approaches | Frames of reference |
|---|---|---|
| Web of rules (output) <br> ↓ <br> Actors <br> (employers/employees/ state agencies) <br> ↓ <br> Environmental context <br> (technology/markets/ power distribution) <br> ↓ <br> Ideology | • Antagonist class relations between labour and capital <br> • Radical conflict of interest between labour and capital underlines what happens in employment relations <br> • An increasing power struggle is an essential feature of employment relations | *Unitarism* <br> Workers and managers united by common interests and values: enterprise is harmonious <br> *Pluralism* <br> Recognising differing interests in the employment relationship: conflict channelled through institutions <br> *Radicalism* <br> Gross disparity of power between the employer and the individual employee (property-less) |

**THEORY**  SYSTEMS THEORY

The first systematic attempt to formulate a theoretical framework of employment relations was John Dunlop's *industrial relations system* (1958). With reference to Parsons' theory of social systems, Dunlop defined the industrial relations system as an analytical subsystem of industrial societies and located it on the same logical plane as an economic system. Dunlop's work had the advantage of positioning the core components of an industrial relations system and made the rules and norms of the workplace and the works community the centrepiece of analysis, as opposed to the then accepted orthodoxy of industrial conflict or collective bargaining.

Dunlop saw the industrial relations system as a web of rules. He identified the basic components of an industrial relations system as: three groups of actors (managers, workers and their respective organisations, and governmental institutions dealing with industrial relations), three different environmental contexts (technology, markets, and economic and power distribution) and an ideology that consists of the common beliefs of the actors and that binds the industrial relations system together. In Dunlop's model the dependent variable is rules that govern industrial relations behaviour at various levels (international, national, sector, etc), whereas the interaction between the actors, contexts and ideology is the independent variable. Dunlop's approach has been subject to a number of criticisms:

- It is simply a statement of how the rules of the workplace are made and cannot be presented as a general theory of industrial relations. It is solely 'a general framework to organise a description of the interaction between the actors, the environmental context and the ideologies'. It merely collapses to an identification of the key elements and components that have to be given weight when analysing an industrial relations system.

- The rationale of a theory is a hypothesis based on one or more cause-and-effect relationship. Dunlop's model does not construct any hypothesis. He did, however, provide a useful conceptual framework that helps identify key features and processes of the industrial relations system.

- Little attention is given to the employment relationship in the model, which is a central variable in any employment relations system. Dunlop regarded industrial relations more expansively to include all relations between workers, management and governmental agencies and in which the central concern is the 'web of rules'.

- A number of important elements are omitted: for example, no account (let alone an analysis) of the processes by which the rules of the industrial relations system are determined is addressed, and only fleeting attention is given to the role of the state in this regard.

- The dimension of conflict and change is underrated. The essential focus of the systems model is stability as the central purpose of the industrial relations system rather than industrial disputes or wage-settling through collective bargaining.

## MARXIST APPROACHES

THEORY

The term 'employment relations' does not exist in the writing of Karl Marx because the regulation of the class struggle through institutional channels of conflict resolution was unknown at the time. The core institutions, however, underpinning industrial relations – free markets and the factory system – were main components of Marx's analysis of industrial capitalism. Marx approved of the growth of trade unions but his intellectual focus was not on their functions as regulators of wages and other employment conditions but on their role as organisers of workers' resistance against exploitation, estrangement and impoverishment, leading the eventual overthrow of the capitalist wage system. For Marxists, the class struggle to achieve this objective has to continue until the final victory of full industrial democracy is achieved either by revolutionary actions or by social reforms. The present-day employment relations theories that can be traced to Marxist origins include two schools of thought: the political economy of industrial relations and the labour process analysis.

THEORY **The political economy of industrial relations**

This approach is best seen in Richard Hyman's textbook *Industrial Relations: A Marxist introduction*, published in 1975. He argued that to define industrial relations in terms of a web of rules was far too narrow and implied that employment relations is all about the maintenance of stability and regularity in industry and how any industrial conflict is contained and controlled. He declared that in this approach the processes through which disagreement and disputes between employers and employees are generated are ignored, and the question of whether existing structures of ownership and control in industry is an intrinsic source of conflict is regarded as merely external to the study of employment/industrial relations. For Hyman, the concept of 'order' and 'regulation' were only one side of employment relations, and instability and disorder must be evaluated as of equal significance in systems theory.

This led Hyman to conclude that the study of industrial relations was not that of job regulation (ie a web of rules) but rather 'the study of processes of control over work relations'. He was convinced, however, that those processes could be theoretically explained only with reference to class structure and the capitalist environment – in particular, the capitalist accommodation and crisis processes – as well as political, social and ideological power relations.

A different Marxist approach to the political economy of employment relations is provided by John Kelly in his book *Rethinking Industrial Relations*, published in 1998, in which he combined a social psychological mobilisation theory with the economic long-wave trade-cycle theory. Taking the Marxist view of the employment relationship as a given, he argues that exploitation and domination by employers give rise to worker-perceived injustice, which in turn leads to a collective response from workers to remove their grievances. For Kelly, workers' interests and their collective identity are the real forces to be mobilised. In this environmental context militants play a key role, acting to help spread the feeling of injustice and to elevate the collective identity of workers. Kelly's thesis, however, recognises that employers do not sit back and let this happen. They counter-mobilise against trade unions with the support of the capitalist state. This, Kelly says, makes it difficult for workers to achieve the status of a class-conscious collectivity.

Kelly postulated the questions 'How do workers come to define dissatisfaction as an injustice?' and 'How do they come to acquire a shared identity with their fellow employees that divides them from their employer?' He found the answer in long-wave trade-cycle theory. He claims that each turning point between upswing and downswing is associated with an upsurge of mobilisation expressed by increased strike activity. This worker mobilisation is said to induce a period of counter-mobilisation by employers and the state, causing a period of increased class struggle. The implication for employment relations is 'a more or less far-reaching re-construction of the relations between labour, capital and the state'. During the ensuing long wave, the new patterns of employment relations are gradually consolidated until the next transition. Focusing on exploitation, conflict, power and collective mobilisation, Kelly's approach provides a framework which may explain change and the long-run trends in the unequal exchange between capital and labour, but which leaves one ignorant about the nature, operation and effectiveness of the institutions, processes and procedures of employment relations.

## The labour process debate

THEORY

Another strand of a Marxist approach is the debate on the character of the labour process. The focus of the discussion is the so-called transformation problem, which Marx had already defined as the transformation of (bought) labour power into performed work or, expressed more simply, the problem of managerial control of labour. The labour process debate stems from the work of Harry Braverman in his book *Labour and Monopoly Capital*, published in 1974, in which he argued that the key task of capitalist management is the continual control of the labour process in order to extract a maximum of surplus value by transforming labour power into work performance. Armed with Taylor's 'scientific management' and the advanced machinery of industrial technology, management commands the optimal means and methods of a nearly complete control of the labour process. Because management adopts Taylor's policy of rigid separation between planning (management) and implementation (workers), together with progressive division and dissection of labour and progressive mechanisation and automation, the process of degradation of work should accelerate not only in factories but also in offices.

Central to Braverman's theories is that management (capital) controls technology and uses it as a management tool to increase capitalist power and exploitation. In short, technology, machinery and equipment are used by management to deprive the workers systematically of their control of the job. Workers become de-skilled, management acquires greater and greater control, and workers become more homogenous. Given the dynamics of exploitation and control, relationships between capital (management) and labour (workers) in the workplace are of 'structured antagonism'. At the same time, management (capital), in order constantly to revolutionise the work process, requires some level of co-operation from the workforce. The result is a continuum of worker responses ranging from resistance to accommodation, compliance and consent. The framework of the labour process approach thus focuses primarily on the workplace, and not institutions.

FRAMES OF REFERENCE

Alan Fox's research paper from the Donovan Commission (1965–8), entitled *Frames of Reference*, identifies a unitary and a pluralist frame of reference by which employment behaviour might be explained. In 1974 he identified a third frame of reference, which he called the 'radical' perspective. The pluralist approach recognises the differing interests in the employment relationship and supports the channelling and institutionalising of these via trade unions, collective bargaining and procedural agreements. Unitarism, by contrast, views the enterprise as a harmonious whole, with workers and managers united by common interests and values. The radical approach emphasises the gross disparity of power between the employer (propertied) and the individual employee (property-less). Between them these three perspectives illustrate sharply contrasting views people may hold of the social and industrial scene and the way in which these views affect their interpretation of employment relations events and consequent behaviour.

Pluralists see the organisation as a coalition of interest groups presided over by a top management which serves the long-term needs of the organisation as a whole by paying due concern to all the interests affected – employees, shareholders, customers, the community and the national interest. This involves management holding the 'right' balance between the divergent claims of all these participant interests. Through collective organisation – for example, in trade unions – employees are seen to mobilise themselves to meet management on more equal terms to bargain on the terms of this accommodation of interests. Pluralists do not claim anything approaching perfection for this system. They accept that in some situations imbalances in the relative bargaining power between employers and employees (unions) or between management and a particular group of employees may be such that for one side or the other, justice (the outcome) is distinctly rough. Such situations, however, are not seen as so numerous or unfair as generally to discredit the system either from the employees' point of view or from that of management.

Unitarists propagate a concept of an enterprise (organisation) in which management is the only legitimate source of authority, control and leadership. The enterprise is viewed as a united team pulling together for the common good. Conflict is seen to be the result of irrational behaviour and of 'troublemakers' having infiltrated the organisation. These external influences are to be resisted and removed from the enterprise. Unitarists therefore deplore concepts of an enterprise which acknowledges the legitimacy within it of organised groups that see their interests as different from those of top management and engage in conflict with management and occasionally with each other. Such concepts, they feel, are bound to strengthen the legitimacy and public acceptance of trade unions thereby strengthening their collective challenge to management's authority and threatening profits, economic progress and the freedom of the individual worker. A trade union is seen, by unitarists, as a purely external self-seeking force trying to assert itself in an otherwise integrated and unified organisation.

In certain circumstances, employers and managers may succeed in persuading employees to share their unitary frame of reference. Such circumstances would include:

- small establishments
- old family firms
- paternalist concerns with many long-service employees and a charismatic figure at the top
- firms in relatively isolated areas where alternative jobs are few and the right of traditional authority still remains
- cultures or subcultures which still fully legitimise the role of 'the boss'.

The starting point for those holding the radical frame of reference is the largely unequal distribution of power between the employer and the individual employee. Lacking property or command over resources, the employee is seen as totally dependent on being offered employment by the owners or controllers of property, and so the dependent relationship between the employer and the employee is a power relationship. From this position of weakness, employees have little ability to assert their needs and aspirations against those of the employer who can, therefore, treat them not as an end in themselves but as a means to the employer's own ends. Employees say that 'radicals' are treated as a commodity. Unlike pluralists, however, the radicals do not see the collective organisation of employees into, say, trade unions as restoring the balance of power (or anything as yet approaching it) between the propertied classes and the property-less.

Some supporters of the radical frame of reference argue that the imbalance of power enables employees to challenge some kinds of management decisions on issues of special or immediate importance for them. But radicals claim that a great imbalance remains evidenced by the fact that there are many other types of managerial decisions which employees might aspire to influence, were they conscious of having the power to do so, but from which they are excluded. Trade unions are viewed by 'radicals' as striving to achieve managerial improvements to the lot of their members and to defend them against arbitrary management behaviour. They are not seen to challenge management on such basic principles as the social and industrial framework of private property, the hierarchical nature of the organisation, the extreme division of labour and the large inequalities of financial reward, status, control and autonomy at work. Unions are also criticised by those handling the radical frame of reference for a failure to challenge the treatment of labour as a commodity to be 'hired or fired' at management's convenience. Thus for 'radicals', while the employees may be able to secure from the employer marginal improvements in their relatively lowly position, that position is essentially imposed upon them by the great structural inequalities of property ownership and economic power officially sanctioned and supported by the economic forces of the state. What, therefore, those who hold the radical frame of reference ask, does the radically minded employee owe the employer to obey organisation rules even when they are 'jointly agreed' and have been negotiated within an unequal power relationship?

This book adopts a pluralist perspective. The authors accept that there are different interests within and between the employment relations actors and their institutions. The actors recognise that if they do not reconcile these fundamental differences of interest, a number of undesirable costs arise – for example, for employees a lack of work and income, and for the employer a lack of product or service to take to the marketplace to gain income and profits for the most efficient and effective delivery of public services. These costs lead the actors ('players') to realise that they have a common interest in trying to ensure that their differences are reconciled. The rules are the outward expression of this reconciliation of the differences of interests between the stakeholders of the employment relations system. We also support the system model of John Dunlop in that it identifies the elementary components of which an employment relations system is composed. Students have to understand these components before they can start to consider the various theories said to explain employment relations behaviour. To do otherwise would be like discussing whether we were observing an Indian or African elephant without knowing what an elephant is. We now turn to examine the different interests between and within the actors and the common interests that lead to the reconciliation of those differences.

## EMPLOYERS' INTERESTS IN THE LABOUR MARKET

Employment relations is a management problem-solving activity designed to establish the rules, regulations and agreement to regulate the workplace and the work community. Employers seek to secure the services of employees on the most advantageous terms they can through offering a package of employment conditions that contains monetary (pay, paid holidays, etc) and non-monetary (opportunities for career development, good working conditions, colleagues) advantages and disadvantages.

### THE EMPLOYER'S EMPLOYMENT PACKAGE

The monetary considerations taken into account by an employer in purchasing the services of employees include:

- pay
- hours of work
- paid holidays
- sick pay schemes
- incentive schemes
- pension arrangements
- the provision of family-friendly policies such as childcare facilities, flexible working arrangements, etc.

In return for the provision of these items, employers expect their employees to provide, depending on the skill and status of the job:

- flexibility between tasks (functional flexibility)
- minimum standards of competency in the task for which they are being hired as expressed in qualifications, training received and the employees' experience
- a willingness to change (aptitude and adaptability)
- an ability to work as a member of a team
- a capability to show initiative
- a talent to give discretionary effort
- a demonstrable commitment to the organisation's objectives.

In recruiting employees, the employer trades off items in a package of conditions. A management that would, for example, like to be able to hire and fire its employees at will (numerical flexibility) may be willing to offer potential employees – depending on the state of the labour market – a higher financial reward to compensate for the reduced job security. However, if jobs are scarce, an employer may not have to make such a trade-off. Employers who prefer to deploy their employees thereby requiring flexibility between various tasks, are likely to offer a package of higher financial rewards in order to attract employees who can adapt relatively easily to change.

If employers wish to take on high-quality employees, in terms of skills, attitude, etc, they may offer a package of financial rewards that is more advantageous than those being offered by employers who are happy to purchase lower-quality employees. In every sector of the economy there are some employers who are more prepared than their competitors to invest in better employment conditions. The argument is that the higher financial rewards given to the employees are more than offset by the increased productivity, lower labour turnover, greater motivation, etc, that result from acquiring higher-quality employees.

In recruiting employees, the employer cannot ignore the longer-term interests of their organisation. Although employers may like to hire and fire employees at will, they nevertheless require a core of permanent employees to provide continuity and some stability if they are to survive in the marketplace. The size of this core workforce, in relation to those hired and fired at will, is a matter for commercial judgement by each organisation.

The package offered, and accepted, by employees may be minimal, consisting of low wages, long hours, few opportunities to acquire and develop skills and little employment security. Employees may be prepared to accept such a package because the alternative is unemployment. However, employees who work under such an employment package are likely to have low morale, perform at standards below their capability and feel no commitment, loyalty or engagement with their employer. Low morale, low commitment and low engagement have adverse consequences for an organisation's economic performance and/or quality of service or products offered to customers. In the long run, the employment of 'poor'-quality employees increases an organisation's costs, reduces its competitiveness in the product market and puts at risk its very survival.

In recruiting and selecting employees, the package of conditions the employer will have to offer is influenced by the relative balance of bargaining power between the two parties. If the relative bargaining power favours the employer, they will offer potential employees a lesser package of conditions than if the power relationship were reversed. If employers abuse this market power by offering unacceptably low wages and conditions, pressures will develop for the state to restrain – by legal regulation – the misuse of such power. It was such behaviour – admittedly, on the part of a small number of employers – that led to the imposition by the UK Government, from 1 April 1999, of a national minimum wage to be paid to all those in paid employment aged over 18. So in offering a package of conditions to employees, employers must have regard to longer-term considerations and not merely to what can 'be got away with' in the short run.

> ## ❓ REFLECTIVE ACTIVITY
>
> Consider a group of employees in your organisation. What package of monetary and non-monetary employment conditions does your organisation offer to attract that group to come to work for it, and to continue to work for it? Why that package?

## EMPLOYEE INTERESTS IN THE LABOUR MARKET

In the labour market, employees seek from employers the best possible available package of monetary and non-monetary employment conditions available. The monetary aspects include wage/salary rates, hours of work, paid holidays, pension schemes, sick pay arrangements, incentive schemes, childcare facilities and flexible working arrangement opportunities. The non-monetary elements involve such items as:

- employment security
- the opportunity to work with good colleagues in a sociable atmosphere
- the potential for advancement and promotion
- access to training and development opportunities to upgrade skills, acquire new skills, etc
- being treated as a human being, not merely a commodity
- job satisfaction in relation to job design, degree of control over the job (empowerment)
- family-friendly employment policies (eg flexible working arrangements) which enable a balance to be achieved between being a family person and the need to take paid employment to provide for that family
- fair and consistent treatment by managers relative to other employees
- influence on the day-to-day operations at the workplace and at policy level (a voice in management).

Like employers, employees also give different weight to the items in the package of employment conditions on offer. They may, for example, be prepared to work for lower wages if this is compensated by greater employment security. Some other employees may, for example, stay with an organisation even though it pays relatively less than other firms because unlike them it practises employee involvement and empowerment and employee engagement by vesting decision-making with the team leaders or promotes self-managing teams.

It is impossible to tell what a 'standard mix' of benefits sought from employment by employees would include. Motivation theory postulates that each individual is stimulated by his or her own package, and that as economic and social conditions change, the pressures on employees alter with them. The balance between the various items in the package depends on many factors, including age, family circumstances, local and industry-specific employment conditions and the national scene. Nevertheless, employees – like any seller in a marketplace – seek the best possible package of monetary and non-monetary employment conditions.

## REFLECTIVE ACTIVITY

What is your monetary and non-monetary package of employment conditions?

Which are the most important to you? Why?

## THE EMPLOYMENT RELATIONSHIP

The employment relationship has some similarities with all transactions. A golden rule of buying is to purchase goods or services of acceptable quality, at the lowest price obtainable. The employee wishes to sell at the highest possible price. To reach agreement, employees and employers must accommodate each other's interests and establish an appropriate package of employment conditions.

However, the employment relationship is more stable and longer-term than that between the buyer and seller of a commodity such as a house or piece of equipment, furniture, etc. In that kind of activity, the buyers and sellers engage in a one-off and immediate exchange relationship. The parties involved in the labour market, on the other hand, are entering what is expected to be a long-term relationship involving terms that will be reviewed periodically and amended if necessary. In short, a particular feature of the employment relationship is that it has a future.

### DIFFERENT INTERESTS WITHIN MANAGEMENT

There are differences of interest within management at all levels of an organisation, including the workplace. Although working to a common end, management is not a united whole. Managers have differences which, like those between the employers and employees, have to be reconciled if corporate objectives are to be achieved.

In larger organisations, common management activities are divided into different functions – for example, marketing, production-operations, personnel and finance. These management interest groups have a common interest in the survival and growth of the business but often have different and competing interests at the same time. While the common aim of all is to ensure that the products or services reach their destinations at the right time, and are of the right quality, internal power struggles (management politics) and competition for shares of a finite resource often play off one management interest against another.

The main aim of production-operations management is usually the achievement of production targets, and to this end they may consider the organisation's best interests are served by employment policies that permit the hiring and firing of employees and the granting of employee demands to prevent production-service disruptions. This approach is likely to conflict with that of people managers, who may consider the organisation's interests are best served by recruiting, selecting and/or dismissing employees in accordance with good personnel practices, and rewarding them on objective criteria rather than in order solely to meet market demand at any cost.

Differences between interest groups within management are resolved by bargaining between themselves or by arbitration by a more senior manager. Using persuasion and perhaps making constructive compromises, managers seek to gain the commitment of their managerial colleagues to their proposed course of action. Should managers at the same level of seniority be unable to settle their differences by bargaining, a more senior level of manager will arbitrate and decide the appropriate course of action to be adopted.

Employment relations professionals cannot take it for granted that what they propose will be accepted at once and without question by other managers. However, differences between managers have to be reconciled in a constructive, not a destructive, manner. Most management differences can be resolved quickly. As an employment relations professional, you will find yourself frequently bargaining with your management colleagues (at the same, a lower or a higher level of seniority) to resolve differences over what constitutes 'good' employment relations policies and practices to be implemented if the organisation is to achieve its objectives.

## REFLECTIVE ACTIVITY

When did you last have a difference with a colleague over how a problem should be resolved? What was the problem about? What were the differences between you?

What was the resolution of the difference?

Why was there a difference in the first place?

## DIFFERENT INTERESTS AMONG EMPLOYEES

Just as there are a plurality of interests within and between groups of managers, so there are within and between groups of employees. In a workplace, different types of employees (technical, professional, clerical, administrative, craft manual, semi-skilled and unskilled, etc) are employed and can have different interests from each other. Non-manual employees usually expect a positive employment conditions differential over manual workers. Skilled manual workers see their interests, relative to those of lesser skilled workers, best served by pay differentials expressed in percentage terms. If this percentage figure is reduced, skilled manual workers usually demand improvements in pay and conditions to re-establish accepted percentage differentials.

Lesser-skilled manual workers (who also tend to be low-paid) view their interests relative to skilled manual workers best served by pay differentials expressed in money terms. They oppose percentage increases in pay on the grounds that such increases widen monetary differentials. Such differences between the various groups of employees continue. These differences of interests between various groups of employees often makes it difficult for them to support each other in differences with the employers.

## THE RECOGNITION OF DIFFERENT INTERESTS

Employment relations aims to resolve differences between the various interest groups regardless of whether these groups comprise different categories of managers or employees. The bottom line is that the activity of the organisation has to continue even if the behaviour to make it happen must alter, depending on the current situation and the underlying climate of employment relations. In organisations, whether non-union or unionised, where the emphasis is on problem-solving, consultation and communications procedures, differences of interests between employers and employees are formally recognised in written statements of policy and procedures and/or in collective agreements with trade unions – as the following example of Clauses 2.3 and 2.4 (General Principles) of a union Recognition Procedural Agreement at a carpet-manufacturing firm in the West Midlands demonstrates:

2.3 The union recognises management's responsibility to plan, organise and manage the company's operation.

2.4 The company recognises the union's responsibility to represent the interests of its members and to maintain or improve their terms and conditions of employment and work within the constraints imposed on the plant by corporate policy and finance.

Another example is the boxed-off Procedural Agreement between a food manufacturer in the west of Scotland and Unite, which states in its preamble:

The company recognises the union as the sole collective bargaining agent in respect of the categories of employees coming within the scope of this agreement.

The union recognises management's responsibility to manage its establishments and accepts that the company must continue with new and improved methods of work and that the company must be able to make free and intelligent use of its labour force to achieve the highest quality of service and obtain maximum efficiency.

Yet another example of the recognition of the difference of interests between employers and employees is seen in the recognition agreement between an electricity cable manufacture in north-east England and Unite (Transport & General Workers Union Section), which contains the following:

### 3  General Principles
The company has the right to manage the business and direct its affairs and workforce in the efficient pursuit of the organisation's business.

The company recognises the union's responsibility to manage its affairs and to represent the interests of its members.

Both parties agree the need to maintain open and direct communications with all employees on matters of mutual interest and concern.

The aim of employment relations is to resolve areas of conflicting interests and to identify and pursue areas of common interest so as to maintain the business organisation. We now turn to these common interests.

## EMPLOYER–EMPLOYEE COMMON INTERESTS

Unless the organisation keeps running, there is nothing to manage, no profit is made, no service is provided for customers and no pay is made because there is no work done. Although employers and employees have different interests, they have a common interest in ensuring that their different interests are reconciled. There are strong economic pressures on employers and employees to accommodate each other's interests rather than to perpetuate their differences.

### COSTS TO EMPLOYERS

If employers fail to reconcile their different interests with their employees, a number of costs arise:

- The employer has no goods/services to sell in the marketplace.
- The employer cannot earn profit or provide services at value for money.
- Goods and services cannot be supplied to the marketplace at the right price, at the right time and at the right quality.
- Customer needs cannot be satisfied.

- Factories, offices and shops, etc, lie idle or close down.
- Customers take their business to competitor firms.

## COSTS TO EMPLOYEES

The consequences for employees who fail to resolve their different interests from employers are equally obvious:

- They do not remain in employment.
- They do not receive a steady income stream.
- They have no power as consumers.
- They cannot enter into long-term financial commitments (eg mortgages, bank loans, hire purchase contracts).
- They accumulate no employment benefits based on continuity of employment (eg paid holidays, sick pay entitlement and pension payments).
- There is no certainty as to the future level of income.

If employees gain no income from employment, they become dependent on the state for a minimum level of income to satisfy their basic needs of housing, heating, lighting, food, etc.

## THE RECOGNITION OF COMMON INTERESTS

Both employers and employees have an enlightened self-interest in ensuring that their differing interests are reconciled. Enlightened self-interest also helps produce a bottom line beyond which it is not worth pushing for one's own self-interest against the interests of the other party. Interest reconciliation potentially brings mutual gain. Employers secure the survival of their enterprises, gain profit or provide services at value for money, and satisfy the needs of their customers. Employees obtain job security and benefit from more income security, consumer power and status from being employed. Both employers and employees have a common interest in ensuring that companies/enterprises are successful. However, there are occasions when this common interest might not seem very common to employees, especially when told by management that they are to be made redundant because cost cuts are required to re-establish the viability of the enterprise.

The recognition of this common interest is important and is frequently formally stated in agreements between employers and employees. For example, the 2007 National Agreement between the Scottish Print Employers' Federation and the Graphical, Paper and Media Union Sector of Unite says:

> **2  Unit Cost and Competitiveness**
> The parties recognise that the whole basis of the market for printed products is changing rapidly, posing new challenges for everyone engaged in the industry. It is of fundamental importance that those challenges are met with a positive response from employers and employees in order to

secure the future of Scottish printing in the face of intensifying domestic and international competition. The parties willingly accept the need for companies to attain the highest standards in meeting customers' requirements, in particular the need for continuous improvement in increasing efficiency at reducing unit costs.

It is therefore agreed that at individual company level, management and chapel [workplace] representatives will co-operate fully in identifying, discussing and implementing any changes necessary to achieve increased output and lower unit costs through the most effective use of people, materials and machines.

It is further agreed that where practical, managements and chapels will agree and implement efficiency and productivity measures sufficient to offset in full additional costs arising from the national wages and conditions settlement. Such measures can be wide-ranging in scope.

No person will be made redundant as a direct result of implementing this clause ...

Similarly, the Constitution and Memorandum of Agreement between Unite and the Road Haulage Association Ltd for the Road Haulage Industry (Hire and Reward) contains the following paragraph:

### Objects and Functions:
3   The objects of the Council should be to promote joint action for their mutual benefit by organisations of employers and working people.

Clauses 6.2 and 6.3 of Section 6, entitled *Competitive Advantage*, of the pay and conditions agreement between Scottish Power, Power Systems, Scotland and Unite, GMB and UNISON state:

6.2   A key part of the competitive advantage strategy will be continuous improvement in all Power Systems activities to ensure that changing business demands can be rapidly met and best working practices, identified through benchmarking and other means, are safely implemented within the normal joint processes so that competitive advantage can be developed and maintained.

6.3   The Division and the Trade Unions agree that to achieve and maintain competitive advantage, continuous improvement and the changes which will result will be implemented on an ongoing basis, subject to the normal joint processes.

One more example of the mutual recognition of employers and trade unions and employees of common interest can be seen in the following clause taken from a recognition and procedural agreement in the further education sector:

College management, trade union and staff representatives have a common objective in the long term of ensuring the efficiency and effectiveness of the college in the interests of the students and the staff ...

The common need for employers and employees to reconcile their different interests to mutual advantage is stressed in the National Joint Council for Local Authority Fire and Rescue Services agreement entitled *Working Together: A joint protocol for good industrial relations in the Fire and Rescue Service*. It contains the following paragraph:

> The National Joint Council (NJC) recognises that Fire and Rescue Service managers and trade union representatives must work together for the benefit of the service, its employees and local communities …

Important principles underlying this objective, at both national and local level, are the joint commitment to the success of the organisation and joint recognition of each other's legitimate interests and responsibilities.

The Papermaking Partnership, signed by the GMB, Unite and the Confederation of Paper Industries in May 2007, contained three 'pillars': work together, grow together and stay together. The *work together* pillar stated:

> Work together in a spirit of co-operation based on mutual trust and respect to maintain harmonious productive and fulfilling workplaces, resolving problems and differences at the earliest possible stage through regular and open dialogue.

One of the methods by which the different labour market interests of employers and employees are accommodated is by negotiation, which involves two parties (employers and employees) coming together to make an accommodation (agreement) by purposeful persuasion (the use of rational argument) and by making constructive compromises (identifying the common ground for a basis for agreement) towards each other's position. There are different types of negotiating situations (see Chapter 11), but the most usual of those that involve employers and employees are:

- grievance-handling to resolve a complaint by an employee that management behaviour has infringed his or her employment 'rights'

- bargaining, during which employers and employees 'trade' items within a list of demands they have made of each other

- group problem-solving, in which the employer and employee settle the details upon which the employees will co-operate with a request from management to assist in obtaining information to help solve a problem of mutual concern.

## ⸮ REFLECTIVE ACTIVITY

Why is it essential for employees and employers to reconcile their differences?

## ALTERNATIVE INTEREST RESOLUTION MECHANISMS

There are, however, other ways in which the conflict of interests is accommodated. In some cases, individuals who find their aspirations (for example, for promotion or for higher pay) cannot be met with their present employer, resign from their employment and go to work for another where their interests can be, or are more likely to be, better accommodated. Although labour turnover represents a peaceful method of resolving the differences of interests between employers and employees, management has to keep voluntary disengagements in such circumstances to manageable proportions, for labour turnover is not without cost to the employer.

In other circumstances accommodation is achieved by the employer dismissing the employee. Here the employer says it is not in the interest of the company to continue to employ the individual concerned. The employee, however, is virtually bound to hold the opposite view and see his or her interest best advanced by continuing in employment with that employer. Such opposing positions cannot be reconciled, so the employer forces the issue by dismissing the employee – who may or may not respond by complaining to an employment tribunal that he or she has been dismissed unfairly. The tribunal must then come to a decision in favour of the employer or the employee – a decision that may stipulate re-instatement, re-engagement or financial compensation. Ultimately, the tribunal resolves the difference of interests between the employer and the individual employee.

In collective disputes, on rare occasions it can prove impossible to reconcile the interests of employers and employees. During the coal-mining dispute of 1984/5 there were many skilled and patient hands at work trying to obtain a compromise settlement. However, none of their efforts served to forestall the decision of the miners to return to work after a 12-month-long strike on the same employment conditions prevailing before the dispute began in March 1984. No acceptable compromise proved available to the parties.

## SUMMARY

This chapter identified the main components of an employment relations system at an organisation, sector or national level. These were:

- the actors (employers and employees) and their institutions and the state agencies (eg ACAS) with employment relations functions
- the processes (eg employee engagement) whereby the rules governing employment relations behaviour are made
- the rules to regulate employment relationship and behaviour at the workplace. It is conventional to group these rules into two broad categories: substantive and procedural
- the internal and external environments (economic, legal and technological) to the organisation in which the employment relations system operates. These contexts influence the relative power relationship between employees and

employers and thereby the content of the rules and the processes used to determine the rules.

We then examined the various theories that have been advanced to explain employment relations behaviour. Three main groups of theories were assessed: systems theory, Marxist approaches – of which the two most important were the political economy and the labour process debate – and Alan Fox's frames of reference, of which he identified three: pluralism, unitarism and radicalism. Pluralists accept that the workplace and society is a coalition of interests, whereas unitarists accept that the organisation has one focus only of authority and loyalty (management), and that conflict is irrational and caused by troublemakers.

The book takes a pluralist view. It accepts that there are differences of interests within and between the actors and their institutions. It also accepts that the actors have common interests, including that they accommodate their differences because not to do so will result in mutual disadvantages – namely, the collapse of the organisation, no product or service to sell in the marketplace, unemployment, etc. The 'web of rules' of the employment relations system are the outward expression of the terms on which the differences of interests between employers and employees are accommodated.

## KEY LEARNING POINTS

- The study of employment relations involves actors (employers and their institutions, employees and their organisations, and state agencies) using various processes (employee involvement, employee engagement, etc) to conclude rules to govern behaviour at the level of the workplace.

- Rule-making does not take place in a vacuum. It is influenced by the internal and external economic, political (legal) and technological environment within which an organisation operates.

- The first attempt to formulate a theoretical framework of employment relations was the use by John Dunlop of systems theory – a web of rules, actors, environmental contexts and ideology (the common beliefs of the actors).

- Alternative theoretical approaches have been set out by Marxists, particularly Richard Hyman, who is prone to case employment relations theory in class terms. For him, between the two classes of labour and capital there exists a radical conflict of interests which underlies everything that occurs in employment relations. An increasing power struggle is, therefore, a central feature of employment relations.

- Fox's theoretical approach to employment relations centres around three contrasting different frames of reference which affect people's interpretation of employment events and consequent behaviour. The frames of reference are unitarism, pluralism and radicalism.

- Management is not homogenous. There are different interests within and between management. This means that management has to gain the commitment of its colleagues to the action that is proposed.

- Although there are differences of interests within and between the employment relations actors and their institutions, the actors realise that if they do not reconcile these differences, a number of undesirable costs arise. Employers, for example, lack a product or source to take to market while the employees lack work and job rewards. The employment relations rules are the outward expression of the reconciliation of the differences of interest between the stakeholders of the employment relations system.

## REVIEW QUESTIONS

1   Discuss the view that employment relations is the reconciliation of the different interests of employers and employees.

2   To what extent do you consider the Marxist perspective on employment relations is relevant to your organisation?

3   Identify at least three different types of non-strike sanctions that can be used by employees. Evaluate their likely impact on employer–employee relations.

4   You have been asked to provide a short briefing to supervisors (first-line managers) that explains the main external environment factors that affect employment relations at your organisation. What will you say, and why?

5   Explain the main features of the unitary and pluralist frame of reference approach to employment relations.

## EXPLORE FURTHER

**Theoretical perspectives on employment relations**

Ackers, P. and Wilkinson, A. (eds) (2003) *Understanding Work and Employment: Industrial Relations in Transition*. Oxford: Oxford University Press, Chapter 1, pp1–25.

Braverman, H. (1974) *Labour and Monopoly Capital: The degregation of work in the twentieth century*. New York: Monthly Review Press.

Chartered Institute of Personnel and Development (2005) *What is Employee Relations?*

Clegg, H. (1975) 'Pluralism in industrial relations', *British Journal of Industrial Relations*, Vol.13, No.2.

Dunlop, J. T. (1958) *Industrial Relations Systems*. New York: Holt.

Fox, A. (1974) *Beyond Contract: Work, power and trust relations*. London: Faber.

Hyman, R. (1975) *Industrial Relations: A Marxist introduction*. Basingstoke: Macmillan.

Institute of Personnel and Development (1997) *Employment Relations into the Twenty-first Century: An IPD Position Paper*.

Kaufman, R. (ed.) (2004) *Theoretical Perspectives on Work and Employment Relationships*. Industrial Relations Research Association Series.

Kelly, J. (1998) *Rethinking Industrial Relations: Mobilization, collectivism and long waves*. London: Routledge.

Kersley, B., Alpin, C., Forth, J., Bryson, A., Bewley, H., Dix, G. and Oxenbridge, J. (2006) *Inside the Workplace: Findings from the 2004 Workplace*

*Employment Relations Survey*. London: Routledge.

Taylor, R. (2000) *The Future of Employment Relations*. Economic and Social Research Council.

**Employment relations institutions**

Advisory, Conciliation and Arbitration Service, *Annual Report and Accounts*.

Central Arbitration Committee, *Annual Report*.

The Certification Officer, *Annual Report*.

Colling, T. and Terry, M. (2010) *Work, the Employment Relationship and the Future of Industrial Relations*. Oxford: Blackwell.

Dundon, T. and Rollinson, D. (2007) *Understanding Employment Relations*. London/New York: McGraw-Hill.

Farnham, D. (2010) *Human Resource Management in Context: Strategy, insights and solutions*, 3rd edition. London: Chartered Institute of Personnel and Development.

Grainger, H. and Crowther, M. (2007) *Trade Union Membership 2006*. London: Department of Trade and Industry.

Kersley, B., Alpin, C., Forth, J., Bryson, A., Bewley, H., Dix, G. and Oxenbridge, J. (2006) *Inside the Workplace: Findings from the 2004 Workplace Employment Relations Survey*. London: Routledge.

MacLeod, D. and Clarke, N. (2009) *Engaging for Success – Enhancing performance through employee engagement: A report to government*.

Millward, N., Bryson, A. and Forth, J. (2000) *All Change at Work?* London: Routledge.

Taylor, S. and Amir, R. (2006) *Employment Law: An introduction*. Oxford: Oxford University Press, Chapters 1–4.

**Website links**

www.acas.org.uk is the official website of the Advisory, Conciliation and Arbitration Service.

www.bis.gov.uk is the website of the Department for Business, Innovation and Skills and outlines the main provisions of employment law legislation.

www.cac.gov.uk is the website of the Central Arbitration Committee.

www.cbi.org.uk is the website of the CBI, the central employers' organisation in the UK.

www.cipd.co.uk is the official website of the Chartered Institute of Personnel and Development.

www.tuc.org is the official website of the Trades Union Congress.

http://en.wikipedia.org/wiki/employersassociations provides useful information of employers associations.

http://en.wikipedia.org/tradeunions provides information on trade unions in the UK, Europe, the USA and Australasia.

http://europa.eu/institutions is the official website for the European Union and provides information on the directives issued in the employment and social field.

## CHAPTER 3

# The Economic and Corporate Environment

## OVERVIEW

The purpose of this chapter is to examine the factors external to the organisation – economic, political (legal) and technological – that when taken together are referred to as the external corporate environment. It points out how the state plays an important part in determining the corporate environment in its role as an economic manager (macro-economic policy management) and a law-maker (legislation). In addition, the state is a direct 'player' in the employment relations system through its role as an employer. In this regard the chapter describes how the philosophy of the Government is to be seen as a 'model employer', leading the private sector by example, although the way this is demonstrated today is very different from how it was 30 years ago. The chapter then examines the objectives of the macro-economic policy of British governments since 1945, noting how the priorities given to one or more of the components of these economic objectives have differed between governments and how governments have used different means to achieve these objectives. The chapter then goes on to outline the two main bodies of economic thought applied to the macro-economic management: Keynesianism and monetarism. Until 1979 the former dominated, but post-1979 the latter has been the preferred approach. Keynesianism centred on full employment whereas monetarism gave the top priority to the control of inflation. Next, the chapter analyses the main changes in the labour market since 1945, drawing special attention to the end of the 'jobs for life' culture, the increased job insecurity, increased flexibility (numerical, functional, temporal and financial), etc, and their impact on the work of the employment relations professional. The chapter then examines the impact of technology on behaviour in the employment relations game. The chapter concludes by demonstrating how the corporate environment in which an organisation operates influences the overall conduct of employment relations.

## LEARNING OUTCOMES

When you have completed this chapter you should be able to:

- describe how the UK Government in its role as economic manager influences employment relations

- understand the principal economic theories that have been applied to the management of the economy since World War II

- explain how changes in the labour market impact on employment relations

- explain how the corporate environment affects the relative balance of bargaining power

- explain the impact of new technology on the working environment.

## INTRODUCTION

In a 1997 statement on employment relations the CIPD drew attention to the need for every organisation continually to improve its performance because of the challenges that were constantly being imposed on it by the corporate environment. Whether those challenges were intensifying product market competition from changes in the world economy or from the spending controls that continue to characterise the public sector, the pressure is much the same for all organisations. That statement is as true today as it was in 1997, and the pressures to which it refers are unlikely in the short term to diminish.

These pressures are external to the organisation, and the purpose of this chapter is to examine those factors which, when taken together, are referred to as the external corporate environment in which all organisations have to operate. It matters not whether the organisation is a large multi-national, a National Health Service trust or a medium-sized service company – their employment relations are influenced, and shaped, by the way in which the external corporate environment impacts on the workplace.

## CONTEXT

In Chapter 1 we noted that the corporate environment needed to be examined in the context of economic management, political/legal influences and technological changes. The legislative influences are more fully considered in Chapter 4, so this chapter will concentrate more on the economic, political and technological factors. These three issues are important to understanding employment relations and why organisations choose to adopt particular policies and how such policies have changed, or might change, over time.

The business environment in which employment relations professionals operate is constantly changing, and it is important for them to be aware not only of specific shifts in employment relations policies resulting from such changes but to monitor the external environment to anticipate possible changes and developments and draw up a plan to deal with these expected changes if and when they arise. Employment relations policies devised and implemented in this context have both a reactive and proactive role – a strategic role that is central to the organisation's growth and survival.

Although each of the elements is crucial in determining the employment relations practices of individual employers, the response of each to the impact on their own business or organisation is likely to be different. For example, a traditional non-union company such as Marks & Spencer is unlikely to have responded in the same way to the legislative changes introduced during the 1980s as a company that was traditionally heavily unionised. Equally, non-union organisations may react in a completely different way to changes introduced by the Employment Relations Act (1999). The statutory rights on union recognition contained within that Act have caused many organisations to have a fundamental re-think in attitudes towards collectivism and the role the workforce may play in the process of change. The 1980s changes to the laws on strikes, picketing and closed shops opened the door to employers who wanted to force through change, and had a major impact on trade union membership and influence.

Although many commentators predicted that the right to request statutory recognition would reverse the decline in union membership, this does not seem to have happened. Certainly, there were a significant number of voluntary recognition arrangements entered into in the immediate aftermath of the 1999 legislation's coming into force, and in 2003 there was a slight increase in union density. However, information from the *Workplace Employment Relations Survey* 2004 suggests that this was not sustained. The *Workplace Employment Relations Survey* (WERS) series has documented and comprehensively monitored the state of employment relations in workplaces in Britain over the past three decades, and the 2004 survey concluded that collective bargaining was clearly decreasing. The survey concluded that 'most striking of all, perhaps, was the continued decline of collective labour organisation' (see Table 3.2 *Pay determination methods 1998 and 2004* below). Employees were less likely to be union members than they were in 1998, workplaces were less likely to recognise unions for bargaining over pay and conditions, and collective bargaining was less prevalent. Even so, the rate of decline appeared to have slowed from that seen in earlier periods, and the joint regulation of terms and conditions remains a reality for many employees in Britain. One-half of employees were employed in workplaces with a recognised trade union, one-third were union members, and 40% had their pay set through collective bargaining. Nonetheless, the picture differed markedly across sectors of the economy and by workplace size, union involvement in pay setting and the joint regulation of the workplace very much the exception in the private sector and in smaller workplaces.

There has also been a decrease in the incidence of joint consultative committees. Although there has been a decline in representative forms of employee voice, there has been some growth in direct forms of communication between management and employees, including wider use of face-to-face meetings with the entire workforce or teams of employees, and greater use of systematic communication through the management chain. These trends are a continuation of changes that can be traced back through the 1990s and late 1980s. Table 3.1 below from the 2004 *Workplace Employment Relations Survey* shows union presence by sector of ownership and management attitudes towards trade unionism. Table 3.2, also from WERS (2004), shows the extent to which collective bargaining declined over the period 1998–2004 as a method of pay bargaining.

Since the WERS 2004 was completed, figures from the Department for Business, Innovation and Skills (BIS) clearly show that union membership and density continues to decline. BIS is responsible, with the Office for National Statistics (ONS), for publishing the national statistics on trade union membership, and as the box below shows, overall union membership continues to fall. You may find the following websites useful: www.bis.gov.uk and www.statistics.gov.uk.

The findings above demonstrate one of the greatest challenges that trade unions face if they are to maintain some reasonable level of density within UK workplaces, attracting younger members. It is significant that union density in the over-50 age-group remains relatively stable, while among young people it continues to decline. Following the 2009 recession, when significant numbers of older workers either were made compulsorily redundant or volunteered for

**Table 3.1 Union presence by sector of ownership and management attitudes as a percentage of workplaces**

| | Aggregate union density | No union members | Union density of 50% or more |
|---|---|---|---|
| | *% of employees* | *% of workplaces* | *% of workplaces* |
| All workplaces | 34 | 64 | 18 |
| *Sector of ownership* | | | |
| Private | 22 | 77 | 8 |
| Public | 64 | 7 | 62 |
| *Management attitudes towards union membership* | | | |
| In favour | 61 | 13 | 51 |
| Neutral | 21 | 77 | 8 |
| Not in favour | 5 | 92 | 1 |
| Actively encourages | 58 | 3 | 62 |
| Actively discourages | 5 | 100 | 0 |

Base: All employees in workplaces with 10 or more employees (column 1), and all workplaces with 10 or more employees (columns 2–3). Figures are weighted and based on responses from 21,540 employees (column 1) and 1,973 managers (columns 2–3).

Table 3.2  Pay determination methods 1998 and 2004

| | Percentage of workplaces | | | | | |
| --- | --- | --- | --- | --- | --- | --- |
| | 1998 | | | 2004 | | |
| | Public sector | Private sector | All | Public sector | Private sector | All |
| *All collective bargaining* | | | | | | |
| Only multi-employer | 28 | 2 | 8 | 36 | 1 | 7 |
| Only single-employer | 19 | 4 | 7 | 12 | 4 | 5 |
| Only workplace-level | 0 | 1 | 1 | 1 | 1 | 1 |
| *No collective bargaining* | | | | | | |
| Only set by management, higher level | 9 | 24 | 21 | 7 | 23 | 20 |
| Only set by management, workplace | 1 | 32 | 25 | 1 | 43 | 35 |
| Only set by individual negotiations | 0 | 6 | 5 | 0 | 5 | 4 |
| Only other methods* | 4 | 3 | 3 | 1 | 1 | 2 |
| (Pay review body**) | – | – | – | (1) | (0) | (1) |
| *Mixture of methods* | 39 | 28 | 31 | 41 | 23 | 26 |
| *All methods* | 100 | 100 | 100 | 100 | 100 | 100 |
| Any collective bargaining | 79 | 17 | 30 | 77 | 11 | 22 |
| Any set by management | 21 | 81 | 69 | 28 | 79 | 70 |
| Any individual negotiations | 1 | 16 | 13 | 2 | 15 | 13 |
| Any other methods* | 39 | 8 | 14 | 32 | 2 | 7 |
| (Pay review body**) | – | – | – | (32) | (0) | (6) |

Base: All workplaces with 10 or more employees. Figures are weighted and based on responses from 2,125 managers in 1998 and 1,994 managers in 2004.

*Notes:*
* In 2004 many responses coded as 'Other methods' in the interview were subsequently back-coded to specific methods, thereby lowering the incidence of 'Other methods' in comparison with 1998.
** In 1998, pay determination via Independent Pay Review Bodies was given as an example of 'other' methods, whereas in 2004 it was separately coded.

a redundancy package, it is likely that this disparity in density among different age groups will widen. If the trends in union membership continue over the next decade, as they have in the last decade, and as the 'baby boomer' generation leaves the active workforce, young workers are unlikely to be as active in trade unions as their older, and former, work colleagues.

Notwithstanding that there has been no increase in membership, many employers still have concerns that the gains made in the last 20 years in eliminating outdated working practices could be eroded. There is concern over a resurgence in trade

---

### Trade union membership 2008: key findings

- The rate of union membership (union density) for employees in the UK fell by 0.6 percentage points to 27.4% in 2008. Among all those in employment in the UK, including self-employed, union density fell from 25.3% in 2007 to 24.9% in 2008.

- Estimates of union membership for UK employees shows that membership in 2008 has fallen by 1.8% to 6.9 million compared to 2007.

- Union density among female employees in the UK fell by 0.4 percentage points to 29.2% in 2008, while for male employees it fell by 0.8 percentage points to 25.6%. For the seventh consecutive year union density of females has been higher than of males.

- Private sector union density fell by 0.6 percentage points to 15.5% in 2008, whereas public sector union density fell 1.9 percentage points in 2008 to 57.1%. The rate of change in public sector union density nearly doubled from −2.3% in 2007 to −4.2% in 2008.

- Union densities of younger age groups have fallen over the past decade. This contrasts with employees aged 50 and above, for whom there is little change in density over the same period.

- The hourly earnings of union members averaged £13.07 in 2008, 12.5% more than the earnings of non-union employees (£11.62 per hour).

- Across all sectors, just under half of UK employees (46.7%) were in a workplace where a trade union was present. One-third of UK employees said their pay and conditions were affected by a collective agreement.

- Collective agreements covered one in five private sector employees, while in the public sector collective agreement coverage was over three and a half times greater, at 70.5%.

Source: Department for Business, Innovation and Skills

---

union militancy driven by the need for all businesses and business sectors to take steps, sometimes unpopular steps, to alleviate the pressures caused by a downturn in economic activity, changes in technology, or an increase in competition. One example of this can be seen in the long-drawn-out postal dispute in 2008/9.

On one side the employers were seeking to deal with a decline in market share while at the same time maintaining their obligation to provide a comprehensive mail delivery service to the public. Their challenge was to drive through changes in working practices, pay and conditions of work in the face of fierce opposition from the workforce who were unable, or unwilling, to see how they would gain any benefit from the changes proposed by their employer. A similar situation faced British Airways in its 2009/10 dispute with cabin crew over staffing levels, pay and benefits.

Both the above disputes were not helped by the need of both organisations to address a huge deficit in their pension funds. Students should be aware that disputes in relation to pensions are likely to increase as organisations in both public and private sectors deal with the impact of increased longevity on funds that are already in serious difficulties. Many organisations have closed or are considering closing their very attractive final salary pension schemes, or at the very least capping benefits or increasing contributions. It is a very emotive subject and one that will create serious tensions in many organisations.

REFLECTIVE ACTIVITY

What are the current pension arrangements in your organisation? If yours is a private sector organisation, is there likely to be a funding deficit? If it is a public sector organisation, what impact will government proposals on changing retirement ages have?

Whatever sector you are working in, do you think that pension issues will impact on employment relations in the near future?

## CHANGE IN ORGANISATIONS

All employers have their own objectives, their own styles of employment relations and their own structures of organisations and associations. These structures have changed in recent times and it is important that the employment relations professional keeps up to date with new trends and developments. For example, the role of employers' organisations (see Chapter 6) has declined in recent years in response to moves to decentralise the levels at which collective bargaining takes place. In the private sector there is now little national bargaining while in the public sector some local authorities have decentralised traditional systems of bargaining in favour of local wage determination.

Organisational structure has changed in both the public and private sector. The structure of the National Health Service today is radically different from what it was 20 years ago. This has meant changes in the way that it manages its employment relations. Changes have also occurred in respect of employees and their organisations. The UK Government's economic policy and changes in legislation have altered the relative balance of bargaining power between employers and employees. This can explain *inter alia* changes in the level of membership of unions, causing individual unions to change their strategies to protect and advance their members' interests – for example, merging with other unions to create a number of 'super-unions'. These issues are discussed in greater detail in Chapter 6.

The role of the state in influencing employment relations has also changed. It has always been a major employer in its own right, and the post-World War II expectation was that it would become a 'model employer' by:

- encouraging collective bargaining
- ensuring that the pay of its employees was in line with that of the private sector
- resolving differences with its employees by arbitration and not the use of industrial sanctions.

This concept has now changed as the whole nature of public sector employment has altered, with former civil servants now working for quasi-private-sector employers. The growth of executive agencies, the outsourcing of local authority services and the spread of privatisation has further diluted the concept of the public servant. This dilution is set to increase as the concept of the public/private sector partnership is widened and expanded.

Most of this change resulted from the objectives of successive Conservative administrations during the 1980s and 1990s to reduce the influence of the Government on people's lives. They saw the role of the UK Government as staying outside the employment relations arena, and although the state remains a large employer, it no longer views collective bargaining, pay comparability and arbitration as central to its employment relations policies. There continues to be a strong encouragement to relate pay increases of government employees to improvements in individual performance. Although successive Labour Governments since 1997 were not as outwardly anti-union as some of their Conservative predecessors were perceived to be, there is significant evidence that the Labour Party's traditional links with the union movement are seen as less important than once they were. While this may change in the future, there is certainly no suggestion that any government will actively promote an increase in collective bargaining in its employment relations policy towards those employees whose terms and conditions of employment it directly or indirectly finances.

All this change has impacted on the nature and style of employment relations processes. As the impact of collective bargaining, and thus collective agreements, has declined, there has been a growth in the use of other employment relations processes. Joint consultation, while not a new concept, has undergone a resurgence, and employee involvement schemes (for example, two-way communication, encouraging employees to contribute their knowledge and experience to operational decisions) have become much more important. This process has been further strengthened by the EU Directive on Information and Consultation, which came into effect from 2005 onwards, depending on the size of the organisation. Additionally, as can be seen by the growing influence of 'engagement' strategies within workplaces, good managers recognise the positive impact of clear, regular and effective communication with their workforce. It is a moot point whether better dialogue and communication would have had a mitigating effect on the two disputes (Post Office and British Airways) that we highlighted above.

The concept of the balance of bargaining power and how important it is to the selection, by the employer, of appropriate employment relations processes was introduced in Chapter 1. This balance is conditioned by changes in the economic, political and technological elements which, taken together, make up the corporate environment. In this chapter the concept is examined in greater detail and linked directly to the economic, legal and technical environment in which organisations exist and compete. The concept of the balance of power is also significant in helping explain changes in the employment relations system over time – for example, why employment relations behaviour now is different from what it was in the 1970s.

**THEORY**

### REFLECTIVE ACTIVITY

List the economic, legal/political and technological factors that have impacted on your organisation in the last five to 10 years.

The economic environment is influenced by the macro-economic policies that a particular government or institutions of government – such as the Bank of England – choose to implement. In the context of the UK, policies regarding the levels of:

- employment
- inflation
- taxation
- interest rates

have a direct effect on employment relations. This is because they have an impact on the relative balance of bargaining power between the buyers and sellers of labour services and thereby the rules and regulations that govern employment conditions. For example, if we are in a period of high inflation, high levels of taxation and high interest rates, the stability of business is threatened. This can in turn lead to higher levels of unemployment and a consequent reduction in employment conditions or redundancies and lay-offs. Even when individuals are in work, a less favourable economic climate will alter their perception of continuing job security and will also have an impact on the relative balance of bargaining power.

However, it would be a mistake to assume that the UK Government has a completely free hand in deciding what economic policies to implement. The first decade of the new century saw two major events that have had a major influence on economic management. Firstly, there was the catastrophic event of 11 September 2001. In the aftermath of the terrorist attacks the financial markets went into what some described as panic mode. The Dow-Jones and FTSE plunged as investors took fright, moving their cash out of shares and into safe havens such as government bonds, and oil prices soared as the world feared a long-drawn-out war. Fortunately, within six months, some of the panic subsided and share prices began to recover – but not before thousands of jobs were lost worldwide, primarily in airlines and other associated businesses. There is no doubt, however, that the aftermath of 11 September influenced, and has continued to influence, the foreign policy of all governments (Iraq/Afghanistan), and that this in turn has had an economic impact (wars do not come cheaply) not just in the UK but also worldwide. Once the impact of 9/11 had receded, it is fair to say that the UK, and other governments, together with individual consumers, went on a massive spending spree. Levels of government, corporate and personal debt spiralled upwards, and this contributed to the initial 'sub prime' debt crisis in the US housing market and the ensuing banking meltdown in late 2008.

The effect of this unprecedented deterioration in banking confidence led, in turn, to one of the worst recessions in living memory. The stock market fell by a significant amount, wiping billions off the value of business; the bank bail-outs implemented by governments raised the level of public debt to record levels, and the supply of credit to businesses and organisations virtually dried up. All of this, not surprisingly, had an impact on the labour market and thus employment relations.

However, whatever the degree of outside influence, the UK Government has the role of an economic manager. Although different political parties may have different ideologies and policies, the objectives of economic management – whichever party is in power – have been broadly similar. These have been:

- price stability
- full employment
- economic growth
- a balance of payments surplus.

However, the priorities given to these four objectives have differed between governments. The Conservative Governments (1979–97) gave the greatest priority to price stability, whereas the Labour Governments (1974–9) put the greatest emphasis on the full employment objective. The objective of Labour Governments from 1997 onwards has been slightly different. Although they have adopted many of the economic disciplines of their predecessor Conservative Governments, their principal aim has been to establish a stable economy. One of the difficulties that Britain has endured since World War II is a propensity to 'boom and bust' in the context of the economic cycle. In order to achieve economic stability the Labour Government took a number of steps, some of them reasonably straightforward (such as controlling public spending) and some of them very radical (such as surrendering the control of interest rates to the Bank of England). Monetary policy was subcontracted to the Bank of England immediately after the 1997 General Election and has, since then, broadly been seen as a success by all the main political parties. The Bank's Monetary Policy Committee now makes decisions on interest rates, and this has helped to provide a degree of stability in Britain's financial markets.

Of course, not everybody can always be satisfied, whoever sets policy, because it would always be possible to make a good argument for cutting rates, for increasing them, and for keeping them the same. Some commentators would argue that our present system is good news for Britain because, unlike the members of the eurozone, at least we still have control over monetary policy. Their interest rates are dictated by the European Central Bank (ECB), which has to have a policy that suits the whole of the zone. This may not necessarily be in the interests of individual countries, whose economies may be growing at a faster rate than some of their euro partners. It is a difficulty used by the anti-euro camp to support their stance over non-membership.

Even though the two main political parties may have similar economic objectives, when in government the policies they implement to achieve them are likely to be different. The employment relations professional needs therefore to understand that the economic policies of a Conservative Government are likely to differ from those of a Labour Government, and that these distinctions in policy can have differing impacts on the relative balance of bargaining power. There are some politicians who believe that Britain should follow a policy of full employment and that the achievement of this goal justifies a degree of direct UK government intervention into the affairs of public and private enterprises. When this approach has been adopted, the outcome has been to give organised labour a relative advantage in the balance of relative bargaining power.

An important aspect of economic policy is the level of public expenditure. The International Monetary Fund (IMF) has repeatedly warned that financial market confidence and long-term interest rates are adversely affected if governments pay insufficient attention to the need to reduce the public sector borrowing requirement. This is an issue which, because of the huge rise in the level of government debt, will dominate debate over the next five years or more. There is no doubt that public spending will have to reduce significantly in the short to medium term to allow the balance between gross domestic product (GDP) and the public sector borrowing requirement (PSBR) to return to a more acceptable level. This is bound to have a major impact on employment relations, particularly in the public sector where, during the period 2002–8, there were major increases in spending by the Labour Government as they tried to deliver on their promise to improve the delivery and quality of public services. Initially, this was good news for supporters of Keynesian economic theories, which taught that fiscal policy should be counter-cyclical. However, there are dangers in this approach because of the impact that external influences can have on government economic policy. For example, if there were a series of adverse events impacting upon the UK economy, the Government's spending plans may be unsustainable and cause a consequent rise in interest rates and unemployment. Actually, there certainly have been a series of adverse events which, while they have not had the damaging impact on employment and interest rates, will have longer-term consequences.

Although there is, at present, no reliable data, one reason that the rise in unemployment has not been as bad as was feared is because of the willingness of employees to accept wage freezes, wage cuts and cuts in their hours in order to remain in employment. However, if the economy fails to deliver reasonable levels of growth, the present record low levels of interest rates cannot be sustained, taxation will almost certainly increase, inflationary pressures will return, and there will be a consequent rise in the numbers unemployed. These pressures will make the job of the employment relations specialist extremely important as they seek to minimise employee conflict and help to raise productivity by playing an important role in the management of change.

Of course, economic downturns – as with periods of growth – are cyclical, and the role of the 'economic manager' (government) is to put in place appropriate policies of which the most important are structural ones that might help insulate us against the ups and downs of the economic cycle. We need to keep ourselves more attractive than our rivals as a place to work and invest. In January 2010 the Labour Government sought to address this with the publication of a strategy document entitled *Going for Growth: Our future prosperity*. This document built on previous strategy documents and has as its core objective the need for government to operate 'intelligently alongside business and the dynamic of the market to strengthen the policies and foundations of British industrial competitiveness'. The view is that:

> to prosper, Britain needs to ensure that policies and investment in skills, infrastructure, innovation and finance for businesses reinforces the fundamentals of our competitiveness. Government must use its role and influence as both regulator and customer to much better effect, and government action must be targeted on those sectors and markets where it can make most difference.

This, they say,

> is the basis for a modern approach to industrial policy, and for public investment in business support, infrastructure, workforce skills and science and research.

The strategy document identified seven core capabilities in the British economy that the Labour Government believed would underpin the drive to restore strong, sustainable, long-term growth.

The seven capabilities are:

- supporting *enterprise* and entrepreneurial activity, including the access to finance required for starting and growing firms
- fostering *knowledge* creation and its application
- helping *people* develop the skills and capabilities to find work and build the businesses and industries of the future
- investing in the *infrastructure* required to support a modern low-carbon economy
- ensuring *open and competitive markets* to drive innovation and rising productivity
- building on our *industrial strengths* where we have particular expertise or might gain a comparative advantage, and where government action can have an impact
- recognising and employing the right strategic role for *government in markets* that allows us as a nation to capitalise on new opportunities.

To view the document in full and to find out about other government initiatives for stimulating economic growth, go to www.bis.gov.uk.

While it is always the role of government to identify the structural policies that are needed to raise productivity and competitiveness, many such policies are slow-burn. Starting a business that will be successful and create jobs does not happen overnight. It takes time. And whatever strategies are put in place for encouraging competitiveness and improving national productivity, the Government's role of economic management will, irrespective of their politics, be extremely difficult over the next five years. Despite the Government signalling an intent to maintain 'front-line services', there will have to be significant reductions in public expenditure or tax increases, or a mixture of both. Failing to deal with the budget deficit could have serious implications for interest rates and inflation.

Translated into employment relations terms, this usually means keeping a tight control over increases in public sector pay. Amongst private sector employers there is always concern over the possibility of any government taking a soft line on public sector pay. For example, the desire to improve rewards for groups such as nurses, the police or teachers in response to public opinion can create a 'knock-on' effect across the board. If the Government is unwilling, or unable, to keep a tight control over public sector pay settlements, then any appeals to the private sector to show restraint will fall on deaf ears. That is why one of the most important skills for the employment relations professional is the art of scanning the political and environmental landscape to establish the extent to which policy shifts may have an impact on employment relations in the future.

### REFLECTIVE ACTIVITY

Whether you are in the private or public sector, what impact will a steep decrease in public expenditure have on your organisation?

THEORY    GLOBALISATION

In economic terms, a further impact on employment relations comes from the growth in multi-national companies and the expansion of the global marketplace. 'Globalisation' is a word that is much in evidence today, but it is difficult to define. A possible all-embracing definition is 'the process of developing markets in new parts of the world for products and services developed in another part of the world, with the intention of increasing profit and spreading opportunity for return on investment'. Using the benefits of technology it is possible to migrate employment around the world to the place where conditions are most ideal for the producer – development in the 'first world', software in India, production in the third world, and a global sales team based in Brussels. Globalisation is said to be breaking down old world divisions and creating new.

The globalisation of markets, products and businesses has been a driver of major change over the past 50 years. Supporters of globalisation would argue that for both consumer and employee it has built bridges, created a greater sense of global community, and provided employment and opportunity for millions, and that this stimulus for change has created actions and events that have, on the whole, had major positive benefits for humankind.

Opponents of globalisation would refute this. Their argument is that, on the whole, companies have invested in the third world in order to take advantage of cheap labour and increase profits that have benefited Western societies. It is not our intention to agree or disagree with either of these views – our concern is with the impact globalisation has on employment relations.

Competition (which usually underpins the urge to globalise) breeds insecurity. Employees have a tendency to feel unsafe when they know that their employer is competing in the global marketplace. At any time a new process, product or service can undermine the very basis of their jobs, and this can breed insecurity. It is certainly true that we live in a world of multi-nationals, and because of the 'credit crunch' 2008/9 we have clear evidence that the intricacies of international finance drill down and have an impact on employment relations at the local level. Indeed, they can influence the location of new employment opportunities and, in some cases, the underlying culture of employment relations practices.

Multi-nationals see wage rates, expansion and investment in the context of the global market, in much the same way that a national company makes decisions after taking into account subsidies from enterprise areas, development corporations, and so on. International competition affects employment relations in other ways. Firms from the USA and Japan who set up in the UK look for qualities such as flexibility and adaptability. This has caused some of the traditional demarcation lines in industry to become blurred or removed to a great extent. The negotiation of such methods of working makes them important in the area of employment relations.

To understand how the UK Government's role as an economic manager can affect employment relations and the relative balance of bargaining power between employers and employees, it is important to review and understand the two principal economic theories that have been applied to the management of the UK economy since the end of World War II. Not least, because a reversal of the economic policies that are currently being applied could result in a high-wage, high-inflation economy.

## THE FULL EMPLOYMENT/ECONOMIC GROWTH ERA                    THEORY

For nearly 30 years after World War II, successive UK governments regardless of their political complexion were committed to a policy of full employment. During this period economic management was heavily influenced by the views of the economist John Maynard Keynes, whose basic ideas included:

- The general level of employment in an economy is determined by the level of spending power in the economy.

- The overall spending power in the economy depends upon the amount of consumption and investment undertaken by individual households and employing organisations as well as UK government expenditure on health, education, social security, defence, industrial assistance, etc.

- Full employment is achieved by the Government regulating overall spending power in the economy by its fiscal (tax), monetary (interest rates), exchange rates (value of the pound relative to other currencies) and public expenditure policies.

- If unemployment rises due to a lack of overall spending power in the economy, the Government should inject spending power by reducing taxes on private and corporate incomes, property, expenditure (VAT, excise duties), by lowering interest rates, and/or by increasing its own expenditure.

Application of the Keynesian model of economic management led to economic growth, increased public provision (in such areas as housing, education and the National Health Service) and personal prosperity for the majority of households. From the perspective of trade unions, full employment provided them with increased bargaining power which, in many instances, led employers to concede inflationary wage settlements. Many of the craft unions – for example, printers and engineers – operated policies aimed to restrict the number of new entrants to their particular craft, which was said to delay the introduction of new working methods or technology. This behaviour created labour shortages in certain occupations or in others led to over-staffing. Attempts to resolve this problem led to considerable organisational conflict and a perception that management was unable to implement effective policies to counteract many of these restrictions. This led, inevitably, to a worsening of management and union relationships.

However, notwithstanding the increase in the overall standard of living, the general level of performance of the British economy was one of slower economic growth compared to its major competitors. This relative economic under-performance had many downside effects, one of which was less than constructive employment relations. By the latter part of the 1960s the effect of high wage settlements, together with union defensive attitudes and poor management, caused many commentators to take the view that this deterioration in competitiveness was a direct consequence of poor workplace industrial relations (Nolan and Walsh 1995). This view was supported by the report in 1968 of the Royal Commission on Trade Unions and Employers' Associations which had been established in 1965 under the chairmanship of Lord Donovan. Thus, the reform of workplace industrial relations became a major public policy priority. However, opinions on the type of reform, and how best to implement it, differed – particularly on the role of the law as a catalyst for bringing about change. Nonetheless, the need for reform was not questioned.

So by the mid-1960s the concerns about the prevailing system of employment relations and its adverse impact on economic competitiveness via relatively higher UK prices and lower labour productivity levels than those of our economic competitors became central to the political agenda. The Labour Government under Harold Wilson, which was elected in 1964, decided to try to re-establish UK economic competitiveness by direct interference in the outcome of employment relations through a productivity, prices and incomes policy designed to control inflation by ensuring that income increases were linked to increases in productivity and not to changes in the rate of inflation or what other workers were receiving.

For followers of Keynesian economics, if creating full employment gave rise to inflation, then the implementation of a productivity, prices and incomes policy was necessary. Because wage costs account for such a significant proportion of employers' total costs, excessive rises in wage levels affect the inflation spiral. As inflation rises, economic policy-makers are tempted to regulate economic activity by stifling demand which, in turn, can lead to rises in unemployment. Keynes argued that increasing unemployment to control inflation could be avoided, and full employment maintained, by the introduction of a productivity, prices and incomes policy.

The history of incomes policy over the period 1948–79 shows that in the short run they were successful but after two or three years broke down, usually in the face of a strike in support of a pay increase in excess of the policy. By the 1970s such policies were proving politically explosive. Such attempts to limit wage settlements was seen by some as a deliberate attempt to shift the balance of bargaining power towards the interests of employers and was resisted by the unions to the point of industrial disputes – the most famous example of which was the miners' strikes of 1972 and 1973/74 and the 'winter of discontent' in 1978/79.

This problem of economic performance is of vital importance when considering any sort of long-term pay deal whether it is a government-imposed incomes policy or a freely negotiated two- or three-year pay deal. If the economy fails to perform in the way that was indicated when the deal was struck, the participants will want to re-examine it. In the 1960s and the 1970s UK management was not always impressed by the arbitrary imposition of government pay norms, particularly when interest rates and inflation were running at very high levels, and they were often happy to work with their employees to find ways round them. Private sector employers were more interested in continuation of production, and some were prepared to pay higher wages to avoid industrial action. While we now live in a highly competitive world economy, where maintaining some form of competitive advantage is essential for most businesses, this was not always the case in the three decades after World War II. During that period a much greater proportion of an organisation's customer base was static relative to today, and therefore they had a much greater ability to pass on increased wage costs in the form of increased prices. In the case of the public sector, there was no serious long-term attempt to limit the growth in public expenditure – and companies and enterprises therefore learned to live with high inflation and its consequent impact on wages and prices.

## ? REFLECTIVE ACTIVITY

Explain the main tenets of the Keynesian approach to macro-economic management. What are its implications for employment relations at the workplace level? Give some appropriate examples.

### 'IRRESPONSIBLE UNION BEHAVIOUR'

Circumventing pay norms was but one example of a wider malaise. By the beginning of the 1960s the balance of power was firmly with the trade unions and – particularly in the car industry – shop stewards at plant level were increasingly exercising this power. They were reluctant to abide by disputes procedures and to subject themselves to control by full-time officials, particularly those national trade union leaders who were prepared to co-operate with some form of pay restraint. Some industries like ship building, car manufacture and the ports had their own agendas that tended to be parochial, and in the opinion of many employers were motivated by political and not industrial objectives. Many employers also questioned whether shop stewards in calling unofficial (not supported by the union) and unconstitutional (failing to follow all the stages of an agreed procedure) strikes truly represented the wishes of all their members. Such views about the internal democracy of trade unions was given credence in that many industrial action decisions were based on voting by a show of hands at mass meetings, rather than by a secret ballot of those being asked to become involved.

One common theme of the 1960s and 1970s was the perception – partly based on strike statistics, and on the trade unions' links with the Labour Party and therefore Labour Governments – that trade union leaders were more powerful than UK government ministers. Given that poor workplace industrial relations were judged to have had a negative impact on economic performance, unions and their alleged 'irresponsible' use of power were seen as major contributors to the UK's relative lack of economic competitiveness. If businesses were not investing sufficiently, this – it was claimed – was the fault of the unions. If new technology was not embraced sufficiently quickly, again the unions were seen as the basis of the problem. If inflation was out of control, it was the fault of the unions.

Although any objective examination of employment relations during this period would show the unions having to accept a large part of the blame, weak management performance during the period was also a contributory factor. There was insufficient investment in training and development, and then, as now, insufficient investment in innovation and research. The debate about skill levels within UK organisations relative to our international competitors is ongoing. Despite the investment in Training and Enterprise Councils, National Vocational Qualifications and the National Curriculum that have taken place over the last two decades, there has been a continuing concern that children still leave school ill-equipped for the task ahead. Chief executives of some of Britain's larger organisations, including the likes of ASDA, have expressed their concern over the lack of basic skills in some of their new recruits. On the other side of the coin there are those employers who do not see any value in investing in people. One problem is a perception that the Government does not have a clear strategy in respect of this problem. Since the beginning of the 1980s there have been various redesigns of our training and development infrastructure. While it is always laudable that governments should try to underpin training and development with some form of statutory intervention, continual tinkering with the infrastructure is confusing for employers and is likely to result in less, not more, training. There is evidence that many organisations have, over time, failed to invest sufficiently in training. Once the pool of available labour decreases, its 'price' goes up. These and other effects are not necessarily the immediate results of a change of UK government, but over time the needs of economic management changes and shifts. The strategic employment relations professional monitors and anticipates such changes, to support and inform the organisation's future plans and objectives.

Clearly, there has been some success in raising skills levels over the past two decades. A report commissioned by the Department for Trade and Industry and the Economic and Social Research Council, by Michael Porter of Harvard Business School, stated that 'an emphasis on skills, innovation and enterprise is needed to ensure that the UK makes the transition to a new phase of economic development.' Porter set out six key areas for improving competitiveness:

- *public investment* – Increase investment in research and development, and boost education and transport spending.

- *the regulatory context* – Improve competition policy, develop a strategy for training in advanced management skills, and improve university/business links.

- *clusters* – Institute a sustained programme of cluster development so that businesses in similar fields benefit from the proximity of partners, suppliers and research.

- *regions* – Decentralise power and address planning issues.

- *roles and institutions* – Form new collective institutions to help the private sector lead development, while the Government reduces its role.

- *management* – Managers must boost innovation and quality with increased investment in R&D, skills, modern production and IT.

These are clearly very worthy objectives, but to what extent we have moved forward since Porter's report is less clear. Yet there is no doubting available evidence which suggests that UK managers at middle and junior levels are less skilled than their counterparts in other competing economies.

## THE RISE OF MONETARISM

THEORY

The so-called 'winter of discontent' of 1978/9, when low-paid public sector employees took strike action to gain pay increases in excess of the then Labour Government pay increase norm, coincided with the end of the five-year electoral cycle. The incumbent Labour Government knew it had to call a General Election during 1979, and although they sought to postpone it for as long as possible, an election was duly held in May 1979. The Conservative Party campaigned on the promise of better management of the economy, lower income taxes, less government expenditure and curtailing union power – all of which they claimed would help the UK economy regain competitiveness. They committed themselves to introducing legislation designed to ensure that trade unions acted responsibly.

During their period in opposition (1974–9), a growing faction within the Conservative Party had begun to question the ability of Keynesian economic policies to provide price stability (commonly referred to as 'sound money'). Instead, those that Keegan (1984: 66) refers to as the 'economic evangelicalists' began to embrace the concept of monetarism as the means to control inflation and improve economic competitiveness. Although monetarism can mean different things to different people, its basic propositions are that:

- If the general level of purchasing power in the economy as a whole grows more quickly than the increase in the general level of goods and services produced in the economy as a whole, firms and households will have more money to purchase goods and services than are available in the economy as a whole.

- There comes a position where there is 'too much money chasing too few goods and services' – when demand is greater than supply. Shortages arise and market prices start to increase as consumers compete with each other for this reduced supply.

- Increasing inflation arouses expectations that future inflation rates will be even higher, resulting in a) higher wage demands and settlements, and b) a wages-prices inflationary spiral in turn resulting in an increase in the general level of unemployment as the competitiveness of firms declines and workers 'price themselves out of jobs'.

- To prevent inflation, the increase in the overall level of purchasing power in the economy as a whole must match the rate of increase in the general output of goods and services in the economy as a whole.

- If the increase in the economy-wide level of purchasing power exceeds the increase in the general level of the supply of goods and services in the economy as a whole, spending power (demand) must be decreased by raising interest rates and reducing the level of UK government (public) expenditure.

For monetarists, unemployment will only fall, in the longer term, if the productive capacity of the economy is increased. Measures to achieve such an increase are usually referred to as 'supply-side' economics. The key to reducing unemployment and controlling inflation is to enhance the ability of the economy to increase the supply of goods and services to the market more efficiently by:

- creating an environment conducive to private enterprise

- creating incentives for individuals to work

- creating incentives for firms to invest, produce goods and services and employ workers

- liberalising product markets

- privatising public-owned enterprises

- reducing taxation

- de-regulating labour markets.

The Conservatives won the 1979 election and began the process of applying monetarist policies to the management of the UK economy. These policies have now been applied in one way or another since that time, and are set to continue. However, since 1997 governments have taken the view that competitive advantage comes from quality and added value and the provision of minimum standards of protection for employees – for example, the minimum wage. It may be that the application of economic policy is now less doctrinaire than in the past. There is a view that Labour endorses and understands the concept of human capital much more than the Conservatives. By spreading opportunities through education and injecting more social justice into the equation, it believes the UK can become a 'knowledge-based economy' capable of competing with the best.

## LABOUR MAKES CHANGES

The make-up of the UK economy changed radically in the last quarter of the twentieth century. One of the visible results of this, for the employment relations professional, has been a much more deregulated labour market. The reforms to the labour market have seen a move from employment in manufacturing to employment in the service industry, which has accounted for an increase in non-manual jobs at the expense of manual ones. Part-time employment has increased while full-time employment has decreased. The rise in part-time employment, when converted to full-time equivalents, does not compensate for this downturn in full-time work. Although it would be an over-simplification to blame all the changes in the labour market on monetarist policies, those policies were the engine by which the reforms were driven. The higher unemployment in comparison with the 1960s and 1970s has had a major impact on employment relations. While trade union influence is lower and industrial disputes have declined, there is a sense that employees feel less secure. This is partly a consequence of the near economic meltdown of 2008/9, but it reflects a trend that has been growing for some time. Some of this reflects the change in how people view their current position – the 'job for life' that underpinned so much of our post-war thinking and strategic decision-making has gone. It is now the accepted wisdom that individuals will move jobs, and even careers, several times during their active working life. At one level this insecurity manifests itself in the number of claims to employment tribunals – over 150,000 in 2008/9 – although the willingness of individuals to enforce their rights may be a result of greater knowledge on their part. More than 75% of people claim they feel well informed about their employment rights, according to figures published by the Department for Business, Innovation and Skills (BIS). Key findings of the 2008 *Fair Treatment at Work Survey* (FTWS) show that 78% of the working population feel well or very well informed about their rights, and 85% claim to know where to find information on their rights if they need it. Whatever the factors involved, employers need to take the issue of employee insecurity very seriously if they are to ensure that they are capable of continually improving their performance. The annual ACAS report provides data on tribunal claims, requests for help and information, and details of mediation and arbitration cases – students would be well advised to make themselves aware of its content. A full copy of the ACAS annual report can be viewed on its website: www.acas.org.uk/publications.

## REFLECTIVE ACTIVITY

Do you monitor the indicators of employee insecurity, such as a rise in grievances, individual or collective, a rise in labour turnover or an increase in sickness absence?

THE LABOUR MARKET

Some commentators have argued that the relative growth in jobs in the service sector relative to the manufacturing sector has led to an increase in 'McJobs' – part-time, badly paid and with low status – which has contributed to the decline in trade union membership and influence. It is argued that the lack of security offered by this type of employment has made people less inclined to join trade unions because they are afraid to challenge their employer. The decline in traditional union strongholds such as mining and ship building has had an effect, but as with most things in employment relations, the reality tends to be more complex.

If we are to understand the significance that the labour market has on employment relations, we need to understand more about the composition of the UK workforce and the changes that have taken and are taking place. As we noted earlier in the chapter, the *Workplace Employment Relations Survey* (WERS) series has documented and comprehensively monitored the state of employment relations in workplaces in Britain over the past two decades. The survey design has remained broadly the same during that period in order that reasonable comparisons may be drawn – although it has always added new elements and discarded others in order to reflect changes in the employment relations landscape. In particular, the 1998 survey had a significant redesign involving a move away from detailed questioning on union organisation and collective bargaining and towards a greater focus on the management of employees. The findings from the 2004 WERS provide the most recent account of the state of employment relations in Britain, and the next survey is due to take place in 2011. As we note in Chapter 4, and as the authors of the 2004 WERS report:

> Since 1997, legislation has been introduced or reformed in a number of areas, including: working hours, rates of pay, union recognition, work and family life, workplace conflict and equal opportunities and, most recently, information and consultation.

After the publication of that report, legislation on age discrimination has also been implemented which in itself is likely to have an impact on the age profile of the working population.

Because WERS 1998 was concluded prior to these legislative changes, the authors of the 2004 survey consider that it provides 'a baseline against which the impact of several key pieces of employment legislation can partly be assessed'. Although the 2004 survey did not seek to assess the impact of the new legislation, it did attempt to highlight where change had occurred in areas affected by government policy.

Notwithstanding the fact that it is more than 10 years since WERS 1998, the data it provided is still very useful in understanding the current labour market. As its authors pointed out, 'Commentators looking at the British labour market often highlight the issue of flexibility', and the tables below provide some useful insights into this issue.

The survey asked whether workplaces had contracted out services which would previously have been undertaken by people directly employed in the organisation, and found that a third of respondents said that this was the case. Furthermore, one-third were using former employees of the workplace as contractors. They found that 11% of employers had transferred some employees to a different employer in the five years preceding the publication of their report, and that this proportion was far higher (22%) in the public sector than in the private sector (6%).

Another area which has had a major impact on the labour market is non-standard employment. This is generally defined as anything that is not permanent full-time work and embraces part-time working, the use of freelancers, outworkers and temporary and fixed-term contract employees.

Critics of labour market reforms have argued there has been a growth in the use of part-time labour to the detriment of full-time jobs. The 1998 WERS provides information on the extent of part-time employment, which is defined as working fewer than 30 hours per week. The survey found that part-time workers accounted for a quarter of all jobs in workplaces with 25 or more employees, but that their distribution varied enormously across workplaces of different kinds.

The WERS disclosed that the use of freelancers (13%) and outworkers (6%) is reasonably significant, but provided some revealing data about temps and fixed-term contract employees. There had been a widely held perception that employers had placed a greater reliance on the use of temporary and fixed-term contract employees. Table 3.3 below shows that this was not the case and that the majority of workplaces did not use temps or employ people on fixed-term contracts.

Table 3.3 The use of temporary agency workers and fixed-term contracts, by occupation

| Occupation | Percentage of workplaces employing | |
|---|---|---|
| | Temporary agency workers | Fixed-term contracts |
| Managers and administrators | 1 | 6 |
| Professional | 5 | 15 |
| Associate professional and technical | 5 | 6 |
| Clerical and secretarial | 17 | 13 |
| Craft and related | 2 | 3 |
| Personal and protective service | 2 | 5 |
| Sales | 0 | 4 |
| Plant and machine operatives | 4 | 2 |
| Other occupations | 5 | 6 |
| None of these workers used | 72 | 56 |

Base: workplaces with 25 or more employees. Figures weighted, based on responses from 1,921 managers.

Whatever the statistics, there is no doubt that 'the ability of managers to adjust the size of their workforces in line with requirements and demand – usually referred to as "numerical flexibility" – appears to be widespread'. Figure 3.2 below shows that during the 1990s there was an increase in the use of non-standard employment.

**Figure 3.2  The changes in the use of different forms of labour**

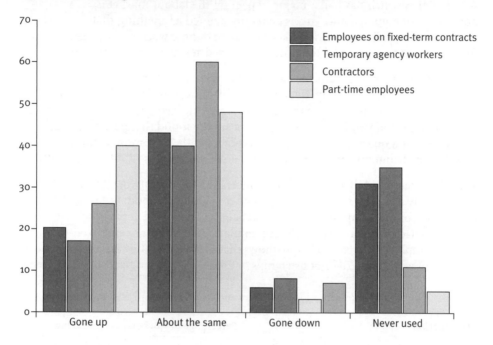

There is a sense, if you simply consider the above data, that the move to greater flexibility is all one way – that changes in the type of working arrangements have benefited the employer more than the employee. But as the 2004 WERS indicates (see Table 3.4), there has since the 1998 survey been a substantial increase in the availability of flexible working arrangements, including home-working, term-time-only working, flexi-time and job-sharing, at least among continuing workplaces.

This data tends to support the view that more and more employers understand their employees' need for more work–life balance. To some extent this acceptance of work–life balance has been driven by legislation. The ability of individuals to seek flexible working arrangements, and the requirement on employers to treat such requests seriously and provide a detailed response to the requesting employee, have helped change attitudes. Being required to explain, in a proscribed format, why a particular job cannot be 'shared' or be done in less time has demonstrated to managers that their opposition to flexible arrangements cannot be sustained.

Table 3.4  Use of temporary agency workers and fixed-term contracts, by occupation

| Occupation | Temporary agency workers | Fixed-term contracts |
|---|---|---|
| | % of workplaces employing | % of workplaces employing |
| Managers and administrators | 1 | 6 |
| Professional | 5 | 15 |
| Associate professional and technical | 5 | 6 |
| Clerical and secretarial | 17 | 13 |
| Craft and related | 2 | 3 |
| Personal and protective service | 2 | 5 |
| Sales | 0 | 4 |
| Plant and machine operatives | 4 | 2 |
| Other occupations | 5 | 6 |
| None of these workers used | 72 | 56 |

Base: workplaces with 25 or more employees.
Figures are weighted and based on responses from 1,921 managers.

Whatever type of organisation you work in, the impact of the labour market changes will have affected the way you do your job. In organisations that still rely on a greater proportion of traditional, permanent, full-time employees there is likely to be pressure for change. Employment costs are still, for most businesses, the most significant item in the management accounts and provide one of the better opportunities to make savings. In the near future, as competition heightens, some form of 'the flexible firm' will have to become a reality for all organisations – but this is not necessarily bad news ... although the pessimistic view of the reformed labour market is the 'McJobs' thesis.

## JOB CREATION

Although many commentators acknowledged that part-time jobs will account for a significant amount of net job creation and that the proportion of women in the workforce will continue to rise, it would be wrong to interpret this as the creation of a second-class labour market. A closer look at the forecasts contained in a 1999 report from the Institute of Employment Research (IER) at the University of Warwick predicted that job creation would take place in two broad categories. One was in 'personal and protective services', which includes security guards and carers. While this could be made to fit the pessimistic (McJobs) thesis, the impact of the minimum wage, the Working Time Regulations, the Part-Time Work and Temporary Workers and Fixed-Term Contract Work Directives have helped to mitigate some of the abuses of long hours and low pay.

The second category was managerial, professional and technical jobs, demanding high levels of education and skill. Later research by IER entitled Working Futures is a series of projections produced by IER in collaboration with Cambridge Econometrics (CE). *Working Futures 2004–14* represents the most detailed and comprehensive set of employment projections ever published for the UK. It focuses upon the future patterns of demand for skills as measured by occupation.

The results are intended to provide a sound statistical foundation for the deliberations of all those with an interest in the supply of and demand for skills, including individuals, employers, education and training providers as well as the various agencies and departments of government. Clearly, research such as this must be read in the context of today's economic conditions. Because it makes reference to projected growth rates and prospects for the economy, including inflation and employment, students must check these against more up-to-date information such as in the Bank of England's quarterly report: www.bankofengland.co.uk.

## THEORY    GREATER FLEXIBILITY

But what does all this structural change in the labour market mean at the level of the individual firm? What is its impact on employment relations? Many of the changes that have taken place over the last two decades have been driven by the increase in the global marketplace and by the need to develop organisations that can respond flexibly to the rapidly changing demands of that market. This has given rise to the concept known as 'the flexible firm', but the data from WERS indicates that the movement towards changing work patterns is at best mixed. Stredwick and Ellis (1998) identified a number of surveys that 'throw light on the reality of the movement towards flexible working'. They concluded that, 'The evidence is strong all round that the move to greater flexibility is gathering pace, and that organisations see it as a means of achieving competitive advantage.' Nothing that has happened in the intervening period has changed that assumption. As we noted above, more and more employees are seeking flexible working arrangements and there is clear evidence that employers are pushing ahead with changes in working practices. The Post Office, British Airways, parts of the NHS, together with countless numbers of less high-profile organisations, have introduced changes to their working arrangements. In the majority of cases, and probably because of high levels of communication and engagement, these have not created the levels of workforce opposition that might have been the case 20 years ago.

Nevertheless, the debate over the future of work will continue, and – given the effects of one of the deepest recessions we have ever experienced – the prospects for work and employment are of major importance not just to policy-makers at the macro level but to policy-makers at organisational level. Issues around the jobs and workplaces of the future need to be carefully considered, and the employment relations specialist must be a key player in this debate. That requires them to constantly be aware of new research, government policy and economic developments. Outcomes from the Future of Work Programme, launched by the Economic and Social Research Council in October 1998, pose some interesting questions.

> Are we poised to witness a radical re-drawing of established divisions between paid and unpaid work? With policy-makers, 'think tanks' and visionaries vying to impose their particular interpretations of the future, there is no shortage of responses to these complex questions. Commentators typically assert that the forces of globalisation and technology are challenging current patterns of working, but find little else on which to agree.

> At the extremes, pessimists conjure a haunting spectre of mass unemployment, growing insecurity and widening social divisions, while optimists claim that the emerging 'new' economy will liberate many employees from the dull, dreary and degrading jobs that stifled working lives in the past. Both scenarios remain ungrounded in any systematic theory or evidence, and a pervasive weakness is the absence in such accounts of an adequate historical perspective.

More details of the programme, together with details of an extensive range of published material, can be found at www.leeds.ac.uk/esrcfutureofwork, which notes that:

> Visionaries of the future portend a radically different workplace from the past. They anticipate a new world in which job structure and broader macro-conditions which provided many workers with a measure of security and career continuity will have a greatly diminished salience.

It goes on to say:

> The stable employment relationships which have come to serve as a reference point for the future are said to be collapsing as the forces of globalisation, privatisation and new technologies are propelling organisations to redefine the rhythms, contractual terms and spatial patterns of work.

Even if the workplace of the future is not as radically different as the visionaries referred to above believe, there will be change – not least because the flexible labour market has been central to UK government policy since 1979 and remains an integral part of ongoing policy decisions.

## THE STATE AS EMPLOYER BEFORE 1979

During the post-war period, the state always sought to give a lead to the private sector as a model and good employer, as expressed in the implementation of particular employment relations policies. Collective bargaining was considered a good and desirable activity. Union membership was encouraged and led to high levels of unionisation in the public sector. Nine out of ten white-collar trade unionists were employed in the public sector. When industries were taken into public ownership, there was an obligation on the public corporation created to recognise, consult and negotiate with trade unions. The state also sought to ensure that its staff received comparable pay and conditions to those doing the same or similar work in the private sector.

Comparability was thus the basis of wage claims and adjustments. For example, in the Civil Service the civil servants were given a Pay Research Unit to look at rates of pay, to compare pay with private sector employees, and to provide the negotiators with information.

**THEORY**    INCREASING THE SUPPLY SIDE

Conservative Governments from 1979 had a different approach to economic management and pursued a twin-track policy to achieve their objectives. They eschewed the prevailing post-war consensus in areas such as the welfare state, UK government intervention in industry, incomes policy, tripartite discussions and keeping unemployment in check, even at the risk of inflation rising. Instead, they made clear their intention of letting the market decide.

Monetarist policies were introduced as a means of reducing inflation, which meant sharp increases in interest rates and in indirect taxes (especially VAT) and cuts in public expenditure. The result was large increases in unemployment, especially in the country's manufacturing industries such as ship building, car manufacture and steel. By allowing unemployment to rise, the UK Government was making it clear that radical measures were needed if the British economy was to re-establish its competitiveness.

In addition, Conservative Governments sought the encouragement of an enterprise culture by the deregulation of product and labour markets, the privatisation of nationalised industries, and the regulation of trade unions' industrial activities. As Blyton and Turnbull (1994: 145) saw it:

> The objectives of UK government policy in the 1980s could be simply stated: namely, to encourage enterprise through the de-regulation of markets, especially the labour market.

They noted that the foundations of Conservative Governments' policy under Mrs Thatcher could be found in the writings of free-market economists such as Milton Friedman and in particular Friedrich Hayek. Of the UK economists who subscribe to the monetarist philosophy, the work of Patrick Minford is a good indicator of why the policy agenda has been developed as it has. Minford argued that trade unions used their power to raise wages above the market rate, which then caused price inflation, which in turn caused further rises in unemployment. This process, he argued, reduced both the efficiency of individual firms and the economy as a whole through the imposition of restrictive practices, demarcation, etc. For the monetarists, then, if employment was to increase, the labour market behaviour of trade unions had to be regulated. Trade unions needed to be restrained from abusing market power, and it was for this reason that Conservative administrations over the period 1979–1997 introduced legislation to free up labour markets from trade union, employer association and government influence.

The restriction on trade union behaviour was two-pronged. The Conservatives made it clear that they were no longer prepared to promote the Government's traditional role as a 'model employer'. The idea that the state should be a model to the private sector remained, but the notion of what constituted a 'model employer' changed, and in 1981 the Government ended the Civil Service comparability agreement which had operated since 1951.

The UK Government became less favourably disposed to collective bargaining and instead argued that employees should be rewarded as individuals. They sought to act against the collective voice because they subscribed to the view that it led to overpriced jobs and consequently to unemployment. The state ceased to encourage people to become members of trade unions or to take part in collective bargaining. Conversely, they also discouraged the traditional role of employers' federations in national wage bargaining. Comparability of pay for public sector employees was terminated because it was thought that pay increases should be related to the ability to pay and the availability of labour resources. Thus the pay of an occupational group should not necessarily be the same in different parts of the country. Differentials should reflect the scarcity of that labour. So wage negotiation at operating unit levels, where the ability to pay and scarcity of labour factors could more easily be taken account of, were encouraged and the traditional 'going-rate' argument discouraged.

## REFLECTIVE ACTIVITY

Outline three main functions of the state in employment relations.

## PUBLIC EXPENDITURE

The UK Conservative Government argued that inflation was the result of money supply increasing faster than the increase in output of goods and services in the economy. Money supply is the total spending power in the economy as a whole, but a major component in this is public expenditure. Given that the UK Government was responsible directly or indirectly for the wages of one-third of the employees in the country, and given that pay is an important part of public sector expenditure, UK governments cannot adopt a neutral stance on public sector settlements. So although the Conservative Governments made it clear that a formal incomes policy with norms and enforcement agencies was not on their agenda, they were prepared to ensure effective controls over the pay rises for public sector employees by the simple expedient of limiting the rise in public expenditure. This approach brought the UK Government into conflict with a number of public sector unions – for example, schoolteachers – who had their collective bargaining rights removed by Act of Parliament.

The labour market reforms since 1979 have seen a progressive diminution of the welfare safety net for unemployed workers. Governments considered that overgenerous welfare provision meant that people had less incentive to work and therefore remained unemployed for longer than was necessary. This so-called dependency culture was tackled by changing the basis on which an individual was eligible for unemployment benefit, and by reducing the length of time such benefit was payable. Because of the fear of unemployment, such changes in the welfare system meant that employees became less resistant to employer control and were less likely to seek reviews of their terms and conditions of employment for fear of losing their jobs.

Although Labour Governments have not reversed the policy initiatives of their predecessors, they have, through a series of interventions, sought to make work pay for a greater number of people, thus reducing the dependency culture. A report by the Institute for Fiscal Studies (IFS) assessed government changes to the tax and benefits system and the introduction of the National Minimum Wage. It concluded that the package of measures would make work pay by between £7 and £13 a week extra. This report, together with the Warwick report referred to above, suggest that we are in the process of creating a labour market where employers are creating new jobs and people are more willing to take them.

## THE IMPACT OF TECHNOLOGY

Every organisation operates within certain technological constraints which impact on its size and structure. In turn, the size and structure of an organisation will undoubtedly have an influence on its culture. Because culture affects relationships between people, it can be seen that technology and technological development are important factors in employment relations.

It is important that employment relations professionals understand the term 'technology'. If it merely implies some form of process or engineering, does it have any relevance outside of manufacturing? Technology is more than an engineering process. From the perspective of an organisation it is about the application of skills and knowledge. It is therefore both relevant and necessary to understand it.

In the context of employment relations it is possible to identify three perspectives from which to view the impact of new technology. One is that new technology, because of its impact on traditional skills, acts as both a de-skilling agent and a creator of unemployment. The second perspective is that new technology is a positive force in that it creates new opportunities for employees who have the chance to learn new skills. A third perspective sees technology as the means whereby previously unpleasant or repetitive tasks can be eliminated. For example, the introduction of robotics into the car industry removed the need for employees to carry out mundane operations, with a consequent improvement in the climate of employment relations in an industry previously dogged by labour problems. Each of these three perspectives is, to some degree, correct, but the impact of new technology varies from industry to industry and from organisation to organisation.

Although most people acknowledge that in general terms technological development has reduced the demand for certain types of labour, it is clear it has presented some significant opportunities for job creation. One example is the large growth in the use of call centres, particularly in the financial services sector. They are clearly technology-driven and rely on a combination of complex computer-based communications technologies, and they employ in excess of 200,000 people.

Technological development based on computers, lasers and telecommunications not only has the capacity to de-skill jobs, it can blur demarcation lines, create an alternative lower-paid workforce for an employer and provide the impetus for changes in work patterns.

It is important for the employment relations professional to recognise where technology requires changes in working patterns or processes and to identify appropriate and available training opportunities. A commonly held view about the impact of technological change is that it creates problems, particularly where trade unions are represented in the workplace, and is often resisted. Of course, when change is on the agenda, both trade unions and employees generally will have fears over job losses, de-skilling and increased management control. The skill of the employment relations professional lies in understanding these concerns and seeking ways of mitigating them. Personnel professionals should have a vested interest in the *management* of change, not just the imposition of change.

Whatever the nature of the technology, its impact – and therefore the response to it by all stakeholders – is inevitably linked to the UK's poor record in skills development and productivity. The Government was so concerned about the lack of skills development that the Performance and Innovation Unit (PIU) at the Cabinet Office set up a task force to examine the problem and to recommend policies to overcome it.

The task force, which reported in November 2001, concluded that 'workforce development' (WfD) can 'help to raise labour productivity and increase social inclusion'. They described WfD as 'a relatively new term for training and skills development [sitting] between training (which has a narrow focus) and education (which is broad), and is firmly grounded in business need'. The PIU adopted the following definition:

> Workforce development consists of activities which increase the capacity of individuals to participate effectively in the workforce, thereby improving their productivity and employability.

The key points from the task force report were:

- A relatively high proportion of the UK population of working age lacks basic and intermediate skills.

- The benefits of education and training are, in large part, captured by individuals through increased earnings and by firms through increased productivity.

- Without basic skills – literacy and numeracy – individuals cannot start to develop a career path and may be trapped in a low pay/no pay cycle.

So far as productivity is concerned, there continues to be concern over Britain's productivity deficit relative to the performance of other advanced economies. The government enquiry on competitiveness referred to above suggested that:

> the sluggish pace of managerial innovation might partly cause and be the result of other shortcomings, such as low investment in capital, research and development and workforce skills development.

And, because many modern management techniques are thought to rely on the availability of skilled workers and state-of-the-art machinery, these will not be in place if investment is low.

> This cocktail could explain the persistent productivity gap and the low level of innovation … relative to the US and the leading continental European economies.

> *People Management* (2003) Vol.9, No.10; page 10

This productivity gap means that British workers produce around 20% less for every hour they spend at work than those in France, Germany and the USA. This is not about a lack of competence on the part of UK workers, but is the consequence of decades of under-investment in plant and machinery and in skills development. Raising the skill levels and closing the productivity gap is a central theme of economic policy, and is another example of how the Government's management of the economy impacts on the employment relations specialist.

This is because whatever skills organisations require in the future, the employment relations professionals will have to recognise that changes in the balance of skills will have a significant impact on their work. In some organisations investment in improved technology may lead to both staff development and redundancies. In some organisations such investment can cause difficulties in recruiting sufficient skilled labour with the consequent pressure that this can bring, particularly in respect of unit labour costs. Overall, it is important to remember that new technology varies in its impact. This is based on a number of variables including the nature of the product or service, the type of organisation involved, the management strategy employed and the attitude of trade unions (where they are represented) and employees.

## REFLECTIVE ACTIVITY

What changes in technology do you expect to affect your organisation, or the sector in which you operate, in the next five years? What is their likely impact on employment relations behaviour?

## THE BALANCE OF BARGAINING POWER

In Chapter 1 we introduced the concept of the 'balance of bargaining power' and said that it was this balance that determines whether employers or employees feel that their interests have been satisfied. We also said that the balance in bargaining power operates at both a macro and a micro level. At the macro level the combination of economic management and political, legislative and technological change influences the overall conduct of employment relations, while at the micro level these factors can have totally different impacts.

The Government's economic and legal policies have major implications for the outcome of employment relations behaviour. If economic policies are directed towards the creation of full employment and the maximising of economic growth, this weakens the relative bargaining power of the employer but strengthens that of the employee. A high level of demand for goods and services in the economy as a whole generates demand for labour to produce/provide those goods and services. If the demand for labour services increases relative to their supply (ie to the extent that shortages develop), then the 'price' employers will have to pay to secure those services will also increase.

If, on the other hand, government economic policies give the highest priority to reducing inflation by lowering household and corporate spending and reducing public expenditure, then the demand (spending power) in the economy will fall and as a consequence, so will the demand for labour. The result will be labour 'surpluses' giving rise to redundancies and increased unemployment. The effect of the supply of labour exceeding demand is downward pressure on the 'price' of labour services. And if labour prices are inflexible downwards, less labour will be employed than previously (ie there will be a rise in unemployment) at the same price. In such situations, the relative balance of bargaining power of employers will be strengthened and that of the employees weakened.

If the Government introduces legislation favourable to employers' interests, the bargaining power of employers relative to employees is strengthened. This is what Conservative Governments did during the period 1980–97 by introducing a series of labour law reforms. If a government introduces legislation favourable to the interests of employees and trade unions, the bargaining power of employees relative to employers is strengthened. Some employers had real fears that the introduction of the statutory recognition procedures contained in the Employment Relations Act (1999) would swing the balance of power towards trade unions, particularly in industries such as media and communications. However, there is no evidence that this happened to any great extent, as we saw earlier in the results from the 2004 WERS and other surveys. Legislation, by setting standards of behaviour by employers to regulate (for example, the right not to be unfairly dismissed) the relationship between an individual employee and his/her employer, also influences the relative balance of bargaining power between employers and individual employees.

The implementation of new technology also impacts on bargaining power. For example, developments in communications have helped to produce global markets which have increased product market competition. This can lead to downward pressure on the 'price' of labour services and a shift in bargaining power towards the employer. The reverse can also be true. By creating new jobs, requiring new skills and making some industries more capital-intensive, the implementation of technological change has strengthened the bargaining power of employees. One only has to look at the advertised vacancies for a whole range of information technology jobs to identify one sector where this is true.

The influence on bargaining power of the wider economic and legal environment surrounding an employment relations system cannot be underestimated, and in this regard the decision-making bodies of the European Union have become increasingly important. The role of the UK Government and European Union Council of Ministers (see Chapter 4) in this context means that representative bodies of employers and employees participate in the political lobbying process to persuade the political decision-makers to introduce economic and legal policies favourable to their interests.

**THEORY**    THE MICRO LEVEL

So far, the relative bargaining power between the buyers and sellers of labour services has been analysed on the macro level. However, analysis at this level cannot explain why some groups of employees retain their bargaining power vis-à-vis the employer despite low growth or high unemployment, and why some employers are in a relatively weak bargaining position despite the economic climate's being in their favour. In many respects what matters for the employer is their bargaining power relative to particular groups of workers at the enterprise level. This is the relative bargaining power at the micro level.

Consider a situation where the national picture is unfavourable to employees in general. Unemployment is rising steeply, redundancies are occurring every day, employers are seeking to restrict wages and general employment conditions, and new, small firms, are replacing more established businesses. However, your organisation could be in a sector where the product or process has a limited shelf-life. If you also have a collective relationship with a well-organised trade union(s), they would be aware of how a trade dispute could have an immediate and costly effect on customer confidence or income generation. Alternatively, your company could be non-union but very high-tech and be experiencing rapid expansion. It requires highly skilled, highly trained and committed employees to produce its products. However, these skills are in short supply because the major employers in the area are in the information industry and other new companies, seeking the same skilled labour, are continuing to move into the area.

In both these situations employees would perceive that, notwithstanding the national (macro) picture, the relative balance of bargaining power was very much in their favour. This situation could be made even worse if the management of the business had no clear employment relations strategy or if policies and procedures were non-existent or out of date.

REFLECTIVE ACTIVITY

Consider the work groups in your organisation and ask yourself the following questions. Which have the most potential power to disrupt the organisation? What is the basis of their power? Do they realise they have this power? If not, why don't they? Do you think they would be willing to use their power?

## BARGAINING POWER AND MANAGEMENT BEHAVIOUR                    THEORY

In general terms, the balance of bargaining power has been in favour of employers over the past years because of the legislative and economic policies of successive governments. When this is the case, it is important that power is exercised in a responsible and not an arbitrary manner.

If the balance of bargaining power favours management, it may achieve its objective despite adopting a management style that is unprofessional and based on an attitude of 'Take it or leave it', 'Go and work for somebody else', and 'There are plenty of other people who would be only too willing to work here.' In such situations the workforce complies with, but is not committed to, management's action and policy. The employees are cowed, have no respect for management, and store up grievances that will come to the surface with a vengeance when the relative balance of bargaining power turns in favour of the employee. There is some anecdotal evidence that some of the claims for union recognition have gained the support of a majority of the affected workforce as a response to previous (bad) management behaviour.

Managing in such a way that employee commitment is not forthcoming is not sustainable in the longer term. It inevitably relies on a crude abuse of power, and this in the long term will be detrimental to the business – which in turn will experience high labour turnover, low employee morale and depressed productivity levels. The employment relations professional manages on the basis of just cause for action, consults and discusses with employees and treats them in a fair, reasonable and consistent manner. Managing on this basis regardless of the relative balance of bargaining between employers and employees, normally gains the respect of the latter even though management invariably gains what it wants.

A further reason why an employment relations professional should not act in an arbitrary manner is that if the bargaining pendulum can swing one way, it can swing back. If you fail to exercise power responsibly when it is in your favour, then you should not expect responsible behaviour from employees when they have the advantage. Bargaining power, as we have noted, is influenced by economic policy and legal intervention. If those policies are changed, a number of variables may be affected. For example, if the predicted increase in managerial, professional and technical jobs becomes a reality and employers do not invest sufficiently in skills training, skills shortages will raise the price of certain types of labour. Statutory rights to union recognition could provide employees with greater bargaining power.

## REFLECTIVE ACTIVITY

Can you identify where the relative balance of bargaining power lies in your organisation? Is this balance static, or is there the potential for any significant shift in power?

## SUMMARY

In the period since 1979, but particularly in the last two decades, changes in legislation, closer integration with Europe and rapidly changing economic circumstances have led, and will continue to lead, to a re-examination of patterns of employment relations. The way in which the employment relationship is managed has changed: managers are now much more aware of the value of good communication and employee involvement in decision-making. We know, from the various Workforce Employment Relations Surveys and other sources, that there has been, and continues to be, a decline in collective bargaining, and that the unions do not seem to have halted the decline in their overall membership. All of this change has been influenced by the 'corporate environment', and this chapter has examined the role of the UK Government as an economic manager in terms of the objectives of macro-economic policy, and how employment relations is affected by the way in which that policy is implemented. In particular, we examined the contrast between the Keynesian and monetarist approaches to economic management and the impact that the change to monetarism has had on the UK economy since 1979.

We noted how the rise in multi-national companies and the growth of 'globalisation' has had an impact on both economic management and individual organisations. We found that globalisation has provided the spur to organisations to take tough decisions, confront performance issues, and create new products so they compete the world over. However, we also highlighted the insecurity that can be a by-product of the drive to do things in new and better ways.

We have looked at the role of the UK Government as an employer and discussed the way in which the concept of the Government as a 'model employer' has changed over time. In the immediate post-war years there was encouragement of collective bargaining and an attempt to ensure comparability of pay between the public and private sectors. From 1979 the emphasis was on a more individual approach to the employment relationship, with a clear discouragement of national pay bargaining.

Finally, we looked at the impact of technological change on the corporate environment and acknowledged that it influences employment relations in a number of ways. We also discussed the need to generate enthusiasm for skills development and to raise UK productivity levels so that they match those of our competitors. We also saw that technology can have negative as well as positive effects – it can create unemployment, it can provide the opportunity for employees to learn new skills, and it can generally improve the working environment.

From whatever perspective you view the corporate environment, there is no doubt that over the last 20 years there has been a radical change in our system of employment relations. This change has manifested itself in changes to working practices, and changes in the labour market with an increase in part-time and temporary working. Reward systems have also changed, issues such as performance-related pay, reward for teams and profit-related pay becoming more prevalent.

Changes in legislation, closer ties with our European partners, rapidly changing economic circumstances all have an impact on the corporate environment and in turn on the established patterns of employment relations.

## KEY LEARNING POINTS

- Changes in economic management and reforms to labour law can cause trade union power and strike activity to decline or increase, and such changes have a marked effect on the balance of bargaining power.

- The role of the state in employment relations has changed, and it no longer seeks an active role in promoting particular practices.

- The way in which the economy is managed has a direct impact on employment relations because it influences such things as price stability, growth, investment and employment levels.

- The continuing globalisation of markets will be a major influence on organisational change and thus employment relations.

- Technological innovation will continue to influence the workplace, and will therefore impact on employment relations practices.

- Management power should be exercised in a responsible manner, and not arbitrarily.

## REVIEW QUESTIONS

1  Your organisation needs to make changes in working practices in order to make significant cost savings caused by the cancellation of orders by a major customer in the public sector. What steps will need to be taken in order to minimise conflict in the workplace when implementing the changes?

2  You have identified an increase in labour turnover within your organisation, which you believe is due to a rised in employee insecurity. Which indicators would help to prove, or disprove, your belief and what measures could be implemented to overcome the problem if it truly exists?

3  Some commentators argue that the pace of technological change must inevitably slow down. Do you think this is a fair statement? If not, where do you see change happening and how is it likely to impact on your organisation?

4  Where does the relative balance of bargaining power lie in your organisation? Do you see this balance as static and, if so, why? Or, if there is potential for a significant shift in power, explain how and why this might occur.

EXPLORE FURTHER

Blyton, P. and Turnbull, P. (1994) *The Dynamics of Employment Relations*. London: Macmillan.

Donaldson, P. and Farquhar, J. (1991) *Understanding the British Economy*. London: Penguin.

Earnshaw, J., Rubery, J. and Cooke, F. L. (2002) *Who is the Employer?* London: Institute for Employment Rights.

Emmott, M. and Hutchinson, S. (1998) 'Employment flexibility: threat or promise?', in Sparrow, P. and Marchington, M. (eds) *Human Resource Management: The new agenda*. London: Financial Times/Pitman.

Farnham, D. (1995) *The Corporate Environment*. London: Institute of Personnel and Development.

Felstead, A., Jewson, N. and Walters, S. (2004) *Changing Places of Work*. Basingstoke: Palgrave Macmillan.

Greenfield, S. (2003) 'Flexible futures', *People Management,* Vol.9, No.21, October; pp52–3.

Healy, G., Heery, E., Taylor, P. and Brown, W. (eds) (2004) *The Future of Worker Representation*. Basingstoke: Palgrave Macmillan.

Houston, D. (ed.) (2004) *Work–Life Balance in the Twenty-First Century*. Basingstoke: Palgrave Macmillan.

Institute for Employment Research (1999/2000) *Review of the Economy and Employment 1998* and *1999*.

Institute for Fiscal Studies (1998) *Entering Work* and *the British Tax and Benefit System*.

Keegan, W. (1984) *Mrs Thatcher's Economic Experiment*. London: Penguin.

Lewis, D. and Sargeant, M. (2001) *Essentials of Employment Law*, 6th edition. London: CIPD.

Marchington, M., Grimshaw, D., Rubery, J. and Willmott, H. (eds) (2004) *Fragmenting Work in New Organisational Forms: Blurring boundaries and disordering hierarchies*. Oxford: Oxford University Press.

Moynagh, M and Worsley, R. (2001) 'Prophet sharing', *People Management,* Vol.7, No.25, December; pp24–9.

Moynagh, M. and Worsley, R. (2001) *Tomorrow's Workplace*. London: CIPD.

Nolan, P. and Walsh, J. (1995) 'The structure of the economy and labour market', in Edwards, P. (ed.) *Industrial Relations – Theory and practice in Britain*. Oxford: Blackwell.

Nolan, P. (2001) 'Shaping things to come', *People Management*, Vol.7, No.25, December; pp30–1.

O'Dowd, J. (2003) 'A new deal', *People Management*, Vol.9, No.10, May; pp38–40.

Roberts, Z. (2003) 'Crossing the divide', *People Management*, Vol.9, No.18, September; pp29–32.

Simms, J. (2004) 'Home or away?', *People Management*, Vol.10, No.11, June; pp35–9.

Stredwick, J. and Ellis, S. (1998) *Flexible Working Practices: Techniques and innovations*. London: Institute of Personnel and Development.

Taylor, R. (2003) 'Generation next', *People Management*, Vol.9, No.18, September; pp38–40.

White, M., Hill, S., Mills, C. and Smeaton, D. (eds) (2004) *Managing To Change? British workplaces and the future of work*. Basingstoke: Palgrave Macmillan.

## CHAPTER 4

# The Legislative Framework

## OVERVIEW

The chapter begins by outlining the process by which UK legislation is approved – parliamentary readings of the Bill followed by Royal Assent as an Act of Parliament – and then goes on to consider the most important and major influences in employment law, namely the *contract of employment,* which defines and regulates the relationship between the employer and the employee. The chapter notes how the state intervenes with this relationship by providing the employee with certain rights against the employer – for example, protection from arbitrary dismissal and the right to a minimum level of pay. Next, the chapter examines the functions of the law in employment relations, drawing on the work of Otto Kahn-Freund, who outlined three functions of the law in regulating employment rights: auxiliary, regulatory and restrictive. It then turns to one of the most dynamic and complex areas of employment law: discrimination law. Because there is no cap on the level of compensation payable and because potentially damaging publicity may arise out of high-profile cases, the chapter argues that employers would be wise to regard the elimination of discrimination, harassment and inequality as a high priority. Then the chapter examines the law relating to unfair dismissal and redundancy. This is particularly important because this area continues to provide the bulk of an employment relations professional's work, involving a right of the individual employee that may be applied not only against employers but, in the case of unionised employees, against their views. The rights of union members – for example, to a secret ballot before being called out on strike – is the next theme of the chapter, which then moves on to examine the nature and jurisdiction of employment tribunals, including the application process, ACAS conciliation, the hearing and the decision. Although it is not specifically a piece of employment legislation, the Human Rights Act (1998) impinges on employment law, and the chapter therefore analyses its impact. The final part of the chapter examines likely future developments in UK employment law.

## LEARNING OUTCOMES

When you have completed this chapter, you should understand and be aware of:

- the importance of the employment contract
- the legislative process
- the principal function of the law
- how the law impacts on relationships at work
- the nature and jurisdiction of employment tribunals
- recent developments in the law.

## INTRODUCTION

There has always been a significant role for the law in the conduct of employment relations, but relative to the last 100 years the present employment law regime now imposes itself on every facet of the employment relationship. However, it is important that the employment relations professional does not view the law as simply a process of compliance. Good employment relations will not be achieved by waving a legal rulebook and stating what people cannot do. Good employment relations will be achieved by the positive actions that employers take to win the trust and confidence of their workforce.

Notwithstanding this approach, we have to recognise that from recruitment to departure every act of the employer is measured against a particular legislative standard. Whether that standard is 'not to discriminate', 'to act reasonably', or to provide a certain level of 'care', it means that employment relations professionals and line managers have to stop and think before taking particular actions. Because of its sheer amount and complexity employment law can often overwhelm even the most experienced of practitioners, and for this reason its range and impact need to be clearly understood.

It is not our intention to provide a detailed explanation of every piece of legislation, and we will not do that. Textbooks such as Lewis and Sargeant's (2009) *Essentials of Employment Law* and frequently updated online facilities such as the CIPD Employment Law Service can do that job in a much more effective way. Our purpose is to examine the legislation in the context of employment relations and to explain how relationships can be influenced by the way in which individual employers apply legislative rules and standards.

## THE LEGISLATIVE PROCESS

There are now two principal sources of employment law with which the employment relations professional must be concerned: legislation that derives from a political decision of the governing party, and legislation that derives from Europe. Notwithstanding this, it is important to recognise that the UK Parliament will be the source of most laws with which the employment relations specialist should be concerned even though the actual legislation might have been directed by, or influenced by, Europe. In Chapter 5 we describe the process by which European legislation is decided and give numerous examples of EU directives that have been transposed into UK law, and it is not necessary to repeat that detail here. We will, however, be looking at some of the developments in European Law. Lewis and Sargeant (2009) provide a detailed explanation of 'the sources and institutions of employment law', but generally, the process by which the legislation is enacted is as follows. The Government of the day might issue a 'Green Paper' followed by a 'White Paper' followed by a 'Bill' which, after the parliamentary process has been exhausted, becomes an 'Act of Parliament'. The first two stages are not obligatory and governments can bypass them if they so wish.

The Green Paper is a consultative document and is used by the Government to obtain the views of interested parties to proposed legislation. This can apply irrespective of whether the proposal is driven by Europe or results from a political decision. Views might be submitted by employers' organisations, trade unions and organisations such as the CIPD. Even individuals can contribute to the consultative process. Recent examples on which the Government has entered into consultation include the implementation of the EU Agency Workers Directive, the extension of paternity leave and pay, the 'blacklisting' of trade unionists and the recast European Works Council Directive.

Once the consultation is complete, the Government will usually issue a White Paper setting out their policy and intentions. A Bill is then introduced into Parliament and, assuming it survives the scrutiny of both the House of Commons and the House of Lords, the agreed Bill becomes an Act – for example, the Employment Rights Act (1996).

One initiative, which has proved to be of great value to employment relations specialists, was a decision by the Department for Trade and Industry – now replaced by the Department for Business, Innovation and Skills (BIS) – to implement changes in employment law on two specific dates each year. These two dates are 6 April and 1 October, and the harmonisation of common commencement dates (CCDs) is intended to ensure that changes to employment policy are made in a co-ordinated fashion and to provide businesses, employee representatives and individuals with greater clarity and awareness about when changes will be made.

At present this initiative is limited to legislative changes on which the BIS is the lead department, and it will therefore not necessarily include changes emanating from the European Union or other government departments. In addition to harmonising dates, the BIS also issues an annual statement of forthcoming employment regulations which comprises five sections. Section A details changes that are due to commence on 6 April; section B details the changes due on 1 October; section C details regulatory changes that are to be implemented outside of the CCDs; section D details changes arising from Europe when the coming-into-force date is different and not aligned to either common commencement date; and finally, section E provides details of other key BIS activity that will impact on the employment law framework in the current year and beyond. This section will be of particular benefit to those charged with drafting employment relations strategies and policies as part of an organisation's long-term planning process. Details of the current annual statement can be found on the BIS website at www.bis.gov.uk.

## REFLECTIVE ACTIVITY

Explain the key stages in the UK legislative process at which employers can attempt to influence the contents of legislation.

Sometimes the distinction between a politically driven development and one that is Europe-driven is not easily identified – as Bercusson (1996) says:

> the dynamic of national labour laws is no longer determined solely or even mainly by domestic developments. It is not merely that UK labour law is required to incorporate EU norms – EU norms are themselves the reflection of the national labour laws of member states.

It is also the case that legislators will often merge these two influences in an attempt to maximise the use of parliamentary time. For example, the Employment Relations Act (1999) contains provisions – on part-time workers, parental leave, etc – that derived from the European process as well as provisions derived from the political process – trade union recognition and the right to be accompanied at disciplinary and grievance hearings. For HR and personnel practitioners, a classic example of how the source of legislation can become confused is demonstrated by the Minimum Wage Act (1998). The proposal for a minimum wage was a clear manifesto commitment of the Labour Party prior to the 1997 General Election and was, in part, a product of their close relationship with the trade union movement. Once they were elected, it became one of their priorities for legislation, and yet many practitioners remain convinced that the minimum wage was introduced because of an EU Directive. Similarly, the current rules concerning statutory union recognition were politically rather than Europe-driven.

### THE LAW AND EMPLOYMENT RELATIONS

Employment relations specialists do not need to be lawyers, but they do need to understand the interaction between the law and employment relations. They need to understand that, because of the many legal developments over the past

30 years, and because we live in a more litigious age, every employment relations decision is potentially capable of legal challenge. Hence, in 2008/9 over 150,000 applications were received by employment tribunals. This is down on previous years, but provisional figures for 2009/10 indicate that the trend is going back up. In the following part of this chapter we have attempted, by referring to some of the principal areas of law, to identify where these challenges are most likely to occur, and how employment relations policies and processes must be capable of managing them.

For example, the psychological contract – seen by many as a key element in the employment relationship – can be seriously affected by how existing and new rights are implemented. Simply doing the minimum required might avoid legal challenge, but might leave individual employees feeling vulnerable or undervalued. Equally, using the statutory provisions as a baseline from which to offer enhancements – such as providing paid rather than unpaid parental leave – can, in appropriate circumstances, pay major dividends in employee commitment to the organisation.

## THE CONTRACT OF EMPLOYMENT

The most important and major influence in employment law is the contract of employment, and the first Contracts of Employment Act was placed on the statute book in 1963. Although that Act has now been repealed, its provisions have been incorporated into the Employment Rights Act (1996) and it is vital that the employment relations professional understands its impact. This is because it defines and regulates the relationship between the employer and the employee. Being an 'employee', or in recent years, a 'worker', is the key determinant in the types of rights an individual enjoys, and it is thus an area which has given rise to a large amount of litigation and case law.

In any business the categories of workers used may include any one or more of the following:

- employees, either full- or part-time
- independent contractors
- agency workers
- casual workers
- fixed-term contract workers
- home-workers.

However, in the UK only certain of these individuals are entitled to all the protection afforded by current employment legislation. These distinctions, while they might seem pedantic, are of crucial importance to the management of individuals. 'Workers' might not have all the rights that 'employees' have, but failure to observe good practice in the management of such individuals could be costly if, for example, they allege that they have been unlawfully discriminated against. In many cases it will be absolutely clear that a person is an employee, but in between these two certainties there exists a wide variety of relationships that exhibit characteristics of both employment and self-employment, and it is *in relation* to these relationships that the difficulties lie.

Section 230(1) of the Employment Rights Act (1996) defines an 'employee' as an 'individual who has entered into or works under (or, where the employment has ceased, worked under) a contract of employment'. Section 230(2) provides that a 'contract of employment' means 'a contract of service or apprenticeship, whether express or implied and (if it is express) whether oral or in writing'. This definition does not provide any guidance as to when an individual may be said to work under a contract of service (as opposed to a contract for services), and in order to determine whether a particular relationship is one of employment (contract of service – referred to in the old cases as a 'master and servant' relationship) or self-employment (contract for services or 'independent contractor') it is therefore necessary to refer to the case law.

There have been many attempts by the courts to provide a simple and easily understandable definition, but in *Montgomery v Johnson Underwood Limited*, the Court of Appeal confirmed that in determining whether a contract of employment exists the 1968 case of *Ready Mixed Concrete (South East) Limited v Minister of Pensions and National Insurance* offers the best guidance. In the *Ready Mixed Concrete* case it was held that a contract of employment exists if three conditions are fulfilled. The first condition is that there exists a 'mutuality of obligation' between the parties. If an individual agrees to provide his or her own work (ie personal service) and skill for the employer when the employer requires him or her to do so, and the employer in return agrees to provide work for the individual and pay a wage or other remuneration for that work, then there will exist a mutuality of obligation. The second condition is that the individual is *under the control* of the employing company. Some of the relevant factors to be considered when determining whether an individual is under the control of the employing company are whether the individual:

- is under a duty to obey orders
- has control over his or her hours
- is subject to the company's disciplinary procedure
- is supervised as to the mode of working
- provides his or her own equipment
- has to comply with the company's rules on the taking of holidays
- works regular hours
- can delegate his or her duties
- can work for others at the same time as working for the particular company
- is integrated into the employer's business – eg is he or she responsible for issuing management instructions, and does he or she have the power to discipline the company's workers?

Finally, and if the first two tests are satisfied, there is the condition that *the other provisions of the contract are consistent with its being a contract of service*. Relevant factors include who has responsibility for tax and National Insurance and whether the individual is in receipt of sick pay/holiday pay. Notwithstanding that these factors may be present, the first two conditions (mutuality of obligation and control) are the 'irreducible minimum' required for a contract of employment. Once these tests have been satisfied and it is clear that an individual is employed under a contract of employment, he or she effectively has the following full rights under all current employment legislation:

- protection from unfair dismissal
- statutory redundancy payment
- maternity leave and statutory maternity pay
- statutory sick pay
- parental and urgent family leave
- a minimum period of notice
- a written statement of particulars of employment.

There will nevertheless be occasions when employers will dispute that an individual is an employee, and in such cases it will be necessary to look at the prevailing case law. A useful source of reference in such circumstances would be the CIPD Employment Law Service.

Unfortunately, such has been the development in individual employment rights that it is now necessary to look beyond the distinction of employee and non-employee to determine what entitlements an individual might have and to take into account the relatively new concept of 'worker'. Section 203(3) of the Employment Rights Act (1996) sets out the definition of a 'worker', but a general definition can be broken down into three parts so that a 'worker' is someone who:

- works under a contract
  - to carry out personal services
    - for another party to the contract.

This definition potentially covers a wide range of individuals who provide personal services under a contract. The great majority of agency workers, home-workers, casuals and freelancers are likely to be workers. Someone who falls within the definition of a 'worker' will enjoy rights under the following legislation (rights which are, of course, also conferred on employees):

- the Working Time Regulations (1998)
- the National Minimum Wage Act (1998)
- the Health and Safety at Work Act (1974)
- the Public Interest Disclosure Act (1998)
- the Part-Time Workers (Prevention of Less Favourable Treatment) Regulations (2000)

- Part 11 of the Employment Rights Act (1996) (the right not to have unlawful deductions made from wages)
- Section 10 of the Employment Relations Act (1999) (the right to be accompanied at disciplinary and grievance proceedings)
- the Race Relations Act (1976), the Sex Discrimination Act (1975) and the Disability Discrimination Act (1995)
- the Fixed-Term Worker Regulations (2002).

> ### REFLECTIVE ACTIVITY
>
> How would you explain to a line manager the importance of issuing employees with a written statement of their terms and conditions of employment?

Aside from the issue of employment status, one area where the contract of employment is of vital importance is in the management of change. In Chapter 3 we discussed change in the context of employment relations strategies, but there is also a legal dimension to this process because, in many instances, the desire for change within an organisation might involve a variation to an individual's contract, and how this variation is managed can have a very significant impact on the employment relationship.

In a strictly legal sense, neither employer nor employee can unilaterally change the terms and conditions of employment because a contract can be changed only by mutual agreement. Actually, organisations change their employees' terms and conditions quite frequently, and very often there are little or no discussions about the change. Certainly, it would sometimes be hard to identify where and when the 'mutual agreement' happened. It is also wrong to believe that such agreement can be implied simply because the employer 'gives notice' of an intent to make changes. The key is consent. Consent can be gained by either individual or collective negotiation or can be implied by the conduct of the parties. Implied consent could be deemed to have occurred if an individual remains at work for a considerable period after a change has been imposed. Where a unilateral change is imposed, and the employee makes it clear that it is unacceptable, he or she is entitled to treat the contract as repudiated. In such circumstances the employee could argue that he or she has been 'constructively dismissed' and seek a suitable remedy from an employment tribunal.

But, as Lewis and Sargeant (2009) state:

> Developments in the law of unfair dismissal make it very difficult for an employee to resist a unilateral variation. Suffice it to say at this stage that employers can offer, as a fair reason for dismissal, the fact that there was a sound business reason for insisting on changes being put into effect.

Provided that the manager, or managers, dealing with the change process operate from a 'good practice' perspective, they should find it is relatively easy to satisfy a tribunal that they have acted reasonably. This is particularly true if the majority of employees affected had been prepared to go along with the employer's proposals. There is one caveat to this – the amount of consultation that took place. While it is not possible to specify what amounts to a 'reasonable' amount of consultation, 'good practice' and common sense would indicate that any consultation would require that employees knew what the changes meant to them personally; what, if any, impact the changes would have on their remuneration, their working time and working arrangements; and what other options were available to them. It would also be expected that they would have sufficient time to consider the proposals and voice any objections. Common sense should tell any manager that presenting somebody with a *fait accompli* is hardly likely to be classed as reasonable.

This may well be the legal reality, and there will be unscrupulous employers who believe that imposing change asserts management's 'right to manage'. They could not be more wrong. There is now overwhelming evidence that individuals work harder, and smarter, when the psychological contract is in a state of high maintenance. Forcing change on people may well be possible, but does it pay dividends? We think not. In this book we continually emphasise the need for 'good practice' in employment relations. To use the law as blunt instrument to drive through change could never be described as 'good practice'. Then again, neither are we naïve – some individuals will always resist change, no matter how much you seek to negotiate or consult with them. In such circumstances, and as a last resort, change might have to be imposed, but at least the employer is seen to have acted in good faith and in the interests of the business.

## THE FUNCTION OF THE LAW                                    THEORY

Notwithstanding the fact that the contract of employment underpins the legal relationship between employers and their employees, this is – as we have said – not a legal text. In the context of employment relations we therefore need to consider the law in a much broader framework. Otto Kahn-Freund in his classic book *Labour and the Law* (1972) stated that the 'principal purpose of labour law [was] to regulate, to support, and to restrain the power of management and the power of organised labour', and he outlined three functions of the law in regulating employment relations that would achieve this purpose. These were:

- the auxiliary function, where the law is designed to promote certain behaviour (for example, collective bargaining) towards certain ends or else the law, in the last resort, will regulate behaviour. The statutory recognition procedures contained in the Employment Relations Act (1999) are a classic example of this function, as the number of voluntary arrangements made since the Act came into force testify

- the regulatory function, where the law regulates management's behaviour towards its employees and trade union officers' behaviour towards their members. This is the area of individual employment rights and the rights of individual trade union members

- the restrictive function, where the law establishes the 'rules of the game' when employers and employees are in the process of making agreements. This type of legislation effectively lays down the circumstances in which employers and trade unions can impose industrial sanctions on each other without the parties having redress to the legal system.

In this chapter we will be linking these three functions to various pieces of employment law so that it is evident how the legislative framework develops over time.

## THEORY    THE AUXILIARY FUNCTION OF THE LAW

From the end of World War II and throughout most of the 1950s and 1960s there was tacit support, by both the main political parties and through the legislative process, for the principle of collective bargaining. However, from the late 1960s and throughout the 1970s, employers and some politicians began to challenge this principle because of what they considered an excess of trade union power. This recognition that collective bargaining, and its manipulation by some trade unionists was a factor in the country's low-productivity, low-output economy was the reason that some people started to lobby for change. The lobbying was certainly successful, and the idea that the law should be used to promote collective bargaining was anathema to successive Conservative Governments from 1979 to 1997. Certainly, the auxiliary function of the law as described by Kahn-Freund did not figure highly in their legislative programme during this period. In fact, the 1980 Employment Act repealed a statutory trade union recognition procedure that had been introduced in 1975 by the Employment Protection Act, and further legislation during this period actively discouraged the process of collectivism. The Employment Relations Act (1999) – which is discussed in more detail in later chapters – with its provisions for statutory recognition and opportunities for trade union representation at discipline and grievance hearings, has to a degree reversed this process.

## THEORY    THE REGULATORY FUNCTION OF THE LAW

This second function of the law has provided the foundation for a series of statutory rights individual employees have, relative to their employer. These began to emerge in the early 1960s. Parliament justified providing such rights on the grounds that private arrangements (for example, by collective agreement) had failed to provide an adequate minimum acceptable level of protection for individual employees against certain behaviour by their employers. Interestingly, the trade unions were initially opposed to such initiatives as the Redundancy Payments Act because they believed it undermined their own role. At the same time, the introduction of individual rights at work sent a clear message to employers that they must act with just cause and be 'fair and reasonable' in the treatment of their employees on those matters where statutory minimum standards were being established for their employees.

A floor of legal rights was created, which has since been expanded and developed, by successive UK governments and the courts, who have been sympathetic to the view that there should be a basic level of employment protection below which no employee should be permitted to fall. These minimum levels can be enhanced by private agreements – for example, via collective bargaining or simply by employers who wish to offer a more attractive employment package. Many organisations now offer maternity pay and leave that goes beyond the statutory minimum, for instance, because they need to attract women back to work after the birth of a child. But this is a matter of policy for individual organisations. What is important for the employment relations professional is to understand the range and importance of these individual rights.

## DISCRIMINATION

Discrimination law in all its guises continues to be one of the most dynamic and complex areas of employment law. Since there is no cap on the level of compensation payable and since potentially damaging publicity may arise out of high-profile cases, employers would be wise to regard the eradication of discrimination, harassment and inequality as a high priority – not just because of the high costs involved, but because unlawful discrimination in any form makes it impossible to foster a climate of good employment relations.

In the UK it is unlawful to treat anyone less favourably on the ground of their sex, their sexual orientation, their race, their age, their religious beliefs, or because they have a disability. Basically, there are two categories of discrimination, direct and indirect. *Direct discrimination* occurs when an individual is treated less favourably because of their sex, race or other protected characteristic as set out in the various pieces of legislation that apply, such as the Race Relations Act, or the Sex Discrimination Act. *Indirect discrimination* occurs when an individual is treated the same way as everyone else, but they do not, or cannot, comply with a rule, condition or requirement of employment that applies to everyone because of their race, sex, marital or family status, religious beliefs, etc, and a higher proportion of people who do not have that characteristic do, or can, comply with it, and there is no valid reason for the rule or requirement. For example, a policy of hiring people only who were able to relocate at short notice may disadvantage people who have family responsibilities – eg persons with young children (women employees).

The requirement not to discriminate applies before and during the employment relationship (and to a limited extent after employment), and therefore would cover less favourable treatment in recruitment, performance review appraisal, training, a compensation package, promotion, or selection for redundancy. Unlike claims of unfair dismissal, in which the level of compensation is capped, discrimination claims are unlimited in the potential amount of the financial award. Moreover, employers can, in appropriate cases, be required to pay compensation for injury to feelings and personal (psychological) injury as well as being required to discharge aggravated or exemplary damages. On top of this, interest can be added to the award of compensation.

For this reason the eradication of discrimination requires a knowledge and understanding of the key legal principles, the ability to monitor changes and developments in the law, and the will to take on board the practical lessons to be learned from decided cases. Since the Equal Pay Act (1970), Sex Discrimination Act (1975), Race Relations Act (1976) and Disability Discrimination Act (1995) came into force, there have been some 700 significant decisions by the appellate courts which have been reported in *Industrial Relations Law Reports* (IRLR), one of the most widely used series of law reports in the field of employment relations, interpreting the statutory provisions.

One of the reasons why we are devoting a significant amount of this chapter to the subject of discrimination is because discrimination cases have assumed increasing prominence and – although they represent only 15% of cases that go to employment tribunals compared to 27% for unfair dismissal – now represent the largest subject area that go before the appellate courts.

The influence of discrimination legislation is one of the reasons behind the decision to replace the three specialist equality bodies – the Equal Opportunities Commission, the Commission for Racial Equality and the Disability Rights Commission – with a single umbrella organisation, the Equality and Human Rights Commission (EHRC) as from 2007. This body is not only carrying on the work of the previous commissions but has also taken responsibility for the sexual orientation, religious discrimination and age discrimination laws.

As well as enforcing the law, the EHRC promotes equal opportunities in society as a whole, in particular the provision of public services. It also provides a 'one-stop shop' for those seeking advice and information on diversity strategies.

One of the Government's reasons for creating the umbrella organisation was that people do not see themselves solely as a woman or black or gay, and therefore neither should equality organisations. This mindset was a key factor behind the decision to introduce an overarching piece of legislation, the Equality Bill (2009), to provide a clearer legal framework on equality matters. The Bill became law in the spring of 2010 and it is of vital importance that practitioners make themselves aware of all its provisions.

For most managers discrimination law can be a minefield. The cost of dealing with complaints of discrimination and harassment and resultant tribunal claims can, relative to claims for unfair dismissal, be prohibitive. Generally, there is more evidence to be gathered, more witnesses to be heard and, of course, no cap on the possible compensation to be awarded. There are also a number of business risks – firstly, to the organisation's reputation, particularly if the case is covered by the press. Secondly, a discrimination claim is also likely to be personally embarrassing and in all likelihood distressing for those managers named in the claim. If they are found to have discriminated, harassed or bullied, managers are likely to be subject to disciplinary action, may be dismissed and may well find that the claim continues to blight their career. Finally, there is the issue of management time. Frequently, in discrimination claims, an employer will be served with a discrimination questionnaire. The time taken to respond to these questionnaires together with the time taken to properly prepare for and attend at a tribunal hearing can be substantial.

Employers and individual line managers are most at risk of allegations of discrimination when making key decisions which will impact on employees on subjective grounds. One of the key elements an applicant must prove if he or she wishes to succeed in a discrimination complaint is the existence of a detriment. What this means in practice, of course, is that when making key decisions about employees, employers must as far as possible base them on objective criteria. By far the best means of minimising the risk of claims is to behave proactively and prevent claims from being brought in the first place. In order to do this it is essential that employers are sensitive to potential issues of discrimination and harassment within the workplace, and that steps are taken at an early stage when a potential problem arises.

It is therefore particularly important that employers watch out for the warning signs of discrimination/harassment – which are likely to include the following:

- grievances (which may themselves seem somewhat petty)
- 'personality clashes'
- high levels of absenteeism
- ill-health (particularly any stress-related illness)
- poor performance (particularly where there has been a sudden downturn in performance following some change in the working arrangements)
- negative comments through peer evaluation/the appraisal process
- high levels of staff departures
- negative comments during exit interviews.

There are very few employers or individual line managers who do not genuinely want to eradicate discrimination and harassment from their workplace. If asked to pinpoint where employers/line managers with the best of intentions have gone wrong, the majority of employment lawyers would tell you that they have waited too long before obtaining advice and assistance from their own personnel specialist. If line managers are facing a difficult personnel issue, are having to make 'high-risk decisions' or believe they have spotted the warning signs of a potential dispute within their team, clearly, the first action they should take – rather than seeking to resolve it themselves – is to pick up the phone and call for help. But for this to happen the employment relations specialist must ensure that he or she enjoys the confidence of line manager colleagues – confidence that is gained through offering reliable, consistent advice.

## REFLECTIVE ACTIVITY

Do you think your organisation has ever avoided taking a decision because of a fear that it might be accused of a discriminatory act?

Time and again the cases indicate that if action is taken at an early stage, potential problems can be resolved. Often, problems can be resolved using an employer's internal grievance procedure – particularly if this allows any grievance to be dealt with confidentially. If, however, potential problems are not dealt with at an early stage, there will be an increasing risk of claims being brought, of potential liability and of the costs already outlined. For this reason, not only should organisations have equal opportunities policies that are more than just bland statements, they need to have a means by which people can raise issues of concern – as the following example, taken from an actual employee handbook, illustrates.

---

### PROCEDURE FOR HANDLING EQUAL OPPORTUNITY PROBLEMS

This procedure explains what to do if you have an Equal Opportunities problem, issue or complaint.

At *Smith & Co. Limited* we understand that it may be hard for you to work to your full capacity if you are being treated unfairly or harassed at work. That is why we support equal opportunity (EO) in this workplace.

If you bring a problem to us, it will be handled confidentially, impartially and speedily.

We have outlined the procedure for handling problems in steps. Not all of these may apply to you, or you may follow them in a different order than shown here.

#### Step 1: Talk to the person / people involved

If you can, it's best to try and resolve issues yourself and to do so as soon as possible after the incident. We understand that you may not always feel comfortable doing so, particularly if you have a problem with your supervisor or line manager.

#### Step 2: Talk to the person responsible for EO

If you would like to talk over an issue or find out what your rights are, make a time to talk to our company's EO representative who will meet with you as soon as possible. In general they will not discuss your problem with anyone else without your permission. The only exception to this is if you tell them something that may affect someone's safety.

Depending on what you decide, and after taking details from you, the EO representative will arrange for the other person(s) involved in the issue to be seen (preferably within two workdays of meeting with you) to obtain their side of the story.

We strongly encourage timely complaint resolution and we will aim to deal with matters as expeditiously as possible. The EO representative will speak to witnesses if they need further information. Witnesses may include people who didn't actually see what happened but who observed your reaction or other related behaviour.

The EO representative will then decide if they have enough information to know whether your allegation happened (using the standard proof that it is more likely than not to have happened). They will then submit a report to the Managing Director or other director with a recommendation about what, if any, further action is needed.

Although our intention is to deal with all complaints in a timely manner, there may be times – during holidays, for example – when the time-scales set out above cannot be adhered to.

Where allegations are proved, the company will resolve the problem by:

- bringing everyone together for a meeting to reach an agreement/resolve issues if the allegation is not of a serious nature

- taking appropriate disciplinary action (such as requiring an apology, counselling, an official warning, transfer, demotion) against the person(s) responsible if the allegation is serious.

They may also arrange training on EO issues for all staff to ensure that everyone knows what is and isn't acceptable.

### Step 3: Contact the Group Human Resources Director

If you are unsatisfied with the decision reached under this procedure, or you do not feel comfortable bringing it to our attention, you can contact the Group Human Resources Director for information and advice about your issue at *[insert details]*.

### How will our company handle your problem?

We will handle your problem:

*1 Confidentially*

Only those directly involved in your issue or complaint (including anyone helping to sort it out) will have access to information about it. Information about the problem will only go on an employee's file if they are disciplined in relation to it.

*2 Impartially*

Everyone involved in the issue will get the chance to tell their side of the story, and will be treated as fairly as possible. The person handling the issue or complaint will not make a decision or take any action until all relevant information has been gathered.

*3 Speedily*

We will handle all issues or complaints as quickly as possible. Where possible, we will try to resolve all issues within 4 weeks.

### WE WILL NOT TOLERATE:

### Victimisation

Less favourable treatment or disadvantage of anyone involved in an issue or complaint being handled under this procedure will be disciplined. Malicious use of this procedure (for example, to lie about someone) will also be a disciplinary matter.

**We will not take any action without proof**

We will investigate all issues before making a decision and/or taking action. We will only take action if we believe that it is more likely than not that the allegations happened.

However, as important as it is to watch out for potentially discriminatory acts, and to take appropriate action, managers must not be inhibited from making fair, objective business decisions simply because an employee might claim that such a decision is discriminatory.

In the case of *Madarassy v Nomura International plc* the Court of Appeal approved the principle that in all discrimination cases the burden of proof is, first of all, on the claimant to demonstrate that they were treated less favourably on the basis of sex, race, disability, etc. It is not sufficient for the claimant to demonstrate simply a difference in status. So if, for example, an employee was facing the possibility of disciplinary action and complained that it was because of a disability, the employer would have to show that the same action would have been taken against an able-bodied employee – ie that the action taken was because of the disciplinary offence, and not because of the disability.

## REFLECTIVE ACTIVITY

Does your organisation have an equal opportunities policy? What are the business case arguments you would use to justify such policies?

## DISMISSAL AND REDUNDANCY

Although discrimination law might be one of the most dynamic and complex areas of employment law, the law relating to unfair dismissal and redundancy continues to provide the bulk of the practitioner's workload. In Chapters 12 (*Employee Performance and Behaviour*) and 14 (*Managing Redundancies*) we look in much greater detail at the skills that are required to manage these two important issues, but in the context of Kahn-Freund's regulatory function these individual rights are a key area for any employment relations professional.

By virtue of section 94 of the Employment Rights Act (1996), an employee who at the effective date of termination (EDT) of employment has continuous service of one year or more with the employer has a right not to be unfairly dismissed and is afforded the right to present a complaint to an employment tribunal. In order to successfully defend an employee's claim for unfair dismissal, an employer must be able to satisfy an employment tribunal of three things:

- that the real or principal reason for the dismissal was one of the potentially fair reasons as set out in section 98(2) of the Employment Rights Act (1996)

- that it was reasonable to dismiss in all the circumstances of the case, and

- that the employer followed a fair procedure.

The potentially fair reasons for dismissal are:

- capability problems (including ill-health) or lack of qualifications

- misconduct

- redundancy

- contravention of statute (eg no work permit for the employee), or

- 'some other substantial reason'.

Concerns often arise when employers seek to attach a label to the 'reason' that they are dismissing an employee, and this is especially true in, for example, cases of persistent short-term absences. Where employees have been dismissed on these grounds, some employers have sought to justify their actions by classifying the dismissal as being for incapability (ie a 'capability' issue) arising from the sickness whereas others have classified the dismissal as being on the basis of conduct relating to the employee's poor attendance record. Understandably, this has caused employers some concern in that they had difficulty in satisfying themselves that they had a potentially fair reason for dismissal. To their relief, the Employment Appeals Tribunal (EAT) sought to resolve this difficulty in the case of *Post Office v Wilson*, in which they indicated that tribunals should consider whether any of the reasons set out in section 98(2) apply to the facts before them but that if none of these categories fitted the facts, the tribunal must then consider whether the employer has established 'some other substantial reason' for dismissal. The burden of proof in establishing the reasons for dismissal lies squarely with the employer, although in most cases this burden is not difficult to discharge.

However, there are a number of circumstances where an employee's dismissal will be held to be automatically unfair, which include where the employee can show that the real reason for dismissal was:

- health- and safety-related

- maternity-related

- related to dependant care/parental leave

- related to the employee's assertion of a statutory right

- related to the participation by the employee in industrial action where it was within the first eight weeks of industrial action

- related to the employee's membership or non-membership of a trade union or to his or her participation in trade union activities

- redundancy, where the employee was selected for redundancy for any of the reasons set out above

- in relation to protected shop workers and betting workers who may not be dismissed for refusing to work on Sundays
- relating to employees appointed as member-nominated trustees of their pension fund, under the Pensions Act, who may not be dismissed for exercising their function as such
- relating to employees elected (or seeking election) as employee representatives for the purposes of consultation over collective redundancies or transfers of undertakings, who may not be dismissed for performing, or proposing to perform, any such functions or activities
- connected with a business transfer to which the Transfer of Undertakings (Protection of Employment) Regulations 1981 apply
- related to the employee's spent conviction or failure to disclose it
- related to a disclosure qualifying under the Public Interest Disclosure Act (1999), or exercising rights under the Working Time Regulations (1998), the National Minimum Wage Act (1998) or Tax Credits Act (1999).

Individual employees enforce their rights on discrimination, redundancy, unfair dismissal and a range of other matters via employment tribunals. We will examine the nature and jurisdiction of tribunals later in the chapter, but suffice to say that they are independent judicial bodies set up with the objective of dealing with employment disputes quickly, informally and cheaply.

The sheer variety of potentially unfair reasons for dismissal, or claims for discrimination, indicates that for the employment relations professional there is no room for complacency. An incorrectly handled dismissal, a failure to deal with a complaint of discrimination, an ill-advised decision in respect of a business transfer or health and safety issue, can mean an appearance before an employment tribunal. Even when things are done properly, the area of law dealing with individual rights at work can still give rise to a vast amount of litigation. Although the statistics on the number of complaints brought by employees (see Tables 4.1 and 4.2) show that the total of accepted claims in the year 2008/9 declined compared to 2007/8, they were still in excess of 150,000. Some of these were made under more than one jurisdiction ('type of claim'), which is why the total of claims accepted and the total by mix of jurisdiction differ. Although many of the applications made are not proceeded with (see Table 4.2), they still represent a degree of work for the employment relations specialist, and of particular concern is the rise in the number of cases alleging a failure to inform and consult over redundancies.

### REFLECTIVE ACTIVITY

Do you think the recession in 2009 was wholly to blame for the increase in some types of claim, or is there a deeper malaise in the approach to employment relations by some managers?

Table 4.1  Claims accepted by employment tribunals

|  | April to March | | |
|---|---|---|---|
|  | 2006/7 | 2007/8 | 2008/9 |
| *Total claims accepted* | 132,577 | 189,303 | 151,028 |
| *Total claims initially rejected* | 10,762 | 9,779 | 10,576 |
| Of the total, those that were resubmitted and subsequently accepted | 3,861 | 3,323 | 2,858 |
| Of the total, those that were resubmitted and not accepted | 6,901 | 6,456 | 7,718 |
| *Jurisdiction mix of claims accepted: Nature of claim* | | | |
| Unfair dismissal | 44,491 | 40,941 | 52,711 |
| Unauthorised deductions (formerly Wages Act) | 34,857 | 34,583 | 33,839 |
| Breach of contract | 27,298 | 25,054 | 32,829 |
| Sex discrimination | 28,153 | 26,907 | 18,637 |
| Working Time Directive | 21,127 | 55,712 | 23,976 |
| Redundancy pay | 7,692 | 7,313 | 10,839 |
| Disability discrimination | 5,533 | 5,833 | 6,578 |
| Redundancy – failure to inform and consult | 4,802 | 4,480 | 11,371 |
| Equal pay | 44,013 | 62,706 | 45,148 |
| Race discrimination | 3,180 | 4,130 | 4,983 |
| Written statement of terms and conditions | 3,429 | 4,955 | 3,919 |
| Written statement of reasons for dismissal | 1,064 | 1,098 | 1,105 |
| Written pay statement | 990 | 1,086 | 1,144 |
| Transfer of an undertaking – failure to inform and consult | 1,108 | 1,380 | 1,262 |
| Suffer a detriment/unfair dismissal – eg pregnancy | 1,465 | 1,646 | 1,835 |
| Part-Time Workers Regulations | 776 | 595 | 664 |
| National Minimum Wage | 806 | 431 | 595 |
| Discrimination on grounds of religion or belief | 648 | 709 | 832 |
| Discrimination on grounds of sexual orientation | 470 | 582 | 600 |
| Age discrimination | 972 | 2,949 | 3,801 |
| Others | 5,072 | 13,873 | 9,274 |
| TOTAL | 238,546 | 296,963 | 266,542 |

## THE RIGHTS OF UNION MEMBERS

As well as a statutory floor of rights for employees, union members have their own statutory rights. These rights, which were considerably extended under the post-1979 Conservative Governments, have been justified on the grounds that trade unions needed to be more democratic, be more accountable to their members and exercise their power more responsibly. As the climate of UK industrial relations worsened in the 1960s and 1970s there was a widespread

**Table 4.2  All unfair dismissal jurisdictions disposed of at a hearing**

|  | Number (000s) | Percentage of | |
|---|---|---|---|
|  |  | Dismissal proceeding hearings | All unfair dismissal cases disposed of |
| *Cases dismissed:* |  |  |  |
| At a preliminary hearing | 1.01 | 10.9 | 2.6 |
| Unsuccessful at hearing | 4.37 | 46.9 | 11.1 |
| All cases dismissed |  | 57.0 | 13.7 |
| *Cases upheld:* |  |  |  |
| Reinstatement or re-engagement | 7.0 | 0.1 | 0.0 |
| Remedy left to parties | 132.0 | 1.4 | 0.3 |
| Compensation | 2.48 | 26.7 | 6.3 |
| No award made | 1.30 | 14.0 | 3.3 |
| All cases upheld | 3.93 | 42.2 | 10.0 |
| *All cases proceeding to a hearing* | 9.31 | 100 | 23.6 |

**Table 4.3  Representation of claimants at employment tribunals**

| Represented by: | 2006/7 | 2007/8 | 2008/9 |
|---|---|---|---|
| Trade union | 9,902 | 29,136 | 8,812 |
| Lawyers | 79,313 | 117,565 | 85,871 |
| No representation information provided | 31,694 | 31,780 | 41,270 |
| Other | 11,701 | 10,814 | 15,075 |
| Total claims | 132,610 | 189,295 | 151,028 |

belief that trade union leaders were, without collecting the views of their members, coercing them to undertake labour market activities (for example, undertaking industrial action) harmful to their employment security – in short, that much strike activity was the result of political idealism on the part of trade union officials, rather than the consequence of a breakdown in collective bargaining.

This view resulted in the enactment of a series of measures to provide positive rights for union members to participate in or restrain union decision-making on specific issues. The main trade union member rights are:

- to participate in regular secret postal ballots, at least once every 10 years, to decide whether or not their union should establish, or retain, a political fund financed by political fund contribution, independent of the normal union subscription

- to elect all voting members of their union's executive (including its president and general secretary) by secret postal ballot at least once every five years

- to participate in a secret ballot before a union takes organised industrial action against an employer
- not to be called upon to participate in industrial action not supported by a properly conducted secret ballot
- not to be disciplined unjustifiably by their union
- to inspect their union's accounting records.

As a means of helping individual union members enforce their rights, the Employment Act (1988) provided the means whereby they could seek assistance if they were considering or taking legal action against their union.

## THE RESTRICTIVE FUNCTION OF THE LAW

**THEORY**

Ever since 1871 trade unions have, except when they were undermined by the *Taff Vale* decision in 1901, enjoyed immunity from actions for civil damages. That is, they have been protected from being sued simply because they took, or were taking, industrial action. The basic immunity framework was contained in the Trade Disputes Act (1906), and this remained in force until 1971 when the Conservative Government introduced the Industrial Relations Act. This limited trade union immunity by the introduction of the concept of 'unfair industrial practices' which, if unions committed them, gave those affected by the action the right to sue for damages.

The Trade Union and Labour Relations Act (1974) repealed the Industrial Relations Act (1971) and re-established the trade unions' immunities position back to that provided by the Trades Disputes Act (1906). The Trade Union and Labour Relations (Amendment) Act (1976) extended trade union immunity to the breach of all contracts for which trade unions were responsible when they called their members out on industrial action. This gave trade unions licence to persuade their members to take secondary industrial action. Secondary action is that taken against an employer with whom the trade union has no dispute but who might, for example, be a key customer of an employer with whom they currently do have an industrial dispute. By taking this type of industrial action the union hopes the secondary employer will put pressure on the employer involved in the main dispute to settle the dispute on terms more favourable than presently on offer.

By 1976, trade unions had a very wide immunity from legal action in the case of industrial disputes. They could call, without a legal liability arising, for industrial action in connection with any kind of industrial dispute, no matter how remote those taking the action were from the original dispute. Nobody seriously challenged this union legislative position until 1979 when, as we noted above, there were moves to clamp down on the unions' abuse of their power. Legislation came at regular intervals, and between 1980 and 1993 there were seven Acts of Parliament designed to restrict trade union activity and behaviour.

- The Employment Act (1980) removed the unions' immunity if their members engaged in picketing premises other than their own place of work.

- The Employment Act (1982) narrowed the definition of a trade dispute, outlawed the practice of pressuring employers not to include non-union firms on tender lists, and enabled employers to sue trade unions for an injunction or damages where they were responsible for unlawful industrial action.
- The Trade Union Act (1984) introduced, *inter alia*, pre-strike ballots.
- The Employment Act (1988) amongst other things effectively outlawed the closed shop.
- The Employment Act (1990) removed unions' immunity if they organised any type of secondary action in support of an individual dismissed for taking unlawful action.
- The Trade Union and Labour Relations (Consolidation) Act (1992) brought together in one piece of legislation much of the law relating to collective provision.
- The Trade Union Reform and Employment Rights Act (1993) made some amendments to existing requirements, most particularly in relation to ballots for industrial action.

These pieces of legislation substantially increased the grounds on which an employer can take legal action against a union. The circumstances in which unions can claim immunity from civil action have been tightened and now include provisions which require full-time officials to repudiate the actions of lay officials if they take actions contrary to the legislation. If immunity is to be maintained, such repudiation has to be meaningful – and the courts can require unions to present evidence of the steps they have taken to bring their members within the law.

## REFLECTIVE ACTIVITY

Outline, with appropriate examples, the functions of the law in employment relations.

There is now no serious argument that these reforms were both necessary and timely. Requiring unions to hold a pre-strike ballot of their members prior to taking industrial action has now become part of the employment relations landscape and is not seriously questioned. Similarly, the requirement that full-time officials should be subject to periodic re-election has become part of the fabric of trade union organisation.

## THE NATURE AND JURISDICTION OF EMPLOYMENT TRIBUNALS

Employment tribunals are independent judicial bodies, 'inferior courts' within the meaning of the Rules of the Supreme Court. For administrative convenience the country is divided into regions, each of which has its own office. Individual tribunals usually comprise three members: an employment judge (a solicitor or barrister of seven years' qualification), an employer representative, and an employee representative (usually a trade union representative). They also have jurisdiction in a wide range of matters derived from various statutory provisions (see Table 4.1 above). Each matter is begun by an application which is subject to its own time limit but which the employment tribunal usually has a discretion to extend, and applications are made to the appropriate tribunal regional office.

The employment tribunal is a statutory body and its composition is governed by the Employment Tribunals Act (1996) as amended by the Employment Act (2002) and, as a consequence of the 2002 Act, the rules for its administration are now set out in the Employment Tribunals (Constitution and Rules of Procedure) Amendment Regulations (2008). These Regulations, together with previous regulations such as the Employment Tribunals (Constitution and Rules of Procedure) Regulations (2004), set out how tribunals operate on a day-to-day basis.

## THE APPLICATION PROCESS

Proceedings are commenced by an applicant (the claimant) who presents a claim form which has to provide details about the claimant and the respondent and other information that will help determine whether the claim can be accepted by the employment tribunal.

Once the application is received and has been accepted by the Secretary to the Tribunals, it is registered and a copy sent to the respondent and also to ACAS. With the copy that is sent to the respondent, the tribunal will send details of how to respond to the claim, the deadline by which the response must be received, and the consequences of not replying. The respondent has 28 days to submit their response form.

Once a claim has been received and properly responded to, the employment judge has powers to manage the proceedings in order to ensure the smooth and efficient running of the case. He or she can issue directions on any matter that he or she thinks is appropriate either from the parties' application/response or at a pre-hearing review.

Either may make an application – or the tribunal may order – that one or other party must provide further and better particulars of any grounds upon which they rely, or any facts or contentions relevant to their claim. The essence of further particulars is to enable a party to know in advance the nature of the case that they must meet at the hearing. Failure to provide further particulars can result in the claim's being struck out. In keeping with the need to provide further and better particulars, a tribunal can order such discovery and inspection of documents and set a time and a place for compliance. As with further particulars, discovery is an important step in the process of enabling the parties to know the nature and extent of the case they have to respond to. The rules of procedure allow tribunals the power to strike out applications, or award costs, when a party to the proceedings does not comply with a directions order. This change has meant that the importance of compliance with any directions made is greatly increased. Costs can be awarded if a party, or its representative, has conducted proceedings vexatiously, abusively, disruptively or otherwise negatively. Costs can be awarded only if a party to the proceedings is legally represented, but there is also a provision within the rules for preparation time orders to be made when there is no legal representation. These orders may be particularly beneficial to those employers who prefer to present their own cases because they also cover the issue of vexatious claims.

## ACAS CONCILIATION

Since its inception, one of the roles that ACAS has played in employment relations is conciliation in tribunal claims. ACAS officers receive details of claims to tribunals and then contact the parties to assess whether a settlement is possible. ACAS has a legal duty to offer free conciliation where a complaint about employment rights has been made to an employment tribunal, and a power to provide conciliation where a claim could be made but has not yet been. The role of ACAS is to help find a solution that both sides find acceptable instead of going to a tribunal hearing. ACAS does not impose solutions but will try to help the parties settle differences on their own terms. Although this process is known as conciliation, it is essentially the same process as mediation.

This conciliation service is voluntary – parties to a tribunal claim only take part if both agree that it can stop at any time. Crucially, it is impartial: ACAS does not take sides or judge who is right or wrong. However, in providing this help, the conciliation officer will seek to offer an opinion to both sides on their likely chances of success. ACAS are not part of the tribunal service, and their involvement does not delay the tribunal process, nor can anything said to the conciliation officer be offered in evidence at a tribunal hearing because it is completely confidential. It should be noted that conciliation might only be available for a limited period for certain types of complaint to an employment tribunal, and that if this applies, the tribunal will notify the parties. Otherwise, conciliation can continue until the case is heard by the employment tribunal. Most practitioners will appreciate that it is often in the days leading up to the tribunal hearing, or at the tribunal door itself, that settlement between the parties is reached. The fact that a significant number of claims do not get to a full hearing is testament to ACAS's success in this area.

One particular point to note in considering the work of ACAS in the field of individual disputes is its ability to offer free and impartial pre-claim conciliation (PCC). Where a problem or disagreement in the workplace is likely to lead to a tribunal claim, ACAS will often be able to help employers and employees find a solution that is acceptable to both, and avoid the costs, stress and time associated with an employment tribunal. The Dispute Resolution Review, published in 2007, highlighted the benefits for both employers and employees if workplace disputes are resolved swiftly and with minimal formality before they escalate into litigation. The ACAS pre-claim conciliation service was expanded in April 2009 to help achieve that aim, and ACAS reports that assistance has been provided in nearly 4,000 cases. Over 80% of the cases in which both employers and employees have agreed to conciliate have been resolved without turning into tribunal claims.

## THE HEARING AND THE DECISION

If ACAS has not been able to help and the case continues to a full hearing, it is the responsibility of the parties to ensure that their witnesses are ready and willing to attend at the tribunal and that they, through the process of discovery, have in their possession all necessary and relevant documents. Every encouragement is given to the parties to agree documents, and tribunals now direct that the parties prepare an agreed 'bundle' of documents for use during the hearing. This responsibility generally falls to the respondent (employer) because it is considered that they will have the appropriate administrative resources and, in the majority of cases, will have in their possession all, or the majority of, the documents.

Individual applicants may appear before a tribunal without representation or may be represented by a lawyer, a trade union official or any other person of their choice. If they are unrepresented, the tribunal does what it can to assist them while ensuring that there is no bias.

Although there is no specific rule that dictates the order in which evidence is given, it usually depends on who has the burden of proof. In unfair dismissal cases where dismissal is admitted, the respondent employer begins. If dismissal is not admitted, or it is incumbent upon the applicant to prove his or her case – for example, in constructive dismissal – the applicant begins. In order to speed up the process of evidence-giving, tribunals' witness statements are generally exchanged prior to the hearing. This helps both parties with their preparation and can avoid lengthy cross-examination.

Once a witness has given their evidence they may be cross-examined by the other side and may also have to answer questions put to them by the tribunal members. Then, when the parties have called all their witnesses, they are given an opportunity to make their final submissions. It is generally the case that the party who presented their evidence first will have the final word. Finally, the tribunal will withdraw to make their decision. They will usually indicate whether they can announce their decision on the day of the hearing or whether it will be given in writing to the parties afterwards. When the applicant is successful, there will often be a need for the parties to make further submissions in respect of the size of any compensation payment, or the type of relief to be granted.

## REFLECTIVE ACTIVITY

You are asked by your line manager to explain the procedure used in employment tribunal hearings. What would you tell him or her, and why?

## THE ACAS ARBITRATION SCHEME

ACAS was empowered by the Employment Rights (Dispute Resolution) Act (1998) to operate an arbitration scheme as an alternative to employment tribunal hearings. The implications of the scheme are far-reaching, and before submitting to arbitration the parties should therefore be aware of the process involved.

The central features of the arbitration scheme are that it is:

- voluntary
- speedy
- informal
- confidential, and
- free from legal arguments.

With these aims, it was thought by many that the scheme would herald a return to the idealism of the original tribunals of the mid-1960s. The scheme is currently only available for unfair dismissal complaints and referral must be by the mutual consent of both parties.

Arbitration under the scheme is on standard terms only. These cannot be varied. If the arbitrator, having regard to the ACAS code of practice, found the dismissal to have been unfair, the awards may be reinstatement, re-engagement or compensation.

### THE HEARING

The arbitrator is responsible for the conduct of hearings. The general principles lay out that the language of the proceedings is in English, there are no oaths or affirmations, and parties are free to engage representatives and bring witnesses if they wish. Note that no special status will be accorded to legally qualified representatives. The arbitrator decides on procedural and evidential matters. His or her approach is inquisitorial and there is no direct cross-examination. Questions between the parties may only be addressed through the arbitrator.

The applicant may withdraw from the process at any time, provided it is done in writing to ACAS or the arbitrator. The parties are also free to reach a private agreement to settle the dispute before the end of the hearing. The arbitrator can endorse such an agreement but not interpret or ratify it in any way. This power is limited to agreements which are in his or her remit – eg unfair dismissal disputes.

The arbitrator's decision is in writing, includes references to general considerations and reasoning taken into account in reaching his or her decision, and will be sent to both parties at the same time within a three-week deadline. The amount of any awards of compensation will be reasonable in the circumstances, taking into account the established practice of and statutory limits imposed on employment tribunals. The arbitrator's decision will not be published nor lodged with the employment tribunal, which makes the process very attractive where the issue is of a sensitive nature or publicity is preferably to be avoided. Given the apparent attractiveness of the scheme, it is strange that it has been woefully under-utilised, suggesting that parties prefer the established employment tribunal route.

## REFLECTIVE ACTIVITY

Explain three advantages and disadvantages to an employer in agreeing to have alleged unfair dismissal claims decided by voluntary arbitration rather than at an employment tribunal.

## THE HUMAN RIGHTS ACT (HRA)

The Convention for the Protection of Human Rights and Fundamental Freedoms (the Convention) was signed by the UK in 1950, and in 1951 the UK was the first to ratify it, but it is only recently that it has been supported by specific legislation. The Human Rights Act (1998), which came into force on 2 October 2000, states in its preamble that it is:

> an Act to give effect to the rights and freedoms guaranteed under the European Convention on Human Rights …

Although it is not specifically a piece of employment legislation, it impacts on employment law in three ways:

- Courts and employment tribunals are obliged to construe domestic legislation compatibly with the European Convention on Human Rights (ECHR) so far as it is possible to do so.
- Courts and employment tribunals must themselves act compatibly with the ECHR, save where they are prevented from doing so by primary legislation.
- Public bodies must act compatibly with the ECHR (this will include in relation to their employment policies and procedures), again save where they are prevented from doing so by primary legislation.

### THE IMPACT OF THE ACT ON DIFFERENT TYPES OF EMPLOYER

The position in an employment context can be summarised as follows. A pure public authority such as central government or the police will be required to act at all times compatibly with Convention rights. Insofar as an employer has acted in breach of a Convention right in respect of a particular employee, that employee can issue proceedings. So far as private employers are concerned, they are not required to act compatibly with Convention rights regardless of what capacity they are acting in.

### THE IMPACT OF THE ACT ON COURTS AND TRIBUNALS

It would be a mistake, however, to assume that the Act does not have implications for a private sector employer or for a public/private sector employer acting in a private context. The Act is still relevant to the actions of such an employer because of its impact on UK courts and tribunals. The Act impacts on UK courts and tribunals in the following ways:

- Courts or tribunals are required to act compatibly with Convention rights (this is because for the purposes of the Act 'public authority' is expressly defined as including courts and tribunals).

- Courts and tribunals are required to take into account European Court of Human Rights jurisprudence when considering an issue relating to a Convention right.

- Courts and tribunals are required to interpret UK legislation in a way which is compatible with Convention rights 'so far as it is possible to do so'.

It remains, however, comparatively early days in the operation of the Act, and it is realistic to say that its impact will be felt over a much longer period yet.

### EXAMPLES OF THE IMPLICATIONS OF THE ACT IN AN EMPLOYMENT CONTEXT

The exact impact of the Act and particular Convention rights will depend upon how UK courts and tribunals interpret their role under the Act and how they interpret particular Convention rights. Notwithstanding this, it is possible to identify potential implications, and although there has been little case law to date, it is probable that, as the law develops, litigants and their lawyers will seek to link Convention rights to employment rights. For example, Article 6 – which provides for the right to a fair trial – might be used to include the admissibility or otherwise of evidence in tribunal hearings. Tribunals will have to consider whether to admit evidence such as evidence from phone-tapping or searches of a company's email system, where that evidence has been obtained in breach of Article 8, the right to respect for private and family life.

In this context, the Court of Appeal in 2004 adjudicated in an unfair dismissal case in which the applicant claimed that his rights under Article 8 had been infringed. The case concerned a charity youth worker dismissed after failing to inform his employers that he had been cautioned for gross indecency in a public toilet. His claim that the dismissal was unfair because it amounted to a breach of his Convention right to respect for his private life failed before the Court of Appeal, as it did in the EAT, on the basis that a criminal offence which happens in a place to which the public has access cannot be regarded as taking place in private. The Court of Appeal acknowledges, however, that if a dismissal was on grounds of an employee's private conduct within Article 8, and was an interference with the right to respect for private life, that will be relevant to the determination of an unfair dismissal claim. This is because under section 3 of the Human Rights Act, an employment tribunal, so far as it is possible to do so, must read and give effect to section 98 and other relevant provisions of the Employment Rights Act in a way that is compatible with Convention rights. 'There would normally be no sensible grounds for treating public and private employees differently in respect of "unfair dismissal", Lord Justice Mummery says in the leading decision. Therefore 'it would not normally be fair for a private sector employer to dismiss an employee for a reason which was an unjustified interference with the employee's private life.' During the course of the decision (*X v Y* [2004] IRLR 625), Lord Justice Mummery laid down guidelines on the correct approach to be adopted when Human Rights Act points are raised in unfair dismissal cases.

1 Do the circumstances of the dismissal fall within the ambit of one or more of the articles of the Convention? If they do not, the Convention right is not engaged and need not be considered.

2 If they do, does the state have a positive obligation to secure enjoyment of the relevant Convention right between private persons? If it does not, the Convention right is unlikely to affect the outcome of an unfair dismissal claim against a private employer.

3 If it does, is the interference with the employee's Convention right by dismissal justified? If it is, proceed to **5** below.

4 If it is not, was there a permissible reason for the dismissal under the ERA, which does not involve unjustified interference with a Convention right? If there was not, the dismissal will be unfair for the absence of a permissible reason to justify it.

5 If there was, is the dismissal fair, tested by the provisions of section 98 of the ERA reading and giving effect to them under section 3 of the HRA so as to be compatible with the Convention right?

Other issues which might come before the courts include Article 10, the freedom of expression. This might be used by employees to sound the death knell for employers' dress codes, but potentially the most contentious issue might arise over Article 11, the freedom of assembly and association. Article 11's principal significance is in relation to trade unions and their activities. The provisions of the Trade Union and Labour Relations (Consolidation) Act (1992) (TULRCA) will have to be interpreted in a way that is compatible with Article 11 insofar as this is possible – although the general view of commentators is that by and large it *should* be possible.

Particular areas where it is felt that Article 11 is likely to be relevant include picketing, where the issue is likely to depend upon whether the existing provisions within section 220 of TULRCA and the code of practice on picketing (Code of Practice: Picketing, 1992) strike a reasonable balance between the right to protest and the interests of those affected by protest. In particular, it has been suggested that although in general these provisions may do this, there may be room for argument that certain provisions – such as, for example, provisions limiting the number of pickets to six – go beyond this. A further issue concerns the right to be a member of a particular trade union/not to join a trade union. It has also been argued that because Article 11 gives a right to form and join trade unions for 'the protection of interests', this must necessarily involve a right to representation. Finally, there is the matter of the 'right to strike'. It has been held that the right to strike is one of the rights protected by Article 11 – but the consensus is that it is likely to be reasonable for a state to impose significant restrictions on this right. However, there is a real possibility that trade unions and their lawyers will seek to use Article 11, particularly if there is any attempt by future governments to limit their rights to picket, strike and represent their members.

## REFLECTIVE ACTIVITY

Has the Human Rights Act made any impact on your organisation or one with which you are familiar?

## DEVELOPMENTS IN THE LAW

For HR practitioners, dealing with the law should be second nature, and taking account of the law in decision-making ought to be automatic. However, throughout the 1960s, 1970s and 1980s the scope of the law was relatively narrow and could be neatly categorised as individual or collective. Latterly, though, that scope has widened. New legislation, amendments to regulations and the decisions of tribunals continue to expand and extend the impact of law in the workplace. This process of change requires the employment relations professional to be particularly vigilant in monitoring what is changing, when it is changing, and what the likely impact is on the workplace. In the concluding part of this chapter we look at some of these developments and seek to identify what their probable impact is likely to be.

### AGE DISCRIMINATION

We have already said that discrimination law is one of the most dynamic and complex areas of employment law, and that its scope and coverage has changed dramatically over the past few years. One significant area of discrimination law that has impacted on business is age discrimination. Although most businesses seem to have come to terms with the need to take a non-discriminatory approach to recruitment and selection, the issue of retirement has caused some considerable problems. The problems have been caused by the Government's insistence on writing a 'default retirement age' (DRA) into the age discrimination regulations. This firstly led to significant litigation that went all the way to the European Court, and has now led to a government review of the DRA. A survey of employers' policies, practices and preferences relating to age has been commissioned, which will provide an insight into employers' use of the DRA. The Government has called on businesses and individuals to submit evidence on the following broad areas:

- the operation of the DRA in practice
- the reasons that businesses use mandatory retirement ages

- the impact of removing the DRA
- the experience of businesses operating without a DRA
- how any costs of raising or removing the DRA might be mitigated.

**REFLECTIVE ACTIVITY**

What will the business implications for your organisation be if the DRA is abolished? Why?

## ABSENCE FROM WORK

For many employment relations specialists and their line management colleagues, managing absence provides a continuing set of challenges. Historically, many of the problems have been caused by the perception that individuals are able to obtain a 'sick note' from their GP with relative ease. In order to address this problem, and the wider issue of an increasing number of disability benefit claimants, the Government has introduced 'fit notes'. These will replace the old doctors' sick note. Following a period of consultation, the Government has decided that:

- The new 'fit note' will list common types of changes that employers can introduce to encourage a return to work, such as a phased return to work, amended duties, altered hours, and workplace adaptations. Practical suggestions will be based on the patient's health condition, rather than being job-specific.

- The new 'fit note' will not have a tick-box allowing the GP to recommend an occupational health assessment. There was a fear that this would become an easy default option for GPs to select.

- The 'fit for work' option has been removed, following the consultation, and GPs will therefore only have two options to choose from: 'unfit for work' and 'you may be fit for work, taking account of the following advice'. The latter option was previously expressed as 'may be fit for some work'. The new wording was changed to reflect the fact that it is not the doctor but the employer, in consultation with the employee, who is best placed to decide whether they can accommodate any changes to facilitate a return to work.

- The maximum duration a medical statement can be issued for has been reduced from six months to three months during the first six months of an illness, because it was thought that the previous six-month period did not encourage people to return to work.

- Only GPs will be able to issue a 'fit note', although the Government has not ruled out allowing other healthcare practitioners to issue statements in the longer term.

However, the new system has not been without its critics. Some HR professionals fear that it will lead to disputes between employers and employees about what constitutes suitable work following a period of sick leave. This concern arises from the ability of doctors to provide an assessment of an individual's fitness for work and their option to state that an individual 'may be fit for work, taking account of the following advice'. The form of the note asks doctors to list any of a variety of workplace adjustments from which the employee might benefit and which might enable a return to work, but it does not ask them to go into detail about exactly what components of the employee's original job the employee will be able to perform. This is of clear concern to HR professionals since it places the onus on employers to decide what patients are capable of doing on their return to work.

One HR director commented that:

> If the employer is left to determine suitable work with only a 'fit for some work note' and a diagnosis, then those without occupational health advice may struggle, and there will inevitably be disputes about what constitutes suitable work.

Despite the concerns of some employers, the CIPD is positive about the changes. The Institute is currently carrying out research with the British Occupational Health Research Foundation into how capable line managers are in managing the return to work of long-term absentees. Ben Willmott, CIPD Senior Public Policy Adviser, said:

> It's not going to be a sudden process, but over a period of years we expect this [the 'fit note'] to lead to more people returning to work than would have done under the previous system. It will provide a framework to encourage GPs to have a conversation about a phased return to work.

## OTHER DEVELOPMENTS

The developments described above concern issues that are, or will be, of direct relevance to employers and employees, but there are always other matters that are not specifically about employment but will nevertheless impact upon the work of the HR professional and must be taken account of and their impact understood.

## SUMMARY

In this chapter we have tried to identify the relationship between good employment relations and the law. We have stressed that employment relations is as much about 'good practice' as it is about legal compliance, but we have recognised that the employment relations professional cannot afford to be dismissive of the law. This is because the law impacts on almost every activity in the workplace. Furthermore, individual employees are very much aware of their 'rights' at work and do not hesitate to use the mechanisms open to them (employment tribunals) to assert those rights.

We have explained that legal intervention derives from two main sources: the political choices of the governing party, and developments within Europe. But additional to this are developments in case law, and as we have explained, some of the major developments in discrimination law have been influenced by the decisions of the appellate courts.

We have examined the role of employment tribunals, with particular reference to the revised rules of procedure, and made it clear that the employment relations specialist must understand their scope and complexity.

Finally, we have looked at some, but not all, legal and other developments that we believe will impact on the work of the employment relations professional.

## KEY LEARNING POINTS

- Because all employment relations discussions have the capacity of legal challenge, it is important for managers to operate good employment practice.

- The scale of legal developments is such that employment relations professionals must continue to monitor changes and develop their own skills to do this.

- Employment relations professionals do not need to be lawyers, but they do need to understand the interaction between the law and employment relations.

- The employment relations professional should not view the law as simply a process of compliance. Good employment relations cannot be achieved by waving a legal rulebook and stating what employees and others cannot do. Good employment relations is achieved by the positive action employers take to win the trust and confidence of their workforce. To use the law as a blunt instrument to drive change could never be described as good employment practice.

- Employment relations professionals have to understand the range and importance of individual employee employment rights – but this is not sufficient. They must, for example, in the event of disciplinary cases, be able to manage the disciplinary procedure.

- Employment law is a function of good HR practice, and not the reverse. A professional employment relations manager will only take action if just cause to do so has been established after a thorough investigation, and will then take action in a fair, reasonable and consistent fashion. Employment law in the individual rights field says that if employers do not act on the basis of just cause and fair, reasonable and consistent behaviour, it will cost them in paying financial compensation to individuals concerned.

## REVIEW QUESTIONS

1 You are scheduled to give a training session to line managers in your organisation on the topic 'Employment law is nothing more than good employment practice'. Explain what is meant by 'good practice' in this context, and how it can ensure that your own organisation is protected against damaging employment tribunal decisions.

2 You have been asked by your chief executive officer (CEO) to provide the senior management team with a briefing note on how employment relations within the organisation might be affected by the age discrimination regulations. The organisation currently has no policy on retirement and has heard that this might

cause some difficulties. Explain, and justify, the employment relations issues you would have to cover in your briefing note.

3  What benefits could employees expect to obtain from a more flexible employment contract? Provide a justification for your answer.

4  A regional manager has asked to meet you to obtain advice on the status of some workers at her division. Three people

have worked on a daily basis as cleaners supplied by an external agency for over 12 months. The regional manager would like to terminate the cleaning contract but has heard that these three workers may now have accrued rights in respect of your company as much as, if not more than, with the agency firm. What advice will you give, using evidence and/or examples to justify what you say?

## EXPLORE FURTHER

Bercusson, B. (1996) *European Labour Law*. London: Butterworths.

Deakin, S. and Morris, G. (2005) *Labour Law*. Oxford: Oxford University Press.

Industrial Relations Service (various dates) *Employment Review: Policy, practice and law in the workplace*.

Kahn-Freund, O. (1972) *Labour and the Law*. London: Stevens, for the Hamlyn Trust.

Lewis, D. and Sargeant, M. (2009) *Essentials of Employment Law*, 10th edition. London: Chartered Institute of Personnel and Development.

O'Dempsey, D., Allen, A., Belgrave, S. and Brown, J. (2001) *Employment Law and the Human Rights Act*. Bristol: Jordan Publishing.

Taylor, S. and Emir, A. (2006) *Employment Law: An introduction*. Oxford: Oxford University Press.

Wells, K. (2003) 'The impact of the Framework Employment Directive on UK disability discrimination law', *Industrial Law Journal*, Vol.32, No.4: 253–73.

**Weblinks**

www.bis.gov.uk is the website of the Department for Business, Innovation and Skills, and will give you access to the main provisions of Acts of Parliament relevant to employment relations.

www.cipd.co.uk for information about the CIPD Employment Law Service.

www.employmenttribunals.gov.uk is the official website of the Central Office of Employment Tribunals.

www.equalityandhumanrights.com is the website of the Equality and Human Rights Commission created by the merger of the Equal Opportunities Commission, the Commission for Racial Equality and the Disability Rights Commission.

## CHAPTER 5

# The Importance of the European Union

## OVERVIEW

The influence of the European Union on HR/personnel management in the UK cannot be overstated. Its powers to determine the rules which regulate workplace relations between employers and employees in member states have grown dramatically since the 1990s. The Single European Market (SEM) established by the Treaty of Rome (1957) is a free trade area in which capital, labour, goods and services have free movement in the market. Competition in the SEM is to be fair competition, and competitive advantage cannot be based on artificial means – for example, by devaluation of the currency, changing interest rates and lowering employment and social standards. Competitive advantage has to be based on improved efficiency and productivity. The SEM also has a social dimension. The Treaty of Rome, enhanced by the Treaty of Maastricht (1993), contains a procedure whereby minimum employment and social conditions can be harmonised within member states. The chapter outlines the development of the social dimension of the SEM via the Treaty of Rome, the Single European Act (1986) and the Maastricht Treaty. It goes on to show how this Treaty involved the EU-wide social partners directly in the employment law-making process of the EU, including the negotiation of collective agreements (Framework Agreements) which can then be transposed into an EU Directive and then into national law. The chapter ends by examining how EU Directives in four areas – equal opportunities, employment protection, employment relations and health and safety – have impacted on the everyday work of the UK HR/personnel specialist.

## LEARNING OUTCOMES

When you have completed this chapter, you should be aware of and be able to describe:

- the influence of the European Union on employee relations management in the UK
- the main developments in the social dimension of the European Single Market
- the key institutions of the European Union
- the legislative processes of the European Union
- the unique role for 'social partner' organisations at the inter-professional and sectoral level to shape, draft and determine the scope of all new EU employment and social legislation (the so-called social dialogue process)
- the Social Chapter of the European Union
- how the Social Chapter of the European Union impinges on the everyday work of the employment relations professional in the fields of equal opportunities, employment protection/working conditions, employment relations and health and safety at work.

## INTRODUCTION

The influence of the European Union (EU) on HR/personnel management in the UK cannot be overstated. Its powers to determine the rules and regulations which govern workplace relations between employers and employees have grown dramatically since the mid-1990s. Examples of where the UK has had to take on board EU initiatives in the employment law field include collective redundancies, transfers of undertakings, acquired rights, the 'burden of proof' in equality cases, information and consultation, part-time work, fixed-term contracts, agency and temporary workers, pregnancy and maternity leave rights, parental leave, working time and equal opportunities. These are all areas in which EU legislation has directly affected the everyday work of the UK HR/personnel professional.

Personnel and HRM specialists have to appreciate that laws made at EU level take precedence over the domestic laws of member states. This applies to employment legislation just as much as legislation in every other field. However, the most important lesson to be learned from the innovations since 1993 is that the two sides of industry – employers and workers – are encouraged to participate in the law-making process when legislation is being enacted in the social and employment field.

The TUC, CBI and CEEP (UK) are members of the ETUC, Business Europe and CEEP (see pages 148–150) respectively, the trade union and employer organisations at EU level. As officially recognised 'social partners' by the EU, the ETUC and Business Europe are given the opportunity to participate in the law-making process by negotiating collective agreements (the 'social dialogue process'), which may then be transposed into legally binding EU Directives. The UK Government can, of course, continue to enact whatever social and employment legislation it wishes domestically, provided that such legislation does not undermine the provisions laid down by EU law. The considerable powers given to the social partners courtesy of the Maastricht and Amsterdam Treaties might well be expected to lead to trade unions and employers playing a much greater role in the determination of social and employment legislation in the future. As a consequence, the TUC and CBI (the UK social partners) – as influential affiliates within the ETUC and Business Europe – are well placed to have an important say in the determination of any such legislation.

Personnel and HRM specialists should also give thought to the consequences if the UK was to join the European Single Currency (the euro). Although there has been much debate over the economic and political merits or otherwise of the UK's joining the euro, little attention has been given to the impact it would have on employee relations. Currency transparency, for example, would inevitably lead to easier comparisons of productivity and labour costs across member states, which in turn would probably lead to further pressure for harmonisation of minimum employment and social standards across member states. In addition, as the 'enlargement' process continues with 'the EU 15' becoming 'the EU 27', the high-skill and low-labour-cost workforce of Eastern and Central Europe will generate even greater calls for a 'level playing-field' in the area of social and employment conditions.

THEORY

As personnel and HRM specialists, you ought to be aware of the impact that the 'European Dimension' has on employee relations and give consideration to how line managers might be persuaded to recognise its relevance.

## THE DEVELOPMENT OF THE EUROPEAN UNION

THEORY

The origins of the European Union date back to the late 1940s and the revulsion which followed the two devastating World Wars. Jan Monnet, an 'ideas man' who had been put in charge of the *Commissariat du Plan* to bring about the economic recovery of France, suggested the pooling of French and German coal and steel production to Robert Schuman, the French foreign minister. Both men were convinced that a prerequisite to a lasting peace in Europe was the reconciliation of the two great enemies, France and Germany. This proposal formed the basis of the Schuman Plan, which led to the Treaty of Paris (1951). Under its terms, Germany, Italy, France, Belgium, the Netherlands and Luxembourg created the European Coal and Steel Community (ECSC, 1952) whose fundamental aim was to allow these six countries on a joint basis to control the production, development and distribution of coal and steel, which were then still major prerequisites for waging war.

Although essentially an economic imitative, both Schuman and Monnet believed that the pooling of French and German coal and steel production would

THEORY

'immediately provide for the first stage of a European federation'. In short, they saw the ECSC as the first step towards an economic and political federal Europe. Schuman was a pragmatic politician and rejected any 'big bang' approach. He believed that the way to European integration was to deal with each sector at a time – hence, coal and steel in 1952, followed by atomic energy in 1957. Ironically, it was the 'big bang' approach that was to succeed. Although we had to wait for some 30 years, the European Economic Community (EEC, 1957) paved the way for the creation of a single integrated European economy in 1987 with the adoption of the Single European Act (SEA, 1987).

The experience of the Coal and Steel Community provided a model for the establishment, via the Treaty of Rome (1957), of two further European Communities: the European Atomic Energy Community (EAEC) and the European Economic Community (EEC), commonly referred to as the 'Common Market' and aimed to develop close co-operation on economic matters.

In 1967 the three Communities and their institutions were rationalised by a Merger Treaty, which created the European Communities (EC). In 1973, the UK, Ireland and Denmark joined the EC, followed by Greece in 1981, and Spain and Portugal in 1986. The EC became the European Union (EU) in 1993 when the Maastricht Treaty on European Union revised and widened the remit to include inter-governmental co-operation between member states on common foreign and security policy and on justice and home affairs. In 1995, Sweden, Finland and Austria joined the EU. The Treaty of Amsterdam (1997) was marked by the then new Labour Government in the UK's signing up to the 'Social Chapter', the terms of which were incorporated for the first time into the main corpus of the Treaty. The Treaty of Nice (2003) paved the way for enlargement of the EU, and on 1 May 2004 10 new states became members of the EU (Slovakia, Estonia, Hungary, the Czech Republic, Slovenia, Latvia, Lithuania, Poland, Malta and Cyprus). In 2007, Bulgaria and Romania also joined the EU, bringing its membership to 27. The 27 member states of the EU constitute the largest economic unit in the world, with a population of over 500 million.

Iceland, Norway and Liechtenstein are part of the European Single Market. They are subject to all EU Single Market legislation under the European Economic Area Agreement (EEAA), including some employment legislation. However, they are not full members of the EU.

## AIMS OF THE EUROPEAN UNION (EU)

The principal aims of the European Union (EU) are summarised as follows:

> The Community shall have as its task, by establishing a common market and an economic and monetary union and by implementing the common policies or activities referred to in Articles 3 and 3a, to promote throughout the Community a harmonious and balanced development of economic activities, sustainable and non-inflationary growth, respecting the environment, a high degree of convergence of economic performance, a high level of employment and of social protection, the raising of the

standard of living and quality of life, and economic and social cohesion and solidarity among Member States.

Official Journal of the European Commission (OJEC) C325/40 24.12.2002

And – most important from a HR/personnel point of view – the treaties commit the member states to ensuring that the EU's citizens receive a share of the benefits accrued from economic integration in the form of an upward harmonisation of living standards and working conditions (see OJEC C325/92 24.12.2002).

These along with other aims, objectives and principles are defined in a series of treaties. The treaties also contain details of the structure and operation of the EU (see below). They are the constitution of the EU and provide a legal basis for legislation and other measures. All members have to abide by these treaties and the legislation agreed under them. All the legislation adopted by the EU since 1957 is referred to collectively as the *Acquis Communautaire*, which all countries wishing to join the EU must accept as a condition of membership.

When there are changes to the treaties, they have to be ratified by all member states. This is done by either a referendum of a member state's citizens or by a majority vote in the member state's national parliament. In both cases, the people, or their representatives, have the last word. However, there is always a price to democracy – namely, delay. Ratification normally takes about 18 months to two years. Changes brought about by treaties do not become binding on member states until the ratification process has been completed.

## THE TREATY OF ROME (1957)

`THEORY`

The founding treaty of the EU is the Treaty of Rome (the European Economic Community Treaty) of 1957, which provided for the creation of a free trade area by removing barriers to the free movement of goods, labour, capital and services (the so-called four great freedoms) between member states. By integrating the economies of the member states, it was hoped that healthy product market competition would stimulate innovation, technological development, increased productivity and increased demand. In line with economic competition, it was envisaged that not only would output increase but consumer prices would fall, stimulating even further demand for goods and services. The 'European economy' would thus be firing on all four cylinders and this 'upward virtuous circle of prosperity' would result in real benefits for everyone within the Common European Market.

Although the bulk of the Treaty of Rome was concerned with removing the barriers to free trade, the increased market competition was to take place on a fair basis. Players in the free trade area would only be able to gain a competitive advantage through improved efficiency and productivity. They would not be able to gain competitive advantage through artificial means such as the devaluation of the currency (hence the need for a single currency – the euro), unilateral changing of interest rates or driving employment and working conditions down to the floor. The Treaty of Rome therefore contained an important chapter that dealt with a whole set of social provisions. This 'Social Chapter', contained in the original Treaty of Rome, distinguished the EU from all other 'free trade agreements' in so much as it gave it a 'social' as well as an 'economic' dimension. (See Treaty Establishing the European Economic Community (EEC), Title lll, Social Policy, 1957.)

The Social Chapter provided for closer co-operation in the 'social and employment field' between member states. One of the tasks it set itself was:

> to promote improved working conditions and an improved standard of living for workers so as to make possible their harmonisation while the improvement is being made.

The Chapter also enshrined, as one of its principles, the right to equal pay for equal work between men and women.

The founders of the EU were not just creating a free trade area but a community in which there would be harmonisation of social and employment conditions. There would be free competition within the free trade area, but this would be within the constraints of minimum social and employment standards across member states. As explained above, unlike any other free trade agreements – for example, the North America Free Trade Association (NAFTA) – the EU has always had a social dimension.

## THE SINGLE EUROPEAN ACT (SEA, 1987)

Progress in moving towards a free market was slow, largely because each proposal to achieve this objective required the unanimous agreement of all member states. There was always at least one member state which objected. A way had therefore to be found to prevent any single member state from stopping the rest from getting on with the job of completing the establishment of a free trade market. In 30 years, the Council of Ministers (see below) had hardly been able to adopt a single important measure designed to achieve the Single Market.

In 1985 the Commission (see below) proposed that member states should speed up the creation of the common market and, by 31 December 1992, adopt 282 necessary measures to achieve the free movement of goods, capital, labour and services between member states. To achieve this, the Single European Act amended the Treaty of Rome in three important ways.

First, for the first time a deadline – 31 December 1992 – was set for finally achieving the 'four great freedoms'.

Second, it introduced a new legal basis to allow member states to agree measures by qualified majority vote (QMV) rather than by unanimous vote. Under this system member states were given a number of votes relating to their populations:

- France, Germany, Italy and the UK: ten votes each
- Spain: eight votes
- Belgium, Greece, the Netherlands and Portugal: five votes each
- Sweden and Austria: four votes each

- Denmark, Finland and Ireland: three votes each

- Luxembourg: two votes.

A qualified majority was 62 of the total 87 votes available. To block proposals, a member state had to gather together 26 votes. Put another way, there had to be opposition from at least three member states to block a proposal. Two large states (for example, France and Germany together) could no longer veto proposals. In the absence of at least 26 votes against, a proposal was accepted and even the member states who abstained or voted against it had to implement it into their national law.

Third, the Act introduced another innovation by formalising the EU's commitment to involve the 'social partners' (employers and trade unions) in its decision-making machinery (see below).

The Single European Act also brought changes to the Social Chapter. It provided that health and safety regulations across the EU member states could be harmonised on the basis of qualified majority voting. This health and safety 'fast track' has been used lavishly and was the basis of the Working Time Directive (1993), which was then transposed into UK employment law via the Working Time Regulations 1998 (see below).

The impact of the Single European Act cannot be overestimated. By removing the veto of a single member state to proposals, it was radical and revolutionary. It meant that Europe would never be the same again. It meant that the EU law-making mechanisms could actually start to work as envisaged by the authors of the Treaty of Rome. Above all, it meant that employment relations professionals had to take Europe seriously because it was now possible to influence the drafting of new EU laws in a way unthinkable within national parliaments.

## THE TREATY ON THE EUROPEAN UNION (TEU, 1993)

In December 1991, the heads of member states met in Maastricht to agree further steps on the road to greater political, economic and monetary integration amongst member states. The eventual outcome was the Treaty on the European Union (1993), which formally changed the name of the EC to the European Union (EU) and provided for the creation of a common currency (the euro) from 1 January 1999, with national currencies being taken out of circulation by 2002. The Treaty also reaffirmed the principal of 'subsidiarity' in EU legislation. Although the principle is interpreted in different ways, it basically provides that the EU should take legislative action solely when the objectives of such legislation can only be achieved, or at least achieved better, at the EU level than at national level. Not surprisingly, however, there is little agreement on when this criterion is met.

The Treaty on the European Union also made two important changes to the Social Chapter. First, all member states (excluding the UK) agreed to extend the number of employment and social issues that might be adopted by QMV. As a result of the UK's objections, no new 'social provisions' were incorporated into the main body of the Maastricht Treaty. However, a compromise agreement was reached whereby member states other than the UK could use EU institutions to introduce additional binding legislation within the social field, on the understanding that any such legislation would not apply to the UK. This was done under a separate Social Policy Agreement which listed the specific social issues upon which the rest of the member states could legislate. This agreement was attached to the Social Protocol annexed to the main Treaty spelling out the arrangements just described.

The second innovation was the formalisation of the EU's commitment to involve the 'social partners' directly in its decision-making machinery. It provided for compulsory consultation with the social partners on social and employment proposals and gave them the option of negotiating Framework Agreements on such issues which could then be made legally binding on member states by transposing them into a Council Directive.

### THE TREATY OF AMSTERDAM (1999)

This Treaty introduced changes thought necessary to help prepare the EU for eventual enlargement to the applicant countries of Central and Eastern Europe, to take account of changing political priorities and to give effect to the need for stronger EU action in areas such as employment, social policy and the environment. The key provisions of the Treaty were:

- It developed further the principles of democracy and individual rights and for the first time established a clear procedure to be followed in the event of 'serious and persistent' breaches by member states.

- The Council of Ministers was provided with new powers to take more effective action to combat discrimination based on sex, ethnic origin, religion or belief, disability, age or sexual orientation.

- It pledged to remove all remaining restrictions on free movement of labour between member states by 2004, the only exemptions being the UK and Ireland, which were allowed to retain frontier controls.

- It introduced a new Chapter, which related exclusively to employment.

- The Agreement on Social Policy was transferred from the annex and incorporated into the main body of the Treaty, and thus became applicable to all member states. This was possible only because of the 1997 General Election in the UK, which brought in a Labour Government committed to rescinding the 'UK opt-out' and 'signing up' to the Social Chapter.

For the HR/personnel professional, the Treaty was significant for four reasons. First, the UK Labour Government agreed to opt in to to the Agreement on Social Policy annexed to the Treaty of Maastricht. As a result, the provisions governing this area were fully incorporated into the Treaty proper, and the UK again took full part in social policy-making and thus became fully bound by EU legislation in this area. The UK also had to adopt those Directives – on parental leave and on European Works Councils – that had been adopted under the Social Policy Agreement.

Second, the principle of equal pay for equal work was extended to 'work of equal value'.

Third, the Treaty provided the EU with competencies to take action to combat any form of discrimination whether based on sex, racial or ethnic origin, religion or belief, disability, age or sexual orientation. All legislation in this field, however, was subject to the agreement of all member states (the 'unanimity' principle).

Four, the Treaty contained an Employment Chapter committing the EU for the first time to take into account the need to achieve high and sustainable employment opportunities when taking decisions related to its commercial and economic objectives. This was the first time the promotion of a high level of employment had been written down as one of the main objectives of the EU. It was to be achieved by co-ordinating the employment policies of the member states to develop a common strategy.

### The Employment Chapter

The Chapter is designed to restore balance in the EU by creating a counterweight to its economic and monetary provisions. It asserts that:

- Employment is a matter of common concern.
- The objective of generating high employment is to be taken into consideration when implementing all other common policies.
- The achievement of this objective is closely monitored.
- The EU considers the employment situation in each member state and in the Union as a whole on an annual basis, and conducts a detailed examination of the steps taken by individual governments to promote employment.
- An employment committee promotes co-ordination of national measures and encourages dialogue between employers and employees.

The Employment Chapter is important because it makes the EU and its institutions for the first time the guardians of an overall employment policy. It is ambitious in the sense that it provides for permanent and regular collaboration within the EU framework.

## THE TREATY OF NICE (2003)

The Treaty of Nice, which came into force on 1 February 2003, paved the way for 10 new countries to join the EU, thus enlarging the EU from 15 to 25 member states. It extended further the issues that could be harmonised on the basis of qualified majority voting, changed the future size and composition of the European Commission and introduced an 'enhanced co-operation' procedure.

The Treaty extended the scope of qualified majority voting (QMV). Some 27 issues changed over completely or partly from unanimity to QMV. The Treaty also re-weighted member states' voting powers in the Council of Ministers to reflect their larger population size. As from 1 January 2005, a qualified majority vote was obtained if a proposal passed two – and in certain circumstances – three tests.

- Test number 1: it receives at least 'a specified number of votes' (this number is termed 'the qualified majority threshold').

- Test number 2: it is approved by a 'majority of member states'.

- Possibly, test number 3: a member of the Council may request verification that the proposal has received at least 62% of the total Council votes. If it has not, the proposal is not adopted. However, this test only applies if it is triggered by a request from a Council member.

The Treaty also limited the size of the European Commission (see below) to one Commissioner per member state, which means that the five large member states had in 2005 to give up their second Commissioner. It also decreed that in the event of the EU's eventually expanding beyond 27 member states, a rotation system for appointing Commissioners would be introduced.

The Nice Treaty also introduced a 'second track' system named enhanced co-operation. In a nutshell, where there are at least eight member states who wish to proceed further and faster on an issue, they will be able to request a formal proposal from the Commission and – subject to agreement of the Council of Ministers acting by qualified majority voting as well as the approval of the European Parliament – the measure would become binding on the member states involved. The Commission, when receiving a request for enhanced co-operation, has to ensure that such co-operation aims to achieve the objectives of the Union, that those objectives cannot otherwise be achieved, and that the proposed enhanced co-operation will not undermine the functioning of the single market. Opting in to enhanced co-operation requires a member state to adopt all decisions previously taken by other member states under enhanced co-operation.

## THE TREATY OF LISBON (2009)

The Treaty of Lisbon came into force on 1 December 2009. There were three fundamental reasons for the Treaty: more efficiency in the decision-making process, more democracy through a greater role for the European and national parliaments, and increased coherence externally. National parliaments are for the first time fully recognised as part of the democratic fabric of the European Union. Special arrangements are made to help national parliaments to become more closely involved in the work of the Union. They are, for example, afforded powers to contest draft EU laws considered to be unnecessary, and have the authority to have a say at a very early stage before a proposal is considered in detail by the European Parliament and the Council of Ministers. The Treaty increases the number of policy areas in which the directly elected European Parliament has to approve EU legislation together with the Council of Ministers. This applies in the areas of judicial and police protection and the adoption of the EU budget, as well as in the existing employment and social areas approved in previous treaties.

The number of Commissioners remains one per member state and the European Parliament may have no more than 751 members. The delegate numbers for each country is fixed at a maximum of 96 and a minimum of six for each member state. A new permanent post of President of the European Council is created, replacing the former system of a six-monthly rotating President. The President has no executive power and is appointed by the European Council for two and a half years. It is hoped that the post will provide greater continuity and stability to the work of the European Council. The Treaty also creates a High Representative of the Union for foreign affairs and security policy, who also becomes Vice-President of the EU Commission. This post is designed to strengthen coherence in external action and to raise the EU profile in the world.

The Treaty also introduces a new voting system for decision-making in the Council of Ministers, on the basis of qualified majority voting. Each member state has one vote. For a decision to be passed on the basis of QMV, two criteria must be passed. First, at least half of the member states must be in favour of the proposal (formerly 15 out of 27 EU countries) and that half must represent at least 65% of the EU's total population. This double majority system will be introduced in either 2014 or 2017, depending on the member states. The Treaty also extends QMV to new areas – for example, energy, security and climate change.

The Treaty contains a 'social clause' whereby social issues (promotion of a high level of employment, adequate social protection, etc) must be taken into account when defining and implementing all policies. It also contains a Charter of Fundamental Rights. These rights are set out in 54 articles and six chapters, and include, *inter alia*, the right to vocational training, to equality of treatment between men and women, to negotiate and conclude collective agreements, and to undertake industrial action, including strike action subject to national law. The UK negotiated an opt-out from the right of EU citizens to take collective action to defend their interests including strike action.

### REFLECTIVE ACTIVITY

Explain the difference between qualified majority voting and unanimous decision-making in the European Union.

## HOW THE EU WORKS

The Treaty of Rome set up four key institutions to achieve its objectives. These were:

- the European Commission
- the Council of the European Union
- the European Parliament
- the European Court of Justice.

## THE EUROPEAN COMMISSION

This is the EU's executive body whose main role is to propose measures and ensure their implementation. It has a monopoly position in respect of the proposing of legislation. Commissioners, who are usually senior and distinguished politicians, are nominated by the member state governments and serve for a period of five years. The President of the Commission enjoys considerable power and influence and sets the agenda for the weekly Commission meetings where new initiatives for making European law are discussed. Each member state nominates one Commissioner who thinks in EU-wide and not in national terms. All policy proposals made by a Commissioner must have the support of a simple majority of all Commissioners before they can be officially launched.

Each Commissioner has a personal 'cabinet' of advisory staff, and each is also in charge of one or more of the policy divisions in the Commission called Directorates-General (DGs). These are sub-divided into Directorates. They are responsible for drawing up proposals for EU action and monitoring the implementation of agreed measures. The Commissioner for Employment and Social Affairs is responsible for employment (including employment relations), social affairs and equal opportunities.

The Commission only consults with EU-wide collective employers (eg Business Europe) or employee organisations (eg the ETUC). It does not consult with any individual company, no matter how large. By this token, it will not deal either with a European Works Council. Individual companies have to deal with the Commission indirectly via an employers' association. For UK companies this will be via an employers' association that is an affiliate of the CBI which, in turn, is affiliated to Business Europe.

## THE COUNCIL OF THE EUROPEAN UNION

The Council comprises 27 members, one representing each member state. It is the EU's decision-making body. Its main function is to adopt measures proposed by the Commission for enactment in the member states.

The Council has several levels. There is the European Council level, which consists of the heads of government of the EU member states and which meets four times a year to discuss major issues and decide on broad areas of policy. There is then the level of the Council of Ministers, which comprises a Minister from each member state according to the subject under discussion. Thus, although each country has a permanent seat in the Council, the personalities who fill these seats change in accordance with the subject being considered. For example, if the Council is discussing employment relations matters, the seats are filled by the respective Employment/Labour Ministers from each of the member states.

## THE EUROPEAN PARLIAMENT

The European Parliament is the EU's main consultative body. Increasingly, in recent years, it has gained co-legislative powers with the Council of Ministers. On all employment legislation at EU level, for example, the European Parliament has joint responsibility with the Council of Ministers to consider and amend the Commission's proposals. It is only when both bodies are agreed that the legislation can be enacted. Its members have been directly elected since 1979. The number of seats allocated to each member state is related to the size of each state's population. Elections to the Parliament are held at five-yearly intervals. Members of the European Parliament (MEPs) take up their seats according to their trans-national political group rather than their nationality. UK MEPs are elected by proportional representation. Labour MEPs sit as part of the European Socialist Group, whereas UK Conservatives sit with the recently formed Conservative and Reformist Group.

The Parliament has a number of specialist committees – such as the Employment and Social Affairs Committee and the Women's Right Committee – which examine issues in depth. The committees draft opinions on Commission proposals and on other issues within their remit, which are debated at the monthly plenary session of the Parliament.

The European Parliament approves the appointment of the European Commissioners, determines the EU budget and proposes amendments to measures initiated by the Commission. Initially, the European Parliament had few powers and was regarded as nothing more than a talking-shop. However, over the years it has acquired greater influence and its powers to influence the legislative process vary according to the procedures governing decision-making in any given area (see below). For example, since the introduction of the co-decision procedure by the Treaty on European Union, the Parliament has significant co-legislative powers. Although the Parliament can reject the annual budget prepared by the Commission, it has only exercised this power on two occasions since 1957.

The Parliament – voting by a two-thirds majority – can dismiss Commissioners, but only *en bloc*. It cannot dismiss a single Commissioner: it is all or none. This power had never been exercised until spring 1999. President Santer and his team of Commissioners resigned *en bloc* – preferring to go voluntarily rather than 'be pushed' by the powers of the Parliament, which on this occasion would most certainly have been used. Santer's Commission collapsed as a result of six cases of mismanagement and petty corruption.

## THE EUROPEAN COURT OF JUSTICE (ECJ)

This Court is the supreme custodian of the EU-enacted laws and its decisions take precedence over any laws or judicial decisions taken in the member states. The size of the ECJ is dependent on the number of member states because each is entitled to one judge, who is appointed for a six-year term. They are assisted by Advocates-General, who deliver preliminary opinions on cases before they are put to the court. A subsidiary court, the Court of First Instance, hears many of the more routine cases. Even so, the average time before a case is heard is 18 months, and the full procedure can take several years.

The European Court of Justice acts as the final arbiter in disputes over the interpretation of the Treaties and over any failure of member states to implement EU laws. It can quash any measures introduced by member states which are incompatible with the Treaties.

The Court has been used by UK individuals, groups and organisations to challenge UK employment legislation on the grounds that it contravenes EU law. For example, the UK Equal Pay Act (1970) was challenged. The Act allowed for equal pay for work of equal value where this was shown to be the case by a job evaluation scheme. Claims by women employees were being rejected after the use of job evaluation. However, a complaint was laid before the European Court of Justice that such claims were failing because the job evaluation schemes being used by UK employers contained gender bias factors. The complaint was upheld, and in 1983 the Equal Pay Act (1970) was amended.

## REFLECTIVE ACTIVITY

Explain the differences in the functions of the European Commission, the Council of Ministers, the European Parliament and the European Court of Justice.

## LEGISLATIVE INSTRUMENTS

Most EU employment and social legislation comes in any of three forms which have important differences from each other:

- Regulations
- Directives
- Decisions.

Regulations are the highest and most rigorous form of EU legislation. They comprise detailed instructions which are immediately applicable throughout the European Union once adopted by the Council of Ministers and are 'directly binding' upon all member states. In other words, Regulations have the same direct status as laws passed by the UK Parliament and must be enforced by the UK courts in the same way. Failure to apply Regulations results in the European Commission making a complaint to the European Court of Justice.

Decisions are more specific in their application (particular member states, sectors or industries) and are immediately binding on those to whom they are addressed. Decisions which impose financial obligations are enforceable in national courts. Decisions are used when the EU wants the full force of European law to apply to individuals, to particular firms or enterprises or to specific member states.

The 'instruments' that the Commission can use are a source of confusion to many people, so a few words of explanation might be helpful. In some cases, primary legislation is contained within the Treaty, such as the provisions that safeguard the rules on product competition, which the Commission has the responsibility to oversee. Should individuals, enterprises or individual member states breach those provisions, the Commission needs instruments to coerce the offenders into compliance. These may take the form of Decisions, which are directly applicable and binding on those to whom they are addressed. However, in the employment and social field, Directives are the main legislative instruments.

Directives set out specific objectives, and each member state is given time (usually two years) to enact legislation within its own Parliament to ensure that the objectives are achieved. Directives, while being less rigid and allowing more flexibility than Regulations or Decisions, are still binding in all member states. In itself, a Directive does not have legal force in the member states but particular provisions may take direct effect if the Directive is not duly implemented. In the UK Directives have been implemented either by being incorporated as they stand into national law or by means of secondary legislation drawn up by the relevant government department or by an Act of Parliament, formulated in the usual way through a Parliamentary Bill.

### Softer instruments

In addition to Regulations, Directives and Decisions, which are 'hard legislation' enforced by the EU, there are other 'softer' instruments that attempt to regulate behaviour in the EU. These are:

- Recommendations
- Opinions
- Resolutions
- Declarations
- Communications
- Memoranda.

Although they all sound formally official, these are not legally binding. They have a moral rather than a legal force, but they can be used as evidence in court. Probably the best known Declaration in the employment relations field is the Community Charter on the Fundamental Rights of Workers, commonly known as the Social Charter (1989).

### Implementation of the instruments

Of the three instruments of European law with real teeth, the most widely used is the Directive. Since 1957, over 60 Directives have been adopted in the social policy field. Over half of these relate to health and safety at work, while the others deal with employment protection/working conditions, equal opportunities, freedom of movement and public health. Almost all of these Directives have been transposed into UK legislation.

If a member state fails to transpose Directives into domestic law by the target date or if EU law is infringed, complaints may be made to the European Commission. Such complaints can be made by individuals, companies, other member states, the European Parliament or pressure groups. The Commission investigates the complaint and asks the member state(s) concerned for an explanation. If this is unsatisfactory, the Commission orders the member states to put the matter right within a specific period of time. If the infringement continues, the matter is referred to the European Court of Justice. If this Court finds against the member state, it passes a judgment with which the member state has to comply. If a failure to comply results in a denial of individual rights, the European Court of Justice may require the member state to pay compensation to the individual.

The important thing about the European Court of Justice is that it takes precedence over all the courts within member states. It has the power to overrule the UK judiciary, including the Supreme Court. When issues and disputes reach the European Court of Justice, it is the end of the road. Once it has made its judgment, there is no further appeal.

## REFLECTIVE ACTIVITY

Outline the difference between a European Union Directive and a Regulation. Which is the more important in employment relations terms?

## THE SOCIAL PARTNERS

Following the ratification of the Treaty of Maastricht, the EU-wide representative bodies of employers and employees (referred to as the 'social partners') now have a role in the EU legislative process. There are four main social partners at the inter-sector level of the EU: the European Trade Union Confederation (ETUC), Business Europe, the European Centre of Employers and Enterprises Providing Public Services (CEEP), and the European Association of Craft, Small and Medium-Sized Enterprises (UEAPME).

### THE EUROPEAN TRADE UNION CONFEDERATION (ETUC)

The European Trade Union Confederation (ETUC) has a dual structure. Apart from the member states, leading national trade union confederations, which are affiliated to the ETUC as full members, it also comprises 12 European sectoral trade unions that until 1995 were called European industry committees but are now known as European industry federations (EIFs). These federations represent individual trade unions from a particular sector. They are recognised by the EU institutions as the sectoral (industry) employees' social partners.

The Confederation was formed in 1973 and today has in membership 82 national trade union confederations from 36 European countries as well as the 12 European industry federations, making a total of 60 million members plus observer organisations in Macedonia, Serbia, and Bosnia and Herzegovina. There are three decision-making bodies which determine ETUC policy: Congress, the Executive Committee and the Steering Committee. The Congress – the highest body – is convened every four years and decides the organisation's policy priorities. The Executive Committee generally meets every three months and takes the policy decisions required to implement the priorities laid down by the Congress. The Steering Committee normally meets eight times a year to decide on urgent action required to implement the strategies laid down by the Executive Committee. The ETUC Secretariat is in Brussels and carries out tasks assigned to it by the Congress and the Executive and Steering Committees. Its principal officer is the General Secretary, who is the head and spokesperson of the Confederation.

## BUSINESS EUROPE

Business Europe was formerly the Union of Industrial and Employers' Confederations of Europe (UNICE), established in 1958. In 2007, just before its fiftieth birthday, UNICE changed its name to Business Europe to reflect more clearly what it does and where it does it. It is the voice of European private business industry. It comprises 40 members from 34 countries including the European Union member states, the European Economic Area countries and some eastern European countries. Its current decision-making structure includes seven main committees involving some 60 working groups. The permanent staff of 45 are based in Brussels under a Director, and the whole organisation works under the leadership of a President. Employment relations matters are dealt with by a working group under the auspices of the Social Affairs Committee. The Council of Presidents, comprising the presidents of all the member federations (including the UK's CBI), is the supreme governing body of the organisation and determines Business Europe's general strategy.

The Executive Bureau brings together representatives of member federations from the five largest countries, the country holding the Presidency, and federations from five smaller organisations on a rotating basis, and meets as necessary. The Bureau monitors the implementation of the organisation's annual programme, stimulating co-ordination with member federations, ensuring that resources are adequate and responding quickly to urgent situations that arise between the meetings of the main committees. The Executive Committee, composed of the Directors-General of all the member federations, translates the Council of Presidents' strategy into activities and tasks for the organisation. Helped by the Executive Bureau, it ensures a balance between tasks and resources. Its policy committees organise the practical work and prepare its position papers on specific policy areas through the working groups. The members of each policy committee are nominated by the member federations.

## THE EUROPEAN CENTRE OF ENTERPRISES WITH PUBLIC PARTICIPATION AND OF ENTERPRISES OF GENERAL ECONOMIC INTEREST (CEEP)

Better known in English as the European Centre of Employers and Enterprises Providing Public Services, CEEP was formed in 1961 and four years later was recognised as the social partner for public sector employers by the European Commission. It seeks to maintain regular consultation with the EU official institutions and consultative bodies, analyses current problems, and contributes to employer-oriented responses on European draft Regulations, Directives and other legislation of interest to its members. Its national sections comprise full members which are enterprises, groups of enterprises or public employers' organisations which to a significant extent undertake activities of public interest. National sections send representatives to the CEEP General Assembly. Individual members are sectoral associations organised at EU level, representing enterprises that undertake activities of public interest. Individual members also send representatives to the CEEP General Assembly. The General Assembly is the principal decision-making body of CEEP. The Council of Administration is the executive management of CEEP, consisting of a minimum of 10 members delegated by the General Assembly. It enjoys the powers required for management and administrative purposes save where such powers are attributed to the General Assembly. The Board of Directors is a group of CEEP members who offer advice to the President, the Executive Vice-Presidents and the General Secretary, discussing contingent strategic options with them, and who themselves have the authority to take decisions in emergency situations.

## THE EUROPEAN ASSOCIATION OF CRAFT, SMALL AND MEDIUM-SIZED ENTERPRISES (UEAPME)

UEAPME (which actually stands for *Union européenne de l'artisanat et des petites et moyennes entreprises*) is the employers' organisation that represents the interests of European crafts, trades and small and medium-sized enterprises (SMEs) at EU level. It is a recognised European social partner, and is a non-profit-seeking and non-partisan organisation. As the European SMEs' umbrella organisation, UEAPME incorporates 83 member organisations from 36 countries, consisting of national cross-sectoral federations, European branch federations and other associate members which support SMEs. It represents more than 12 million enterprises which employ some 55 million people across Europe. The main functions of UEAPME include monitoring EU policy, keeping its members informed on all matters of EU policy, promoting the interests, needs and opinions of its member organisations to EU institutions, and supporting its members academically, technically and legally on all areas of EU policy. As a social partner it acts as an 'agenda setter' in the area of European SME policy. It has a direct role in all EU policies that have any effect on SMEs.

## THE LEGISLATIVE PROCESS

### LEGISLATIVE PROCEDURES

The Treaty of Amsterdam streamlined the EU's decision-making procedures so that there are now two main procedures for adopting EU legislation: the 'Co-operation' and 'Co-decision' procedures. In addition, in the social and employment field, a third procedure is used, known as the 'Social dialogue' procedure (see below).

**Figure 5.1  The 'Co-operation' procedure (Article 252)**

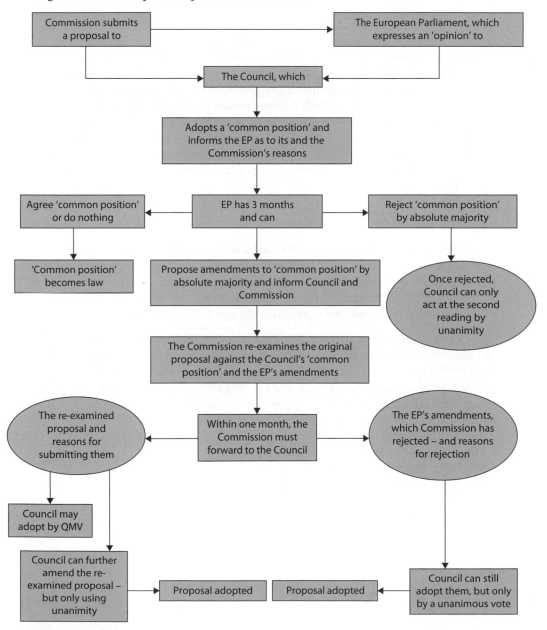

Common to all procedures is that the initiative should be taken by the Commission, which has the sole right to do so. In practice, however, many Commission proposals emanate from direct requests or indirect pressure from member states, other EU institutions or interest groups.

## THE 'CO-OPERATION' PROCEDURE

Under the terms of the Co-operation procedure, legislation may be adopted by QMV in the Council, following two readings by the European Parliament. After the Parliament's first reading, the Council adopts a so-called 'common position'. Parliament may then propose amendments to this common position or reject it outright. If the Council wishes to maintain its common position, despite Parliament's objections, it may only do so unanimously. Following the Parliament's second reading, the Commission will re-examine its original proposal along with the Council's common position and the Parliament's amendments. If the Council wishes to make amendments to this re-examined proposal, it may do so only by unanimity. If it does not wish to do so, the proposal may be adopted by QMV. In short, under the Co-operation procedure the Parliament has the power to reject legislation after the second reading. The Council can, of course, decide to ignore Parliament and still go ahead with the legislation, but it can only do this if it can achieve a unanimous vote amongst all Council members. It only takes one vote against, and the legislation is blocked (see Figure 5.1).

## THE 'CO-DECISION' PROCEDURE

Under the terms of this procedure, the Parliament's legislative powers are significantly enhanced in that the Council can only adopt legislation jointly with the Parliament. The procedure is considerably longer than the Co-operation procedure and it includes a final stage in which an attempt is made to reconcile potentially diverging positions of the Council and the Parliament.

The Co-decision procedure works in the same way as Co-operation – except in one very important way: the Parliament's decision cannot be overruled, even if the Council votes unanimously to reject it. This means that under the Co-decision procedure the Council and the Parliament must seek a compromise which they are jointly prepared to support if a proposal is to become law. If agreement cannot be reached, a Conciliation Committee is created made up equally of representatives of the Council and the Parliament and overseen by the Commission. The Conciliation Committee is given the mandate of creating an agreed text, but if this fails, the European Parliament has the right to veto the piece of legislation outright (see Figure 5.2).

**Figure 5.2 The 'Co-decision' procedure (Article 251)**

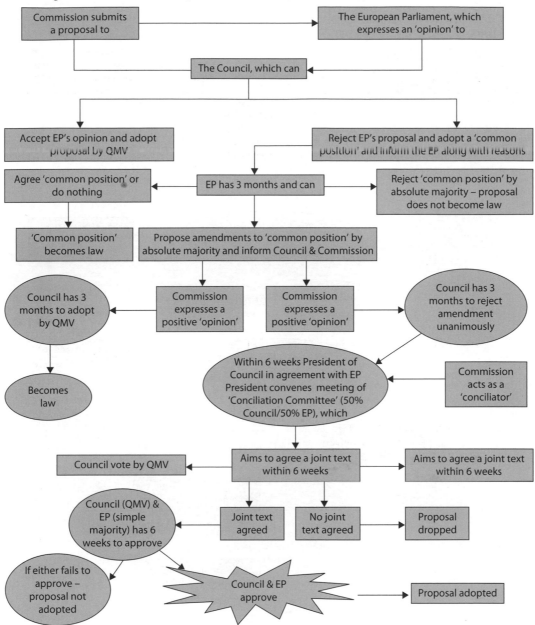

## THE 'SOCIAL DIALOGUE' PROCEDURE

**Figure 5.3 The 'Social dialogue' procedure**

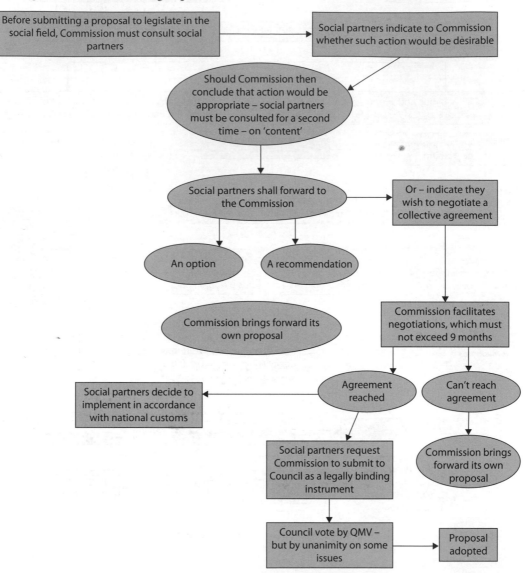

### Inter-sectoral

The Treaty of Amsterdam saw Maastricht's 'Agreement on Social Policy' included into the main body of the Treaty. This stated that the European Commission must consult with the social partners (ETUC, Business Europe, CEEP and UEAPME) about both the direction and the content of EU legislation in the social and employment field. The Treaty also provided for the social partners, should they so wish, to negotiate Framework Agreements as a substitute for legislation. The social partners were also given powers to engage in negotiations under their own initiative. This process is known as 'social dialogue' and operates as follows:

- When considering proposed legislation in the social field, the Commission must first consult the social partners on whether there is a need for legislation. The social partners will typically have six weeks within which to submit their views.

- If the Commission, after consultation with the social partners, concludes that a need for legislation exists, it then consults the social partners for a second time with a view to establishing their views on the possible scope of such legislation. The social partners are given the opportunity to negotiate an agreement as a substitute for Commission legislation. This second period of consultation is normally a six-week period.

- If one or both of the social partners reject the negotiations option, the Commission, then has the powers to bring forward its own proposals for legislation under the 'Co-decision' procedure. If, however, the social partners opt for the negotiations route, they have up to nine months, with the possibility of an extension, within which to negotiate a Framework Agreement.

- If the social partners successfully negotiate a Framework Agreement, they have to submit that agreement to the Commission with a recommendation that it be put forward as a formal legislative proposal to be adopted by the Council of Ministers.

- Should the social partners fail to reach a voluntary agreement, a fall-back position comes into play. The Commission may submit its own proposals under the 'Co-decision' procedure by which the Council of Ministers takes decisions on the basis of QMV.

The negotiation of an EU-wide Framework Agreement that has thereafter been transposed into a Directive has happened successfully in the case of parental leave (the Parental Leave Directive), part-time working (the Part-Time Work Directive) and fixed-term contracts of employment (the Fixed-Term Contracts Directive). In 2009, the social partners negotiated a revision to the 1995 Parental Leave Directive that will result in the Council of Ministers issuing a revised Directive.

The social partners have also concluded voluntary agreements on:

- teleworking (2003)
- work-related stress (2006)
- harassment and violence at work (2007)
- the lifelong development of competencies and qualifications (2002)
- gender equality (2005).

The social partners decided not to ask the Commission to transpose these agreements into a Directive but opted for the 'voluntary' route whereby member states would implement the terms of the agreement in accordance with their own customs and procedures. The Teleworking Agreement provided protections and laid down regulations governing the working practices of teleworkers. The Harassment and Violence at Work Agreement endeavours to increase awareness and understanding of the problem, and provides a framework for dealing with it. The Agreement requires enterprises to publish a clear statement to the effect that harassment and violence in the workplace will not be tolerated, also specifying the procedure to be followed in the event of problems.

The social partners attempted to use the Social dialogue procedure with respect to temporary and agency workers. Negotiations for a Framework Agreement between the social partners broke down and the Commission brought forward its own proposals under the Co-decision procedure. However, on three issues – European Works Councils, the burden of proof in sex discrimination cases, and information and consultation at the national level – the social partners decided not to enter into negotiations and the Commission brought forward its own proposals, which were eventually adopted by the Council.

Framework Agreement negotiations are arranged, and appropriate venues and interpreters provided, by the Commission, which also provides a chairperson to facilitate the negotiations between the social partners. All the costs associated with the negotiations – travel, accommodation, etc – are met by the Commission. The employer and trade union sides usually negotiate against very tight mandates from their respective constituents. Once agreement is reached, the social partners' affiliated organisations must ratify the agreement.

### Sectoral

The same Social dialogue procedure that exists for inter-sectoral purposes is also available for social partners within the EU industrial sectors to establish minimum social and employment standards for a particular sector. The social partners in the sectoral social dialogue are the European industry federations affiliated to the ETUC and the sector-based employers' organisations. Sectoral social dialogue has so far led to well over 100 joint texts, covering such issues as vocational training, employment and working conditions. The weight of these texts varies from joint opinions expressing views on EU proposals for legislation and general policy in the sectors to specific agreements on issues reached by collective bargaining. These agreements commit the national partners as members of the signatory organisations but have no binding force.

An example of a sector-wide Framework Agreement is the agreement limiting annual working time in the civil aviation industry to 2,000 hours and flying time to 900 hours. This was the third agreement of its kind in the transport industry. The other two agreements were negotiated in 1998 and related to sea transport and the railways. In 2002, voluntary guidelines on supporting age diversity in commerce were negotiated by EuroCommerce (employers) and UNIEuropa Commerce (trade unions), and in the agricultural sector, a European agreement was made on vocational training. The social partners of the telecommunications sector also undertook the first review of the implementation of their teleworking agreement, which had been concluded in February 2001.

**REFLECTIVE ACTIVITY**

Framework agreements have been negotiated at a European level. Briefly explain:

- who the parties are that negotiate such agreements

- how long the parties may take to reach such an agreement

- how such agreements are enforced throughout the member states of the EU.

## THE SOCIAL DIMENSION OF THE EUROPEAN UNION

### THE SOCIAL CHAPTER

The founders of the European Union did not just create a free trade area in which people, goods, services and capital could move freely. They were establishing a political and economic community in which there would be social regulation/protection in its free trade area. Product and service market competition would take place on a 'level playing-field' of minimum social and employment conditions in all member states. To this end, the Treaty of Rome contained a Social Chapter (Title III Social Policy), subsequently amended by the Single European Act (1987) and the Treaty on the European Union (1993) and regrouped in the Treaty of Amsterdam under the heading 'Social Policy, Education, Vocational Training and Youth'. The objectives of the Social Chapter are :

> the promotion of employment; improved living and working conditions; proper social protection; dialogue between management and labour; the development of human resources with a view to lasting employment; and the combating of social exclusion ...

It also commits member states, as a condition of membership, to ensure and maintain the application of the principle that men and women should have equal pay for equal work or work of equal value. The UK became fully covered by the Social Chapter on 1 May 1999, when the Treaty of Amsterdam came into force. That treaty also empowers the EU to take action to combat any form of discrimination whether based on sex, racial or ethnic origin, religion or belief, disability, age or sexual orientation. Finally, when making social policy, the EU may draw inspiration from the European Social Charter signed in Turin on 18 October 1961, and from the 1989 Community Charter of the Fundamental Social Rights of Workers (Article 136) – see below.

The Social Chapter is not a set of detailed regulations. It is a mechanism which allows the member states to make new rules and legislation at the EU level on a wide range of social and employment issues. As we have seen, it allows common rules to be introduced by the Council of Ministers by:

- a unanimous vote

- a qualified majority vote

- a Framework Agreement negotiated by Business Europe, UEAPME, CEEP and the ETUC and/or their sectoral equivalents

which may then be issued as a Directive and transposed into national legislation.

The Framework Agreement procedure limits the power of the European Parliament or member states in the Council of Ministers to make any amendments. This ability of collective bargaining to shape both the direction and content of legislation is considerable and unique. The CBI, CEEP (UK) and TUC are the UK members of Business Europe, CEEP and ETUC respectively. As a result, they have acquired a special significance as organisations in the UK. All three are respectively representing the interests of UK companies (private and public) and employees in the drafting of legislation that can then become legally binding in the UK and apply equally to unionised and non-unionised companies/ establishments.

### Qualified majority items

Under the Social Chapter procedures, legislation in any of the following areas can be adopted by qualified majority voting:

- improvements in the working environment to protect workers' health and safety
- working conditions
- information and consultation with workers
- the integration of persons excluded from the labour market
- equality between men and women with regard to labour market opportunities and treatment at work.

### Unanimous vote issues

The Social Chapter mechanisms can be used to introduce EU-wide legislation on the basis of unanimity amongst member states in the following areas:

- social security and the social protection of workers
- the protection of workers where their employment contract is terminated
- the representation and collective defence of workers' and employers' interests, including co-determination
- conditions of employment for third-country nationals legally resident in the EU.

### Excluded issues

However, certain subjects – namely, pay, the right of association, the right to strike and the right to impose lock-outs – are formally excluded from harmonisation by legislation based on Social Chapter procedures.

Critics of the EU nevertheless point out that although some areas are formally subject to unanimity or even excluded altogether, this is by no means a secure safeguard. They argue that past experience suggests EU institutions will seek to apply the broadest possible interpretations in order to maximise the scope for adopting measures by qualified majority voting despite possible objections from individual member states. The Social Chapter mechanisms are seen as having the risk of costly, far-reaching and unforeseeable legislation being imposed on the UK. It is viewed by its opponents as mirroring the more interventionist approach common in much of the EU and contrary to a deregulated approach to the operation of labour markets.

## THE SOCIAL CHAPTER IN PRACTICE

There are four areas of employment relations management in which EU laws have, and will continue to have, a direct impact on the work of the UK HR/personnel specialist:

- equal opportunities
- employment protection/working conditions
- employment relations
- health and safety at work.

Employment relations professionals must obtain copies of the actual Directives (see the box below) and the implementing UK legislation in these areas rather than depend on summaries. It must be borne in mind that many Directives are not simply transposed into UK law by one piece of legislation. For example, in areas such as equal opportunities, the requirements of a Directive have been transposed into several separate legal instruments within the UK.

---

**EU Employment and Social Directives that impact on the work of UK employment relations professionals**

*Equal opportunities*

- Equal Pay Directive (1975)
- Equal Treatment Directive (1996)
- Parental Leave Directive (1996)
- Sex Discrimination Directive (1997)
- Part-Time Worker Directive (1997)
- Fixed-Term Contract Directive (1999)
- Agency Worker Directive (2008)

*Employment protection*

- Collective Redundancy Directive (1975)
- Transfers of Undertakings Directive (1977)
- Insolvency Directive (1980)

- Proof of an Employment Relationship Directive (1992)
- Posting of Workers Directive (1996)

*Employment relations*

- European Works Council Directive (1994)
- European Works Council (UK Extension) Directive (1997)
- Information and Consultation Directive (2002)
- European Company Statute (2001)

*Health and safety*

- Working Time Directive (1993)

## EQUAL OPPORTUNITIES

### Equal pay

The 1975 Equal Pay Directive sought to improve the effectiveness of equal pay for men and women as laid down in the Treaty of Rome by reducing differences between member states in the application of this principle through approximation of member state laws on the subject. The Directive stated that the principle of equal pay required the elimination of all discrimination on the grounds of sex with regard to all aspects and conditions of remuneration for the same work or for work to which equal value is attributed. It also provided that any job classification (evaluation) system used for determining pay must be based on the same criteria for both men and women, and must be drawn up so as to exclude discrimination on grounds of sex.

In 1983 the Equal Pay (Amendment) Regulations were introduced in the UK to comply with this Directive. These Regulations *inter alia* introduced provision for 'independent experts' to undertake job evaluation exercises independently of the employer in the case of claims for equal pay based on work of equal value.

### Parental leave

In 1995, the social partners (Business Europe, ETUC and CEEP) concluded a Framework Agreement on parental leave which was then issued as the Parental Leave Directive (1996). It provided an individual right for parents to take up to three months' unpaid leave after the birth or adoption of a child before its eighth birthday. Employees are protected from dismissal for asking for the leave and have the right to return to work on the same conditions as before. The Directive also entitled individuals to a certain number of days off work for urgent family reasons in the case of sickness or accident. The UK Government transposed this Directive into national legislation via the Maternity and Parental Leave Regulations (1999).

In June 2009 the European social partners, including UEAPME, which had not been a party to the 1995 Agreement, negotiated a revision to the 1995 Framework

Agreement providing for an increased period of leave and encouraging fathers to take some leave by making parts of the leave non-transferable. Specifically, the revised agreement provisions:

- increased the length of parental leave from the previous three months to four months
- made part of the leave non-transferable in order to encourage fathers to take advantage of parental leave
- offered a right to request flexible working when returning from parental leave
- called on member states to establish notice periods that workers should give in exercising the right to parental leave.

At the time of writing, the next step will be for the Commission to propose to the Council of Ministers implementation of the revised agreement as a Directive, and then for the UK Government to enact the revised Directive into UK domestic law.

### Equal treatment

The Equal Treatment Directive (1976) was designed to give effect to the principle of equal treatment for men and women with regard to access to employment, promotion, vocational training and working conditions, including the conditions governing dismissal. As a result of this Directive, the UK had to introduce legislation to equalise the retirement ages for men and women, to remove the difference whereby men could receive statutory redundancy payments up to the age of 65 but women up to 60, and to ensure that occupational pensions are equal for men and women. The provisions of the Directive were made binding in the UK initially under the Sex Discrimination Act (SDA) (1975), and the Equal Pay Act (EPA), which came into force in 1975. Each Act has been amended a number of times since it came into force, the latest amendment to both being in 2003.

### The burden of proof

Measures laid down in respect of the burden of proof in cases of discrimination based on the Sex Discrimination Directive (1997) sought to improve the effectiveness of national implementation of the principle of equal treatment by enabling all persons to have their right to equal treatment asserted by judicial process after possible recourse to other competent bodies. The Directive provides that where a complaint to a tribunal establishes 'facts from which it may be presumed that there has been direct or indirect discrimination', the employer has to prove 'that there has been no breach of the principle of equal treatment'. The Directive thus places the burden of proof on the employer to demonstrate that the principle of equal treatment has not been breached, rather than obliging the employee to prove that an infringement has taken place. This Directive was implemented in the UK in October 2001 by the Sex Discrimination (Indirect Discrimination and Burden of Proof) Regulations.

## EMPLOYMENT PROTECTION/WORKING CONDITIONS

### Part-time workers

In 1997, UNICE (now Business Europe), ETUC and CEEP negotiated a Framework Agreement on part-time work designed to remove discrimination against part-time workers, to improve the quality of part-time work, to facilitate the development of part-time work on a voluntary basis, and to contribute to the flexible organisation of working time in a manner that takes into account the needs of employers and workers. A part-time worker is defined as a worker whose normal average weekly hours of work calculated over one year are less than those of a comparable full-time worker. If no comparable full-time worker exists within the same establishment, reference is made to applicable collective agreements or national law.

The social partners agreed that part-time workers should be treated no less favourably with regard to employment conditions except where justified on objective grounds. Employers are to facilitate the transfer between full-time and part-time work by providing information on available work within the establishment and by greater access to vocational training. Member states and national social partners were urged to identify and eliminate obstacles to part-time work. The Framework Agreement was transposed into a Directive with an implementation deadline of 20 January 2000. In April 1998 this Directive was extended to the UK and came into force in June 2000 under the Part-Time Workers (Prevention of Less Favourable Treatment) Regulations. This gave part-time workers in the UK rights to be treated no less favourably than full-time workers and to receive the same hourly rate of pay, the same access to company pension schemes, the same entitlements to annual leave and maternity/parental leave on a pro rata basis, the same entitlement to contractual sick pay, and no less favourable treatment in access to training.

### Fixed-term contracts

In 1999, the EU social partners concluded a Framework Agreement on fixed-term contracts. These negotiations had been initiated by UNICE (now Business Europe), who had proposed such negotiations in February 1998. This was unique in that it was the first time UNICE had proposed, and initiated, legislation in the social and employment field under the Social dialogue provisions. The agreement generated an EU Directive discouraging the promotion of fixed-term contracts and limiting their use. Fixed-term employees are:

- not to be treated less favourably than permanent employees doing similar work for the same employer at the same establishment
- protected against unfair dismissal without a qualifying requirement
- no longer able to waive their right to claim redundancy pay when their contract expires
- entitled to terms and conditions equivalent to permanent staff, on a pro rata basis.

The UK gave effect to this Directive in 2002 via the Fixed-Term Employees (Prevention of Less Favourable Treatment) Regulations.

## Agency workers

More than 1 million agency workers are employed in the UK. Their jobs can last a matter of hours, months, or in some cases more than one year. They have a key role in the UK's flexible labour market, and it is vital that business is able to bring in extra people quickly and easily. There are benefits to agency work in that it is a flexible option for some, and can be an important route back to work for the unemployed. Following the breaking down of the Framework Agreement negotiations on agency workers, the Commission brought forward its own draft Directive designed to put an end to the situation in which agency staff can work in a company for a long time but never receive equal treatment with full-time workers. To this end, the Directive proposed that agency workers receive the same employment rights to basic pay and other employment conditions as full-time workers once they have spent six weeks in a specific post.

In June 2009 the Commission, under pressure from the UK's TUC and CBI, agreed that agency workers should receive equal treatment with permanent employees after 12 weeks in a specific job. This therefore means that after the 12-week period, agency workers should have the same pay, holidays and other working conditions, such as overtime and breaks, as directly recruited staff. But sick pay and pensions are excluded. The UK Government had reached a deal on a 12-week period with the CBI and TUC in May 2008. In the following month these three bodies persuaded the Commission to incorporate the 12-week threshold into the Directive, which was then accepted by the Council of Ministers. The UK Government gave effect to this Directive via the Agency Worker Regulations (AWR) in October 2011.

## Redundancy

The Collective Redundancy Directive (1975) introduced the requirement for consultation, in good time, with employee representatives on mass redundancies with a view to reaching an agreement. The consultations must cover ways and means of avoiding collective redundancies or limiting the number of workers affected, and of mitigating the consequences through help for redeployment or retraining workers made redundant. The employer must provide the workers' representatives with certain information – for example, the reason for the redundancies, the number and types of workers to be made redundant, and the criteria proposed for the selection of workers to be made redundant.

This Directive was transposed into UK legislation in the Employment Protection Act (1975). The Directive was amended slightly by a further Directive (1992), which was implemented in the UK in June 1994 in the Trade Union Reform and Employment Rights Act (1993). This ensured that consultation takes place at the workplace affected, even if the redundancy decision has been taken by a controlling body in another country.

## Transfer of undertakings

The Transfer of Undertakings/Acquired Rights Directive (1977) sought to protect employees in the event of a change of employer through takeover or merger. It introduced the principle that when a business is sold, employees should transfer to the new owner on the same basic terms and conditions of employment and could not be dismissed for reasons connected with the transfer. In transposing the Directive into UK law (the Transfer of Undertakings and Protection of Employment Regulations – TUPE) the Government excluded the public sector.

However, in 1992 the European Court of Justice confirmed that the Directive applied to employees in both the private and non-profit sectors. The UK law was therefore amended by the Trade Union Reform and Employment Rights Act (1993) to include public sector employees. In 1998, an amendment to the 1977 Directive was introduced to limit existing law by clarifying that transfer of undertakings legislation applied only when an 'economic activity' which retains its identity is transferred. The UK implemented this amendment in July 2001. A further Directive was adopted in 2001 and, as a consequence, amendments to the TUPE Regulations followed.

## Contracts of employment

The Proof of an Employment Relationship Directive (1992) imposed an obligation on an employer to inform employees of the conditions applicable to the contract or employment relationship. By doing so, it was hoped to provide employees with improved protection against possible infringements of their rights and to create greater transparency in the labour market. The Directive required all employees working over eight hours per week for more than one month to receive written confirmation of the main terms and conditions of their employment within two months of starting work. Changes to written particulars must be notified in writing within one month. It also required conditions for overseas postings to be provided in writing. Implementation of the Directive in the UK was via an amendment to the EPCA (1978), now the Employment Rights Act (1996).

## Insolvency

The Insolvency Directive (1980) requires member states to set up insolvency funds to guarantee reimbursement of outstanding pay to employees if a business collapses. It was implemented in the UK without change to existing law, which was already established by the then Employment Protection (Consolidation) Act (1978). Further protections of employees in the event of their employer's insolvency were provided for in the Employment Rights Act (1996) and the Pension Schemes Act (1993).

## The posting of workers

The Posting of Workers Directive (1996) aims to ensure minimum protection of workers posted temporarily to a member state other than the one in which they normally work. It is also designed to ensure fair competition and to provide minimum employment conditions for these employees. A posted worker is guaranteed such terms and conditions as laid down in the law and in applicable collective agreements in the member state to which he or she is posted, in particular, maximum work periods and minimum rest periods; minimum paid annual holidays; minimum rates of pay, including overtime rates; health and safety; the conditions of hiring out workers, particularly temporary employment agencies; protective measures concerning the employment of pregnant women, new mothers, children and young people; equality of treatment between men and women; and other non-discrimination measures.

Member states are required to establish adequate procedures to allow workers and/or their representatives to enforce the provisions of the Directive. A posted worker can bring a claim under the Directive in the host country, without affecting any right to do so elsewhere. This Directive was transposed into UK law via the Employment Relations Act (1999) and the Equal Opportunities (Employment Legislation) (Territorial Limits) Regulations (1999).

## EMPLOYMENT RELATIONS

### The European Works Council Directive

This Directive (1994), and its extension to take in the UK in 1998, provides for a Europe-level information and consultation system to be set up in all organisations with more than 1,000 employees in member states and employing more than 150 people in each of two or more of these. A Works Council (or an alternative system) has to be agreed between the central management of the organisation and a special negotiating body (SNB) of employee representatives. If no agreement is reached within three years, a fall-back system applies. This requires the establishment of a European Works Council of employee representatives with the right to meet central management at least once a year for information and consultation about the progress and prospects of the company, and to request extra consultation meetings before certain major decisions are taken affecting more than one member state.

European information and consultation systems already in place before the set deadline implementation date of 22 September 1996 – or 15 December 1999 in the case of the UK – were exempted. Effect was given in the UK to the European Works Council (UK Extension) Directive (1997) by the Transnational Information and Consultation of Employees Regulations (1999).

### Information and consultation at national level

The aim of the Information and Consultation Directive (2002) was to establish a general framework setting out minimum requirements for the informing and consulting of employees in undertakings or establishments within the European Community. Its requirements apply to undertakings employing at least 50 employees in any one member state or establishments employing at least 20 employees in any one member state. An 'undertaking' is defined as a public or private undertaking carrying out an economic activity whether or not operating for gain. An 'establishment' means a unit of business in accordance with national law and practice. In short, a multi-site UK company employing at least 50 individuals across a number of plants in different geographical locations would be deemed an undertaking. An enterprise could be any of these individual plants provided that it had a workforce of at least 20 employees. The right to information and consultation covers information on the recent and probable development of the undertaking's or the establishment's activities and economic situation; on the situation, structure and probable development of employment within the undertaking/establishment; on any anticipatory measures envisaged, in particular where there is a threat to employment; and on decisions likely to lead to substantial changes in work organisation or in contractual relations. This information is to be given at such time, in such fashion and with such content as is appropriate to enable employees' representatives to conduct an adequate study and, where necessary, prepare for consultation.

Under the Directive, consultation should take place at the relevant level of management and employee representation and in such a way as to enable employees' representatives to meet with the employer and obtain a response, and the reasons for that response, to any opinion they might formulate. In addition, consultation must take place with a view to reaching an agreement on decisions within the scope of the employer's powers likely to lead to substantial changes in work organisation or in contractual relations.

Member states also have to provide for appropriate measures in the event of non-compliance by employers or employees' representatives with the provisions of the Directive, and ensure that adequate administrative or judicial procedures are available to enable the obligations deriving from the Directive to be enforced. Member states must also provide for adequate penalties to be applicable in the event of any infringement of the Directive. Such penalties are to be proportional to the seriousness of the offence.

Member states had until early 2005 to implement the requirements of this Directive. Implementation of the required provisions by a voluntary negotiated agreement between labour and management was witnessed. In member states such as the UK and Ireland, where there is no general, permanent and statutory system of information or consultation, or of employee representation at the workplace, the Directive was introduced in stages as follows:

● Undertakings with at least 150 employees (or establishments with at least 100 employees) had to be covered no later than 23 March 2005.

● Undertakings with at least 100 employees (or establishments with 50 employees) no later than 23 March 2007.

● Undertakings with 50 employees (or establishments with 20 employees) no later than 23 March 2008.

### The European Company Statute

In October 2001 the EU adopted a Regulation establishing the European Company Statute (ECS) and an accompanying Directive on the involvement of employees in the European company. In terms of the development of EU social and employment legislation, this event was historic, bringing to a close after 31 years what was probably the longest legislative process in this field. It was in 1970 that the European Commission had first proposed giving companies the option of forming a European company which could operate on a Europe-wide basis and be governed by Community law directly applicable in all member states (rather than national law). For many years the proposal failed to gain approval in the Council of Ministers, largely due to disagreement over the worker involvement provisions to apply in a European company.

A European company may be formed by two or more EU companies through merger or formation of a joint subsidiary or holding company, or by the transformation of a single existing EU company. Employee involvement arrangements – information and consultation, plus board-level employee participation in some circumstances – must generally apply in all types of European companies.

Companies participating in the formation of a European company must negotiate with the employees via a special negotiating body (SNB) made up of employee representatives. The negotiations are expected to result in a written agreement on the employee involvement arrangements. If these arrangements include a reduction of existing board-level participation rights that apply to a certain proportion of employees, this must be approved by a two-thirds majority of SNB members (from at least two member states). The SNB may decide not to open talks or decide to terminate talks in progress – in which case existing national information and consultation rules will apply. Where the SNB and the management reach an agreement, the result should be the setting up of an EWC-like 'representative body' or an information and consultation procedure. If the parties so decide, the agreement may also set out rules for board-level participation. SNB negotiations must be completed within a six-month period. This may, however, be extended by mutual agreement to a total of one year. If no agreement is reached, or the parties so decide, a statutory set of 'standard rules' apply, providing for a standard 'representative body'. The standard rules also provide for board-level participation in certain circumstances where this existed in the participating companies.

In October 2003, the then Department for Trade and Industry (DTI) published a consultative document entitled *The Implementation of the European Company Statute: The European Public Limited Liability Company Regulations 2004*. The consultation period ended in January 2004, and the UK Government implemented the Directive in October 2004.

### Industrial action and posted workers

In December 2007, the European Court of Justice made an important ruling in the so-called *Viking* and *Vaxholm/Laval* cases. Both these cases involved the substitution or replacement of workers in one country with workers from another country. The ruling centred on circumstances in which the desired outcome is to reduce labour costs through the offer of less generous terms and conditions to a workforce which is not the original workforce.

In 2003, to cope with operational losses, the Finnish passenger ferry operator Viking Line attempted to reflag its ship, the *Roselia*, to operate under an Estonian flag with the intention of hiring an Estonian crew to replace the existing Finnish crew. This would have significantly reduced the company's labour costs. Following a threatened strike by the employees, the company withdrew the proposal. In 2004, anticipating that when the current collective agreement ended, it would wish to return to the solution of reflagging its ships, the company brought an action before the UK courts seeking an injunction to stop the International Transport Workers' Federation and the Finnish Seamen's Union from attempting to interfere with the Viking Line's rights to free movement. The UK Court of Appeal referred the matter to the European Court of Justice (ECJ).

The *Laval* case concerned a Latvian construction company that had posted Latvian workers to work on Swedish building sites. The Swedish Building Workers Union sought a collective agreement for these workers to comply with the existing industry agreement. Having failed to obtain this, it began collective industrial action by blockading all Laval building sites in Sweden. Subsequently, Laval brought proceedings before the Swedish courts against the trade unions, and – as in the *Viking* case – questions were referred by the national courts to the ECJ because the issues concerned were fundamental principles of EU law.

Both cases raised the issue of whether EU law can restrict trade unions in one member state from taking industrial action or if it can restrict the application of collective agreements in a host member state. The ECJ ruled that the right of trade unions to take collective action, including strike action, was a fundamental right which formed an integral part of the general principles of Community law. It went on to say that this right to collective action be balanced against the free movement of services in the European Single Market and the freedom of establishment. The ECJ's ruling therefore limited the possibilities for trade unions to achieve better terms and conditions for posted workers. Its decision said that unions can only use industrial action to force a company from another member state to conclude collective agreements on matters listed in the Posted Worker Directive – for example, maximum work periods, minimum paid holidays and minimum rates of pay. The judgment means that unions cannot ask for more favourable employment conditions than in national legislative rules for minimum protection. They cannot ask for an undertaking to comply with terms and conditions in collective agreements which are usually better than minimum standards established by legislation. The judgment also means that if a member state does not have a legal minimum wage, a system for declaring collective agreements universally binding or transparent central collective agreements with minimum wages, trade unions cannot take industrial action to force a company coming from another member state to pay the collectively bargained minimum rates of pay. The EU's decision also implies that trade unions can never, by means of collective action, demand more than the minimum rate of pay from a company coming from a different member state. It also means that member states cannot have laws that permit unions to take collective action against companies entering their country that have concluded a collective agreement in their own country unless similar conditions also apply to domestic companies.

## HEALTH AND SAFETY

Several Directives were adopted in the 1970s and 1980s setting minimum standards for the control of noise, vibration, asbestos and other agents, as well as Directives harmonising safety signs. Today, over 40 Directives have been adopted, making health and safety at work the most regulated area of EU social policy. These Directives have largely been incorporated into UK law via the Control of Substances Hazardous to Health (COSHH) Regulations (2002). However, the majority of these Directives are so-called 'daughter' Directives, aimed at implementing in specific areas the provisions laid down in the 1989 Framework Directive, which itself was intended to encourage improvements in the health and safety of workers at work.

An important EU measure in the health and safety area is the Working Time Directive (1993), transposed into UK law via the Working Time Regulations, which became operative on 1 October 1998. The Conservative Government (1992–7) challenged the legality of the Directive before the European Court of Justice, on the basis that it was an employment measure rather than a health and safety issue and thus ought to be subject to unanimous voting in the Council of Ministers instead of being decided by QMV. The rationale behind the challenge was that the UK was exempt at that time from voting when the QMV procedure was operated, because of the Maastricht opt-out, whereas under the unanimity principle the UK would have been allowed to exercise its veto and thus block the measure. In the event, the ECJ confirmed the Commission's position that 'working time' was indeed a health and safety measure, and the UK was instructed to transpose the Directive into domestic legislation. A further consequence of this ruling was that the ECJ spelled out a new and much wider definition of what was a health and safety issue, opening the door to the Commission's bringing forward many more proposals to legislate on what hitherto would have been considered employment issues, which required unanimous voting. As health and safety measures, such proposals could henceforth be adopted by QMV. (Note that because the UK opt-out still applied at that time, such measures could have been adopted by the Council of Ministers without the UK's being present.)

The Working Time Regulations introduced a range of significant new rights and entitlements, such as a minimum of four weeks' paid annual leave (but which can include bank holidays). There is significant scope in the Regulations for employers and employees to enter into collective agreements on how the working time rules will apply in their own particular circumstances. Collective agreements can be made with an independent trade union, while 'workforce agreements' can be made with workers who are not covered by collective bargaining. Certain activities, or sectors of activities, of workers are excluded from the Regulations. These include those whose working time is under their own control – for example, managing executives, family and religious workers, domestic servants and trainee doctors. However, a new so-called 'horizontal amending Directive' (HAD) was adopted by the Council of Ministers extending the Directive on the organisation of working time to the previously excluded sectors and activities (road, rail, air, sea, inland waterways and lake transport, sea fishing, offshore work and junior doctors). These measures were implemented over the period 2003/4.

Broadly, worker entitlements under the Regulations (eg rest periods and paid annual leave) are enforced by an individual complaint to an employment tribunal. In the case of the mandatory 'limits' on working time (such as the weekly working time and night work limits), employees' rights are enforced by health and safety authorities (the Health and Safety Executive and local authorities). However, workers have protection against detrimental treatment or unfair dismissals for, amongst other things, refusing to work in breach of an acceptable working time limit. Employers are required to keep adequate records, going back two years, to show that the working time limits have been honoured. The transposition legislation which gave force to the original Directive was the Working Time Regulations (1998).

In September 2004 the European Commission issued a draft Directive revising the Directive concerning certain aspects of the organisation of working time. Progress on discussing the draft Directive was slow. Nonetheless, in 2008 it was agreed that the UK opt-out from the maximum 48-hour working week should continue, but where an individual opted out, an upper limit of a 60-hour maximum week would apply, calculated over a three-month period. This means that employers will have to keep working time records even for opted-out workers. At the time of writing, the UK Government is still to translate this amendment to the Working Time Directive (see below) into UK legislation.

## REFLECTIVE ACTIVITY

Explain, with appropriate examples, the impact of at least three pieces of European Union-derived law on your organisation. What implementation problems did they give rise to? How were these overcome?

## CASE STUDY

### The European Union

Planet Corporation employs 4,500 workers who produce a wide range of electronic domestic appliances for the European and North American markets. It is a UK-based multi-national company and – apart from the UK, where it employs 1,500 workers – it has establishments in France (1,000 employees), Germany (1,500 employees), Italy (100 employees) and Hungary (400 employees).

The UK workforce feels strongly that their wages are well below what the company can afford. This feeling has grown stronger since the European plants with which they identify most closely (France, Germany and Italy) became part of the euro zone. It is easier now to compare pay and conditions plus living standards with workers in these countries, and it certainly seems to the UK workforce that their colleagues there are getting a much better deal.

The UK trade union that is recognised and is well organised in the plant has asked to meet with the management of Plant Corporation to put forward a claim for an improvement in pay and conditions. This in itself is not unusual because pay and conditions agreements usually last 12 months and the time for a review is approaching in any case. On this occasion there are a number of significant issues which the chief executive officer of the UK operation has highlighted. They are:

- Plant Corporation's central management has been informed that the European Works Council (EWC) has tabled an item for discussion at the next EWC meeting which is scheduled to take place in two weeks' time. The item focuses on pay differentials and general rewards and policies throughout the company's European operations.

- The UK site is more profitable than other sites in Europe.

- Last year, the organisation invested £3 million in new equipment in the UK plant and as a result attracted new and lucrative business from North America which could develop into a long-term revenue-generating arrangement. However, delivery dates, quality, maintenance and price are all important considerations. The contract with the North Americans has just been signed.

- The only other site belonging to Plant Corporation which could technically fulfil the USA requirements is the one in Budapest. Although labour costs are much lower there, their current performance in terms of productivity and delivery reliability are not good.

**Activity**

The central management has asked your CEO to attend a strategy meeting to discuss a number of key issues, of which the question of pay and conditions and employee relations in the UK – along with the North American contract – are the most important. As the HR manager you should use your knowledge and understanding of contemporary research and employee relations policy and practice in other organisations to produce an employment relations strategy, which should include the following:

1 an analysis of the problem

2 possible solutions with associated costs and benefits, and

3 justified options/recommendations.

## EUROPEAN UNION DECLARATIONS

### The Social Charter

In the field of employment relations there is only one major Declaration. This is what is most often in English called the Social Charter.

The Community Charter on the Fundamental Rights of Workers, commonly known as the Social Charter, was adopted by all member states except the UK in December 1989. It was introduced as a result of political pressure to provide benefits for employees as a balance to what was seen as the advantages for companies provided by the Single European Act (1987) and the coming into force of the Single Market on 1 January 1993. The Charter is a Declaration and has no legal force in itself. It is in essence a 'wish list' of social objectives.

The Charter proposes a floor of basic common employment rights and objectives which should be established and implemented without discrimination at appropriate levels across all member states to ensure that:

- the right of free movement in the EU becomes a reality
- workers are paid a sufficient wage to ensure a decent standard of living
- adequate social security protection is provided by all member states
- basic law on working time, the provision of contracts, the treatment of part-time and temporary workers, and collective redundancies is improved and harmonised
- all workers have the right to join or not to join a union, negotiate collective agreements and take collective action, including strike action
- all workers have access to continuous vocational training throughout their working life
- equal treatment and equal opportunities between men and women are developed, particularly to enable men and women to reconcile family and work responsibilities
- information and consultation are developed along appropriate lines, taking into account national practices, particularly in European enterprises
- health and safety protection is improved
- young workers are given access to training and fair treatment
- the elderly are guaranteed an adequate income
- measures are taken to improve the social and professional integration of people with disabilities.

The Charter emphasises that the implementation of these 12 principles would contribute not only towards the improvement of living and working conditions provided in the Treaty of Rome (1957) but would also lead to a more effective use of human resources across the EU and therefore improve economic competitiveness and job creation. Although not in itself a legally binding document, the Charter has nevertheless formed the basis for much EU action in the area of social policy – for example, the Working Time Directive, the European Works Council Directive and the Part-Time Work Directive. The Charter's incorporation into the Treaty of Amsterdam strengthens its standing as an important basis for EU social and employment policy.

## SUMMARY

This Chapter has:

- identified the growing importance of the European Union on employment relations management in the UK
- explained how the European Single Market in which goods, services, people and capital can move freely (the four great freedoms) also has a social

dimension, known as the Social Chapter, to provide for the harmonisation of minimum social and employment conditions between member states

- outlined the main role and function of the legislative institutions of the European Commission, the Council of Ministers, the European Parliament and the European Court of Justice

- pointed out how the introduction of the qualified majority voting (QMV) procedure in 1987 removed the veto of member states over Commission proposals in certain areas and meant that Europe could never be the same again and its law-making mechanisms could actually start to work as envisaged in 1957

- explained how the Treaty of Maastricht (1993) provided for compulsory consultation by the European Commission with the social partners (both at the inter-sectoral and sectoral levels) on any social and employment proposals, and permitted the social partners the option to agree voluntarily to negotiate a Framework Agreement on the issue, and for that Agreement to be made binding on member states via its transposition into a Directive

- noted that Framework Agreements collectively bargained by the inter-sectoral social partners and then issued as a Directive and then transposed into UK legislation have been concluded in eight areas – parental leave, part-time work, fixed-term contracts, teleworking, work-related stress, harassment and violence at work, lifelong development of competencies and qualifications, and actions on gender equality

- described how European Union social and employment legislation comes mainly in the form of Directives which set out specific objectives, and how each member state is given time (usually two years) to enact legislation within its own Parliament to ensure that the objectives are achieved

- detailed how, under the Social Chapter procedures, some issues (eg working conditions, the information and consultation of workers) can be harmonised by qualified majority voting, some (for example, protection of workers where their employment contract is terminated, Co-determination) on the basis of unanimity amongst member states, and yet others (for example, the right to association, the right to strike and the right to lock-out) are formally excluded

- spent time outlining how and where European Union laws have had, and will continue to have, a direct impact on the work of the employment relations professional in the UK

- noted, above all, that UK legislation arising from the European Union exists in the following areas: equal opportunities (equal pay, parental leave, equal treatment and the burden of proof in cases of sex discrimination); employment protection/working conditions (redundancies, transfer of undertakings, insolvency, part-time work, agency workers, fixed-term contract workers); employment relations (information and consultation with employees in multi-national companies operating within the EU, in European companies and in member-states-based companies, industrial action, and the principles of free movement) and health and safety (the Working Time Regulations).

- The Single European Market (SEM) was the vision of the authors of the Treaty of Rome (1957), but it did not become a reality until 1 January 1993 after the Single European Act (1986) removed the veto of member states on economic and health and safety matters. It is a free trade area, and capital, labour, goods and services have freedom of movement in the market.

- Although the SEM is based on the advantages of the theory of market competition, this competition takes place on a fair basis. Members of the market cannot compete by devaluing their currencies, unilaterally changing interest rates or reducing employment and social conditions to the bottom.

- To protect employees, the SEM contains a social dimension (the Social Chapter) whereby minimum employment and social standards can be established in the market (Treaty of Rome, Treaty of Maastricht (2002) and the Treaty of Amsterdam (1997)).

- An important decision-making process in the EU is the Social dialogue process, which involves the EU-wide social partners (Business Europe, CEEP and ETUC) directly in the EU law-making process. If the Commission proposes legislation in the employment and social field, the social partners have the option to negotiate a Framework Agreement (collective agreement), which can be then transposed into an EU Directive and into national law.

- To date, the social partners have negotiated three Framework Agreements (parental leave, fixed-term contracts and part-time work) which have been transposed into EU Directives. In addition, they have negotiated five voluntary agreements (eg teleworking, stress, harassment and violence at work).

- If the social partners opt not to negotiate a Framework Agreement, the Commission may bring forward a draft Directive on the issue concerned to become a Directive via the Co-decision procedure.

- EU Directives in the areas of equal opportunities, employment protection, employment relations and health and safety have had a direct impact on the day-to-day work of the UK HR/personnel specialist.

## REVIEW QUESTIONS

1 Your line manager has recently attended a CIPD meeting at which the speaker argued that collective bargaining involves four classic features – ie parties, an agreed procedure governing the process of bargaining, outcomes (agreements) and the ability to impose sanctions. She has asked you to explain to her how the European Union Social dialogue process – which she understands is a form of collective bargaining at a European level – meets these criteria. Outline, and justify, what you would say in reply to her query.

2 You have been asked to explain to a senior colleague the different legislative instruments open to the Council of the EU. Choose up to three individual EU Directives and explain how they have impacted on your organisation, and justify the action taken.

3 Your company is fed up with having to implement employment and social legislation from the European Union. Your chief executive officer wants to influence this legislation so that it is more favourable to employers. You have been asked by

the CEO to produce a paper outlining and justifying what your company must do to influence employment and social legislation from Europe more effectively.

4 Explain the Social dialogue process. Why should employees want to negotiate Framework Agreements?

5 Explain how the Social Chapter has developed since the Treaty of Rome (1957).

## EXPLORE FURTHER

Chartered Institute of Personnel and Development (2000) *Europe: Personnel and development*. London: CIPD.

Department of Trade and Industry (1996) *The Social Chapter – the British and Continental approaches*. London: DTI.

European Economic Commission (1993) *White Paper on Growth, Competitiveness and Employment*. Brussels: EC.

*European Industrial Relations Review* is a monthly journal covering employment relations news in the European Union.

European Union Commission (annual publication) *Industrial Relations in Europe*.

Gennard, J. (2008) 'The Vaxholm/Laval case: its implications for trade unions', *Employee Relations*, Vol.30, No.5.

Gennard, J. (2009) 'Is social Europe dead?', *Employee Relations*, Vol.30, No.6.

Hall, M. (1994) 'Industrial relations and the social dimension of European integration', in Hyman, R. and Ferner, A. (eds) *New Frontiers in European Industrial Relations*. Oxford: Blackwell.

Hoffman, R. and Mermet, E. (2001) 'European trade union strategies on Europeanisation of collective bargaining', in Schulten, T. and Bispinck, R. (eds) *Collective Bargaining Under the Euro*. Brussels: European Trade Union Institute.

*Industrial Relations Journal* (various dates) Annual European Review.

Industrial Relations Services and Industrial Relations Research Unit,

Warwick Business School (various dates) *European Works Council Bulletin*. This is a regular bulletin dealing with developments in European Works Councils.

Keller, B. (2005) 'Europeanisation at sectoral level. Empirical results and missing perspectives', *Transfer: European Review of Labour and Research*, Vol.11, No.3: 397–408.

Keller, B. (2003) 'Social Dialogue – the state of the art after Maastricht', *Industrial Relations Journal*, Vol.34, Issue 5.

Marginson, P. and Sisson, K. (2004) *European Integration and Industrial Relations*. Basingstoke: Palgrave.

Marginson, P. and Sisson, K. (2002) 'European integration and industrial relations: a case of convergence and divergence', *Journal of Common Market Studies*, Vol.40, No.4.

*People Management*, a fortnightly journal for CIPD members which covers major developments in employment and social matters in the EU. Legislative matters covering employment arising from EU Directives are covered in its Law at Work section.

### Weblinks

http://europa.eu/institutions is the group website of the EU Commission, the Council of the EU, the European Parliament and the European Court of Justice

www.eurofound.europa.eu is the website of the European Foundation for the Improvement of Living and Working Conditions

www.eurofound.europa.eu/EIROnline is the website of the European Industrial Relations Observatory, which offers news and analysis of European industrial relations by country and topic

www.businesseurope.eu

www.ceep.eu

www.ueapme.com

www.etuc.org is the ETUC website that also provides information on the 15 European industry federations which represent workers in individual sectors including, for instance, journalism and entertainment

## CHAPTER 6

# Employment Relations Institutions

## OVERVIEW

The actors in the employment relations system form institutions to protect and advance their interests. The state also establishes institutions to ensure that the actors behave within acceptable standards in their employment relations activities. This chapter analyses these two sets of institutions. It begins by examining the role and function of employers' associations – dispute resolution, advisory services and political lobbying. The chapter then goes on to to look at the purpose and objectives of trade unions, the reason for the decline in union membership, the future for trade unions, and the job-centredness of UK trade unions. Next, the role and functions of staff associations are explained. The chapter then turns to the institutions established by the state to regulate the behaviour of the actors. The Certification Officer ensures that the employers and trade unions comply with statutory requirements concerning elections, mergers, finance and political funds. The Advisory, Conciliation and Arbitration Service (ACAS) seeks to promote good employment relations practice, provide information and advice, conciliate in individual employment rights disputes and provide conciliation, mediation and arbitration in collective industrial disputes. The Central Arbitration Committee (CAC) arbitrates, *inter alia*, in disputes over trade union recognition.

## LEARNING OUTCOMES

When you have completed this chapter, you should be aware of and able to describe:

- why some organisations join employers' associations and others do not
- how employers' organisations can help personnel professionals in their day-to-day work
- why trade unions behave as they do
- the role and functions of staff associations
- the role of the Advisory, Conciliation and Arbitration Service, the Central Arbitration Committee and the Certification Officer.

## INTRODUCTION

This chapter is concerned with the institutions of employment relations – employers' associations or federations, trade unions and staff associations, their peak organisations the CBI and the TUC, their international and European equivalents (see Chapter 5), and the state organisations of the Advisory, Conciliation and Arbitration Service (ACAS), the Central Arbitration Committee (CAC) and the Certification Officer. Both employers and employees have a range of options open to them by way of external organisations which might be useful to them and about which they have to make choices.

For example, should an employing organisation join its sector association or federation? Should it join peak organisations such as the Confederation of British Industry (CBI) or the Institute of Directors (IoD)? If it does decide to join their sector organisation, does it – assuming that the organisation it is thinking of joining is one which gets involved in collective bargaining in the first place – allow that organisation to bargain on its behalf? Does becoming a member bind it to a particular course of action? Even if the reasons for contemplating membership are nothing to do with collective bargaining, what sort of services are available to employers – and how are they paid for?

On the other side of the coin there is a need for employers to hear the voice of their employees so that there is a two-way dialogue enabling staff to influence what happens at work. This in turn raises the question of what institution embodying that employee voice might be appropriate. Is it a trade union? A Works Council? Or should employee voice not be viewed any longer in terms of collective representation? And again, in turn this raises issues such as why employees join or do not join trade unions.

## EMPLOYERS' ORGANISATIONS

Employers' associations are voluntary, private bodies which exist to provide information and co-ordination in areas of common interest. There are many different associations covering overlapping areas of geographical spread and industrial sector, and grouping large or smaller organisations. The Annual Report of the Certification Officer, which lists employers' associations, shows that since 1983 the number of employers' associations has declined. In 1983 there were 375 employers' associations on the Certification Officer's List, but by 2003 that number had fallen to 91, by 2005 to 85, and by 2009 to 80. The decline is the result of mergers and of companies going out of business. For example, 2008 saw the amalgamation of the 10 employers' associations involved in all the English-based Engineering Employers' Federation to form one new organisation – the EEF. In 2005, the Scottish Knitwear Association, the Food Manufacturers' Industrial Group and the Stourbridge Crystal Glass Manufacturers Association disbanded themselves, and in 2008/9 the National Bookmakers' Federation and the Scottish Grocery Trade Employers' Association did the same.

Employers' associations vary in size and influence from the very small with no full-time staff to large and highly influential organisations such as the EEF (over 5,000 member organisations), the Road Haulage Association (9,437 members) and the Retail Motor Industry Federation Ltd (9,492 members). The EEF is the manufacturers' organisation that helps thousands of companies to evolve and compete in a fast changing world. It boasts that:

> The EEF is the most powerful force backing UK manufacturing. Powering its growth with potent thought leadership making it fit for the future – and effective in the present – with switched on business services and representing its interests at the heart of government. When manufacturing gets moving, the EEF is its engine . . .

The EEF is the only membership organisation dedicated entirely to the manufacturing industry – an industry that is responsible for 55% of UK exports and whose productivity regularly outpaces economic growth. Around a quarter of the manufacturing businesses are members of the EEF. The Newspaper Society represents the interests of provincial newspaper publishers, whereas the British Printing Industries Federation protects and advances the interests of, *inter alia*, general, carton, security and magazine printers. The major employers' organisation are listed in the box below.

---

**Main employers' associations**

Association of Colleges
EEF
Electrical Contractors Association
Heating and Ventilating Contractors Association
Road Haulage Association
British Printing Industries Federation
Chemical Industries Association
National Federation of Retail Newsagents
Construction Confederation
Newspaper Society
Federation of Master Builders
National Pharmacy Association Ltd
Confederation of Paper Industries
Glass and Glazing Federation
Retail Motor Industry Federation
Dairy UK
England and Wales Cricket Board Ltd

---

In the public sector, the Local Government Association (LGA) is a lobbying organisation that acts as the voice of the local government sector and an authoritative and effective advocate on its behalf. In 1997, local government came together and created the Local Government Association to be its voice in the national arena – 424 authorities make up the Local Government Association, and it covers every part of England and Wales. Together the LGA represents over 50 million people and spends around £113 billion per year on local services. The

LGA assists its members to shape public debate and influence policy and practice in public services, and ensures that the sector attracts, retains and develops staff with the skills it needs.

The Convention of Scottish Local Authorities (COSLA) is the representative voice of Scottish local government and also acts as the employers' association on behalf of all Scottish Councils. The Association of Colleges provides its members with a number of services including benchmark surveys – for example, the Career Services Survey and salary surveys. It also provides advice on standards and ethics. Its Principle for Professional Practice Committee offers a review of the law regulating employment, considers relevant ethical issues, identifies the key role of career centres and makes recommendations for resolving individual situations fairly.

In common with trade unions, employers' associations that wish to have their legal status confirmed must be registered on a list kept by the Certification Officer (see below). Employers' associations are required to keep proper accounting records, to establish and maintain a satisfactory system of control of their accounting records, and to submit an annual return to the Certification Officer. An employers' association must submit its annual returns and accounts to this Officer before 1 June each year. The Certification Officer can investigate the financial affairs of an employers' association.

## REFLECTIVE ACTIVITY

Is your organisation in the membership of an employers' association?

If not, why not? If it is, why is it?

## THE IMPORTANCE OF EMPLOYERS' ASSOCIATIONS

Employers' bodies, whether in the public or private sector, organise themselves in different ways. The priority each gives to employment relations, as opposed to trade matters, differs according to tradition, the nature of the industry it represents and the degree of unionisation in its particular sector. Generally, it remains true that those associations that are most concerned with employment relations are those involving companies that make use of semi-skilled and skilled labour in areas where there is a high concentration of a single industry, such as engineering or printing.

There are three types of employers' associations:

- national federations to which local employers' associations are affiliated – eg the EEF, which is a federation of six autonomous organisations
- single national bodies such as the British Printing Industries Federation (BPIF), which is divided into six regions for administrative and representational purposes

- single associations with a national membership such as the British Ceramic Confederation.

Employers' associations consist of companies of varying sizes, from the very small to the very large. The largest are sometimes organised into either autonomous local associations (for example, Scottish Engineering) or non-autonomous district associations, such as the British Printing Industries Federation. Some employers' associations have a similar organisational structure to trade unions such that their ultimate decision-making authority is a national council or the equivalent. The basis of representation on such a council varies from association to association. Except for those with local autonomy, in most employers' organisations local and regional associations are consultative rather than decision-making bodies.

Although organisations of employers have existed for a very long time, there is some evidence that in recent times their prominence and influence over employment issues has declined. The 2004 *Workplace Employment Relations Survey* confirmed that in their role as sources of advice and information and as the employers' side of industry-wide or regional negotiating bodies, employers' associations had diminished in importance since the 1980s, indicating that more and more managements seemed to be assuming responsibility for their own employment relations. In 2004, the common sources of external advice for managers were lawyers (29%), ACAS (26%), accountants (17%) and the CIPD (16%). Nevertheless, there are still a significant number of employers' associations which continue to negotiate collective agreements at national level. In the private sector national agreements still exist – for example, in electrical contracting, paper-making, construction, road haulage and general printing. In the public sector national pay arrangements still exist for fire-fighters and local government manual workers, while the National Association of Health Authorities and Trusts – an employers' body – provides evidence to the appropriate pay review body. Yet in many industries national agreements have become less extensive as the percentage of employees covered by collective bargaining has fallen from 70% of employees in 1994 to 40% in 2004 and even lower today. National agreements tend to remain in industries dominated by small companies that operate in very competitive labour and product markets. For these companies, which usually do not have the resources to establish an HR/personnel function, the national agreement is still regarded as significant in taking labour out of competition and in providing an employment relations infrastructure for the sector via the procedures (eg disputes and grievances) contained in the agreement.

The Social dialogue procedure at the inter-professional and sector level of the European Union (see Chapter 4) has, however, given an added importance to the collective bargaining role of employers' associations. Employer organisations that wish to influence the social regulation of the labour market in the EU can only do so by joining an employers' association and then trying to shape the policy of that association so that in turn that body attempts to get that policy adopted as the view of its EU-wide equivalent either at the sector or inter-professional level. If British companies wish to influence the position of Business Europe (which is the only EU-wide inter-professional private sector employer voice recognised by the EU Commission) on the social regulation of the Single Market, they must be members, directly or indirectly, via the Confederation of British Industry (CBI), which is a major affiliate of Business Europe. If UK engineering companies wish to shape EU social regulation of the EU-wide engineering industry, they have to be members of the EEF, which in turn affiliates to the Western European Metal Trades Employers' Organisation, which is the only EU-Commission-recognised EU-wide engineering sector employer voice for consultation and negotiating purposes.

## NATIONAL AND OTHER REPRESENTATIVE BODIES

The best-known UK-wide employers' organisation in the UK is the Confederation of British Industry (CBI), whose roots go back to 1915 with the formation of the National Union of Manufacturers, later renamed the National Association of British Manufacturers (NABM). Within five years, two further organisations – the Federation of British Industries (FBI) and the British Employers' Confederation (BEC) – were formed. The CBI, as an organisation, was the result of a merger in 1965 between these three bodies. Its membership includes individual companies and national and regional trades and employers' associations. It sees as its overall task the promotion of policies for a more efficient mixed economy. It is estimated that around half of the total workforce are employed in organisations affiliated to the CBI. An important political lobbying organisation, the CBI's major function is to provide for British industry the means of formulating, making known and influencing general policy in regard to industrial, economic, fiscal, commercial, labour, social, legal and technical questions.

The ultimate governing body of the CBI is its Council – although in practice the Council has delegated the majority of its decision-making powers to its Chairmen's Committee and the CBI Board. The former, of which at least 10% of its members represent SMEs, takes the lead responsibility for setting the CBI's position on all policy matters. The CBI Board takes the lead responsibility for all operational and financial matters. The President's Committee advises the President on the CBI's aims and objectives as well as negotiations and relationships with other public and private bodies. The CBI consults and supports its members through a regional organisation of 13 regions. There are also 16 standing committees of the CBI charged with supporting specific areas of policy or members. Through this regional and standing committee structure, the CBI is able to consult its members and involve them in policy formulation.

However, although it does not specifically engage in employment relations activities, the CBI's lobbying activities can (and do) have an impact on issues that affect workplace employment relations. In recent years, the CBI has lobbied successfully on behalf of employers on issues such as the National Minimum Wage, statutory trade union recognition procedures, the reform of the employment tribunal system and the implementation, in the UK, of EU Directives. As an organisation, the CBI does not engage in negotiations with employee representatives but it does maintain a direct working relationship with the Trades Union Congress (TUC) as well as an indirect one via joint membership of bodies such as ACAS and the Health and Safety Executive.

## REFLECTIVE ACTIVITY

Outline the main services the Confederation of British Industry provides for its members.

## THE ACTIVITIES OF EMPLOYERS' ORGANISATIONS

Employers' organisations can assist the HR/personnel professional in his or her day-to-day work through the services they offer to their members. These services fall into five areas:

- collective bargaining with trade unions
- assisting in the resolution of disputes
- providing members with general advice
- representing members' views to political decision-making bodies
- representing member companies at employment tribunals.

### COLLECTIVE BARGAINING

Collective bargaining services carried out for members have declined. Multi-employer bargaining, which greatly diminished in importance in the 1980s became – according to the 1998 *Workplace Employee Relations Survey* – even more of a rarity in the 1990s. In workplaces with recognised trade unions, multi-employer negotiations affected the pay of some or all employees in 68% of workplaces in the 1980s. By 1990 this had fallen to 60% – but in 1998 it was down to 34%. Over three broad sectors of the economy, the fall over the period 1980–98 was substantial. In public services, the drop was from 81% to 47%, while in private manufacturing the fall was from 57% to 25%. The most dramatic fall, however, was in private services. In 1984, in this sector, 54% of workplaces were affected by multi-employer negotiations. By 1998 the figure had fallen to just 12%.

The *Workplace Employee Relations Survey* for 1998 reported that when the falling proportion of workplaces with a recognised union was taken into account, the demise of multi-employer collective bargaining was even more apparent. Among all workplaces with 25 or more employees, multi-employer bargaining directly affected 43% of workplaces in 1980, 31% in 1990 and just 14% in 1998. The public sector emerged as the only major sector of the economy where multi-employer bargaining remained common: in 1998, 41% of public sector workplaces were affected by it. In the private sector, the proportion in 1998 was a mere 4% of workplaces, down from over 25% in 1980. Private sector employers have effectively abandoned acting jointly to regulate the terms and conditions of employment.

## DISPUTE RESOLUTION

The provision of dispute resolution services has links with national bargaining arrangements in that most national agreements provide access to an established dispute procedure. Such procedures tend to stipulate a number of stages through which a dispute are to be processed. Stage 1 may include the involvement of a local employers' association representative, a union branch secretary, lay union officials from within the organisation in dispute, and the organisation's management. If the dispute is not resolved at this stage, it may – depending on the employers' association and the union involved – move up to a district or regional level. Some of the players will stay the same as at the first stage, but the full-time officials will probably differ. The third stage involves national officials of the employers' association and the appropriate trade unions. If there is no resolution of the differences at this stage, some disputes procedures provide for the involvement of an independent third party whose decision will be binding. Such dispute procedures usually contain provisions stating that 'no hostile action' is to be taken by either side or that the status quo must prevail while the dispute is going through its various stages.

## ADVISORY AND INFORMATION SERVICES

During the years when national collective bargaining was in the ascendancy, many employers' organisations became bureaucratic and unimaginative. They had a captive membership and paid little attention to membership retention, or to the range of services that they offered members. All this changed as companies began to prefer bargaining at a more local level. This in turn led employers to examine what else they were receiving from their associations, in return for not insignificant levels of subscriptions. Some employers' organisations quickly realised that if they were to continue to have an employment relations influence, they had to provide their members with a package of benefits and services that would be seen to add value to businesses. In this context, many employers' associations widened their existing advisory services on good practices and model procedural agreements on issues such as disciplinary, dismissal and redundancy procedures. Their ability to market such services was helped by the growth, particularly in the 1970s and 1980s, of employment legislation that added to employees' 'rights at work'. Unfair dismissal, health and safety and equal pay are just three examples. In the 1990s and the early years of the twenty-first century, a raft of legislation from the European Union Council of Ministers added to the advisory and information services that employers' associations now provide for their members.

The recruitment literature of many of the large employers' associations places greatest emphasis on the employment advice and support services it can offer to members. For example, the Construction Confederation offers its members advice and support on wage rates and conditions of employment, disciplinary procedures, redundancy procedures and representation at employment tribunals, and provides a regular bulletin outlining relevant developments in employment law. Most employers' organisations also provide employee relations information services. Prominently featured in such information are pay and benefits data based on regularly conducted surveys which are useful for salary and pay comparisons and for use in local negotiations. However, such surveys can be problematic, because the associations have no means of enforcing individual returns. Nevertheless, provided that the employment relations professional recognises these limitations, such surveys can be a valuable tool. Other topics on which employers' associations provide information include labour productivity and UK government and EU policy developments in employment relations.

Employers' associations not only provide advice for small company members on issues such as managing employee disciplinary matters but may also represent them at employment tribunals when such company members are faced with alleged unfair dismissal from employers. It is not necessary to employ a leading law firm with the level of high costs associated when the expertise is readily available and proven through employee association membership. Some of the larger employers' associations also provide training services for their members. By tailoring a series of training programmes for each member company they can deliver specific courses best suited for the business and for individuals. These customer-designed training courses can be workshops over a period of time and/or day courses.

Now read the case study below, about Fibercore.

## CASE STUDY

### Fibercore and the EEF

*Background:*

Fibercore Ltd

- produces optical fibres
- employs 25 people
- has an annual turnover of £9 million.

*Services supplied by the EEF:*

- bespoke training
- industry intelligence
- HR and legal advice and support
- networking
- policy and representation.

*Overview:*

Fibercore and EEF have worked in partnership since 2003. During this time, the managing director has been instrumental in his role as an EEF regional board member.

> Our relationship with the EEF allows us to keep on top of best practice and up to date with legislation and information – benefitting both our business and our employees.

Fibercore uses a lot of the information the EEF provides both online and in print – the latest surveys on management and engineering pay scales, for example:

> We receive high-quality no-nonsense and detailed information on a regular basis from the EEF and use several of their services. Being fully informed has allowed us to ensure that we operate the highest level of HR and employment welfare for our existing staff.

*Outcomes:*

The EEF has facilitated a direct link between businesses and the policy-makers, enabling Fibercore to contribute to the ongoing development of policy and legislation – ensuring that manufacturing-related issues are at the heart of the Government's agenda.

The EEF has provided in-depth research and practical market information allowing Fibercore to operate the highest level of HR and employment welfare.

The EEF's range of tailored training programmes has helped to keep Fibercore on the front foot – adding value to its business.

The EEF has provided access to authoritative up-to-the-minute management information that Fibercore has utilised in its approach to forge relationships with academic institutions – gaining recognition early and attracting entrepreneurial and inventive candidates to the business.

By providing expert advice and guidance through membership, the EEF has successfully assisted Fibercore with the necessary processes to avoid an employment tribunal.

**Activity**

1   What are the main lessons you take from this case study on how employers' associations can help add value to organisations?

2   If Fibercore were not a member of an employers' association, could it have achieved the same outcomes? If it could, how could it? If it couldn't, why couldn't it?

## THE REPRESENTATION OF MEMBERS' INTERESTS

A major growth area of activity has also been the representation of members' views to a range of other organisations, particularly political bodies – UK government departments, local authorities, the institutions of the European Union and political parties. These political lobbying activities may be of particular interest to the large company whose inclination might otherwise be to leave an association if its only purpose was the negotiation of a national agreement. Now that many large organisations operate in a European and worldwide market, they know that their only means of influencing UK government or European Union policy is through a collective voice. The EEF, for example, reports regularly to its members on its representations to the major political parties to try to ensure the employment policies that such parties develop, and adopt, to meet the needs of the engineering industry. The UK Government and the EU Commission find employers' organisations useful in obtaining a collective employer view on a wide range of consultative documents. Examples include proposed UK employment legislation, the EU Commission reviews of the Working Time and European Works Council Directives, the McLeod and Clarke Report on employee engagement and the EU proposed Directive on Agency Working.

### REFLECTIVE ACTIVITY

Why might organisations wish to be members of an employers' association?

## NON-MEMBERSHIP OF EMPLOYERS' ASSOCIATIONS

First, not all organisations view employers' associations in a favourable light. Why is that? Some companies view employers' associations as too restrictive and see membership as an obstacle to independent action to introduce innovation in employment relations policies and practices. Such companies regard innovation, whether in operational matters or people issues, as an essential managerial activity in today's economic climate. They therefore feel the need to be responsible for, to co-ordinate and to control their own employment relations activities. Nevertheless, it is important to remember that even those companies which bargain unilaterally, or independently of the appropriate employers' association, cannot ignore when deciding their own employment relations policies and practices what is happening more generally in the sector in which they are operating. An important part of the employment relations function is to take account of other wage settlements, particularly within the sector in which their organisation operates. Not being aware of such settlements, many of which affect their competitors, could seriously weaken their own bargaining position and impact adversely on their competitiveness.

Second, there are those companies who do not take out membership of an employers' organisation because they see it as incompatible with their non-recognition of trade union policy and philosophy. These companies perceive employers' associations as very much part of a collective approach to employment relations. They prefer to relate to their employees on a more individual basis.

There are businesses which, despite their feelings, join employers' organisations because of their more traditional trade association activities. A number have arbitration schemes to resolve differences between supplier and customer, whereas others have the ability to remove an organisation from membership if they do not meet agreed standards on, for example, the quality of service or product provided for the customer. This can be an effective sanction for a company which relies on the 'badge' of the trade association to help secure business, as is the case with some of the building trades or electrical contractors.

## TRADE UNIONS

### PURPOSE AND OBJECTIVES

Trade unions are organised groups of employees who:

> consist wholly or mainly of workers of one or more description and whose principal purposes include the regulation of relations between workers and employers.
>
> Section 1 of the Trade Unions and Labour Relations (Consolidation) Act

The primary purpose of trade unions is to protect and to enhance the living standards of their members. The principal methods they use to achieve this objective fall broadly into two categories: industrial and political. Industrial methods include the negotiation of agreements with employers and all that belongs to collective bargaining, grievance procedure, industrial action, use of third-party intervention, joint consultation, etc.

Political methods, on the other hand, cover all types of union participation in the political process including 'pressure group' activities in relation to the UK Government and the EU decision-making bodies, whether they are conducted by campaigns, delegations, lobbying or sitting on governmental and EU advisory committees. Pressurising the UK Government to pass legislation favourable to trade unions is usually done by the Trades Union Congress (TUC). EU political lobbying is done through the activities of the European Trade Union Confederation and/or the European Industry Federation for the sector (see Chapter 5). Trade unions also lobby the International Labour Office (ILO), which is a United Nations agency, to obtain minimum labour standards on a global scale. This lobbying is undertaken by the International Confederation of Free Trade Unions (ICFTU), which was formed in 1949. Its membership consists of 241 affiliated organisations in some 156 countries on five continents, with a membership of 155 million, 40% of whom are women. The ICFTU thus has a close relationship with the ILO, which is made up of government, employer and worker representatives. The ILO has established many minimum labour standards (known as ILO Conventions) to operate globally to protect workers' rights and which all governments in membership of the United Nations are expected to enact in their national legislation.

At the international level, trade unions also lobby inter-governmental bodies via Global Union Federations, of which there are 13. They link together, at international level, as nationally based trade unions from a particular trade or sector. They share a common determination to organise, to defend human rights and labour standards, and to promote the growth of trade unions for the benefit of all working men and women and their families.

## REFLECTIVE ACTIVITY

What are the main purposes of trade unions?

### TRADE UNION MEMBERSHIP LEVELS

#### Overall

Total union membership in the UK peaked at an all-time high of 13.2 million members in 1979, made up of 12.1 million members in TUC-affiliated unions and just over 1 million in non-TUC unions. In 2008/9, the total trade union membership – as reported by the Certification Officer – was 7.7 million. Trade union density is much larger in the public sector (60%) than the private sector (16%). In the former sector, three employees in every five are trade union members, but in the latter it is fewer than one in five (Metcalf, 2004). In the manufacturing sector, union density at 27% is below that for the economy as a whole (28%). However, in the manufacturing sector there is still a high union presence, especially amongst skilled manual workers. Trade union membership remains low in private sector services (financial, retail), amongst private sector non-manual employees, in small firms and in foreign-owned firms.

### Trade union membership decline

THEORY

The traditional explanations of the decline in trade union membership include:

- the composition of workforce and jobs – If employment declines in traditional areas of high union membership, then as a matter of arithmetic, total union membership falls. Booth (1989) attributes over two-fifths of the decline in union membership in the 1980s to such compositional factors. That composition factors play a minor part in explaining changes in union membership has been confined by Machin (2002)

- the business cycle – Membership is said to increase at times of low and/or falling unemployment

- the role of the state – The state can influence membership directly through laws on recognition and the closed shop, and indirectly by creating the environment in which employee–management relations are conducted. In this way the state can undermine or promote collectivism. Freeman and Pelletier (1990) calculated a 'legislation index' according to how favourable or unfavourable various strands of labour laws were to unions in each year. The changes in the law in the 1980s were held to be 'responsible for the entire decline' in union membership. There are, however, those who argue that the state today so regulates the employment relationship – for example, working time, family-friendly policies – that in both the short run and the long run the activities of the state undermine the rationale for unions. For example, in the mid-1960s the trade unions opposed the Redundancy Payments Act, arguing that the obtaining of financial compensation for the inevitable loss of a job was the legitimate concern of trade unions, not the state

More recently, it has become accepted that these three explanations of changes in union membership give insufficient weight to the role of employers, individual employees and unions themselves:

- the role of employers – Some argue that employers have become more hostile to unions. To examine this view one could look at plant closures, de-recognition activity and the new recognition of trade unions. There is no research evidence to support the hypothesis that union activity has resulted in a higher rate of plant closures amongst unionised workplaces relative to their non-union counterparts, nor that management embarked on the wholesale de-recognition of trade unions. Research by Machin (2000, 2003), however, demonstrates that union decline is mainly explained by the inability of unions to achieve recognition in newer workplaces (see below)

- the role of individual employees – An important advantage to the individual who joins a trade union is the wage premium compared with an equivalent non-member. In the 1980s, economists estimated the mark-up in wages for a union member relative to a non-member to be around 10%. Today, the premium is estimated at best to be half this level. Indeed, some studies show there is no longer any wage plus to joining a union. The loss of a wage premium is a reason cited by Metcalf (2004) for individuals not to join unions and to help explain why union membership is also falling in those sectors of the economy where unions are recognised

- Millward *et al* (2000) argue that workers have lost their taste for belonging to a union, but others (for example, Towers, 1997) believe there is a 'frustrated demand' for membership which results in a 'representation gap'. Over the last 20 years there has been a large rise in the proportion of the workforce that has never been a union member – up from 28% in 1983 to 60% in 2004 – suggesting that unions are experiencing difficulties in getting individuals to take out membership in the first place. Research also suggests (see below) that younger employees are much less likely to belong to a union than older workers, and that this gap in membership rates by age has grown sharply in recent years. This 'withering of support' for trade unionism thesis has been questioned by Towers (1997), who argued that many non-unionists would join a union if one were available in the workplace.

- the role of unions themselves – This involves questions such as what the impact is on membership gains, for example, of the trend to large conglomerate unions, of recent emphasis by unions on 'organisation', and of moves away from traditional adversarial industrial relations towards greater co-operation with employers via partnership (Heery *et al*, 1999; see also Chapter 8).

THEORY    **The new workplace/young worker thesis**

Machin's research (2000, 2003) shows that union recognition in workplaces with 25 or more employees fell from 64% in 1980 to 42% in 1998. In 1980, establishments less than 10 years old had a recognition rate of 0.59 – almost as large as the fraction of workplaces aged 10 or more years which recognised unions. He also shows, however, that over the next 20 years, unions found it increasingly more difficult to organise new workplaces. By 1998, just over a quarter of workplaces under 10 years of age recognised a trade union – only half the corresponding figure of older workplaces. This inability of unions to make an impact on new workplaces is not, as often thought, restricted to the private services sector. Only 14% of manufacturing workplaces opened after 1980 recognised a trade union, compared to 50% of those establishments in 1980 or before. This 36% gap in union recognition rates in manufacturing compares with a corresponding figure of 10 percentage points for private services. There is no significant recognition gap for public sector workplaces.

Some of the difficulty in achieving recognition in younger/newer workplaces is due to the fact that they tend to be small, relatively more female-intensive and more likely to be in the private sector. Machin's (2003) research demonstrates clearly that workplace age is a central factor in explaining the decline in union membership over the past 30 years. It also indicates that lower recognition rates in newer workplaces is not the end of the story, since he also shows that even where union recognition is achieved, union density is some 11 percentage points lower than it is in older workplaces.

Research by Bryson and Gomez (2003) and Machin (2003) shows that young workers are now much less likely to be in a trade union than at any time since 1945. Their 'age of employee' effect corresponds to the 'age of workplace' factor discussed above. In 1975, 55% of employees aged 18–64 were union members, but by 2001 this figure had fallen by 29%. Membership rates were lower in both years for employees aged below 30. In 1975 union membership density was only 11 percentage points lower for younger people (48% compared to 59%) but by 2001 the gap had risen to 19 points (15% compared to 34%). Union density among young men has fallen by 39 points over the last quarter of a century, and that for young women by 23 points.

`THEORY`

One reason for the increasing gap between membership rates between younger and older workers is said to be the transmission of membership across generations. Machin and Blanden (2003) have shown that there is a 30% higher probability of being a union member if your father is also a union member. Fewer parents are union members today than was previously the case so – given the cross-generation correlation in trends of taking up union membership – fewer younger people are likely now, and in the future, to join trade unions.

`THEORY`

Two main features in the decline of trade union membership since 1979 are thus that fewer young workplaces have union recognition agreements and/or arrangements and fewer young workers are members of unions. In sectors of employment dominated by new firms, there is less likely to be a union to join. Younger workers are particularly affected because they are more than likely to be employed in young workplaces. In 1998, for example, in workplaces established before 1980, only 10% of the workforce was aged under 25, whereas among those set up in the 1980s and the 1990s, the corresponding figure was 17%. Metcalf (2004) argues that young workers probably are the main factor in explaining falling union density in workplaces where unions are recognised. Between 1983 and 1998, he points out, in workplaces where unions are recognised, the density of those aged 30 remained virtually unchanged at 70%, but the density of those aged 18–25 almost halved from 67% in 1983 to 41% in 1998.

## THE FUTURE OF UNIONS

`THEORY`

The review of contemporary research on trends in trade union membership indicates that future membership trends of trade unions will depend on the unions' ability to persuade employers to recognise them and to convince employees to take up membership. One route by which trade unions might revive their membership is to engage in more intensive organising activities, and another would be to improve their attraction to both employers (for example, by partners and arrangements – see Chapter 8) and potential members. With respect to their organising and servicing of members' activities, trade unions cannot neglect their existing membership. This will involve unions maintaining and advancing their terms and conditions of employment, providing them with services such as advice on employment matters, promoting lifelong learning, representing their interests in grievance and disciplinary procedures, and representing them before employment tribunals and third-party intervention bodies. Presently, the percentage of workers covered by collective bargaining (see Chapter 8) but not members of a union is 38%. If trade unions are to increase their membership in the future, they will have to make serious endeavours to organise this group of workers. Future membership will also be boosted if unions succeed in organising a significant proportion of the estimated 14 million employees who are not presently members and who do not have their terms and conditions determined by collective bargaining.

Heery *et al* (2000) surveyed major unions and found that most have formal organising, recruitment and retention of membership policies, have invested additional resources in organising activity and have attempted to organise groups of workers who they had hitherto forgotten. Contemporary research shows, however, that all this organising activity has met with limited success. The impact of the trade union recognition procedures of the Employment Relations Act (1999) has been modest (Gall, 2004). After gaining recognition relatively easily in the first two years of the operation of the Act, unions are now meeting stronger resistance to recognition demands from employers (Industrial Relations Service, 2006). The loss of union members from redundancy, plant closures, etc, continues to far exceed the number of new members obtained from organising activity. The future for unions therefore looks bleak.

**THEORY**    EXPLAINING TRADE UNION BEHAVIOUR

The classic work of Alan Flanders of some 40 years ago on this question is as relevant today as then. For Flanders (1968), union behaviour was characterised by:

- 'sword of justice' objectives

- the advancement of job interests and not class interests

- according the highest priority to delivering their objectives by industrial methods rather than political methods

- pragmatism – dealing with matters in a sensible, flexible and realistic manner rather than being influenced by fixed theories or ideology.

Flanders has demonstrated that throughout their history trade unions have sought for their members not only more income, more leisure time and more security but also an enhancement of their status by establishing employment rights for them – for example, the right to a certain wage, the right not to have to work longer than so many hours, the right not to be subject to arbitrary dismissal. For this reason, Flanders contended that trade unions can be viewed as a 'sword of justice' seeking fairness of treatment for their members from employers and from the state. This 'sword of justice' behaviour is seen in the impact of trade union behaviour, for example, on pay distribution, on the event of accidents in the workplace, on the provision of friendly-family policies and in the promotion of equal opportunities. Metcalf (2004) has estimated that if there were not trade unions in the labour market, the wage differential between male and female employees would be 2.6% higher than its present level. The corresponding figures he presents for non-manual/manual worker differentials and between white and black workers are +3.0% and +1.4% respectively. An aspect of union behaviour is to seek to be an egalitarian influence on the workings of the labour market.

Flanders (1968) also helps us to understand trade union behaviour when he described them as being 'job-centred' and not 'class-centred'. The basis of trade union membership in the UK is the job the individual performs. The main function of a trade union is to protect the employment conditions and status of their members from 'invasion' by employers, other groups of workers and their trade unions. Trade unions represent a sectional interest in society in that they further the common interests of employees performing certain jobs to the exclusion of other groups of job performers.

One of the consequences of job-centred trade unionism is the existence of different types of trade unions. Although in the light of trade union mergers it is becoming less and less relevant, it is still the convention to divide trade unions in the UK into three broad main types: occupational (or craft), industrial, and general. However, today few occupational unions exist, and those that do are relatively small in size. Examples include the British Air Line Pilots Association (BALPA) and the Associated Society of Locomotive Engineers and Firemen (ASLEF) and the Professional Footballers Association (PFA). Such unions recruit members selectively, on a job-by-job basis, irrespective of where they work. It is the employee's occupational status, job skills and qualifications or training that determine whether or not an individual qualifies for membership, not the industry or the organisation that employs him or her.

Industrial unions will organise any workers, regardless of their status and skills, who are employed in a particular industry. They recruit vertically within an industry but will not recruit from groups working in much the same way in a different industry. In short, they recruit members vertically from among all employment grades, normally including both manual and non-manual workers within a single industry. However, in the UK because of the constantly changing and evolving structure of industry, it is not a simple matter to define the boundaries between industries. Examples of single-industry-based unions in the UK are now very few.

General unions will recruit any workers (both manual and non-manual) horizontally across industries and vertically within industries. Such unions seek to regulate labour markets by trying to establish a monopoly over the supply of employees. The best example of a general union in the UK is the GMB.

Another consequence of job-centred unionism is the existence of a large number of individual trade unions. In the UK, trade union structure is characterised by a small number of very large unions co-existing with a large number of small unions. In 2008/9, the Annual Report of the Certification Officer noted that there were 185 registered independent trade unions in the UK. Of these, 14 (all with membership of 100,000 or more) accounted for 86% of total trade union membership but accounted for only 8% of the total number of trade unions. 89 trade unions had membership of less than 1,000. They accounted for 38% of the total number of unions but only 0.3% of the total membership of trade unions. The 14 largest unions in 2008/9 are shown in Table 6.1.

**Table 6.1 Trade unions with a membership of 100,000 or more in 2008**

| Union | Membership |
|---|---|
| Unite | 1,952,226 |
| UNISON: The Public Service Union | 1,344,000 |
| GMB | 590,125 |
| Royal College of Nursing | 393,865 |
| National Union of Teachers | 374,170 |
| Union of Shop, Distributive and Allied Workers | 356,046 |
| National Association of Schoolmasters; Union of Women Teachers | 313,350 |
| Public and Commercial Services Union | 304,829 |
| Communication Workers Union | 236,679 |
| Association of Teachers and Lecturers | 208,568 |
| British Medical Association | 138,359 |
| Union of Construction Allied Trades and Technicians | 129,065 |
| University and College Union | 117,597 |
| Prospect | 102,695 |

Over the last 30 years, as a result of trade union mergers, the number of unions affiliated to the TUC has fallen from 112 in 1979 to 53 in 2008. These mergers have been driven by the implementation of technological change and changing product and labour markets. The impact of these changes has been a loss of trade union membership, continuing employer opposition to recognition in key economic sectors, difficulties in financial viability, and inter-union competition for members. The trend in union mergers is towards the formation of 'mega-unions' aspiring to represent whole sectors of the economy. This trend was confirmed by the merger in 2007 of Amicus (1.2 million members), which represented all the interests of employees in the private sector of the economy, and the Transport and General Workers Union (900,000 members) to form Unite, with 2 million members. UNISON has aspirations to become the union which represents the interests of all employees employed in the public sector.

July 2008 saw a new development when Unite and the United Steelworkers – North America's largest private sector union – concluded an agreement creating what they described as the 'world's first global union'. It is a federal union with its principal office in London. The concept of transnational unions is represented by the union for maritime professionals: Nautilus International changed its name from Nautilus UK to enable a merger with its Danish equivalent.

A consequence of the unwieldy trade union structure resulting from job-centred unionism is inter-union conflict over the recruitment of employees (membership jurisdiction) and industrial policy. Skilled workers, for example, prefer to see their wage differential over lesser-skilled workers expressed in percentage terms. The lesser-skilled workers, on the other hand, prefer wage differentials expressed in absolute monetary terms. Equal percentage increases in wages widen money differentials. Equal monetary increases (commonly referred to as flat-rate increases), on the other hand, narrow percentage differentials.

Job-centredness also results in differences in attitudes to macro-economic policy issues. Trade unions whose members are working in firms engaged very much in foreign trade favour UK entry into the euro currency because this would protect their members from experiencing downward pressures on their employment conditions as the value of the pound fluctuates against the euro. Membership of the euro, however, removes from governments the ability to regulate the economy by changing interest rates and devaluing the pound sterling. Euro membership also commits member country governments to keep their debts within 3% of the gross national product. Given these restraints, public sector unions fear that when their economies experience difficulties, governments are likely to react by cutting public expenditure. Such a government policy would not be in the interests of the members of public sector unions. So we can see why private-sector-based unions perceive euro membership to favour the job interests of their members whereas public sector unions, on the whole, see such membership as contrary to the job interests of *their* members.

Job-centred unionism also has implications for trade union solidarity. There is a tendency to think – especially among left-wing romantics – that unions automatically support one another when involved in an industrial dispute with employers. In reality, this is far from the case. Solidarity action occurs only when the job interests of the different trade unions concerned coincide. Then, and only then, do they show support and solidarity for each other. In 2003 the Royal Mail decided to discontinue transporting mail on the railways. The effect of this was to transfer work from the railways to the road. The Rail, Maritime and Transport Union (RMT) members stood to lose jobs from this move. The Communication Workers Union (CWU) members employed by the Royal Mail stood to gain – the mail carried on the railway network was now to be transported by road in Royal Mail vehicles. When the RMT sought the support of the CWU to get Royal Mail to change their decision, the CWU remained unchanged in its attitude.

Flanders (1968) also showed that unions accord the priority to the industrial methods, over political methods, in advancing the interests of their members. This is still as true today. When they have a choice, trade unions invariably prefer to rely on industrial, rather than political, methods to achieve their aims. This does not mean that they despise political action. On the contrary, they are as a rule very ready to use political lobbying – but to support and to supplement their industrial methods, never to supplant them. This was seen in the attitude of trade unions to union recognition and the National Minimum Wage legislation, both of which are supportive – as opposed to being restrictive – of collective bargaining.

At a minimum, unions have to engage in political action to obtain freedom from legal constraints upon the exercise of their main industrial functions – freedom of association, the right to undertake industrial action. However, trade unions have enough industrial strength to regulate their relationships with employers by direct negotiation – they do not seek government assistance. If, though, trade unions are too weak to do this – as we witnessed in the 1990s – they give a higher priority to regulating their relationship with employers by UK and EU legislation.

Why, then, do trade unions prefer industrial methods to political methods to achieve their objectives? Their members join because they value the services trade unions provide in enlarging and protecting their rights in the workplace. There is also the basic point that the vast majority of trade union members are much less interested in political issues than they are in industrial issues. Given this, how many members would trade unions be able to recruit and retain if all they had to offer was their political activities?

## THE TRADES UNION CONGRESS

The TUC was established in 1868. In 2008 it had 53 affiliate unions with a total membership of 6.8 million. It performs two broad roles. First, it acts as the collective voice of the UK trade union movement to governments, inter-governmental bodies and international trade union bodies. Second, it attempts to influence the behaviour of its affiliated unions. However, the sanctions it possesses to influence its affiliates are limited. When the TUC was established, it was very much the voice of the craft unions, which jealously guarded their autonomy. As a result, in devising the TUC constitution, they were not prepared to devolve much power or resources to it, nor to allow it to interfere in their activities. This limitation remains, and the autonomy of affiliated unions is still regarded as paramount, particularly in the area of wages and employment conditions. The TUC has limited authority over its affiliates and little resources. It has to persuade its affiliates of the rightness of its decisions. It is not always successful.

The supreme authority in the TUC is its Annual Congress, which is held in September, and to which affiliated organisations send delegates on the basis of one for every 5,000 members or part thereof. Congress policy is decided on the basis of motions, submitted by affiliated unions, being accepted by a majority vote of delegates. The implementation of policy decided at Congress is the responsibility of the General Council, which is serviced by the General Secretary. Unions over a certain membership size have automatic representation on this Council. There is also reserved representation for women and black unionists.

### THE TUC'S ROLE

The TUC has authority from its affiliates to act in three areas: industrial disputes, inter-union disputes, and the conduct of affiliates. In the case of a dispute between an affiliate union and an employer, the TUC does not intervene unless requested to do so by the affiliate involved. However, if negotiations break down (or are likely to break down) and the ensuing dispute might result in the members of another affiliated union being laid off, then the TUC General Secretary can intervene to try to effect a settlement.

The TUC can intervene in the case of disputes between affiliated unions over membership and job demarcation issues. A complaint by one affiliate against another is investigated by a Disputes Committee, which can recommend that a union that has poached members from another affiliate must give those members back. If the union fails to comply with the recommendations of a Disputes Committee, the General Council can suspend the union from membership until the next Congress, at which it may be expelled from membership.

The TUC can also investigate complaints that an affiliated union is engaging in conduct detrimental to the interests of the trade union movement or contrary to the declared principles or declared policy of the Congress. Should such a complaint be upheld, the General Council will recommend to the union concerned what it must do to put the matter right. Should the union fail to do this, the General Council will recommend its suspension from membership until the next Congress, at which it will be expelled unless it complies with the recommendation.

## REFLECTIVE ACTIVITY

Outline the main functions of the TUC.

## STAFF ASSOCIATIONS

Staff associations are usually established within a single organisation and for a particular group of employees. Their funding and/or office accommodation is therefore often dependent on the employer. They are not regarded as trade unions in the traditional sense and stand apart from mainstream trade unionism even if they are not actually hostile to it. Staff associations included on the Certification Officer's list of independent trade unions have historically been strongest in banking and insurance. However, such staff associations are small in membership size in that more than half have fewer than 500 members. The main causes of the formation of independent staff associations relate to the employees' wish to:

- respond concertedly to a specific event (eg threatened redundancies)

- have their own rather less formal type of union

- replace an existing consultative body by one that has negotiating powers

- establish collective representation where no representative system previously existed.

They also sometimes fulfil employer desires for a management-dominated consultative body or a management-inspired association.

Independent staff associations are characterised by high membership density. For example, the coverage rate within the top 10 building societies typically averages around 70% to 80%. They typically represent all the white-collar employees of a company, from managers to clerks and word-processor operators. However, a substantial minority limit their membership to specific groups, the two most common being managers and executives, and agents, representatives and salespeople.

Although the largest staff associations may act as independent unions, the effectiveness of the smaller ones is limited by their narrow membership base and weak financial resources. Many operate from a modest financial base. The majority of staff associations are recognised by employers for negotiating and representational purposes. Most agreements they conclude follow the normal pattern and cover such issues as recognition, provision of facilities, joint negotiating machinery, consultation, and grievance and discipline procedures.

The ability of independent staff associations to represent the interests of their members may be questioned. An organisation whose membership is confined to the employees of a single employer is exposed to pressures that are much less effective against a broad-based organisation. It will also find it difficult to bargain on equal terms with that employer, particularly if the size of the undertaking places strict limits on its membership and financial resources. The fact that senior managers can, and do, belong to a staff association leads some to question their genuine independence from employer interference.

In addition to staff associations which have a Certificate of Independence from the Certification Officer (see below), there are a much larger number of bodies which bear the title of 'staff association' and which make no claim to be a trade union even in an informal sense. Such bodies usually have a consultative rather than a bargaining function, and little or nothing in the way of independent resources. Membership is usually automatic for all non-manual employees, and there is often no membership subscription since the employer meets any expenses incurred by the association.

## REFLECTIVE ACTIVITY

Explain the difference(s) between a staff association and a trade union.

Professional associations, such as the British Medical Association or the British Dental Association, often represent the interests of their members in negotiation with the relevant employers but also function as organisations responsible for the education and certification of practitioners and the maintenance of professional standards among members. The dual role of negotiators and professional standard-bearers can sometimes conflict, as the medical and nursing professions have found. It can be difficult to take legitimate action in support of an industrial dispute without coming into conflict with a professional code of conduct.

## STATE AGENCIES

In this section we look at those state agencies that have a statutory role in employment relations, whether that role is in respect of individual or in respect of collective issues. In the UK there are three major agencies of this kind: the Certification Office for Trade Unions and Employers' Associations, the Advisory, Conciliation and Arbitration Service (ACAS) and the Central Arbitration Committee (CAC).

### THE CERTIFICATION OFFICE

The post of Certification Officer was established in 1975, although its origins go back to before World War I when it was originally known as the Register of Friendly Societies. The Officer is appointed by the Minister for Business, Innovation and Skills after consultation with ACAS. The Certification Officer is responsible for:

- maintaining a list of trade unions and employers' associations

- ensuring compliance with statutory requirements and keeping records available for public inspection

- determining that a trade union is independent of employer control, domination or interference – the principal criteria used by the certification officer for this purpose are: history, membership base, organisation and structure, finance, employer-provided facilities and negotiating record

- dealing with complaints concerning trade union elections (for example, the election of the executive committee, the president and/or the general secretary), certain other ballots and certain breaches of trade union rules

- ensuring the observance of statutory requirements governing mergers between trade unions and between employers' associations

- overseeing the political funds and finances of trade unions and employers' associations.

The Employment Relations Act (1999) extended the Certification Officer's power to deal with:

- complaints by trade union members that there has been a breach, or that a breach is threatened, of the rules of a trade union relating to the appointment, election or removal of an office-holder

- disciplinary proceedings

- ballots of members other than in respect of industrial action

- the constitution or proceedings of an executive committee or other decision-making meeting.

## THE ADVISORY, CONCILIATION AND ARBITRATION SERVICE (ACAS)

The state provided third-party intervention in industrial disputes long before ACAS was established (Mumford, 1996). Such measures were previously the responsibility of the Department of Employment and its predecessor Ministries (eg the Ministry of Labour). The credibility of third-party intervention depends on the disputant parties' being confident that the third party is independent of government (or any other political) influence and therefore totally independent.

In the 1960s and 1970s the credibility of government-provided third-party intervention services became seriously compromised. This came about because Ministers – often as a condition of making the third-party services available to the disputant parties – made it clear that they expected the independent arbitrator to have due regard to the Government of the day's incomes policy. Indeed, on occasions, the Minister refused joint requests from employers and unions for third-party intervention on the grounds that the employer's offer was already in excess of the limits of the Government's incomes policy. The clash between the Government's role as an industrial peacekeeper and its role as an economic manager became most acute in 1968 when the newly created Department of Employment and Productivity – which was responsible, *inter alia*, for the provision of third-party intervention services – was also given responsibility for ensuring that the Government's incomes policy was applied effectively.

The early 1970s therefore saw increased demands by unions and employers for a third-party intervention service that was formally independent of the state, and in particular of the whims of different governments' prices and incomes policies. The strength of this feeling was seen when the TUC and CBI established their own private third-party arrangements. In September 1974, the then Labour Government created the Advisory, Conciliation and Arbitration Service (ACAS) as a Royal Commission. It was established as a statutory body on 1 January 1976 under the provisions of the Employment Protection Act (1975).

ACAS is independent of direct ministerial intervention although its sponsoring Ministry is the Department for Business, Innovation and Skills. ACAS is governed by an executive body known as 'the Council', which originally consisted of a chairperson and nine ordinary members – three chosen in consultation with the CBI, three in consultation with the TUC, and the remaining three independent people with specialist knowledge of employee relations. In 1992 the Council became 11 ordinary members, the additional two members representing the interests of small businesses and non-TUC unions.

ACAS seeks to:

- promote good practice
- provide information and advice
- conciliate in complaints to employment tribunals
- conciliate in the case of collective disputes
- prevent and resolve employment disputes.

### Promoting good practice

ACAS organises conferences and seminars on topical employment and employment relations issues. For small businesses, ACAS also runs self-help workshops where employment policies and procedures are discussed. Unlike the other services provided by ACAS, which are free, there is a charge for conferences, seminars and small-firm workshops. ACAS also sells a range of booklets offering practical guidance and advice on employment and industrial relations topics – for example, on discipline, job evaluation, recruitment and induction, employee appraisal, hours of work, teamworking and employee communications and consultation. During 2008/9, 23,182 delegates benefitted from an ACAS-organised training course, while a further 840 delegates attended other ACAS conflict-management-related training courses. 1,214 organisations of various sizes benefitted from ACAS-delivered tailored in-house training courses. These training courses made an important contribution to ACAS's objective of disseminating good practice and assisting in the formulation of sound policies for the employment relationship. They are also part of a service ACAS has developed to help SMEs which, because of pressures of work, can often find it difficult to keep up to date with good employment practice.

ACAS also has issued three Codes of Practice. Its Code of Practice on Disciplinary and Grievance Procedures provides practical guidance on good practice in disciplinary and grievance matters in employment and is obligatorily taken into account by arbitrators appointed by ACAS to determine cases brought under the ACAS Arbitration Scheme (see Chapter 11).

The ACAS Code on the Disclosure of Information to Trade Unions for Collective Bargaining Purposes sets out good practice in this area, and its Code on Time Off for Trade Union Duties and Activities provides guidance on time off for trade union duties, time off for training of trade union officials, and time off for other standard trade union activities. It also covers the responsibilities which employers and trade unions share in considering reasonable time off, and outlines the advantages of reaching formal agreements on time off.

These Codes impose no legal obligations on an employer. Failure to observe the Code does not, by itself, render anyone liable to proceedings – the provision of the Code on Disciplinary and Grievance Procedures may, however, be taken into account in proceedings before an employment tribunal and in an arbitration hearing under the ACAS Arbitration Scheme. The Disclosure of Information Code is taken into account by the Central Arbitration Committee when arbitrating on a complaint that an employer has failed to disclose information for collective bargaining purposes.

### Providing information and advice

ACAS provides information and guidance on a wide range of employment relations matters. It does this primarily through the ACAS helpline, which can be contacted by anyone. It has a team of 100 advisers based throughout Great Britain. The service is free, confidential and impartial, and is designed to assist employers and people at work. It provides a useful and cost-effective advisory service, particularly for small firms and individuals to help them clarify the range and increasing complexity of employment legislation, and thereby avoid difficulties at work. Most enquiries are dealt with by telephone, but a small number are answered by letter or personal interviews, usually by prior appointment.

In 2008/9, ACAS Helpline advisers answered 726,306 telephone calls, on every aspect of employment relations. The most frequently asked questions related to discipline and dismissal issues. Other topics of regular questions are requests for flexible working, maternity, paternity and adoption leave, and pay. The Working Time Regulations are also a regular subject of questions. For many organisations the ACAS helpline is often the first point of contact with ACAS. Sometimes their enquiry raises issues which cannot readily be answered by telephone, and in such cases the problem is addressed by face-to-face contact with ACAS field staff.

### Conciliating in individual employment rights disputes

ACAS has a statutory duty to act as conciliator in a wide range of individual employment rights complaints, including unfair dismissal, breach of contract (eg

**Table 6.2 Individual complaints concerning employment rights 1985–2009**

| Date | Unfair dismissal | Total complaints received |
|------|-----------------|--------------------------|
| 1987 | 34,572 | 40,817 |
| 1988 | 36,340 | 44,443 |
| 1989 | 37,324 | 48,817 |
| 1990 | 37,654 | 52,071 |
| 1991 | 39,234 | 60,605 |
| 1992 | 44,034 | 72,166 |
| 1993 | 46,854 | 75,181 |
| 1994 | 45,824 | 79,332 |
| 1995 | 40,815 | 91,568 |
| 1996 | 46,566 | 100,399 |
| 1997 | 42,771 | 106,912 |
| 1998 | 40,153 | 113,636 |
| 1999 | 52,791 | 164,525 |
| 2000/1 | 51,721 | 166,153 |
| 2001/2 | 53,994 | 163,409 |
| 2002/3 | 49,424 | 162,932 |
| 2003/4 | 39,766 | 102,559 |
| 2004/5 | 34,864 | 81,883 |
| 2005/6 | 35,944 | 109,712 |
| 2006/7 | 35,583 | 105,177 |
| 2007/8 | 33,352 | 151,249 |
| 2008/9 | 43,028 | 138,535 |

Source: ACAS Annual Reports, 1985–2008/9

non-payment of termination payments or commission), or discrimination on grounds of sex or race or in equal pay, or a failure to provide statutory benefits. However, for individuals and organisations to participate in this conciliation is voluntary. It is impartial, confidential, free of charge and independent of the employment tribunals. The number of complaints handled by ACAS concerning alleged breach of employment rights is shown in Table 6.2.

When making a complaint to an employment tribunal, a person must first complete form IT1 and send it to the appropriate employment tribunal office, which then passes a copy to ACAS. The case is then allocated to a conciliation officer whose responsibility it is to attempt to help the parties settle the complaint without the need for a tribunal hearing, if that is their wish and if both parties are willing to accept conciliation. The officer's role is to help in a neutral and independent way, and involves making both parties aware of the options available to them so that they may reach informed decisions on how best to proceed. The conciliation officer explains tribunal procedures and the ACAS Arbitration Scheme (see below) as well as relevant law, but does not make decisions on the merits of the case or impose or recommend a particular settlement. Any settlement terms are the responsibility of the parties concerned. The conciliation officer conveys the views of one party to the other. If there is information one party wishes to keep from the other, then so long as the party explains that to the conciliation officer, the information will not be passed on. Where a case is not settled before the date fixed for the tribunal hearing, the employment tribunal will resolve the matter.

In unfair dismissal cases, the conciliation officers have the statutory duty to explore first the possibility of re-instatement, or of re-engagement on suitable terms, before seeking to promote a monetary or other form of settlement. The Employment Rights (Disputes Resolution) Act (1998) empowers conciliation officers, if both parties agree, to draw up binding settlements in which both parties opt out of the employment tribunal system in favour of resolving the employee's complaint of unfair dismissal through voluntary arbitration – the ACAS Arbitration Scheme (see Chapter 11). The underlying principle behind this Scheme is to make the resolving of unfair dismissal claims by voluntary arbitration as similar as possible to the arbitrations currently undertaken by ACAS in settling trade disputes (see below). By 2009 ACAS had accepted 61 cases for resolution under the Scheme. The main barriers to the use of this Scheme continue to be opposition from the legal profession and a lack of understanding on the part of individuals, trade unions and employers of the benefits of the process and its outcome compared to the more confrontational tribunal process. ACAS also has an Arbitration Scheme for resolving by voluntary arbitration – rather than at an employment tribunal – disputes over alleged unreasonable refusal by an employer to grant an employee's request for more flexible working.

ACAS's role is to attempt to settle cases without the need for a tribunal hearing, recognising that not all cases are capable of a settlement and that some parties may wish to have their cases decided in a legal setting. On average, three out of four claims for employment rights breaches are either settled or withdrawn following ACAS intervention after which there is no need for a tribunal hearing. In the case of discrimination claims, the withdrawal/settlement rate is over 80%.

ACAS involvement is normally welcomed by the parties because it provides a means of settling their differences without the need for what can be expensive, stressful and lengthy legal hearings. An important part of the conciliation officer's job is to diffuse the tension and reduce the acrimony that often exists between the parties so as to enable them to focus realistically on the options open to them.

Nevertheless, an organisation that has acted without just cause against an employee is unlikely to be interested in seeking an ACAS-conciliated settlement with the individual concerned. If the employer has complied with good employment practice, there would be no business case for settling the complaint via ACAS conciliation. The organisation would be confident of having its case upheld. Only organisations that, for example, dismiss employees without complying with good employment practice are likely to see advantages in an ACAS-brokered pre-tribunal settlement.

Some disputes between individual employees and their employers or between individual colleagues or groups of colleagues do not involve actual or potential claims to an employment tribunal. In these situations ACAS statutory conciliation service is not appropriate. ACAS can, however, provide, for free, individual mediation to help resolve disputes of this kind. In 2008/9 ACAS mediators took on 230 new assignments, the vast majority at the request of the employers concerned, and successfully completed 195. This form of mediation is where an impartial party, the mediator, helps two or more people in a dispute to attempt to reach an agreement. Any agreement comes from those in dispute, not from the mediator. The mediator is not there to judge, to say one person is right and the other wrong, or to tell those involved in the mediation what they should do. The mediator is in charge of the process of seeking to resolve the problem, not the outcome. The mediators may be employees trained and accredited by an external mediation service who act as internal mediators in addition to their day jobs. ACAS, for example, provides mediators and mediation training, including the Certificate in Workplace Mediation. Mediators can work individually or in pairs as co-mediators.

Individual mediation distinguishes itself from other approaches to conflict resolution in a number of ways. It is informal, flexible, voluntary, binding in honour only, has no legal status, and the individual employee concerned is unrepresented. Individual mediation seeks to provide an informal and speedy solution to workplace conflict and can be used at any point in the conflict cycle. The process offers a safe and confidential space for participants to find their own answers – for example, by exploring the issues, feelings and concerns of all participants, by giving participants insights into their own behaviour and by allowing those involved to understand and empathise with the feelings of those with whom they are in conflict.

There are distinct phases in the individual mediation process. The first stage deals with the parties separately, while the remaining stages are dealt with during joint sessions (hearing and explaining the issues, building and writing an agreement). There may be a need to separate the parties at various points and speak to them individually – for instance, if there appears to be an impasse or the mediator feels that one side is unwilling to divulge information that might help to break the deadlock. There are occasions when 'shuttle mediation' – the mediator moving between the parties and relaying the views of each – has to be used because the parties will not sit in the same room with each other, or because at certain points it is more effective to do so. But the aim is to bring them together eventually. Although individual mediation is generally assumed to take place face to face, it can also be carried out via email, video link or over the phone. There are, however, no hard and fast rules when individual mediation can or cannot be used.

## REFLECTIVE ACTIVITY

How effective has ACAS been, do you think, in preventing individual complaints against alleged arbitratory behaviour by an employer going to employment tribunals?

## Conciliating and mediating in collective disputes

Collective employment disputes are very costly both to the employers and to the employees, so it is sensible to resolve workplace problems before they develop into disputes. ACAS employs two principal methods to help organisations avoid costly disputes:

- workshops in which employer and employee representatives discuss and agree on potential barriers to the achievement of long-term organisational goals. Such workshops are useful for exploring problems where the underlying causes are not clearly known. Once these are identified, courses of action can be agreed to rectify the problems

- joint working parties in which employer and employee representatives work together to devise and implement practical solutions to specific problems by, for example, collecting and analysing information and evaluating options.

ACAS staff normally chair the working party. However, although prevention is better than cure, employment disputes inevitably occur. When this happens, ACAS can help the parties by offering:

- conciliation

- mediation

- arbitration.

## The conciliation process

Requests for conciliation in collective disputes normally come from employers, trade unions or employee representatives in organisations where there are no trade unions or employee representatives. Before it agrees to conciliate, ACAS checks that the parties have exhausted any internal dispute resolution procedures they may have. In coming to conciliation, no prior commitment is required from the parties, only a willingness to discuss the problem(s) at issue. Conciliation is an entirely voluntary process and it is open to either party to bring discussion to an end at any time – although effectively management remains in control of deciding whether to continue with the process or to withdraw from it.

ACAS conciliators help the parties in dispute settle their differences by agreement and, if possible, in a long-term way. The conciliator remains impartial and independent, makes constructive suggestions to facilitate negotiations, provides information at the request of the parties and gains the trust and confidence of both parties so that a sound working relationship is developed. The first step in conciliation in a collective dispute is to discover what the dispute is about – a fact-finding process that usually requires the conciliator to meet with both sides separately, although occasionally information may be obtained at joint meetings. Almost all conciliations involve a mixture of side meetings at which the conciliator explores issues separately with the parties, and joint meetings at which the parties can explain their position face to face. The exact mix of side and joint meetings is determined by the conciliator in discussion with the parties.

Where it is clear a settlement might be achieved, the conciliator seeks to secure a joint agreement, usually in the form of a signed document, which finalises the terms of the settlement. Any agreements reached in conciliation are the responsibility of the parties involved, and ACAS has no power to impose or even to recommend settlements. In collective disputes there is no time-limit to the conciliation process, and ACAS continues to assist the parties as long as they wish it to and there appears a chance of reaching an agreed settlement. The role of the conciliator is to keep the two sides talking and to help facilitate an agreement.

**The mediation process**

In a collective dispute, if a settlement is not reached through conciliation, ACAS can arrange to try to resolve the issue through mediation. In this case, both parties agree that an independent person or a Board of Mediation should mediate between them. The process of mediation involves each side setting out its case in writing, followed by a hearing at which the two sides present, in person, their evidence and arguments. Hearings are usually held at ACAS offices or at the premises of the employer or the trade union. The mediator (or the Board of Mediation) makes formal, but not binding, proposals or recommendations to provide a basis for settlement of the dispute. The parties are free to accept or reject the mediator's proposals or recommendations. In mediation, as in conciliation, the employer remains in control of the situation and can withdraw at any stage. A settlement cannot be imposed by a third party. The employer remains free to accept or reject.

## The arbitration process

If the parties to a collective dispute decide to take their differences to arbitration for settlement, they appoint a jointly agreed arbitrator to consider the dispute and to make a decision to resolve it. Occasionally, arbitration may be by a Board of Arbitration with an independent chairperson and two side members drawn from employer and trade union representatives. It is the arbitrator who makes the award resolving the dispute, and not – as many seem to think – ACAS. Unlike conciliation and mediation, in arbitration the employer does not retain control because before ACAS will facilitate arbitration both parties must agree to abide by the arbitrator's decision. This is a long-established principle of arbitration, and in practice arbitration awards are invariably accepted and implemented.

### REFLECTIVE ACTIVITY

Explain the differences between conciliation, mediation and arbitration.

## What issues go to the arbitrator?

Table 6.3 shows the extent to which conciliation, mediation and arbitration has been used in the UK in collective disputes since 1979. It indicates that in general there has been a fall in the use of all three processes. However, the table indicates a slight but irregular rise in the incidence of conciliation since the late 1980s and early 1990s. In the case of mediation and arbitration, the figures have been relatively static for a decade. The type of issues that are the subject of arbitration are what are often referred to as disputes of rights, which are issues arising from the parties' rights under collective agreements. Arbitration is rarely used in what are referred to as disputes of interest – issues that arise from the negotiation of new or revised collective agreements.

An analysis of ACAS statistics (see its Annual Reports) over the last 30 years reviewing the types of issues under dispute at arbitration shows a dominance of three: job grading, dismissal and discipline, and other pay and conditions of employment (not annual pay increases). This demonstrates that employers have been prepared to go to arbitration on issues:

- that are important to them – but not so important that they are prepared to impose industrial sanctions on the union
- where the cost of losing is bearable
- where there is unlikely to be adverse publicity from the arbitrator's award.

## Why is arbitration so little used?

Arbitration is the accepted instrument of the last resort, but employers – whether in the private or public sector – continue to be sceptical about the principle of arbitration even on disputes of rights, let alone disputes of interests. Trade

Table 6.3 The use of third-party intervention in industrial disputes 1979–2009

| Date | Completed collective conciliation | Mediation | Number of arbitration hearings |
|---|---|---|---|
| 1979 | 2,284 | 31 | 394 |
| 1980 | 1,910 | 31 | 281 |
| 1981 | 1,716 | 12 | 245 |
| 1982 | 1,634 | 16 | 235 |
| 1983 | 1,621 | 20 | 187 |
| 1984 | 1,448 | 14 | 188 |
| 1985 | 1,337 | 12 | 150 |
| 1986 | 1,323 | 10 | 174 |
| 1987 | 1,147 | 12 | 133 |
| 1988 | 1,053 | 9 | 129 |
| 1989 | 1,070 | 17 | 150 |
| 1990 | 1,140 | 10 | 190 |
| 1991 | 1,226 | 12 | 144 |
| 1992 | 1,140 | 7 | 155 |
| 1993 | 1,118 | 7 | 156 |
| 1994 | 1,162 | 8 | 148 |
| 1995 | 1,299 | 5 | 136 |
| 1996 | 1,197 | 4 | 113 |
| 1997 | 1,166 | 11 | 60 |
| 1998 | – | – | – |
| 1999/2000 | 1,247 | 1 | 63 |
| 2000/1 | 1,472 | 5 | 55 |
| 2001/2 | 1,371 | 5 | 61 |
| 2002/3 | 1,353 | 9 | 71 |
| 2003/4 | 1,245 | 6 | 63 |
| 2004/5 | 1,123 | 7 | 51 |
| 2005/6 | 952 | 2 | 55 |
| 2006/7 | 949 | 2 | 44 |
| 2007/8 | 917 | 2 | 39 |
| 2008/9 | 960 | 3 | 25 |

Source : ACAS Annual Reports, 1979–2009

unions essentially remain pragmatic in their approach to accepting arbitration. They are in the bargaining business and are suspicious of anything that impedes their ability to gain by whatever means the best possible deal for their members. Although many trade unions profess to love 'free and unfettered' collective bargaining, their objections to arbitration are as much pragmatic as principled. However much they might be opposed to it in other circumstances, trade unions whose bargaining power is weak sometimes propose arbitration if and when they sense they could not secure approval for industrial action. In the 1980s and

1990s, unions anxious to maintain or expand their membership base showed a willingness to enter into so-called 'new-style' agreements in which pendulum arbitration (see Chapter 1) and/or a partnership agreement (see Chapter 8) were perceived as the basis of avoiding a need for strike action.

Employers can also be similarly guided by pragmatism. Whatever the principal argument of companies that they should negotiate within their procedure agreements and then, if there is a final 'failure to agree', stand up to the consequences without third-party intervention, the fact remains that many companies faced with the prospect or reality of industrial action themselves seek the conciliation – and at times, arbitration – route.

However, a major reason in employers' reluctance to resort more readily to arbitration is the reputation of the arbitration process itself – that the employer cannot retain control of events and must accept whatever the arbitrator may award, and that the arbitrator will 'split the difference' between the parties. Arbitration is first and foremost a process which transfers the ultimate responsibility for certain key business decisions from management to an independent third party. This is in contrast to collective bargaining, conciliation and mediation, in which each side retains considerable authority over events. Either party can exercise the prerogative of walking away at any time. There is little evidence to support the view that in disputes of interests the arbitrator always splits the difference. Yet however undeserved it is, arbitrators have this reputation. Until ACAS can effectively nail this misconception, any extension of the arbitration process into disputes of interest is unlikely to be achieved.

In disputes of interest there is also the criticism that the arbitrator usually improves upon the final offer made by the employer in direct negotiations. In doing this, arbitrators are likely to be acting on two assumptions. First, that the union would not be coming to arbitration unless it felt it could secure more for its members, and second, that in agreeing to arbitration the employer is anxious to avoid the alternative of industrial action and all its associated costs. The employer might well therefore be willing to pay a little more if such action can be avoided. An award handed down by an independent arbitrator holds out greater certainty of this than an improved offer by the employer.

Arbitration will remain a vital and indispensable instrument of last resort in dispute resolution. It can never be ignored – but it is unlikely to become more extensively used.

### REFLECTIVE ACTIVITY

Explain the circumstances in which an employer might be prepared to go to arbitration to resolve a dispute with the employees. What are the main dangers to an employer of using arbitration to resolve collective and/or individual disputes with employees?

## THE CENTRAL ARBITRATION COMMITEE (CAC)

The Central Arbitration Committee's roots go back to the 1919 Industrial Courts Act, which established the Industrial Court as a permanent and independent body for voluntary arbitration in industrial disputes. In 1971 the Industrial Relations Court changed its name to the Industrial Arbitration Board, which in turn became the Central Arbitration Committee under the Employment Protection Act (1975). The CAC is a permanent independent body with statutory powers. Its main functions are:

- hearing complaints from a trade union of an employer's failure to disclose information for collective bargaining purposes

- disposing of claims and complaints regarding the establishment and operation of European Works Councils in Great Britain

- dealing with complaints arising from the European Public Limited Liability Company Regulations (2004) (in respect of a European company), from the European Co-operative Society Regulations (2006) or from the Companies Cross-Border Mergers Regulations (2007)

- adjudicating on applications relating to statutory recognition and de-recognition of trade unions for collective bargaining purposes where such recognition or de-recognition cannot be agreed voluntarily

- hearing complaints concerning information and consultation under the Information and Consultation of Employees Regulations (2004)

- providing voluntary arbitration in industrial disputes. This function has, however, not been used for some years.

The Committee consists of a chairperson, 11 deputy chairpersons, 28 members experienced as representatives of employers and 26 members experienced as representatives of workers. All members of the Committee are appointed by the Secretary of State after consultation with ACAS. Decisions are made by panels of three committee members appointed by the chairperson and consisting of either the chairperson or a deputy chairperson, one member whose experience is as a representative of employers and one member whose experience is as a representative of workers.

The CAC is thus a specialist body which can approach its legislative responsibilities in a variety of ways, assisting the parties to reach voluntary agreements but making legally enforceable decisions when necessary. It is this flexibility which sets it apart from traditional courts (Burton, 2002). The CAC seeks to ensure that the parties have every opportunity to state their case, and issues decisions that take full account of the parties' views, explaining clearly the reasoning behind every decision. CAC decisions do not and cannot, however, set precedents because each case is different and has to be treated on its merits. No panel of the CAC is bound by a decision of another panel, and decisions are not circulated, although all are available on the CAC website.

In the case of the trade union recognition procedure, the CAC has powers to decide on:

- whether an application should be accepted
- which groups will be included in any recognition agreement (the bargaining unit)
- whether to hold a ballot, and on the conduct of the ballots
- the method of collective bargaining if the parties cannot agree this themselves.

The CAC arbitrates on disputes between employers and a trade union over whether the appropriate bargaining unit is compatible with effective management. If there is a CAC-imposed bargaining unit and the union still wishes to proceed to obtain recognition, the CAC has to decide whether the union has majority support. Except where the union has already recruited the majority of employees in the bargaining unit, the CAC will arrange for a secret ballot which can – at the discretion of the CAC – be at the workplace or be by post to the employees' homes. If the union has a majority on a vote of at least 40% of the whole bargaining unit, the CAC declares the union recognised. If the employer persists in failing to recognise the trade union, the CAC can impose trade union recognition for collective bargaining purposes by means of an agreement that then becomes legally binding on the parties. The CAC also plays a similar role in the trade union de-recognition procedure contained in the Employment Relations Act (1999).

The TUC Report on union recognition deals covering the period November 2004 to October 2005, published mid-2006, revealed a sharp drop in both voluntary recognition agreements and statutory awards. During this survey period, 49 new voluntary recognition deals were signed – significantly fewer than the previous year's figure of 154. In addition, 12 statutory agreements were awarded in the same period. These figures represented a decline in activity compared with the previous year when there were 25 CAC statutory awards. The decline in trade union recognition activity was also noted in the 2008/9 CAC Annual Report, which stated that during that year the number of applications for statutory trade union recognition had been 42, compared with 64 in 2007/8 and 2006/7.

## REFLECTIVE ACTIVITY

Explain the differences between ACAS and the CAC in terms of their roles and functions.

## SUMMARY

- The main services employers' organisations offer to their members are assistance in the resolution of disputes, representation at employment tribunals, advisory and information services ('good practice', model agreements, salary data, etc) and the representation of members' views to political and other decision-making bodies.

- The primary purpose of trade unions is to protect the jobs of their members and to enhance their pay and employment conditions principally by the use of collective bargaining and political lobbying.

- The UK trade union organisation is characterised in membership terms by a small number of very large unions and a large number of very small unions.

- Over the last 30 years trade union membership has declined due, *inter alia*, to structural factors (eg a switch of employment from manufacturing) and public policy initiatives unsupportive of trade union organisation.

- Although there are those who believe that trade unions are in terminal decline, the early 2000s has seen some increase in total trade union membership.

- Staff associations are usually established within a single organisation and are characterised by high membership density.

- The majority of large staff associations are recognised by employers for bargaining and representational purposes, and most agreements to which they are a party cover such matters as recognition, the provision of facilities, consultation, and grievance and disciplinary procedures.

- In addition, there are a much larger number of staff associations which are employer-dominated and have only a consultative function.

- The Certification Officer performs a number of functions including determining that a trade union is independent of the employer, dealing with complaints by members, seeing that union merger procedures are observed, and overseeing trade union political funds.

- ACAS promotes good practice (via Codes of Practice), provides employee relations information and advice, conciliates and mediates in individual complaints to employment tribunals, and in the case of collective disputes, conciliates and facilitates mediation and arbitration.

- The Central Arbitration Committee arbitrates on industrial disputes, on complaints from trade unions of an employer's failure to disclose information for collective bargaining purposes, on complaints over the establishment and operation of European Works Councils in the UK over information and consultation with employees, and on disputes over trade union recognition and de-recognition. It also deals with complaints arising from the application of the European Public Limited Liability Company Regulations (2004) and the Company Cross-Border Mergers Regulations (2007).

## KEY LEARNING POINTS

- Employers and employees form collective organisations (such as employers' association and trade unions) to protect and enhance their interests.

- The state has created organisations (such as ACAS and the employment tribunal system) to ensure that employers and employees behave in line with accepted standards.

- It is lobbying, advice and information provision, networking and the ability to influence the European Commission employment and social legislation via indirect membership of EU-wide multi-sector-wide organisation that gives added value to companies from membership of an employers' association.

- The main causes of the decline in trade union membership over the last 30 years include changes in: the composition of the workforce and jobs, the business cycle, the attitude of the state, the role of the employer, the attitude of individual employees, and the role of the trade unions themselves.

- Trade union behaviour is characterised by seeking fair treatment for their members by employers and the state, by the advancement of job interests and not class interests, by giving the highest priority to achieving objectives by industrial rather than political methods, and by pragmatism.

- The main state agencies are the Advisory, Conciliation and Arbitration Service (ACAS), the Central Arbitration Committee (CAC), the Certification Officer and the employment tribunal system.

## REVIEW QUESTIONS

1 Explain the differences between the Central Arbitration Committee and the Advisory, Conciliation and Arbitration Service.

2 Your organisation is a small to medium-sized firm and has recently been invited to join a well-known and respected employers' association for the industry. The owner is sceptical of what value the association could add to the organisation. Explain to him or her the main functions of employers' associations and, using evidence, show the possible value to employment relations in the company.

3 You have been invited to give a talk at a one-day workshop organised by the local branch of the Chartered Institute of Personnel and Development on the future of trade unions. You have been asked to give a manager's perspective on the differences between 'union organising' and 'union servicing' strategies. Outline, with appropriate evidence, what you would include in your talk.

**EXPLORE FURTHER**

Advisory, Conciliation and Arbitration Service (various dates) Annual Reports.

Advisory, Conciliation and Arbitration Service/Chartered Institute of Personnel and Development (undated) *Mediation: An employers' guide*. London: ACAS/CIPD.

Booth, A. (1989) 'What do unions do now?', Discussion Paper in Economics, No 8903. Uxbridge: Brunel University.

Brown, W. and Tower, B. J. (2000) *Employment Relations in Britain: 25 years of the Advisory, Conciliation and Arbitration Service*. Oxford: Blackwell.

Bryson, A. and Gomez, J. (2003) 'Buying in to union membership', in Gospel, H. and Wood, S. (eds) *Representing Workers: Trade union recognition and membership in Britain*. London: Routledge.

Burton M. (2002) 'The principles and factors guiding the CAC', *Employee Relations*, Vol.24, No.6.

Certification Officer (various dates) Annual Reports.

Central Arbitration Committee (various dates) Annual Reports.

Flanders, A. (1968) 'What are unions for?', reprinted in Flanders, A. (1970) *Management and Unions*. London: Faber & Faber.

Freeman, R. and Pelletier, J. (1990) 'The impact of industrial relations legislation on British union density', *British Journal of Industrial Relations*, Vol.28, No.2.

Gall, G. (2004) 'Trade union recognition in Britain 1995–2002: turning a corner?' *Industrial Relations Journal*, Vol.35, No.3: 249–70.

Gennard, J. (2009) 'Voluntary arbitration: the unsung hero', *Industrial Relations Journal*, Vol.40, No.4.

Gennard, J. (2002) 'Employee Relations Public Policy Developments, 1997–2001:

a break with the past?', *Employee Relations*, Vol.24, No.6.

Heery, E., Simms, M., Delridge, R., Salmon, J. and Simpson, D. (2000) 'Union organising in Britain: a survey of policy and practices', *International Journal of Human Resource Management*, Vol.11, No.5.

Heery, E., Simms, M., Delridge, R., Salmon, J. and Simpson, D. (1999) 'Organising unionism in the UK', *Employee Relations*, Vol.22, No.1.

Industrial Relations Service (2006) 'Decline in union recognition deals', *European Industrial Relations Review*, No.390, July.

Industrial Relations Service (1995) 'Staff Associations: Independent unions or employer-led bodies?', *Employment Trends*, No.575, January.

Machin, S. (2000) 'Union decline in Britain', *British Journal of Industrial Relations*, Vol.38, No.4.

Machin, S. (2002) 'Factors of convergence and divergence in union membership', Centre for Economic Performance, Discussion Paper No.554. London: London School of Economics.

Machin, S. (2003) 'Trade union decline: new workplaces and new workers', in Gospel, H. and Wood, S. (eds) *Representing Workers: Trade union representation and membership in Britain*. London: Routledge.

Machin, S. and Blanden, J. (2003) 'Cross-generational correlations of union status for young people', Centre for Economic Performance, Discussion Paper No.553. London: London School of Economics.

Metcalf, D. (2004) 'British unions: resurgence or perdition?', Centre for Economic Performance, Discussion Paper. London: London School of Economics.

Millward, N., Bryson, A. and Forth, J. (2000) *All Change at Work? British employment relations 1980–1998, as portrayed by the Workplace Industrial Relations Survey series*. London: Routledge.

Mumford, K. (1996) 'Arbitration and ACAS in Britain: a historical perspective', *British Journal of Industrial Relations*, Vol.34, No.2.

Towers, D. J. (1997) *The Representation Gap: Change and reform in the British workplace*. Oxford: Oxford University Press.

### Weblinks

www.acas.org.uk is the official website of the Advisory, Conciliation and Arbitration Service

www.businesseurope.eu is the web address of Business Europe

www.cac.gov.uk is the website of the Central Arbitration Committee

www.cbi.org.uk is the official website of the Confederation of British Industry

www.ceep.eu is the website for the public sector employers social partner, CEEP

www.certoffice.org is the website of the Certification Officer

www.cosla.gov.uk is the website for the Confederation of Scottish Local Authorities

www.eef.org.uk is the website of the Engineering Employers Federation

www.employmenttribunals.gov.uk is the website of the employment tribunals

www.etuc.org is the website of the multi-sector employee social partner, the European Confederation of Trade Unions

www.lga.gov.uk is the website of the Local Government Association

www.tuc.org is the website of the Trades Union Congress

www.union-networks.org is the website of Union Network International (UNI), the largest global union federation

www.unitetheunion.org is the official website of Unite, which is the largest trade union in the UK

## CHAPTER 7

# Employment Relations Strategies and Policies

## OVERVIEW

This chapter is divided into five main parts. The first part deals with the formulation of an organisation's strategy, concentrating on the main elements of business strategy, the levels at which strategic decision-making takes place – the corporate level, the business-unit level, and the levels appropriate to the different functions of the business (marketing, production, HR, etc) – and the matching between an organsation's activities and its resources. The second part looks at the associated employment policies necessary to achieve the strategic objective. The third part analyses the role of the management style (authoritarian, paternalistic, consultative, constitutionalist and/or opportunist) on strategy formulation and associated employment relations to achieve the required outputs. It argues that although external constraints on employment relations policy formulation are an important element, the internal constraints are probably of greater significance. The fourth part of the chapter is concerned with the management of change, including why attempts to introduce change often fail (no clear vision, poor communication, looking for quick fixes, etc) and how important it is for managment to be able to articulate a clear vision of the objectives of the change programme and to gain the commitment of the workforce to the proposed changes. The final part of the chapter notes that one of the policy choices an organisation can make centres on the question of its relationship, or not, with a trade union and whether management style will cause different managers to have different approaches to the role and involvement of unions.

## LEARNING OUTCOMES

When you have completed this chapter, you should be aware of and able to describe:

- what strategy is, and the role that strategy plays overall in defining employment relations strategies and policies
- how strategic choices can be driven by the values, preferences and power of those who are the principal decision-makers
- why the choice of particular employment policies is often a strategic decision
- the concept of management style and its importance to the process of employment relations
- why some organisations continue to embrace collective relationships and others prefer to remain non-union or anti-union.

## INTRODUCTION

In Chapter 2 the main components of employment relations were identified, and we noted that the balance of bargaining power is affected by the economic, legal and technological environments, and that this in turn can influence prevailing management style. In the following chapters we develop these issues further as we examine the corporate environment, the legislative framework and the European Union, and how these are important to employment relations professionals. In this chapter we discuss the importance of employment relations strategies, and the type and style of employment policies that flow from such strategies.

The management of people is one of the most challenging areas of business management and most organisations would argue that it is taken very seriously. Nonetheless, in many organisations it is the poor relation in terms of importance and profile. This is despite the large amount of research and analysis that shows how important it is in differentiating between organisational performance.

Writing in *People Management* in 2001, Simon Caulkin pointed out that there had been over 30 studies conducted in the USA and UK since the early 1990s that had left little doubt that the management and development of people has one of the most powerful effects on overall business performance, including overall profitability.

THEORY

Reviewing the evidence on behalf of the CIPD, Caulkin stated that:

> it would be hard to overestimate the importance of this finding. The empirical results that prove the business case slot the final piece into a new business model that has people squarely at its centre. It completes a historic transition from a mechanistic view of the company to one that sees it as a living system where Tayloristic task management gives way to knowledge

management; the latter seeking to be cost-efficient by developing an organisation's people assets, unlike the former which views labour as a cost to be minimised.

Caulkin believed that the findings opened up:

> huge opportunities for competitive improvement through learning, managing and developing people more effectively. The same goes for the UK economy as a whole, where people management has the potential to turbo-charge investment in skills, R&D and new technology, offering a way to jolt the economy out of its low-skills/low-quality equilibrium and claw back the productivity advantage held by its competitors.

**THEORY**  The work reviewed by Caulkin, and his conclusions, were supported in a report produced by John Purcell *et al* and published by the CIPD in 2003. The report, *Understanding the People and Performance Link: Unlocking the black box,* was the culmination of six years of study and was developed to overcome criticism of earlier studies, which were seen as flawed because they 'had been carried out in manufacturing, where issues such as productivity were easier to manage'.

The Institute therefore developed a programme of work with three specific aims:

- to improve the evidence linking people management to business performance or organisational competitiveness

- to provide accessible information on which managers can act through effective choices and decisions

- to improve understanding of why and how people management practices influence business performance.

Despite the plethora of research into the HR/business performance link, one of the most difficult tasks facing HR/personnel professionals is opening the minds of their management colleagues to adopting different, but proven, approaches to managing people. An earlier CIPD report, *Voices from the Boardroom* by David Guest *et al,* noted that 'most senior executives are, at best, only dimly aware of recent research on people management and performance.' Such a lack of awareness carries the danger that the employment relations specialist, who ought to be aware of new ideas and approaches, will attempt to implement a new idea without ensuring that his or her management colleagues have a full understanding of what is proposed.

That is why, in this book, great stress is laid on the need to gain commitment from senior management colleagues to employment relations initiatives. Yet gaining commitment is not something that happens in isolation. In order to obtain it you have to ensure that a proper business case is made for the adoption of new techniques or new approaches. It is easy to be critical of managers for not embracing new ideas, but if they are simply invited to buy in to them as an article of faith, they will not make available the necessary investment in time and resources.

So before seeking to change people management processes within an organisation, there has to be a business case made that will demonstrate that such change is necessary. In making this business case it is important to show that there is a link between the delivery of business performance, human resource management generally, and, in the context of this book, employment relations specifically.

To be successful, the business case must flow from the organisation's overall strategy. And to understand this connection we need to look at the whole concept of strategy – a subject that is the subject of intense discussion and debate, and that has become increasingly more important to managers in both the public and private sector. This has happened because although organisations have always had strategies, 'only since the 1960s has it been common to address explicitly the question of what their strategy should be' (Kay, 1993; p.6). This change in emphasis was one consequence of the fluctuations in economic performance that characterised the decades between the end of World War II and the new millennium. Similarly, the growth in the intensity of competition, either at home or abroad, during this period forced organisations to recognise that there is a need to continually change themselves – not necessarily a revolutionary change, but certainly a process of evolution. Such evolutionary change has to be managed and requires that organisations develop clear business strategies that will then drive functional strategies, one of which is human resources generally, and more specifically the management of employment relations. However, it is not only senior managers who must concern themselves with the strategic direction of an organisation: it is essential for all levels of management.

THEORY

If the latter part of the twentieth century taught us anything, it is that the pattern of employment relations has, for the most part, changed. Forty years ago employment relations was dominated by the relationship between management and unions. That is no longer the case. Not only have unions declined in terms of membership, they have also changed in terms of attitude and approach. Similarly, managers have also changed, and where unions are recognised, they are, in most organisations, seen more as partners than opponents. Recent disputes at Royal Mail and British Airways might suggest that when times are more turbulent management and unions revert to a more adverserial approach; such a view would not necessarily reflect the genuine willingness of both parties to work together.

THEORY

One reason for this changed relationship has, quite clearly, been the impact of the pace of change to which most businesses have been exposed, and which has created a need for directors and senior managers to look more carefully at their approach to employment relations management, both strategically and through day-to-day management activities. They have come to accept that there are advantages to be gained in identifying employee attitudes through enhanced communication, and then attempting to reshape those attitudes for the benefit of the organisation and the people that work in it. Later chapters on employee involvement and engagement will explore these themes in greater detail. Attitudinal change is of particular importance as organisations, in both the public and private sectors, have sought to maximise efficiency as a means of securing a competitive advantage. Such advantage is now as important an issue for the public sector as it is for the private sector, particularly as the levels of public spending that have been a feature of Labour Governments' economic management since the turn of the century are, as a consequence of the serious recession of 2008/9, set to fall. Whoever is in power over the next 10 years, public sector organisations – whether schools, hospitals, local authorities or whatever – are likely to have more competition forced upon them as the Government insists on their being more customer- and quality-focused in order to achieve greater value for money and help in the process of reducing public expenditure. Competition, and hence the need for change, are very often linked to new technology or to the growth of the global economy. Whatever the challenge, it will impact on and dictate the type of employment policies that the management of an organisation will seek to implement.

## WHAT IS STRATEGY?

The origin of the concept can be traced in military history back to the Greek word for an army commander: *stratēgos*. In the context of public or private organisations it is about the way that the senior management lead the organisation or business in a particular direction. The development of strategic objectives enables leaders to influence and direct an organisation as it conducts its activities. There are many definitions of strategy, and students of employment relations must be aware that there is no model answer. Notwithstanding this, it is hard to argue against the view (Tyson, 1995) that:

> Strategy may be described as the attempt by those who control an organisation to find ways to position their business or organisational objectives so that they can exploit the planning environment and maximise the future use of the organisation's capital and human assets.

Clearly, this is but one definition of strategy, and there are many texts on strategy and strategy formulation. Different authors such as Mintzberg (1987 and 1994) and Ansoff (1991) have sought to define strategy in a way that is relevant to all tiers of management, and students are encouraged to seek out these various texts to ensure that their own view of strategy formulation is not one-dimensional.

However, one of the most comprehensive and detailed texts on strategy is the work by Johnson, Scholes and Whittington (2008), who have tried to provide an understanding of what corporate strategy is and why strategic decisions are important. They view corporate strategy in two ways – as a matter of economic analysis and planning, and as a matter of organisational decision-making within a social, political and cultural process. Overall, the authors have identified a number of characteristics that are usually associated with the terms 'strategy' and 'strategic decisions', and these are:

- Strategic decisions are likely to be concerned with or affect the long-term direction of an organisation.

- Strategic decisions are about trying to achieve some advantage for the organisation – for example, over the competition.

- Strategic decisions are therefore sometimes conceived of as the search for effective positioning to provide such an advantage in a market or in relation to suppliers.

- Strategic decisions are likely to be concerned with the scope of an organisation's activities.

- Strategy can be seen as the matching of the activities of an organisation to the environment in which it operates.

- Strategy can be seen as building on or stretching an organisation's resources and competences to create opportunities or capitalise on them.

- Strategies may require major resource changes for an organisation.

- Strategic decisions are likely to affect operational decisions.

- The strategy of an organisation will be affected not only by environmental forces and resource availability but also by the values and expectations of those who have power in and around the organisation.

All together, the authors would say that if a definition of strategy is required, the above characteristics provide the basis for the following one:

> Strategy is the direction and scope of an organisation over the long term which achieves advantage for the organisation through its configuration of resources within a changing environment, to meet the needs of markets and to fulfil stakeholder expectations.

If they are correct in the way they describe these characteristics, it means that the whole process becomes very complex. This is particularly true if the organisation operates in a wide geographical area – a multi-national, for example – or has a wide range of products, or operates in the public sector – a health trust, for example. Throughout this text we make the point that employment relations cannot stand alone, that it has to be integrated with other management and HR/personnel functions. The same is true of strategy: it requires an integrated approach to managing the organisation. Managers must cross functional and operational boundaries in order to engage with strategic problems and reach a consensus with other management colleagues who will, inevitably, have different interests and perhaps different priorities.

As we explain in Chapter 11, this will often involve negotiation over the use of resources with management colleagues and is one of the reasons why negotiation skills are so important.

## STRATEGIC FORMULATION

THEORY

To understand further the nature of strategy it is helpful to obtain some understanding of the process of strategy formulation. A team at the the Aston Centre for Human Resources (Aston University, Birmingham) in 2008 stated that a classic strategic management process consists of a series of steps:

- establishing a mission statement and key objectives for the organistaion

- analysing the external environment (to identify possible opportunities and threats)
- conducting an internal organisational analysis (to examine its strengths and weaknesses and the nature of existing management systems, competencies and capabilities)
- setting specific goals
- examining possible strategic choices/alternatives to achieve the organisational objectives and goals
- adoption/implementation of chosen choices
- regular evaluation of all of the above.

Taking this classic process and the Johnson, Scholes and Whittington view as a starting point, we can link these common themes to the different approaches to strategy formulation.

One of the oldest and most influential portrays strategy as a highly rational and scientific process. This approach is based on one of the characteristics identified above – namely, the importance of the fit between an organisation and its environment. Analyses are made of a firm's environment to assess likely opportunities and threats, and of its internal resources to identify strengths and weaknesses. This process is often referred to as a SWOT analysis, and it is argued that through rigorous planning, senior managers can predict and shape the external environment and thus the organisation itself.

Other approaches to strategy formulation argue that the complexity and volatility of the environment may mean that a SWOT analysis is both difficult and inappropriate. This evolutionary approach believes that organisations are at the mercy of the unpredictable and hostile vagaries of the market. The environment in which they operate may be changing so frequently that any data they use, either historical or current, may be worthless.

Some writers argue that it is not possible to apply either a rational or an evolutionary label to the process of strategy formulation, but that it is behavioural – that strategic choice results from the various coalitions that are to be found within organisations. The most dominant of these coalitions will be at senior management level, and it is they who have to 'create a vision of the organisation's future' (Burnes, 1996; p.168).

The extent to which managing people is given a high profile within the organisation will be driven by the values, ideologies and personalities of those in positions of power and influence and those individuals who formulate strategy and the long-term direction of the organisation. When we talk about the organisation in strategy terms, we very often mean the chief executive, whose values and beliefs will ultimately shape the culture of the organisation and will consequently decide the type and style of employment relations policies that it tries to follow. In essence, what we are talking about here is leadership – that strategy is moulded by the personality of an individual or individuals and the way in which he, she or they is/are able to motivate people to change.

Similarly, the values and beliefs of such chief executives will have a significant impact on the long-term direction of a business, and there are those who believe that leadership is a key success factor. However, not everybody takes this view. David Butcher and Mike Meldrum (*People Management*, 28 June 2001) question whether leadership is really important in business. They suggest that 'where chief executives do preside over successful businesses, it is sometimes because they are the beneficiaries of decisions taken long before they landed the top job.'

Keith Grint (2005) from the Lancaster University Management School takes this view a stage further. He writes that 'We have yet to establish what [leadership] is, never mind whether we can teach it or predict its importance.' He identifies four quite different ways of understanding what leadership is:

**THEORY**

- person – is it *who* leaders *are* that makes them leaders?
- result – is it *what* leaders *achieve* that makes them leaders?
- position – is it *where* leaders *operate* that makes them leaders?
- process – is it *how* leaders *get things done* that makes them leaders?

From this brief summary of strategy and strategy formulation it is clear that there is no one right way. We have noted that there are a number of approaches that can be adopted by an organisation, but it is equally clear from the consistent references to environment, the identification of objectives, etc, that there is a closeness about them all. So what is the best approach? Jenkins and Ambrosini (2002) suggest that:

> a useful way is to consider the different elements of strategy and use these to form an agenda that gives managers a reasonably clear set of concepts.

They identify eight primary subjects ('the eight Cs') which cover the diverse and complicated aspects of strategy that can be considered by an organisation.

---

**The eight essential elements of business strategy**

*Context*
Issues concerned with an organisation's external environment: how the external environment is perceived, how it is studied, what the organisation can do to control it and to change it. Context also refers to industry and market structure, and strategic groups.

*Competing*
Issues concerned with how organisations gain customers, how they identify their competitors and how they outperform them. This section is also about the competitive strategies organisations can implement to achieve sustainable advantage, and about co-operation and collusion.

*Corporate*
Corporate strategy typically addresses the multi-business context. So this heading deals with questions of alliances, diversification, mergers, globalisation, corporate parenting, etc.

*Choice*
Issues concerned with decision-making and the degrees of freedom for an organisation to

determine a particular strategy. This section deals with questions and issues surrounding the choices made by firms in following a particular trajectory.

*Competences*

Issues concerned with the organisation's resources, such as skills, know-how, organisational knowledge, routines, competences and capabilities. This section focuses on the role of a resource in an organisation, and in generating competitive advantage. It also deals with issues such as the transferability and the immutability of resources.

*Culture*

Issues concerned with an organisation's internal environment. It includes the role of organisational culture, its importance and its influence on employees.This heading also covers how culture is created or changed, and how employees perceive organisational culture.

*Change*

Issues concerned with the types of change an organisation can implement, and how change can take place, or how change is constrained. This section also includes the reasons for change, the change process, and the possible outcomes of change programmes.

*Control*

Organisational structure, power relationships and the way managers control what is happening in their organisation. Control describes the role of managers in the organisation, the extent to which they can 'manage' what is happening inside organisations, and the extent to which they know what is happening around them.

Source: Jenkins and Ambrosini (2002) *Strategic Management: A multi-perspective approach*

Whatever method of strategy formulation is adopted, it is important to understand that it will be constrained by societal, environmental, industry-specific and organisational factors, many of which will conflict with each other. Take, for example, societal factors. There can often be significant national differences in the way people approach work, and with the growth in multi-national companies and globalisation this can have a major impact on workplace culture. It is often the case that changes in society have a greater impact on organisations than changes in management.

The environment within which any organisation operates will, without doubt, constrain strategic choice. This may be a relatively stable and predictable environment in which planning and predicting the future is not a particularly hazardous exercise. Alternatively, as we witnessed during the last two years of the so-called 'noughties', an organisation might have to develop strategy in an unpredictable and uncertain environment in which planning is almost impossible. Turmoil in financial markets, in corporate life and in the funding of our public instituitions reinforced the reality that, whatever the environment, most organisations have to operate in a constantly changing world. Their fundamental challenge is to cope with a scenario in which, having developed what they believe to be an appropriate strategy, the world steps in and changes the rules. This external interference, whether it comes from currency exchanges, increases in energy prices or terrorism, often has a far bigger impact on companies than managerial issues. The name of the game is how quickly they can adapt their business model to those changes, because it is the change process that provides the link between business strategy and employment relations strategies. And while environmental considerations may provide the stimulus for change, there is a clear consensus that the success or otherwise of individual change programmes is governed by the people in each organisation.

### REFLECTIVE ACTIVITY

Consider the environment in which your own organisation has had to operate over the past five years and what changes it has required to be made to business plans and strategic objectives. How would you describe the whole situation?

## LEVELS OF STRATEGY    THEORY

It is important to consider not only the sort of strategic choices that organisations can make but also the levels of strategic decision-making. There are three levels with which we need to concern ourselves (Burnes, 1996):

- corporate-level strategy, which concerns the overall direction and focus of the business

- business-unit-level strategy, which is concerned with how to compete in a particular market

- functional-level strategy, which is concerned with individual areas such as personnel, marketing, etc.

All these levels are interrelated, but equally, each of them has its own distinctive strategic concerns. We now need to look at them in a little more detail.

### CORPORATE-LEVEL STRATEGY    THEORY

Corporate-level strategy concerns itself with a number of questions and is usually formulated at board level. One of these questions will be about the overall mission of the organisation: what is the game plan? How should the business portfolio be managed? Should you make acquisitions or dispose of parts of the business? What priority should be given to each of the individual parts of the business in terms of resource allocation? How is the business to be structured and financed?

In the CIPD research conducted by Purcell *et al*, they noted that:

> One of the keys to the HR-performance link is the existence of a 'big idea', a clear mission underpinned by values and a culture expressing what the organisation stands for and is trying to achieve.

According to Purcell *et al*, organisations with a big idea displayed five common characteristics: the idea was embedded, connected, enduring, collective, and measured and managed. The big idea therefore means more than just having a formal mission statement. It means that the values are spread throughout the organisation so that they are embedded in policies and practices. These values interconnect the relationships with customers (both internal and external), culture and behaviour, and provide the basis upon which employees should be managed.

However, even taking on board the processes espoused by Purcell *et al*, the mission will fail unless it is capable of being achieved. This means that three things are necessary. Firstly, the mission must be expressed in language that is understandable to the bulk of employees, which means that attention must be paid to the communication process. Secondly, it must be attainable. That is, employees should recognise that the organisation has some chance of achieving the objectives it has set itself. Thirdly, the mission must be challenging. It needs all of those involved in its achievement to be stretched, for their individual performances to be a condition of the mission's overall success. That is why the current focus on employee engagement, and to a lesser extent employee involvement – which we examine in more detail in later chapters – is so vital to organisational success.

## REFLECTIVE ACTIVITY

If the organisation in which you work has a declared mission, how does it fit with the criteria we describe? If it doesn't fit those criteria, how would you express a mission for it that does meet the need to be understandable, attainable and challenging? Alternatively, if no mission has been articulated, what do you think it should be (again fitting it with our declared criteria)?

## THEORY  BUSINESS-UNIT-LEVEL STRATEGY

Competitive or business-unit-level strategy is concerned with the way a firm or business operates in particular markets – what new opportunities can be identified or created? Which products or services should be developed? In this context, strategy is concerned with gaining an advantage over the competition. Porter (1985) sees this as seeking to obtain a sustainable competitive advantage – which markets should the organisation attempt to compete in, and how does it position itself to achieve its objectives? How does it achieve some form of 'distinctive capability' (Kay, 1993)? What should its product range or mix be? Which customers should it aim for? Decisions about products, markets and customers were central to some of Porter's (1985) theories about strategy. He argued that there are only three basic strategies that dictate the choice to be made. These are:

- cost leadership that aims to achieve lower costs than your competitors' without reducing quality

- product differentiation based on achieving industry-wide recognition of different and superior products and services compared to those of other suppliers

- specialisation by focus – in effect seeking out a niche market.

This type of distinction is fine in the private sector, but what about the public sector? All the decisions that Porter says are important have an effect on employment relations in that they impact on the way that the organisation structures itself internally and on the way that relationships are managed. For this reason it is important for public sector organisations to adapt these principles to their own service in order to create their own business strategies.

## FUNCTIONAL-LEVEL STRATEGY

**THEORY**

Functional-level strategy is, in a sense, fairly straightforward. At this level strategy is concerned with how the different functions of the business (marketing, human resources, finance, production, customer services, etc) translate corporate- and business-level strategies into operational aims. In HR terms this means that there has to be a clear alignment between business and HR strategy, and in Figure 7.1 we demonstrate how this leads to the formulation of an employment relations strategy – that business strategy drives HRM strategy, which in turn drives employment relations strategy, and that from this process are derived the practices and policies that influence the employment relationship. Once you have reached down to this level of functional strategy, it is important that the various functions pay attention to how they organise themselves, not only in order to achieve their aims but to ensure synergy with the rest of the business.

**Figure 7.1 Strategic employment relations management: an overview**

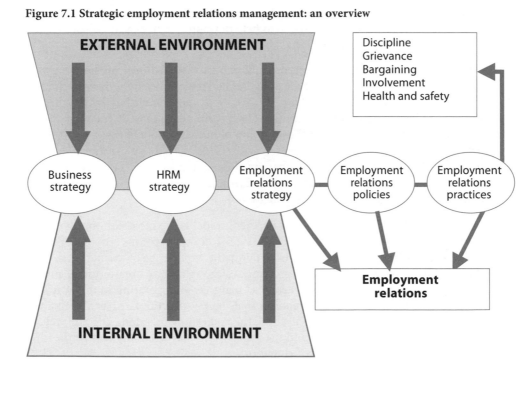

We now turn specifically to the strategic issues concerning the management of people.

## REFLECTIVE ACTIVITY

What external factors over the next five years are likely to impact on corporate strategy, both in the wider business context and in the specific challenges that your own organisation is likely to face? How, if at all, will these impact on your employment relations strategy?

### PEOPLE STRATEGY

One aspect of strategy concerns the match between an organisation's activities and its resources. These resources can be physical (equipment, buildings) or they can be people. Strategies in respect of physical resources may require decisions about investment or even about the ability to invest. Strategies about people also require decisions to be made about investment, but it is a different type of investment decision – not the type that fits easily into the process usually reserved for capital expenditure. It is more likely to be the sort of investment that we examined in Chapter 3, such as investment in skills development.

There is no doubt that over the past two decades the employment landscape has changed significantly. As this evolutionary process has taken place, and such clichés as 'Our people are our greatest asset' have found their way into organisational mission statements, the role of HR and employment relations have also changed beyond recognition. Today's HR professionals are expected to be much more proactive than reactive – to help develop practices and policies that deliver the means for organisational objectives to be met.

**THEORY**    HR functions within organisations are now expected to demonstrate how they can 'add value'. There is now a more enlightened view, driven by writers such as Ulrich (1997), Ulrich and Brockbank (2005), by research published by the then Institute of Personnel and Development (1997) and by Deloitte & Touche (1998) that shows a clear link between the adoption of human resource management practices and enhanced business performance. This has led to a greater awareness of the need for clear HR strategies that are aligned to business strategies and for HR to transform itself into a more focused business partner that can provide line managers with clear advice and information.

According to the CIPD the 'business partner' model is the most commonly adopted HR service delivery model, almost 50% of organisations employing business partners in their ranks. It is certainly the experience of the authors that the business partner model is growing – although many organisations and practitioners will not necessarily recognise that they are operating in this way. Operating as a business partner requires that the HR practitioner has a deep and broad understanding of the organisation, the ability to work alongside all levels of management, self-awareness and the expertise to play a leading role in the development and management of change.

Whatever HR management model is in use, there are very few managers that would not subscribe to the view that significant improvement in both productivity and profitability can be achieved if they ensure that people are satisfied with their jobs, rewards, working conditions and career prospects. This, then, requires the development of a clear and focused strategy for managing people, which must at its heart have policies and practices to involve people in the business, and a clear investment in communication and strategies in respect of recruitment and retention, people development, succession planning and strategies for managing and rewarding high performance.

Some of these requirements have a clear link with employee engagement and employee involvement, which will be discussed in depth in later chapters, but because they are key features in the development of strategy we will summarise them here.

In taking a strategic view of managing people it is imperative to ensure that people are at the centre of strategic planning for the organisation. Key questions about the organisation's people must be addressed in planning business strategy. Are the right knowledge, skills and competencies available within the organisation – and if they are not, can they be acquired? Are people capable of taking forward new directions in business strategy? Can the knowledge, skills and competency available be deployed in a way that opens up new business opportunities?

It is also important in developing strategy to take account of company culture. This is a complex area and employee attitude surveys that have been conducted by the authors demonstrate that it is important to undestand how the organisation is perceived by its various stakeholders. These surveys – carried out within the media, leisure and property sectors – reinforced findings from the 1998 Deloitte & Touche survey that to understand company culture you must focus on:

- the artefacts and symbols of the organisation, such as the layout of the working environment, the technology used, the use of information and reporting:

    While it is not always apparent, stakeholders – particularly employees – can be hugely influenced towards achieving organisational goals if they believe their working environment is considered to be important by key decision-makers. In one survey, one of the overwhelmingly negative responses was that 'the company does not care about our working conditions'. When the company embarked on a programme of redecoration and renewal of equipment, the response was very positive.

- the stories and myths that are commonly shared in the organisation and indicate success and failure:

    Despite a huge investment in training and development, the perception in one organisation that 'we never receive any personal development' was a huge shock to management and pinpointed a clear failure of communication.

- the rites and rituals that reinforce behaviour patterns and demonstrate the organisation's values:

  In one example there was a view that information was only available to a privileged few – that the majority of staff were, as a consequence, not valued.

- the rules, systems and procedures that set the parameters for behaviour and action:

  While policies, procedures and practices are important, they can, if an organisation becomes too bureaucratic, constrain people's willingness to 'go the extra mile', which is generally to the detriment of the organisation.

- the organisational heroes and heroines that act as role models for people:

  Our surveys showed that the quality of management paid huge dividends in the achievement of organisational objectives.

- the beliefs, values and attitudes that are expressed and displayed in everyday activity:

  People expressing the view that they were not treated as adults with opinions and ideas was one of the more common responses to our surveys. This has a damaging effect on morale and, therefore, performance.

- the ethical standards that guide the boundaries of what is acceptable and what is not acceptable:

  It was clear from the feedback to our surveys that people who believe they work for a 'good employer' will always produce a higher level of productivity.

- the basic assumptions that are made about human behaviour, human nature, relationships, reality and truth:

  If employees believe that they are not trusted, they will respond negatively. In one organisation there was an assumption, by some but not all managers, that all staff claiming sick pay were 'not usually incapable of attending work'. This went to the core of that organisation's employment relations problem. People who feel they are not trusted will very rarely give of their best.

The second requirement for developing a 'people strategy', involving people in the business, needs attention to be paid to job design, with a particular emphasis on teamworking whereby teams have a high degree of autonomy and freedom for self-management. To be effective, teams need clear objectives and targets and the autonomy to plan and undertake work, acquire resources, and improve processes, products and services. Parameters must be specified so that integration with the organisation as a whole is not compromised, but these must be as wide as possible.

There are very few managers who would disagree with the third main activity: investing in communication. Successful businesses invest heavily in communications and there are three aspects of communication that distinguish high-growth businesses from the less successful. These are:

- communicating business strategy to all employees
- regularly giving feedback on performance measures to all employees
- using a wide range of communication methods.

None of this should come as a surprise to HR professionals, but persuading management colleagues to invest their time and/or monetary resource in improved communication with the workforce, or to seek to be more 'engaged', can be – and often is – very difficult. To be successful it is necessary to do more than preach the latest HR mantra – it is vital to demonstrate practical outcomes. In an article for *People Management* (26 February 2009), Billie Alban and Barbara Benedict Bunker made the point that 'employees want to be treated like adults.' Our own experience in talking to employees in both unionised and non-unionised organisations is that they want to know if there are difficulties within the organisation, for if there are problems and challenges ahead, they want to be allowed to contribute their own ideas to finding a solution. This is borne out by the results of the surveys we conducted, as noted above.

One wonders if the many problems facing British Airways in its long-running dispute with cabin crew do not stem from a failure to communicate, to properly engage with the workforce. At heart, the majority of employees want their organisation to succeed, but not at any price. Contrast the BA experience with that of many other organisations during 2009 whose employees accepted wage cuts, reduced hours and changes in working practices as a means of maintaining their own, and the organisation's, security.

The final elements in a successful people strategy revolve around recruitment and retention, people development, succession planning and the management and reward of high performance.

Failing to pay sufficient attention to the management of performance can cause significant employment relations problems. This does not have to mean a reliance on a bonus culture, but people perform best if they know what they have to do, how well they are doing it, what they have to improve, how the improvement is going to be achieved, and, crucially, how they are going to be rewarded. Setting clear, individual objectives for employees is a critical element in any successful organisation, and linking that to a clear, transparent and equitable reward structure is of paramount importance. For people not to know what is expected of them, or for them to believe that, relative to other colleagues, they are treated less equitably, can lead to dissatisfaction, low morale, high labour turnover and high levels of absenteeism – all of which are classic employment relations problems.

Finally, it is vital to focus on employees as individuals, and while the use of terms such as 'human resources' and 'human capital' encourages a view of an organisation's employees as a homogeneous group, they can diminish the view of employees as individuals. Yet high-performing organisations do focus on people as individuals and use techniques of communication, engagement and involvement that are designed to encourage satisfaction and commitment.

The comments we highlighted above from the various surveys we conducted demonstrate how vital it is that negative perceptions about how people are trusted and valued do not become the accepted norm within an organisation.

Everything we have outlined above is important in formulating strategy, but nothing must be viewed in isolation – as the following example from a private sector organisation demonstrates. It has not been possible to publish the document in full, but the extract demonstrates that it is vital to ensure that the whole range of people management activities – recruitment and selection, reward and recognition, training and development, and employment relations – are integrated into the strategic planning process.

## FIVE-YEAR HUMAN RESOURCE PLAN

### Executive summary

The environment in which all our companies have to operate has, because of the recession, changed beyond recognition. In recent months we have had to go through the painful process of reducing our headcount while at the same time continuing to be very competitive in our various marketplaces. Our staff are, with good reason, feeling insecure and nervous about the future and, in this context, it is important to recognise the importance of the 'people contribution'.

People's contribution is influenced by the way that they are managed and whether they perceive that they are valued for their individual contributions. To this extent it is vitally important that managers, at all levels, acquire, and develop, expertise and knowledge in management skills. To achieve these aims means that we must:

- take a strategic view of managing people
- involve people in the business
- continue to invest in communication
- manage people's performance effectively
- focus on employees as individuals.

If we do these things, we are much more likely to develop enhanced employee commitment. In turn, this will mean that individuals are encouraged to move beyond their basic contractual commitment and develop a strong sense of loyalty to the organisation. Creating the climate where people are prepared to give more by 'going the extra mile' will ensure that their contribution to the business is maximised. But by itself this is not enough. We need to concentrate on certain key factors, which can be summarised as follows.

*Employee reward systems*
Our basic reward system is currently a combination of basic pay, performance- or profit-related bonus (for some individuals) and an optional pension benefit. If we want to motivate individuals to deliver our declared

business strategies, we have to develop our current reward system so that it is capable of meeting individual employee aspirations. To achieve this, we need to ensure that we have a reward system that is both flexible and fair and that is perceived as such by employees. Although our ownership structure does not allow for any 'equity share' arrangements, we need to expand on the successful Long-term Incentive Plan (LTIP) that has been in place in one subsidiary for the past five years. Part of the HR remit over the lifetime of this plan is to ensure that 'reward' is related to real growth in our businesses and not simply to the short-term attainment of artifical budgetary targets.

### Recruitment and selection

There are two major issues that we need to be concerned with. One is to ensure that the level of labour turnover in each part of the business is properly managed and kept within acceptable norms. The second is the need to attract sufficient numbers of high-calibre candidates for declared vacancies. Because of the changing nature of the labour market we must consider what changes we need to make in our employment practices if we are to meet this objective.

### Performance management

The recent difficulties in trading across the whole group have highlighted the need to constantly improve levels of individual performance. This can only be achieved if we seek ways to 'engage' staff so that they feel valued. Without developing strategies for the effective engagement of people, we will not improve organisational performance generally. Staff engagement therefore has to be a key priority. This is a complex process with no easy solutions, and there are number of steps that can be taken to enhance both individual and collective performance.

### Career development

If we are to retain competent employees within our workforce, we need to develop the process of career planning. While this will not be appropriate for everyone, it will be an important factor for some in deciding whether to remain in our employment. Added to this will be a continuing requirement to develop the skills of all our employees. Every group business should have a development plan and provide appropriate budgets for this purpose, which should be driven by the appraisal process. Beyond this, there is also a need to develop those individuals who might have the capability of taking on senior management roles in the future. Our annual succession planning exercise is crucial to meeting this objective, but we also need to provide a senior management development programme.

### Employment relations

It is clear that developments in employment law will not slow down and that during the lifetime of this plan further changes will take place, either because of government intervention (new statutes) or through the development of case law. Cases relating to holiday pay, sickness and retirement ages might require us to amend policies and practices. While relationships with our principal trade unions remain relatively benign, we cannot take these relationships for granted. Union representatives must be part of the communication process.

Overall, our human resource activities over the lifetime of this plan have to meet the following objectives:

- to generate commitment of all employees to the success of the organisation
- to enable the business to better meet the needs of its customers and adopt to changing market requirements
- to help the business to improve performance and productivity, thus generating appropriate levels of growth
- to improve the satisfaction that employees get from their work
- to provide all employees with the opportunity to influence and be involved in decisions which are likely to affect their interests.

The importance of adopting an integrated approach, as demonstrated above, is supported by the research carried out for the CIPD and others. This confirms that companies which are achieving the best results in productivity, profitability and growth have people management strategies that make a real difference. The conclusions of Purcell *et al* are compelling. They state that:

The most successful organisations were those that could sustain their performance over the long term and demonstrate a robust association between people management and performance.

## STRATEGY AND EMPLOYMENT POLICIES

Having examined the process of strategy formulation, we now turn to look at how this links into employment relations in particular – but not forgetting that there must be a link with other aspects of the employment relationship: employee resourcing, employee reward, employee development.

Whatever means organisations choose for formulating their strategy, either at corporate or business level, maximising the organisation's competitive advantage has to be a major issue. This inevitably means that an organisation must constantly re-evaluate itself in order to sustain any necessary improvements. Organisations are therefore concerned with the design and management of employment policies and processes that will deliver and sustain business improvement. The process of change, and its impact on the development of strategy, presents many challenges for the employment relations professional. For example – as we discuss later – there is the issue of trade unions and the provisions on recognition. Where trade unions already exist and are recognised within an organisation, the trends towards individualism, as opposed to collectivism, mean that strategic choices must be made about whether those unions are encouraged or marginalised. Where they do not exist and requests for recognition are received, are these resisted or accepted voluntarily?

Overall, strategies and policies on employment relations must have a direct relationship with the business strategy and must be imaginative, innovative, clear and action-oriented. They need to be formulated by a continuing process of analysis to identify what is happening to the business and where it is going. In this context, the relevance of clear business objectives, as expressed through the medium of a mission statement, cannot be overstated. The key is to develop an employment relations strategy that is responsive to the needs of the organisation, that can provide an overall sense of purpose to the employment relations professional and assist employees to understand where they are going, how they are going to get there, why certain things are happening, and most importantly, the contribution they are expected to make towards achieving the organisational goals.

An interesting example can be found in the experience of the McLaren Group. Although a collection of seven companies with around 1,500 employees, McLaren are famous for their involvement in Formula One Grand Prix motor racing and, in the more recent past, for their association with Lewis Hamilton and Jenson Button. As Patrick Bermingham, McLaren Group HR Director, told *Personnel Management* (June 2009), the group needed to revamp 'its approach to engagement, development and succession planning'. When he joined McLaren, Bermingham says that he found a small HR department 'hungry to take on the more strategic approach' that he had been hired to deliver. 'There was a lot of talk about values, but nobody was explicit about what they were.' In order to develop some coherence to the values, Bermingham set about the task of discovering what people felt about the organisation and what the values should be. He did this by talking to the board, by organising some focus groups and by speaking to 15% of employees randomly selected from across the group. Once this exercise was finished, the values were crystallised into five action statements:

- We win.
- We make things happen.
- We take it personally.
- We work together.
- We enjoy what we do.

The McLaren experience demonstrates that the mission statement does not have to be a bland document, written by senior management, posted on the notice board and then immediately forgotten. It can, as is seen above, contain statements that individual employees can relate to. In McLaren's case 'We win' is the big one. As Bermingham states:

> The concept of winning is palpable. You can almost touch it. If McLaren wins, people are joyous. If there's a bad race, they are desolate and self-critical – but even more determined to win next time.

As the McLaren example demonstrates, once it is clear what the overall philosophy of an organisation is, the employment relations specialist can use this knowledge to put together the employment relations policies for the business.

The needs of an organisation in terms of its employment relations policies are potentially infinite, but could emanate from two specific areas. One – the 'management of change' – could encompass issues as diverse as improving productivity, enhanced employee engagement, changing reward systems or changes to working methods. The other is the organisation's attitude towards trade unions.

**THEORY**    FUTURE CHALLENGES

If we examine some of the challenges facing the HR/personnel specialist both now and in the future, we can identify some of the important links between the various personnel disciplines. In the area of employee resourcing, organisations face continuing challenges in developing policies on recruitment and selection. In employee reward there are continuing and continuous challenges to the personnel practitioner. Stimulating employee commitment, motivation and enhancing job performance are matters which will be discussed in other chapters, but among the issues that must be considered is the balance between pay and non-pay rewards and individual versus collective bargaining. But reward policies must (Armstrong, 1996) be:

> developed and managed as a coherent whole. They need to be integrated with one another and, importantly, with the key business and personnel processes of the organisation.

So far as employee development is concerned, the personnel practitioner faces three challenges, all of which impact on employment relations. Firstly, is it in the company's interests to buy in or to develop their own staff? Where do the long-term interests of the business lie? If you get the balance wrong and buy in too much labour, there is a risk that existing employees will become disillusioned and assume that the organisation is not interested in investing in their future.

Secondly, what sort of employees are required? Generalists or specialists? Personnel professionals have a significant role to play in helping to identify what value there is to the organisation in particular types of employee. Although it is popular to support the idea of multi-skilling, this concept does not always serve the organisation's best interests. Too many people may want to be trained in specific skills, some of which may never be fully utilised. This can then lead to resentment or resistance to further training interventions.

Finally, if investment is to be made in employee development, is it simply a question of training people to carry out the current tasks that they are required to fulfil, or is it strategically valuable to create a 'learning environment', as many organisations have done?

All of these challenges are strategic issues that are interlinked and have an impact on employment relations. In each case they will be conditioned in their scope and their impact by the type and size of the organisation.

## REFLECTIVE ACTIVITY

What challenges will your organisation face over the next five years, and how will these impact on employment relations strategy?

You should have looked at any trends in your organisation's business strategy that might have an impact, such as:

- plans for expansion

- proposals for new investment

- the need to improve profitability or productivity.

You need to consider the impact of changes to your employment relations strategies on the other policy areas – for example, resourcing, reward, health and safety, development. Finally, you need to consider the impact of external influences such as political (a change of UK government, or even Prime Minister), economic (interest rates, inflation, recession, exchange rates, unemployment), societal (demographic trends, the age profile of the population), new technology, and any possible changes in legislation, particularly European influences.

## MANAGEMENT STYLE

THEORY

We said above that the organisation's attitude to trade unions could have a significant impact on employment relations strategy. We have already noted the impact that the values and preferences of organisations' dominant management decision-makers have on strategy formulation. These values and perceptions will in part be determined by whether the organisation adopts a unitary or pluralist approach to its employment relations. The unitary approach emphasises organisations as harmonious and integrated, all employees sharing the organisational goals and working as members of one team. The pluralist approach recognises that different groups exist within an organisation and that conflict can, and does, exist between employer and employees.

These are broad definitions, and it must be noted that simply because an organisation is described as unitarist does not mean that management and employees share the same agenda.

Unitarist organisations can be either authoritarian or paternalistic in their attitudes, and this can have a major impact on management style. Pluralism, while generally used to describe an organisation that embraces collective relationships, can emphasise co-operation between interest groups, not just conflict. It is this distinction in approach to the management of people that leads to variations in employment relations policies, ranging from the paternalistic no-union approach of Marks & Spencer through the single-union no-strike philosophy of Japanese firms such as Nissan, to the multi-union sites of companies such as Ford.

Although external constraints on employment relations policy formulation are an important element, the internal constraints are probably of greater significance. Factors that often determine management style are organisational size, ownership and location. Style can be an important determinant in defining an employment relations policy, and is as much influenced by organisations' leaders as is business strategy. Since Fox first categorised management and employment relations as unitarist or pluralist, others have sought to define the topic in greater detail. In particular, Purcell and Sissons identified five typical styles:

- authoritarian
- paternalistic
- consultative
- constitutional
- opportunist.

The authoritarian approach sees employment relations as relatively unimportant. Although policies and procedures may exist, they are often there because of some legislative necessity (eg grievance, discipline), and as a consequence people issues are not given any priority until something goes wrong. Typically, firms with an authoritarian approach can be small owner-managed businesses, and it is not unusual to find that the things that go wrong revolve around disciplinary issues. In many of the small firms that we have contact with, complaints against them of unfair dismissal are a common problem. For example, an employer who has paid little attention to setting standards of performance dismisses an employee who makes a mistake, and then finds that the dismissed employee wins a tribunal claim for compensation. This is usually because no previous warnings were issued and no disciplinary procedure is followed. An analysis of the size and ownership of organisations appearing in tribunal cases would support this view.

Paternalistic organisations share many of the size and ownership characteristics of the authoritarian type, but they tend to have a much more positive attitude towards their employees. Employee consultation is a high priority, irrespective of whether unions are present in the workplace, and staff retention and reward are seen as key issues.

The type of constitutional organisation described by Purcell and Sissons assumes a trade union presence. Although sharing some of the characteristics of the previous types of organisation, management style in employment relations is often more adversarial than consultative.

In the opportunist organisation, management style is determined by local circumstances. These would determine whether it was appropriate to recognise trade unions or not, or the extent to which employee involvement was encouraged.

Purcell (1987; p.535) moved the analysis of management style forward and redefined it as:

> the existence of a distinctive set of guiding principles, written or otherwise, which set parameters to and signposts for management action in the way employees are treated and particular events handled.

This principle of setting parameters is of vital importance in the management of people. Hilary Walmsley (*People Management*, April 1999; p.48) argued that 'to get the most out of people, managers need to adapt their styles to fit different situations.' However, she went on to say that:

> Managers typically use the same personal style to handle a range of situations. Usually they do this out of habit. Some are not clear about the array of potential styles available to them. Even those who are aware that there are, for example, different ways of developing and motivating people, or of approaching problem-solving, often fail to apply this knowledge to their day-to-day activities. Those who do want to apply new styles can feel confused about where and when they should try them.

Our own research would suggest that the Purcell definition is still valid, but that very often the 'guiding principles' to which he refers will be those of the chief executive. The style employed by these individuals is very closely linked to the issue of leadership.

## INDIVIDUAL AND COLLECTIVE DIMENSIONS

THEORY

Purcell suggested that management style has two dimensions – individualism and collectivism – each dimension having three stages. Individualism is concerned with how much policies are directed at individual workers and whether the organisation takes into account the feelings of all its employees and 'seeks to develop and encourage each employee's capacity and role at work'. The three stages in the individual dimension are:

- commodity status
- paternalism
- resource status.

In the first, the employee is not well regarded and has low job security; in the second, the employer accepts some responsibility for the employee; in the third, the employee is regarded as a valuable resource.

The collectivist dimension is, in a sense, self-explanatory. It is about whether or not management policy encourages or discourages employees to have a collective voice and collective representation. The three stages in this dimension are:

- unitary
- adversarial
- co-operative.

At the unitary stage, management opposes collective relationships either openly or by covert means. The adversarial stage represents a management focus that is on a stable workplace, where conflict is institutionalised and collective relationships limited. The final, co-operative, stage has its focus on constructive relationships and greater openness in the decision-making process.

However, as the process of recovering from one of the worst recessions we have encountered as a nation continues, we need to recognise that management style is not something that can always be easily categorised. Management style is part of the whole leadership process. Holbeche (2009) writes that:

> leadership and management capacity will be of great importance in establishing environments where innovation can flourish. Transformational leadership, as exercised by senior management, will be a key ingredient in engaging employees, harnessing employees' initiative and achieving innovative solutions to business problems.

Tellingly she states that the:

> turn-off factor of inappropriate management styles will become a risk factor for organisations since it is a primary reason for people wishing to leave their organisations.

## REFLECTIVE ACTIVITY

Can you identify the management style that operates within your organisation? Do you think that it changes to meet different needs, or is it static?

Remember, identifying a particular management style is not simply a question of labelling an organisation 'individualist' or 'collectivist'. Purcell points out that the interrelationship between the two is complex, and that simply because an organisation is seen to encourage the rights and capabilities of individuals does not necessarily mean that it is seeking to marginalise any representative group.

## SELECTING EMPLOYMENT RELATIONS POLICIES

The ability to identify which policies are suitable and which are unsuitable for particular types of organisations is an important skill for the employment relations professional to develop. Two issues that must be taken into account in drafting employment relations policies and then implementing them are external and internal factors and their influences. We identified some of the external factors in earlier chapters – in particular, existing and future legislative constraints – but there are other influences. It is important to be aware of the type of policies other employers in your sector or industry are pursuing. These may have an impact in your own organisation – for example, the other organisations' taking a particular stance on employee involvement as a means of retaining key employees could impact on your own ability to retain staff.

Then there is the question of what is considered to be prevailing good practice. In this context 'good practice' means identifying those acts or omissions that distinguish the good employer from the perceived 'bad' employer. For example, if you fail to operate your disciplinary procedure in line with natural justice, you may find that your ex-employees constantly file complaints against you with tribunals – and not only that, but they win compensation as well. Many employers when drafting policies and procedures only scratch the surface. They either do not consider how the policy might operate in practice and whether it will meet the needs of their employees, or are careless in its operation, with the result that it fails to meet the criteria of 'good practice' – which is a standard that we pursue throughout this book. Whatever the policy, therefore, it is important to incorporate monitoring mechanisms within it so that checks can be made on its effectiveness.

All organisations need to have policies on grievance, discipline, equal opportunities, health and safety, pay and benefits, and sickness absence, and these should always be written down and consistently applied. It is also important to acknowledge that although each of the policies mentioned above might differ in scope and depth from one organisation to another, no one – irrespective of the type of organisation that he or she worked in – would seriously question their selection in the range of employment policies adopted.

However, where we do need to examine questions of selection seriously is in respect of those policies which have a clear impact on corporate and business strategies and which can severely affect relationships at work. That an organisation's approach to strategy formulation – and thus its approach to employment relations – will continue to be influenced by UK government actions and also by consumer preferences will impact on its decisions on the way that it manages people and the policies that underpin these management processes.

In earlier chapters we noted that, for well over a decade, the main thrust of industrial, economic and legislative policy has been to create a market-driven economy, and that 'from an industrial relations perspective, the most telling feature of this policy has been the successive pieces of legislation designed to limit the role and rights of trade unions' (Guest, 1995; p.110). Because the question of why some firms willingly recognise trade unions and others do not is so important to employment relations, it is dealt with separately within this chapter. For the moment we will concentrate on policy choices in other areas.

For many organisations that try to link policy choices in employment relations to their business strategies, the real issue is not about individualism or collectivism but about ensuring that their workforce is committed to the organisation. Obtaining employee commitment is one of the principal ways organisations can position themselves in order to achieve a competitive advantage – one of the necessary prerequisites of a successful business. However, employees will only give their commitment if they feel secure, valued and properly motivated – a sense of well-being that is in part derived from the type of employment policies that are adopted and the way in which they are applied. Such policies must be capable of 'adding value' to the business. For the employment relations professional who may be trying to decide on the advice he or she gives in respect of a particular policy, this is of some importance.

In respect of trade unionism, the question is not about pro- or anti-union stances, it is whether entering into a relationship with an appropriate trade union can add value to the business. It would be wrong to assume that the answer to this question will always be no. The search for competitive advantage and employee commitment are key issues and are linked to the management of change in an organisation.

Managing change may require variations in organisational culture, the introduction of flexible working practices, empowerment or some form of teamworking. If any of these routes, or a combination of them all, is followed, the devising and implementation of policies to support them will be required. This is where the involvement of the employment relations professional can be of crucial importance – and before we examine the subject of change, it is important to recognise that the process of designing and implementing policies to support change requires the employment relations professional to develop certain skills. It may be that you have been asked by the board to establish whether a particular initiative will be suitable for your organisation, and proper evaluation is of critical importance because there is a danger that organisations will invest in new ideas that are not suitable for them.

## MANAGING CHANGE

The management of change is something that most organisations have to undertake at some time or other, and during the change process employment relations can be under tremendous stress. In most change programmes it is safe to assume that no more than 25% to 30% of people will be in favour, that up to 50% will probably sit on the fence to see what happens, and that up to a quarter of people will actively resist any changes. That is why, as Machiavelli said,

> There is nothing more difficult to plan, more doubtful of success, nor more dangerous to manage than the creation of a new system. For the initiator has the enmity of all who profit by the preservation of the old institutions, and merely lukewarm defenders in those who would gain by the new ones.

But why does change fail? After all, most organisations that embark on a change programme do so with honourable motives. They want to make life better, both for the organisation and for the people who work in it. Although it is always dangerous to generalise, the cause of the failure comes from within the company. The reasons are varied, but examples include:

- misunderstanding what change is
- lack of planning and preparation
- no clear vision
- looking for quick fixes
- poor communication
- a legacy of previous change programmes.

Given the importance of people to the change process, it is essential that management are able to articulate a clear vision of the objectives of the change programme. To gain commitment to change, that vision has to be expressed clearly and unambiguously so that commitment can be obtained if management take the right steps in managing the process.

The type of steps we have in mind would include the managers' persuading the employees of the need for change. We have acknowledged that a consensus cannot always be achieved when change becomes necessary, but it is a basic principle of good employment relations that consent, however grudgingly given, is better than force. In this context managers might have to accept that change will sometimes have to be negotiated, with or without trade unions. Even without negotiation, it is absolutely true that seeking employee thoughts about the change is much more likely to lead to effective implementation than the management's adopting an attitude of 'We know best.'

Organisations of all shapes and sizes are embroiled in change, and increasingly that includes changing the established culture. This means asking questions such as, 'How can we get our people to be more innovative, more focused, more assertive, more in line with our values?' In some cases a whole new culture is needed in order to fit a new set of values to meet the organisation's intentions. This is particularly important following a major change such as a merger or takeover.

This was the challenge facing Jacky Simmonds, HR Director for the UK and Ireland at TUI Travel (*People Management*, March 2009). TUI Travel was the outcome of a merger between First Choice and Germany's TUI, owner of UK holiday brand Thomson. Simmonds, who had been HR Director at First Choice before the merger, worked with her counterparts at TUI to identify the main people challenges the newly merged organisation would face. Not least among these was the requirement to combine two very different corporate cultures (loud, brash First Choice and venerable Thomson), deciding key locations, determining a new organisational structure, and selecting people for key roles. A very important factor in ensuring success in such circumstances is the quality of communication, and a few weeks into the merger Simmonds commissioned an employee survey. 'A key recommendation was that line managers needed to communicate more with their teams.' Although, as Simmonds says, a great deal of energy was put into ensuring good internal communications, in her view 'You can never do enough.' The merger took place in 2007, and after 18 months the big changes had been made and some of the cost benefits were being delivered. However, as Simmonds found, the benefits of change can be difficult to convey and it is important to recognise that all change, no matter how minor, can create tension and difficulties among the workforce.

Simmonds notes how surprised she was about 'just how much emotion the merger aroused – even among quite senior people'. Among the workforce of the newly merged business there were those who were 'not able to cope with uncertainty', and who:

> found it difficult to change or adapt to a new boss. It wasn't that they didn't think the merger was right, but they had an inability to lead. We had to help them understand what they can do, such as focusing on short-term goals.

However, as with many of the issues that we have covered in this chapter, managing change, altering behaviour and creating a new culture requires clear leadership. As Angela Baron, CIPD Adviser, Organisation Development and Engagement, states in introducing early findings from the CIPD's Shaping the Future research project:

> Organisations that minimise barriers to decsion-making and develop effective leaders who communicate to employees how their roles contribute to strategic priorities are more likely to unlock sustainable performance.

**THEORY** Other research on leadership conducted by Alan Hooper of Exeter University identified five key themes:

- Effective leaders create an understanding in the company about why change is necessary. They are clear thinkers and highly effective communicators, able to define a clear strategy, but with the flexibility to adapt to changing circumstances. Very good listeners, they are aware of the importance of unlocking others' potential, and are passionate and motivating.

- They set a personal example, demonstrating integrity, truth, openness and honesty. When Archie Norman took over as chief executive of the struggling supermarket chain Asda in 1992, he adopted an open communications policy and always spoke his mind. During the early days of restructuring this won him grudging respect and then a growing momentum of support.

- Good leaders ensure good succession. Jack Welch spent 15% to 20% of his time on leadership development at GE.

- They share their experiences with their people. For example, Ken Keir, the managing director of Honda UK, spends three and a half days a week in the factory with his workforce.

- Effective leaders pace themselves, more akin to a marathon runner than to a sprinter. This means good time management, good discipline, effective delegation and a good work–life balance. They are also sensitive to the effect of change at work on the people they are responsible for.

It seems clear that the way in which an organisation is led has a major impact on the management of change. In the same way, the decision-making process is also important. Because the introduction of most new initiatives will be an evolutionary process, overseeing the pace of change is an increasingly important issue for successful management, and this requires effective decision-making. Decision-making in this context is both an end to achieve and a mechanism that can be used deliberately to shift people's behaviour and perspective over time.

Unfortunately, in many organisations the expectation of change creates an uncertainty regarding the immediate and long-term future that can be difficult to manage or placate. If left to manage itself, this uncertainty can quickly fester to become an institutionalised insecurity that can undermine effective decision-making and create a range of employment relations problems. We are not suggesting that a focus on decision-making alone will mean the effective management of change, but clear decision-making with specific decisions allocated to relevant roles will underpin the support employees need to cope with it.

A further factor to be taken into account is that during the change process responsibilities might have to be altered and the boundaries of jobs clarified. This may mean examining organisational structure because some change programmes will challenge traditional hierarchies – a change that can give rise to considerable resentment and individual resistance. It is also important to ensure that other policies that might be required to underpin change are themselves in place – for example, equal opportunities or single-status workforce. With any new policy there will always be those who oppose it, sometimes openly and sometimes covertly, and the employment relations professional will recognise this. He or she will not assume that the process is complete just because an initiative has been properly evaluated and then properly communicated to all employees. He or she will monitor implementation and seek ways to reinforce the initial communication about the policy change.

## MANAGEMENT AND TRADE UNIONS

Although the influence of trade unions has been declining steadily since 1978, the question of trade unionism *per se* is very important to the employment relations professional in trying to determine policies and procedures for his or her own organisation. Some companies seem to manage extremely well by being non-union; some organisations appear to be happy to embrace unions; some actively resist them. And, as we have already noted, one of the policy choices an organisation can make is the question of its relationship, or not, with a trade union. Moreover, as also noted elsewhere in this chapter, management style and philosophy will cause different managers to have different approaches to the role of and involvement of unions. This will range from encouragement to active resistance and refusal – but the 1999 Employment Relations Act now makes it more difficult, if not impossible, to say no.

However, before making the assumption that some existing non-union firms will become unionised, we must understand what we mean by the term 'non-unionism'. Salamon (1998) explains that the term can be used to explain two different types of organisation:

THEORY

Type A: where an organisation has a policy not to recognise unions for any employees or for particular groups of employees (such as managers), and therefore it is a distinct aim or element of management's employment relations strategy to avoid any collective relationship (ie non-unionism results from management decision);

and

THEORY

Type B: where union membership within the organisation or group of employees is low or non-existent, and therefore unions are not recognised because of the absence of employee pressure for representation (ie non-unionism results from the employees' decision not to join unions).

Clearly, type B organisations have little to fear from current union recognition legislation unless something happens in the working environment that fundamentally alters the status quo. If, for example, the company has a history of treating its employees badly and those employees have now succumbed to the blandishments of a union recruiting drive, something will have changed for the worse in the employment relationship. If it is possible to identify a causal act, can something other than union recognition remedy it? Suppose that in a type B organisation there was a sudden rush to join a trade union, the organisation would have to ask itself some very searching questions. Have recent redundancies created a climate of uncertainty? Has there been a change in management style? Have grievances been ignored or badly handled? Any of these could trigger a change in employee attitudes to collective representation such that if management want to remain non-union, they will have to consider how such issues are managed (Judge, 1997).

**THEORY**    NON-UNION ORGANISATIONS

One of the unsubstantiated myths in employment relations has been the idea that non-unionism is the panacea for business success, with organisations such as Marks & Spencer and IBM put forward as prime examples of the concept. The shareholders and customers of M&S might take a contrary view, given that organisation's depressed performance over the past five years. There will always be a debate between those who see trade unions as a negative influence and those, like most of our European partners, who see rights at work (including trade union membership and collective bargaining) as part of an important social dimension to working relationships. It is this polarisation that results in many politicians and business leaders being antagonistic towards the social dimension of the European Union. Post-World-War-II industrial relations has allowed some commentators the opportunity to promote non-unionism as the ideal state to which all businesses should aspire, and to suggest that to allow interventions from Europe would be a massive step backward.

While the debate about unionism versus non-unionism continues, the real question tends to be ignored. That is, is it easier to manage with unions or without unions? Personal prejudice should not come into the process of effective management, but many managers' attitudes towards trade unions have been conditioned either by their own negative experiences during the 1970s and 1980s – a period when the unions contributed to their negative image with some self-inflicted wounds – or by a perception that unions somehow stop managers managing. In some cases the negativity is a result of union representatives being allowed to take the initiative because of poor management. There may be two reasons for this:

- poor training in core skills such as negotiation, communication and interviewing

- a lack of clear policy guidance.

It is because this lack of skills can have such a negative impact on the whole process of employment relations that the second part of this book concentrates on the development of skills such as bargaining, negotiating, managing grievances and handling discipline.

As personnel practitioners ourselves we have received many requests for help from organisations who are having difficulty in managing their employment relations in a collectivist environment. In almost all the cases, blame is laid at the door of the union and there is no recognition that poor management might also bear some responsibility. When appropriate training interventions have been agreed and implemented, we find that there is a complete turnaround. Not only do managers seize responsibility but they find that they are able to do so with little or no union resistance. In truth, union representatives have merely been filling a vacuum that nobody else was interested in. These experiences have caused many managers to become very biased against unions, and many of those that we speak to believe genuinely that without the unions business success would be guaranteed.

Recent disputes involving British Airways and the Post Office have, once again, helped to polarise views. Many observers feel that the inability of Post Office managers to drive through change is a direct result of unfettered trade union power in individual sorting offices. This is too simplistic a view. Listen to many Post Office workers and you will discern a willingness to change – provided, that is, that management also change. Anecdotal evidence suggests that the allegations of bullying by Post Office managers, and the impact that this has on a willingness to change working practices, are too commonplace to be ignored. As we say above, poor management contributes to poor employment relations.

This faith in managing without unions has meant that some of the larger non-union firms within the UK have become the focus of attention for developments in employment relations. Companies such as Marks & Spencer and IBM have always been held up as exemplary non-union employers, but now others have joined the list. At the risk of overgeneralisation, the generic characteristics of these non-union companies tend to be (Blyton and Turnbull, 1994; p.234):

> a sense of caring, carefully-chosen plant locations and working environments, market leadership, high growth and healthy profits, employment security, single status, promotion from within, an influential personnel department, competitive pay and benefit packages, profit-sharing, open communications, and the careful selection and training of management, particularly at the supervisory level.

How many of the companies who yearn for non-union status would be prepared to make the investment in people management that the organisations that they envy have done? The real issue is how well a business is managed – *that* is what determines success.

Notwithstanding the influence of large organisations, data from the 2004 *Workplace Employment Relations Survey* found that non-union establishments are more likely to be small single-plant establishments located in the private services sector. This result is not all that surprising, given the great encouragement that the small firms sector has received and continues to receive. The number of business start-ups has risen, and many of the new organisations have not been able to see the relevance of trade unions. Many of their employees may have been the victims of redundancy in older, traditionally unionised, industries and a reluctance to embrace the supposed cause of industrial decline (trade unions) may be understandable.

However, one must also question how active trade unions have been in trying to recruit from new industries and the new workforce. Have the unions been so busy defending the interests of their existing members that they have not been able to devote sufficient resources to recruitment? Another question that ought to be asked is, 'How will employees' feelings of insecurity about their long-term job prospects act as a feeding-ground for trade union recruiters?'

These and other questions link back to the questions of policy choice. If a business wishes to be, or to remain, non-union, it must be clear about the relationship it will have with its employees. To be a Marks & Spencer you need to be very people-oriented, with great importance placed on respect for employees. This means highly developed and effective leadership skills – and this requires an investment in people. Gaining commitment and becoming a harmonious and integrated unitary workplace requires more than words: it can mean changing the established order.

Alternatively, a business can be a type A organisation as identified by Salamon. These organisations must be prepared to deal with a request for recognition. While the idea might be anathema to an anti-union organisation, having an identifiable policy relating to trade unionism and trade union recognition could be very helpful. We are certainly aware of organisations that have been traditionally non-union, who are taking steps to prepare for a recognition claim – by, for example, training their managers in bargaining skills.

## UNION RECOGNITION

The 1998 *Workplace Employee Relations Survey* (WERS) found that in 47% of workplaces there were no union members at all – 'a substantial change from 36% of workplaces in 1990'. The survey found that there are 'strong associations between the type of union presence and workplace employment size', but as we have noted elsewhere, 'even stronger associations with management attitudes towards union membership'.

By the end of the 1990s trade union recognition had fallen to the point where only 45% of workplaces recognised trade unions, compared to 66% in 1984 and 53% in 1990. But, as we have noted elsewhere – particularly in Chapter 6 – the decline in union membership seems to have been halted. For some, this is a consequence of the Employment Relations Act (1999), but Gregor Gall (*People Management*, 14 September 2000) considers that 'the industrial relations landscape had already begun to change' before the ERA became law. Noting that between 1995 and mid-2000 there were nearly 800 recognition agreements signed, Gall points out that this is not simply a numbers game. For him:

The kinds of new deals being signed – and where, by whom and under what conditions – are also important. They will influence not only the conduct of industrial relations in those organisations themselves, but also the behaviour of other organisations.

Clearly, the numbers of recognition deals that have been signed owes something to the influence of the ERA, but according to Gall:

> Increasing numbers of employers are realising that there is a positive business case for dealing with their workforces through unions, and that it is more efficient, effective and democratic than treating employees as a collection of atomised individuals.

Taking such a stance is clearly a strategic choice for many businesses, who recognise that signing a voluntary deal allows them much more influence over the content of the agreement and saves a damaging confrontation with their workforce.

What is clear is that membership gains have been achieved and unions are now poised to take advantage of the provisions of the ERA in order to reassert their influence in the workplace. How employers respond will be a mixture of strategic choice and policy formulation.

### Obtaining union recognition

The Employment Relations Act (1999) sets out the basis on which employees can obtain recognition. In summary, those provisions are:

- Any independent trade union seeking recognition must apply to the employer in writing requesting recognition. The employer has 10 working days in which to respond. If by the end of the 10-day period the employer has not responded or has rejected the request, the union may apply to the Central Arbitration Committee (CAC) for a decision on the 'appropriate bargaining unit' and/ or whether a majority of the workers support recognition for collective bargaining.

- If, however, the employer indicates during the 10-day period that, while not accepting the request, it is prepared to negotiate to agree the bargaining unit and recognition for it, a negotiation period of 20 working days (or longer, if mutually agreed) is available. If these negotiations fail, the union may apply to the CAC as above, but may not apply if it has rejected or not responded within 10 days to an employer proposal for ACAS to assist.

- Once a recognition claim is referred to the CAC, it must try to help the parties reach agreement within 20 working days (or such longer appropriate period as it may determine). If agreement is not reached within that period, the CAC then has 10 days (or a longer period where it specifies the reasons for extension) to decide the appropriate bargaining unit.

- In respect of an application to decide the appropriate bargaining unit and whether the union(s) has the support of the majority of the workers in it, the CAC must not proceed unless it decides that:

- members of the union (or unions) constitute at least 10% of the workers constituting the proposed bargaining unit, and
- there is *prima facie* evidence that a majority of the workers constituting the proposed bargaining unit would be likely to favour recognition of the union(or unions) as entitled to conduct collective bargaining on behalf of the bargaining unit.

- In deciding the appropriate bargaining unit, the CAC must take these matters into account:
  - the need for the unit to be compatible with effective management
  - the matters listed in sub-paragraph (4), so far as they do not conflict with that need.
  - Those matters are:
    - the views of the employer and of the union (or unions)
    - existing national and local bargaining arrangements
    - the desirability of avoiding small fragmented bargaining units within an undertaking
    - the characteristics of workers falling within the proposed bargaining unit and of any other employees of the employer whom the CAC considers relevant
    - the location of workers.

If the union (or unions) shows that a majority of the workers in the bargaining unit are members of the union, the CAC must declare the union recognised, unless one of the following three conditions applies:

- The CAC is satisfied that a ballot should be held in the interests of good industrial relations.

- A significant number of the union members within the bargaining unit inform the CAC that they do not want the union (or unions) to conduct collective bargaining on their behalf.

- Membership evidence is produced which leads the CAC to conclude that there are doubts whether a significant number of the union members within the bargaining unit want the union (or unions) to conduct collective bargaining on their behalf.

If the union (or unions) cannot show majority membership – or can, but one of the three conditions above applies – the CAC must arrange (through a qualified independent person) a secret ballot of the workers in the bargaining unit, asking whether they wish the union to conduct collective bargaining on their behalf.

If the ballot result shows that the union is supported by a majority of those voting and at least 40% of those in the bargaining unit, the CAC will declare the union recognised.

Note that the CAC must not proceed with a recognition application from more than one union unless:

- the unions show that they will co-operate with each other in a manner likely to secure and maintain stable and effective collective bargaining arrangements, and

- the unions show that if the employer wishes, they will enter into arrangements under which collective bargaining is conducted by the unions acting together on behalf of the workers constituting the proposed bargaining unit.

Where the CAC declares a union recognised, the parties have a negotiating period of 30 working days (or longer if mutually agreed) to agree a method for conducting collective bargaining. If they have not reached agreement by then, they can seek CAC assistance during a further period of 20 working days (or longer if mutually agreed with the CAC). If they still cannot agree, the CAC must specify the method by which the parties must conduct collective bargaining (which they can vary by written agreement) and which will be a contract legally enforceable through the courts, by orders for specific performance, with which failure to comply will constitute contempt of court.

### Employer concerns

Writing in *People Management* (January 1999; p.54), Mike Emmott, IPD Policy Adviser on Employment Relations, stated that 'One thing is clear beyond any doubt: most employers are opposed to the idea of a law on trade union recognition.' Many of these concerns centred on the time-scales within the recognition procedure, but this has been less of an issue owing to the overwhelming number of voluntary recognition deals that have been struck. Of more concern is the perception that many organisations have about the CAC – about whether the CAC adopts an even-handed approach to union recognition claims. The fact that its approach in some disputed cases has been criticised is not necessarily surprising – organisations that have resisted union claims are unlikely to be favourably disposed to the body that granted the disputed recognition. Whether the CAC does give trade unions preferential treatment is largely a matter of perception, but if it is to maintain the confidence of organisations, it must ensure that its independence is clearly maintained.

The Government, as is to be expected, takes a much more benign view of the legislation. They see unions, 'where they are run efficiently along modern lines, as important partners for employers in promoting competitiveness and good practice' (Ian McCartney, *People Management*, 17 September 1998; p.38). This view is supported by Gall, who believes that:

> the Labour Government has helped to engender a climate in which many employers are less inclined to behave unilaterally, and this has legitimised a union role in organisations.

This may of course have little to do with the Government, but may be more a pragmatic reaction, on the part of employers, in realisation that the legislation on union recognition is here to stay, at least for the foreseeable future.

Notwithstanding this, the negative view of the CAC will not necessarily diminish, and as Gall and Cooper report (*People Management*, 12 July 2001), the 'unequivocal legal backing [given to the CAC in the first disputed case to reach the courts] may deter other aggrieved employers from going down this costly avenue'. There is certainly a danger that employers will grant recognition in the belief that the CAC is pro-union, and this will have a consequential negative effect on employment relations.

## EMPLOYERS AND THEIR USE OF THE LAW

The laws that are now on the statute book impact on employment relations in a number of ways, and changes in legislation have meant that trade unions are much more responsible for the actions of their members than they used to be. This in turn means that it is potentially much easier for employers to seek a legal remedy when industrial action is taken against them. There is a much stricter definition of what constitutes strike action, and it can only be lawful if it follows a properly conducted ballot, relates wholly or mainly to matters such as pay and conditions, and takes place between an employee and his or her direct employer. This is intended to rule out sympathy or secondary action by those not involved in the main dispute.

Other provisions in the legislative package include restrictions on the numbers of people that can mount a picket outside a workplace, and compulsory ballots to test union members' support for contributions to a political fund. The law has also outlawed the closed shop – which is not to say that *de facto* closed shops do not still exist, because they do, most notably in the printing industry.

Against this background we must consider the employers' use of such laws. Why do some employers seek legal assistance in the resolution of disputes and others do not? Much has been made of the rights that employers now have to take legal action against their employees, either to sue for damages caused by industrial action or to seek injunctions prohibiting action from taking place.

Although the occasional high-profile case hits the headlines (eg the British Airways cabin crews), there is no evidence to suggest that employers seek to exercise their legal rights every time they are faced with disruptive action. Indeed, there is probably more evidence to suggest that most employers resist the temptation to use the law. This is because they enjoy reasonably good employment relations and are more interested in maintaining those relationships in the long term than they are in short-term victories. This is not to say that some organisations, in industries such as transport, set out deliberately to alienate their workforce. It is simply that there are often other considerations. If they were not seen to challenge 'unnecessary' strikes, they would run the risk of losing, perhaps permanently, many of their customers. For this reason, any employer faced with the threat of industrial action would have to take seriously concerns voiced by its customers and seek to balance these against its long-term relationship with its workforce.

The circumstances in which an employer might have to consider using the law usually follow a breakdown in negotiations with a recognised union. Such a breakdown could lead the union to seek a formal mandate from its members supporting industrial action, or there could be some form of unofficial industrial action encouraged by lay officials. The response that an employer makes in such circumstances is extremely important and can have a critical effect on employment relations.

## REFLECTIVE ACTIVITY

Consider how you would respond to a ballot for industrial action in your organisation and what factors you would take into account.

### INDUSTRIAL ACTION BALLOTS

If, for whatever reason, negotiations with a recognised union have broken down, there is every possibility that the union will seek to organise a ballot of its members. The union may do this not just because members have a desire to take industrial action but because a positive vote can be a very useful means of forcing the employer back to the bargaining table. If you are faced with a ballot for industrial action, there are a number of steps to be taken to check that it complies with all the legal requirements. Firstly, was the ballot conducted by post? Before any form of industrial action can commence, all those employees who it is reasonable to believe will be called upon to take part in the action must have been given a chance to vote. Secondly, were you as the employer given seven days' notice before the ballot took place? Thirdly, has the union appointed independent scrutineers to oversee the ballot? Finally, did you receive notice of the result, and was this at least seven days before any proposed action?

Let us assume that all the legal requirements have been complied with. What are the legal options? Can any action be taken against the union? Not really, unless it can be demonstrated that the proposed action would not be a lawful trade dispute within the meaning of the legislation. There used to be a right to take sanctions against individuals, but the 1999 Employment Relations Act has changed this. The legislation makes it automatically unfair to dismiss workers taking part in protected (lawful) action within eight weeks of the action beginning. Furthermore, after eight weeks it will still be unfair to dismiss if the employer has not followed an appropriate procedure for the resolution of the dispute – an 'appropriate procedure' being one established in a collective agreement. What happens when the union or its members are in breach of an agreed procedure?

Now let us examine a second scenario. Let's say that the ballot for industrial action was not conducted properly. In these circumstances, and before seeking a legal remedy, it is important to consider all the options. Decisions on using legal intervention should never be taken without a full and extensive evaluation. Firstly, it might be appropriate to sit down with those who organised the ballot to discuss concerns about its validity. It is possible that they are already aware of its flaws, but are merely seeking to demonstrate the depth of feeling about a particular issue in order to get a resumption of negotiations. Alternatively, it might be appropriate to talk to those who might have been excluded from a ballot. They may be prepared to back the company in any dispute and it is possible their votes, in a re-run ballot, might overturn the original result. The third option is to seek an injunction against the union restraining its members from taking any action until a proper ballot is conducted. Again this can be a high-risk strategy because in a re-run ballot those who previously voted against the union might vote with them on the basis of solidarity.

Ultimately, as with many aspects of employment relations, whether particular employers choose to seek a legal remedy to constrain the actions of their workforce will depend on management style and whether there is a desire to maintain good working relationships.

## SUMMARY

In this chapter we have noted:

- the link between corporate and business strategies and functional activities such as HR/personnel. This has enabled us to see the relationship between the decisions of the board and the role of line managers in translating those decisions into actionable policies

- the process of strategy formulation and have seen that a number of different approaches are available. Methodologies employed will inevitably differ, and it is important that you understand the various models and their critical components. Equally, it is important that the HR professional understands the goals of his or her organisation and what his or her role is in contributing to the strategic agenda. This will require some more detailed reading both of the texts that have been referred to and of the various case studies that have been highlighted

- that employment relations – like every other function within the business – does not operate in a vacuum. This means that there has to be a relationship with employee development, reward and resourcing

- that there are a number of issues which must be taken into account when drawing up an employment relations policy and managing change. We looked at the skills required in selecting and applying particular policies to the organisation, and the skills needed to manage change effectively. In the context of gaining commitment we highlighted a number of core skills that we feel are an absolute necessity for the professional personnel practitioner

- that different organisations have different approaches to the role and involvement of unions, and we examined the causes of non-unionism. We looked at some examples of non-union firms and whether their success was due to good management or to the fact that they kept unions at arms' length. We concluded that good management was the most important factor. We identified the role that the law can play in management–union relationships and what factors employers must consider before they use the legal processes against trade unions or trade union members

- that there has to be an alignment between business needs and HR needs in order to develop the HR strategy and to determine what HR interventions are required
- that it is important to incorporate monitoring mechanisms into employment relations policies and instigate a robust performance review process
- that it is important to evaluate new initiatives and ideas and gain overall commitment to particular policies before seeking to implement them
- that management style has a major role to play in the determination of an employment relations policy in respect of trade unionism, union recognition, or non-unionism
- that decisions on whether, and when, to use the law against trade unions or trade union members can be quite complex and should not be taken lightly.

## KEY LEARNING POINTS

- Strategy is about the way that senior management lead their organisation or business in a particular direction. The development of strategic objectives enables leaders to influence and direct an organisation as it conducts its activities.

- Whatever method of strategy formulation is adopted, it is important to be aware that it will be constrained by societal, environmental, industry-specific and organisational factors, many of which will conflict with each other.

- The key is to develop an employment relations strategy that is responsive to the needs of the organisation, that can provide an employment relations professional with an overall sense of purpose, and that will assist employees to understand where they are going, how they are going to get there, why certain things do not happen, and most importantly, the contribution they are expected to make towards achieving the organisational goals.

- Management style can be an important determinant in defining an employment relations policy and is much influenced by the values and preferences of the organisation's leader(s) as is business strategy. However, the ability to select which policies are suitable and which are unsuitable for particular types of organisations is an important skill for the employment relations professional to develop. Two important issues here are external and internal factors and their influences.

- In the light of the importance of people to successfully managing change, it is essential that management are able to articulate a clear vision of the objectives of the change programme. To gain commitment to change, that vision has to be expressed clearly and unambiguously. Commitment will thus be obtained if management take the right steps in managing the process.

- Management style and philosophy will cause different managers to adopt different approaches to the role and the involvement of unions. This will range from encouragement to active resistance and refusal – although the statutory trade union recognition procedure contained in the Employment Relations Act (1999) now makes the latter more difficult.

## REVIEW QUESTIONS

1 Describe the strategic planning process. Why is it important for the employment relations professional to be aware of this?

2 Why do some employers manage with the trade unions yet others do not? Why might employers be indifferent as to whether they manage with unions or not?

3 Drawing on research, identify and explain the different employment relations styles in your organisation.

4 Your line manager tells you that the orgnisation is likely to be planning major changes to the organisation in the coming months. She tells you that she wants you to be a member of the Change Team. In this regard she would like you to produce a proposal outlining how the commitment of the employees to this organised change might be obtained. What will you say in your paper, and why?

EXPLORE FURTHER

Allen, D. (2003) 'Testing times', *People Management*, Vol.9, No.8, April.

Ansoff, H.I. (1991) Critique of Henry Mintzberg's the design school: reconsidering the basic premises of strategic management. *Strategic Management Journal. Vol.12, No.6. 449–461.*

Armstrong, M. (1996) *Employee Reward*. London: Institute of Personnel and Development.

Blakstad, M. and Cooper A. (1995) *The Communicating Organisation*. London: Institute of Personnel and Development.

Blyton, P. and Turnbull, P. (1994) *The Dynamics of Employment Relations*. London: Macmillan.

Burnes, B. (1996) *Managing Change: A strategic approach to organisational dynamics*. London: Pitman.

Butcher, D. and Meldrum, M. (2001) 'Defy gravity', *People Management*, Vol.7, No.13, June.

Caulkin, S. (2001) 'The time is now', *People Management*, Vol.7, No.17, August.

Deloitte & Touche (1998) *Business Success and Human Resources*. Management Survey.

Emmott, M. (1999) 'Collectively cool', *People Management*, Vol.5, No.2, January.

Gall, G. (2000) 'In place of strife', *People Management*, Vol.7, No.18, September.

Gall, G. and Cooper, C. (2001) 'Court upholds CAC recognition award to steel union', *People Management*, Vol.7, No.14, July.

Grint, K. (2005) Leadership: Limits and possibilities, Houndmills, Palgrave Macmillan.

Guest, D. (1995) 'Human resource management, trade unions and industrial relations', in Storey, J. (ed.) *Human Resource Management: A critical text*. London: Routledge.

Guest, D., King, Z., Conway, N., Michie, J. and Sheehan-Quinn, M. (2002) *Voices from the Boardroom – A Research Report*. London: Chartered Institute of Personnel and Development.

Holbeche (2009) *Holbeche, L. Aligning Human Resources and Business Strategy.* Butterworth-Heinemann.

Institute of Personnel and Development (1997) *The Impact of People Management Practices on Business Performance*. London: IPD.

Jenkins, M. and Ambrosini, V. (2002) *Strategic Management: A multi-perspective approach*. Basingstoke: Palgrave.

Johnson, G. and Scholes, K. (2003) *Exploring Corporate Strategy*, 6th edition. London: Prentice-Hall.

Johnson, Scholes and Whittington (2008) *Johnson G., Scholes, K. and Whittington, R. (2008) Exploring Corporate Strategy 8th Edition* . London, Prentice Hall.

Judge, G. (1997) 'United firms stand, but divided they fall', *The Guardian*, 29 April.

Kay, J. (1993) *Foundations of Corporate Success*. Oxford: OUP.

Kelly, J. and Gennard, J. (2007) 'Business strategic decision-making: the role and influence of directors', *Human Resource Management Journal*, Vol.17, No.2.

Kersley, B., Alpin, C., Forth, J., Bryson, A., Bewley, H., Dix, G. and Oxenbridge, S. (2006) *Inside the Workplace: Findings from 2004 Workplace Employment Relations Survey*. London: Routledge.

Marchington, M. and Wilkinson, A. (1996) *Core Personnel and Development*. London: Institute of Personnel and Development.

McCartney, I. (1998) 'In all fairness', *People Management*, Vol.4, No.18, September.

Millward, N., Stevens, M., Smart, D. and Hawes, W. R. (1992) *Workplace Industrial Relations in Transition: the ED/ESRC/PSI/ ACAS Surveys*. London: Gower.

Mintzberg, H. (1987) Crafting Strategy. *Harvard Business Review. July–August 66–75*.

Mintzberg, H. (1994) Rethinking strategic planning part 1: pitfall and fallacies. *Long Range Planning. Vol.27, No. 312–21*.

Persaud, J. (2003) 'Mutual appreciation', *People Management*, Vol.9, No.17, August.

PM article by Alban and Benedict Bunker (Feb. 2009) *26th February 2009*.

Porter, M. (1985) *Competitive Advantage: Creating and sustaining superior performance*. New York: Free Press.

Purcell, J. (1987) 'Mapping management styles in employment relations', *Journal of Management Studies*, Vol.24, No.5: 535.

Purcell, J., Kinnie, N. and Hutchinson, S. (2003) 'They're free!', *People Management*, Vol.9, No.10, May.

Purcell, J., Kinnie, N., Hutchinson, S., Rayton, B. and Swart, J. (2003) *Understanding the People and Performance Link: Unlocking the black box – A Research Report*. London: Chartered Institute of Personnel and Development.

Purcell and Sissons (in Marchington & Wilkinson 1996) *Marchington, M. and Wilkinson, A. (1996) Core Personnel and Development. London, Institiute of Personnel and Development*.

Salamon, M. (1998) *Industrial Relations Theory and Practice*, 3rd edition. London: Prentice-Hall.

Scarbrough, H. and Elias, J. (2002) *Evaluating Human Capital – A Research Report*. London: Chartered Institute of Personnel and Development.

Tyson, S. (1995) *Human Resource Strategy: Towards a general theory of human resource management*. London: Pitman.

Ulrich, D. (1997) Human Resource Champion: the next agenda for adding value and delivering results. Boston Mass: *Harvard Business Review. Vol.76, No.1, 124–134*.

Ulrich, D. and Brockbank, W. (2005) The HR value proposition. Boston, Mass: *Harvard Business School Press*.

Walmsley, H. (1999) 'A suitable ploy', *People Management*, Vol.5, No.7, April.

**Weblinks**

www.bis.gov.uk for access to law surrounding trade union negotiation

www.cac.gov.uk is the website of the Central Arbitration Committee and gives access to its annual reports and decisions in trade union recognition cases

## CHAPTER 8

# Employee Involvement

## OVERVIEW

This chapter begins by outlining the theory of the benefits to be gained by an organisation from investing in employee involvement and participation (EIP) – improved economic performance, improved quality of product/service, increased productivity, and a better informed workforce that is more likely to accept the legitimacy of management action. It then outlines the different employee involvement and participation mechanisms in terms of their breadth and depth (eg the amount of time allocated to employee questions during team briefings, the frequency of meetings, methods of selecting employee representatives, etc) and the alleged advantages and disadvantages of each separate mechanism. In its third part, the chapter analyses what constitutes meaningful consultation, and the role and function of joint consultative committees. Next, contemporary research on organisational policy and practice is examined to assess whether employee participation and involvement delivers the positional benefits its supporters claim. The law surrounding employee involvement and participation, especially the Information and Consultation Regulations (2004), and its impact is assessed. The chapter finally goes on to examine 'good employment practice' (how to do it) in the implementation of employee involvement and participation practices – training and development, selecting the practices, commitment by top management, adequate resources, monitoring and review, etc.

## LEARNING OUTCOMES

When you have completed this chapter, you should be aware of and able to describe:

- the business case for involving employees in the affairs of the business
- the strengths and weaknesses of the main direct employee Involvement and participation practices
- the relevance of the main indirect employee involvement and participation practices
- the likely impact of the implementation of information and consultation on employee commitment to the organisation and on employee job satisfaction
- how to devise, and implement, appropriate employee involvement and participation practices for an organisation
- the legal framework surrounding the provision of information and consultation arrangements.

## INTRODUCTION

The term 'employee involvement and participation' (EIP) best captures a range of techniques. EIP takes several forms, ranging from direct EIP, which requires the participation of each individual – for example, team briefings or problem-solving groups – to indirect or representative participation – for example, through workplace committees. These types of EIP vary according to the level of influence they give to employees, the scope of the subject matter for discussion and the level in the organisation at which the mechanisms operate. The amount of influence employees have in decision-making, in particular, is regarded as important because it is likely to affect the degree of impact that EIP has on employee and broader organisational outcomes (Marchington *et al*, 1992).

EIP practices are initiated principally by management and are designed to increase employee information about and commitment to the organisation. Employee involvement concentrates on individual employees and is designed to produce a committed workforce more likely to contribute to the efficient operation of an organisation. By introducing employee involvement mechanisms, management seek to gain the consent of the employees to their proposed actions on the basis of commitment rather than control (Walton, 1985). These mechanisms are thus aimed at enabling individual employees to influence management decision-making processes.

Employee participation, on the other hand, concerns the extent to which employees – often via their representatives – are involved with management in the decision-making machinery of the organisation. This includes joint consultation, collective bargaining and worker representation on the board. These systems focus on collectively representative structures.

It is management, however, who make the final decision over whether employees are to be involved, and to participate, in management decision-making. Employee involvement, unlike collective bargaining and worker representation on the board, is not about employees' sharing power (jointly regulating) with management. The decision whether to accept, or reject, the views of the employees rests with management alone.

## REFLECTIVE ACTIVITY

Explain the difference in meaning between the terms 'employee involvement' and 'employee participation'.

Some commentators who have charted and sought to explain the use of EIP mechanisms have argued that their use varies over time (Ramsay, 1996). These writers argue that managers are seen as key agents in the process, and that management interest in EIP mechanisms is driven by the belief on the part of managers that harnessing employees' ideas and suggestions could improve organisational performance (Dundon *et al*, 2004).

## THEORY | WHY INVOLVE EMPLOYEES? THE THEORY

The control-oriented approach to workforce management associated with F. W. Taylor took shape in the early part of the twentieth century in response to the extending division of labour into jobs for which individuals were considered accountable. To monitor and control effectiveness in these jobs, management organised themselves into a hierarchy of specialised roles supported by a top–down allocation of authority and status symbols to position within the hierarchy. At the centre of this workforce control method was the desire to establish order and to inculcate efficiency in the employee – who was expected to obey, and not challenge, management instructions.

However, increasing international competition and technological change in the last 30 years have meant that higher skills and far greater flexibility are required of the employee. According to Walton (1985), in this environment a commitment strategy towards the workforce is required. Following this strategic approach to managing, the workforce jobs are designed to be broader than before (job enlargement), to combine planning and implementation, and to include efforts to upgrade operations, not just to maintain them. The responsibilities of individual employees are expected to change as conditions change (functional flexibility) and teams – not individuals – are accountable for employee performance. The teams control how they will deliver their output objectives. Employees are thus said to be empowered. A commitment strategy therefore involves dispensing with whole layers of management and minimising status differentials so that control depends on shared goals and expertise rather than on a formal position that carries influence with it.

Under an employee commitment strategy, according to Walton, performance expectations are high and serve not to establish minimum standards but to emphasise continuous improvement and reflect the requirements of the marketplace. As a result, pay and reward strategies reflect not the principles of job evaluation but the importance of group achievement and concerns for gain-sharing and profit-sharing. Equally important, argues Walton, is the challenge of giving employees some assurance of security by offering them priority in training and retraining as old jobs are destroyed and new ones created, and providing them with the means to be heard on such issues as production methods, problem-solving, and human resource policies.

Underlying all these policies is a management philosophy that accepts the interests of an organisation's multiple stakeholders – owners, employees, customers and public. At the heart of this approach is an acceptance that growing employee commitment will lead to improved performance. No organisation in today's modern world can perform at peak levels unless each employee is committed to the corporate objectives and works as an effective team member. Employees want to use and develop their skills, enhance their careers and take pride in their work. The commitment strategy involves employees contributing their own ideas as to how their performance and the quality of product or service they provide can be improved. There is clear evidence that employees want to be part of a successful organisation which provides a good income, and an opportunity for development and secure employment.

The theory of employee involvement and participation postulates economic efficiency gains. There are a number of reasons for such an outcome. First, employees generally are better informed about their work tasks and processes than their managers, and are therefore better placed to achieve enhanced performance. Second, advocates of employee involvement and participation hypothesise that its associated practices provide employees with greater intrinsic rewards from work than from other forms of workplace management such as collective bargaining. It is said that these rewards will increase job satisfaction and in turn enhance employee motivation to achieve new goals. Then it is also hypothesised that by granting workers greater access to management information, mutual trust and commitment will be increased, thereby reducing labour turnover. In addition, empowering workers reduces the need for complex systems of control and hence leads to improved efficiency. Fourth, if employees' views are sought and acted upon by management, employees are more likely to be committed to their organisation and satisfied with their work because they believe managers are sincere in their efforts to involve employees.

There is thus an important assumption behind employee involvement theory – namely, that employees are an untapped resource with knowledge and experience which can be used by employers if they provide opportunities and structures for worker involvement. Wilkinson (2001) has also pointed out that the theory assumes that participative decision-making is likely to lead to better-quality management decisions, so that empowerment represents a win/win situation with gains available to both employers (increased efficiency) and employees (job satisfaction).

**THEORY**

Financial forms of employee involvement are said to improve productivity performance for a number of reasons. First, it is postulated that employees will work more co-operatively because they can all gain by co-operating with each other rather than competing amongst themselves. Second, some argue that performance-related pay schemes indirectly enhance employee effort and commitment by improving communication about company performance and by educating employees about the significance/importance of profitability. There are also those who suggest that such payment schemes increase employees' identification with the organisation.

**THEORY**    The research of Marchington *et al* (2001) demonstrated that employers in the 18 organisations they studied valued the voice of the employee in contributing to management decision-making because they believed it contributed to business performance. Employee voice (by communication systems, project team membership and joint consultation) was perceived to contribute to business performance via better employee contributions, improved management systems and productivity gains. This was seen to be the result of the number of ideas that emerged through employee feedback and joint problem-solving teams.

---

The outcomes of employee involvement and participation

The involvement of and the participation by employees in any organisation has the following outcomes:

- generate commitment of all employees to the success of the organisation
- enable the organisation better to meet the needs of its customers and adopt to changing market requirements
- help the organisation to improve performance and productivity, adopt new methods of working to match new technology
- improve the satisfaction employees get from their work
- provide all employees with the opportunity to influence and be involved in decisions which are likely to affect their interests.

---

**THEORY**    Ramsay (1996) hypothesises that the improved economic performance stemming from employee involvement participation is the result of employers' being able, on behalf of their employees, to change their attitude, to increase their business awareness, to improve their motivation, to enhance their influence/ ownership and to involve their trade unions (see box on Management objectives in introducing employee involvement practices, below). This is not an exhaustive list of variables but nevertheless demonstrates the need for careful definition of those variables. Vague and general definitions such as 'changed attitudes' or 'greater incentive' are inadequate for evaluating the causation between employee involvement and participation practices and their outcomes – for example, increased productivity. Ramsay points out that there is also potential conflict (or at least strain) between these variables. As he remarks:

> To exemplify this last point, a general sense of unity and belonging may sit poorly with the need to sharpen individual competition and incentive, and

it may be advisable to use distinct kinds of scheme to achieve each if both require enhancement ...

For Ramsay (1996), if the business's awareness of employees can be improved, they are more likely to be better and more accurately informed, the rumour 'grapevine' will be reduced, and there is a higher probability that they will have greater job interest, improved knowledge and understanding of the reasons for management decisions and greater support for (or resistance to) management action. The box below suggests that by using employee involvement schemes to increase employee influence/ownership, management are more likely to provide their employees with greater job control and, at the same time, via financial participation schemes, create increased employee ownership in the company and enhanced employee ties to company performance and profitability.

**THEORY**

---

**Management objectives in introducing employee involvement practices**

**Attitudes**
Improved morale
Increased loyalty and commitment
Enhanced sense of involvement
Increased support for management

**Business awareness**
Better, more accurately, informed
Greater interest
Better understanding of reason for management action
Support for/reduced resistance to management action

**Incentive/motivation**
*Passive*
Accept changes in working practices
Accept mobility across jobs
Accept new technology
Accept management authority

*Active*
Improve quality/reliability
Increase productivity/effort
Reduce costs
Enhance co-operation and team spirit

*Personal*
Greater job interest
Greater job satisfaction
Employee development

**Employee influence/ownership**
Increase job control
Employee suggestions
Increase employee ownership in the company
Increase employees' ties to the company performance and profitability

**Trade unions**
*Anti-union*
Keep unions out
Representative needs outside union channels
Win hearts and minds of employees from union

*With union*
Gain union co-operation
Draw on union advice
Restrain union demands

Source: Ramsay, H. in Towers, B. J. (ed.) (1996) *The Handbook of Human Resource Management*, 2nd edition.

Ramsay (1996) also predicts that if management can change employee incentive and motivation in a positive direction, it may have passive, active and personal impacts. The employees may benefit from greater job interest, enhanced job satisfaction and increased opportunities to develop themselves. Active advantages may arise for the organisation stemming from improved quality/reliability of the product or service, increased labour productivity and effort, reduced costs, and enhanced co-operation and team spirit. Amongst the probable passive advantages accruing to the organisation that Ramsay notes are a greater willingness on the part of employees to accept changes in working practices, flexibility across jobs, the implementation of new technology and enhanced front-/first-line management authority.

If management can achieve a positive change in employee attitudes, it is likely to improve not only the morale of employees but also their loyalty and commitment to the organisation. Their sense of belonging and involvement is also likely to be enhanced. In addition, there will be more probability that employees will give greater support to management's position. Employee involvement and participation practices are thus an important means by which management can bring about organisational cultural change. However, such cultural change can only be achieved in any organisation on an incremental basis – the full benefits to the organisation from cultural change arising from the successful implementation of involvement methods will not accrue immediately. The attitudes of every employee, or manager, will not change in a positive direction at the same moment in time. Some will take longer than others to develop a positive change in attitude towards the actions of management. Management must be aware of this phenomenon of incremental cultural change when reviewing and monitoring the impact of the introduction of employee involvement and participation practices on employee outcome.

### REFLECTIVE ACTIVITY

Outline the business case for introducing employee involvement practices to an organisation.

## EMPLOYEE INVOLVEMENT PRACTICES

### THE DIFFERENT PRACTICES

Marchington *et al* (2007) point out that EIP practices take many forms (the breadth). They can include:

- direct downward communication from managers to employees:
  - newsletters
  - email
  - intranet
  - noticeboards

- direct two-way communication between management and employees:
  - team briefings
  - workplace meetings
  - staff newsletters
  - cascading of information via the management team

- direct upward feedback from employees:
  - problem-solving groups
  - suggestion schemes
  - employee/staff attitude surveys

- direct financial participation
  - profit-related bonus schemes
  - deferred profit-sharing schemes
  - employee share ownership schemes

- indirect participation:
  - employee representative structures, eg Works Councils
  - joint consultative committees.

Ramsay (1996), however, divides employee involvement and participation initiatives into four broad types:

- communications and briefing systems – which include downward and upward communications systems

- task and work group involvement – which includes teamworking, quality circles and total quality management programmes

- financial participation – which embraces profit-sharing, profit-related pay and share ownership schemes

- representative participation.

In this chapter, the Ramsay classification is used.

## THE DEPTH OF EMPLOYEE INVOLVEMENT AND PARTICIPATION PRACTICES

Marchington *et al* (1992) also describe the depth of EIP practices. Indicators of depth include:

- the proportion of employees participating in problem-solving groups. This reflects management's commitment to involving as many people as possible in EIP and employee interest in participating

- the amount of time allocated to employee questions during team briefings. This reflects management's willingness to give employees opportunity to clarify their understanding of information received and to hear employee views. It can also indicate the degree of employee willingness to voice their opinions and their level of trust in management

- the frequency of team briefings. Greater frequency may indicate greater importance of the group. Less frequency may indicate waning interest in them or the onset of using them only for considering less urgent priorities

- the permanence of problem-solving groups. This indicates commitment to sustaining EIP over time and perceived utility to management

- a free and open method of selecting employee representatives for joint consultative committees (JCCs). This demonstrates management's willingness to let employees choose their own representative and is indicative of commitment to fairness and efforts to build trust

- the frequency of JCC meetings. Greater frequency may indicate greater importance of the JCC. Less frequency may indicate waning interest in it or the onset of using JCCs only for considering less urgent priorities.

### REFLECTIVE ACTIVITY

What employee involvement and participation practices operate in your organisation (or one with which you are familiar)? How, and why, have the various practices been introduced?

Has the distribution of the employee involvement practices changed over time? If it has, why has it? If it hasn't, why hasn't it?

## COMMUNICATIONS AND BRIEFING SYSTEMS

### COMMUNICATION SYSTEMS

Employee communications involves the provision and exchange of information and instructions which enable an organisation to function effectively and its employees to be properly informed about developments. It covers the information to be provided, the channels (both upwards and downwards) along which it passes, and the way it is relayed. Communication is concerned with the interchange of information and ideas within an organisation.

Whatever the size of an organisation and regardless of whether it is unionised or non-unionised, employees only perform at their best if they know their duties, obligations and rights and have an opportunity of making their views known to management on issues that affect them. With the trend towards flatter management structures and the devolution of responsibilities to individuals, it is increasingly important that individual employees not only have an understanding of what they are required to do and why they need to do it but also have the opportunity to influence what happens to them at work. Marchington *et al* (2001) have shown that companies rate the views of their employees as a critical business issue and are establishing mechanisms for listening to their employees – not because they are being forced to do so but because it seems essential if they are to meet business objectives. These mechanisms engender a two-way dialogue which gives employees the opportunity to influence what happens at work.

Good communication and consultation are central to the management process. All managers have to exchange information with other managers, which necessitates lateral or inter-departmental communications. Failure to recognise this need is likely to result in inconsistency of approach or application. The ACAS advisory booklet on *Employee Communications and Consultation* lists the advantages of good employee communications as:

- improved organisational performance – time spent communicating at the outset of a new project or development can minimise subsequent rumour and misunderstanding

- improved management performance and decision-making – allowing employees to express their views can help managers arrive at sound decisions that are more likely to be accepted by the employees as a whole

- improved employee performance and commitment – employees will perform better if they are given regular, accurate information about their jobs, such as updated technical instructions, targets, deadlines and feedback. Their commitment is also likely to be enhanced if they know what the organisation is trying to achieve and how they as individuals can influence decisions

- greater trust – discussing issues of common interest and allowing employees an opportunity of expressing their views can engender improved management–employee relations

- increased job satisfaction – employees are more likely to be motivated if they have a good understanding of their job and how it fits into the organisation as a whole, and are actively encouraged to express their views and ideas.

## EMPLOYEE COMMUNICATIONS STRATEGY

When devising an employee communications strategy, the following questions must be addressed:

- Why should the company communicate?
- What is to be communicated?
- Who are the audience(s)?

- How is communication to be handled?
- Who is responsible?
- How will success be measured?

As we have seen, a variety of communication methods (spoken and written, direct and indirect) are available for use by management. The mix of methods selected will be determined by the size and structure of the organisation. Two main methods of communication can be distinguished. First, there are face-to-face methods that are both direct and swift and they enable discussion, questioning and feedback to take place. However, it is often advantageous to supplement these methods with written materials, especially if the information being conveyed is detailed or complex. The main formal face-to-face methods of communications are:

- group meetings – meetings between managers and the employees for whom they are responsible

- cascade networks – a well-defined procedure for passing information quickly, used mainly in large or disparately widespread organisations

- large-scale meetings – meetings that involve all employees in an organisation or at an establishment, with presentations by a director or senior managers; these are a good channel for presenting the organisation's performance or long-term objectives

- inter-departmental briefings – meetings between managers in different departments that encourage a unified approach and reduce the scope for inconsistent decision-making, particularly in larger organisations.

Second, there are written methods. These are most effective where the need for the information is important or permanent, the topic requires detailed explanation, the audience is widespread or large, and there is a need for a permanent record of it. The chief methods of written communications include company handbooks, employee information notes, house journals and newsletters, departmental bulletins, notices and individual letters to employees. Electronic mail is useful for communicating with employees in scattered or isolated locations, and audio-visual aids are particularly useful for explaining technical developments or financial performance.

Communications strategies, policies and techniques need senior management support and they require discipline to follow them through. Industry and commerce are littered with communications schemes that have been introduced with the best of intentions before other matters became priorities and a briefing session or a newsletter was missed. The outcome is the development of cynicism amongst employees. It is also true that strategies, policies and tools tend not to be effective without the support and interest of staff. Think of it this way:

> If I am not a big enthusiast, preferring to laze around the house at weekends, the existence of a toolbox in the house is unlikely to persuade me to put in a couple of shelves. However, if I am very enthusiastic about DIY and very keen to put up a couple of shelves, the fact that I have no

toolbox will not deter me. I will simply borrow or buy a toolbox. It is my enthusiasm that is the driver, not the toolbox ...

## MONITORING

It cannot be taken for granted that communications systems are operating effectively, nor can it be assumed that because information is sent it is also received. The communications policy and its associated procedures need regular monitoring and review to ensure that practice matches policy, the desired benefits are accruing, the information is accepted, received and understood, and the management communicators know their roles. Monitoring is largely dependent on feedback from employees through both formal and informal channels, although other indicators include the quality of decision-making by management, the involvement of senior management and the extent of employee co-operation. In monitoring and reviewing an organisation's communication policy, the criteria for assessing its effectiveness are related to the outputs from the operation of the policy. For example, has employee morale improved? Has productivity increased? Is there a greater willingness to accept change on the part of employees and managers? Do the employees have an improved understanding of the company and business generally? Review and monitoring should take place on a regular periodic basis – for example, quarterly or annually – depending on the size of the organisation.

### REFLECTIVE ACTIVITY

Explain the criteria you would use to assess whether an organisation's communications strategy is operating effectively for management's interests.

## BRIEFING GROUPS

The dangers of the use of such groups, from a management perspective, are that as the information cascades down, it becomes watered down, hedged around with rumour, out of date, and imprecise. Many communications policies are less effective than they might be because a lot of information passed down from the top to the bottom of the organisation concentrates on the wider perspective, with the result that the local receivers of the information do not take note of it because it relates to issues which to them are remote and marginal to their interests and concerns.

Of all the communication methods in use, team briefing is perhaps the most systematic in the provision of top–down information. Information cascades down through various management tiers, being conveyed by each immediate supervisor or team leader to a small group of employees, the optimum number being between four and 20. In this way employee queries are answered. This takes place throughout all levels in the organisation, the information eventually being conveyed by supervisors and/or team leaders to shopfloor employees.

On each occasion the information received is supplemented by 'local' news of more immediate relevance to those being briefed. Meetings tend to be short but designed to help develop the 'togetherness' of a workgroup, especially where different grades of employees are involved in the team.

Each manager is a member of a briefing group and is also responsible for briefing a team. The system is designed to ensure that all employees from the managing director to the shop floor are fully informed of matters affecting their work. Leaders of each briefing session prepare their own brief, consisting of information that is relevant and task-related to the employees in the group. The brief is then supplemented with information passed down from higher levels of management. Any employee questions raised that cannot be answered at once are answered in written form within a few days. Briefers from senior management levels are usually encouraged to sit in at briefings being given by more junior managers, while line managers are encouraged to be available to brief the shopfloor employees. The employment relations professional will explain management's view to the employees in a regular and open way, using examples appropriate to each workgroup. Although team briefing is not a consultative process and is basically one-way, question-and-answer sessions can take place to clarify understanding. Feedback from employees is very important.

There are, however, practical problems to be borne in mind in introducing team briefing. First, if the organisation operates on a continuous shift-working basis, is it technically feasible for team briefings to take place, since the employees are working all the time except for their rest breaks? Second, management has to be confident that it can sustain a flow of relevant and detailed information. Third, if the organisation recognises unions, the management cannot act in such a manner that a union believes management is attempting to undermine its influence. Team briefing is highly unlikely to succeed if the relations between management and the representatives of its employees are distrustful.

## EMPLOYEE ATTITUDE SURVEYS

As we have already noted, these surveys are an important upward channel of communication from the employees to management. Such surveys are questionnaire surveys of staff on a one-off or regular (say, annual) basis designed to discover their levels of satisfaction/dissatisfaction with particular aspects of work. The *Workplace Employee Relations Survey* provides evidence of a steady rise in the use, by employers, of employee attitude surveys. In 2004 managers in 42% of workplaces said, as we have noted above, that they, or a third party, had conducted a formal survey of their employees' views or opinions during the previous two years. In most cases (80%), the results of the survey had been fed back to employees in written form.

Management normally uses an employee attitude survey to obtain specific data on employee perceptions of fairness, pay systems, training opportunities and employee awareness of an organisation's business strategy and long-term goals. Employee attitude surveys can:

- provide managers with early warning of issues of concern before they lead to major employment relations difficulties
- help managers make internal comparisons of employee morale and behaviour across a number of departments and sites
- provide employee views on specific HRM/personnel policies such as the operation of the disciplinary and grievance procedures
- provide data that can be used in problem-solving, planning and decision-making.

Many organisations use the information obtained from employee attitude surveys to benchmark employee morale and satisfaction against other organisations. Such information is, however, only likely to be helpful if it is used in conjunction with other information obtained in a different way, and not used in isolation.

Two other important forms of upward communications from employees to management are suggestion schemes and project teams. The former are a formal process established to enable employees to communicate their ideas to management on how working methods, etc, might be improved. Employees are rewarded if their ideas are deemed acceptable for implementation. Such schemes can be electronic or paper-based. In project teams, groups of individual employees are brought together on a regular basis (or an *ad hoc* basis) to consider issues relating to the organisation of work but also wider questions about the vision and mission of the site. They also examine manufacture excellence or a review of operation.

## TASK AND WORK GROUP INVOLVEMENT

The objective of these employee involvement and participation practices is to tap into employees' knowledge of their jobs, either at the individual level or through the mechanism of small groups. These practices are designed to increase the stock of ideas within the organisation, to encourage co-operative relations at work and to justify change. Task-based involvement encourages employees to extend the range and type of tasks they undertake at work. It is probably the most innovative method of employee involvement in that it focuses on the whole job rather than concentrating on a relatively small part of an employee's time at work. Such employee involvement and participation practices include job redesign, job enrichment, teamworking and job enlargement. Job enrichment involves the introduction of more elements of responsibility into the work tasks. Job enlargement centres on increasing the number and diversity of tasks carried out by an individual employee, thereby increasing his or her work experience and skill.

Teamworking is seen by its advocates as a vehicle for greater task flexibility and co-operation as well as for extending the desire for quality improvement. Geary (1994) remarked that:

THEORY

> In its most advanced form teamworking refers to the granting of autonomy to workers by management to design and prepare work schedules, to

monitor and control their own work tasks and methods, to be more or less self-managing. There can be considerable flexibility between different skills categories, such that skilled employees do unskilled tasks when required and formerly unskilled employees receive additional training to be able to undertake the more skilled tasks. At the other end of the spectrum, management may merely wish employees of comparable skill to rotate between different tasks on a production line or the integration of maintenance personnel to service a particular group of machines. It may not result in production workers undertaking tasks which were formerly the preserve of craft people or vice versa. Thus flexibility may be confined within comparable skills groupings. In between, there is likely to be a diversity of practice.

The two most advanced forms of teamworking are semi-autonomous groups and fully autonomous groups. In the latter group, the team members work with one another, have total responsibility for the specific product or service, jointly decide how the work is to be done, and appoint their own team leader. Semi-autonomous groups are characterised by members working with one another, having responsibility for a specific product or service and jointly deciding how the work is to be done. There are teams in which members only work with one another and have no responsibility for products or services, for deciding how tasks would be done or for selecting their team leader. This is in addition to teams in which members work with one another and have responsibility for a specific product or service.

Team size is usually seven to ten, although some teams are much larger. Task flexibility and job rotation can, however, be limited, partly by the sheer range of tasks and partly by the nature of the skills involved. Organisations that operate teamworking arrangements see major training programmes as a necessary accompaniment. Teamworking provides management with the opportunity to remove and/or amend the role of the supervisor and to appoint team leaders. However, research by Gapper (1990) has indicated that management time saved in traditional supervision and control may be more than offset by the need to give support to individuals and groups.

## REFLECTIVE ACTIVITY

What is the extent of teamworking in your organisation? Why is it that?

### QUALITY CIRCLES

A quality circle aims to identify work-related problems that are causing low quality of service or productivity in a section of the workplace, and to recommend solutions to those problems. It provides opportunities for employees to meet on a regular basis (eg once a month, fortnightly) for an hour or so to suggest ways of improving productivity and quality and reducing costs. A quality circle typically involves a small group of employees (usually six to eight) in discussions under the guidance of their supervisor. The members select the issues or problem they wish to address, collect the necessary information and make suggestions to management on ways of overcoming the problem.

In some cases the group is itself given authority to put its proposed solutions into effect, but more often it presents formal recommendations for action, which management then consider whether or not to implement. Quality circles encourage employees to identify not only with the quality of their own work but also with the management objectives of better quality and increased efficiency throughout the organisation. Members of a quality circle are not usually employee representatives but are members of the circle by virtue of their knowledge of the tasks involved in their jobs. They are under no obligation to report back to those of their colleagues who are not members of the circle.

If quality circles are to be effective, a strong commitment from management is necessary. Management do not supply members to a quality circle but allow time and money for its members to meet, and provide the members with basic training in problem-solving and presentational skills. A professional management always treats all recommendations from a circle with an open mind, and if it rejects a proposal will explain the reasons for that decision to the circle. If the organisation recognises trade unions, it is advisable to consult the workplace representatives on the establishment of quality circles and to encourage their support for a device which, if operated properly, contributes to constructive employment relations.

After a dramatic increase in their number – such that by the mid-1980s more than 400 such circles were known to be in existence – the popularity of quality circles declined rapidly. Quality circles fail either at their introduction or after a short period of operation mainly because of a lack of top management commitment, because of the absence of an effective facilitator to promote and sustain the programme, because of management reluctance to bear the costs of operating circles in terms of time (including training time for participants, when employees are inevitably off the job) and/or because of a lack of any follow-up action by management on suggestions put forward by the circles.

## TOTAL QUALITY MANAGEMENT (TQM)

THEORY

Total quality management programmes derive from a belief that competitive advantage comes from high and reliable quality, achieved through the associated welding of more stable and mutual relationships between suppliers and customers. The total quality ethic is a philosophy of business management, the aim of which is to ensure complete customer satisfaction at every stage of production or service provision. Although TQM was initially driven by the demands of external customers, the concept was evolved into a more wide-ranging principle to encompass internal operations. TQM programmes are designed to ensure that each level and aspect of the organisation is involved in continuously improving the effectiveness and quality of the work to meet the requirements of both internal and external customers.

Whereas quality issues were traditionally assigned to specific departments, TQM requires that the quality of products and services be the concern of every employee. Quality management offers service management an effective way of organising and increasing employees' responsibility while meeting the interests of employees at every level, offering them an opportunity to become more involved in the decision-making process. The Prudential Assurance Company, for example, claimed in the mid-1990s that TQM had produced many benefits for them, including a reduction of 45% in the average time in dealing with a life assurance claim.

Others (for example, Geary, 1994) have pointed out that TQM places considerable emphasis on enlarging employees' responsibilities, reorganising work and increasing employee involvement in problem-solving activities, and that this search for continuous improvement is a central thrust. He further notes that:

> The manufacture of quality products, the provision of a quality service and the quest for continuous improvement is the responsibility of all employees, managed and manager alike, and all functions. TQM requires quality to be built in to the product and not inspected by a separate quality department. Where employees are not in direct contact with the organisation's customers, they are encouraged to see their colleagues at successive stages of the production process as internal customers. Thus a central feature of TQM is the internalisation of the rigours of the marketplace within the enterprise.

A second feature of TQM follows on from the first. Because each employee and department is an internal customer to the other, problem-solving necessitates the formation of organisational structures designed to facilitate inter-department and inter-functional co-operation. A consequence of this is that problems are best solved by those people to whom they are most immediate. Employees are to be encouraged and given the resources to solve problems for themselves. Employees, it is contended, will embrace such job enlargement and undertake activities conducive to an improvement in the organisation's efficiency.

Ramsay (1996) argues that total quality management subsumes quality circles or teamwork arrangements into a more integrated approach and concentrates on stressing change throughout the entire organisational system. It is essentially a top–down management-driven process. If total quality management is to succeed, again top management commitment is essential. Departments have to be persuaded that resistance to integration is self-defeating and the employees must have it clearly demonstrated to them that total quality management is not a cover for job rationalisation and redundancies. In short, the employees require evidence that there is a stake for them in the total quality management world – that is, that TQM is superior to their present world.

## FINANCIAL PARTICIPATION

Offering employees a direct stake in the ownership and prosperity of the business for which they work is one of the most direct and tangible forms of employee involvement and participation. By giving employees the chance to participate in financial success, employees can acquire and develop a greater sense of identity with the business and an appreciation of the business needs. Employers also benefit. It is argued that a financial stake gives employees increased enthusiasm for the success of the organisation and often for a voice in its operation. In its most developed form, employee share ownership means that employees become significant shareholders in the business, or even their own employer.

Financial employee involvement and participation schemes link specific elements of pay and reward to the performance of the unit or the enterprise as a whole. They provide an opportunity for employees to share in the financial success of their employing organisation. The main forms of financial participation are:

- deferred profit-sharing schemes, by which profits are put in a trust fund to acquire shares in the company for employees
- profit-related pay
- employee share ownership plans.

### PROFIT-SHARING

These schemes aim to increase employee motivation and commitment by giving employees an interest in the overall performance of the enterprise. In this way management hopes to raise employee awareness of the importance of profit to their organisation and to encourage teamworking by demonstrating that rewards accrue from co-operative effort even more than from individual effort. Profit-sharing schemes ensure that employees benefit from an organisation that makes profits.

However, there are practical problems that must be addressed if profit-sharing schemes are to have the desired effect. A scheme has to contain clearly identifiable links between effort and reward. Individuals must not feel that no matter how hard they work in any year, that effort is not reflected in their share of the company's profits. There is also the issue of whether there is a clearly understood formula for the sharing of any profits so that employees can calculate their share. Profits cannot be assessed quickly enough to secure early movements in pay in response to rapidly changing market conditions. Due account has to be taken of employees or there is a risk of inter-group dissatisfaction in that some employees might believe other groups have received the same profit-share payment but have made less effort.

### PROFIT-RELATED PAY

Profit-related pay is a mechanism through which employers can reward employees for their contribution to the business. It works by linking a proportion of employees' pay to the profits of the business for which they work. Employees are encouraged in this way to strive for commercial success. Employers who have introduced such schemes argue that as well as helping to create a more motivated and committed workforce, profit-related pay provides greater flexibility in the negotiation of pay settlements.

## SHARE OWNERSHIP

Share ownership takes financial involvement a step further by giving employees a stake in the ownership of the enterprise. It grants them shareholder rights to participate in decisions confined to shareholders who vote at the Annual General Meeting. Employee share ownership schemes seek to give individual employees a long-term commitment to the organisation and not just to a short-term financial gain from a sharing of profit. Such schemes are usually linked to profit but the employees' portion is distributed in the form of shares, either directly to each individual or indirectly into a trust which holds the shares on behalf of all employees. Distributing shares to employees involves them in a tax liability that has restricted the development of employee share ownership schemes. One way to avoid this tax liability is an employee share ownership plan (known as an ESOP). Such plans were given a boost when the UK Government in the late 1980s provided important tax concessions for investment in such schemes.

In employee share ownership plans the company shares are initially bought, using borrowed money, by a trust representing the employees. They may not be required to put down a cash stake. The transfer of a portion of the company profits to the trust over subsequent years, as laid down in the initial agreement, enables the trust to pay off the loan and to allocate shares to individual employees.

Employee share ownership plans are clearly a means of promoting employee involvement in ownership. They give individual employees democratic control over significant holdings of company shares. They also have limitations. Employees may view the shares as simply a source of income and so lose the thread of the 'shared ownership' concept. Financial participation shares money, and on its own is unlikely to give rise to a greater commitment on the part of the individual employee to the interests of the organisation.

## REFLECTIVE ACTIVITY

Do you have any financial participation schemes in your organisation? If you do, why were those particular schemes chosen? To what extent and why are they effective? If your organisation does not have any financial participation schemes, why doesn't it?

## REPRESENTATIVE PARTICIPATION

The main form of representative participation is joint consultation, which is a process by which management and employees or their representatives jointly examine and discuss issues of mutual concern. It involves seeking acceptable solutions to problems through a genuine exchange of views and information. Consultation does not remove the right of management to manage – management must still make the final decision – but it does impose an obligation that the views of employees will be sought and considered before that final decision is taken. Employee communication is concerned with the interchange of information and ideas within an organisation. Consultation goes beyond this and involves management actively seeking and then taking account of the views of employees before making a decision. It affects the process through which decisions are made in so far as it commits management first to the disclosure of information at an early stage in the decision-making process, and second to take into account the collective views of the employees.

Consultation does not mean that employees' views always have to be acted upon – there may be good practical or financial reasons for not doing so. However, whenever employees' views are rejected, the reasons for rejection should be explained carefully. Equally, where the views and ideas of employees help to improve a decision, due credit and recognition should be given. Making a practice of consulting on issues upon which management has already made a decision is unproductive and engenders suspicion and mistrust about the process among employees.

Consultation requires a free exchange of ideas and views affecting the interests of employees. Almost any subject is therefore appropriate for discussion. However, both management and employees may wish to place some limits on the range of subjects open to consultation – because of trade confidences, perhaps, or because they are considered more appropriate for a negotiation forum – but whatever issues are agreed upon as being appropriate for discussion, it is important that they are relevant to the group of employees discussing them. If consultation arrangements are to be effective, discussing trivialities is to be avoided. This is not to say that minor issues may be ignored.

Although the subject matters of consultation are a matter for agreement between employer and employees, there are a number of laws and regulations that specifically require an employer to consult with recognised trade unions and other employee representatives. These include:

- The Health and Safety at Work Act (1974) places a duty on employers to consult with safety representatives appointed by an independent recognised trade union.

- The Transfer of Undertakings (Protection of Employment) Regulations (1981) provide for trade unions to be consulted where there is a transfer of a business to which the Regulations apply. This consultation must take place with a view to reaching agreement on the measures taken.

- The Trade Union and Labour Relations (Consolidation) Act (1992) requires employers to consult with trade unions when redundancies are proposed. Such consultation must be undertaken by the employer with a view to reaching agreement and must be about any possibilities of avoiding the dismissals, reducing the numbers to be dismissed, and mitigating the consequences of any redundancies.

- The Social Security Pensions Act (1975) requires employers to consult with trade unions on certain matters in relation to the contracting-out of the state scheme by an occupational pension scheme.

- The Transnational Information and Consultation of Employees Regulations (2000) permit employee representatives the right to meet central management at least once a year for information and consultation about the progress and prospects of the company on a pan-European basis. These Regulations provide for European Union-wide information and consultation machinery to be established in all organisations with more than 1,000 employees in European Union states and employing more than 150 people in each of two or more of these. A Works Council (or an alternative body) must be negotiated between corporate representatives and those of employees elected from the various EU countries in which the company has productive capacity or service provision.

- The Information and Consultation Regulations (2004) established a general framework setting out minimum requirements for the right to information and consultation of employees employed in organisations employing 50 employees. Employees have a right to be informed about a company's economic situation and to be informed and consulted on employment prospects and decisions likely to lead to substantial change in how work is organised and on contractual relations. Information and consultation must take place at the relevant level of management. Employers and employees can agree different procedures from those set out in the Regulations via existing agreements on information and consultation. Employers may withhold information if its disclosure would seriously harm the business. Companies employing 150 or more employees had to comply with the Regulations by March 2005, those employing 100 or more by March 2007 and those with 50 or more by March 2008. The implications of these Regulations for organisations are considered below.

## JOINT CONSULTATIVE COMMITTEES

Joint consultative committees (JCCs) have long been used as a means of employee consultation. They are composed of managers and employee representatives who come together on a regular basis to discuss issues of mutual concern. They usually have a formal constitution which governs their operations. The number of members on a JCC depends on the size of the organisation. Management in organisations that operate over a number of different establishments sometimes prefer to consult with employees on a multi-site basis rather than have a consultative committee for each establishment. These are referred to as 'higher-level committees'. The 2004 *Workplace Employment Relations Survey* reported that 25% of workplaces had a multi-issue consultative committee that operated at a level higher than the establishment – for instance, at regional, divisional or head office level. The equivalent figure in 1998 was 27%.

However, as a general rule the size of the committee should be as small as possible still to be consistent with ensuring that all significant employee groups are represented. It is necessary, in order to demonstrate management's commitment to consultation, that the management representatives on the committee include senior managers with authority and standing in the organisation and who attend its meetings regularly.

Every meeting of the JCC should have as its focus a well-prepared agenda and all members should be given an opportunity of contributing to that agenda before it is circulated. The agenda is normally sent out in advance of the meeting so that representatives have a chance of consulting with their constituents prior to the committee meeting. Well-run JCCs are chaired effectively. It is important that employee representatives know exactly how much time they will be allowed away from their normal work to undertake their duties as a committee member and the facilities to which they are entitled. Employee representatives should not lose pay as a result of attending committee meetings. If joint consultation is to be effective, the deliberations of the committee must be reported back to employees as soon as possible. This can be done via briefing groups, news-sheets, noticeboards and the circulation of committee minutes.

In some organisations, institutions established to inform and consult with employers have titles other than 'joint consultative committee'. Such alternative titles include 'Works Council' and 'employee representative council'. In Marks & Spencer, consultation arrangements are referred to as 'business involvement groups'. There is such a group in each store and area of business, and the number of representatives on the group reflects the size of the business unit/area/store. Each group is made up of representatives elected by employees and has a clear remit and support across the business. In addition, there are regional business involvement groups made up of the chairpersons for each local group. They meet periodically to share and debate issues and ideas that have a wider impact on the business. Marks & Spencer sees its system of business involvement groups as an important part of the communication and involvement process, a means for ensuring that employees are up to date with key issues and events, an opportunity for employees to contribute ideas that might improve business performance and a forum to discuss issues that impact on the employees' working lives. In short, the business involvement group system enables employees to become involved in the way Marks & Spencer develops its business in the future.

## REFLECTIVE ACTIVITY

Do JCCs exist in your organisation? If so, what forms do they take, and are they successful? How could they be improved? If there are no JCCs, what mechanisms are in place to consult with the workforce? Would a JCC be useful? *Why* would it – or why *wouldn't* it?

## THE EXTENT OF EMPLOYEE INVOLVEMENT PRACTICES

The main sources of information about the extent of employee involvement and participation in employee involvement practices are the Workplace Industrial Relations Survey series which relate to 1980, 1984, 1990, 1998 and 2004.

### The Workplace Industrial Relations Survey series

In recent years, direct information and consultation methods (for example, team briefings and workplace meetings) have been growing in popularity whereas indirect methods (for example, joint consultative committees) have been declining. In terms of the breadth of information and consultation methods there was little change in the type of information relayed by managers to employees between 1998 and 2004. Over half of workplaces in 2004 provided information on investment plans, on the financial position of the workplace and on organisational and staff plans in a similar proportion to that provided in 1998.

Joint consultative committees were present in 14% of workplaces in 2004. Their incidence varied markedly according to the size of the workplace. JCCs were rarely present in workplaces with fewer than 25 employees, where managers may find it easier to consult directly with staff, but they were a normal feature of establishments with 200 or more employees. Committees were also more common in the public sector than among private sector workplaces. Within the private sector, the two industry sectors with above-average incidence of consultative committees were manufacturing (19%) and transport and communications (18%). There had been a decline in the incidence of consultative committees at workplace level since 1998, when one-fifth of establishments had such agreements for consulting their staff. The decline was primarily evidenced amongst workplaces with fewer than 100 employees, in which the proportion of workplaces with on-site committees fell from 17% in 1998 to 10% in 2004. Around 62% of workplaces were not covered by a joint consultative committee in 2004, compared with 53% in 1998.

In 2004 three-quarters of committees had met at least four times in the previous 12 months (eg quarterly). A further 21% had met twice or three times, while the remaining 4% had met only once in the year or not at all. In 1998 82% of committees had met on at least four occasions, 14% twice or three times, and 4% met only once or not at all. In 2004 most committees addressed financial issues, employment issues, work organisation and future plans. However, financial issues *in relation to* future plans were less commonly discussed than other issues, more than likely reflecting a reluctance on the part of managers to share such financial information with employee representatives on consultative committees. Only three-fifths of managers said they shared commercially sensitive information with representatives on the committee. Pay issues were discussed by about 50% of all committees in 1998, rising to 66% in 2004, but health and safety issues were less commonly dealt with in 2004 (80%) compared with 1998 (88%). Forty-three per cent of managers in 2004 said that their usual approach was to look to the committee to provide solutions to problems, while a further 45% said that they usually sought feedback from the committee on a range of options put forward by management. The remaining 11% said that they usually sought feedback on preferred options. Overall, 25% of managers considered that the consultative committee was 'very influential' in respect of managers' decisions affecting the workforce at the establishment, 62% considered it 'fairly influential', and 12% viewed it as 'not very influential'. The proportion of managers viewing the consultative committee at their workplace as 'very influential' had decreased markedly since 1998, when 41% gave this response. In 66% of the committees in 2004 the representatives were elected by the employees, whereas in 10% of them representatives were selected by managers. Overall, 11% of committees were composed wholly of union representatives, 67% composed wholly of non-union representatives and 22% were 'mixed constituency' committees.

One of the most common forms of direct communication between managers and employees are face-to-face meetings between senior management and the whole workforce. In 2004, such meetings took place in 79% of all workplaces. The incidence of workforce meetings was slightly higher in the public sector than among private sector workplaces (see Table 8.1). In 25% of cases, workforce meetings took place at least once a month, and in 26% they happened at least once every three months. The proportion of time made available in workplace meetings for employers to ask questions of senior managers or offer their views was lower in large workplaces. On average, 87% of meetings made at least 16% of the meeting time available for employees' questions on views, and 59% afforded

Table 8.1 Direct employer employee communication, by sector of ownership, 2004

| Form of communication | Percentage | | |
|---|---|---|---|
| | Private sector | Public sector | All workplaces |
| *Face-to-face meetings* | | | |
| Meetings between senior managers and the whole workforce | 77 | 89 | 79 |
| Team briefings | 68 | 81 | 71 |
| Any face-to-face meetings | 90 | 97 | 91 |
| *Written two-way communication* | | | |
| Employee surveys | 37 | 66 | 42 |
| Email | 36 | 48 | 38 |
| Suggestion schemes | 30 | 30 | 30 |
| Any written two-way communication | 62 | 84 | 66 |
| *Downward communication* | | | |
| Noticeboards | 72 | 86 | 74 |
| Systematic use of management chain | 60 | 81 | 64 |
| Newsletters | 41 | 63 | 45 |
| Intranet | 31 | 48 | 34 |
| Any downward communication | 80 | 97 | 83 |

Source: 2004 *Workplace Employment Relations Survey*

at least a quarter of the time. A variety of issues were discussed at workforce meetings, the most popular being future plans and matters that were directly or indirectly related to production or the service delivered.

Team briefings took place in 71% of workplaces. Their incidence was positively related to the size of the workplace – they took place in 59% of workplaces with fewer than 25 employees but in 82% of workplaces with 25–49 employees. Team briefings tended to take place on a frequent basis. In almost half of all instances they took place at least once a week, and in a further third took place at least once a month. They also commonly included time for employees to ask questions or offer views (see Table 8.2).

**Table 8.2 Issues discussed at team briefings, 2004**

|  | Percentage of workplaces |
|---|---|
| Production issues | 82 |
| Future plans | 72 |
| Work organisation | 71 |
| Training | 64 |
| Health and safety | 64 |
| Financial issues | 50 |
| Employment issues | 43 |
| Leave and flexible working | 39 |
| Welfare services and facilities | 34 |
| Pay issues | 31 |
| Government regulations | 29 |
| Equal opportunities | 19 |

A number of further arrangements in 2004 provided the opportunity for upward communication from employees to managers in written form. These included the use of email, suggestion schemes and employee surveys. Managers in just over two-fifths of workplaces said that they or a third party had conducted a formal survey of their employees' views or opinions during the previous two years. Employee attitude surveys were more likely to have taken place in larger workplaces than smaller ones, and were more likely to have been conducted in workplaces belonging to large organisations. They were almost twice as common in the public sector as in the private sector. Thiry-eight per cent of workplaces made regular use of email to communicate or consult with employees. Finally, just under one-third made use of suggestion schemes – a proportion that had not changed since 1998. Suggestion schemes were slightly more common in workplaces that used problem-solving groups as a means of identifying improvements to production processes or service delivery.

The 2004 *Workplace Employment Relations Survey* asked questions about the use of noticeboards, newsletters, intranets and the systematic use of the management chain. Each of the four practices was common in larger workplaces and in the public sector. Overall, however, noticeboards were the most common of the four arrangements, being used in 74% of workplaces. Least common was the posting of information on a company intranet. There were increases since 1998 in the use of the management chain and newsletters. In both cases, the increase was proportionately larger in the private sector than in the public sector. In summary, two-thirds of all workplaces provided regular meetings with a substantive opportunity for employee feedback (see Table 8.3). These workplaces employed 67% of all employees. A further 30% of workplaces did not provide meetings of this type but did provide meetings on a regular basis but with less opportunity for feedback or with an opportunity instead of upward communication in writing. A further 4% of workplaces had formal arrangements for downward communications, whereas only 2% of the workplaces had a formal arrangement for direct communication with employees.

**Table 8.3 Summary of direct communication arrangements, 2004**

| | Percentage of workplaces | | | Percentage of employees | | |
|---|---|---|---|---|---|---|
| Form of communication | Public sector | Private sector | All workplaces | Public sector | Private sector | All workplaces |
| Regular meetings with feedback | 59 | 81 | 63 | 64 | 77 | 67 |
| Other meetings or written two-way communication | 33 | 17 | 30 | 32 | 22 | 30 |
| Downward communication only | 5 | 1 | 4 | 3 | 1 | 2 |
| No formal arrangements | 3 | 0 | 2 | 1 | 0 | 1 |

Source: 2004 *Workplace Employment Relations Survey*

The proportion of all workplaces with any form of employee representation fell from almost three-fifths to around a half between 1998 and 2004. Arrangements for direct communication, on the other hand, were widespread and where it was possible to chart changes since 1998 seemed to have generally become more prevalent over the period. Employee representatives – particularly union representatives – continue to play a valued role in assisting employees to obtain pay increases, raise grievances and respond to disciplinary charges.

## THE IMPACT OF EIP MECHANISMS

Based on an analysis of the *Workplace Employment Relations Survey,* Marchington *et al* (2007) found a strong positive link between the 'breadth' and 'depth' of some information and consultation practices and employee commitment. Employee ratings of the helpfulness of some consultation and communication methods were positively linked to job satisfaction and commitment. Employee ratings of managers' effectiveness in consulting employees and employees' satisfaction with their involvement in decision-making were also positively linked with job satisfaction and commitment, suggesting that the way in which information and consultation are implemented is just as important as the type of practice used.

A good deal of research has been done to investigate the links between the use of information and consultation methods and organisational performance. Much less is known about the links between them and broader employee outcomes such as organisational commitment and job satisfaction. These may be important as part of the links in a chain by which information and consultation methods can ultimately influence organisational performance. Marchington *et al* (2007) found that there were no links between any single information and consultation method and employee commitment and job satisfaction in workplaces with 25 or more employees in 2007. However, significant and positive links were found between the 'breadth' of information and consultation (the number of different practices used together in a workplace) and the 'depth' of direct communication methods and employee commitment. Using a range of complementary EIP practices may be important because a single EIP practice is likely to have less impact on its own than a number of practices operating together. An individual EIP practice can be more easily dismissed as 'bolted on' or out of line with other HR practices and not be taken seriously by workers. In contrast, a multiplicity of EIP mechanisms may complement each other and provide opportunities for employees to be involved at work in different ways. For example, information received by employees from a team briefing may be useful when they are working in problem-solving groups.

No links were found between the breadth of information and consultation methods and the depth of direct communication methods and job satisfaction. A negative association was found between the depth of indirect communication methods and job satisfaction. Employee perceptions of the helpfulness of most methods of keeping them informed about the workplace were positively linked to employee job satisfaction and commitment in workplaces with 25 or more employees. For workplaces with 10 to 24 employees, positive significant links were found between employee perceptions of the helpfulness of noticeboards and meetings and organisational commitment and job satisfaction. Very strong positive links were found between employee perceptions of managers' effectiveness in consulting employees, employees' satisfaction with their involvement in decision-making and job satisfaction and organisational commitment in both small and larger workplaces. The results of the research of Marchington *et al* (2007) suggest that the way in which information and consultation methods are implemented is just as important as the type of practice used. There are two reasons why management style and approach matter. There is a continuing trend in increasing workplace coverage of direct EIP. This means that individual managers are being given increasing responsibility for the implementation of EIP practices. Second, the links between management effectiveness in consultation through either formal or informal EIP and employee outcomes are particularly noticeable. The cross-sectoral nature of Marchington's data means that a direct causation in the relationship cannot be proved – that is, whether or not effective management implementation of EIP leads to improved organisational commitment and job satisfaction or vice versa.

## THE INFORMATION AND CONSULTATION OF EMPLOYEES REGULATIONS

These Regulations give effect to the EU Directive establishing a general framework for informing and consulting employees in the European Union. They came into force on a sliding scale, depending on the number of employees in the organisation. From 23 March 2005 the Regulations applied to undertakings with at least 150 employees. From 23 March 2007 they applied to undertakings with at least 100 employees. From 23 March 2008 they related to undertakings with at least 50 employees. Undertakings employing fewer than 50 employees are exempt from the Regulations. An 'undertaking' means a legal entity such as an individually incorporated company, whereas an 'establishment' is a physical entity such as a factory, plant, office or retail outlet. The UK Government decided to apply the Directive to undertakings rather than establishments. When calculating the number of employees for the purposes of these thresholds, the number taken is the average number employed in each month over the previous 12 months. Part-time workers may be counted as half a person, although the employer is under no obligation to work on this basis.

### NEGOTIATED AGREEMENTS

#### Requests for information and consultation arrangements

The Regulations require that where employees request the establishment of information and consultation arrangements in their undertakings, the request must be made in writing by 10% of the employees in the undertaking, subject to a minimum of 15 and a maximum of 2,500 employees (see Figure 8.1). The Directive itself, however, gives no guidance on trigger mechanisms. The Regulations do allow two or more requests from different parts of the workforce to be combined. In addition, if the employees making the request wish to remain anonymous, they may submit the request via the Central Arbitration Committee or a qualified independent person. An employer has one month in which to challenge the validity of this request. Grounds for such a challenge can include:

- too few employees have made the request
- the request is not in writing
- the undertaking does not fall within the scope of the Regulations.

If there are any disputes about the validity of the employees' request, the final decision rests with the CAC.

#### Requests in the case of existing agreements

In a case where a valid request has been made by less than 40% of the workforce but an agreement providing for information and consultation already exists, the employer may, if he or she wishes, hold a ballot of the workforce to determine whether or not the workforce endorses the request. The ballot should be held as early as practicable but no earlier than 21 days after the request was made. If 40% of the employees endorse the employee request in the ballot, the employer

**Figure 8.1 Procedures for establishing information and consultation agreements**

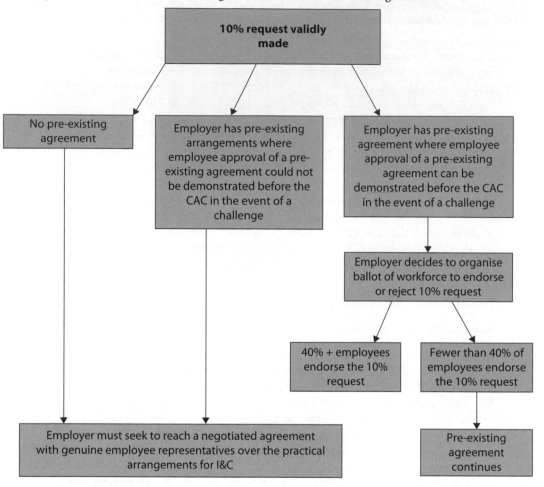

is obliged to negotiate a new agreement on information and consultation. If fewer than 40% of employees endorse the request, the employer is under no obligation to negotiate a new agreement. Complaints may be brought to the CAC concerning the fact that there is no valid pre-existing agreement in place or that the ballot requirements have not been met.

The Regulations also permit the employer to take the initiative to enter into negotiations for an information and consultation agreement without waiting for a request from employees. The negotiation process must start within one month of the employer's notifying the workforce of the intention to negotiate an agreement.

**The three-year moratorium**

There are a number of circumstances in which an employee request (or an employer notification of an intention to negotiate an agreement) is not valid. These include where there has already been a request that has resulted in a negotiated agreement, or where, in the case of existing agreements, a request was not endorsed by a workforce ballot. Here, subsequent requests would not be allowed for a period of three years, unless there are material changes to the organisation or to the structure of the undertaking. This moratorium is intended to avoid repeated requests being made by employees and to prevent the employers from unilaterally overturning agreed agreements.

### Negotiations

Where a valid request has been made or an employer has notified the workforce that it intends to start negotiations, the employer must take the necessary steps to trigger the process. This includes making arrangements for employees to appoint or elect negotiating representatives. All employees must be entitled to participate in appointing or electing representatives and must be represented by one of those appointed or elected. Negotiations are required to start within one month of the request/notification and may last for up to six months. This period can be extended without limit by agreement between the negotiating parties. ACAS and other organisations can help the parties in reaching agreements.

The Regulations also set out a number of requirements that negotiated agreements must meet. These are that they must:

- be in writing and dated
- cover all the employees of the undertaking
- set out the circumstances in which employees will be informed and consulted – this may be either directly or via information and consultation representatives
- be signed by or on behalf of the employer
- be signed either by all or by a majority of the negotiating representatives and approved in writing by at least 50% of the employees or by 50% of employees who vote in a ballot.

Where the parties do not reach an agreement within the six-month time-limit, or any extended period agreed by the parties, standard information and consultation provisions become applicable. The default requirements require the employer to inform/consult elected employee representatives on business developments, employment trends and changes in work organisation or contractual regulations, including redundancies and business transfers. They also require the employer to arrange for a secret ballot to elect one information and consultation representative for every 50 employees or part thereof up to a maximum of 25.

### Enforcement

Enforcement of agreements reached under these statutory procedures, or of the standard information and consultation provisions where they apply, is via complaints to the CAC and the Employment Appeals Tribunal. The maximum penalty that can be awarded against employers for non-compliance is £75,000. Employee representatives must not disclose information or documents designated by the employer as confidential. Employers may withhold information or documents if their disclosure could seriously harm or prejudice the undertaking.

**Voluntary agreements**

The Regulations accept that there is no single static model for information and consultation – no 'one size fits all'. The underlying principle of the Regulations is that UK experience in the area of information and consultation is built up through a wide variety of existing practices all of which should be accommodated. Essentially, individual organisations are encouraged to develop their own arrangements as tailored to their particular circumstances, by means of voluntary agreements. Accordingly, the general thrust of the Regulations is on voluntarily negotiated agreements. However, in the final analysis, if such negotiations fail, employers come under an obligation to inform and consult in accordance with a set of fall-back (default) provisions.

## REFLECTIVE ACTIVITY

What has been the impact of the Information and Consultation of Employees Regulations in your organisation? How do you account for what has happened?

### THE IMPACT OF THE REGULATIONS

After strong lobbying by UK employers and the Government to block the introduction of the EU Directive on national information and consultation, its implementation in the form of the Information and Consultation of Employees Regulations (2004) grabbed few contemporary headlines. Yet things did happen, and are still happening. Research shows that nearly 40% of UK-based multi-nationals revised their information and consultation arrangements between 2006 and 2009, prompted by the Regulations, while in the first high-profile case in 2007, the publisher Macmillan was fined £55,000 for failure to respond to an employee request for a staff consultative committee.

THEORY    Research – sponsored by the Department for Business, Enterprise and Regulatory Reform, ACAS and the CIPD – looked at 13 private sector companies with 150 or more employees where change was taking place. Varying in size from 240 to 6,000 employees, and in the manufacturing, service and the voluntary sectors, eight recognised unions whereas five did not. The researchers found that the key driver for the introduction or overhaul of information and consultation arrangements in virtually all cases was an interest in effectively managing a crisis or major change, and that the companies studied had histories of commitment to employee involvement. For them the Regulations provided both a stimulus to overhaul and extend information and consultation arrangements and an indication of the direction and nature of the reform.

Management – in particular, HR management – drove the detailed change, with little or no influence exerted by employees or unions. Voluntary arrangements (pre-existing agreements), often drawn up by management with little employee input, were the preferred route. The new structures, providing representation on a new or changed forum for all employees, reflected strong, managed acceptance of the link between effective employee participation and corporate performance through building trust and improving two-way communications. Employer commitment was reflected in the participation of top management. The new structures were not to be trivial bodies dealing only with second-order issues but were to discuss key strategic issues.

Other factors shaped management behaviour, most particularly the presence of trade unions. Where unions were well established and accepted, little changed. Terry *et al*, however, found cases where management hoped to use the new arrangements to move beyond trade-union-based 'bureaucratic' relationships into a wider and more flexible set of arrangements. This did not go down well with the trade unions. They also found other cases where employers were resisting attempts at union organising – where the new arrangements were explicitly described as useful in providing employees with a non-union alternative form of representation.

The interaction between the new information and consultation arrangements and the views Terry *et al* found gave rise to several interesting developments. Generally, where unions were recognised, companies agreed – not always readily – that existing union-based structures for negotiation should be protected and operate alongside the new, universal systems: a novel sort of 'dual channel'. A further conclusion was that information and consultation bodies established as part of union-exclusion strategies were engaging in extensive discussion of pay-related issues as part of a demonstration that they constituted viable alternatives to union-based arrangements. Most universal companies developed hybrid representation systems, with union representation sitting alongside others representing non-union employees. Terry *et al*'s research concluded that despite some initial misgivings, the union and non-union representatives appeared to work well together, sharing information and experience. The researchers pose the question whether such developments represent a toe in the door for unions to extend their influence, as some employers fear, or whether they constitute a demonstration that unions are redundant since an equivalent representative function can be performed without them, as some unions fear. Perhaps instead the emergence of hybrid bodies corresponds to a new departure in UK employment relations.

The information and consultation systems appeared to be appreciated by most managers and representatives, union and non-union, interviewed in the Terry *et al* research. Employee representatives felt better informed. The new forums presented, in some cases for the first time, an opportunity to raise and resolve employees' concerns – eg mobile telephone allowances, car parking arrangements – for which there had previously been no obvious place to air them. Quick agreement on such matters raised the standing of the new arrangements in the eyes of affected employers. On the other hand, a number of employee representatives complained that on larger issues they were not being consulted – merely informed of decisions already taken. This is a major issue on which the new arrangements might founder. Some managers complained that after an initial flurry of interest, employee representatives were no longer raising agenda items and the system was increasingly employer-driven – again posing a risk to its long-term viability.

The big question for the companies involved in the research involved was whether the new arrangements improved performance. Despite the significance of this, no companies had established review systems to estimate performance effects, and few had undertaken any sort of cost–benefit analysis of the new structures. Managerial commitment to this objective and to the new structures remains vital if they are to prove enduring and not just another passing fad.

## THE IMPLEMENTATION OF EMPLOYEE INVOLVEMENT AND PARTICIPATION PRACTICES

### General principles

> **Principles underlying the implementation of employee involvement schemes**
>
> - A scheme should be capable of general application to all organisations in which people are employed.
> - Arrangements and procedures should be appropriate to the organisation. There is no one best scheme.
> - There should be joint employer–employee agreement on participation.
> - Where trade unions are recognised, there should be the involvement of trade unions.
> - Leadership in the scheme should be taken by management.
> - The scheme should be inclusive of all employees.
> - Education and training should be given to enable participants to fulfil their role in a constructive manner.
> - Management must retain the responsibility for business decisions.
> - Employees' rights and trade unions' responsibilities may not be prejudiced.

In implementing employee involvement and participation practices, the employment-relations-oriented business performer has to bear a number of basic principles in mind (see the box above). Among the most important are that:

- The arrangements and procedures must be appropriate to the needs of the organisation.
- Agreement on arrangements should normally be arrived at jointly with the employees.
- The arrangements involve trade unions where they are recognised by the organisation.
- The lead in establishing, operating and reviewing arrangements should be taken by management.

- All employees in the organisation must be covered by the arrangements.
- Education and training must be provided to enable those participating in the arrangements to perform effectively.
- Management must retain full responsibility for business decisions.
- Employees' rights and trade unions' responsibilities must not be prejudiced.

## THE NEEDS OF THE ORGANISATION

The employee involvement and participation practices selected by management should be compatible with the characteristics of the organisation, including the nature of its activities, structure, technology and history. Processes and structures appropriate to older industries will not necessarily match the needs of newer organisations formed in a different social, industrial and commercial context. There is no one way of implementing employee involvement and participation practices, and the sole guiding principle should be that practices proposed for introduction are compatible with the organisation's circumstances. It is not essential, for example, to introduce employee involvement and participation practices to help improve product and/or service delivery quality if the organisation operates in a product market where competitive advantage rests with price and not the quality and reliability of the product.

## JOINT AGREEMENT

Employee involvement and participation arrangements in organisations are best developed by joint agreement between management and the employees. If arrangements are introduced on a jointly agreed basis, employees have some ownership of them and have a greater commitment to ensuring the success of the schemes. If management simply impose the arrangements, the employees have no ownership of them and therefore no stake in ensuring their success. Joint agreement by management and employees means joint commitment to operate the arrangements in good faith and as intended. Both parties have an interest in ensuring that they succeed. It is something they have jointly created. In addition, employees see advantages in their representatives being involved in the management decision-making processes, if for no other reason than to act as the custodians of their interests and to ensure management accountability. Employees desire that all levels of management take notice of their views and concerns.

It makes sense, on the basis of the joint agreement/joint commitment argument, that good practice in introducing employee involvement and participation schemes in organisations where trade unions are recognised is that union representatives be involved in deciding the appropriate arrangements and in their operation. This will reassure the trade unions that management's real agenda is not to undermine their influence. In initiating the necessary action to implement effective schemes, the lead must come from management. Employee involvement and participation will not occur or develop of its own accord.

## TRAINING AND DEVELOPMENT

Two other key principles are that opportunities must be available for all employees – including managers – to participate in employee involvement and participation schemes, and that appropriate training and education should be provided for such participants. The former principle involves all employees having the confidence that their views (which are being actively sought) will be taken into account by management before a final decision is made, and not afterwards. An important consideration in this regard is the quality of relationships between individual employees and their immediate superiors and managers. If the quality of decisions made by management is to be improved, they must gain information by listening to what their employees have to say and by asking them appropriate questions. By the same token, employees require information from employers. Both employees and employers require training in communication, presentational and meeting/chairing skills.

Employee involvement and participation arrangements do not relieve management of their responsibility for making business decisions that fall within the area of their own accountability or for communicating such decisions, with relevant background information, to the employees. The quality of management business decisions is likely to be improved if, before a decision is made, the views of the workplace are taken into account. However, the employees do not have a veto on management decisions. The prerogative to make business decisions continues to remain with management.

## SELECTING THE PRACTICES

### Context

There is no single model for the successful implementation of employee involvement and participation practices. Many considerations have to be taken into account by management in deciding which practice(s) to select (see the box below). Individual organisations have to develop and adapt arrangements to fit their own needs. These can vary over time as the organisation's size, structure and activities change. There is no single blueprint for success.

---

**Factors to be considered in implementing appropriate employee involvement and participation practices for an organisation**

**Context**
The practices should be introduced as part of a coherent and consistent strategy.
The practices should preferably not be introduced as 'crisis' management.

**Single v multiple arrangement**
The mix can vary.
A greater mix does not necessarily mean a greater quality of arrangements.

**Integration**
There should be integration between the mix of arrangements (horizontal integration).
There should be integration with the strategic objectives of the organisation as a whole (vertical integration).

**Success elsewhere**
Why have such practices been successful elsewhere?
Could they be transplanted successfully elsewhere?

**Legal requirements**
Transnational Information and Consultation Regulations (2000)
Information and Consultation Regulations (2004)

**Good employee relations**
Good employee relations is a necessary pre-condition.

**Commitment by top management**
Top management must demonstrate a belief in employee involvement and participation schemes.

**Resources**

**Monitoring and review arrangements**

Consideration has to be given to the context in which the arrangements will be introduced and operated. If they are to be introduced as part of a coherent and consistent strategy to improve the performance of the enterprise, the proposed arrangements should be the result of a full evaluation of all the possible practices. On the other hand, if they are being introduced to deal with a crisis situation, then it is likely that the arrangements selected will have been ill-thought-out and possibly rationalised on the flimsy basis that the proposed employee involvement and participation arrangements have been successfully implemented in other organisations. Without any detailed assessment and evaluation, the management will be assuming that the arrangements can be transplanted successfully into their own organisation. Arrangements introduced without proper analysis and evaluation are unlikely to be successful or to provide management with the advantages that might accrue from the implementation of employee involvement and participation schemes.

## Multiple arrangements

Research by Marchington *et al* (1993) into the operation of employee involvement and participation practices revealed that single measures designed to enhance employee commitment to the organisation are much less likely to succeed than the existence of a multiplicity of practices. Nevertheless, whatever the mix of employee involvement and participation practices adopted, they must be appropriate to the organisation's needs as revealed by a thorough assessment and evaluation. Marchington *et al* (1993) also found, for example, that in some small companies the mix of employee involvement arrangements was no more than one or two different practices, whereas in some larger manufacturing organisations there were as many as eight or nine different schemes for enhancing employee involvement and participation. However, they warn that it is dangerous to assume that the greater the number of employee involvement and participation arrangements an organisation introduces, the greater will be their overall quality. They point out that multiple techniques can lead to potentially conflicting pressures and confusions or communication overload for the staff subject to these arrangements.

## Integration

If a multiplicity of different employee involvement and participation schemes is appropriate, not only must they integrate with each other (horizontal integration) but they must be integrated with the strategic objectives of the organisation as a whole (vertical integration). This may require schemes to be customised so that they are relevant and appropriate for the organisation's needs and practices (see below). Since a wide range of employee involvement and participation practices are available to organisations, giving careful consideration to all of them before attempting to implement them makes common sense. If employee involvement and participation arrangements are to make an impact, integration with business objectives and consistency with other management practices is essential.

## Success elsewhere

Just because employee involvement practices have proved to be successful in one organisation, there is no guarantee they will work as successfully in another which is operating in a quite different context. Copying those arrangements that are perceived to be successful elsewhere is a poor basis for selection. A full analysis and investigation of their appropriateness to another organisation is essential. Information is required on what factors made them successful in the first organisation. Do these factors exist in 'copying' organisations? Are there factors at one organisation that would prevent a practice from being successfully transplanted in another organisation?

## Legal requirements

The business-oriented 'thinking performer' employment relations professional, when implementing employee involvement and participation schemes, must also comply with legal requirements surrounding such practices. This can sometimes be a secondary consideration for the thinking performer, since compliance may not give rise to competitive advantage. However, not to comply with legal requirements can give rise to competitive disadvantage. The major pieces of legislation that apply to employee involvement and participation schemes have been outlined above and need not be repeated here.

## Good employee relations

Employee involvement schemes are more likely to be introduced successfully where there is a willingness on the part of both management and employees to be open in their attitude and behaviour. Employee commitment will not be gained in an atmosphere of lack of trust and motivation. Schemes cannot operate effectively in a background of disputes and confrontation. Insufficient motivation on the part of management and employees to make involvement and participation practices work, or insufficient mutual trust to allow them to work, is more likely to be the cause of their failure than the substance of the practices. If management introduce employee involvement and participation schemes but shortly afterwards change their style to one that is less open and participative, the employees are likely to regard this behaviour as an attempt by management to undermine the schemes. Employee scepticism towards the employee involvement and participation practices under which they work will emerge, and the schemes will be less effective.

Good employment relations is thus a necessary precondition for the effective implementation of employee involvement and participation schemes. An open style of management in which employee support for proposed action is gained by consent, and not by coercion, is essential. However, by itself a good employment relations environment is not a sufficient condition for the successful implementation and operation of involvement and participation schemes. It also requires unquestioning commitment from top management.

### Commitment by top management

This is a key condition – but again is not sufficient on its own to deliver involvement and participation schemes that operate effectively. All schemes are unlikely to be effective unless top management, by its own behaviour, demonstrates a belief in them. Top management's commitment requires not only to be felt positively but also to be seen by employees. Managers should accept the value of employee involvement and participation schemes and not give the impression that they are supporting a mere fad in management practice or are speaking rhetoric behind which there is no substance. Whereas a good committee structure may be important for some involvement and participation schemes to be effective, it is totally irrelevant if individual managers are not committed to the schemes' success. Support for introducing employee involvement and participation schemes needs to be secured throughout the whole management structure. If management are not committed to their success, employees will view the arrangements as 'tokenism' and disregard attempts to gain their commitment, loyalty and support.

If managers wish employee involvement schemes to succeed, there can be no loss of momentum following the initial enthusiasm on their introduction. Management commitment has to last longer than just the introduction of schemes, since many are costly in management time if they are not run properly. Nothing destroys employee involvement and participation initiatives more quickly than management action that is inconsistent with the philosophy of worker empowerment. This is particularly so when management's behaviour strongly suggests to the employees that management really consider employment involvement and participation of little significance and something to be quickly dropped when there is short-term production/service provision pressure to meet the customers' needs. Care must be exercised by management in deciding the timing of meetings. If they are scheduled late on a Friday afternoon and there is, for example, little opportunity to explore issues in sufficient depth, employees will question management's commitment to employee involvement initiatives as a means of improving management decision-making. The same applies if employees feel that their views do not really count since their contributions are dismissed without serious examination.

Two important causes of failure of employee involvement and participation practices are the attitudes of middle and lower managers to such schemes and what Marchington *et al* (1993) call the 'lack of continuity caused by the dynamic career patterns of managers who are the driving force behind the schemes'. Middle and front-line management often lack commitment to, and fail to support the development of, employee involvement and participation initiatives. Some regarded them as mechanisms by which senior/top managers pander to the employees and that at the same time undermine front-line managers' authority over employees. They perceive top management's support for the continuation of employee involvement and participation practices as being 'soft' on employees, who they perceive as only too pleased to be paid while not working, and who, as a result, will always have issues they want to discuss with employers.

Frequently, in large multi-plant/-product firms, senior managers expect to stay at an establishment only for a short period of time, and such duration is regarded as part of their development package en route to senior management positions. Marchington *et al* (1993) refer to this type of character as the 'mobile champion', reflecting a picture of the manager who introduces a scheme then moves on to other duties, generally at another site, or to employment elsewhere. His or her successor often has different priorities, and the employee involvement initiatives that were the 'baby' of the predecessor lapse because of operational difficulties or because the successor expects no praise from his or her senior managers for administering another individual's creation.

The introduction of employee involvement and participation arrangements on the basis of fashion and fad will quickly create feelings of disillusionment among employees and a suspicion that management have no real focus to their current and future activities. However, a management committed to the introduction and successful operation of employee involvement initiatives is highly unlikely to select arrangements on the basis of fad over what is appropriate to the organisation's commercial and business needs. Proper analysis of the objectives desired from any employee involvement and participation arrangements before their introduction prevents any possible confusion or conflict between the different practices introduced. This is particularly important when the organisation is introducing a multiplicity of practices. Rather than just select any scheme, it can be helpful if management give extremely careful consideration over how the arrangements will apply and modify any schemes introduced to the needs of the workplace. Schemes which are customised (see above) offer better prospects for success than those that are lifted down from the shelf and which may clash with production or service provision considerations.

An all too common mistake by management in introducing involvement and participation scheme initiatives is to become seduced by the prevalence of public relations accounts into believing that any scheme(s) introduced will be a panacea to solve all their product market problems. The impact of employee involvement and participation in securing a positive change in employee attitudes and behaviour is less profound and permanent than is often claimed if the schemes selected turn out to be inappropriate to that organisation's needs. An inappropriate choice of systems is most noticeable, Marchington *et al* (1993) claim, amongst companies which bring in consultants to advise them on how to implement a new scheme and do so without establishing its relevance or the purpose of the scheme. A company might decide, for example, to introduce a system of monthly team briefings. However, it is a waste of time to do so without having assessed whether there will be sufficient information to sustain it on that basis or whether the front-line manager has the necessary skills or motivation to make it work. This difficult problem becomes further complicated when different management functions or levels in the management structure have a responsibility for introducing employee involvement initiatives, often at the same time and with conflicting objectives. It is a situation particularly current in service sector companies where the issue of customer care often falls within the province of both the HR/personnel and the marketing departments.

A management fully committed to the successful operation of employee involvement and participation practices is going a long way to ensure that those participating in such practices have access to a free flow of information to permit them to operate effectively. This flow of information is most effective if it is up, down and across the organisation. A ready willingness to listen, evaluate and act on views expressed by employees is a sensible approach. There are many pitfalls into which management can stumble with respect to the information they make available in the workplace to participants in employee involvement schemes. Management must strike a balance between providing too little information and providing too much information, or employees can become confused. Managers have to avoid too much 'tell and sell', since this triggers employee mistrust of involvement and participation schemes, especially if most information is bad news and is accompanied by rallying calls for belt-tightening and restraint.

The effective operation of employee involvement and participation practices involves two-way communication. To focus on downwards communication carries the risk that employees and/or their representatives might feel they are only being informed of changes or decisions after the event, rather than before. This may seem an obvious statement, but unfortunately for many managers, common sense is not common practice. A further problem management face is the tendency for employee involvement and participation schemes once implemented to regress, rather than grow and develop, from their original position with respect to their anticipated objectives. Several employee involvement and participation practices that have been successful in one organisation have come apart in another because in the latter their scope collapsed to the level of 'canteen tea discussions'. When the subjects discussed become non-controversial or less interesting, employee indifference, if not scepticism, develops. So despite the fact that employees are the principal objects and recipients of many employee involvement and participation practices, this is potentially the most common cause of failure. A management fully committed to involvement and participation initiatives, introducing it for the right reasons, and having selected the schemes appropriate for its business objectives, is unlikely to concede opportunities for employee scepticism to arise.

A professional management is motivated to ensure that involvement and participation schemes do not become ineffective because their operation produces adverse impacts on the workings of other employment relations institutions in the organisation. Some of the most successful involvement and participation practices have been established in unionised companies with the joint involvement of management and unions. In contrast, arrangements set up independently of trade unions, where they are recognised and are fully representative of their members' views, have often led to difficulties. This can happen because unions – especially those that are weakly organised – regard the introduction of an independent system of employee involvement as an attempt to bypass them and to undermine their relationship with their members. In strongly unionised organisations, employee involvement and participation practices are unlikely to be used to undermine the normal bargaining process with the unions. Attempts to bypass or undermine established trade union channels are likely to backfire and founder on union opposition taken to the point of withdrawal – for example, a refusal to sit at the same table as non-unionists. In non-union companies, the danger that employee involvement schemes may adversely affect other employment relations institutions is less likely to be a potential hazard for management.

A management committed to the effective operation of employee involvement and participation schemes will adopt an open and participative style of management, select appropriate schemes tailored to the organisation's needs, ensure that there is a full flow of information up, down and across the organisation, and will commit the necessary resources in terms of time, finances, people and equipment to support the operation of the employee involvement and participation schemes.

## REFLECTIVE ACTIVITY

Is the management in your organisation fully committed to the successful operation of their employee involvement and participation schemes? Give full reasons for your answer.

### Resources

If employee involvement and participation schemes are to operate effectively, resources are required to meet the direct and indirect costs (time lost, production/service foregone, meetings, training, paid leave, etc) associated with introducing, operating and monitoring them. An uncommitted management is likely to regard them as a cost without any benefit, and to seek to ensure that there is insufficient business to be discussed by those participating in the schemes. The business-oriented thinking performer employment relations professional has an obligation to persuade his or her colleagues to view employee involvement and participation practices that operate in the organisation in a positive light, and to demonstrate to them the value the practices add to the business if they are embraced fully by all levels and functions of management.

The effectiveness of employee involvement and participation practices is often diminished by a lack of skills or knowledge on the part of the participants. It is important for both managers and employees to be provided with training in the skills required to manage employee involvement and participation practices effectively. This involves acquiring and developing the skills of chairing meetings so that employees keep to the agenda and put forward suggestions that are appropriate to the subject matter under discussion. Managers also require training in presentational skills to present information by word of mouth or in writing and by the use of visual aids. In addition, they require interviewing skills to question employees to gain information and/or to seek clarification of employee views. Listening skills are essential, for consultation involves management's listening to what the employees have to say. In participating in employee involvement and participation practices, managers should limit their contributions and allow the employees to do most of the talking. By listening, employers acquire additional information. Managers also require the skills of negotiation to gain the commitment of their managerial colleagues at all levels, and in all functions, and of the workforce to the effective operation of employee involvement and participation mechanisms. If the organisation's management do provide training for their managers and employees to prepare them to participate in employee involvement practices, it is sound business sense periodically to evaluate the effectiveness of the training provided.

Spending resources on training for all involved in the operation of employee involvement and participation practices represents an investment by management. It demonstrates openly to all concerned their commitment to the schemes. To do otherwise invites employee disillusionment with the schemes. A serious and continuing commitment to employee involvement and participation practices is not easy to achieve and requires significant support from the highest levels of management. The gaining of employee commitment, via employee participation and involvement initiatives, is a time-consuming process. It is much easier to undermine the operation of the schemes than to sustain them. Financial resources are necessary to ensure that training is executed effectively and efficiently, and that sufficient time – balanced against production and customer service needs – is set aside for joint consultation meetings, briefing groups and regular management walkabouts.

Management must be aware of the potential problems that face employees working under involvement and participation arrangements. For example, employees may lack knowledge of the subjects under discussion and may have problems coping with the social situation of rubbing shoulders with top management. They may also experience undue pressure from their constituents who have unreal expectations of what employee involvement and participation initiatives can achieve in protecting and advancing the interests of the employees. A business-oriented thinking performer employment relations professional assists employee representatives and individual employees to overcome these problems by providing the necessary facilities for them to keep communication channels open between themselves and their constituents. It will add little value to an organisation committed to the successful operation of employee involvement and participation practices to have employee representatives who are unable to represent their members or to report back to them, or to have union representatives who suspect that management are really opposed to their activities.

### Monitoring and review arrangements

The establishment of mechanisms for the regular monitoring and reviewing of the operation of employee involvement and participation practices is essential. Monitoring is a means of assessing whether the schemes are producing the desired outputs of improved efficiency, productivity, quality of service, a greater willingness on the part of employees to accept change, etc. The effectiveness of employee involvement and participation practices is measured against the outputs of their operation in terms of contributing to the achievement of the overall objectives of the organisation.

Assessing effectiveness in this way avoids the simple acceptance by management and employees of a public relations story describing the alleged success of the operation of one group of employee involvement practices. Nevertheless, it is not easy to quantify the contribution of employee involvement and participation practices to the achievement of corporate objectives (see below). There are problems, *inter alia*, of identifying appropriate benchmarks and isolating the influence of other factors.

The results of any monitoring exercise are best discussed with employee representatives and, where appropriate, recognised trade unions. If the monitoring process exposes weaknesses, remedial action can be taken. Regular monitoring and review also enables an organisation to assess the cost-effectiveness of its employee involvement and participation schemes.

### HIGH-PERFORMANCE WORKPLACES

If an organisation implements employee involvement and participation schemes, what does contemporary research and organisational practice tell us about the expected outcome? The potential rewards are claimed to be substantial. Many organisations have publicised the benefits of the introduction of such schemes. An *Industrial Relations Services Survey* (1999) of 49 organisations' experiences with employee involvement and participation practices over the period 1992 to 1999 reported that:

- around three-quarters believed it had enhanced employee commitment and motivation
- a similar proportion considered that their employment relations had improved
- approximately six in ten said that the quality of products manufactured had improved
- over half claimed that there had been advances in labour productivity
- just under a half believed that their employees' job satisfaction had increased
- the same proportion claimed that their organisational profits or performance had increased

- one-third said that involving employees had lowered absence rates
- just under 30% believed that switching to more participative working arrangements had improved their capacity to attract and retain employees.

The former Department for Trade and Industry publication *High-Performance Workplaces: Informing and consulting employees* (2003) reported a round-table response by employer and employee representative organisations on the benefit of information and consultation arrangements. At a general level, many employers' response was that commitment, motivation and enthusiasm were the outcome of investing in, and valuing, the workforce. From that, it was argued, came a sense of shared purpose, ownership and values and a shared interest in the success of the business. The employers also contended that a major ingredient of the success of information and consultation machinery was mutual trust and respect between management and the workforce and a clear understanding of what was expected from employees. In short, their view was that if the people were not on-side, the business plan could not be delivered. Information and consultation was seen by many participants in the round-table discussion as a catalyst for the development of innovative workplace processes and practices which helped establish trust and thereby facilitated cultural change. Some respondents stressed the importance of two-way communications – that there was more to it than simply keeping staff informed of what was going on: the decision-making itself could be improved through a process of genuine dialogue through which minds could be changed.

Participants in the discussion were in agreement that there were benefits both to the employees themselves and to the business they worked for in informing and consulting staff. The benefits for employees were said to stem from their having a greater say in the way the business was run. This was perceived as having direct benefits in terms of a better and safer working environment, improved work organisation and working conditions and better training. By helping staff to feel valued and involved, it was hypothesised, information and consultation machinery could lead to higher employee morale and motivation. In turn, this could lead to fewer recruitment problems, less absenteeism, lower staff turnover, a willingness to take on responsibility and, if necessary, an acceptance of or ability to adapt to changes whether in ways of working or as a result of large-scale reorganisation.

Many participants in the former DTI round-table discussion believed that the benefits of information and consultation for business included improved communications across the organisation, access to a wider pool of knowledge, experience and ideas, staff who better understood what they were doing and how it fitted into the overall business, and a greater responsiveness and less resistance to change. Many respondents accepted that there was a link between information and consultation and improved productivity. Some saw a direct link – for example, employees were perceived to be more responsive to customer demands as a result of information and consultation arrangements. Others considered that better company decisions could be made by tapping into the knowledge and ideas of the wider workforce. Some business organisations, however, urged caution in that there are costs as well as benefits to business – too much consultation, for example, might introduce delays and confusion into decision-making, or informing and consulting too early over possible job losses might create uncertainty and damage morale among the workforce.

**THEORY**  High-performance work systems are said to yield performance levels above those associated with more traditional workplace and employee relations practices (Godard, 2004). According to proponents these practices achieve this largely by enabling and motivating workers to develop, share and apply their knowledge and skills more fully than do traditional practices, with positive implications for the quality of jobs as well as for performance. In the employment relations literature there are many who argue that the implementation of high-performance systems also creates opportunities for union renewal, enabling unions to discard their traditional adversarial role in favour of a new partnership one. As Godard (2004) says:

> Thus the high-performance paradigm is best practice not only for employers but also for workers, and, potentially, for their unions …

A wide variety of practices are associated with high-performance workplaces. To gain the improved productivity over traditional work practices, innovative human resource management practices are necessary in certain combinations or 'bundles'. These practices then have an impact on employees – and it is, in large part at least, through this impact that improvements in organisational performance are realised. A high-performance work system strategy entails management's ceding a degree of control to employees and introducing a range of progressive methods which increase employee welfare.

**THEORY**  High-performance work systems fall into two broad types of human resource practices. The first is often referred to as alternative work practices, and includes autonomous and semi-autonomous work teams, job enrichment, job rotation and participatory practices such as quality circles, problem-solving groups, briefing groups, attitude surveys, profit-sharing schemes, joint consultation machinery and employee share ownership. The second group of practices is referred to as high-commitment employment practices and includes high-quality selection, recruitment and training systems, performance appraisal, job security, Investors in People accreditation and single status. Most supporters of high-performance work systems argue that these practices, when successfully implemented, are of universal benefit to employers. A general assumption is that the productivity/performance benefit over more traditional employment relations management practices increases with the number of practices adopted. High-performance workplaces are said to gain competitive advantage primarily through the high performance of people stemming from the implementation of a number of different but complementary human resource management practices.

There is, however, a general recognition in contemporary research findings that there is no single template for creating a high-performance workplace. The introduction of the various human resource management practices is not enough by itself. Many other factors are important. These include:

- good leadership
- a clear vision
- a commitment to continuous improvement
- a culture that encourages innovation
- capital investment
- customer focus
- a recognition that change is inevitable and must be embraced
- taking a long-term strategy view of where the organisation is going.

The relative importance of these and other factors differs between organisations depending on their individual circumstances, but whatever the mix it is important to be consistent in pursuing them and to keep reinforcing the approach.

**THEORY**

Godard (2004), however, argues that the view that high-performance work systems yield superior performance outcomes may be unwarranted, and that their implications for both workers and unions are at best uncertain. Ramsay *et al* (2000) challenge the view that the superior performance resulting from the implementation of high-performance work practices operates through the incentive and motivation effects captured as 'high-commitment' or 'high-involvement' employee outcomes. They examine an alternative explanation of the relative better performance of high-performance work systems, postulating that the gains arise from work intensification, offloading of task controls and increased job strain. Using data from the *Workplace Employee Relations Survey* of 1998 they tested models based on high-performance work systems and labour process approaches. They conclude:

> However, the widely-held assumption that positive outcomes from HPWS flow via positive employee outcomes has been shown to be highly questionable. Nor do our results suggest we should accept the simple counter-argument that gains to management always come at the expense for labour of degradation of work. On the basis of our analysis, this assumption is no more tenable than that of orthodox theories of HPWS ...

They account for their findings of no adequate explanation of the outcomes of the implementation of high-performance work systems, *inter alia*, in terms of the limitations of the WERS 1998 data, suggesting that the statistical models of the relationship between high-performance work practices and organisational outcome are perhaps too simple to capture the complex reality of the implementation and operation of such practices.

**SUMMARY**

- By the introduction of employee involvement initiatives, management seek to gain consent from their employees for their proposed actions on the basis of commitment rather than control.

- Employee involvement and participation covers a wide range of practices designed to increase employee information about the organisation, and thereby to produce a committed workforce.

- It is management, however, who make the final decision over whether employees are to be involved, and to participate in management decision-making.

- Employee involvement and participation practices are designed to change the attitudes of employees, enhance their business awareness, improve their motivation, and enhance their influence/ownership in the business.

- Employee involvement and participation practices can be direct (communications, problem-solving groups and financial participation) or indirect (forum of employee representatives).

- The incidence of employee involvement initiatives has risen as the frequency of collective bargaining has fallen.

- In implementing employee involvement practices, a number of general principles apply – the needs of the organisation, the provision of education and training, multiple arrangements, top management commitment and adequate resources.

- Important initiatives on employee involvement and participation requirements have come from the European Union, particularly the National Information and Consultative Directive (2000), which has been transposed into UK law via the Information and Consultation with Employee Regulations (2004). These have potentially far-reaching implications for all organisations.

- Employee communications mechanisms involve the provision and exchange of information which enable an organisation to function effectively and its employees to be informed properly about developments.

- Task and work group involvement schemes encourage employees to extend the range and types of tasks they undertake at work; teamworking is the best example of such schemes.

- Total quality management is designed to ensure continuous improvement of the effectiveness and quality of the work to meet the requirements of customers.

- Financial participation schemes (profit-related pay/share ownership, etc) enable employees to acquire and develop a greater identity with the business and its needs.

- The main form of representative participation is joint consultation, which is a process by which management and employees (or their representatives) jointly discuss issues of mutual concern.

- The introduction of employee involvement and participation schemes with sophisticated HR practices is said to produce high-performing workplaces. Such workplaces are more productive and efficient than workplaces managed by more traditional employment relations practices. Some research suggests, however, that this view may be overstated.

- Employee involvement concentrates on individual employees and is designed to produce a committed workforce more likely to contribute to the efficient operation of an organisation. Employee participation is concerned with the extent to which employees are involved with management in the decision-making machinery of the organisation.

- Growing employee commitment brought about by the implementation of employer participation and involvement mechanisms is said to lead to improved organisational performance.

- The objective of employee involvement and participation mechanisms is to tap into employees' knowledge of their job, either at the individual level or through the mechanism of small groups. These practices are designed to increase the stock of ideas within the organisation, to encourage co-operative relations at work and to justify change.

- Meaningful consultation involves a) providing employees with complete information on management's proposed actions, b) giving the employees sufficient time to consider this information, c) receiving the employees' response to management's proposed actions, d) giving careful consideration to the employees' views and thereafter explaining fully why some views have been taken on board and, more importantly, why some have not – or alternatively explaining why management have genuinely not made up their minds about the proposed action, and e) seeking to come to an amicable and altogether mutually beneficial agreement.

- Contemporary research and existing organisational policy and practice finds a strong positive link between the breadth and depth of some information and consultation practices and employee commitment. Significant and positive links have been found between the breadth of information and consultation (the number of different practices used together in the workplace) and the depth of direct communication methods and employee commitment.

- In implementing employee involvement and participation practices, the employment relations business-oriented thinking performer has to bear in mind a number of basic principles. These include: ensuring that arrangements and procedures are appropriate to the needs of the organisation, providing education and training to enable those who participate in the arrangements to perform effectively, selecting the appropriate EIP mechanisms, and obtaining adequate resources and commitment from top management.

## REVIEW QUESTIONS

1 Using research evidence and your knowledge of organisational policy and practice to formulate your answer, what is the value of employee involvement and consultation for your organisation?

2 Your organisation is regarded as a good non-union employer that utilises employee involvement mechanisms. Your line manager asks you to explain the organisational objectives for such mechanisms. What would you say – and why?

3 You have received an email from an HR colleague: 'There is a growing misunderstanding between union representatives and line managers about what constitutes information-sharing and what consultation is.' Why does this difference in perception exist, do you think? In your reply, use evidence to explain why it might be the case.

4 At a recent management awayday meeting, a few of the newly appointed line managers were talking about the Information and Consultation Regulations (2004). One of the line managers is a bit of a 'backroom lawyer' and said that he thinks the Regulations are permissive. In other words, individual companies can choose whether or not to implement them – and in any case, companies can alter the wording and content to suit the way they want to do things. You have been asked to comment on his understanding of the situation. Drawing on appropriate evidence, what would you say?

5 As part of the organisational plan to review employee procedures and practice, senior management are considering introducing a more systematic approach to employee involvement and participation. You have been asked to produce a briefing paper for the senior management team explaining the likely benefits to the organisation of implementing employee involvement and participation. Drawing on contemporary research, explain and justify the contents of your briefing paper.

## EXPLORE FURTHER

Advisory, Conciliation and Arbitration Service (2005) *Information and Consultation: Good practice advice*. London: ACAS.

Advisory, Conciliation and Arbitration Service (1995) *Employee Communications and Consultation*. London: ACAS.

Beaumont, P. B. and Hunter, L. C. (2003) *Information and Consultation: From compliance to performance*. London: Chartered Institute of Personnel and Development.

Cox, A., Marchington, M. and Suter, J. (2007) *Embedding the Provision of Information and Consultation in the Workplace: A longitudinal analysis of employee outcomes in 1998 and 2004*, Employment Relations Series No.72, February. London: DTI.

Department for Trade and Industry (2003) *High Performance Workplaces: Informing and consulting employees*. London: DTI.

Department for Trade and Industry (2002) *High Performance Workplaces: The role of employee involvement in a modern economy*. London: DTI.

Dundon, T., Wilkinson, A. and Marchington, M. (2004) 'The meanings and purpose of employee voice', *Int. Journal of HRM*, Vol.15, No.6: 1149–70.

Gapper, J. (1990) 'At the end of the honeymoon', *Financial Times*, 10 January.

Geary, J. (1994) 'Task participation: employees' participation enabled or constrained?', in Sissons, K. (ed.) *Personnel Management*, 2nd edition. Oxford: Blackwell.

Godard, J. (2004) 'A critical assessment of the high-performance paradigm', *British Journal of Industrial Relations*, Vol.42, No.2.

Gospel, H. and Williams, P. (2005) 'Changing patterns of employee voice', in Storey, J. (ed.) *Adding Value Through Information and Consultation*. Basingstoke: Palgrave.

Hall, M., Hutchinson, G., Parker, J., Purcell, J. and Terry, M. (2007) *Implementing Information and Consultation: Early experience under ICE Regulations*, Employment Relations Research Series No.88. September. London: Department for Business, Enterprise and Regulatory Reform.

Harley, B., Hyman, J. and Thompson, P. (2005) *Participation and Democracy at Work*. Basingstoke: Palgrave Macmillan.

Marchington, M. (2005) 'Employee involvement patterns and explanations', in Harley, B., Hyman, J. and Thompson, P. (eds) *Participation and Democracy at Work – Essays in Honour of Harvie Ramsay*. Basingstoke: Palgrave.

Marchington, M., Wilkinson, A. and Ackers, P. (1993) 'Waving or drowning in participation?', *Personnel Management*, March: 46–50.

Marchington, M., Goodman, J., Wilkinson, A. and Ackers, P. (1992) *New Developments in Employee Involvement*, Employment Department Research Series, Employment Department Publication, No 2.

Marchington, M., Wilkinson, A., Ackers, P. and Dundon, T. (2001) *Management Choice and Employee Voice*. London: Chartered Institute of Personnel and Development.

Marchington, M. P., Cox, A., Suter, J. (2007) *Embedding the Provision of Information and Consultation in the Workplace*. Department for Trade and Industry.

Ramsay, H. (1996) 'Involvement, empowerment and commitment', in Towers, B. (ed.) *The Handbook of Human Resource Management*, 2nd edition. Oxford: Blackwell.

Ramsay, H., Scholarios, D. and Harley, B. (2000) 'Employees and high-performance work systems: testing inside the black box', *British Journal of Industrial Relations*, Vol.38, No.4.

Walton, R. E. (1985) 'From control to commitment in the workplace', *Harvard Business Review*, March–April.

Wilkinson, A. (2001) 'Employment', in Redman, T. and Wilkinson, A. (eds) *Contemporary Human Resource Management: Text and cases*. London: *Financial Times*/Prentice-Hall.

**Websites**

www.acas.org.uk is the ACAS website and gives access to ACAS publications on employee involvement and participation, including its *Employee Communications and Consultation* advisory booklet and its *Teamwork: Success Through People* booklet, plus its *Getting It Right* (communications with your employees) factsheet.

www.ipa-involve.com is the official website of the Involvement and Participation Association, which specialises in assisting both unionised and non-unionised organisations to develop effective information and consultation processes and workplace partnership.

## CHAPTER 9

# Employee Engagement

## OVERVIEW

This chapter begins by explaining the purpose of employee engagement – to ensure that employees are committed to their organisation's goals and values, motivated to contribute to organisational success, and able to enhance their own sense of well-being. It then looks at the extent of employee engagement, looking at both *how much* employees are engaged (enough for them to 'go the extra mile') and *with whom* they are engaged (the employer/the organisation). The chapter then analyses why some employees feel disengaged, and examines the view that it is difficult to assess in any useful way the level of employee engagement without systematically consulting the employees themselves. This leads on to the outlining of 10 key steps in conducting an effective and authoritative employee engagement survey – eg obtaining top management support, encouraging everybody to participate, ensuring confidentiality, etc. The chapter then describes a number of public and private organisations that have successfully implemented employee engagement and outlines four main barriers to its implementation (lack of employee awareness, uncertainty about starting, inappropriate organisational culture and underestimating the effort and resources required for engagement). The chapter concludes by analysing the factors that are critical to gaining employee engagement – leadership, engaging managers, employee voice and organisational integrity.

## LEARNING OUTCOMES

When you have completed this chapter, you should be aware of and able to describe:

- what employee engagement is
- the case for organisations engaging with their employees
- the barriers to the introduction of employee engagement
- the necessary conditions to make employee engagement a success
- the outcomes of engaging with employees
- the techniques and processes of employee engagement
- the benefits to the individual employee of employee engagement.

## INTRODUCTION

The management of the employment relationship is central to good human resource management practice, and many professional practitioners (for example, the CIPD) believe that employment relations now needs to focus on gaining and retaining employee commitment and engagement. Employment relations skills and competencies are still seen as critical to achieving performance benefits through a focus on employee involvement and commitment. Engaging employees' hearts and minds can be a major challenge for many organisations since in today's increasingly competitive global market 'good practice' with regard to progressive employment practices is not sufficient. The mix of human resources and other factors of production are vital to sustained business performance. More and more companies and enterprises are viewing employee engagement as the key to adopting high-performance work practices. It is, however, not the only term used to describe positive attitudes and behaviour of employees at work. Other terms commonly used are 'commitment', 'organisation citizenship behaviour' and 'the psychological contract'. The policy and practice implications of employee engagement are often captured in 'high-involvement work practices' and 'high-performance working'. The United Kingdom Commission for Employment and Skills has defined high-performance working (HPW) as:

> a general approach to managing organisations that aims to stimulate more effective employee involvement and commitment in order to achieve high levels of performance.

The Commission went on to point out that, importantly, the HPW approach is specifically designed to enhance the discretionary effort employees put into their work and to utilise and further develop the skills that they possess. HPW is thus concerned with the efficient and effective use of the workforce but with an important emphasis on creating good-quality work rather than simply focusing on making employees work harder. This is the central premise of employee engagement.

There is clearly still a significant role for human resource management professionals in most workplaces to drive the engagement agenda at senior and executive management level and translate it into everyday reality. The causal relationship between HR practices and improved business performance is not clear. It is said to operate through employee perceptions and attitudes. High-performance work practices cannot simply be imposed by the top managers but is reliant upon developing employee security, trust and their buying in to the goals and values of the organisation. The achievement of business goals and financial returns is becoming increasingly dependent upon delivery by front-line employees. Engagement, going to the heart of the workplace relationship between employee and employer, is said by its supporters to be a key unlocking productivity and to transform the working lives of many people for whom a Monday morning is an especially low point of the week. If it is the workforce performance that explains to a significant extent whether companies, enterprises or organisations survive and grow, then whether or not the workforce is positively encouraged to perform to its best should be a major consideration for every business leader and manager and be put at the heart of business strategy.

The MacLeod and Clarke report *Engaging for Success* (2009) argued that in a world where most factors of production are increasingly standardised, where a production line or the goods on a supermarket shelf are much the same the world over, employee engagement is 'the difference that makes the difference' – and could make all the difference as organisations and companies face the reality of global competition. In short, there is an increasing recognition amongst all functions of management that people are the source of productive gain and competitive advantage. For the advocates of employee engagement, it is about establishing mutual respect in the workplace for what people can do – establishing the right context as individual employers, as companies and organisations, and as consumers of public services, to serve everybody. It is a triple win, therefore, for the individual at work, for the enterprise or service and for the country as a whole.

---

**THEORY**     **WHAT IS EMPLOYEE ENGAGEMENT?**

To its supporters – for example, MacLeod and Clarke (2009) – employee engagement is about:

- unlocking people's potential at work and the measurable benefits of doing so for the individual employee, the organisation and the UK economy

- retaining and building on the commitment, energy and desire to do a good job to maximise individual and organisational performance

- making the employees' commitment, potential creativity and capability central to the operation of the organisation – it is how people behave at work that can make the crucial difference between business success or failure

- enabling people to be the best they can at work, recognising that this can only happen if they feel respected, involved, heard, well-led and valued by those they work for and with

- employees' having a sense of personal attachment to their work and organisation – they are motivated and able to give their best to help it succeed, and from this will flow a series of positive benefits for the organisation and the individual

- ensuring that employees are committed to their organisation's goals and values, are motivated to contribute to organisational success and are able at the same time to enhance their own sense of well-being

- providing clear evidence of trust and fairness based on mutual respect through which two-way promises and commitments between employees and management are understood and fulfilled

- being a two-way process: the organisation must work to engage the employee who, in turn, has a choice about the level of engagement to offer the employer – each reinforces the other.

There is, however – as we saw in Chapter 2 – no agreed definition of employee engagement. MacLeod and Clarke (2009) report that in the course of their work they came across more than 50 definitions, one of which (submitted by Professor Katie Truss) was:

> Engagement is about creating opportunities for employees to connect with their colleagues, managers and the wider organisation. It is also about creating an environment where employees are motivated to want to connect with their work and really care about doing a good job . . . it is a concept that places flexibility, change and continuous improvement at the heart of what it means to be an employee and an employer in a twenty-first-century workplace.

The Chartered Institute of Personnel and Development publication *The New Rules of Engagement* (Johnson, 2004) described employee engagement as a combination of commitment and organisational citizenship. It saw the recipe for success lying in job security, respect, organisational purpose, feedback, recognition and teamwork. It pointed out that engaged employees demonstrated commitment, made a willing contribution, helped others, were less absent from work and were less inclined to resign from their employment. The implication of this is that the HR function in organisations is critical to convincing boards of directors and senior managers of the need to focus more on their employees and customers, and not just on their shareholders.

## REFLECTIVE ACTIVITY

Two line managers approach you and tell you that they have been hearing a lot about employee engagement. They tell you they are uncertain what the term means. They ask you to explain it to them. What would you tell them?

The CIPD views employee engagement as a workplace approach designed to ensure that employees are committed to their organisation's goals and values, motivated to contribute to organisational success and able to enhance their own sense of well-being. It sees employee voice and involvement as key components of engagement, and argues strongly for employers' aligning their employment relations strategies with their wider workforce approaches. Barriers to be overcome in the absence of engagement in organisations often include a lack of awareness and managers' reluctance to open up and give feedback. The MacLeod and Clarke report (2009) highlights the need for real and sustained understanding and buy-in from senior echelons, for managers at all levels to receive effective training in engagement and people skills, for employees' voice to be sought and listened to, and for trust and authenticity where the espoused values of an organisation are lived for real. For the CIPD, employee engagement places the way people are managed at the centre stage of organisations. The CIPD sees that the ability of employee engagement to measure the attributes and behaviours of a workforce is what distinguishes it from people management in general. The key drivers of successful employee engagement are, the CIPD notes, the quality of managers' leadership, good-quality line management, employee voice, and integrity in that behaviour throughout the organisation is consistent with shared values, leading to trust and a sense of moral confidence. As a business issue, employee engagement is not the exclusive preserve of the HR profession. However, HR has a major role to play in implementing employee engagement, and thus presents a significant opportunity for the profession to demonstrate its business-focused credibility.

There are a number of theoretical approaches that underpin employee engagement, including motivation theory. It is consistent with employment relations theory (pluralism) in that although employers and employees have an inherent difference of interests, these are often superseded by common interests which give rise to mutual advantage. From the successful implementation of employee engagement the employer gains, *inter alia*, increased productivity, increased profitability, lower labour turnover and reduced employee absence rates. Employees, meanwhile, gain more opportunities for personal growth, work in teams that support one another, suffer lower levels of stress and have a better work–life balance.

Employee engagement is also consistent with human capital theory, which postulates that if organisations invest in their workforce (the factor of production labour) – for example, by providing training (for both employees and managers), career development procedures and practices, flexible working, and by engaging in meaningful joint consultation and information-giving activities – this will increase output, labour productivity and the financial reward gained by employees to a higher level than would be the case in the absence of such investment in the workforce.

Organisational psychology theory can also be called upon to explain employee engagement in that it recognises that at the heart of the employment relationship is reciprocity. The theory postulates that if employees believe that they are, and will be, supported by the employer, and particularly their line manager, in getting what they desire out of work, beyond just money, they will reciprocate with positive behaviour. Perceived organisational support from management is said to lead, on the part of the employee, to reciprocal discretionary behaviour. The chain which links employment policies through management behaviour to organisational performance is held together by employee responses and behaviour.

## REFLECTIVE ACTIVITY

Do you think employee engagement is just another management fad? Is it something new or simply old wine (a longstanding management approach) in new (fashionable management-speak) bottles? Justify your answer.

## IS EMPLOYEE ENGAGEMENT JUST ANOTHER FAD?

The ACAS policy discussion paper on *Building Employee Engagement* (2010) puts forward two reasons for suggesting that the focus on employee engagement is likely to be more important and more long-lasting than other management initiatives such as quality circles. First, it has been accepted for many years that employees who are committed to their work and to their employer have a higher probability of behaving in positive, co-operative ways, to the benefit of the firm and of themselves. They are also less likely to take sickness absence or quit. Second, the concept of engagement stems from a recognition that work in the modern enterprise is more complex and changes more frequently than it used to, given the current emphasis on 'brain' rather than 'brawn'. This makes the task of management more challenging. Command-and-control management styles in most companies are now much less effective since employees tend to know the intricacies of the job better than managers do. More and more what makes a competitive difference is not technology but the way in which employees choose to undertake their job in terms of how co-operative, how innovative, how caring and how responsive to customers they are. Putting employees at the centre of the policy and practice debate means that the emphasis is placed on the management behaviour required to build engagement more than on rules and regulations. Together with case evidence (see below) and statistics, this – the ACAS discussion document argues – is why employee engagement is important, does make a difference, and is unlikely to go away.

The ACAS document, however, predicts that employee engagement will be a short-lived fad if it is used by employers to get their employees merely to work harder. Exception has been taken, for example, by some trade unions to the engagement agenda because its emphasis on discretionary behaviour can be seen as no more than inveigling people simply to do more, to make more of an effort – for example, in unpaid overtime. It is also the case that in the implementation of high-performance working, there have been incidences of increased stress and intensification of work. There is also evidence that some managers think that engagement is just about listening to their employees via an engagement attitude survey as a form of two-way communication. This, the ACAS document suggests, will kill off any interest in employee engagement quickly as the employees realise it is a phoney form of communication. Employee engagement, its supporters contend, is about much more than this. It is about building trust, involvement, a sense of purpose and identity in respect of which the employees' contribution to business success is regarded as essential.

## THE EXTENT OF EMPLOYEE ENGAGEMENT

The MacLeod and Clarke survey (2009) demonstrates that there is a wide variation in engagement levels in the UK within and between organisations and companies. It notes that the Corporate Leadership Council (CLC) reported that the highest-scoring companies describe 23.8% of their employees as 'highly engaged', while in the lowest-scoring companies only 2.9% of their people are in the 'highly engaged' category, using the same measurement techniques. It also points out that an Institute of Employment Studies survey found that engagement in organisations varied between age groups, between the type of organisation, and between different job roles. The 2004 *Workplace Employment Relations Survey* likewise indicated that job-related satisfaction varied across workplaces, implying that it was partly determined by the workplace itself and not just by demography or by job-related characteristics. The MacLeod and Clarke report (2009) also draws attention to a 2006 study by Professor Katie Truss and the Kingston Business School, carried out on behalf of the CIPD, which found that only three in ten of UK employees were actively engaged with their work – findings echoed by a YouGov survey for the Trades Union Congress in 2008. Recent work for the CLC has indicated that one in five UK workers might be engaged, but only 4% exhibited the highest levels of engagement.

**THEORY**  The MacLeod and Clarke study (2009) found that within the public sector the levels of engagement were comparable with those in the private sector. Towers Perrin pointed out that 12% of UK public sector staff are 'highly engaged', and 22% 'disengaged' – figures borne out by results from the Annual National Health Service staff survey. McLeod and Clarke are convinced that even if these figures are only indicative, they suggest that overall levels of engagement in the UK are lower than they could be. They also report that managers appear to be increasingly less likely to encourage and support employees to try new things. And they point out that:

- From 2008 to 2009 the number of employees who said that their manager supported new ways of doing things declined from 51% to 40%.

- The number of employees who reported that managers were encouraging them to develop their own ideas declined from 51% to 43%.

- Those who reported that their manager encouraged them to actively try out new ideas declined from 48% to 38%.

- No fewer than 42% of employees said that they would refuse to recommend their organisations as an employer to friends and family.

- Only 24% of private sector employees believe that change is well managed in their organisations, compared with 15% in the public sector (Ipsos MORI).

- There is increasing evidence that individuals' skills are being under-utilised at work – a significant source of disengagement for the individuals affected. The 2004 *Workplace Employment Relations Survey* found that over half of employees surveyed considered that the skills they possessed were higher than those required to do their jobs.

- Concern over engagement levels is widely shared. From a global sample of 60 companies, the Corporate Leadership Council found that over 80% of senior HR professionals agreed that employee engagement was a high priority for 2009 and for future years.

If higher engagement is correlated with improved economic performance and increased competitiveness, the relatively low levels of engagement in the UK are evidently impacting adversely on the UK economy. Gallup estimated that in 2008 the cost of disengagement to the UK economy was between a low of £60 billion and a high of £65 billion. The IES/Work Foundation also reported in 2008 that if organisations increased their investment in a range of good workplace practices relating to engagement by just 10%, they would increase profits by £1,500 per employee per year.

How do we explain the relatively low extent of employee engagement in the UK? The MacLeod and Clarke report (2009) points to four reasons. First, there are still too many chief executives and senior managers who are unaware of employee engagement or have still to be convinced of its benefits. Many are put off by evidence that the benefits of investing in employee engagement approaches may take time to show through in performance. Others dismiss the concept as 'soft and fluffy' rather than a bottom-line issue. Second, even those who are interested in the concept frequently do not seem interested in addressing the topic or know where to go to get practical advice and support. Getting started, comment MacLeod and Clarke, can be a challenge. Third, there persists a managerial mindset that demeans human beings as human resources and human capital, as opposed to creative and productive people who are the wellspring of success. Finally, there is poor management leadership, which gives rise in turn to poor management practice and to line managers' failing to engage with their staff. MacLeod and Clarke argue that poor management skills in dealing with employees lies behind many of the causes of disengagement, and they remind us that people join organisations – but they leave managers.

## REFLECTIVE ACTIVITY

To what extent does employee engagement operate at your workplace? Why is engagement at this level, do you think? What might be done to increase it?

## ENGAGED WITH WHAT OR WHOM?

Engagement is a combination of attitude and behaviour. The attitude is commitment, and behaviour is action to co-operate – sometimes referred to as 'going the extra mile'. But committed or engaged with what or whom? The ACAS discussion document draws attention to the importance of this, since the policy implications vary according to the nature and direction of engagement. Management consultants who undertake employee engagement surveys give the impression that engagement is mainly or wholly to do with engagement *with the employer and the organisation* for which people work. It is normally measured as the extent to which employees wish to stay with their employer, are proud to work for the firm, and are prepared to exert extra effort on behalf of the organisation. This can sometimes be brought together as an 'engagement index'. Although correct, it is too narrow an interpretation. Commitment to a supervisor has a stronger link to performance than does commitment to the organisation. In reality, employees have multiple loyalties. In some circumstances, employees such as a lawyer or a teacher may be indifferent towards an employer but be passionate about their job, team leader and customers.

THEORY This multi-faceted nature of employee engagement has been noted by researchers at the Employee Engagement Consortium at Kingston University. They point out that central to the concept of employee engagement is the idea that all employees can make a contribution to the successful functioning and continuous improvement of organisational processes. They view employment as being about creating opportunities for employees to connect with their colleagues, managers and the wider organisation. It is, for them, about creating an environment in which employees are motivated to want to connect with their work and really care about doing a good job. The Kingston researchers report that there is evidence that engaged employees perform better than others, take less sick leave and are less likely to leave their employer. They distinguish between three types (or dimensions) of employee engagement:

- *intellectual engagement* – the extent to which individuals are absorbed in their work and think about ways in which performance can be improved

- *affective engagement* – the extent to which people feel positive emotional connections to their work experience and thus with the company

- *social engagement* – the extent to which employees talk to colleagues about work-related improvements and change.

An implication of this research is that employee engagement has a number of dimensions and that what motivates one group of employees to be engaged may differ from another. As Kinnie *et al* (2005) point out, one size does not fit all, and this means that employers have to understand the different motivators of engagement in different sections of their business – especially differences between occupations. At the same time, there are key common factors linking the experience of work to organisational commitment and engagement for all employees, or the vast bulk of them (Purcell *et al*, 2009). Using the 2004 *Workplace Employment Relations Survey*, the ACAS policy discussion document on *Building Employee Engagement* argued that it is possible to distinguish between eight main occupational groups and, using regression analysis, identify factors significantly linked to positive commitment for all or most occupations. These are:

- employee trust in management (significant for all occupations)

- satisfaction with work itself (significant for seven of the eight occupations)

- satisfaction with involvement in decision-making at the workplace (significant for six out of the eight occupations)

- the quality of relationships between management and employers, often referred to as the 'employee relations climate' (significant for five of the eight occupations)

- satisfaction with the amount of pay received (significant for five of the eight occupations)

- job challenge (significant for five of the eight occupations)

- satisfaction with the sense of achievement obtained from work (significant for four of the eight occupational groups).

Trust in management was highly significant for all occupations. closely followed by job satisfaction (doing the work itself) and involvement in decision-making, sometimes referred to as 'employee voice'. These factors are basic building-blocks for employee engagement.

## DISENGAGEMENT

Not all employees are engaged and, indeed, the number who are 'fully engaged' – meaning that they score highly in every dimension – is often unexpectedly small, in many cases less than one in five. As the ACAS policy document points out, the search for the fully engaged employee may be a distraction, since an employee can be highly engaged in one or two aspects of their work, less so in others, and yet still be very effective and committed.

The factors associated with disengagement or low levels of engagement can expose basic failings in employment policy and practices. It is accepted, for example, that where people work in jobs with very short task cycle times, perhaps a minute or less (as found in some telephone contact centres and some manufacturing assembly work), where there is high stress related to little autonomy and inflexibility, and where there is a feeling of job insecurity, employees will tend to have lower engagement levels. These factors point to the need for 'good jobs' through better job design. Lower levels of engagement are also more likely to be found where there is perceived unfairness in rewards, where there is bullying and harassment, and where people believe they are stuck in their jobs and feel cut off from open communications. This has clear implications for line manager behaviour.

## THE EMPLOYEE ENGAGEMENT SURVEY

In 2004 the *Workplace Employment Relations Survey* reported that 42% of workplaces employing 10 or more people had conducted an employee survey in the two years prior to the *Workplace Survey*. The incidence was greater in workplaces where there was a specialist HR manager. Surveys were more likely in the public sector (over two-thirds) than the private sector (37%) and were more frequently found in large workplaces. It is difficult to assess in any useful way the level of employee engagement without systematically consulting the employees themselves. The upside of surveys is that they not only provide data which gives evidence on levels of employee engagement and variations between parts of the organisation, but can also highlight the factors that contribute to engagement, supported by statistical evidence. Survey results can, when used constructively alongside other data – for example, absence and labour turnover, customer satisfaction, quality measures – help to explain differences in the data. The MacLeod and Clarke report (2009) provided interesting data from the Nationwide Building Society showing the difference in the business performance of 41 areas according to whether the staff engagement scores were high, medium or low.

Since April 2008 the Nationwide Building Society has produced an Area Directors' Measurement Pack that includes information on business performance (for example, lending, business insurance, savings and banking), customer experience, operational and regulatory risk, staff performance review results, voluntary employee turnover and absence rates. The retail areas are then divided into three categories (high, medium and low) according to staff engagement scores, which enables the company to compare 41 areas on a scale in which the 14 areas with the highest engagement levels are classed as 'high engagement', the next 14 as 'medium engagement', and the bottom 13 as 'low engagement'. It shows that those areas with high engagement score 14 percentage points higher on the sale of banking products than those with low engagement scores, and are 34 percentage points higher on the sales of general insurance. In terms of customer service, Nationwide found significantly higher scores for customer experience in areas of high engagement. There was a difference of 8 percentage points between 'high' and 'low'. Those retail areas within Nationwide's branch network with high engagement had a voluntary employee turnover rate of just over 10%, whereas in those with low engagement it was some 18%. Nationwide also found that retail areas in the top third of their relative engagement index had lower absence levels. They calculated that if all retail areas brought their engagement scores up to those in the top third, and there was a parallel improvement in the number of days lost, it could represent a financial saving of £800,000 per year.

The engagement survey has to be effective and well designed and have the confidence of the employees as well as the senior managers. The ACAS document on *Building Employee Engagement* sets out 10 key steps in running an effective and authoritative employee engagement survey.

## TEN STEPS TO RUNNING AN EFFECTIVE EMPLOYEE ENGAGEMENT SURVEY

### 1 Obtain active support from top management

There must be strong support from top management for conducting the survey, publishing the results and taking action in the light of the issues identified. Top management must also be committed to repeating the survey at regular intervals. The survey's aims and design, and the actions to be taken following the results, should be on the agenda of the executive board and/or the board of directors.

### 2 Ensure alignment with the business strategy

The survey must be closely aligned with the business strategy so that key areas of importance to the business can be identified. This could be innovation, leadership, quality, absence, or whatever. To do this will involve discussions with appropriate senior managers.

### 3 Involve employees in the design

Equally, the survey needs the support of the employees and should cover items of importance from their perspective. This means discussing the survey with the recognised trade union or employee representatives. Focus groups with employees can help identify key issues that should be covered in the questionnaire.

### 4 Decide on the arrangements for the survey

The decision must be taken whether to survey all employees or to rely on a sample. In very large organisations sampling is possible although the authenticity of the survey then tends to suffer in the eyes of the employees, since people may say 'Well, they didn't ask *me.*' Will the survey be filled in by hand on hard copy or be completed online? Employees may be given a choice over which method suits them best. It is useful for around two weeks to be afforded to complete the survey.

### 5 Encourage everyone to take part

Deliberate and considered action must be taken before and during the survey to publicise it and encourage everyone to take part. Most surveys can achieve a response rate of around 60% to 70% if there has been a concerted effort via all communication media to 'sell' the survey. One of the key issues is to ensure confidentiality. Stories abound of managers whose pay is linked to response rates on survey results either bullying staff to complete the survey and to answer questions in a certain way so as to minimise bad news, or giving rewards during the survey period.

### 6 Ensure confidentiality

Confidentiality is essential. Staff must be confident that their answers cannot be traced back to them, and that they are able to say what they really think and feel. Using an external agency to conduct the survey helps protect confidentiality. If the survey is online and an agency is not being used, a remote external server is essential. Confidentiality is also achieved by following the rule that data is never broken into groups of fewer than 10 people. Although it may be important to collect some demographic data such as ethnicity, age, gender and disabilities, it is vital to ensure that this does not inadvertently identify someone from a minority group.

### 7 Take care in selecting the questions to ask

The range of questions should include measures of engagement and those key parts of people management and employment relations which theory and practice suggest are likely to be causal factors. These are likely to include:

- attitudes towards the nature of the work (autonomy, discretion, responsibility, control)

- attitudes towards the nature of the job (workload, pace, monitoring, skills)
- attitudes towards management and unions (communication, involvement, representation)
- attitudes towards management (trust and the climate of employee relations)
- attitudes towards the company (advocacy, pride, loyalty).

### 8 Benchmark the questions to compare results

The design of the survey should not be seen as a one-off event but as part of a continuous effort to monitor and build employee engagement. It is important to be able to benchmark the results over time to plot changes in levels of engagement and compare the results with those in the same sector and the economy as a whole. External survey agencies can provide this service and ensure that the questions replicate those asked elsewhere. An important additional reason for using standard questions is that they are likely to have been tried and tested. This suggests that a core number of questions will be used in every survey. It is possible to add additional questions to cover areas of particular concern or interest. The only caveat is that the questionnaire should not take more than 15 minutes overall to complete, or response rates will fall. Most surveys use a five-point scale giving the respondents a choice of how satisfied or dissatisfied they are, plus a neutral position.

### 9 Analyse the results

Simple descriptive analysis of the results provides a basis for understanding the overall picture of employee engagement. More sophisticated statistical analysis will allow questions to be grouped together to explore patterns of behaviour and attitudes, what factors contribute to engagement, and how these differ – for instance, between types of employee, department or locations.

### 10 Report back and take action

It is good practice to report the results of the engagement survey within two months of the closing date. Full results must be reported to senior management and in some instances to union or employee consultative committees. There must be discussion of areas in which action should be taken to help build levels of engagement or deal with weaknesses identified through the survey results. It is common practice – and a good one – for the results to be relayed to employees using various forms of company media but especially via team meetings or briefings at which there can be a discussion of the measuring of the results and reports on planned actions. Some employers make the engagement results one of the key performance indicators for line managers.

The employee engagement survey provides very useful information to support the search for better alternatives. Concentrating on developing employee engagement has the advantage that it frequently does not require the introduction of new policies or employment practices. It is not, for example, like calls for a new pay and rewards system that might require the organisation to invest in new computer software.

## THE CASE FOR EMPLOYEE ENGAGEMENT

The MacLeod and Clarke report (2009) points out that the growing currency of engagement has generated a large number of studies from academics, consultancies and organisations that look at the impact of high levels of engagement on outcomes for the business or organisation. It further remarks that this research, together with anecdotal evidence, covers a wide range of industries, and suggests that there is a strong story to be told about the link between employee engagement and positive outcomes. In particular, there are a number of studies that demonstrate that private sector organisations with higher levels of employee engagement enjoy a better financial performance, and that high levels of engagement are also associated with better outcomes in the public sector. Research into the extent to which reliable associations can be found between levels of engagement and performance outcomes is increasingly available. As John Purcell told the MacLeod and Clarke researchers:

> Despite the difficulties and weaknesses, it is hard to ignore the volume of studies which show, to varying degrees, with varying sophistication, a positive relationship between high-performance/-involvement work practices and outcome measures ...

At the same time, however, caution is necessary in the assessment and interpretation of 'evidence' about the processes and benefits of engagement. Many studies of the subject lack empirical detail and devote excessive attention to the views of those who have a vested interest in reporting progress and success. Watch out for any tendency towards overblown rhetoric. Employee engagement, if properly understood, carefully implemented and objectively measured, is however a powerful tool for delivering positive reputational and 'bottom-line' outcomes.

### THE PRIVATE SECTOR

We next consider three private sector case studies illustrating the advantages of employee engagement.

CASE STUDY

## The law firm Fairfields Bruckhaus Deringer

Employee engagement is fundamental to Fairfields' approach to retaining and developing people. As a way to ensure that they continue to improve in this area, they launched an Associate Engagement Group (AEG) in their London Office in 2007.

Currently made up of 11 associates and five partners, the AEG is aimed at facilitating changes to help associates become more engaged in the business and in the way the London Office operates. The firm sees this as an important step towards giving associates more involvement in decisions that affect them and more opportunities to play a wider role in the firm.

It means that the associates examine working practices in detail and challenge them, addressing an enormous range of issues, from revamping the London Office reception area to evaluating their career path.

The AEG gathers feedback from roughly 600 London associates through a survey and face-to-face meetings, identifying key issues and forming the year's agenda, culminating in a one-day forum at which all associates can meet and talk to partners.

Topics usually include appraisals, feedback and mentoring, career prospects and communications. One associate describes it as 'a great chance to discuss the London-wide issues that have been identified as the most important to us, the company, and to have partner input into how improvements can be made'.

AEG working groups make recommendations to management and to the forum. The issues they tackle are categorised as 'quick fixes', 'rapid-focus' or 'longer-term'. Quick fixes can be as simple as replacing paper cups with china mugs, while rapid-focus groups concentrate on areas of substantive concern such as associate involvement in business development. The work of the longer-term groups covers issues such as career paths and planning, and is ongoing.

Source: *People Management*, 5 November 2009

CASE STUDY

## Engagement at Sainsbury's

Most companies would be aware that in order to improve performance you need motivated, engaged people. But you need to define what 'engagement' means for your organisation.

For Sainsbury's, colleague engagement does not start and finish at the checkout. The company has 150,000 people working for it and recognises that it will only achieve its goal if everyone pulls together.

In 2005 the company developed a sales-led recovery programme, 'Making Sainsbury's Great Again', that refocused on the core elements of its brand – 'great food at fair prices delivered by great colleagues'. A cornerstone of this was the creation of a new goal and values. The company wanted to give colleagues back a voice through listening to their opinions and ideas and demonstrating that it believed their contribution made a difference.

Colleagues Councils exist in every Sainsbury's location, giving people a chance to voice their opinions on everything from facilities to charity fundraising. In August 2004 Sainsbury's launched its 'Tell Justin' scheme. This received over 27,000 suggestions from colleagues, many of which were adopted. The company also organised 'The Big Pitch', which encouraged colleagues to put forward ideas to improve the business. Nearly 650 took part, and 12 were selected to present their ideas to a judging panel led by Chief Executive Justin King.

The results of the opinion survey clearly showed the impact engagement has in relation to business performance. The company's 10 highest-performing stores on engagement outperform on sales, service, availability and absence, while those with the lowest engagement scores remain below target on some measures.

Increasingly, Sainsbury's is learning that it is not only what we do internally that influences engagement. Over the past two years it has focused on community initiatives and found that these also make a difference.

Source: *People Management*, 5 November 2009

## CASE STUDY

### TUI UK and Ireland

*The team:* HR

*Number in team:* 100

*Number of staff for which responsible:* 17,000

*The organisation:* Travel company TUI, UK and Ireland, created in 2007 by a merger of First Choice and Thomson

*The challenge:* To implement an effective employee engagement strategy, bringing together staff from the two merged companies that were previously competitors

*What the organisation did:*

- asked for employee feedback for a new vision, values and strategy
- created an employee brand 'Be special'
- aligned HR processes with the company vision

- developed communication channels to suit the company's range of demographics and role
- launched a 'Work in partnership' (WIP) initiative to give staff a role in the decision-making process

*Benefits and achievements:*

- Fifteen months after the merger, 97% of the top 700 managers said they would work over and above what is expected of them.
- Decisions made in the WIP forums meant that the deadlines for integration were achieved.
- 'Be special' is now more than a brand and has come to represent the newly merged entity's culture.

Source: *People Management*, 27 October 2009

## REFLECTIVE ACTIVITY

What lessons can you draw from these three private sector studies?

The Sainsbury's case study is an example of an effective employee engagement strategy that evolved in developing new vision and values and created an employer brand to use as a basis for behavioural and cultural change. The three case studies also demonstrate that employee engagement places not the managers but the people who are managed at the centre stage of the organisation. They also emphasise the need for good leadership and management, and demonstrate that engagement brings a clear win for the individual employee. Because it is achieved by making changes that impact positively on how employees think and feel about what they experience at work, it is likely to impact positively on their well-being too.

**THEORY    PUBLIC SECTOR**

The MacLeod and Clarke study (2009) found that 78% of highly engaged employees in the UK public sector said they could make an impact on public service delivery or customer service, as against 29% of the disengaged. Two of the data reports in this sector found that one key characteristic of employee engagement – staff advocacy – was strongly associated with better organisational performance as measured by external regulators. A survey conducted by Ipsos MORI of staff in local councils found that councils rated 'excellent' by the Audit Commission were more likely to have higher levels of staff advocacy (ie staff who would speak highly about the authority to others outside the organisation) than those rated 'weak'. A similar finding emerged when the ratings of hospital trusts by the Healthcare Commission were compared to the staff survey results.

The conclusion from the evidence available of the impact of successful employee engagement in practice is that the relationship between engagement, well-being and performance is too strong and is repeated too often for it to be a coincidence. By engaging their staff through a series of techniques and processes, organisations (both private and public) have succeeded in changing the emphasis from direct supervision of employees to self-managed teams, to leadership training, to meaningful consultation (communication/voice), recognition, continuous improvement and employee well-being. Especially important is communications, in that senior staff of the organisation have a clear vision of the organisation and can articulate it to the staff, enabling them:

- to understand how their role (job) fits into the bigger picture of the organisation
- to provide staff with feedback on their performance
- to listen to their concerns
- to give staff autonomy and control by giving them the opportunity to show initiative and to input their own ideas
- to be fully confident in the senior management team and in that team's concern for the employees.

The evidence also shows that in unlocking discretionary effort from staff, not only is exceptional communication necessary but so is respected leadership and a strong sense of community centring on shared values. There is thus no shortage of evidence about people management policies and practices (for example, employee voice and teamworking) that contribute to the building of employee engagement. A survey by Towers Perrin of employee attitudes in six European countries found that a key component in securing workforce engagement was visible commitment and involved senior leaders who communicated frequently and believably on a range of business and organisational issues. Communication is the factor which makes policies real and without which they are ineffective. It is not enough that messages are delivered. They have to have been received and understood or there will be no impact on employees' hearts and minds. Employees who work for engaging organisations are with an organisation they feel proud to work for, have managers who are more likely to listen and care for them, have leaders who listen to and inspire them, have more opportunities for personal growth and development, and work in teams that support each other. They are highly likely to perceive the deal they get from the employer as positive, and they experience lower levels of stress and a better work–life balance.

## BARRIERS TO ENGAGEMENT                                    THEORY

MacLeod and Clarke (2009) identified four broad barriers to effective management by an organisation's leaders. These barriers occurred across both the private and public sectors, and were:

- a lack of awareness of employee engagement
- not knowing how to address the issue
- the negativity of managers and of the consequential organisational culture
- great variability in the views of managers and leaders and their commitment to employee engagement.

To this list can be added resistance to change.

### LACK OF AWARENESS

Some leaders are not aware of employee engagement. Others do not believe that it is worth considering or do not fully understand the concept and the benefits it could have for their organisation. Accenture reported that 75% of leaders have no engagement plan or strategy even though 90% said that engagement impacts on business success. Uncertainty over engagement is also reflected in a fear that engagement might be seen as too 'soft and fluffy' or as 'not the British way'. As the law firm Fairfields Bruckhaus Deringer told MacLeod and Clarke:

> We could have come out from a fluffy approach but it wouldn't have worked. So we put the performance metrics up front …

This lack of appreciation at the most senior level of what employees contribute is underscored by Accenture's finding that over half of the chief financial officers surveyed had little more than a minimal understanding of the returns on their investment in human capital. Some argue that a greater awareness of the benefits of employee engagement will only come after 'ditching the centuries-old dominance of accountancy as the way of understanding the organisation'.

## UNCERTAINTY ABOUT STARTING

Other leaders who are interested in employee engagement do not know how to address the issue within their organisation. This lack of certainty about how, and where, to start can be compounded by the feeling that employee engagement is something that it is 'out there' – a product one buys, often at great expense. It is not always helpful to focus on employee engagement as a product. In itself it can be a barrier to action. MacLeod and Clarke (2009) also point out that there are those who have a tendency to confuse useful thinking with positive action on employee engagement.

## MANAGERS AND ORGANISATIONAL CULTURE

Even when leaders place great emphasis on the idea of employee engagement, managers may not share the belief, or may be ill-equipped to implement engagement strategies. As a result, the organisational culture is unable to deliver engagement. The Kingston Business School identified these deficiencies as:

- reactive decision-making that fails to address the problem in time
- inconsistent management style based on the attitude of individual managers which leads to perceptions of unfairness
- lack of fluidity in communications and the knowledge of sharing due to a rigidity in communication channels or in cultural norms
- low perceptions of senior management visibility and the quality of downward communication
- poor work–life balance due to a long-hours culture.

Many respondents told MacLeod and Clarke of the need for better training for managers in so-called soft or people skills, both as part of the current syllabus for business qualifications and more generally. A large proportion of them felt that current skills training concentrated too heavily on qualifications and too little on how people skills were implemented within the workforce. As one respondent remarked:

> Too often managers are promoted because of their competence in the job they last did – not because they've the right skills for the new one.

## UNDERESTIMATING ENGAGEMENT

Among those leaders who are concerned with employee engagement, there is great variability in their views and commitment to it. Often, the potential of engagement is underestimated. For some, engagement is an annual staff survey of which the results may be acted upon. For others, a survey is no more than one tool in an overall approach that places employee engagement at the core of the organisation's strategy. Respondents to the MacLeod and Clarke survey (2009) expressed concern that some senior managers regarded employee engagement as another job on the to-do list that could be ticked off once an annual staff survey had been carried out, and the results perhaps delegated to HR and line managers to fix. This misses the point that keeping employees engaged is an ongoing process that has to be hard-wired into the organisation's DNA. Nor is engagement something that can be achieved overnight – a need for quick results does not sit easily with the extent of culture change that might be required. To copy out a survey and then not follow it through by implementing changes based on that survey's results is more likely to disengage staff than not doing the survey in the first place. It is important to take soundings and discover what the state of play is within an organisation. A staff survey may be a useful means of testing out levels of engagement, but it is not enough by itself – particularly if it leads to trying to change the engagement score rather than really fix the issues that make up the score.

## RESISTANCE TO CHANGE

Another reason often given for lack of action on employee engagement is resistance to change. The impression can be given that building employee engagement means that action is needed on every aspect of people management. This may include designing better jobs, building more effective employee voice systems, adopting a radical change in the manner in which line managers are selected, rewarded and trained, or transforming top management vision, values and leadership. This, then, becomes too daunting a list and it is unclear how long it would take for positive improvement to feed through.

### REFLECTIVE ACTIVITY

How do you think these barriers to engagement outlined above can be overcome?

## ENABLERS OF ENGAGEMENT                                          THEORY

According to the MacLeod and Clarke survey (2009), there are four 'broad enablers/drivers' which are critical to gaining employee engagement:

- leadership
- engaging managers
- employee voice
- integrity.

MacLeod and Clarke were themselves struck in the course of their work by how often the same four enablers/drivers were cited as being critical to employee engagement.

## LEADERSHIP

Leadership provides a strong strategic narrative which has widespread ownership and commitment from managers and employees at all levels. A strong narrative provides a clear shared vision for the organisation at which is the heart of employee engagement. It is an expressed story about what the purpose of an organisation is, why it has the broad vision it has, and how an individual contributes to that purpose. Employees must understand not only the purpose of the organisation for which they work but also how their individual role contributes to that vision.

## ENGAGING MANAGERS

Engaging managers are at the heart of organisational culture. They facilitate and empower rather than control or restrict staff. They treat their staff with appreciation and respect and show commitment to developing, increasing and rewarding the capabilities of those they manage. Engaging managers offer clarity for what is expected from individual members of staff, which involves some stretch and much appreciation and training. They treat their people as individuals with fairness and respect and with a concern for the employee's well-being, and have a very important role in ensuring that work is designed efficiently and effectively. Employees need managers who are themselves engaged and who are seen to be committed to the organisation and who need to 'know, focus, care and inspire' employees. Engaging managers offer clarity, appreciation, positive feedback and coaching to their employees.

Given the crucial role of the line management relationship in the gaining of employee engagement, the Institute of Employment Studies (IES) embarked in 2009 on a research project entitled 'The Engaging Manager' to understand how managers who inspire and engage their teams to perform well behave in their dealings with people. The project involved seven organisations: the Association of Chartered Accountants, Centrica, Corus, HM Revenue and Customs, the London Borough of Merton, Rolls-Royce and Sainsbury's. Researchers identified 25 'engaging managers', and the IES interviewed them, their own managers and their teams. The interviews centred on engaging behaviour rather than on personality. The 25 managers had little in common except their ability to engage their teams via very similar behaviours. Their jobs and roles varied, their span of control ranged from four people to over 5,000, and they were very different in terms of personality, background and training.

All the managers interviewed said that an important way to learn about management was to observe others. One remarked:

> I think my style is more looking at managers I worked with before, and stealing the bits that work for me and losing the bits that don't.

A very strong theme was the belief that they should be clear about goals and expectations, as summed up by the comment:

> I try to encourage people to think of the wider objectives and how they fit in ...

The managers in the IES research had been selected by their organisations because their teams had high engagement scores. Yet it soon became apparent they were also high-performing managers with high-performing teams. It was additionally noticeable that the managers were good at the difficult matters – tackling poor performance quickly and effectively and breaking bad news. The consensus was that honesty and openness were essential, along with empathy and demonstrating that the manager had an understanding of the possible impact on staff.

Because the engaging managers were mostly in middle or senior posts, their own line managers were almost all more senior managers. Most had seen changes in the engaging manager's style – an important finding because it shows that managers can acquire new behaviours and become more engaging. Several described their engaging managers as gaining increased self-awareness, often alongside modified behaviour. Senior managers valued their engaging manager's ability to communicate and to motivate and involve the team, enabling people to give their best. They also felt that their engaging manager had a good approach to managing performance with a focus on clarity of expectation.

There was a feeling amongst engaged teams that they were happy and enjoyed their work, and that there was a good atmosphere, compared with other teams. An important feature was teams' openness and ability to discuss a wide range of topics. Comments included, 'You can almost see a visual difference between the teams', and 'There's an openness which doesn't happen elsewhere.' As well as describing engaging behaviours, respondents were asked to describe disengaging managerial behaviour (see Table 9.1). Lastly, team members were asked to draw a picture that represented how they saw their manager. Several themes emerged. The most popular picture of all, however, was of a sun or a smiling face.

**Table 9.1 Top behaviours of engaging and disengaging managers**

| The top behaviours of engaging managers | The top behaviours of disengaging managers |
| --- | --- |
| Communicates, makes clear what is expected | Lacks empathy/interest in people |
| Listens, values and involves team | Fails to listen and communicate |
| Is supportive, backs team/you up | Is self-centred |
| Is target-focused | Doesn't motivate or inspire |
| Has clear strategic vision | Blames others, doesn't take responsibility |
| Shows active interest in others | Is aggressive |
| Displays good leadership skills | Lacks awareness |
| Is respected | Doesn't deliver |

Source: *People Management*, 5 November 2009

## EMPLOYEE VOICE

In an organisation that affords effective and empowered employee voice, the views of employees are sought out. They are listened to and the employees see that their opinions count and make a difference. Employees speak out and challenge management when appropriate. A strong sense of listening and of responsiveness permeates the organisation, enabled by effective communication.

According to many surveys, feeling listened to is the most important factor in determining how much employees value their organisation. Being heard reinforces a sense of belonging within an organisation and a belief that one's actions can have an impact. But of course employers must act upon what they learn from their employees. A key driver of engagement, according to MacLeod and Clarke (2009), is the ability for employees to feed their views upwards, feeling well-informed about what is happening in the organisation and thinking that one's manager is committed to the organisation. Action by management on feedback is critical. There are synergies between engagement approaches and partnership agreements working between unions and employers where trust, co-operation and information-sharing are key.

## INTEGRITY

Behaviour throughout the organisation should be consistent with stated values, leading to trust and a sense of integrity. Most organisations have stated values and all have accepted behavioural norms. Where there is a gap between the two, the size of the gap is reflected in the degree of mistrust within the organisation. If the gap is closed, high levels of trust usually result. If an employee sees the stated values of the organisation being lived up to by the leadership and by colleagues, a sense of trust in the organisation is more likely to be developed thereby constituting a powerful enabler of engagement. Examples of the kinds of gaps between espoused values and what actually happens in practice might include having a sign outside the office which reads 'The employees are our most important asset' while tolerating a culture of bullying.

This list of enablers of employee engagement is not based on statistical research but rather emerged from the numerous conversations MacLeod and Clarke had on their visits and meetings around the country. The enablers come from the practical experience of a large number of organisations, big and small, private and public, which are trying to build engagement. The list of four drivers is more powerful because of this. The ACAS discussion document *Building Employee Engagement* concludes – summarising from many studies – that engagement is closely related to effective commitment, such that an engaged employee might say:

> I have a sense of belonging: I feel I am part of something, able to contribute in a climate of co-operation. It is backed by my experience that the organisation supports me and encourages my development, asking me to do an interesting job which can be worthwhile and challenging. The leaders of the organisation, and especially my line manager, are people I can trust and are good to work with, my opinions are listened to and my contribution is respected. I like working with able and committed work colleagues. It is good to work for a successful organisation or one that is striving to be so, with a clear mission and purpose, and I know what I do contributes to this ...

If employers are to address issues of employee engagement, they need a mechanism for measuring the concept. This can be achieved via a structured survey. The lists of drivers outlined by MacLeod and Clarke and other research findings provide the basis for selecting both what questions should be asked and what actions should be taken in responding to the survey results. There is also the issue of what policies and practices are likely, if effectively implemented, to build employee engagement.

## SUMMARY

- More and more companies are viewing employee engagement as the key to adopting high-performance work practices. The policy and practice implications of employee engagement are often captured in 'high-involvement work practices' and 'high-performance working'. High-performance work practices cannot be imposed by senior managers but is reliant upon developing employees' security, trust and their buying in to the goals and values of the organisation.

- There is an increasing recognition amongst all functions of management that people are the source of productive gain and competitive advantage. Employee engagement is 'the difference that makes the difference' and can make *all* the difference.

- Employee engagement is about unlocking people's potential at work. It builds on employee commitment to do a good job and makes it central to the operation of the organisation, enables employees to be the best they can at work, ensures that employees are committed to the organisation's goals and values, provides for trust and fairness based on mutual respect, and is a two-way process in which employer and employee reinforce each other.

- As a business issue, employee engagement is not the exclusive preserve of the HR profession. HR has a major role to play, however, in implementing engagement and thus forwards a significant opportunity for the profession to demonstrate its business-focused credibility.

- There are a number of theoretical approaches by which employee involvement can be analysed, including motivation theory, employment relations theory (pluralism), human capital theory (investment in individual employees) and organisational psychology theory (reciprocity theory).

- The MacLeod and Clark report (2009) shows that there is a wide variation in employee engagement levels in the UK within and between organisations. Its extent varies between age groups, different types of organisations and different job roles. Levels of engagement in the public sector were comparable with those in the private sector. The relatively low level of engagement in the UK is due to many senior managers being unaware of the benefits of engaging employees and/or being put off by the fact that the benefits may take time to show through in performance.

- There are three types of employee engagement – intellectual engagement, affective engagement and social engagement. The implication of this is that engagement has a number of dimensions and that what motivates one group of employees may differ from what motivates another. One size does not fit all.

Managers have to understand the motivators of engagement in the different parts of the business.

- Disengaged employees all feel job insecurity, have little autonomy in doing their work, feel they are treated unfairly, especially in rewards, may be subject to bullying and harassment, and are not listened to or respected.

- It is difficult to assess in any useful way the level of employee engagement without systematically consulting the employees themselves. Employee engagement surveys demonstrate the factors that contribute to building engagement. A survey must be effective and well designed. There are 10 steps in running an effective and authoritative employee engagement survey – top management active support; alignment with business strategy; involving employees in the design; deciding on the arrangements for the survey; encouraging everyone to take part; ensuring confidentiality; selecting the questions to ask; benchmarking the questions in order to compare results; analysing the results; and reporting back and taking action.

- There is a strong story to be told about the link between employee engagement and positive outcomes – better financial performance, lower absence and sickness rates and higher productivity. By engaging their staff through a series of techniques and processes, organisations (both private and public) have succeeded in changing the emphasis from direct supervision of employees to self-managed teams, to leadership training, to meaningful consultation and information-giving, recognition, continuous improvement and employee well-being. The research shows that in unlocking discretionary effort from staff, not only is exceptional communication necessary but so is respected leadership and a strong sense of community centring on shared values.

- The main barriers to increasing the extent of employee engagement in the UK are: a) lack of awareness of employee engagement on the part of senior management; b) managers who have interest in the concept do not know how to address the issue; c) negativity of managers and organisational culture (managers ill-equipped to implement engagement strategies); d) great variability in the views of managers and leaders and their commitment to employee engagement; and e) resistance to change.

- MacLeod and Clarke (2009) identify four broad enablers/drivers which are critical to successfully building employee engagement. These are leadership, engaging managers, employee voice (views are sought, consequent action is taken), and integrity (management's behaviour is consistent with the organisation's stated values).

## KEY LEARNING POINTS

- Engagement is about enabling people to be the best they can at work, recognising this can only happen if they feel respected, involved, well-led and valued by those they work for and with.

- In reality, employees have multiple loyalties – to their job, team leaders, customers, employer. They may be passionate about some of these but indifferent to some.

- It is difficult to assess in any useful way the level of employee engagement without systematically consulting the employees themselves – hence the importance of running an effective and authoritative employee engagement survey.

- By engaging their staff through a series of techniques and processes, organisations (private and public) have succeeded in changing the emphasis from direct supervision of employees to self-managed teams, to leadership training, to meaningful consultation, continuous improvement and employee well-being. Especially important in communications is that senior staff of the organisation have a clear vision of the organisation and can articulate it to the rest of the staff.

- Engaging managers are at the heart of organisational culture. They facilitate and empower rather than control or restrict staff. Feeling that they are listened to is the most important factor in determining how much employees value their organisation. They see that their opinions count and make a difference.

## REVIEW QUESTIONS

1   Using arguments that draw on appropriate evidence, explain how you would persuade your organisation that investment in improving employee engagement would be beneficial.

2   You have been asked by your line manager to carry out an employee engagement survey. What would you include in this survey? Justify your answer.

3   Outline the main barriers to effective management by an organisation's leaders and explain what action you might be able to take to overcome these barriers.

4   Explain why leadership and employee voice are critical 'enablers' to gaining employee engagement.

5   At a recent meeting of managers in your workplace it was remarked that in a recession employee engagement has little or no relevance. Your line manager asks you whether you agree with this view. What would you tell your line manager – and why?

**EXPLORE FURTHER**

Advisory, Conciliation and Arbitration Service (2010) *Building Employee Engagement*, Policy Discussion Paper, January. London: ACAS.

Barker, G. (2006) 'The benefits of an engaged workforce', *Personnel Today*, October.

Chartered Institute of Personnel and Development (2005) *What is Employee Relations?* London: CIPD.

Emmott, M. (2006) 'Hear me now', *People Management*, November.

Johnson, M. (2004) *The New Rules of Engagement, Life–Work Balance and Employee Commitment*. London: Chartered Institute of Personnel and Development.

Kersley, B., Alpin, C., Forth, J., Bryson, A., Bewley, H., Dix, G. and Oxenbridge, S. (2006) *Inside the Workplace: Findings from the 2004 Workplace Employment Relations Survey*. London: Routledge.

Kinnie, N., Hutchinson, S., Purcell, J., Rayton, B. and Swart, B. (2005) 'Satisfaction with HR practices and commitment to the organisation – why one size does not fit all', *Human Resource Management*, Vol.15, No.4: 9–20.

MacLeod, D. and Clarke, N. (2009) *Engaging for Success: Enhancing performance through employee engagement: a report to government*. London: Department for Business, Innovation and Skills.

O'Reilly, C. and Pfeffer, J. (2000) *Hidden Value: How great companies achieve extraordinary results with ordinary people*. Boston, MA: Harvard Business School.

*People Management* (2009) 'Research on managers', November.

*People Management* (2009) 'The award for employee engagement', October.

Purcell, J., Kinnie, N., Swart, J., Rayton, B. and Hutchinson, S. (2009) *People Management and Performance*. London: Routledge.

Robinson, D. and Hayday, S. (2009) *Engaging Managers*. London: Institute of Employment Studies.

**Websites**

http://engagement.accorservices.co.uk/website/employee-engagement-whitepaper-form.html

www.cipd.co.uk/research is a website that gives access to CIPD research and documents on employee engagement

www.idea.gov.uk is a web resource that would help anyone planning, implementing or reviewing a programme of action to improve employee engagement

www.youtube.com for an employee engagement video

## CHAPTER 10

# Other Employment Relations Processes

## OVERVIEW

This chapter begins by analysing the theoretical approaches to collective bargaining of the Webbs (an economic institution), of Alan Flanders (a political process) and of Neil Chamberlain. It then examines the neo-classical economic view that collective bargaining is the cause of unemployment and poverty. Next, the chapter looks at the conditions necessary for collective bargaining to take place, and at its dimensions (level, scope, etc). This is followed by a detailed analysis of a special type of collective bargaining agreement – namely, partnership agreements. The section explains the principles underpinning such agreements and gives examples of them from the papermaking industry, the general print sector, the fire and rescue service and the Scottish Prison Service. The benefits to management of these agreements are then discussed, as are the contemporary research findings on the outcome of such agreements. Next, the chapter analyses the decline, over the past 30 years, in the use of industrial action. If collective bargaining breaks down, the differences between the social partners may be settled peacefully by the use of the disputes procedure and/or the use of third-party intervention (conciliation, mediation and arbitration). The chapter explains these processes fully. The final part of the chapter examines the strategies a management might adopt to minimise the disruption to an organisation caused by the imposition of industrial sanctions by the employees.

## LEARNING OUTCOMES

When you have completed this chapter, you should understand and be aware of:

- the main theoretical approaches to collective bargaining
- the dimensions of collective bargaining in terms of its coverage, scope and level
- the main types of bargaining arrangements – for example, single-table, multi-union

- the main advantages and disadvantages to employers of partnership agreements
- the importance of collective bargaining as a pay determination mechanism
- trends in collective industrial conflict in the UK
- how to justify the use by employers of conciliation, mediation and arbitration to resolve disputes
- the processes of conciliation, mediation and arbitration
- the strategies and policies managers might adopt to minimise the likely effects of the imposition of industrial sanctions against their organisation.

## INTRODUCTION

Collective bargaining, in spite of a major decline in its use, nevertheless still remains an important employment relations process. The 2004 *Workplace Employment Relations Survey* found that around 27% of workplaces set pay for at least some of their employees through collective bargaining with unions. In organisations employing between 200 and 499 employees and those employing 500 or more, the corresponding figures were 57% and 65% respectively. The greater incidence of collective bargaining in larger establishments meant that the overall percentage of employees who had their pay set through collective bargaining was higher (40%) than the percentage of workplaces with at least some collective bargaining. In the public sector 83% of workplaces set pay for at least some of the employees through collective bargaining with a union.

## THEORY | COLLECTIVE BARGAINING

### THEORETICAL APPROACHES

The major theoretical approaches to collective bargaining are those of:

- Sidney and Beatrice Webb, who in their classic work *Industrial Democracy*, published in 1902, regarded collective bargaining as an economic institution
- Alan Flanders, who in his classic article entitled 'Collective bargaining: a theoretical analysis' in the *British Journal of Industrial Relations*, November 1968, viewed collective bargaining as a political institution
- Neil Chamberlain in his classic 1951 book entitled *Collective Bargaining*. This work produced a generic definition of the institution encompassing twentieth-century developments in its character
- neo-classical economic theory, which sees the effects of collective bargaining as increased unemployment and worker poverty.

## Sidney and Beatrice Webb

For the Webbs, collective bargaining was one of three methods by which trade unions sought to maintain and improve the living standards of their members. It was perceived as an alternative to the methods of mutual insurance (ie providing their members with various benefits such as unemployment, strike and sickness payments) and legal enactment (ie pressing for legislation which favoured their interests). The Webbs did not provide a definition of collective bargaining, arguing that it could best be understood by a number of examples. They put forward the following comparison by way of explanation:

> In organised trades, the individual workman, applying for a job, accepts or refuses the terms offered by the employer without communication with his fellow workmen and without any other consideration than the exigencies of his own position. For the sale of his labour, he makes with the employer a strictly individual bargain. But if a group of workmen concert together and send representatives to conduct the bargaining on behalf of the whole body, the position is at once changed. Instead of the employer making a series of separate contracts with isolated individuals, he meets with a collective will, and settles, in a single agreement, the principles upon which, for the time being, all workmen of a particular group, or class, or grade, will be engaged ...

For the Webbs, collective bargaining was exactly what the words imply – a collective equivalent and alternative to individual bargaining. Where employees were willing and able to combine, they preferred it to bargaining as an individual with their employer because it enabled them to secure better terms of employment by controlling competition amongst themselves. For the Webbs, collective bargaining is an economic institution.

Flanders (1968) was critical of the Webbs' approach. First, he thought they ignored the employers' interest in collective bargaining and assumed that collective bargaining was something forced upon employers against their will by strikes and other union sanctions. Although this may be true in some cases, it is undeniable that some employers do see advantages in engaging in collective bargaining (see Chapter 2). Second, Flanders argued that the Webbs were not comparing like with like. The individual bargain (agreement) between the employer and the employee, and which is given legal status in the form of an employment contract, provides for an exchange of work for money (wages and other employment conditions). It sets out the conditions of exchange. A collective agreement, however, as Flanders points out, does not commit anyone to buy or sell labour services. Its function is to ensure that when labour services are bought and sold, the employment conditions offered will, at least, match with the terms of the agreement. For Flanders, a collective agreement is essentially a body of rules to regulate the labour market, and as he points out, 'This is a feature which has no proper counterpart in individual bargaining.'

## Alan Flanders

For Flanders, collective bargaining is a political institution. It is, for him, a rule-making and rule-administration process. The parties to collective bargaining negotiate procedural as well as substantive agreements (see Chapter 1) to regulate their own relationships, as distinct from the employment relationship between the individual employee and the individual employer. For Flanders, the joint making of procedural rules is very much part of the collective bargaining process, and he therefore regarded everything concerned with avoiding and/or resolving conflicts between the buyers and sellers of labour services – including grievance settlement – as collective bargaining. Unlike the Webbs, Flanders also regarded collective bargaining as involving a power relationship between organisations. He saw collective bargaining as being distinct from other rule-making processes such as legislation and third-party intervention in the authorship of collectively bargained rules. Such rules are jointly determined by representatives of employers and employees who, as a result, share responsibility for their content and observance.

Flanders was also critical of the Webbs for ignoring any consideration of the social achievements of collective bargaining. He argued that for those employees on whose behalf a trade union acts in collective bargaining, the impact of its actions extends beyond the securing of economic advancement to the establishment of rights in industry:

- the right to a defined rate of wages
- the right not to have to work longer than a certain number of hours
- the right to be paid for holidays.

The rules of collective bargaining may also regulate issues such as dismissal, discipline, promotion or training. Rules in a collective agreement by defining rights (and obligations) are also a means of preventing favouritism, nepotism, victimisation and arbitrary discrimination. In negotiating collective agreements, for Flanders, trade unions are acting jointly with employers as private legislators to promote the 'rule of law' in employment relations. Collective bargaining is received as an institution freeing employees from being too much at the mercy of the market.

Flanders also considered the Webbs' approach limited in that they envisaged that the only type of conflict to be settled by collective bargaining was economic. They failed to recognise that unions and employers when meeting collectively to decide the rules to regulate their relationship are inevitably involved in resolving other types of conflict. Flanders argued that collective bargainers are interested in the distribution of power between themselves as well as the distribution of income, and so the impact of collective bargaining is not confined to labour markets. In collective bargaining there are also non-material interests at stake – for example, law and order, feelings of equity, employment security, status. A further area of non-economic conflict referred to by Flanders was the role of collective agreements in restraining the exercise of managerial authority in deploying, organising and disciplining the workforce. These issues, he pointed out, are often as much conflicts over values as over interests.

## Neil Chamberlain

Chamberlain considered that all the various theories surrounding the nature of collective bargaining could be reduced to three. They are that collective bargaining is:

- a means of contracting for the sale of labour
- a form of industrial governance, and
- a method of management.

He called them respectively the marketing, governmental and managerial theories. He viewed collective bargaining as the process which determines on what terms labour will continue to be supplied to a company by its present employees or will be supplied in the future by newly hired workers. This marketing theory is based on the principle that collective bargaining is necessary to redress the balance of bargaining inequality between employers and employees.

The governmental theory accepts the contractual nature of the bargaining relationship but views the collective agreement as a 'constitution' on the basis of which is established an industrial government for the plant, the company or the industry. The principal function of the 'constitution' is:

> to set up organs of government, define and limit them, provide agencies for making, executing and interpreting laws for the industry and the means for their enforcement.

The need for some balance of bargaining power is accepted, but that balance is seen as resting firstly on the mutual dependency of the parties, and secondly on the power of each to veto the actions of the other. So the principle underpinning the governmental theory is the sharing of industrial sovereignty. Collective bargaining is a constitutional system for an industry. The union shares sovereignty with management over the workers and, as their representative, uses that power in their interests.

The managerial theory views collective bargaining as a system in which the union joins the company officials in reaching decisions on matters in which both have vital interests. The presence of the union enables the workers, through union representatives, to participate in the determination of the policies which guide and rule their working lives. Collective bargaining by its very nature involves union representatives in decision-making roles. They are 'actually *de facto* managers'. The principle that underpins this managerial theory is that of mutuality. Once the collective agreement has been concluded, its terms cannot be amended or rescinded except by a renegotiation of the agreement. Union representatives alone are powerless to modify its terms. Management (company) representatives are equally devoid of authority to alter the joint agreement. It is subject to change only by the mutual agreement of these two groups of representatives. The managerial theory of collective bargaining recognises that the ownership of property does not give unfettered authority to exercise power in industry. Responsibility towards other stakeholders in the business/organisation provides the basis for insisting that managerial authority be shared with their representatives in the manner collective bargaining can achieve.

Chamberlain's three theories are an attempt to produce a generic definition of collective bargaining. In separating these theories he did not consider them sharply distinguished from one another or that they were mutually incompatible alternatives. He claimed that they represent stages of development of the bargaining process itself, that they constitute stages of recognition of what collective bargaining is, that they represent different conceptions of what the bargaining process should be and that they suggest different emphases on various aspects of collective bargaining. Chamberlain's three theories are useful tools of analysis in examining employment relations problems and useful guides to explaining union–management relationships.

THEORY    ### Neo-classical economic theory

The Webbs, Flanders and Chamberlain all viewed collective bargaining as a good and desirable activity both in terms of its content, processes and outcomes and particularly in its social achievements. Neo-classical economic theory, however, sees the outcomes of collective bargaining as undesirable in that they cause unemployment and the existence of low pay in the non-unionised sector of the economy.

Figure 10.1 represents the unionised sector. The supply of labour curve (SW) is L-shaped, showing that the collectively bargained wage rate is the minimum at which the members of the union will supply their labour services. In the initial equilibrium at the collectively bargained wage rate of OW, the employer(s) demands OQ quantity of the union's membership. If the demand for labour falls, the demand curve shifts to $D_1D_1$.

**Figure 10.1 The unionised sector**

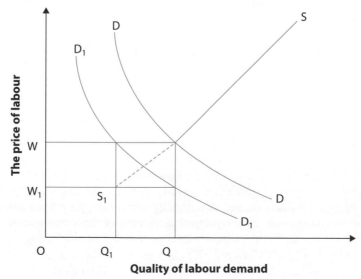

Because of the terms of the collective agreement, the wage rate is inflexible downwards, so employers are now only prepared to employ $OQ_1$ of the union's membership. $Q_1Q$ members of the union become unemployed. For OQ of its membership to remain employed, the wage rate would have to fall to $OW_1$. The union is not prepared for this to happen, so the employer adjusts to the change in labour demand by declaring redundancies amongst unionised members. Neo-classical economists thus argue that the downward inflexibility in wage rates under a collectively bargained system of pay determination causes unemployment.

Figure 10.2 represents the non-unionised sector. The sector wage is in equilibrium at a wage rate of OW and an employment level of OQ. The $Q_1Q$ unemployed in the unionised sector now seek employment. Being unable to obtain employment in the unionised sector, they seek employment in the non-unionised sector. The supply of labour to the unionised sector thus increases to $S_1S_1$. The effect of this is to reduce the equilibrium wage rate in the non-unionised sector to $OW_1$ and to widen the wage differential between the unionised and non-unionised sectors. It is in this way that neo-classical economists argue that collective bargaining causes low pay in the non-unionised sector.

**Figure 10.2 The non-unionised sector**

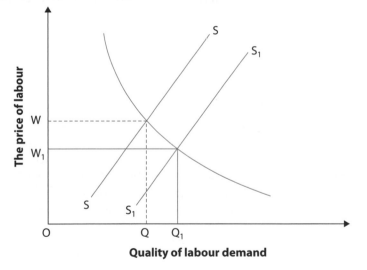

## CONDITIONS FOR COLLECTIVE BARGAINING

THEORY

For collective bargaining to exist at any level (see below), four conditions must be met. First, there must be organisation on the part of the employers and employees. Second, there must be a substantive agreement. Third, there must be a procedural agreement. Finally, both the employers and employees must be able to impose sanctions (costs) upon each other so that they can reassess their positions towards each other in terms of the demands they make of each other. The negotiation of Framework Agreements, for example, under EU social dialogue processes, meets these criteria. There is organisation on the part of employers (Business Europe, CEEP) and employees (the ETUC). There is a clear procedure on how the parties relate to one another in bargaining. There is a substantive agreement (the Framework) and the sanction is that if the parties fail to make any agreement, the Commission will bring forward its own Directive on the subject. The parties will thus have, or not have, influence over this Directive.

---

### REFLECTIVE ACTIVITY

Why has the coverage of collective bargaining declined in the last two decades, do you think? What has happened to collective bargaining coverage in your organisation (or one with which you are familiar)?

---

## DIMENSIONS OF BARGAINING

### The level of bargaining

An important decision for a management which recognises and negotiates with one or more unions centres on the level at which bargaining is to take place. There are a number of bargaining levels available from which to make a strategic choice:

- multi-employer level
- single employer level (ie company level)
- enterprise level
- a combination of all three levels.

Multi-employer bargaining has conventionally combined two levels – bargaining on establishment of framework terms and conditions at industry level, and bargaining on other matters left to individual companies. The general print industry, for example, has two-tier bargaining. The employers' association the British Printing Industries Federation negotiated with the graphical paper media sector of Unite a national agreement to set out minimum conditions to operate in the industry. These minimum terms can be enhanced by bargaining at the plants between the individual company and the GPM sector of Unite. The actual distribution of responsibility between the two tiers varies between industries and also changes over time. Company bargaining is where all terms and conditions of employment are negotiated at the central company level. Bargaining at this level enables pay and conditions to be related to the economic circumstances of the company as a whole and provides standardised conditions across the company for similar jobs. Amongst the many firms that negotiate only at the whole company level include the Ford Motor Company, British Aerospace, Rolls-Royce, Tesco, Honda, Toyota and Bombardier Aerospace.

Enterprise bargaining (or plant bargaining) is where terms and conditions are negotiated between management and union representatives at each plant or business unit of the company. Such bargaining tends to be either autonomous to each plant or co-ordinated across all plants. In the former case, each plant has the authority to settle all terms and conditions locally. In the latter case, bargaining is co-ordinated at plant level within limits set by the corporate centre. Enterprise bargaining has the attraction of enhancing management's ability to respond flexibly to employment relations policies by introducing pay, conditions and incentives related to local conditions. On the other hand, it requires management to have a competency in bargaining skills which might not exist at plant level and can increase the danger of claims for wage parity by different groups of workers.

Over the past 30 years, the trend in bargaining levels has been towards decentralised bargaining within organisations. The 2004 *Workplace Employment Relations Survey* reported that in only 15% of workplaces was pay determination influenced by industry-wide agreements. In the public sector, the corresponding figure was 47%. Today, in most of the private sector, collective bargaining takes place at either the company or workplace level. The public sector has also witnessed a decentralisation of collective bargaining.

Towers (1996) argues that the choice of bargaining levels can be guided by well-established criteria. He points out that multi-employer bargaining is an attractive option in industries which are geographically concentrated (for example, the ceramics industry), are dominated by a large number of companies of relatively small size (for example, the general printing industry), are faced by strong competitive pressures, have a high degree of trade union membership and have high labour costs. Small employers with limited time, resources and expertise are attracted to bargaining arrangements which secure negotiating skills, limit the influence of the union in the workplace, reduce vulnerability to competitive pay pressures in circumstances of labour intensity and set industry-wide standards. Towers suggests that more generally, company (corporate level) bargaining is most likely to be chosen where all or most of the following are present:

THEORY

- a single product market
- a stable product market
- a centralised organisational structure
- a preference for centralised functions
- standardised terms and conditions across operations
- preference for negotiating with national union officials.

In contrast, enterprise bargaining is likely to be favoured in the opposite set of conditions – for example, in a multi-product company, in the face of unstable product markets with a multi-divisional organisational structure, and with a preference for decentralised functions. The decentralised organisational form allows organisations to respond with sensitivity to different market changes across its product range.

**REFLECTIVE ACTIVITY**

What arguments would you use to convince a line manager that the level of the enterprise (establishment) is the right level at which to conduct collective bargaining?

### The scope of bargaining

The scope of bargaining relates to the subject matters covered by collective bargaining agreements. Such agreements are likely to include some or all of the following:

- pay levels and structures

- other terms and conditions of employment (hours of work, paid holiday entitlement, sick pay, pensions and health and safety)

- working agreements (staffing levels, allocation of work, etc)

- flexible working

- training

- redundancy.

The Fire Service pay and conditions agreement of 2003 included the following elements:

- a preamble setting out the role and responsibilities of a modern fire service

- pay

- integrated risk management plans and working time arrangements. Risk management plans not only included the provision of appropriate personnel and equipment to respond to fire and other emergencies but also took into account other factors such as legislative and community fire safety and the training of fire-fighters and emergency control staff

- other conditions of service in the national agreement – health and safety, occupational health, family-friendly working arrangements, maternity provisions and fairness at work

- a disputes procedure

- disciplinary arrangements

- negotiating machinery – by the end of November of that year working group representatives of the Fire Service stakeholders were to propose revisions to the constitution of the National Joint Council for local government services.

In 2004 the *Workplace Employment Relations Survey* reported that collective bargaining determined pay rates for an average of 90% of employees in unionised workplaces and in 27% of all workplaces. These workplaces were mainly in the private services sector of the economy. This non-pay scope of collective bargaining probably reflects two trends. First, some employers respond to falling or low union density by unilaterally setting employment conditions that treat the union recognition agreement as irrelevant. Second, it may also reflect the fact that employees leave the union when management begins to set wages unilaterally, even if the management still formally continues to recognise the union.

## BARGAINING AGREEMENTS

### Number of unions

Multi-unionism is now less of a feature for a significant number of unionised workplaces since as a result of union mergers the existence today of a large number of unions in a workplace is comparatively rare. In 2004 in nearly half (49%) of workplaces there was only one union present, although in the majority of cases this situation was the result of a formal agreement to recognise only that union.

Multi-unionism is said by some to have contributed to the UK's labour productivity deficit relative to its major international competitors. Others have argued that it is not multi-unionism as such that has a negative productivity effect but fragmented bargaining structures. In the last 30 years, many organisations – especially when opening a 'greenfield site' – have adopted a policy of dealing with one union only or a number of unions collectively. The main planks of this tidying up of bargaining arrangements have been:

- single-union arrangements
- single-table bargaining arrangements.

### Single-union arrangements

Single-union arrangements are those that occur where a company recognises only one union for collective bargaining purposes. In workplaces which recognise only one union, this situation has arisen through a formal single-union agreement rather than happening simply by chance. The 2004 *Workplace Employment Relations Survey* reported that among the 30% of workplaces that recognised unions, around half (49%) recognised a single union. Rather less than one-third (29%) recognised two unions, and one-fifth (21%) recognised three or more. The recognition of a single union was also more likely in the private sector than in the public sector. In both cases, however, the differences were due to union members in smaller workplaces and in private sector establishments being more likely all to belong to the same union.

Single-union arrangements have nonetheless existed in the UK retail sector for many years. In the 1980s their growth was most prominent on 'greenfield sites'. During this period, their growth was also controversial, especially in circumstances where an employer sought to achieve single-union bargaining arrangements by de-recognising existing unions and it turned out that the employer's preferred union was chosen after a so-called 'union beauty contest'. In some cases, the selected union had no tradition of membership in the company or industry, and in extreme cases had no members employed at the establishment concerned. Single-union arrangements are particularly beneficial in organisations that aim at teamworking, product/service quality and flexibility amongst its workforce, since the presence of one union reduces the likelihood of employee opposition to the introduction of such practices on the grounds that they threaten the job territory claimed by trade unions.

### Single-table bargaining arrangements

In single-table bargaining, all trade unions recognised by the management come together to discuss and agree their position before sending a single team representing all the unions' interests to the bargaining table to meet with the employer. This team thus bargains on behalf of all employees from every union. Such arrangements save management time and resources and minimise inter-union strife. All this makes for a more efficient operation and for a more effective management of the enterprise. The employees are likely to end up having similar employment deals, or single-table arrangements cannot work. Terms and conditions must be at least close in terms of pay, sick leave, holidays, pensions and other fundamentals. Single-table bargaining shortens the communications chain and can be used to unify and to harmonise working conditions as well as making the introduction of new practices – for example, flexible working – more easy to achieve. The 2004 *Workplace Employment Relations Survey* found that single-table bargaining took place in 60% of the workplaces surveyed that recognised more than one union.

However, single-table bargaining is not always the right practice to introduce. There has to be commitment to the concept from the top management. In addition, it must be remembered that there are specific levels of negotiation which have to be maintained for particular groups below the level of the single table. Managers have to be prepared to open up all employee issues – for example, fringe benefits which previously may have been restricted to one or two groups.

Amongst unionised workplaces, single-union agreements and single-table bargaining arrangements are equally common but found in different types of workplaces. Single-table bargaining arrangements are over three times more likely in the public sector than in the private sector. Over half the unionised workplaces in the wholesale and retail and financial services and the community services have a single-union agreement.

### REFLECTIVE ACTIVITY

From the viewpoint of a management which recognises more than one union, what are the advantages of insisting on single-table bargaining?

## PARTNERSHIP AGREEMENTS

In the face of increasing global competition, thriving business depends upon improving conditions and upon constant change. To achieve this, the co-operation of all those involved in the enterprise is required. It was shown in Chapter 2 that the idea of management, employees and trade unions working together for their mutual benefit and to secure the future of the enterprise is the very essence of employment relations. In the mid-1990s, some trade unions, in an effort to reverse the decline in their membership and to gain the acceptance of employers, began to give greater emphasis to the notion of working together with employers to achieve common goals. This took the form of negotiating partnership agreements with employers.

### PRINCIPLES

Such agreements are not a form of bargaining – they are a sophisticated form of employment relations in which management and trade unions commit themselves to shared responsibility for meeting business objectives within a framework for jobs, pay security and good conditions of employment. The TUC document *Partners for Progress*, published in 1997, set down six key principles to underpin partnership agreements at the workplace. These are:

- *Principle 1 – commitment to the success of the enterprise*
  Effective partnership agreements are based on a shared understanding of, and commitment to, business goals of the organisation of/to its lasting success, including support for flexibility and a willingness to embrace 'good practice' ideas from outside. In some instances, the operation of this principle may mean the replacement of a previously hostile and adversarial atmosphere of employment relations.

- *Principle 2 – recognising legitimate interests*
  This principle demands a recognition that at any one time there might be quite legitimate differences in interests and priorities between the partners to the agreement and an acceptance that ultimately each party will respect the others' needs to do their best for their own constituencies. Partnership agreements, if working effectively, should build up trust between the parties and should assist the resolution of differences between the parties.

- *Principle 3 – commitment to employment security*
  This principle is usually embodied in partnership agreements by a combination of measures to maximise employment security within the enterprise (for example, limiting the use of compulsory redundancy, joint agreement on staffing levels) and measures designed to improve the employability of staff beyond it (for example, by improving the transferability of skills and qualifications).

- *Principle 4 – focus on the quality of working life*
  This principle is a recognition that successful enterprises should invest in the personal development of their employees by strengthening the talent pool of the enterprise and by opening up opportunities for personal growth

(including vocational and non-vocational development) that have hitherto been unavailable to employees.

- *Principle 5 – transparency*
  If partnership agreements are to be meaningful and not a sham exercise in participation, they must be based upon a real sharing of hard information and on openness to discussing plans about the future when they are at the formulation stage. The process of consultation must be genuine, with the management committed to listening to business cases from the employees for alternative plans.

- *Principle 6 – adding value*
  This principle is a recognition by the parties to partnership agreements that they should access sources of motivation, commitment and resources that were not accessed by previous employment relations institutions at the workplace. For example, this may involve adding value beyond the immediate workplace through providing the hub of a training process that meets the enterprise's skill requirements but also puts something back into the wider talent pool of the sector.

There are other factors that are essential for successful partnership agreements. One is leadership on both sides. Successful partnerships are often based nominally on the personal leadership skills of a few individuals who often take significant risks in moving relationships onto a new footing. Another factor is a clear understanding of the case for change. Whether the spur is a shift in product markets, the advent of new business goals or the impossibility of continuing a tradition of adversarial employment relations, it has to be closely understood. Building a relationship requires both employees and managers to invest time and effort. Partnership agreements are by definition based on high-trust relationships, and where they supersede antagonism there is no way to shorten this lengthy process.

### EXTENT

Partnership agreements and arrangements are now well established in organisations in every sector of the economy. They exist in many organisations that are household names, including Tesco, the Co-operative Bank, Scottish Power, Legal and General, United Distillers and Vintners, the Inland Revenue, British Gas, UNISYS, Scottish Water, Alstom, the Fire and Rescue Service and the Scottish Prison Service. The Papermaking Partnership, the GPM Sector of Unite and the BPIF Partnership and Code of Practice are unique in that they are the only partnership agreements that cover complete industries. Brown (2004) described the extent of partnership agreements as follows:

> Partnership agreements in contemporary Britain range from some that are thinly veiled devices to limit and constrain union influence through to some that do indeed seek to nurture trade unions as genuinely representative and independent, albeit on a co-operative basis. In much of employment where there are strong traditions of collective bargaining,

employers and unions are developing co-operative relationships that meet the TUC's definition but avoid the increasingly politically charged word 'partnership'...

It would, however, be wrong to give the impression that partnership is the defining characteristic of a majority of organisations. Partnership agreements and arrangements do not mean the end of conflicts of interests between employers and employees. Conflicts of interests will inevitably remain – but where partnership arrangements exist at the workplace, some would argue that such conflicts will be much easier to resolve when employee relationships are most likely to be based on trust and mutual respect rather than on hostility and suspicion.

## REFLECTIVE ACTIVITY

Explain the principles that underpin partnership agreements and arrangements at the workplace. Which do you think is the most important? Why?

### EXAMPLES OF PARTNERSHIP AGREEMENTS

We now look at four actual partnership agreements: papermaking, general print, a fire and rescue service and a prison service.

**The papermaking partnership**

The Confederation of Paper Industries has jointly developed a partnership agreement with the GPM sector of Unite and GMB so that the parties can work together to further the interests of employers and employees and to effectively resolve any conflicting interests. The partnership agreement is industry-wide and sets out minimum standards across the industry. The partners are committed to supporting successful companies in setting higher standards in the workplace. The background to the agreement, signed in 2007, was the desire of the employers' association and the trade unions to modernise their then existing national agreement.

The employers and the employees forged a partnership to work together, to grow together and to stay together – the three pillars of the partnership – so that the papermaking industry remains a successful part of the UK's manufacturing sector. The agreement is intended to support a partnership where everyone works through issues together to achieve mutually beneficial sustainable outcomes. It must be interpreted in the spirit of partnership and of anticipating that no one should be expected to gain or lose through the differing interpretation of words or through manipulating outcomes. The partnership pillars, principles and its appropriate sections are shown in Table 10.2 below. The CPI and the unions work together to sustain and improve partnership across the papermaking industry and to promote the interests of the industry by joint approaches to the media, the

Government in the UK, Europe and internationally, and key stakeholders and external partners via the Partnership Committee. This provides a forum to:

- assess the effects of external changes upon the national agreement, such as new social or employment legislation, White Paper/consultation exercises or European Directives and proposals
- share information on the state of the industry
- consider the value of joint lobbying of government at both national and European level to further the interests of the industry
- resolve disputes over the interpretation or the application of the national agreement based on the principle of partnership.

Table 10.2  The papermaking partnership

| Partnership pillar | Partnership principle | Agreements |
|---|---|---|
| **Work together** in a spirit of co-operation, based on mutual trust and respect, to maintain harmonious, productive and fulfilling workplaces, resolving problems and differences at the earliest possible stage through regular and open dialogue. | The CPI and trade unions will work together to sustain and improve partnership across the interests of the industry by joint approaches to media, government (in the UK, Europe and internationally) and key stakeholders and external partners. The CPI and trade unions perform a key role in representing the interests of employers and employees respectively. People will work together to resolve differences speedily and avoiding conflict and dispute, firstly tackling the problems together locally and then nationally, and exploring every opportunity to prevent hostilities. Employers will actively engage employees in the running of the business by sharing information and through regular and genuine consultation. Everyone is entitled to be treated with dignity and respect, to be free from discrimination, bullying and harassment, and to feel a valued part of the papermaking community. | Partnership Committee Recognition agreement appointment/ facilities for trade union reps Disputes procedure Information and consultation Dignity at work Privacy |

| Partnership pillar | Partnership principle | Agreements |
|---|---|---|
| Through partnership, **grow together**, to maintain a successful papermaking industry as part of the UK manufacturing economy and strive for continuous improvement to the performance and profitability of companies and to the living standards and quality of life of employees. | Companies must be profitable and highly productive if the UK papermaking industry is to compete in the world market.<br><br>To be profitable and highly productive the partners in their company will need to work together in partnership to meet the needs of stakeholders and customers.<br><br>The partners recognise the demands of everyday life, and will work together to achieve an effective work–life balance. | Pay<br><br>Efficiency and productivity<br><br>Working hours<br><br>Work–life balance |
| **Stay together**, working in partnership and overcoming short-term obstacles to achieve security of employment through successful companies employing a well-trained, fully utilised and flexible workforce. | The partnership creates a joint responsibility for the long-term success of the papermaking industry.<br><br>The most effective route to secure employment is through profitable and highly productive companies.<br><br>Where job losses become necessary there will be full consultation so that the partners can work together to achieve a dignified outcome and find ways to minimise or avoid redundancy.<br><br>The partnership recognises the need for the active and committed involvement of everyone in the industry in the development and promotion of a comprehensive approach to health and safety. | Learning and skills<br><br>Temporary staffing<br><br>Lay-off and short-time<br><br>Health and safety<br><br>Sickness<br><br>Cancer screening |

Source: Confederation of Paper Industries

The Partnership Committee consists of equal number of senior representatives of employer companies and trade unions (normally totalling four to six people) together with specialist advisers on any relevant agenda subject. The Committee has an independent chairperson and meets on an *ad hoc* basis. It can make recommendations on the broad content of the agreement, industry codes of practice or guidance notes where it is agreed that inclusion in the national agreement is the best means of meeting the industry's needs.

The partnership agreement then contains sections on:

- the Partnership Committee, which provides a forum for the partners to, *inter alia*, share information on the state of the industry and resolve disputes over the interpretation or application of the national agreement

- recognition and procedure, providing formal recognition of the unions that form the partnership

- trade union representatives, their appointment and facilities, and ensuring that union representatives are adequately trained to act in a representative capacity

- the procedure for avoiding disputes

- information and consultation, setting out the importance of information and consultation in securing effective partnership and improved productivity

- dignity at work, to ensure that employment practices reflect modern values (eg that bullying and harassment is unacceptable) and best practice in workplace relations

- privacy at work, setting out the rights of employees in relation to data held about them to ensure fairness of treatment in the workplace

- wages and payment, to establish the basic parameters for an industrial minimum wage structure and for the application of any general wage increase

- efficiency and productivity, involving trade unions, employees and their representatives in planning productivity improvements and cost-reduction programmes to ensure that their interests are addressed and that the plans are workable; to ensure that commitments to the customer are met, that machines are fully utilised, that employees are properly deployed and that disruptions from problems such as absence or breakdown are minimised

- working time and leisure time, defining working patterns and arrangements for leisure breaks including annual and public holiday entitlements

- work–life balance, to enable employees to balance the demands of personal life with their obligations to their work

- learning and skills, to ensure that employees are properly trained and fully skilled, and to ensure that the knowledge and expertise of the employer and the employees are utilised to the highest degree – to be competitive as an industry requires a well-skilled and properly deployed workforce

- temporary staffing, stating the need for flexibility at the local level to determine the use of non-permanent staff

- protection against lay-off and short-term working, to provide the opportunity to accommodate unexpected and temporary loss of work while protecting the earnings of employees and safeguarding permanent employment

- health and safety, ensuring the adoption of best practice in achieving a healthy and safe working environment in the industry

- the sick pay scheme, defining basic sickness payment entitlements for those employees covered by the national agreement

- cancer screening, guaranteeing the right to time off with pay for employees to undergo tests and cancer screening – a potentially life-saving employee benefit provided at minimal cost to the company.

**The Fire and Rescue Service**

In 2007, the National Joint Council for Local Authority Fire and Rescue Services agreed to operate, from 2008, a Joint Protocol for Good Industrial Relations in the Fire and Rescue Service, designed to develop and improve upon industrial relations across the service UK-wide. It is recognised that Fire and Rescue Service managers and trade union representatives must work together for the benefit of the Service, its employees and local communities. To this end, the partnership agreement set out the following principles:

- joint commitment to the success of the organisation
- joint recognition of each others' legitimate interests and responsibilities
- joint focus on the quality of working life
- joint commitment to operating in a transparent manner
- joint commitment to continuously improving industrial relations
- joint commitment to reaching agreement within appropriate time-scales
- joint commitment to ongoing dialogue and the exchange of views, including face-to-face meetings
- joint commitment to a 'no surprises' culture.

In support of the above principles, the employers agreed to engage trade union representatives early in consultation/negotiation on issues which have workforce implications; share full and appropriate and timely information to enable full consultation or negotiation to take place; take on trade union views, providing full and frank feedback on how that process influenced their subsequent position; and put in place reasonable trade union facilities in accordance with statutory requirements and ACAS good practice guidance in order to support this inclusive approach. The Fire Brigades Union (FBU) agreed to take an active and constructive part in discussion at an early stage to facilitate reaching agreement within the appropriate time-scale; to provide a considered response to proposals, including alternative options in accordance with a locally developed time-scale or those contained in the national model procedures as appropriate; and to share with managers relevant and appropriate information to assist discussions.

Under the agreement, all parties:

- recognise their common interests and joint purpose in furthering the aims and objectives of the organisation and in achieving reasonable solutions
- will behave respectively towards each other at all times
- accept the need for joint consultation or negotiation in securing their objectives
- will identify at the outset the appropriate time-scale for discussion
- respect the confidential nature of the, at times, sensitive information exchanged
- actively work together to build trust and a mutual respect for each others' role and responsibilities

- ensure openness, honesty and transparency in communications
- provide top-level commitment to the principles set out in the joint protocol
- take a positive and constructive approach to industrial relations
- commit to early discussion of emerging issues and to maintaining dialogue in order to ensure a 'no surprises' culture
- commit to ensuring high-quality outcomes
- where appropriate, seek to agree public positions.

To assist all parties at local level the National Joint Council (NJC) has agreed model consultation and negotiation procedures which are contained in the scheme of conditions of service (the 'Grey book') that promotes joint solution-seeking. In addition, the NJC Joint Secretaries have a role in assisting dispute resolution at local level. Such issues have to be jointly referred in writing, and the parties locally have to demonstrate that consultative or negotiation processes have been exhausted at local level. All of the principles and the commitments in the Joint Protocol are intended to encourage and support a joint approach to ensure efficient and effective industrial relations in the UK Fire and Rescue Service.

**The Scottish Prison Service**

The Voluntary Industrial Relations Agreement in the Scottish Prison Service was signed in December 2007 on behalf of the Scottish Prison Service and the Prison Officers Association (Scotland), the Public Commercial Services Union and Prospect, which comprise the Scottish Prison Service trade union side (TUS). Paragraph 2.2 of the Agreement states:

> The agreement is underpinned by a partnership approach to solving industrial relations issues, with all parties being committed to the success of the Scottish Prison Service (SPS) as described by its vision, goals and values.
>
> The overall intention is to create a climate of relations between the parties in which there is no occasion or necessity for the recognised constituent unions within the TUS to consider industrial action.

The purpose of the agreement is to ensure that all collective disputes, whether at local or national level, are dealt with effectively and that differences are resolved without disruption to the operation of the Prison Service. The principles of the voluntary industrial relations agreement are:

- to resolve any dispute at the lowest competent level
- recognition of the rights of all parties
- an obligation to behave responsibly towards each other
- to consult respective parties at an early stage
- to provide each other with all necessary information required for meaningful consultation and negotiation
- that all parties should work within the agreed procedure

- that throughout the procedure it is incumbent on all parties to maintain commentaries at all levels with a view to resolving the issue
- that all parties are committed to jointly providing an agreed and effective training package for managers and union representatives in order to ensure a common understanding of the content and practice of this agreement
- that substitutes should attend meetings if any of the parties are unable to meet on the set date.

The content of the agreement sets out the scope, a procedure for processing disputes, situations in which the status quo may be temporarily suspended, and general provisions, clauses among which commit the SPS and TUS to working in partnership so that all proceedings and interactions between them are conducted respectfully and with dignity as exemplified in, and in accordance with, the SPS Standards of Behaviour for Relationships at Work.

### The general print sector

The new national partnership agreement, with its associated code of practice, between the British Printing Industries' Federation (BPIF) and the Graphic, Paper and Media section of Unite came into effect on 16 November 2005. It was the result of over 15 months' work by both parties under the joint BPIF/AMICUS Sector Partnership at Work Project. This began in November 2003 following the former DTI's approval of funding for a major initiative to improve the printing industry's productivity and working environment through a new partnership between employers and the unions at national level. Both parties recognised that there were increasing signs that the national bargaining framework was in need of a major overhaul if it were to adequately address the challenges the industry would face in the coming years. In particular, it needed to address issues relating to skills development and the work–life balance of people working in the industry and to enable companies to respond to increasing competition arising from the development of new media and the sourcing of plants overseas.

The Partnership Agreement and the Code of Practice is in five parts: general; nationally agreed wage increases; holiday agreements; hours – overtime, shift working and flexible working; and part-time, temporary and agency workers. The Code of Practice seeks to set out best practice in employment conditions rather than minimum entitlements. The introduction of the Code reflects the view of both parties that companies and chapels must work together to achieve the highest possible standards of employment relations. The Code supplements the national agreement by setting out standards that the parties consider BPIF member companies should be seeking to achieve in the following areas:

- learning and skills
- health and safety
- privacy at work
- information and consultation

- childcare guidelines
- preparation for retirement
- redundancies and business transfers
- flexible patterns of work
- controlling sickness absence and enhancing employees' pay entitlements
- the induction checklist for new temporary workers.

The General part of the partnership agreement covers 38 different issues. Some of the areas that might be regarded as particularly significant are:

Part 1.2  Partnership – sets out a definition of partnership, lists areas of common interest to both employees and employers (eg profitability, a safe working environment, the provision of information and consultation, training) and lists a set of principles that should be adopted to secure effective partnership at work (common understanding of the performance of the business, building of trust, etc)

Part 1.4  Dignity at work – sets out the rights of employees in relation to equal opportunities and treatment, reflecting developments in legislation, and details the procedures to be followed in the event that an allegation of harassment is made by an employee

Part 1.9  Privacy at work – outlines the rights of employees in relation to data held about them, whether paper-based or held electronically

Part 1.10  Learning and skills – commits companies to plan their future skills requirements and the actions necessary to address these in consultation with the workforce, and to allocate an amount equal to 0.5% of their payroll costs to training within their companies

Part 1.12  Full cost recovery – sets out requirements for employees to recover additional costs arising from national settlements in full by efficiency and productivity improvements at company level

Part 1.17  Redundancies and business transfers – documents agreements to deal with redundancies and business transfers through consultation and negotiation in accordance with the procedures set out in the Code of Practice

Part 1.29  Preparing for retirement – encourages companies to assist employees to prepare for retirement by providing appropriate counselling and a phased reduction in working time in the three months prior to retirement, supported by guidance in the Code of Practice

Part 1.30  Pensions – advocates the provision of good pension schemes and states an expectation that employers will make a contribution to company pension schemes in circumstances where employees do so.

Part 2 of the partnership agreement gives the wages increases due to the year covered by the current national agreement together with the new nationally agreed rates that result from the application of these. Part 3 sets out arrangements for accruing and taking annual holiday entitlement and the total holiday entitlement (five weeks and one day, paid on the basis of average weekly earnings) due in a full year. Part 4 contains the provisions relating to working hours (37½ hours per week), overtime, shift-working (night, double-day, treble, four shifts and five shifts and permanent weekend shifts) and flexible working. The final part of the partnership agreement defines the terms and conditions under which part-time, temporary and agency workers are to be engaged, supported by an induction checklist for temporary workers contained in the appropriate Code of Practice.

Ken Iddan, a Past President of the BPIF, claims that the partnership agreement is a significant step towards enhancing the future profitability of print. He said that it took a quantum leap in building a progressive working relationship between companies and their employees and union representatives, and offered the potential for the printing industry to achieve a substantial competitive advantage relative to other European printing industries.

## REFLECTIVE ACTIVITY

What are the main principles of a partnership agreement? Why should employers want to sign such an agreement?

Our four examples of partnership agreements show that, operating within a unionised context, they vary in content and style. However, in all four some contemporary employment issues are covered. These include:

- business-focused consultation and communications arrangements
- joint working groups
- employee commitment to business goals
- long-term pay deals
- employment security
- the sharing of information
- training and development
- a focus on local problem-solving activities
- the harmonisation of employment conditions and single status.

Unlike conventional collective agreements, partnership agreements are much more comprehensive in scope and specifically accept that employers and employees have fundamental differences in interests but have overriding common interests in ensuring that the organisation remains competitive and survives and grows.

Those who favour the partnership approach to employment relations point to a number of advantages to employers. Involving employees in a partnership arrangement gives them greater say in decision-making and therefore a greater commitment to the enterprise. This in turn should improve the morale of employees and so help employers achieve the higher work performance they desire. In both the private and public sectors, organisations cannot rise to the challenge of increased competition and demands for improved products and services unless all those working for the organisation feel they have a stake in the success of the business. It is argued, therefore, that partnership agreements will help employees to deliver better products and services.

Advocates of partnership agreements also claim that they are an advantage to unionised employers in that they mean that simply saying 'no' cannot be the first response of the workforce to employer proposals for change. They point out that when entering into a partnership, a union must recognise that change is inevitable, that change is not necessarily a threat, and associate themselves with good practice, continuous improvement, high productivity and enhanced competitiveness. Supporters of partnership-based employment relations also point to research which shows that workplaces with partnership agreements are one-third more likely than others to achieve average financial success and labour productivity (see *Partnership Works*, TUC – information available at www.tuc.org.uk/partnership/tuc).

Partnership agreements present employers with important challenges, however – the greatest being that partnership agreements allow unions to exercise much greater influence over strategic decisions. Partnership also requires some rethinking of management roles – in particular, the responsibilities of middle managers. The partnership approach is designed to give workers more autonomy, and this must mean some relinquishing of control by immediate managers, supervisors and team leaders. There is always the danger that some managers may see these developments as a threat rather than a need to move from a culture of direct intervention in relatively simple tasks to a culture of coaching, problem-solving and facilitation.

**THEORY**    THE OUTCOME OF PARTNERSHIP AGREEMENTS

Views on the actual outcomes of the operation of partnership agreements are divided. Haynes and Allen (2000) note, from their study of partnership agreements in Legal & General and Tesco, that these led to a strong workplace union presence and an increase in union membership. Taylor and Ramsay (1998), on the other hand, contend that management may use trade unions, via partnership agreements, to increase the rate of exploitation of workers through their involvement in HRM techniques. Partnership, therefore, they argue does not actually guarantee a strong workplace presence for trade unions.

The debate in the academic research literature is not solely confined to the impact of partnership on trade unions. Kelly (2001) evaluated the actual improvements emerging from partnership in terms of union membership, wages and conditions and union influence. He argues that in terms of membership there were only two partnership companies in which it had increased, and that there is little support for the view of the TUC that partnership companies offer 50% higher wages than non-partnership companies. He also claims that job security is not as widely available in partnership companies as supporters would suggest, and that the extent of union influence over decision-making in partnership companies is low.

Oxenbridge and Brown (2002) analysed the relationship between collective bargaining and what they refer to as the 'new' industrial relations of partnership. Based on case study data, they argue that there is a continuum of styles and relations. First, there are those production-oriented companies in which relations between unions and employers still focus on conventional bargaining relations. In these situations, partnership is mainly implicit and nurtured by the role of formal and informal union–management relations. In contrast, Oxenbridge and Brown also identify companies that used partnership agreements to constrain the influence of trade unions and in which workplace trade unionism was relatively weak. Unions concluded the partnership agreements owing to more aggressive management approaches, and partnership therefore appeared to be related to the enhancement of management control. In short, for Oxenbridge and Brown the outcomes of partnership agreements are less clear-cut than supporters and opponents contend. Johnstone *et al* (2004), on the basis of a case study in a British utility company, reported that management claimed that on balance their partnership agreement had had a positive impact, the benefits including improved industrial relations, quicker pay negotiations and increased legitimacy of decision-making. The trade union representatives also believed that partnership had brought benefits, including greater disclosure of information, greater influence, inter-union co-operation and more local decision-making. The views of employees on the perceived outcomes of the partnership agreement were found to be more mixed.

**THEORY**

Research shows that unless a union can demonstrate to its membership that they gain from partnership relationships, there are likely to be serious internal union tensions but, worse still, membership apathy, cynicism and loss. Perhaps most significant is the research evidence that the procedural support offered by co-operative relationships is of considerable importance to the union in the day-to-day work of representing members. As Brown (2004) remarks:

> Unions may have lost much of the capacity to coerce management, but co-operative relationships offer them, at least, increased access to management and the opportunity to build an influence on behalf of their members that is built on trust. For employers, especially private sector employers, this requires a commitment to mutuality, to sustaining the union's role even when the collective strength that may once have enforced it is all but gone …

Many of the critics of the partnership agreements, especially academics, fail to recognise that most unions faced with developing a partnership relationship were not given the option of retaining or building, strong bargaining positions. The alternative to a partnership agreement is, for most, either incrementally diminished influence leading to effective de-recognition, or outsourcing to non-unionised sites in the UK or overseas. In the view of Brown (2004) it is wholly misleading to pose robust, traditional negotiation as a hypothetical alternative for most contemporary partnership agreements.

The divided views in academic research on the outcomes of partnership agreements can be put down to a number of factors. These include the use of different research methods (for example, the use of case studies as opposed to surveys), the complex interaction of specific contextual factors such as the business context, sectoral differences (for example, relatively negative outcomes in traditional but declining industries and relatively optimistic outcomes reported in expanding sectors such as retailing and finance). There are also definitional problems. There is no one accepted definition of a partnership agreement. For some observers (including the authors of this book) they must conform to the TUC's six principles, whereas others include the so-called 'sweetheart' agreements between employers and unions. This raises the possibility that researchers into the outcomes of partnership agreements are not comparing like with like.

## MECHANISMS FOR RESOLVING CONFLICT

If agreement cannot be reached in the collective bargaining process and negotiations break down, there are a number of choices available to the employer and the employees. First, the matter can be referred to the disputes procedure (sometimes called an 'avoidance of disputes' procedure) which sets out several stages available to attempt to resolve a dispute peacefully. If a settlement can be reached using the collective disputes procedure, that procedure may have a final stage providing for third-party intervention in the form of conciliation, mediation and arbitration. These processes were explained in Chapter 6. What happens, then, if the parties decide to take their dispute to conciliation and/or arbitration?

| Typical Procedure for the Avoidance of Disputes | |
|---|---|
| If a collective issue raised at the Advisory Committee is unresolved then the following procedure will apply. | |
| Stage One: | Item raised on the agenda of the Advisory Committee by a Shop Steward or the Company. Every effort must be made to resolve the issue at this stage. |
| Stage Two: | If the matter remains unresolved, it will be referred to the appropriate full-time officer of the Union and appropriate senior management of the Company. |
| Stage Three: | If the matter remains unresolved, it will be referred to the National Secretary of the Union and appropriate senior management of the Company. |
| Stage Four: | If the mater is unresolved at Stage Three and in consultation with ACAS it is agreed that the matter could be resolved by conciliation, then that process will be initiated. |

## CONCILIATION

ACAS conciliators try to help the parties settle their differences by agreement – if possible, for the longer term. Conciliation staff of ACAS remain impartial and independent at all times, understand the dispute and the attitude of the parties to it, gain the trust and confidence of both parties, make constructive suggestions, if appropriate, to facilitate negotiations, and provide information at the request of the parties. The first step for the conciliator is to find out what the difference between the parties is about and to ascertain the attitude of the parties to that difference. This fact-finding stage usually involves the conciliator meeting each of the sides separately, although occasionally he or she may gather information at a joint meeting.

Although the details of conciliation vary from case to case, the process normally proceeds via a series of 'side meetings' in which the conciliator explores the issues with each party, and joint meetings at which the two sides can explain their position face to face. No time limits are set and the ACAS conciliator continues to help the parties as long as they wish and there is some chance of achieving an agreement. Where it appears clear that a settlement might be achieved, the conciliator looks to secure an agreement, usually in the form of a signed statement. Once an agreement is reached, it is the responsibility of the parties to implement it. ACAS has no powers to enforce the agreement.

If conciliation fails, then the parties might agree to settle their differences by arbitration.

## ARBITRATION

### Terms of reference

If both parties voluntarily agree to arbitration, the first task is to agree terms of reference for the arbitrator. ACAS will assist the parties in this task. The terms of reference are important because they tell the arbitrator what it is the parties wish the arbitrator to do. They set limits to the arbitrator's powers, which are usually constrained to within the range of the parties' claims. They prevent the arbitrator from wandering into issues that the parties do not wish the arbitrator to get into – for example, commenting on deficiencies in the procedures. In arbitration, the terms of reference are usually worded in a simple manner. Typical terms of reference would be:

> to determine if the company applied its policy in full with reference to redundancies announced on XX May 2009

> to determine whether the meal break on night shift in company X should be extended to the operator group

> to determine the appropriate grading in respect of library assistants in the department.

The terms of reference give the arbitrator flexibility within their limits.

However, in the case of pendulum (or final offer) arbitration, the terms of reference confine the arbitrator's award to either the employer's final offer or the employees' (the union's) final claim. The arbitrator must make an 'either/or' decision, and no other settlement can be awarded. This is made clear in the terms of reference.

Below is an example of the terms of reference in a pendulum arbitration case:

The arbitrator is asked to decide between the following differences in the employer's offer and the union's claim

*The employer offer*
From 1 January XXXX a 5.3% increase on basic pay, bonuses, overtime and all allowances

*The union claim*
From 1 January XXXX a 7% increase on basic pay, bonuses, overtime and all allowances

Pendulum arbitration has been favoured by electronics firms where a strike would run the risk of losing markets because adjustments cannot be made quickly enough to product/services in the light of rapidly changing customer demand and technology. Manufacturing companies whose main customers are the large supermarket chains have also favoured pendulum arbitration, believing that a strike runs the risk of a permanent loss of business to what is the company's main customer. Pendulum arbitration is usually written in as the final stage of an agreed dispute procedure. It is argued by those who favour pendulum arbitration that prohibiting arbitrators from occupying the middle ground between a final employer offer and final union claim encourages the parties to make more reasonable offers and claims, since the alternative is to enter a win-all or lose-all situation. Indeed, it is argued that eventually both sides will be so close together that the gap becomes bridgeable in negotiation and arbitration becomes unnecessary. In other words, the main assumption behind pendulum arbitration is that it puts such pressures on the employer and trade union to make an agreement that the process is unlikely ever to be used.

A great disadvantage of pendulum arbitration lies in the assumption that one side is 100% right and the other is 100% wrong. Why should compromise be an acceptable and justified principle in the collective bargaining processes and yet be ruled out in the arbitration process? Second, there are longer-term employee relations consequences if one side is found to be comprehensively right and the other just as comprehensively wrong. There are further disadvantages. An arbitrator may be faced with two complicated packages, and unless he or she is very lucky he or she will find *both* packages unsatisfactory. If the arbitrator cannot select the best items from each package and award accordingly, he or she has to weigh the two packages and choose the least objectionable.

### ? REFLECTIVE ACTIVITY

What do you consider to be the advantages and disadvantages to an employer of favouring pendulum arbitration over conventional arbitration?

### Choice of arbitrator

The next stage in the process is for the two sides to agree jointly the name of the independent person to arbitrate on their differences. Again, ACAS facilitates this by making available to the parties its 'panel of arbitrators' but it does not provide any information about previous cases to disputant parties. Sometimes the parties are content to allow ACAS to appoint the arbitrator. Mumford (1996) reports that the vast majority of the individuals on the ACAS panel are academics (or retired academics), over 45 years of age and grammar-school-educated but interested in the practicalities of industry and employment relations. In short, they do not 'live in ivory towers'. ACAS strives to maintain long tenure amongst its arbitrators in order that they accumulate experience which helps them develop the skills in conflict management, so helping dispute resolution. The parties thus jointly determine the independent person to whom they are prepared to hand over the decision on how to resolve their differences.

### Written submission to the arbitrator

After the terms of reference have been clarified and the independent person has been selected, the next step in the process is the setting of the date and the venue for the arbitration hearing. The types of venue vary but most hearings are held on the company's premises. Other popular venues are hotels and the appropriate ACAS regional office.

The venue is agreed between the parties and the arbitrator, although it is ACAS that implements these arrangements. Before the hearing date, both sides submit to the arbitrator a written statement of their case and arguments. The parties also exchange their respective written cases with each other before the date of the hearing. It is essential that all information given to the arbitrator is known to the other side. Written statements, together with any supporting documents and a list of those attending the hearing, are submitted to the arbitrator at least one week before the hearing.

Arbitrators reach their conclusion only after considering all the facts and arguments put to them by the parties, and they always study the written statements very carefully. Each written statement normally covers the background information about the company and its products, union representation, etc; an explanation of the history and background of the dispute, including an account of the sequence and outcome of any relevant meetings or discussions; the arguments supporting or opposing the claim; and a brief summary of the case which brings together the essential points the arbitrator is being asked to consider. Relevant agreements, procedures or rules are attached as appendices. In the case of a job-grading dispute, for example, full details are given of the grading scheme in operation – whereas in a disciplinary case, details of any disciplinary rules or procedures are provided.

In certain circumstances, before the hearing date there may also be a site visit. This is highly likely in the case of differences between parties concerning the degree of skill required by a job, the physical conditions under which the work is carried out or the assessment of piecework, prices or times. In all these cases it is of value for the arbitrator to see the work in progress.

**The arbitration hearing**

The procedure outlined below is standard practice in the use of voluntary arbitration to settle:

- trade disputes
- claims of allegedly unfair dismissal
- the allegedly unreasonable refusal by an employer to accept an employee's request for flexible working.

The hearing is informal and confidential, the parties usually being represented by those responsible for conducting normal negotiations. It is generally completed in two to three hours, is held in private, and the procedure to be followed is a matter for the arbitrator to agree with the parties. However, the stages of a typical arbitration hearing are (Gennard, 2009) :

1 The arbitrator explains his or her role and then reads out the terms of reference to ensure that both parties place the same interpretation on their scope or meaning.

2 The arbitrator checks that the parties have exchanged their written statements and have had sufficient time to give the statements proper consideration.

3 The arbitrator normally invites the party making the 'claim', or seeking to change the status quo, (say, Party A) to put its case uninterrupted and to include a critique of the written submission of the other party (say, Party B). This is usually done by one person but other members of the team may be called upon to give supporting statements.

4 The arbitrator then invites Party B to ask questions about Party A's statement. Such questioning can be effected either directly by the leader of Party B to Party A or through the arbitrator.

5 The arbitrator invites Party B to put its case uninterrupted and to include a critique of the written submission of Party A. This again will be carried out by one person but with other members of the team giving supportive statements.

6 The arbitrator then invites Party A to ask questions about Party B's statement. Again, such questioning can be effected directly to the other party or via the arbitrator.

7 The arbitrator will then ask questions of each party in turn or put the same questions to both parties. The party to whom the question is directed may respond through the team leader or nominate another member of the team to respond. The person who answers the question may call upon another member of the team to make a supporting statement. Each time one party responds to a question, the other party is given the opportunity to comment on the response. One party can ask questions of the other through the arbitrator.

8 Before inviting the parties to make their closing statements, the arbitrator

normally obtains a formal assurance from each party that everything it wished to say has been said and that it has had sufficient opportunity to comment on or attempt to rebut what has been said by the other side.

9 The arbitrator will then invite each side to make its closing statement. These are normally taken in reverse order to the opening presentations. The formal (or closing) statement is a summary of the main points the party wishes the arbitrator to take into account in reaching his or her decision and should contain no new evidence. (This is the last opportunity for the parties to convince the arbitrator that if he or she is a reasonable and fair-minded person, he or she can only award in their favour.) The arbitrator cannot accept any further evidence after the hearing.

## The award

The arbitrator does not announce the award on the day of the hearing. The arguments of the parties are taken away and given serious consideration. The parties receive the award, via ACAS, usually within two to three weeks of the hearing. All awards are regarded as confidential to the parties and are not published unless the parties agree otherwise. The arbitrator's report sets out the issues that have influenced his or her award. The important consideration is that neither party is left with a strong feeling of resentment so that the dispute, although ended, continues to fester. A typical award is presented as follows:

### The Award

Having given very careful consideration to the arguments very well presented to me by both parties, both orally and in writing, I award that:

THE JOB OF CLERICAL OFFICER IS CORRECTLY GRADED AT LEVEL 4

Arbitrators do not give reasons for their decisions because to do so could give rise to further dispute between the parties. They do, however, indicate the factors (or considerations) they took into account in reaching their decision (award). Those factors may be complex and manifold, and include the need for the parties to continue in a working relationship after the award, the need to bring the dispute to a final conclusion, the potential 'knock-on' effects of an award on other groups of workers, the ability of the employer to finance the award, and the credibility of the negotiators – particularly where the employer's pay offer has been rejected, against the advice of the union negotiators, by the employees concerned. In short, these collapse to three major considerations: equity, economics and expediency (pragmatism).

A wise arbitrator (C. W. Guillebaud) once stated about arbitration that:

If at all possible, neither side should be left with a strong feeling of resentment so that the dispute continues to rankle – for the arbitrator will not then have achieved the objective of settling the matter satisfactorily and improving relations for the future.

In other words, the arbitrator's award should seek to minimise aggregate dissatisfaction. In addition, the parties are not always interested in the rationale behind the arbitrator's decision since they have come to arbitration after a long process and by this time are just relieved that the matter has been resolved and satisfied that they have been able to state all the arguments in favour of their position.

The award of the arbitrator is not legally binding – but it is virtually unknown for an award not to be implemented by the parties. It would be difficult (or require very exceptional circumstances) for one of the parties not to want to implement the award. They are morally bound to do so. After all, they have gone to the arbitration of their own volition, shaped the terms of reference for the arbitrator, selected the arbitrator and had every opportunity to state their case to the arbitrator.

## INDUSTRIAL ACTION

Large-scale industrial disputes can have a disproportionate effect on the statistics of working days lost. In 1984, for example, the coal mining dispute accounted for 83% of the 27,135 days lost. In 1996, one dispute in the transport, storage and communication sector accounted for 61% of the total days lost over the year. Again, in 2002, two disputes accounted for 60% of the total days lost over the year.

There has been a substantial decline in strike activity over last 30 years. The number of stoppages has been on a downward trend. In 2002 it fell beneath the relatively narrow band it had been in since 1992. The number of working days lost per 1,000 employees is the standard method that has been used to convert working days lost into a strike rate that takes account of the size of the labour force. It also enables comparisons to be made across industries and regions that differ in size. Because the number of employee jobs has not changed dramatically over the past 30 years, the rates for the UK as a whole show the same pattern of general decline, with occasional peaks that can be seen in the working days lost series. In the latter half of the first decade of the twenty-first century, the major national dispute was in Royal Mail when the management were accused by the Communication Workers' Union of imposing change to modernise the Royal Mail without proper consultation and negotiation. In December 2009, a threatened strike by British Airways cabin crew was averted when the courts ruled that there had been irregularities in the strike ballot held by the Unite union.

How do we account for the decline in strike activity over the last 30 years? Economic factors have been important. Until the late 1990s and in the economic crisis of 2008/9, economic conditions were characterised by rising unemployment, increased product and labour market competition, and changing technological developments. In such economic conditions the probability of strikes occurring is considerably reduced. The ability of the employees to impose economic costs on the employer via the withdrawal of their labour is limited. If strikes occur in such economic conditions, they are likely to last for a long time thereby increasing the economic cost to the striking employees.

Following the re-election of the Blair government in 2001, there was a significant increase in public spending but especially in the health service and education sectors. One effect of this was to increase the demand for labour in the public sector. This quickly led to labour shortages. Excess demand for labour tends to produce economic conditions in which the probability of strikes occurring increases. Such economic conditions are also likely to give a positive outcome for the strikers because the economic costs of the industrial sanctions imposed on the employer are high. The employer is more likely to concede to the union's demands. Prior to this expansion in public expenditure, the pay of public sector employees had tended to lag behind that of the private sector. Public sector employees and their unions saw the change in their balance of bargaining relative to their employers as an opportunity to catch up with, and preferably overtake, pay movements in the private sector. It is not surprising, therefore, that recent years have witnessed significant incidences of industrial action in the public sector. Such groups have included local government manual workers, schoolteachers, fire-fighters, nursery nurses and Royal Mail employees.

Another important factor in the decline of strike activity over the last three decades has been the trend in real wages – ie the amount of goods and services that an employee's pay can actually purchase. In periods of rising real wages, strike action tends to fall. The rising expectation of employees for increased living standards can be accommodated. In general, the last 30 years – apart from the economic recessions of the early 1990s and of 2008/9 – have seen significant increases in real wages for those who have remained in employment. Workers have not felt aggrieved and have seen no reason to want to impose industrial sanctions against their employers.

## REFLECTIVE ACTIVITY

What factors, other than economic ones, do you believe help explain the decline in the frequency of collective industrial action over the last 30 years?

## COPING WITH INDUSTRIAL ACTION

Although every employer's focus is to concentrate on steps to avoid disputes turning into industrial action with sanctions, such disputes can and do happen. In this event, it is essential that management implements a strategy and policy that maintains as much normality as possible. There is a set of strategic options available to management to minimise the likely disruption from the application of industrial sanctions to the organisation. However, not every one applies in every case to every organisation. They are to:

- keep materials and supplies coming in

- find alternative sources of labour. In the 2008 Royal Mail dispute, the employer recruited 5,000 temporary staff in an effort to maintain an acceptable level of service to the customer during the Communication Workers' Union selective strikes. This employer action met with varying degrees of success. In 2010, in anticipation of a BA cabin crew strike, the BA management raised the prospect of staffing entire planes with new recruits on different pay and conditions – in effect creating a new fleet within the airline. This alternative workforce was to be created from volunteers from baggage-handling and check-in agents. The BA Chief Executive wrote to staff saying:

  I am asking for volunteers to back BA by training to work alongside cabin crew who choose not to support a strike so that we are ready to keep our customers flying as much as we possibly can if the strike goes ahead.

- maintain output or a level of service to satisfy demand
- maintain the distribution of the product or service to the customer.

Management need to evaluate critically each of these choices. In the case of a retail organisation that needs to keep supplies coming in, the critical questions that have to be answered are:

- Will a picket be mounted?
- Who will unload and store the goods?

When considering an alternative supply of labour, the critical questions are whether the organisation can get other staff and new part-timers. With respect to the maintaining of a minimum level of service, the vital considerations are:

- Can orders be advanced or dealt with cumulatively?
- Is there any current overstocking that can be used up first?

As regards the distribution of the goods, operational issues include whether customers could themselves come to the organisation, and if so, whether they would be met by pickets. Could customers be telephoned when deliveries are being despatched? Could working hours be temporarily altered to expedite matters?

### ? REFLECTIVE ACTIVITY

Imagine you are the manager of a transport operation. You believe that current negotiations with your employees are going to break down and the employees are going to impose industrial sanctions upon you. What key questions would you ask yourself with respect to the strategic options open to you?

Making sure that supplies keep coming and going is critical. If a business cannot continue to service the market or continue to receive materials, the organisation will have difficulties in maintaining output or some minimal level of service. Recruiting an alternative workforce is more than just getting in extra people. It may be that the alternative workforce is already in your organisation. Managers and team leaders/front-line managers may be able to do the work of the potential strikers. Perhaps the work to be done can be covered by other workers who are members of other trade unions not involved in the dispute or who are not unionised at all. Maintaining output to satisfy demand is often possible in the period before the dispute starts. Overtime can be increased, production switched to other plants or companies, and priority tasks be tackled first.

## SUMMARY

- The distribution of collective bargaining in the UK fell from 70% in 1984 to 40% in 1998 to 34% in 2006.

- A strategic choice for a management involved in collective bargaining is the level at which bargaining takes place – multi-employer level, company level, enterprise level or some combination of these levels.

- Over the past 30 years, the trend in bargaining levels has been towards decentralisation within organisations.

- There has been relatively little change in the scope of collective bargaining over non-pay issues amongst establishments that recognise trade unions.

- There has been a substantial increase in the proportion of unionised workplaces where pay bargaining does not take place.

- Untidy bargaining structures have been seen to have an adverse effect on the efficiency of organisations. Managements have tried to overcome this by introducing single-union arrangements or single-table bargaining arrangements.

- Partnership agreements are a sophisticated form of employment relations in which management and trade unions commit themselves to share responsibility for meeting business objectives within a framework for jobs, pay security and good conditions of employment.

- The key principles underpinning partnership agreements are: a commitment to the success of the enterprise, recognising legitimate interests, a commitment to employment security, a focus on the quality of working life, transparency, and adding value.

- Partnership agreements are said to bring benefits to employment, employers and trade unions, and they are now well-established in organisations in every sector of the economy.

- If agreement cannot be reached in the collective bargaining process and negotiations break down, there are a number of choices available to the employer – notably to refer the matter to the disputes procedure, and/or to seek third-party intervention in the form of conciliation, mediation or arbitration.

- Although the details of conciliation vary in each case, the process usually proceeds via a series of side meetings where the conciliator explains the issues with each party and a joint meeting at which the two sides can explain their positions face to face.

- Arbitration involves the parties determining the terms of reference for the arbitrator, selecting the arbitrator, presenting submissions to the arbitrator, attending an arbitration hearing, and receiving and implementing the arbitrator's award.

- In jointly agreeing to go to arbitration, the parties may decide to opt for pendulum arbitration in which, unlike conventional arbitration, the terms of reference confine the arbitrator's award to the employer's final offer or the employees' final claim, and in which no other settlement can be awarded.

- If the breakdown of the collective bargaining process cannot be resolved by the use of the disputes procedure or by the use of third-party intervention and the employees impose industrial sanctions, it is important for management to implement a strategy and associated policies that will minimise the impact of such sanctions on the organisation.

## KEY LEARNING POINTS

- Collective bargaining, in spite of a major decline in its use in recent years, still remains an important employment relations process, especially in the public sector. It is an effective problem-solving mechanism.

- Collective bargaining can be analysed in terms of its coverage, dimensions (level, scope, etc) and arrangements (single-union/single-table).

- Partnership agreements are not a form of bargaining but are a special type of collective agreement. They are underpinned by six principles (success of enterprise/recognition of legitimate interests, etc), are found in every sector of the economy, are more comprehensive in scope than conventional agreements and specifically accept that although employers and employees have differences of interests, they have overriding common interests (eg the success of the enterprise).

- Contemporary research shows that the views on the actual outcome of partnership agreements is mixed. Some research is favourable, some unfavourable, and others are uncommitted.

- If relationships between employers and employees break down, disputes can still be resolved peacefully by the use of the disputes procedure and/or third-party intervention – conciliation, mediation or arbitration.

- On the other hand, the breakdown of relations may lead to the employees imposing industrial sanctions against the employer – overtime ban, strikes, etc. The incidence of strikes over the last 30 years has declined. If industrial action arises, there are strategic options available to the employer to minimise its likely impact.

## REVIEW QUESTIONS

1 The employees have recently approached your Chief Executive Officer with a view to establishing a partnership agreement. He is scheduled to meet the employee representative tomorrow to discuss their proposals. He needs you to give him the 'bare bones' of what partnership agreements are all about and what the negotiation of one would mean for your organisation. Drawing on contemporary research, outline and justify what you will tell him.

2 Explain the approaches of the Webbs, Flanders and Chamberlain to the role and purpose of collective bargaining.

3 As an employee relations manager, you have been invited to outline to the board of directors the relevance of collective bargaining. Bearing in mind that union membership is high at the company and there has always been a healthy union–management relationship, the directors would like to know the purpose and functions of collective bargaining in today's commercial environment. Justify what you will say.

4 Define 'partnership' and, using contemporary research, explain the key features that make it different from an adversarial approach to employment relations.

5 Both employers and employees say they value the existence of the availability of voluntary arbitration but they rarely make use of this employment relations process. Why do you think this is the case?

## EXPLORE FURTHER

Brown, W. (2004) 'The future of collectivism in the regulation of industrial relations', *Human Resource and Employment Review*, Vol.2, No.4.

Chamberlain, N. W. (1951) *Collective Bargaining*. London: McGraw-Hill.

Cully, M., Woodland, S., O'Reilly, A. and Dix, S. (1999) *Britain at Work as Depicted by the 1998 Workplace Employee Relations Survey*. London and New York: Routledge.

Flanders, A. (1968) 'Collective bargaining: a theoretical analysis', *British Journal of Industrial Relations*, November.

Gennard, J. (2009) 'Voluntary arbitration: the unsung hero', *Industrial Relations Journal*, Vol.40, No.4.

Haynes, P. and Allen, M. (2000) 'Partnership as union strategy: a preliminary evaluation', *Employee Relations*, Vol.23, No.2.

Industrial Partnership Association (1996) *Towards Industrial Partnership: A new approach to relationships at work*. London: IPA.

Industrial Partnership Association (1997) *Towards Industrial Partnership: New ways of work in British companies*. London: IPA.

Industrial Relations Services (2002) 'When all else fails', *Employment Review*, No.719, January: 12–16.

Johnstone, S., Wilkinson, A. and Ackers, P. (2004) 'Partnership paradoxes: a case study for an energy company', *Employee Relations*, Vol.26, No.5.

Kelly, J. (2001) 'Social partnership agreements in Britain: union revitalisation or employer counter-mobilisation', in Martinez Lucio, M. and

Stuart, M. (eds) *Assessing Partnership: The prospects for and challenges of modernisation*. Leeds: Centre for Industrial Relations and Human Resource Management.

Millward, N., Bryson, A. and Forth, J. (2000) *All Change at Work?* London and New York: Routledge.

Mumford, J. (1996) 'Arbitration and ACAS in Britain: a historical perspective', *British Journal of Industrial Relations*, Vol.34, No.2.

Oxenbridge, S. and Brown, W. (2002) 'The two faces of partnership? An assessment of partnership and co-operative employer/trade union relationships', *Employee Relations*, Vol.24, No.3.

Taylor, P. and Ramsay, H. (1998) 'Unions, partnership & HRM: sleeping with the enemy', *International Journal of Employment Studies*, Vol.6, No.2.

Towers, B. (1996) 'Collective bargaining levels', in Towers, B. J. (ed.) *A Handbook of Industrial Relations Practice*. London: Kogan Page.

Trades Union Congress (1998) *Partners for Progress: New unionism in the workplace*. London: TUC.

Webb, S. and Webb, B. (1902) *Industrial Democracy*. London: Longmans Green.

**Web links**

www.acas.org.uk

www.britishairways.com (2010 dispute)

www.britishprint.com (general print partnership agreement)

www.paper.org.uk (papermaking partnership agreement)

www.wers2004.info (website of 2004 *Workplace Employment Relations Survey*)

www.ebu.org.uk (partnership agreement in Fire Service)

www.postoffice.co.uk and www.guardian.co.uk (for 2009/10 Post Office dispute)

www.sps.gov.uk (website of Scottish Prison Service)

www.tesco.com

www.tuc.org.uk

www.unitetheunion.org.uk

## CHAPTER 11

# Negotiation (Including Bargaining)

## OVERVIEW

This chapter explains the purpose, the common elements and the different types of bargaining situations in which a management may find itself. It then outlines the stages involved in the negotiating process, the interpretation of hidden language and the use of adjournments. Negotiation involves two or more parties coming together to make an agreement by purposeful persuasion (argument backed by evidence) and constructive compromise. The chapter then identifies the different negotiating situations a management may find itself involved in – between managers, grievance-handling, bargaining (with a unionised or non-unionised workforce) and group problem-solving. But the main negotiation situation most managers are involved in is with their management colleagues over various issues – for example, a proposed course of action – so this chapter is very relevant to your work situation. Grievance-handling also involves two or more parties coming together to resolve the employee grievance by persuasion and compromise. Again, you are likely to be involved in this management activity. Bargaining is often thought to be confined to unionised environments, but this is not the case. Bargaining takes place in non-unionised firms, especially large ones. So the bargaining skills outlined in this chapter, if they are not of immediate relevance to you now, are likely to become relevant to you sometime later in the development of your HRM career. The chapter explains the stages of bargaining – preparation, presentation, searching for common ground, concluding the agreement, and writing up the agreement – and you are finally introduced to the technique of the aspiration grid.

## LEARNING OUTCOMES

When you have completed this chapter, you should be aware of and able to describe:

- the purpose of negotiations
- each of the different negotiating situations in which management may find itself
- how employee relations negotiations differ from commercial negotiations
- the different stages in the negotiating process
- what is involved in preparing for bargaining
- how to justify the activities involved in conducting and concluding bargaining
- what is involved in writing up an agreement
- the different outcomes of bargaining.

THEORY     THE PURPOSE OF NEGOTIATIONS

Negotiation involves two parties (such as individuals, companies, employers, trade union representatives, employee representatives) coming together to confer with a view to concluding a jointly acceptable agreement. It is a process whereby interest groups resolve differences between, and within, themselves. The term can therefore apply to a number of different situations ranging from, at one extreme, resolving a difference between two managers as to how a problem might be best solved, to, at the other extreme, a meeting with a trade union to determine the year's annual pay increase.

If both parties to an agreement do not have the same understanding about what they have agreed, they run the risk of spending time – time that could be used for more fruitful purposes – resolving disputes between themselves over whether one party or the other is behaving in accordance with what was agreed. Making an agreement commits the parties to behaving within its parameters until they agree jointly to change the terms of the agreement. So what has been agreed must be capable of effective implementation and operation.

**Common elements**

Negotiation involves two main elements:

- purposeful persuasion
- constructive compromise.

Each party attempts to persuade the other to accept its own case (request) by marshalling arguments backed by factual information and analysis. However, the probability that one party can persuade the other to accept its case (requests) completely is extremely low. If an agreement is to be reached, both parties must attempt to accommodate their demands of each other. To do so, they must identify parameters of common ground within and between their requests of each other. Constructive compromise can then be made within these parameters. Compromise is only possible if sufficient common ground exists between the two parties. The overriding objective of any negotiation is for the parties to reach a mutually acceptable agreement and not to continue their differences nor to score debating points off each other. Negotiation is a problem-solving technique.

So we can define negotiations as:

> two parties coming together to confer with a view to making a jointly acceptable agreement by the use of purposeful persuasion and constructive compromise

– see Figure 11.1. This definition does not confine negotiation to set-piece bargaining situations. It demonstrates that a negotiating situation arises where any two parties have a difference but have a common need to reconcile it, and so have to meet together and find an acceptable solution to their difference(s) through persuasion and compromise.

**Figure 11.1  The definition of negotiation**

THEORY

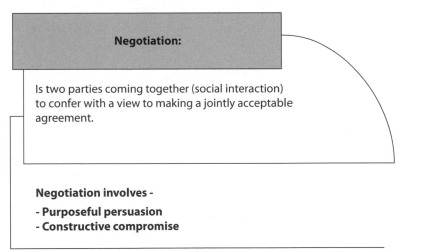

## DIFFERENT TYPES OF NEGOTIATING SITUATIONS

Figure 11.2 identifies four main types of negotiating situations in which managers may find themselves:

- between managers – this involves a negotiated settlement to an issue usually confined to an individual (for example, at an appraisal interview establishing a manager's objectives for the coming year, or resolving a difference between two managers as to how a problem with an employee might best be overcome)

- grievance-handling to resolve a complaint by an employee that the behaviour of someone else at the workplace has affected them unfairly, thereby causing feelings of injustice if not an intolerable situation; grievances normally relate to individual employees, but if they are not handled with care, they can develop to concern a group of employees

- bargaining that results in a negotiated agreement to resolve issues of collective concern to employers and employees (for example, pay, hours of work, holidays and working practices). It can also take place within the management team (or union teams) to establish a common position to be presented to the other party in forthcoming bargaining sessions. This is often referred to as intra-organisational bargaining (see below). However, bargaining can, and does, take place between management and individual employees (for example, in a non-union environment, particularly amongst middle management) resulting in a personal contract

- group problem-solving that results in a negotiated agreement to resolve issues such as the conditions on which one party will co-operate with a second party in relation to action initiated by that second party.

**Figure 11.2  Different types of negotiating situations**

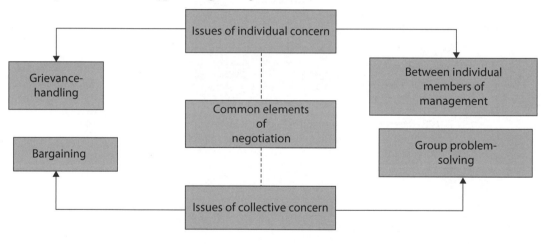

## BETWEEN INDIVIDUAL MANAGERS

The most common negotiating situation in which employment relations managers/professionals are likely to find themselves is the one shown in the top right-hand quadrant of Figure 11.2 – negotiation with their management colleagues. Each day managers find themselves negotiating with their colleagues, either in the same management function or in another management function (for example, marketing, finance, sales, operations management). These managers can be of the same, higher or lower status than themselves. Negotiations between individual members of management are likely to be over such issues as:

- suggested courses of action (for example, how to deal with an employee complaint against management behaviour)

- the introduction of new employment practices and procedures (for example, the introduction of an appropriate incentive scheme)
- securing the allocation of additional financial, staffing and equipment resources to support the people function
- gaining the commitment of managerial colleagues to a proposed course of action, particularly in the context of employee relations initiatives.

Negotiations between individual managers involve parties protecting the same economic and political interests, so the style of negotiations in such situations is generally friendly and constructive   and certainly not adversarial.

### Courses of action

Two or more managers may disagree over how a problem should/might be resolved. In such a situation each manager will seek purposefully to persuade the other of the merits of his or her proposed solution to the problem. If one is able to persuade the other that his or her proposed solution (or some compromise) is acceptable, that is the agreement that will be implemented to solve the problem. However, if managers with different views on how a problem might be resolved cannot be persuaded to accept one or other desired approach, or they cannot agree a compromise solution between them, a senior manager will have to intervene and impose a resolution to the problem.

### Obtaining resources

Employment relations managers also frequently negotiate with senior managers to gain resources to enable them to implement new policies, procedures and practices which they have devised on their own initiative or as requested by a more senior manager. In such circumstances a junior manager seeks to persuade the senior manager to allocate the necessary resources. The outcome may be an agreement in which the junior manager obtains some resources – not perhaps what he or she would ideally like, but nevertheless sufficient to implement the new policies, procedures and practices. On the other hand, the senior manager may not be persuaded by the junior manager's arguments and may prefer instead to allocate resources to an alternative project that he or she considers to have a higher priority.

### Gaining commitment

Managers in any management function and at any level of seniority cannot assume that their proposed actions, policies and arrangements will be accepted without question by their management colleagues. There is likely to be some opposition from those management colleagues who have different interests and priorities. Financial pressures may mean that one manager's progress is another's hold-up, and such inter-departmental rivalries can be a problem in organisations. So if unanimous management commitment to and support for proposed changes to policy and/or strategy (for example, a major change in reward strategy or a new training and development strategy) are to be gained, some manager has to make a persuasive case that carries his or her colleagues along. An agreed management position to which all are committed (ie have bought in to) is thus likely to emerge via the process of intra- or inter-management negotiation involving persuasion and often compromise.

Negotiation then is not – as is popularly thought – an activity confined to relationships between managers and employee representatives. It is a daily activity in which all managers, inside and outside the employment relations function, are involved. Negotiations take place day in and day out between managers of different and similar levels of executive authority and between the different managers from the different management functions. Nevertheless, some managers have difficulty viewing such circumstances as negotiating situations, preferring to regard them as a process of 'influencing others' and/or gaining the support/commitment of others.

## REFLECTIVE ACTIVITY

When were you last involved in a negotiating situation where the other party was a management colleague? What was the issue? What arguments did you use to persuade your colleague that your view of handling the issue might be the right one? What counter-arguments did your manager colleague put forward? How were your differences of approach to solving the problem overcome?

## GRIEVANCE-HANDLING

### What is a grievance?

A grievance is a complaint, real or ill-founded, by an employee that the behaviour of management or that of another employee has impacted upon them in an unfair manner, creating feelings of injustice. Such complaints, however, may be unjustified. If management believe that the employee's complaint is unfounded – perhaps because the employee has simply misunderstood the situation – then management must explain to the employee why it considered this to be the case. Not to do so carries the danger of adding another complaint to the original one, as well as sending a message to the employee that management is not taking their complaint seriously.

Grievances are important to the individuals concerned. Each grievance has to be treated on its merit. One person's grievance cannot be traded off against that of another individual. Two separate grievances should not be linked. In managing grievances, it is not good practice for management to say 'We shall concede the grievance of individual $y$ if you will drop the grievance of individual $x$.' Individual $x$'s grievance must be resolved before consideration is given to the complaint of individual $y$.

### Grievance issues

Complaints about management's behaviour tend to come from individual employees and can range over a wide number of issues, such as that:

- a bonus payment has been calculated incorrectly
- a disciplinary penalty is too harsh
- promotion has been denied unreasonably
- access to a training opportunity has been refused
- the job is currently under-graded
- the employee has been sexually harassed/bullied by another employee or manager
- there are insufficient car parking spaces in the company car park
- working conditions – eg heating, lighting, space – are unpleasant
- overtime opportunities are restricted to particular individuals rather than distributed equally across all employees in the department/section
- a request for more flexible working arrangements has been unreasonably denied.

Although complaints about management behaviour usually come from individual employees, if they are not handled sensitively they can (and do) develop into collective employee complaints. The resolution of an employee grievance involves negotiation in that both management and the complaining employee seek to persuade each other that their own suggestion to resolve the grievance is the better one. However, such persuasion is rarely successful and a mutually acceptable solution will involve the parties' making concessions towards each other's positions.

### Most grievances are not referred to the procedure

Most organisations have a grievance procedure. Employment relations managers must be familiar with this procedure. However, when an employee raises a grievance against management behaviour, the matter does not automatically trigger the full procedure. The vast majority of employee grievances are settled either informally or by a voluntarily negotiated and agreed settlement before the procedure is triggered. Informal settlements can include an apology by the employer or perhaps an admission of error by the employer, who then rectifies the mistake that is the cause of the employee's complaint. Alternatively, the employer may explain to the employee why his or her grievance is ill-founded – an explanation that the employee then accepts.

 REFLECTIVE ACTIVITY

What are the main issues of employee complaints in your organisation? Do these tend to get resolved informally, or do they require the full procedure?

In most academic literature, the words 'negotiation' and 'bargaining' are taken to mean one and the same thing. This is incorrect. Bargaining is only one of a number of different negotiation situations in which a management may find itself. The tenor and style of negotiating in bargaining is likely to be more adversarial than in grievance-handling and group problem-solving situations (see below) since in this situation the representatives of the employer and the employee are seeking to protect and advance the interests of their constitutuents.

There are, however, different bargaining situations, which have been classified by Walton and McKersie in their classic book *A Behavioral Theory of Labor Negotiations* as:

- integrative bargaining
- distributive bargaining
- intra-organisational bargaining.

**Integrative bargaining**

Bargaining is a situation in which the parties involved have a 'shopping list' of demands of each other. One party (usually the employees, collectively) proposes a list of improvements to pay and other employment conditions (for example, a shorter working week, longer holidays) and the other (normally the employer or an organisation of employers) responds with a set of counter-proposals covering changes in working practices and changes in the pattern of working hours, etc.

For example, in the 2002/3 annual pay negotiations between the Fire Brigades Union and the Fire Service employers, the former had the following shopping list:

- an improvement in the basic pay for fire-fighters to £30,000 per year – an increase of 39.3%
- emergency control staff to receive the same wage as fire-fighters
- fire-fighters working the retained and volunteer duty systems to be trained to the same standards as fire-fighters and to receive the same pay and conditions
- the introduction of the more 'appropriate and relevant' Fire Service National Pay Formula
- the settlement date to be 7 November 2002.

The Fire Service employers presented the following counter shopping list:

- any improvement in pay to be subject to central government's providing the funding
- a commitment to national pay scales in the Fire Service
- the introduction of a new National Pay Formula, based on automatic indexation to pay increases in the economy as a whole, and which could accommodate special allowances without depressing national pay increases

- control staff conditions to be dealt with through job evaluation, reflecting the employer's belief in the principle of equal pay for work of equal value
- an inquiry to be established by the Government on the basis that this represented the only way of securing additional funding: the inquiry to examine pay and modernisation of working practices and to report in time for any new agreement to be implemented on 7 November 2002.

A bargaining situation involves issues of collective interest to the workforce, unlike an employee's grievance, which normally involves an issue of interest only to that individual. In many bargaining situations, a constructive compromise is achieved by 'trading' taking place over the items that each party has flagged up to the other for negotiation. In these situations identifying which items in their shopping list the parties are prepared to trade is a key activity in preparing for the bargaining (see below).

The parties come to an agreement in these bargaining situations by trading items in their respective shopping lists. The aim of the parties is to use trading to advance, or protect, their own interests and thus create new 'prices' (new rules) at which employee services will be bought and sold. This bargaining situation in which the parties accommodate each other's interests by trading items in their shopping lists with a view to both parties gaining something from the bargaining is categorised by Walton and McKersie as integrative bargaining.

In the 2002/3 Fire Service dispute, the employers traded:

- a wage increase of 16% over 31 months, staring with 4% from 7 November 2002, a further 7% from 7 November 2003, and a further 4.2% from 1 July 2004, to give an annual pay of £25,000 for qualified fire-fighters
- a settlement date in future of 1 July
- a new National Pay Formula.

In return they received (gained):

- the new National Pay Formula to be subject to review
- an increase in the agreed 16% above 4% to be dependent on the modernisation of working practices with its achievements in intended efficiency validated by the Audit Commission
- the establishment of a Technical Advisory Panel to broker agreement in the case of local disputes over the introduction of alternative duty systems to the cherished two-shift system that had been in place for many years.

### Distributive bargaining

Distributive bargaining is nevertheless still to be found even in the private sector, as illustrated by the following example taken from a bargaining outcome in a newspaper publishing company in East Anglia. The company received the following claim from the National Union of Journalists (NUJ) on behalf of its journalist employees:

- parity of pay rates with a competitor newspaper plus 2%

- an increase in paid holiday entitlement
- sabbatical leave for staff employed by the company for a number of years
- consideration to be given to childcare arrangements in association with a nearby nursery
- the adoption of a new health care scheme
- the provision of a staff canteen
- an increase in the mileage rate above the current level of 40p per mile.

The company did not put forward a set of counter-proposals and entered into bargaining sessions with the NUJ. The eventual outcome was that the company conceded new rates of pay as follows:

- the annual salary for journalists who had satisfactorily completed their training was raised to £16,600
- a minimum annual salary of £16,600 for senior journalists was created with further increments dependent on responsibility and experience
- individuals whose salaries did not increase as a consequence of the changes to banding to receive an increase of 1.6% or £300, whichever was the greater.

In return for this increase in its labour costs, the company received from its journalists no concession in working practices. It was a classic 'something for nothing' agreement involving a transfer of scarce economic resources from the company to its employees.

THEORY    **Intra-organisational bargaining**

The two different bargaining situations outlined above relate to the reconciliation of differences/interests between management and its employees' representatives. Walton and McKersie distinguished a third type of bargaining situation in which bargaining takes place within the two bargaining parties to arrive at a consensus as to what would be requested from the other party. They referred to this as intra-organisational bargaining. It deals with resolving conflict which occurs between each bargaining team. Usually, the management team participating in bargaining has within it a number of different interest groups each of which may want something different (or have different priorities) in terms of concessions from, or concessions to, the other party. Disagreements within the management team can exist over the bargaining outcome aims, the items in the shopping list to be traded, the strategy and tactics to be adopted and whether an offer from the other party should be accepted (see below).

These internal conflicts can occur before, during, and at the end of the bargaining process. A consensus has to be struck within the bargaining team to resolve these internal differences. Intra-organisational bargaining within a management team can take place at a number of different levels:

- the workplace – The different interests here have to be accommodated and a common position agreed

- the company – All the different workplaces that make up the company have to reconcile their differences

- the industry – In multi-employer bargaining (or industry-wide bargaining) all the companies in the industry have to negotiate a common position acceptable to companies of different sizes, containing different components of the industry and having experience in differing degrees of product market competition

- the European level – In negotiating Framework Agreements under the EU Social dialogue process (see Chapter 5), the public and private sector employers' organisations from each of the member states engage in bargaining to reach a consensus position with regard to negotiating with the ETUC.

The higher the level at which negotiations are to take place, the greater the number of conflicting interests there will be within the management team, and the greater the difficulty in establishing a common acceptable position. For example, Business Europe has 31 member organisations, whereas the British Printing Industries' Federation – which bargains annually over pay and employment conditions with the Graphic, Paper and Media sector of Unite – has to bargain a common position with over 1,000 member companies before commencing negotiations with the union.

### Attitudinal structures

An important part of the bargaining process is the attitude that the two parties adopt towards each other. The attitude may be adversarial or it may be co-operative, or it may be of mutual professional respect and trust. The bargainers may change their attitudes towards each during the bargaining stages (see below) depending on such factors as changes in the economic environment and personalities. The bargainers may also attempt to influence the expectations of the other parties over what the outcome of the bargaining might be, or indeed, what their original proposal's offer might be.

An example of such behaviour by an employer is shown in the case study below. Here, the chief executive is clearly attempting to condition the employees to expect little in the way of improved wages and employment conditions in the forthcoming pay negotiations. As we have already noted, the style and attitude of the parties towards each other is also likely to vary depending on the negotiating situation in which the parties find themselves. All this points to the employment relations professional acquiring and developing the good practice of getting to know his or her opposite number on the other side. For example, how does he or she think? Is he or she prone to exaggerate? And so on.

### The chief executive officer reviews the prospect for the forthcoming negotiations

At a time when the company has been busy and the employees have seen much overtime, it is important to remember that this reflection of high levels of activity and 'just-in-time' requirements makes it more difficult than usual for us to plan output effectively. Because of our continuing over-capacity, price competition remains fierce and margins continue to be eroded.

Our quarterly economic survey shows that in six of the last seven quarters we have achieved poorer margins. In the light of the increasing product market competition, an increase in the price of our products is impossible. Against such an uncertain economic background there is simply no ability to pay for any improvements in terms and conditions and certainly no question of any reductions in working time through increases in holidays or a shorter working week.

## REFLECTIVE ACTIVITY

Explain the difference between integrative, distributive and intra-organisational bargaining.

## GROUP/JOINT PROBLEM-SOLVING

This is a situation in which two or more parties negotiate the details whereby one party will co-operate with the other. Such negotiation takes place most commonly in a situation where management is endeavouring to initiate some action to resolve a problem of common concern to both parties. Let us consider another case study example.

### Co-operation with consultants?

An organisation is currently performing comfortably in terms of sales, profitability, etc, but recognises that in the near future product market competition will become more intense. The top management has started to consider suitable policy initiatives that might be introduced to minimise any adverse consequences in terms of sales and so forth when the greater product market competition becomes a reality.

As a first step, the organisation has decided to invite a team of consultants to examine its work organisation and systems and to produce a feasibility study on what action/policies it might introduce, and what their effect might be on improving its future product market competitiveness. The management has committed itself to implement none of the report's recommendations until the workforce has been consulted and involved in thorough discussions on the report.

However, if the consultants are to obtain a full picture for their report, they will have to speak to, and have the co-operation of, the workforce. The company believes that the best way to achieve this is for the consultants to go into the departments and to speak to the employees on an individual basis. But the consultants will have to inform the supervisor/team leader and the representative of the employees of what they intend to do in the department. Supervisors/team leaders have accordingly been told to release employees from their workstation so that they can speak to the consultants.

The workforce has an interest in seeing the organisation's efficiency improve because it will enhance their job security. They are therefore prepared to co-operate with the work of the consultants – but they have some concerns. First, they know that in other firms where this consultancy organisation has done work, redundancies have been declared shortly afterwards.

Second, the employee representatives are worried that management wish them to have no role when the consultants are speaking to their constituents. They would prefer to be present at any interviews the consultants carry out with individual employees in the various departments.

The workforce is not against the use of consultants as the matter of principle, but its representatives have decided to approach the management about its concerns. The ensuing negotiations between the parties are over:

- whether the firm of consultants preferred by management to produce the feasibility report will be used, or whether another firm of consultants could be brought in

- the procedure to be adopted by the consultants when in the departments – will they have direct access to employees? Will employee representatives be present at interviews?

The example illustrates the manner in which a group problem-negotiating situation operates. Management are normally seeking the co-operation of their workforce to some proposed action to gain information which can then be used to solve a problem jointly with the employees, to mutual gain. As a result, the management's negotiating style (attitude) will not be adversarial. Management want something from the employees so they will start by demonstrating to them that there is an advantage in co-operating. For management to bang the table and be insulting in the negotiations towards the employee representatives would be inappropriate to the context and unlikely to secure management's primary objective, which is to gain employee co-operation with the work of the consultants.

### REFLECTIVE ACTIVITY

Has there recently been a joint problem-solving situation in your organisation? If there has, what was it about? What were the terms on which the employees co-operated? If there has been no recent joint problem-solving situation in your organisation, why has that been the case?

## STAGES IN THE NEGOTIATION PROCESS

All negotiating situations involve the stages shown in the bullet-point list below, although the length of time each stage lasts and the degree of formality in each stage will vary. For example, a negotiating situation between managers on how to deal with a problem is unlikely to be written down except perhaps in the form of a letter and/or an internal memorandum to management colleagues. In all negotiating situations, the preparation stage lasts the longest time. The amount of time the two parties spend in actual bargaining – perhaps in a face-to-face situation across the table – is small, relative to the total time spent by both sides in the whole negotiating process.

The stages in the negotiation process are:

- preparation and analysis
- presentation
- searching for and identifying common ground
- concluding the agreement
- writing up the agreement.

## PREPARING FOR BARGAINING

### Selection of the bargaining team

The size of the management team will vary, but there are advantages in its being small and of an uneven number. If the team is small, it is easier to maintain discipline among its members. An odd number means that if the bargaining team has to take a vote to determine its position, there is always a majority view to prevail. A team of three will always at least split two to one, and one of five will at least divide three to two. A team of two might divide one against one, and one of four may split two against two. The management bargaining team should represent all major interest groups in the business.

At least three functions have to be carried out by a negotiating team who will work together under the guidance of its leader. The leader will be the main spokesperson and the principal negotiator in heading the negotiations. In addition, the leader will call for an adjournment if management considers one to be necessary, and will hold the chair during adjournments. It is the team leader who will enter corridor (private) discussions with the leader of the other side. The leader will also be responsible for finalising the agreement on behalf of management.

Leaders require a number of attributes. They have to have good interpersonal skills to build the team as a coherent whole, and they have to be acquainted with the employees' attitudes and, if appropriate, the policies and problems of any organisation which represents the employees. It is imperative that the leader shows leadership and is respected by the other members of the team. In addition, the leader must be firm, be capable of exercising good judgement, be patient, be a good listener and be skilful in communicating ideas and getting points across.

The negotiating team also requires a note-taker whose important role in negotiations cannot be stressed enough. The note-taker's role includes:

- in adjournments, informing the negotiating team whether the negotiations are making progress or just going round in circles
- advising the negotiators whether the agreed strategy and tactics (see below) are being observed
- recording the proposals made by the other party
- indicating whether the negotiating team has – say, through lack of concentration – missed an offer/proposal from the other side (if this is happening, the negotiating team can return to it in the next or subsequent bargaining sessions)
- ensuring that all issues are addressed; the note-taker summarises to the negotiating team what issues have been settled and what issues are still outstanding, and prevents issues that are on the negotiating agenda from being forgotten or overlooked
- supplying a complete and accurate record of what has been agreed, from which management drafts the agreement.

The team also requires a strategist whose role is to monitor the strategies of both sides and to identify and seek to confirm the anticipated basis of common ground and of constructive compromise for both sides. The strategist also provides any additional information or details that may be required by the team. In addition, he or she monitors and assesses any proposal as and when it is made by the other party.

Some negotiating teams also find it is useful to have a member whose sole purpose is to listen to what is being said and to make no spoken contribution in the bargaining sessions. Other teams may also like to have a person whose role is to watch the body and facial reactions of the members of the other side when they are receiving proposals from management or making proposals to management. These reactions can convey useful information and reveal the extent to which the other party is committed to its own proposals and open to counter-proposals from the management side.

Regardless of the size of the management's negotiating team and the division of labour between them, it is imperative – prior to both the first meeting with the other side and to meeting again after an adjournment – that each member of the management team be given the opportunity to contribute to the discussion and agree on the bargaining objectives, strategy and tactics (see below). Ideally, the negotiating team should determine these issues. This provides each team member with an insight into the overall plan and strategy, and thereby generates commitment amongst the whole team to its objectives. So while the role of the team leader is most important during negotiations, the role of the whole team is very important in determining policies and strategies.

### Team discipline

Members of the management team should conduct themselves during the negotiations in line with the agreed position(s) established in the analysis stage (see below), so that the team in the actual negotiations is united and purposeful. It is important before meeting with the other side that the team agrees that only one member should speak at a time in the bargaining sessions, and that the team leader should not be interrupted unless it is absolutely necessary. However, all members of the team should be prepared to speak when called upon to do so by the team leader. If members of the team other than the leader are to make a spoken contribution during the bargaining sessions, it should happen as part of a predetermined strategy, the leader having indicated to the other party that they are speaking by invitation from the leader.

It is also important before meeting with the other party that the team reminds themselves of the importance of not disagreeing as a team in front of the other side, and that if team discipline begins to break down, the leader should seek an adjournment so that the necessary action to re-establish discipline can be taken (even to the extent, if necessary, of excluding a member of the team from participating any further in the face-to-face negotiating sessions). The maintenance of team discipline is easier if all members are fully acquainted with the negotiating objectives and the necessary arguments and tradable items (see below) regarded as essential to achieving those objectives. It may help if before meeting with the other side the team has agreed a non-verbal method of communicating with each other (eg signals, passing notes, etc) during bargaining sessions.

The arguments from the management bargaining team have to be consistent and, despite any provocation or unprofessional behaviour on the part of the other side, should not deviate from the agreed format. If during negotiations the other side attempts to disrupt the discipline of the management team by trying to bring in another speaker from the management side against the planned sequence of contributors, the team leader must intervene immediately to make clear to the other side that their remarks be addressed to him or her. He or she should tell the other side to address all their remarks through him or her as the team leader. If a member of the management bargaining team begins to talk out of turn, the leader must carefully restrain him or her, using appropriate language in the right tone of voice. It may, for example, only be necessary to tell the team member to keep quiet or to calm down for discipline to be restored – but if this does not work, an adjournment may be necessary during which discipline can be restored.

The members of the negotiating team must remain within their agreed roles and speak only when invited to do so, unless a change of plan is agreed during adjournments in the negotiations. However, the team members should endeavour to help each other out of difficulty if the team comes under pressure. Getting rattled transmits to the other side a clear message that management may not be totally united in its commitment to its case, and that unexpected gains may be made by playing to these perceived differences.

## REFLECTIVE ACTIVITY

What considerations should management take into account in selecting its team for bargaining with its employees' representatives? Justify your answer.

## THE ANALYSIS STAGE

A management negotiating team goes through three stages in preparing for bargaining. These are:

- analysis

- the establishment of aims to be achieved in the forthcoming bargaining sessions

- planning the strategy and tactics to achieve these aims.

The analysis stage of preparing for bargaining involves management's undertaking research to collect information to substantiate their proposals to be put to the employees' representatives and/or to provide counter-arguments to the justification of the proposals from the other party. The employment relations professional must therefore be familiar with sources of information. Such information will be available from within the organisation (internal sources) or provided by outside organisations (external sources) such as the National Statistics Office, government departments, non-government organisations (eg ACAS, the Certification Office, the Health and Safety Executive), employers' associations, private research organisations (for example, Industrial Relations Services and Incomes Data Services) and academic institutions. Information from internal sources is likely to cover such issues as:

- labour productivity trends

- profitability

- labour turnover

- absenteeism

- total sales

- investment

- pay changes

- orders pending

- the cash flow position

- employment trends.

Employers' associations are an important external source of information. They keep records about the types of agreements that exist in a sector and collect data on the size of pay increase settlements being granted by member companies. Many employers' associations are also trade associations and as such collect information on the sector for a number of subjects – eg total sales figures, the balance of foreign trade (export/import trends) and unit labour costs.

The analysis stage also involves the management negotiating team in checking on the relevance to the forthcoming negotiation situation of existing arrangements such as:

- collective or individual agreements
- custom and practice.

The employment relations manager should be familiar with the meaning and content of those policies that give effect to such rules, arrangements and to accepted custom and practice.

In pay bargaining, purposeful persuasion arguments and counter-arguments usually relate to the company's ability to meet the employees' wages claim, labour market shortages and surpluses for particular occupations, pay relativities in terms of what other workers in other companies/other sectors are obtaining in wage increases (commonly referred to as 'the going rate'), changes in occupational and industrial/sector pay differentials (often referred to as 'the earnings league table') and changes in inflation since the last pay increase was granted (ie the need to keep real wages at least maintained).

These arguments by employee representatives for improvement in wages and employment conditions are illustrated by the following trade union wage claim in an engineering company in the Midlands of the UK:

Our 5% wage increase is a justifiable claim on behalf of our members. Since the wages and condition settlement last year, the rate of inflation – as shown by the Index of Retail Prices – has increased by 1.5%. Our members therefore require an increase of 1.5% in wages to maintain their real purchasing power. You have been experiencing difficulty in recruiting labour over the last 12 months and the number of people leaving your employment has increased. This reflects that your pay and conditions are out of line with your labour market competitors. To overcome this staff shortage problem and to make your pay rate competitive, our members require a further 2.5% in addition to the 1.5% inflation protection increase. The additional 1% is justified by the increase in the company's sales, profitability and productivity over the past 12 months. In addition, the company forecasts continuing growth over the coming year and has reported to its shareholders an average 4.5% increase in sales and an average of 7.1% increase in operating profits over the past 12 months.

A further example can be given of a wage claim to a company based in Cambridge:

A 3.8 percentage increase is claimed in line with increases nationally. Average weekly earnings for the whole economy rose by 3.7% in the year to September, up from 3.6% in August. A further 3% increase on basic salary is justified by productivity increases, this increase to be applied and financed wholly through this year's productivity gains (self-financing). There have been many increases in productivity this year. Those that spring to mind are that the company has reduced staffing levels over the last two years from 550 to 500. In some areas, staffing levels have been reduced by 50%, while mailroom staff have taken on extra work – that of leaflet-counting. A further 1% on basic salaries is justified by 'the Cambridge phenomenon', or as it is regularly described by the media, 'Silicone fen'. The people of southern Cambridgeshire know of its existence only too well. They have to pay its extra costs daily. The price of petrol is a good example. Cambridge Council already pay an allowance of 2% and many other companies are being approached by staff to consider this when reviewing staff wages.

Those involved in annual pay bargaining must therefore be familiar with external sources of information covering inflation, pay trends and labour market indicators. Employment relations professionals – particularly those involved in bargaining – need to be knowledgeable about the extent and quality of information (data) available from the following sources:

- Industrial Relations Services
- Incomes Data Services
- *Labour Market Trends*
- the New Earnings Survey.

You should consult these sources of information and acquaint yourself with the information they contain, and be aware how useful this might be to you. The New Earnings Survey is, however, particularly important – and we now take a look at what is in it.

**The New Earnings Survey**

The New Earnings Survey (NES) is the most comprehensive source of earnings information in Great Britain. It is absolutely essential that you consult this source of pay data during your studies of employment relations. It is a survey of earnings of all those in employment in Great Britain carried out in April of each year. The survey is based on a 1% sample of employees who are members of PAYE income tax schemes, and is designed to represent all categories of employees in businesses of all kinds and sizes. The sample each year comprises all those whose National Insurance numbers end with a specific pair of digits. The sample pair of digits has been used since 1975. Employers are then contacted to give details on the identified employees. The method covers about 90% of the sample. The remaining 10% is obtained directly from large employers. This sample can include some employees not in a PAYE scheme. The coverage of full-time adults is virtually complete. The coverage of part-time employees is, however, not as comprehensive.

The NES provides an annual snapshot of earnings and hours worked, analysed by gender (equal pay) industry (from which an earnings league table can be calculated), occupation (skill differentials can be worked out from this series), age group, regions, county and collective agreements. Its results are published in six parts:

- Part A is a streamlined analysis giving selected results for full-time employees in particular wage negotiation groups, industries, occupations, age groups, regions and sub-regions.
- Part B provides analyses of earnings and hours for particular wage bargaining groups.
- Part C analyses hours and earnings for particular industries.
- Part D provides the same analysis for particular occupations.
- Part E provides the same analysis for regions and counties.
- Part F provides an analysis of the distribution of hours, joint distribution of earnings and hours, and an analysis of hours and earnings for part-time women employees.

The earnings data covers the level of earnings, the make-up of total earnings (basic pay, overtime pay, shift premiums, incentive payments, etc) and the distribution of total earnings (by decile, quartile and median).

## REFLECTIVE ACTIVITY

Take a look at the New Earnings Survey. Write a report on how pay and conditions in your organisation compare with the national average. How would you account for any differences found?

## THE IDENTIFICATION OF TRADABLE ITEMS

The most important activity for the management team in preparing for bargaining, however, is the identification of the key issues involved in the forthcoming bargaining sessions and the identification from among them of which of these issues management are prepared to trade. It also involves anticipating which of the issues the employees' side is prepared to trade on and which it is not. By identifying possible tradable items, the management bargaining team establishes the parameters within which it expects to be able to identify common ground with its employees and thereby the basis for a compromise agreement. In making these decisions about the possible tradable items, management weigh up the significance of the issues at stake for the protection and advancement of their, and the employees', economic interests.

In negotiations, at any given time, some of the issues are tradable and others are not. Let us give another example.

Management have just received a list of demands from the employees that includes a 2.5% increase in basic rates, the introduction of a productivity bonus, an increase in holidays, changes to paternity leave arrangements and the removal of non-strike arrangements. After long consideration, management decide – because of market conditions – that any increase in basic rates and any removal of 'no strike' arrangements are not tradable items. However, they are prepared to trade the introduction of a productivity bonus if this can be made self-financing, an improvement in holiday entitlement and changes to existing paternity benefits.

Having decided which items they are prepared to trade, the management negotiating team now starts the task of anticipating which issues it believes the employees (the union) will be willing to trade. In doing this, management must assess the strength of feeling of the employees about each of the items on the negotiating agenda, including whether they feel sufficiently strongly that at the end of the day they would be willing to impose industrial sanctions against the organisation. Let us say, for example, that management anticipate that the employees and their representatives feel most strongly about the introduction of a productivity bonus and gaining an increase in holiday entitlement (ie that these are their non-tradable items). So in this case, management anticipate that the employees are willing to trade basic pay rate increases, the no-strike clause and paternity arrangements (that these are their tradable items) to obtain improvements in holiday entitlement and the introduction of a productivity bonus. Management thus see a basis for agreement around a productivity bonus, an increase in holiday and paternity leave changes in return for the retention of a no-strike clause and no change in basic rates.

## ESTABLISHING BARGAINING AIMS

The next phase of the preparation stage is the establishment by the management negotiating team of the objectives it wishes to achieve in the forthcoming negotiations. This phase also requires management to anticipate the negotiating aims and objectives of the employees and/or their representatives. It is a task that can be done more competently if the management know and understand what motivates the representatives of the workforce with which it has to deal. Getting to know them does not mean agreeing with their position. However, it is only by knowing 'what makes them tick' (for example, their attitudes, their reaction to pressures upon them, their personalities) that management can predict/anticipate with any reasonable degree of certainty:

- how the employees' representatives might react to management proposals
- the issues they are prepared to trade in bargaining
- the bargaining style they are likely to adopt
- the strategy and tactics they might develop.

By setting objectives, the negotiators know what they are trying to achieve. Bargaining is about compromise and flexibility, so it is normally unrealistic to set inflexible objectives because that usually gives only two options: win or lose. Negotiators have to arrive at some sort of prioritised approach. It is standard practice for bargainers to establish three positions for each item involved in the negotiations. These positions are:

- What would management ideally like to achieve?
- What do management realistically believe they can achieve?
- What is the least for which management will settle (the fall-back or sticking position)?

The fall-back position represents the lowest package for which management will settle. It is the minimum that can be accepted without failing to meet the negotiators' objectives. If this position cannot be achieved, management may prefer to enter into a dispute situation with its employees. It means that management are prepared to withstand industrial sanctions that the employees may take against them rather than settle for less than their fall-back position. Management as part of preparing for negotiations must therefore also draw up plans to minimise/offset any costs that may accrue to the organisation should a failure to agree result in industrial action by employees.

## THE ASPIRATION GRID

Having established their negotiating objectives, the next step for management is to anticipate the bargaining aims/objectives of the other party along the same lines – what is likely to be their ideal, realistic and fall-back positions on each issue involved in the negotiating situation? Having considered which items they are prepared to trade, having anticipated the tradable items of the other party, having established their own bargaining objectives and having anticipated those of the other party, management can now construct an aspiration grid which sets out the parameters for the expected outcome of the negotiation. Such a grid shows the issues management are prepared to trade as well as management's anticipation of the issues they expect the employees will be willing to trade. It gives the parameters within which the forthcoming bargaining might be expected to develop. It helps management identify the information they require from the other party and the information required to be conveyed to the other party.

An example of how an aspiration grid can be used is shown in Table 11.1. An **X** indicates that a party is not prepared to trade that item. An **O** indicates that the party is prepared to trade that item. This grid is based on the most recent example cited in the text above. If both parties have an **X** against the same item in their fall-back column, it indicates that there will be no accommodation on that issue and the expectation must be that the negotiations will break down. There can be no basis for an agreement. Management would then have to give consideration to whether they are prepared to bear the costs that a failure to agree would involve. If they decide they are not, management will have quickly to reassess their position on that issue.

Table 11.1  An aspiration grid

| Items for negotiation | Management | | | Employees/union | | |
|---|---|---|---|---|---|---|
| | Ideal | Real | Fall-back | Fall-back | Real | Ideal |
| Basic rate increase of 2.5% | X | X | X | O | O | X |
| Introduction of productivity bonus | X | X | O | X | X | X |
| Increase in holiday entitlement | X | O | O | X | X | X |
| Changes to paternity leave | X | O | O | O | O | X |
| Retention of no-strike clause | X | X | X | O | X | X |

The grid shows that management would ideally like to trade no items with the employees. However, they know that this is unrealistic. The grid shows that management has therefore established a 'realistic' position of wishing to trade increases in holiday entitlement and changes to the paternity leave arrangements for no changes in pay and to the no-strike arrangements, and for there to be no productivity bonus introduced. The management fall-back position is to introduce a productivity-based bonus scheme, to increase holiday entitlement and to change existing paternity leave arrangements in return for no increase in basic rates and the retention of the no-strike clause. The bottom line for the management bargaining team is to trade a productivity bonus, an increase in holiday entitlement and changes to paternity leave arrangements in return for no increase in pay and retention of the no-strike clause.

The grid also shows what management expect to be the negotiating objectives of the employees' representatives. Management know that the representatives would ideally like to trade no items. Management are of course aware that the employee representatives will view this as unrealistic. The grid therefore shows that management anticipate the employees' realistic bargaining aim to be one of trading pay and changes in existing paternity leave arrangements in return for the introduction of a productivity-based bonus scheme, increased holiday entitlement and the removal of the no-strike clause. The grid further shows that the management bargaining team anticipates that the bottom line for the employees' representatives is likely to be to trade no increase in pay, no changes to the paternity leave arrangements and the retention of the no-strike clause in return for the introduction of a productivity-based bonus scheme and an increase in holiday entitlement.

The grid thus suggests that there is a basis for agreement between the parties. This is indicated in that the fall-back positions of the two parties do not have **X**s against the same issue. Management are not prepared to trade a basic rate of pay increase and the removal of the no-strike clause. Management anticipate that the employees are prepared to trade these issues. The employees are expected by management not to be prepared to trade the introduction of a productivity-based bonus scheme and an increase in holiday entitlement. However, management have assessed that they can live with trading these issues. The management negotiating team now has a structure of how the bargaining can be expected to develop and evolve. In the face-to-face sessions with the representatives of the employees, it will have to pass information to them about what issues management are prepared to trade and at the same time seek to gain information from the employees' side which confirms management's expectations of what the employees are prepared to trade.

The aspiration grid enables a negotiating party to structure its own position systematically and to record the expected outcomes of the other party's position. It sets out each side's objectives, known or anticipated, and their three positions. The grid gives an expected structure to bargaining sessions prior to their beginning. It indicates the information the parties require to obtain and transmit to each other during the forthcoming bargaining sessions to confirm (or readjust) their expectations of the other party's position. If information received during the bargaining sessions suggests that expectations about the other party's intentions are inaccurate, the aspiration grid has to be re-analysed and amended.

The aspiration grid gives management a picture of how the bargaining sessions are likely to develop. In the actual bargaining sessions, management can test out whether their anticipation of the employees' bargaining objectives is correct or must be re-assessed by ensuring that the employees and their representatives receive clear information as to management's bargaining objectives.

If management enter bargaining without having established objectives, the probability of reaching an unsatisfactory outcome or entering into a dispute situation is increased. It is essential that in establishing their 'realistic' and 'fall-back' bargaining objectives, management take proper, and due, account of the relative balance of bargaining power between themselves and their employees (see Chapters 1 and 2). The management negotiating team must take all these factors into account. If the balance of bargaining power favours the employer, the aspiration grid will be different from one that relates to a situation in which the bargaining power lies with the employees and their representatives.

## PLANNING STRATEGY AND TACTICS

The third phase of the preparation stage is when the negotiating team plans its strategy and tactics to deliver its bargaining objectives. This involves:

- deciding before meeting with the other party who is to speak, in what order, and on what issues
- anticipating arguments and counter-arguments.

### Anticipating arguments and counter-arguments

An important part of planning the strategy and the tactics to achieve the bargaining objectives is to anticipate the arguments most likely to be used by the other party against your case, and to consider how they might be countered. In this regard it is helpful if a member of management's negotiating team can 'play the devil's advocate' and probe management's case for its weak points, exploring how the employees' and/or their representatives' arguments against management's case may be exposed and answered. Plans can then be made as to how they might be answered.

**Communicating with the team**

During the negotiating sessions, the team may find it necessary to communicate without the need to call for an adjournment. Any agreed method of communication will have to be non-verbal. Research shows the most common method used in negotiating teams is the passing of notes.

In conducting negotiating, the preparation stage is the longest and most important stage in the process. If management's analysis of the information they have gathered – whether by interview techniques or from statistical data – is incorrect, it will establish inappropriate bargaining objectives and develop an unrealistic strategy and tactics, with the result that the chances of achieving management's bargaining objectives will be significantly reduced. If it does achieve those objectives, despite inadequate preparation, it is likely to be because management holds the upper hand in the relative balance of bargaining power stakes or by sheer good fortune. Good luck is not, however, a management skill. A 'seat of the pants' approach to a bargaining situation is understandable – but any competent negotiator will tell you that there is no substitute for preparation. The golden rule to remember when preparing for bargaining is:

Failure to prepare

is

preparing to fail.

If management fail to prepare adequately, however, disaster does not follow automatically. The situation can be rescued if management re-assess their negotiating analysis, objectives and strategy and tactics in the light of new information they obtain which was not available at the preparation stage. In short, they amend their original aspiration grid. Indeed, it is essential that management re-assess their bargaining objectives, their aspiration grid and the analysis upon which they based it, every time they obtain information they did not have, or did not take into account when getting ready for the next bargaining session. During any negotiating adjournments, management should frequently monitor and review their bargaining objectives (including a review of the aspiration grid) in the light of how the negotiations are developing and progressing.

## REFLECTIVE ACTIVITY

'Failure to prepare is preparing to fail.' Explain the importance of this statement for employment relations managers who are involved in bargaining.

## THE PRESENTATION STAGE

At the first meeting with the other side, if the negotiators are unknown to each other, it may be necessary to break the ice by having the teams introduce themselves to each other. On the other hand, if the bargainers are well known to each other, some other form of general meeting might help to start things off on the right foot.

### Management begin the meeting

If management are making the initial presentation, the leader of the management team first gives a general summary of their proposals by the use of such language as:

> Today, we want to put to you proposals in six areas – increased holidays, reduced working hours, increased pay, enhanced childcare facilities, changes in working practices and the conditions surrounding the operation of the sick pay scheme …

After informing the employee(s) or their representatives of the issues they are going to raise, management then substantiate the case already outlined by adducing supporting facts and figures emphasising the rationale behind the proposals and trying to suggest the strength of their feeling towards each of them. So the first part of the presentation stage of negotiating involves both parties' telling each other what they ideally would want from each other.

Although it is perhaps not common practice, it is good practice for each party to put on the table all the issues it wishes to be dealt with in the forthcoming negotiation/bargaining sessions and not just to present its views on selected issues. This avoids the possibility of a set of long negotiating sessions over many issues ending in apparent agreement only for one party to then say 'Oh, by the way – we need to talk about [a new issue] as well.' Some negotiators believe that there can be advantages in 'keeping something up your sleeve to hit them with later', but bearing in mind that the purpose of negotiation is to come to an agreement, this is a dangerous tactic because:

- The hidden issue might be a non-negotiable issue for the other side or one on which it is prepared to trade only if the alternative is no agreement at all. If this is the case, there is a high probability that the negotiations will break down, losing with them the issues on which an accommodation has already been made.

- It can destroy the mutual trust between the leaders of the respective negotiating teams. Negotiators do not like to have negotiated in good faith and to have openly raised all the issues to secure an agreement only to find that the other party has behaved differently.

- If one party behaves consistently in this way, the other party will come to regard it as part of that party's negotiating ritual and take it into account in future bargaining sessions. Any new supposed surprise thereafter, hoping to evoke further improvements in the offer/claim by the other side, is undermined.

At best, a management may get away with the 'keep something up your sleeve' tactic once. The employment relations professional should be an open, and not a devious, negotiator who puts all of his or her cards on the table to be considered in any negotiation from the outset.

**Management receives proposal(s)**

If management are receiving one or more proposals from their employees' representatives, they listen carefully to what they are saying and do not interrupt the presentation. When the employee side has completed its presentation, it is good management practice to avoid an unconsidered (ie knee-jerk) response. By the same token, it is unwise for management to respond with immediate counter-proposals unless they have been agreed beforehand. If management are receiving proposals for the first time, their response should be confined to asking questions to seek clarification of the employees' proposals so that they can be confident that they genuinely understand what those proposals actually mean. Typical questions might be:

- What does the actual proposal on item X really mean? Could you please give us more details?

- What is the source of the information on the statistic for the wage rates/inflation rate, etc, that you have quoted?

- When you refer to average earnings, what kind of average do you mean – mode, median, unweighted arithmetic?

It is essential that at the end of the presentation of the employees' proposals, management are 100% certain about what has been proposed and what it is the employees' proposals actually mean. It is therefore good practice, before the employees' presentation session concludes, for management to summarise back in a neutral manner what they understand has been proposed on behalf of the employees. At the end of the employees' presentation, management should arrange to meet with the employees at a future date so that a full and measured response to the employees' proposal(s) can be given.

We can illustrate this point by use of the following typical measured response from CEN Ltd to a list of demands from its employees for changes in their wages and employment conditions.

### RESPONSE TO WAGE CLAIM

Thank you for your claim, which has been given very careful consideration by the company.

Before addressing the principal part of your claim – an increase in wage rates – I would like to deal with the other items that you put forward for consideration.

*Increased holidays*

Currently, all staff working for CEN enjoy five weeks' annual holiday. This compares favourably with other organisations across a range of industries and in particular with the majority of our competitors. It is also important to emphasise that holiday entitlement for one group of staff is not something that the company would decide in isolation. When we agreed to recognise the union for collective bargaining, it was made clear that being a member of a trade union would not bring any better, or worse, benefits to individuals. Similarly, those areas of the company that have chosen not to go down the collective bargaining route will likewise be no better or worse off.

Because the company can see no justification for increasing holiday entitlement across the board, we are unable to agree to this aspect of your claim.

*Sabbaticals*

Similar arguments about common benefits also apply to this issue. However, we do note that in your claim you are not specific about how sabbaticals would operate. While we do not believe that such a system would be workable across the company, we are prepared to listen to any detailed ideas that you want to present before ruling this matter out completely.

*Childcare provision*

Again, this is an area in which you have provided no detail. For example, how many people would want to take advantage of any provision? Would those people be prepared to make a contribution to the cost? Clearly, the company can see some advantages – staff retention, for example – that might flow from such a provision, but again it is not something that can be considered for one group of staff in isolation. What we therefore propose is that the Personnel Director carries out an evaluation of costs, local provision, etc, and that the matter is revisited as a potential company-wide benefit. If you would like to submit ideas, the possible number of interested participants, etc, to this evaluation, the Personnel Director would be delighted.

*Healthcare*

Together with colleagues across the company you will, either tomorrow or Thursday, be receiving a letter from David Smith advising you of the company's intention in this area. As I am sure your colleagues in the union have advised you, this is something that the Personnel Director has been evaluating since earlier this year, and it has always been the intention that any scheme would be delivered across the group.

*Canteen*

We are afraid that this element of your claim cannot be accepted. There is no evidence to suggest that staff are prevented from taking a proper lunch break, and there are numerous local outlets serving hot and cold food at affordable prices. The suggestion that staff are somehow forced down the road of eating unhealthy snacks does not stand up to any sort of close scrutiny. However, if you can provide evidence of any member of staff who is prevented from taking their lunch break on a regular basis, please do so. It will then be addressed.

### Staffing levels

Management are not fully aware of any 'ongoing crisis situation', but if you can provide details of your concerns, they will be looked at and responded to.

### Motoring expenses

We do not understand your comment about an absence of motoring expenses. Any member of staff who uses their own car for business use is reimbursed at the rate of 33p per mile. We acknowledge that this might need to be reviewed and are prepared to discuss this with you. However, for the record, there is no 'Inland Revenue rate' of 43p.

### Air conditioning/pool cars

Please provide us with details of your concerns.

### Investors in People

Your comments on the decision to apply for the IiP standard are noted. So far as job descriptions are concerned, Colin has already written to individuals about this, and we now consider that the matter has been dealt with.

### Pay

First of all we would like to make it clear that these negotiations are between CEN Ltd and Union X. Other companies within the Group will carry out their own negotiations and arrive at their own conclusions. We have no intention of linking these quite separate matters.

We are solely concerned with pay levels at our establishment and what is right for this business.

We note your comments regarding an increase of 5% across the board because, you say, that it is increasingly costly to live in Mid-Anglia. While we appreciate that gaining a foothold on the housing ladder in this region can be difficult, this does not apply to those already living here. For those individuals already resident in the area, the rise in the cost of living is 2.1%. The Bank of England, in its latest inflation report, does not expect it to rise significantly above this level over the next two years. Clearly, such economic data has to be taken into account by the company when setting its budgets for both revenue and costs – particularly wage costs. For example, it is unlikely that our advertisers would accept an increase in our rates that was significantly higher than the prevailing rate of inflation. We therefore have to keep budgeted increases in revenue within inflationary targets, which limits our ability to budget for unsustainable increases in our costs.

For this reason, we are unable to accept your claim for an across-the-board increase of 5%. However, we do understand the need to increase our overall salary rates for your group of employees so that they properly reflect the market in which we operate. We therefore make the folowing proposals:

1   We could increase the starting rate for trainees from £12,250 to £13,000 – an increase of 6.1%. This would also mean that since 2000 the starting rate for trainees would have increased by 27%. We also intend to increase the final year rate for trainees from £14,250 to £15,000 – an increase of 5.3% since last year, and an increase since 2000 of 22%.

2   At present, we have a 0–2-year qualified band of £14,250 to £15,750 and a 2+ years' qualified rate for seniors that starts at £15,500. It is our intention to abolish the 0–2-year qualified rate and simply have a senior staff rate instead.

3   With effect from 1 January next year, trainees will go on to the higher level (£15,000) once they have obtained their qualification. This usually occurs approximately 21 months after they commence training. Once they have satisfactorily completed their training, they will move on to the newly established senior rate which, with effect from 1 January next year, will be £16,500 for senior qualified staff. This represents an increase of 6.45% for 2+ years qualified staff and 15.8% on the starting rate for newly qualified staff. At the beginning of 2000, the starting rate for newly qualified staff was £11,750, so our proposals would represent an increase over three years of 40%.

4   For individuals who fall outside the changes I have already detailed, we propose to increase salaries in 2003 by 2.5%. This, as in previous years, represents a rise in salary above the prevailing rate of inflation. Overall, the changes we propose for next year will bring significant increases to over 50% of our staff, the average increase for your members being 4.7%.

So by the end of the presentation stage both parties will have put to each other their ideal positions. There is unlikely, at this stage, to be much common ground between them. However, the issues to be resolved during the bargaining sessions will now be known to both parties, who can now forthwith begin the task of seeking confirmation of their anticipated common ground.

## IDENTIFYING COMMON GROUND

The emphasis and tone of the negotiations now switches from concentrating on differences to identifying points of common ground that can form the basis of a possible agreement. The juncture has now been reached at which both parties must seek to confirm the expected common ground from which an agreement can be built. Each team needs to obtain, in future bargaining sessions with the other party, information that will enable it to confirm whether its expectations of the location of the common ground are correct.

Each subsequent bargaining session must be used constructively by both parties to gain this necessary information. Management must supply information to the other party so that the employees can assess the correctness of their expectations of management's position on the issues that are the subject of the negotiations. Bargaining sessions which do not provide the information required by the two parties to confirm (or disprove) their anticipated areas of common ground are not a constructive use of time. Negotiating sessions do happen in which neither party gains relevant information. This generally occurs when either party tries to:

- score points off the other
- lay blame
- issue threats
- shout down the other side or be sarcastic
- interrupt
- talk too much
- attack personalities on the other side.

Management can seek to confirm their expectations of where the common ground with the other side lies by a number of techniques. The most important of these are:

- the 'if and then' technique, which involves using such language as 'If you are prepared to move closer to our position on issue $y$, we are prepared to move closer to your position on $x$' – A positive response to this means that $x$ and $y$ have been identified as tradable items. The technique deliberately emphasises the requirement of the other side to move. It is a conditional offer

- open discussion within broad parameters – For example, management may indicate that an issue may be considered, but only in return for something – say, a different set of employee representative arrangements. Management would then outline these arrangements so that they form the basis of discussion and negotiation

- questioning (interviewing) for clarification of the other side's position

- watching the body language of the other party (frowns, glances, nods, etc) as the members react to the proposals put forward

- listening carefully to what is being said, including any conditions placed on any offers/proposals

- every now and then, using neutral language, summarising the other party's position on an issue – This is particularly helpful if the issue concerned is complex. Such a summary might well begin with something like '… So what you are saying is that you understand our offer on issue $x$ means that [at this point there is a complex example given of how the party believes what the other party has proposed will operate] and we both have no problems with that.' Each separate negotiating meeting should begin with one or the other party's summary of the stage the negotiations have reached. Such a summary usually outlines the areas upon which agreement has been reached and the issues upon which an agreement has still to be reached

- linking the issues so that specific issues may together be precisely identified as ones the parties are prepared to trade or not – Linking issues also ensures that the negotiations maintain momentum

- seeking agreement in principle before discussing details – It is pointless discussing the details of, for example, how the flexibility of employees between different tasks will operate if one party is totally opposed to employee flexibility.

If the use of the techniques outlined above draws out new information, an adjournment can be called – if thought necessary – to consider the implications of the new information, including whether there is a need to re-assess negotiating aims (ie amend the aspiration grid), to reopen analysis or to revise strategy and tactics.

**Summary of Techniques to Confirm Common Ground**

- the 'if and then' technique
- open discussion
- asking questioning, seeking clarification
- watching the body language
- listening to what is said and how
- periodic summarising
- linking of issues
- looking for a general agreement before a detailed one

## Listening for disguised messages

In negotiation situations, listening skills enable a negotiation team to decode signals hidden within the spoken language. Let us look at some example statements:

- 'At this stage, we are not prepared to consider that,' means 'That is a tradable item but at this stage it is not thought necessary to trade it.'

- 'We would find it extremely difficult to meet that demand,' means 'Meeting that demand would not be entirely out of the question.'

- 'I am not empowered to negotiate on that point,' means 'You will have to talk about that to my boss.'

- 'We can discuss that point,' means 'It is negotiable.'

- 'These are standard company terms,' means 'These terms are negotiable up to a point.'

- 'It is not our policy to make bonus payments, and even if we did, they would not be as large as 10%,' means 'We will let you have 2%.'

- 'It is not our normal practice to,' means 'We might do that, if you make it worth our while.'

There is information significant enough to confirm tradable items in these statements. If either negotiating team neglects to listen for the true meaning hidden within such statements, it may miss out on learning what it needs to know.

### The importance of momentum

Confirmation of what is the common ground gives the bargaining sessions a momentum. If they then become bogged down on a particular issue, the momentum can be sustained by switching to a new issue. This reinforces the importance of the negotiators putting all issues on the table from the outset. A thorny issue can be returned to later, and if it is then the only outstanding issue preventing an agreement being secured, the parties are more than likely to re-adjust their attitudes towards that issue to a more accommodating one. Both sides at that stage are faced with a stark choice. Either an accommodation is reached on the one outstanding issue or no agreement is made – the agreements on issues that have been reached will then fall by the wayside. The party that has the stronger feelings on the remaining, but difficult, issue is thus faced with the very real possibility of throwing the baby out with the bathwater.

---

### REFLECTIVE ACTIVITY

Outline the various techniques by which a management bargaining team can search for the common ground and thereby the basis for an agreement with representatives of the workforce. Which of these techniques do you consider to be the most important, and why?

---

## ADJOURNMENT

In bargaining, the use of adjournments is useful in ensuring that the bargaining sessions are proceeding as planned. The number and frequency of adjournments depend upon the normal practice of bargaining sessions in the environment in which they are being undertaken. Although adjournments may be suggested at any time, there are at least three constructive uses of the *ad hoc* (as distinct from the scheduled) break:

- to give the parties an opportunity to withdraw and review progress amongst themselves or consider a proposal tabled by the other side

- to provide a break if the negotiations have reached an impasse or become bogged down in trivia or personal argument such that team discipline is in danger or has broken down

- to provide an opportunity for one or two members of each side to talk informally with each other away from the negotiating table in a manner that would not be appropriate in the formal bargaining sessions. This equally gives the leaders of the two teams a chance to meet away from the negotiating table to discuss, without commitment, what it would take to unblock the impasse. The words 'without commitment' are normally used in such situations to reassure the other members of the two teams that their leaders will not strike any formal deal without prior reference back.

Adjournments thus enable one or both parties to reconsider their position in private, and are very much part of negotiating situations. Their main purpose is to provide space in which to review and assess progress against the negotiating objectives and against the perceived objectives of the other party. They provide an opportunity to update the negotiating strategy in respect of how the negotiations are progressing. If the adjournment is taken to consider a specific proposal, it is important to remember that such adjournments create expectations of a response in the minds of the other party. Reading what is going on is vital, and keeping the mind focused on the negotiating objectives is essential. In such situations, the warning by Cairns (1996) is salutary:

> If the adjournment is to consider a new offer, don't take ten minutes
> to reject it and 50 minutes discussing sport or the previous night's TV.
> Management may get the signal that if you took an hour to consider their
> offer, they are close to an agreement.

Adjournments should also be sought by management wherever they have any doubts about how the negotiating session is progressing or team discipline is about to break down (or has already broken down). The golden rule for management is:

> If in doubt, get out.

## CONCLUDING THE AGREEMENT

Entering this stage of the bargaining process is a matter of timing and judgement. The ability to recognise the best deal that in the circumstances can be reached and will be acceptable to the constituents represented is an important skill for the employment relations professional to acquire. In negotiating situations where increases in pay and other conditions are being offered in return for changes in working practices, the last item to be decided is what the amount of the increase in pay will be. There are a number of reasons for this.

First, the employer wants to know exactly what it is going to get in terms of increased work effort for the pay increase. It is only when an amount is on offer that the employer can make a considered judgement whether the 'price' for the changes in working practices gained is worth it. The same applies to the employees. It is only when they know what they have to do for it (ie the price they have to pay) that they can make a considered decision on whether the proposed pay increase offer is adequate compensation.

Second, if the pay issue is put on the table early in the negotiations, the negotiations themselves are likely to become deadlocked. The momentum to the negotiating session will come to a halt. Neither of the parties could accommodate each other's interests because it would not, at this stage, be able to assess whether the price was worthwhile.

Third, by negotiating over pay after all other issues have been agreed, the negotiators are faced with a stark choice. If they cannot accommodate each other over pay, the whole agreement collapses. What has been agreed concerning the other items in the respective shopping lists is withdrawn. The parties have to weigh up whether they want to throw out the baby with the bathwater. Neither will want to see all its earlier hard work go to waste. Attitudes are thus more attuned to compromise than if there were more than one outstanding issue. Both sides also have to weigh up whether – if an agreement fails to materialise over the one outstanding issue of pay improvement – they are prepared to bear the costs that go with the other party's imposing industrial sanctions against them.

### Factors to consider in concluding the agreement

There are a number of considerations management should bear in mind when closing the negotiations. First, they must be satisfied that all the issues have been discussed and agreed and that both parties fully understand what they have accepted. If there is a misunderstanding over what has been agreed, the negotiating process must recommence. It is crucial that both sides have the same understanding of what they have agreed, or when the agreement is implemented the parties will become embroiled in frequent disputes over how one party or the other is interpreting and/or applying the agreement.

Second, management have to convince the other party that their final offer *is* final. Management must be extremely careful not to allow any suggestion that what is effectively a bluff is its final position or that what is genuinely its final position is no more than a bluff. A series of 'final' offers from management will destroy their credibility with the other party and undermine their ability to convince the workforce that the bottom line has been reached. Management gain little by telling the employees that there can be no further improvement on their offer if the threat of industrial pressure from the employees – for example, by a ballot supporting industrial action – brings a further concession. In such circumstances, management have demonstrated to the other side that they have not reached their fall-back position and the employees will begin to expect even further improvement. When management tell the employees that their offer is final, then that must be the case.

The authors once heard a personnel director referring to the fact that he always had four sets of final offers, each hidden away in one of his pockets. This may sound amusing, but when he pulls out these four offers he will destroy his negotiating credibility with the employees and their representative body. To tell them that management have reached their final offer will not be believed, because what the director was saying was that he was prepared to raise his final offer at least four times. What would he do if the fourth offer were not believed? A management negotiator has to retain the respect and credibility of the other party. 'Final final final' offers will not achieve this.

Third, management should avoid being rushed into concluding a final agreement, no matter how tempting the offer/proposal from the other side sounds. Management must make sure that they have all the information they require from the employees (or their representatives) and then seek an adjournment. This will enable the management negotiating team to examine the final offer and to identify any potential problems that may have gone unnoticed before.

## WRITING UP THE AGREEMENT

Once management have an oral agreement, they should run through a summary of the proceedings with the employees' representatives noting precisely what has been agreed, and thereafter secure an agreement that what has been summarised is indeed what was agreed. It should then be written up in 'draft form'. The written agreement should state:

- who the parties to the agreement are
- the date it was concluded
- the date upon which it will become operative
- which groups/grades of employees are covered by the agreement
- the contents (clauses) of the agreement
- the duration of the agreement
- whether the agreement can be reopened before this end date, and if so, in what circumstances
- how disputes over its interpretation and application will be settled (through the existing grievance/disputes procedure?)
- which other agreements, if any, it replaces.

The written agreement should contain the signatures of representatives of the parties covered by the agreement.

## REFLECTIVE ACTIVITY

Explain why recording the negotiating process is vital. Outline the techniques that can be used for this purpose and what the advantages of each are.

The agreement is usually drafted by management and then sent to the other party, which will usually initial the clauses of which it accepts the wording. Only when both sides are happy with the wording will the agreement be printed and formally signed.

There are some pitfalls management should avoid when writing up the agreement. First, they should check the wording very carefully. One word can make a big difference to the meaning of a clause in the agreement. There is, for example, a vast difference in meaning between a clause which states that 'The management may provide ...' and a clause which states that 'The management will provide ...'. The first implies that in certain circumstances management may not provide. The second leaves no room for doubt.

Second, they should retain full concentration in the latter stages of the negotiations. It is likely that by then the negotiating process will have been going on for some time. There is a danger that the management negotiating team will relax once they have an oral agreement, thinking perhaps that the hard work is over. However, management should bear in mind that the details of what was said in negotiations may all too quickly be forgotten. What has been agreed will be what is down in black and white on the signed agreement.

Third, the agreement must be straightforward and easy to understand. Unless it is fully understood by both parties and its wording and intent clear, its operation will cause endless disputes over its interpretation and application.

Fourth, it is important for the management negotiating team to keep an accurate record of what was agreed. It may turn out to be management's only protection against an attempt by the other party to insert into the agreement something that was not agreed during the negotiations. Fortunately, attempts to cheat when writing up an agreement are extremely rare among management and employees' bargaining representatives. To behave in this way would be to try to 'pull a fast one' over the other side. A party may get away with this type of behaviour once – but the cost could be high in terms of lost professionalism and of lost trust with the other party.

So throughout the stages of negotiation there is a gradual movement towards common points of agreement. At the end of the presentation stage there is little common ground between the parties, but at each subsequent meeting there should emerge – via an exchange of information – an increasing degree of common ground. Each meeting of the two parties should make progress towards a constructive compromise (see Figure 11.3).

**Figure 11.3 The reconciliation of differences over time**

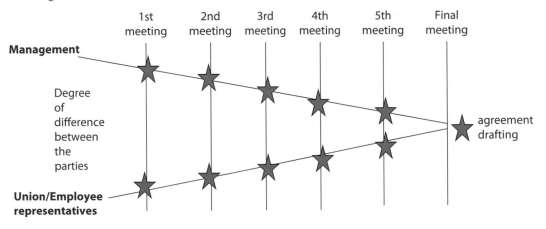

## THE OUTCOME OF NEGOTIATIONS

The best outcome of the bargaining process is one in which both parties make some gains – the so-called win/win situation. This is normally achieved by professional negotiators who concentrate on achieving well-prepared objectives, on maintaining long-term relationships with the other party, on emphasising a pragmatic approach, and on making an agreement which meets the needs of both parties. However, the relative balance of bargaining power between the two parties still heavily influences the outcome of the bargaining regardless of the professionalism the management bargaining team displays.

The opposite outcome is the lose/lose situation, which arises from a lack of professionalism on the part of the negotiators. The result is that:

- neither party achieves its objectives
- no agreement is secured
- long-term relationships are soured
- the constituents of the negotiators no longer respect/trust them
- both parties become disillusioned with the negotiating process.

A third possible outcome is the so-called win/lose situation in which one party dominates the other and secures something from the other party without giving anything in return. We saw above that where this is the outcome it is referred to as distributive bargaining. Such bargaining outcomes are characterised by an 'us and them' distinction between the parties. The bargaining teams' energies are directed towards victory ('I win: you lose'), a strong emphasis on immediate solutions regardless of their long-term consequences, sometimes even personalised conflicts rather than the considered assessment of facts, information and arguments, and little consideration of the quality of future relations between the parties after the negotiations are over.

## SUMMARY

- Negotiations can be defined as what happens when two or more parties come together to make an agreement by purposeful persuasion and by making constructive compromises.

- Four different negotiating situations can be identified – between managers, grievance-handling, bargaining, and group problem-solving.

- The most common negotiating situation in which employee relations professionals are likely to find themselves is negotiating with their managerial colleagues over various issues – for example, to determine the appropriate course of action to solve a problem.

- Grievance-handling is resolving an individual employee's complaint that management behaviour (or that of another person) has impacted unfairly upon them.

- Integrative bargaining is where the parties involved reach an agreement by trading items in the list of demands they make of each other.

- Group problem-solving is a situation in which two or more parties negotiate the details whereby one party will co-operate with action proposed by the other that is of common interest to both parties.

- The main differences between employment relations negotiations and commercial negotiations lie in the choice of negotiating partner, face-to-face relationships, adjournments, the status of agreements reached, and the need to consider the quality of future relationships.

- There are five stages to the bargaining process – preparation and analysis, presentation, searching for the common ground, concluding the agreement, and writing up the agreement.

- The most important stage is preparation and analysis, and its importance can be summed up in the sentence 'Failure to prepare is preparing to fail'.

- An aspiration grid shows the issues the parties expect to trade with each other, and helps identify the common ground likely to be the basis of reaching a compromise agreement.

- There are techniques available to management through which they can confirm their expectations of where the common ground lies.

- These techniques include the 'if and then' technique, questioning, body language, listening and summarising.

- In writing up the agreement, clear wording is important if future disputes over the interpretation and operation of the agreement are to be avoided.

---

**KEY LEARNING POINTS**

- Negotiation is two parties or more coming together to make an agreement by purposeful persuasion and constructive compromise (common elements).

- There are therefore a number of different negotiation situations – between managers, grievance-handling, bargaining, and group problem-solving. The most common negotiation situation in which managers find themselves is negotiating with management colleagues to gain their commitment to a particular course of action. This requires persuasion and compromise.

- Grievance-handling also involves two parties coming together to resolve an employee's grievance by purposeful persuasion and constructive compromise.

- Walton and McKersie (1991) have provided a theoretical underpinning of bargaining with their concepts of integrative bargaining (both parties gain), distributive bargaining (one party gains) and intra-organisational bargaining (bargaining by groups within one bargaining party to arrive at a consensus as to what would be requested from the other party).

- Bargaining is usually associated with unionised situations, but in fact bargaining currently often takes place in non-unionised environments, especially in large non-union firms in which bargaining may be carried out with employee representatives.

- There are five main stages to bargaining situations: preparation, presentation, searching for the common ground, concluding the agreement, and writing the agreement. The most important of these is the preparation stage, which involves three steps: analysis, establishing the bargaining aims, and planning the strategy and tactics to achieve these aims.

- The preparation stage involves the construction of an aspiration grid which sets out the parameters for the expected outcome of the negotiation. It shows the issues management are prepared to trade on (constructive compromise) as well as management's anticipation of the issues they expect the employees will be willing to trade on. It helps management identify the information they require from the other party and the information required to be given to the other party. If the information from the other party is different from what management were expecting, the aspiration grid must be re-assessed and amended accordingly.

- Incorrect analysis results in unrealistic bargaining or the establishing of incorrect objectives, quite likely also resulting in the devising of the wrong strategy and tactics in the endeavour to achieve those incorrect objectives. Failure to prepare is preparing to fail.

- The use of adjournments is useful in ensuring that the bargaining sessions are proceeding to plan.

## REVIEW QUESTIONS

1 The aspiration grid is a useful tool for professional bargainers. Your senior manager has not come across the term and asks you to explain what it means and how it can be used in the forthcoming pay negotiations with the employee representatives.

2 What is the most important skill required of an effective management bargainer? Why is it so?

3 The HR director has added two managerial members to the company's negotiating team which is about to bargain with the recognised trade union over a forthcoming pay grading issue. The director has asked you to brief the two new members, ensuring that they understand both distributive and integrative bargaining tactics and how to identify these during negotiations. What will you say? Justify your explanation.

4 'Failure to prepare is preparing to fail.' Explain the importance of this statement in preparing for bargaining.

5 Explain, with examples, why gaining the commitment of other management colleagues to a specific course of action is a negotiation situation.

**EXPLORE FURTHER**

Cairns, L. (1996) *Negotiation Skills in the Workplace: A practical handbook*. London: Pluto Press.

Industrial Relations Services (twice monthly) *Employment Trends*.

Industrial Relations Services (monthly) *Pay Intelligence*.

Incomes Data Services (twice monthly) Report.

Incomes Data Services (three times a year) *Pay Directory*.

Office for National Statistics (annually, in six parts) *New Earnings Survey*.

*People Management* (2009) 'How to negotiate with trade unions', November: 41.

Singh, R. (1992) 'Negotiations', in Towers, B. J. (ed.) *A Handbook of Industrial Relations Practice*, 3rd edition. London: Kogan Page.

Walton, R. E. and McKersie, R. B. (1991) *A Behavioral Theory of Labor Negotiations*, 2nd edition. Ithaca NY: ILR Press.

Walton, R. E., Cutcher-Hershenfeld, J. E. and McKersie, R. B. (1994) *Strategic Negotiations*. Cambridge MA: Harvard Business School Press.

**Web links**

www.statistics.gov.uk is the official website for national statistics on the labour market (National Statistics Office)

www.elmrems.gai.gov.uk is the web address of the Earnings and Labour Market Review, an unparallelled source of up-to-date and relevant commentary, analysis and data for users of both labour market and economic statistics

www.incomesdata.co.uk is the website of Incomes Data Services, an independent research organisation. Its publications and information services are used by those responsible for personnel and related issues in thousands of companies, voluntary organisations and public sector organisations

## CHAPTER 12

# Employee Performance and Behaviour

## OVERVIEW

In this chapter we examine the practices that are required if employee behaviour and performance is to be effectively managed. This includes the principles of discipline-handling, the characteristics of a fair and effective disciplinary procedure, the legal aspects of discipline and dismissal, and the monitoring and evaluation of disciplinary procedures. The chapter stresses that a fair and effective disciplinary procedure is one that concentrates on improving or changing behaviour, and not one that relies on the principle of punishment. The chapter explains the law surrounding the management of the disciplinary process and then looks at the concept of 'good practice' in relation to performance and behaviour at work, including the steps that should be taken when managers are trying to alter existing behaviour or performance, and how to ensure that all employees are treated fairly. Next, the chapter examines 'good employment practice' once the formal stage of the disciplinary process has been entered – keeping records, delivering warnings and advising employees on what will happen thereafter if the desired changes to performance or behaviour are not made. The procedure should allow all employees to understand what is expected of them in respect of conduct, attendance and job performance. The chapter then examines the use of the disciplinary procedure, stressing that it is important to ensure that its application cannot be challenged. It therefore offers guidelines which are broken down into three stages (investigation, disciplinary hearing, appeals) to help guarantee a consistent and fair approach. The chapter ends with a discussion of how to manage employee absence and the appeals stage of the procedure.

## LEARNING OUTCOMES

When you have completed this chapter, you should be aware of and able to describe:

- the development of disciplinary procedures
- how the law supports the use of disciplinary procedures and protects individuals from unfair treatment
- the importance of clear rules about conduct
- the importance of counselling to the disciplinary process
- how to use the disciplinary process to manage different disciplinary problems
- the importance of setting clear performance standards for individuals.

## INTRODUCTION

This chapter and the one that follows cover two related topics: discipline and grievance. Although they are to be dealt with separately, it is important to recognise that both are a two-way process and concern complaints, real or imagined, by one party against another. Both are covered by a specific code of practice, which is examined in detail later in the chapter. However, because of the way that the law has intervened in the discipline process (unfair dismissal legislation), disciplinary issues have tended to have a much higher profile within organisations than grievances, which are not as legally regulated.

### WHAT IS DISCIPLINE?

THEORY

Discipline is an emotive word in the context of employment. The dictionary offers several definitions of the word *discipline*, ranging from 'punishment or chastisement' to 'systematic training in obedience'. There is no doubt that discipline at work can be one of the most difficult issues with which a manager has to deal. It brings to the forefront matters relating to an individual's performance, capability and conduct, and in the context of employment the most appropriate definition to adopt might well be (Collins Concise Dictionary):

> to improve or attempt to improve the behaviour, orderliness, etc, of by training, conditions or rules.

In this chapter we examine the practices and skills that are required if employee behaviour and performance is to be effectively managed. This includes the principles of discipline-handling, the characteristics of a fair and effective disciplinary procedure, the legal aspects of discipline and dismissal, and the monitoring and evaluation of disciplinary procedures. A fair and effective disciplinary procedure is one that concentrates on improving or changing behaviour, and not one that relies on the principle of punishment.

## MANAGEMENT PROBLEMS WITH THE DISCIPLINARY PROCESS

Many managers have a problem with managing employee behaviour and performance because they believe that the methodology available to them – the disciplinary process – is cumbersome and ineffective or that the law on employment rights is heavily biased in favour of the employee. This can often result in problems being ignored because it is felt that effective action against individual employees either takes too long or is liable to mean an appearance before an employment tribunal at which the employee is more likely to be successful. Many managers share this basic misconception, and it is the responsibility of the employment relations professional to advise and guide their managerial colleagues through what, to many, is a minefield.

## GOOD PRACTICE

It is important for managers, at all levels, to appreciate that the effectiveness of the business can be undermined if issues relating to conduct, capability and performance are not handled professionally and consistently, or, even worse, if such matters are ignored altogether. This chapter *inter alia* looks at the concept of 'good practice' in relation to performance and behaviour at work, at the steps that should be taken when managers are trying to alter existing behaviour or performance, and at how to ensure that all employees are treated fairly. 'Good practice' is a concept that many managers have difficulty with because it is a term that is difficult to define. In the context of discipline at work, it is about acting with just cause, using procedures correctly, acting consistently, following the rules of natural justice – it is all four of those things – and more. It is also about developing those good management habits which ensure that you do follow procedure, you do act consistently and you do take account of the rules of natural justice when taking disciplinary action. Good practice is therefore an important principle. Not only does it help to ensure fairness and consistency but it makes good business sense and can add value.

## THE ORIGINS OF DISCIPLINARY PROCEDURES

Up to the beginning of the 1970s employers had almost unlimited power to discipline and dismiss individual employees – and in many instances they were not slow to exercise this power. While it was possible for a dismissed employee to sue for 'wrongful dismissal' under the common law, this was rarely a practical option because of the time and heavy costs involved. The only time that this employer power was likely to be restricted was where trade unions were present in the workplace and dismissal procedures were established through the collective bargaining process.

This changed with the Industrial Relations Act (1971). This Act gave individual employees the right, for the first time, to complain to an industrial tribunal that they had been unfairly dismissed. Industrial tribunals themselves had only been established in 1964, so in 1971 they were a relatively new feature of business life. They were renamed 'employment tribunals' with effect from 1 August 1998 by the Employment Rights (Dispute Resolution) Act (1998), and this change has been carried through to all pre-existing enactments. As well as introducing the right not to be unfairly dismissed, the 1971 Act also introduced, in 1972, the Industrial Relations Code of Practice. This introduced the idea that there was a right and a wrong way to deal with issues of discipline. It was subsequently superseded by an ACAS Code of Practice on *Disciplinary Practice and Procedures in Employment*, and this has now in turn been superseded by a Code of Practice on *Disciplinary and Grievance Procedures* (see below).

The 1971 Act was a turning point in the relationship between employer and employee. The relative informality of the then industrial tribunals and the fact that access to them did not depend on lawyers or money meant that for many employees the threat of dismissal without good reason disappeared or diminished. This does not mean that employees cannot be unfairly dismissed. They can. The law has never removed from management the ability to dismiss whoever it likes, when it likes, and for whatever reason it likes. All that has happened since 1971 is that where employers are deemed to have acted unreasonably and unfairly in dismissing employees, they can be forced to compensate an individual for the consequences of those actions. Most employers have accepted this legal intervention without serious complaint, and seek to manage performance and behaviour issues in as fair a way as possible. Some clearly do not, and take a cavalier attitude to individual employment rights. Others suffer from a misconception over what they can do and how the law impacts upon their actions.

## THE CURRENT LEGAL POSITION

Up until 1996, the law relating to discipline and dismissal was contained in the Employment Protection (Consolidation) Act (1978). In August of that year the Employment Rights Act (1996) came into force, consolidating provisions contained in the 1978 Act together with provisions of the Wages Act (1986), the Sunday Trading Act (1994) and the Trade Union Reform and Employment Rights Act (1993; TURERA). The Employment Relations Act (1999) and the Employment Act (2002) have made further changes.

The starting point for the disciplinary process is to be found in section 1 of the 1996 Act, which deals with an employee's right to a statement of employment particulars. Section 3 of the Act declares that any statement of particulars must also specify any disciplinary rules applicable to the employee or must refer the employee to the provisions of a document specifying such rules which is reasonably accessible to the employee. The Employment Act (2002) inserted a further requirement that the statement must also include information about any procedures applicable to the taking of disciplinary decisions.

The section goes on to declare that the statement of particulars must also specify who an employee can appeal to if they are dissatisfied with any disciplinary decision that is made.

Sections 94 to 134 of the Act deal specifically with unfair dismissal, and these set out:

- the legal definition of dismissal
- the specific reasons for which it is fair to dismiss an employee
- the position of shop workers who refuse to work on a Sunday
- the position of trade union officials
- the position of health and safety representatives
- the position of pension trustees.

## FAIR DISMISSALS

There are three ways in which an individual can be legally dismissed. One: their employment is terminated with or without notice. This is the most common situation and includes circumstances in which somebody is summarily dismissed for gross misconduct or simply given notice of dismissal. Two: they are employed under a fixed-term contract and that contract comes to an end without being renewed. Three: they resign (with or without notice) because of the employer's conduct – a situation more usually known as 'constructive dismissal'. This book is not intended as a legal text, and more detail on the meaning and applicability of these three definitions can be found in *Essentials of Employment Law* by David Lewis and Malcom Sargeant (2009) or in the CIPD Employment Law Service, which has been specifically designed to aid all practitioners with the legal aspects of their work.

Subsection 2 of section 98 of the Employment Relations Act (1996) defines a number of reasons for which it can be fair to dismiss an employee. These are:

- lack of capability or qualifications
- bad conduct
- redundancy
- breach of a statutory provision
- 'some other substantial reason'.

Dismissals relating to 'capability' (performance or absence) and 'conduct' (behaviour), together with 'some other substantial reason' (which is explained below) are probably the most common, and have the most links with the disciplinary process. Dismissals for redundancy are discussed in detail in Chapter 14. However, for a reason for dismissal to be considered fair, it has to pass the test of 'reasonableness' set out in section 98 of the Employment Rights Act. This states in subsection 1 that:

> In determining ... whether the dismissal of an employee is fair or unfair,

it is for the employer to show a) the reason for the dismissal and that it is either a reason falling within subsection 2 (see above), or that it is for some other substantial reason.

Subsection 4 then goes on to say that:

the determination of the question whether the dismissal was fair or unfair, having regard to the reason shown by the employer shall depend on whether, in the circumstances (including the size and administrative resources of the employer's undertaking), the employer acted reasonably or unreasonably in treating it as a sufficient reason for dismissing the employee; and that the question shall be determined in accordance with equity and the substantial merits of the case.

The requirement to act reasonably has been central to the operation of unfair dismissal legislation for some considerable time, and one of the acid tests that an employer defending a case at tribunal can be judged on is the quality and fairness of its disciplinary procedures. This concept is supported by the legal validity given to the ACAS Code of Practice on *Disciplinary and Grievance Procedures* and by the case of *Polkey v A E Dayton Services Ltd* [1987] IRLR 503. In the *Polkey* case the House of Lords effectively stated that failing to follow a proper procedure was unlikely to succeed as an effective defence unless the employer could prove that the outcome would have been no different irrespective of the procedure followed – a prospect that is, according to their lordships, fairly remote.

For some, leaving tribunals to decide on the quality and fairness of an employer's disciplinary policies and procedures was too subjective. A skilled advocate could make out a case for the probity of even the weakest of procedures, and as a consequence there was pressure for change.

Change came in the shape of the Employment Act (2002), which took the principle of procedural fairness a step further. It contained a section on dismissal and disciplinary procedures, which detailed how disciplinary matters were to be handled. These procedures – known as the 'three-step dismissal and disciplinary procedure' (see the box below) – were then incorporated into a new section 98A of the Employment Rights Act (1996).

---

Standard (three-step) dismissal and disciplinary procedure

*Step 1*
The employer must set down in writing the nature of the employee's conduct, capability or other circumstances that may result in dismissal or disciplinary action, and send a copy of this statement to the employee. The employer must inform the employee of the basis for his/her complaint.

*Step 2*
The employer must invite the employee to a hearing at a reasonable time and place where the issue can be discussed. The employee must take all reasonable steps to attend. After the meeting, the employer must inform the employee about any decision, and offer the employee the right of appeal.

*Step 3*

If the employee wishes to appeal, he/she must inform the employer. The employer must invite the employee to attend a further hearing to appeal against the employer's decision, and the final decision must be communicated to the employee. Where possible, a more senior manager should attend the appeal hearing.

The standard dismissal and disciplinary procedure applies when an employer is contemplating dismissal (including dismissal on grounds of capability, conduct, redundancy, non-renewal of a fixed-term contract and retirement). Failure to follow the above procedure when it applies makes any consequent dismissal automatically unfair. Because it was recognised that there would be occasions (cases of gross misconduct, for example) when it was not possible, or appropriate, to follow the standard three-step procedure, a modified two-step procedure was also built into the process (see the box below).

Modified (two-step) dismissal procedure

*Step 1*

The employer must set down in writing the nature of the alleged misconduct that has led to the dismissal, the evidence for this decision, and the right to appeal against the decision, and send a copy of this to the employee.

*Step 2*

If the employee wishes to appeal, he/she must inform the employer. The employer must invite the employee to attend a hearing to appeal against the employer's decision, and the final decision must be communicated to the employee.

Although, as we explain below, these statutory procedures have now been repealed, the introduction of a clear three-step approach to a disciplinary matter reminded managers of some very important principles. The 2002 Act also introduced the possibility that compensation in unfair dismissal cases could be increased, or reduced, dependent on how far from the three-step principle the parties to a claim had strayed.

Unfortunately, the three-step procedure did not do what its designers had intended, which was to bring transparency to the disciplinary process and speed up the disposal of tribunal claims. Instead, it delivered some unforeseen consequences and more, not less, casework for tribunals. One flaw in the new procedures was the requirement for employees to raise a grievance with their employer before they could bring an unfair dismissal claim. Not surprisingly, many employers argued that their former employee had not done so, and therefore their claim ought to be struck out. Another flaw was the attempt by many claimants to argue that their former employer had failed to follow the statutory procedure, thus rendering their particular dismissal automatically unfair. Because both parties to a claim were arguing such procedural points, cases were not being dealt with speedily. The first stage in many cases – before the facts of the matter could be considered – concentrated on whether the proper procedure had been followed.

A further problem occurred in respect of dismissals for redundancy, which were also covered by the new procedure. By the very nature of redundancy consultations, however, such dismissals did not fit easily into a procedure designed to deal with disciplinary matters. Whatever else it might be, redundancy is not a disciplinary matter, and employers were constrained in the way they handled redundancy consultation by the need to fit into a procedure that was designed for a different purpose.

Consequently, by virtue of the Employment Act (2008), what had become highly controversial statutory procedures were repealed and replaced by a revamped ACAS Code of Practice (see below) that took effect in April 2009. Some of the implications of the repeal were that:

- a procedural breach on the part of an employer no longer renders a dismissal automatically unfair

- employees are again able to bring a claim to a tribunal without first raising a grievance with their employer

- the power of tribunals to raise or lower awards by up to 50% because of procedural breaches and to extend the time-limit for bringing claims has been removed.

However – as we will see when we examine the ACAS code in more detail – the principle of raising or reducing compensation has not been entirely lost.

Finally, it is important to remember that the Employment Rights Act (1996) does set minimum qualifying periods of employment for the acquisition of employment rights – limits that can be and have been changed. For example, on 1 June 1999 an employee's minimum period of continuous service with an employer to qualify for unfair dismissal was reduced from two years to one year. It is always disturbing when we hear, as we do, managers talk of having a free hand to take whatever actions they like during an individual's first months of employment. Making distinctions about how to deal with performance or behaviour issues based on an individual's length of service is to invite the possibility of inconsistency creeping into the process, and to lay the organisation open to legal challenge. To avoid this possibility it is prudent for all managers and employment relations professionals to ignore an individual's length of service and treat all disciplinary issues in exactly the same way. Generally, if recruitment, induction and the probationary period are thorough and well managed, then any issues in the early part of an individual's employment ought to be resolved without the need for disciplinary action.

## DISCIPLINARY PROCEDURES

### THE ACAS CODE OF PRACTICE

The ACAS Code of Practice on *Disciplinary and Grievance Procedures in Employment* is of significant importance in the management and resolution of disciplinary issues. While breach of the Code of Practice is in itself not unlawful, its provisions and impact are central to the understanding of the disciplinary process. The latest edition of the Code, which is issued under section 199 of the Trade Union and Labour Relations (Consolidation) Act (1992), came into effect in April 2009. Its importance to the process is fundamental and underpins the whole approach to managing conflict at work, for although a failure to follow any part of the Code does not in itself make a person or organisation liable to any proceedings, employment tribunals do take the Code into account when considering relevant cases. Tribunals are also able to adjust any awards made in relevant cases by up to 25% either way if they consider that any party has unreasonably failed to follow the guidance set out in the Code.

Given such a very clear statement of the Code's status, it is a foolish organisation that does not take seriously the need to invest time in ensuring that its own disciplinary procedure and practice are appropriate and meet the minimum requirements set out in the legislation.

Because of the importance that ACAS places on drawing up disciplinary procedures and company rules, it has produced a guide, entitled *Discipline and Grievances at Work*, which provides advice on dealing with disciplinary matters. The guide – which can be downloaded from the ACAS website www.acas.org.uk – complements the ACAS Code of Practice on *Disciplinary and Grievance Procedures* and provides good practice advice for dealing with discipline and grievances in the workplace. Students and practitioners alike will find it of immense assistance containing, as it does, extracts from the Code of Practice, which are reproduced to reinforce the guidance that is offered.

The guide looks at:

- the need for rules and disciplinary procedures
- handling a disciplinary matter
- holding a disciplinary hearing
- deciding and implementing disciplinary or other action
- the appeals process.

## THE DISCIPLINARY PROCEDURE

For a number of years, disciplinary procedures commonly observed a specific sequence:

- an oral warning
  - followed by a written warning if the required improvement was not forthcoming
    - followed by a final written warning if conduct or performance was still unsatisfactory
      - potentially followed, finally, by dismissal.

Under this type of procedure employers routinely issued oral warnings that were anything but 'verbal'. More often than not, such warnings were followed up in writing and placed on an employee's personnel record – thus, in effect, making them a written warning in everything but name. The latest ACAS guide recognises this contradiction and suggests that cases of minor misconduct or unsatisfactory performance are dealt with informally. In the informal stage, which effectively replaces the oral warning, managers are seeking an agreement with the employee on how to ensure that the misconduct (perhaps in timekeeping) is not repeated or that steps are taken to overcome the performance issues. There is no reason why, if agreement is reached on the way forward, that it is not confirmed in writing. If managers do this, however, it is important to confirm that nothing that has been said, done, or agreed constitutes disciplinary action.

It is only if the informal approach does not work, or matters are too serious for such an approach, that employers are recommended to move into the formal stage. The formal stage, which provides for a written warning or final written warning, has not changed in any material way over the years, but a good employer would still recognise the principles introduced by the three-step statutory approach referred to above. These stated that in order to meet the standards imposed by the Code of Practice you must invite an employee to a properly constituted disciplinary hearing, you must hold that hearing, and – assuming the decision is to impose a disciplinary sanction – you must provide the right and the means to appeal.

Once a situation has entered the formal stage of a disciplinary process, there are a number of important points to note. Firstly, it is important that a record be kept of every disciplinary warning issued. Secondly, it is important to advise individuals on how long a warning will remain 'live'. 'Live' in this context indicates the length of time that a particular disciplinary sanction will stay on the record. Warnings can be taken into account if further disciplinary issues arise, but warnings that have expired cannot. Many organisations will have different time-scales for different levels of warning. For example, a written warning might only be 'live' for six months, whereas a final written warning might be live for 12 months. Finally, it is important that employees are advised of what will happen next if the desired changes to performance or behaviour are not made. One important point to note at this stage is the rights that individual employees now have under data protection legislation. Under the provisions of this legislation, employees have the right to see anything that the employer holds in their personnel file – and this would include any notes made as part of the disciplinary process. It is therefore important to ensure that a professional approach is taken to the writing of such notes, and that they do not contain malicious or defamatory remarks.

The purpose and scope of a disciplinary procedure should be very clear. It should allow all employees to understand what is expected of them in respect of conduct, attendance and job performance, and set out the rules by which such matters are governed. The aim is to ensure consistent and fair treatment for all.

### REFLECTIVE ACTIVITY

To what extent does your organisation's disciplinary procedure meet the criteria of clarity? Does it set out the time for which individual warnings will remain 'live', and is it capable of ensuring consistent and fair treatment for all employees? You may consider it worth reviewing your procedure against these benchmarks.

## PRINCIPLES UNDERLYING DISCIPLINARY PROCEDURES

When we examine handling discipline, you will note that the only way to ensure consistency is by taking a 'good practice' approach and recognising that a disciplinary procedure is more than just a series of stages. You should also recognise that there are a number of principles that underlie the procedure which are extremely important and help to ensure good personnel management practice. As with the mechanics of the procedure itself, ACAS offers guidance on good disciplinary procedures which, it says, should:

- be in writing
- be non-discriminatory
- provide for matters to be dealt with without undue delay
- provide for proceedings, witness statements and records to be kept confidential
- indicate the disciplinary actions which may be taken
- specify the levels of management which have the authority to take the various forms of disciplinary action
- provide for workers to be informed of the complaints against them and, where possible, to see all relevant evidence before any hearing
- provide workers with an opportunity to state their case before decisions are reached
- provide workers with the right to be accompanied
- ensure that except for gross misconduct, no worker is dismissed for a first breach of discipline
- ensure that disciplinary action is not taken until the case has been carefully investigated
- ensure that workers are given an explanation for any penalty imposed
- provide a right of appeal – normally to a more senior manager – and specify the procedure to be followed.

The right to be accompanied by a shop steward or other trade union official only used to apply to workplaces where there was a recognised union. However, the Employment Relations Act (1999) has now provided all workers with the statutory right to be accompanied at disciplinary and grievance hearings. The right applies where the worker is required or invited by his or her employer to attend certain disciplinary or grievance hearings, and when he or she makes a reasonable request to be so accompanied. In Chapter 3 we examined the concept of 'workers' and how certain employment rights had now been extended to apply to them. This right is one of them, and the statutory right to be accompanied applies to *all* workers, not just employees working under a contract of employment.

Whether a worker has a statutory right to be accompanied at a disciplinary hearing will depend on the nature of the hearing. When a problem first surfaces, employers often choose to deal with it initially by means of an informal interview or counselling session. So long as the informal interview or counselling session does not result in a formal warning or some other action, it is often more appropriate to try to resolve matters with just the worker and the manager present. Equally, employers should not allow an investigation into the facts surrounding a disciplinary case to extend into a disciplinary hearing. If it becomes clear during the course of the informal or investigative interview that formal disciplinary action may be needed, then the interview should be terminated and a formal hearing convened at which the worker should be afforded the statutory right to be accompanied.

It is important to note that the right to be accompanied applies to every individual, not just union members, and it is of no consequence whether the organisation recognises unions or not.

The statutory right to be accompanied applies specifically to hearings which could result in:

- the administration of a formal warning to a worker by his or her employer (ie a warning, whether about conduct or capability, that will be placed on the worker's record)
- the taking of some other action in respect of a worker by his or her employer (eg suspension without pay, demotion or dismissal), or
- the confirmation of a warning issued or some other action taken.

## AFTER LIVE WARNINGS EXPIRE

Although it is to be hoped that any disciplinary problems within an organisation can be resolved at the earliest opportunity, and without recourse to all levels of the procedure, the world of work is not so simple. Many managers complain that having given an individual an oral warning or, in some cases, having got all the way through to final written warning stage, the problem to which the disciplinary action related resurfaces once the warning ceases to be 'live'. It is then assumed, mistakenly, that the whole process must begin again.

This is not so – and three points must be considered. Firstly, for what length of time do warnings stay 'live'? If it is for too short a time, you run the risk of only achieving short-term changes in behaviour. On the other hand, you do not want it to go on too long. A sanction that remains on an employee's record for an excessive period of time relative to the original breach of discipline can act as a demotivating influence. Secondly, has the warning been too narrow? Very often, it makes more sense to issue a warning in such a way that an employee is left in no doubt that 'any further breaches of the company rules will result in further disciplinary action'. The ACAS Code of Practice makes it clear that the procedure may be implemented at any stage. If you have an employee against whom you constantly have to invoke the disciplinary procedure, or the offence is serious but does not amount to gross misconduct, then it may be appropriate to begin with a written rather than an oral warning. In extreme cases, a final written warning could be appropriate. However, it might be appropriate to ask why somebody constantly faces disciplinary action. Has there been a failure of management, or a lack of management action?

## GROSS MISCONDUCT

Before leaving procedural requirements it is necessary to examine what the concept of gross misconduct means. You will have noted above that according to the ACAS principles it is permissible to dismiss an individual without notice if he or she has committed an act of gross misconduct. Gross misconduct can be notoriously difficult to define and often difficult to prove, and ACAS very helpfully provides a list of actions that would normally fall into this category. They are:

- theft or fraud
- physical violence or bullying
- deliberate and serious damage to property
- serious misuse of an organisation's property or name
- deliberately accessing Internet sites containing pornographic, offensive or obscene material
- bringing the organisation into serious disrepute
- serious incapability through alcohol or the influence of illegal drugs
- causing loss, damage or injury through serious negligence
- a serious breach of health and safety rules
- serious acts of insubordination
- unlawful discrimination or harassment
- a serious breach of confidence.

While that is quite an extensive list, it is also notable for its lack of clarity. For example, what is an act of serious insubordination? Would it cover the refusal to carry out instructions received from a supervisor? What is serious negligence or serious incapability through alcohol? For example, although attitudes have changed and people tend not to socialise so much during their breaks, drinking at lunchtime still happens. How do you decide when a lunchtime drink crosses the threshold? One of the difficulties managers face in dealing with this type of disciplinary issue is ensuring that they do not impose their own moral standards on other people.

Inevitably, in matters of gross misconduct there will sometimes be a lack of clarity over when somebody has overstepped the mark. The potential difficulties caused by this lack of clarity mean that whatever procedure you establish, it reflects the organisation's structure and culture – the norms and beliefs within which an organisation functions. This is where the writing of clear company rules is so important. Not only do they help to distinguish between ordinary and gross misconduct but they provide employees with clear guidelines on what is acceptable in the workplace, in terms of both behaviour and performance.

### REFLECTIVE ACTIVITY

How sure are you that your organisation's procedure is working as it should? What criteria would you use to assess whether it is or is not?

## RULES IN EMPLOYMENT

Rules should be written for the benefit of both employer and employee. Their purpose should be to define and make clear exactly what standards of behaviour are expected in the workplace. Typically, rules cover the following areas:

- timekeeping
- absence
- health and safety
- misconduct
- the use of company facilities
- confidentiality
- discrimination.

There are some (including ACAS) who would argue that rules about poor performance should also be included, but there are some practical difficulties about writing rules in respect of poor performance. Individuals need to know what is expected of them in respect of performance, but this ought to be done through a clearly written job description that sets out their prime tasks and responsibilities and how their performance will be measured. Clearly, if rules relating to behaviour are broken, and as a consequence performance is impaired – for example, by drunkenness – it is easy to see a link between poor performance and rule-breaking, and that the disciplinary procedure might be used to correct the problem.

But if someone is simply not competent to carry out the tasks for which he or she has been employed, it is hard to identify what sort of rule has been broken, notwithstanding the fact that the disciplinary procedure may be used as a means of correcting the problem. This, however, is a minor point. The important point is to ensure that the following principles are followed, whatever rules are established:

- They are clear.
- They cannot be misinterpreted.
- They are capable of distinguishing between ordinary misconduct and gross misconduct.

However, not withstanding the difficulties in writing rules about performance, many companies now include a section on capability within their disciplinary procedures. While many procedures content themselves with identifying the various procedural stages and a definition of gross misconduct, others are including sections such as those in the following example.

### CAPABILITY

We recognise that during your employment with us your capability to carry out your duties may vary. This can be for a number of reasons, the most common ones being that either the job changes over a period of time and you have difficulty adapting to the changes, or you change (most commonly because of health reasons).

*Job changes*

a   If the nature of your job changes and we have concerns regarding your capability, we will make every effort to ensure that you understand the level of performance expected of you and that you receive adequate training and supervision. This will be done in an informal manner in the first instance and you will be given time to improve.

b   If your standard of performance is still not adequate, you will be warned, in writing, that a failure to improve and to maintain the performance required will lead to disciplinary action. If this were to happen, the principles set out in paragraph 2 above will apply. We will also consider a transfer to more suitable work, if possible.

c   If we cannot transfer you to more suitable work and there is still no improvement after you have received appropriate warnings, you will be issued with a final warning that you will be dismissed unless the required standard of performance is achieved and maintained.

*Personal circumstances*

a   Personal circumstances may arise in the future which do not prevent you from attending work but which prevent you from carrying out your normal duties (eg a lack of dexterity or general ill-health). If such a situation arises, we will normally need to have details of your medical diagnosis and prognosis so that we have the benefit of expert advice. Under normal circumstances this can be most easily obtained by asking your own doctor for a medical report. Your permission is needed before we can obtain such a report, and we will expect you to co-operate in this matter should the need arise. When we have obtained as much information as possible regarding your condition, and after consultation with you, a decision will be made as to whether any adjustments need to be made in order for you to continue in your current role or, where circumstances permit, a more suitable role should be found for you.

b  There may also be personal circumstances which prevent you from attending work either for a prolonged period or periods or for frequent short periods. Under these circumstances we will need to know when we can expect your attendance record to reach an acceptable level, and again this can usually be most easily obtained by asking your own doctor for a medical report. When we have obtained as much information as possible regarding your condition, and after consultation with you, a decision will be made as to whether any adjustments need to be made in order for you to continue in your current role or, where circumstances permit, a more suitable role should be found for you.

## THE IMPORTANCE OF CLEAR RULES

THEORY

Failure to be clear and failing to make a proper distinction between types of misconduct has caused many organisations to suffer losses at employment tribunals. It is no good having a very clear procedure, laying down the type and number of warnings that an individual should receive, if the rules that are being applied are imprecise or do not reflect the attitudes and requirements of the particular business. As Edwards (1994; p.563) says:

> How people expect to behave depends as much on day-to-day understanding as on formal rules. Workplaces may have identical rule-books, but in one it may be accepted practice to leave early near holidays; in another, on Fridays; in a third, when a relatively lenient supervisor is in charge; and so on.

There is also a need to ensure that rules reflect current industrial practice, as is illustrated by the following case. The applicant, who was a union representative, had been dismissed for gross misconduct for gaining unauthorised access to his employer's computer system. He had accessed a part of the system that would normally not be available to him by using another employee's password. In his defence it was argued that 'he had only been playing around' with the system, and that there had been no intent to obtain information to which he was not entitled. Furthermore, that although he might have been doing something wrong, it was not 'gross misconduct' and could have been covered by a disciplinary warning. In upholding the dismissal for gross misconduct (*Denco v Joinson* [1991] IRLR 63) the Employment Appeals Tribunal (EAT) stated:

> The industrial members are clear in their view that in this modern industrial world if an employee deliberately uses an unauthorised password in order to enter or to attempt to enter a computer known to contain information to which he is not entitled, then that of itself is gross misconduct which *prima facie* will attract summary dismissal, although

there may be some exceptional circumstances in which such a response might be held unreasonable.

In essence the EAT were making the same point that had been made some years earlier in *C A Parsons & Co Ltd v McLaughlin* (1978) IRLR 65, that some things should be so obvious that it ought not to be necessary to have a rule forbidding it. However, for the avoidance of doubt, the EAT went on to say in the *Denco* case that:

> It is desirable, however, that management should make it abundantly clear to the workforce that interfering with computers will carry severe penalties. Rules concerning access to and use of computers should be reduced to writing and left near the computers for reference.

While the comments of the Employment Appeals Tribunal about certain things being obvious may seem perfectly reasonable, it should be remembered that employers have an absolute duty to demonstrate that they have acted reasonably when they dismiss somebody. In *Denco*, the EAT acknowledged that there might be circumstances in which an employer's particular response might be 'unreasonable' even about something which is supposedly obvious. The message is very clear. If something is not allowed, say so – and spell out the consequences of breaching the rule. Because technology, or the ownership of businesses, can change, what may have been acceptable once may now be frowned on. A classic example is information technology (IT) which, since the *Denco* case in 1991, has moved forward at a remarkable pace. Nowhere is this more evident than in the case of Internet access and the use of email where personal use is difficult, and time-consuming, to monitor, but which, if inappropriately used, can bring an organisation into serious disrepute. For some organisations the problems of unacceptable email use have been overshadowed by the growth in social networking sites and the potential harm they bring to a business.

These developments have caused many organisations to rethink their policies on computer use and to recognise that clear guidance has to be given to employees. The following extract from an IT policy is one example.

### IT Resources Policy *[extract]*

Please read this document carefully.

Failure to comply with this policy may not only result in disciplinary proceedings (including summary dismissal for acts of gross misconduct) but may also result in criminal and/or civil liability for you and/or the Company. Breach of those rules shown below will be considered by the firm to be acts of gross misconduct.

*Business and non-business use of the firm's IT resources*

The Company's IT resources, including but not limited to computer hardware, software, telephones, fax machines, voicemail, email, intranet and Internet access (the 'IT resources'), are intended primarily to assist you to conduct the Company's business (the 'Business') in accordance with your duties as an employee of the Company.

You may make reasonable personal use of the Company's IT resources provided that:

- you do so in your own time and it does not materially affect the amount of time you and your colleagues devote to your or their duties respectively

- it does not interfere with or adversely affect the Company's Business and/or reputation, and

- it is in accordance with this policy.

You may use the IT resources in your own time for reasonable non-business purposes – but please note that you have no legal right to do so under the terms of your employment or otherwise. In any event, your use of the IT resources (whether for personal or business use) may be monitored. Use of the IT resources for non-business use remains subject to the Company's discretion and rules and regulations, and may be withdrawn by the Company on a temporary or permanent basis at any time.

*Use of the Company's IT resources*

Whether you use the IT resources for business or for personal use, there are things you must NOT DO and things that you must DO.

These are listed below:

. . . . . . . . . . . . .

. . . . . . . . . . . . .

. . . . . . . . . . . . .

Some managers argue that personal use of email at work should be outlawed, but this can be very difficult. Better, as the example above shows, to accept personal use but to manage it properly. However, there is a growing trend for employers to go further with social networking sites and ban the use of them completely during working hours. In some professions – teaching being a good example – staff have even been warned about who they should, and should not, have as friends on Facebook.

As we stated above, there are a number of variables – such as technological developments – in the drafting of company rules, and the prudent employment relations professional will ensure that in his or her organisation they are the subject of regular monitoring so that they properly reflect the organisation's current values and requirements.

The need to be clear about the behavioural standards that are expected in any workplace, and about the sanctions that will be applied for non-compliance, is particularly important in distinguishing between gross and ordinary misconduct. Frequently, organisations commit the error of making vague statements in their company rules to the effect that certain actions 'may' be treated as gross misconduct, or that the failure to do something 'could' leave an individual liable to disciplinary action. For example, many rules on theft that we have seen simply state that 'Theft may be considered to be gross misconduct'.

This sort of wording can only leave room for doubt and confusion. If an employee stole a large sum of money from the company, there is little doubt that they would be charged with gross misconduct and, if the allegation was proved, dismissed without notice. What, though, would happen if the alleged theft was of items of company stationery or spare parts for machinery? Would every manager treat the matter as one of gross misconduct and dismiss, or would the value of the items taken be a consideration? Employment relations professionals have to be aware of these potential contradictions when helping to frame rules that govern the employment relationship. If it is normal practice to turn a blind eye to the misappropriation of items such as stationery, this can cause problems when someone is accused of a more serious theft. We have already highlighted the importance of discipline being applied fairly and consistently. It can be questioned if this is happening if different managers are given the opportunity to apply different standards to the same actions. Allowing different managers to take a different view about the seriousness of certain acts of theft brings inconsistency into the process. This could prove very costly at an employment tribunal. One way to avoid this problem is to make positive statements – for example, that theft *will* be treated as gross misconduct.

A better rule on theft might be:

*Theft:*

Stealing from the company, its suppliers or fellow employees is unacceptable, whatever the value or amount involved, and will be treated as gross misconduct.

Using this style of wording should help to ensure that every employee in the organisation knows the consequences of any dishonest action on their part. Ensuring that managers apply the sanction consistently is another problem, and one that we will deal with later in the chapter.

## REFLECTIVE ACTIVITY

How often are the rules in your organisation reviewed, and when were they last updated? Do you know whether different standards are utilised in the application of the rules?

Theft, whatever standards different organisations might apply, is usually associated in the public mind with gross misconduct, notwithstanding the problems of definition that we have just discussed. The distinction between gross misconduct and other serious infractions of the rules can often be harder to identify. The first thing to acknowledge is that no clear distinction exists, but it is possible to apply common sense to the issue. For example it is easy to understand that a serious assault on another person ought to be treated as gross misconduct whereas that of poor timekeeping would not. While a consistent failure to observe timekeeping standards might ultimately lead to dismissal, the two offences clearly initially provoke different outcomes – namely, immediate dismissal in the first case and normally an initial, informal, warning in the second. Perhaps one way in which a distinction might be drawn, therefore, is by reference to the expected outcome of the disciplinary process and to the relationship of trust that has to exist between employer and employee.

Although we do not wish here to explore the wider issues relating to the contract of employment, it is implied in every contract that for an employment relationship to be maintained there has to be mutual trust and confidence between employer and employee. When issues of discipline arise, that relationship is damaged. One of the purposes of disciplinary action is to bring about a change in behaviour, and if the offence is one of poor timekeeping, there is usually no question of a total breakdown of trust: the expected outcome of disciplinary action is of improved timekeeping and a rebuilding of the relationship. If the cause of the disciplinary action is a serious assault on another employee, perhaps a manager, a disciplinary sanction might bring about a change in behaviour or ensure that the offence is not repeated, but there is a high probability that the relationship of mutual trust and confidence might be damaged beyond repair, and it might be impossible for the employment relationship to be maintained.

## HANDLING DISCIPLINARY ISSUES

The way in which managers and employment relations professionals approach disciplinary issues will be subtly different, depending on the nature of the problem. Most organisations will have some form of disciplinary procedure, and probably some company rules, but the use and application of the procedure may vary from company to company and from manager to manager. In some organisations disciplinary action is very rarely taken, either because standards are clear and accepted by employees or because standards are vague and applied haphazardly. In others, standards are maintained by an over-reliance on automatic procedures, which usually acts as a demotivating influence on the workforce.

The purpose of any disciplinary procedure should be to promote good employment relations and fairness and consistency in the treatment of individuals. As the current ACAS Code of Practice on *Disciplinary and Grievance Procedures* puts it:

> Fairness and transparency are promoted by developing and using rules and procedures for handling disciplinary and grievance situations. These should be set down in writing, be specific and clear ... It is also important to help employees and managers understand what the rules and procedures are, where they can be found, and how they are to be used.

Good, well-communicated disciplinary procedures do enable organisations to influence the conduct of workers and deal with problems of poor performance and attendance, thereby enhancing organisational efficiency. The principles of fairness and consistency are at the heart of 'good practice', and the aim of all managers should be to handle disciplinary issues in as fair and equitable a way as is possible. They should do this because it represents 'good practice' in terms of management skill, not just because of the influence of the law. If managers are only concerned with legal compliance, they will not be as effective as those who are driven by the need to operate 'good practice'. The law on unfair dismissal is now so ingrained into the fabric of the workplace that only by maintaining such standards does it cease to become an issue. Good managers have nothing to fear from the laws relating to individual employment rights. That is not to say the law should be ignored – but neither should it be feared. In an ideal world managers would act in such a way that they avoid accusations of unfair treatment. But this is not an ideal world and even the best managers can find themselves defending their actions before an employment tribunal. This is why it is important for the concept of 'good practice' to become part of an organisation's ethos.

Not only does this allow organisations to demonstrate consistent and fair treatment for all, but it ensures that they meet their absolute duty to act reasonably, as is set out in section 98(4)(a) of the Employment Rights Act (1996). Furthermore, such an approach not only makes good business sense, it fits the concept of natural justice that is so important in handling disciplinary issues.

The 1996 Act identifies the reasons for fairly dismissing an employee as (poor) conduct, (lack of) capability and 'some other substantial reason', and all of these would require the implementation of a disciplinary process in order for any action taken to be reasonable. However, before reaching for the disciplinary procedure, a good manager will consider whether some other route would be more appropriate. Maintaining good standards of discipline within an organisation is not just about applying the rules or operating the procedure. It is about the ability to achieve standards of performance and behaviour without using the 'big stick'. One way this might be done, and to avoid becoming embroiled in the disciplinary process, is counselling, which might provide the required change in behaviour without making the individual concerned feel that he or she was some kind of dissident.

## COUNSELLING

Counselling is more than simply offering help and advice. It is helping an individual, in a non-threatening way, to come to terms with a particular problem. The problem may be about performance, about timekeeping, about drug or alcohol abuse or about another employee – for example, an accusation of sexual harassment. Counselling an employee, whatever the nature of the problem, needs careful preparation. In a situation involving the abuse of a drug or alcohol, managers may not have the necessary skills to carry out such a sensitive task, but even if they conclude that specialist assistance is required, they can still help to bring the problem out into the open. In other cases, provided the problem is approached in a systematic way, this type of intervention may avoid disciplinary action.

One example of where counselling might be an appropriate first step would be in respect of an allegation of sexual harassment or bullying. Provided that the complainant has not suffered any physical assault and, most importantly, that the complainant is happy for the matter to be handled in an informal way, counselling can be very helpful – not only to the alleged harasser but also to the victim. Without wishing to minimise or condone what can be a very serious problem in some workplaces, it can often be the case that the alleged harasser or bully does not realise that their behaviour or actions are causing offence or fear. Sitting down with an individual and explaining to them that some of their words or actions are causing distress to another employee can often be very effective. However, it is important not to leave it there but to monitor the situation, ensure that the behavioural change is permanent, and see that the complainant is satisfied with the action taken and the eventual outcome. If you do not do this, you may find yourself dealing with a formal grievance or even a claim for constructive dismissal.

## REFLECTIVE ACTIVITY

Does your organisation's disciplinary code say anything about equal opportunities or discrimination? Is there, for example, a clear rule that says sexual harassment or racial discrimination will not be tolerated? Do you have a code of practice that gives guidance on how to manage these sorts of problems?

Similarly, if the problem concerns poor performance, 'good practice' would be to discuss the problem with the employee concerned rather than go straight into the disciplinary procedure. The first step would be to speak to the employee, in private, explaining what aspects of performance were falling short of the desired standard, and most importantly, what actions were required by the employee to put matters right. The golden rule to remember is to set clear standards. If the employee does not know what is expected of them, how can they deliver the performance that is required? Another step in this process might be to consider whether some additional training might be an option. All of this might be best dealt with under a formal appraisal scheme, if one exists within the organisation.

### THE FORMAL APPROACH

However, if after following the counselling route there are still complaints of harassment, or the quality of work being carried out still falls below standard, it may then be necessary to begin disciplinary proceedings. Again it is important to remember the principle of 'good practice'. The operation of the disciplinary procedure can often lead to managerial disenchantment because they claim that 'it takes too long', particularly when you have to advise them to proceed cautiously. It is our experience that managers are often unable to view a disciplinary issue with any real objectivity, and this can cause them to rush to judgement – often with calamitous effect at a tribunal. This is where the employment relations professional has a clear duty to advise and guide management colleagues. Since starting down the disciplinary path can, ultimately, lead to a dismissal, it is important to remember the requirement that in taking a decision to dismiss somebody you should act reasonably and in accordance with natural justice.

It is easy to understand the frustration a line manager might feel if the disciplinary process takes too long, but it is the employer who is in control of the process and can determine the timings. The question of fairness relates not to how long the process takes but to the quality of the procedures followed. For example, say you had an experienced employee who was responsible for carrying out a very important task within the organisation and which had serious cost implications if it was not carried out efficiently. If the task was not being performed satisfactorily, the amount of time you could allow the employee to improve their performance would be limited. Alternatively, if the employee was inexperienced and performing a task that was less cost-sensitive and important, the time allowed for improvement should be longer.

It is also necessary to consider how long the substandard performance has been allowed to continue unchallenged, because it may be the case that a previous manager was prepared to accept a lower standard of performance. What is important in either of these scenarios is that the employee is made aware of the standard that is required and understands the importance of achieving that standard in whatever time-scale is agreed. Under the ACAS Code it is acceptable to miss out stages in the procedure, and this may be the more obvious solution if the consequences of the poor performance are so serious.

## USING THE DISCIPLINARY PROCEDURE

Whatever the nature of the problem, once the decision has been taken to invoke the formal disciplinary procedures it is important to ensure that its application cannot be challenged. The following guidelines – which are broken down into three stages – help to ensure a consistent and fair approach.

### INVESTIGATION

In the majority of cases of alleged misconduct it is vitally important that a proper investigation is carried out. Such an investigation should take place in a timely and sensitive fashion and must be seen to be fair and thorough. The manager selected to carry out the investigation has an obligation to explain to the individual being investigated that the process will involve an objective and non-judgemental inquiry into the facts of the alleged misconduct – that the purpose is not to build a case against the employee but to search for evidence which confirms or refutes the allegation.

As we note below, where possible and practicable the investigation should be undertaken by a person different from the one who might hear any consequent disciplinary case. As with all employee relations activities, it is advisable to keep clear notes of any interviews with witnesses and the accused employee. A thorough investigation should take account of any relevant work documents, policies and procedures and seek to establish whether any relevant training had been carried out.

## PREPARING FOR THE DISCIPLINARY HEARING

If the outcome of any investigation is that the disciplinary procedure should be invoked, then – as with all management activities – the preparatory process is of particular importance. There are various steps that must be taken in preparing to conduct a disciplinary interview, and a number of points to consider, some of which are a statutory requirement:

1 Prepare carefully, and ensure that the person who is going to conduct the disciplinary hearing has all the facts. As we stated above, if the organisation is of sufficient size and has the appropriate resources, this person should be different from the individual who conducted the investigation. This sounds straightforward, but it is not always possible to obtain all the facts. Frequently, the evidence of alleged misconduct is no more than circumstantial, particularly in cases involving theft. However, the guiding principle is to ensure that, where appropriate, a thorough investigation has taken place and that whatever facts are available are presented – including, where appropriate, written witness statements. Sometimes, people will ask to remain anonymous when providing information during a disciplinary investigation, and this has to be treated with a great deal of care. If possible, seek some form of corroborative evidence and try to check whether the anonymous informant's motives are genuine.

2 Ensure that the employee knows what the nature of the complaint is. This again sounds straightforward but is often the point at which things begin to go wrong. For example, it would not be sufficient to tell an employee that they are to attend a disciplinary hearing in respect of their poor performance. They have to be provided with sufficient detail so that they can prepare an adequate defence and so that the employer can demonstrate that it has met the statutory requirements set out in the procedure outlined above.

3 Arrange a suitable time and place for the interview. This would seem to be obvious, but as with so many things in employee relations, what may seem obvious to the specialist is not always apparent to the busy line manager. There is a tendency for managers to arrange meetings within their own offices where the potential for being interrupted is more pronounced or privacy less easily guaranteed. It is also important to remember that the employee might request an alternative date to the one suggested, particularly if their chosen companion or trade union official cannot attend.

4 Ensure that the employee knows the procedure to be followed. Simply because an individual was provided with a copy of the disciplinary code when they commenced employment does not imply that they know the procedure to be followed. It is always wise to provide them with a new

copy of the disciplinary procedure – not least because there may have been amendments since they received their version.

5 Advise the employee of their right to be accompanied (see above). Where individuals work in a unionised environment this tends to be automatic, with an invitation to attend the meeting sent directly to the appropriate union official. However, in non-unionised environments people are not always sure who would be an appropriate person to accompany them or whether they want to be accompanied at all. As a matter of good practice it is wise to encourage somebody to be accompanied, but if they refuse, it has to be respected. When that does happen, the fact that the employee wishes to attend a disciplinary interview on his or her own should be recorded.

6 Enquire if there are any mitigating circumstances. What is or is not a mitigating circumstance will be dictated by each case. It is not for the employer to identify matters of mitigation, but it is important to ask the employee who is facing a disciplinary sanction whether there are any particular circumstances that might account for their actions. Whether an individual manager accepts what may seem to be no more than excuses is a question of fact determined by individual circumstances. For example, an employee with a bad timekeeping record might be excused if they were having to care for a sick relative before attending work, whereas another employee might put forward a less acceptable excuse, such as a broken alarm clock.

7 Are you being consistent? This is where the employment relations professional can provide the line manager with invaluable assistance. Most line managers deal very rarely with disciplinary issues and may not be aware of previous actions or approaches that have been taken in respect of disciplinary issues. The employment relations professional can provide the advice and information that ensures a consistent approach.

8 Consider explanations. This is not the same as mitigating circumstances or excuses. This is the opportunity that you must give to an employee to explain their acts or omissions. For example, if the hearing was about poor performance, the employee might want to point out factors that have inhibited performance but which might not be immediately apparent to the line manager conducting the hearing. There may be issues around the quality of training received or the quality of instructions given.

9 Allow the employee time to prepare their case. The question here is how much time should be allowed. It is important that issues of discipline are dealt with speedily once an employee has been advised of the complaint against them, but it is important for the employee not to feel unfairly pressured in putting together any defence that they have.

10 Ensure that personnel records, etc, are available. This covers more than basic information about the individual and includes records relating to any previous disciplinary warnings, attendance, performance appraisals, etc.

11 Where possible, be accompanied. It is very unwise for a manager to conduct a disciplinary interview alone because of the possible need at some future

time to corroborate what was said. It also helps to rebut any allegations of bullying or intimidation that may be made by a disgruntled employee.

12  Try to ensure the attendance of witnesses. This should not be a problem if the people concerned are in your organisation's employ, but can prove difficult when they are outsiders.

The importance of careful preparation cannot be stressed too strongly, for it is at this stage that things often go wrong. Where tribunals, for example, often express concern is in the preliminary stages of the disciplinary process. Employers are often criticised for failing to give sufficient information to the employee about the nature of the complaint against them. We have certainly found examples of employers who have deliberately withheld information to prevent employees from constructing plausible explanations for their conduct or actions.

## THE DISCIPLINARY INTERVIEW

Good preparation helps the third part of the process – conducting the actual disciplinary interview. There are a number of points to remember at this stage:

1  Introduce those present – not just on grounds of courtesy, but because an employee facing a possible sanction is entitled to know who is going to be involved in any decision. In a small workplace this may be unnecessary, but it can be important in larger establishments.

2  Explain the purpose of the interview and how it will be conducted. This builds on the need to ensure that the employee fully understands the nature of the complaint against them and the procedure to be followed. As with any hearing, however informal, what it is for, what the possible outcomes are, and the method by which it is to be conducted are important prerequisites for demonstrating that natural justice has been adhered to. If it is apparent that, for whatever reason, the employee does not fully understand the nature of the complaint against them, you must halt the proceedings until they are clear – even if this means postponing to another day.

3  Set out precisely the nature of the complaint and outline the case by briefly going through the evidence. This may seem like overkill, but it is important to ensure that there are no misunderstandings. It is important to ensure that the employee and their representative or companion, if they have one, are given copies of any witness statements and afforded a proper opportunity to read them.

4  Give the employee the right to reply. Put simply: no right of reply – no natural justice.

5  Allow time for general questioning, cross-examination of witnesses, etc. If this did not happen, it would be difficult to persuade a tribunal that the test of reasonableness had been achieved.

6  No matter how carefully you prepare, or how well you are conducting a disciplinary hearing, things might not always proceed smoothly. People can get upset or angry and the whole process becomes very emotional. In such

circumstances it might be advisable to adjourn and reconvene at a later date. If this happens, it is important to make it clear to the employee that the issue cannot be avoided and a hearing must be held.

7  Sum up. There is a need to be clear about what conclusions have been reached and what decisions are to be made, and for this reason it is better to adjourn so that a properly considered decision can be made. One of the biggest handicaps the employment relations specialist can face is the manager who pre-judges. It is not uncommon to be asked to assist at a hearing where the manager wishes to administer a particular, predetermined, type of warning. It is the job of the professional adviser to counsel against this approach.

Careful preparation and a well-conducted interview are not guarantees that individuals will not complain of unfairness, but they are essential if the test of reasonableness is to be satisfied.

## MISCONDUCT DURING EMPLOYMENT

There are two distinct perpetrators of misconduct: the persistent rule-breaker and the individual who commits an act of gross misconduct. In most instances, dealing with the persistent rule-breaker is relatively straightforward, provided that the disciplinary code is applied in a sensible and equitable manner. Assuming that it has been possible to go through some form of counselling with the employee but the required change in behaviour has not been forthcoming, it is likely that the only alternative is to begin the disciplinary process. The likely first step would be a written warning followed, if necessary, by the subsequent stages in the procedure, leading ultimately to dismissal.

Although the dismissal of an employee is never an easy task for a manager, it can – if the steps outlined above are followed – be a relatively straightforward process. Furthermore, individuals who are dismissed for persistent infringements of the rules, for which they have had a series of warnings and the opportunity to appeal, rarely go to employment tribunals. It is difficult for an individual to claim that the employer acted unreasonably when they have been given a number of opportunities to modify their actions. The only complaint that an individual might have in such circumstances is that the procedure itself was unfair or had been applied contrary to the rules of natural justice. This could happen if some people were disciplined for breaches of the rules and others were not, or if employees could demonstrate that they were being asked to achieve unreasonable standards.

### REFLECTIVE ACTIVITY

Imagine that your organisation had dismissed somebody for bad timekeeping and unauthorised absences, and the employee had challenged this in an employment tribunal. What evidence would you need to present in support of your organisation's action?

## GROSS MISCONDUCT

Gross misconduct, on the other hand, presents totally different problems for the manager. Earlier, some of the issues surrounding the concept of gross misconduct were examined, as was the need to be absolutely clear what breaches of the rules *will* mean, as opposed to 'might' mean. For the manager who is called upon to deal with a case of alleged gross misconduct it is vitally important that all procedural steps are strictly adhered to, because mistakes can be costly. For obvious reasons, managers are often under extreme pressure to resolve matters quickly. This is not just because it is much fairer to the accused individual that the matter is resolved, but because other colleagues may have already prejudged the outcome. Pressure cannot always be avoided, but it is necessary that in such circumstances the requirement to investigate thoroughly, prepare properly and conduct a fair hearing is met on every occasion.

Some cases of gross misconduct are very clear-cut, and the employee concerned either admits the offence or there are sufficient witnesses to confirm that the alleged offence was committed by the employee in question. In such cases the first decision for the employer is to decide whether to treat the matter as gross misconduct – for which the penalty is summary dismissal without notice or pay in lieu of notice – or to take a more lenient line. Such decisions are made easier if the company rules are clear and unambiguous about what constitutes gross misconduct. But in our experience, many cases of gross misconduct are not clear-cut and managers are very unsure about how to deal with them. Some of the cases in which we have been asked to assist include suspected theft of goods or money, suspicion of tampering with time-recording devices, suspected false expense claims and seeking payment of sick pay while fit for work. One reason why managers can be unsure about these type of offences is that some of them could lead to criminal charges being laid against the employee or employees concerned.

One way to approach this sensitive issue is by ensuring that the 'Burchell rules' are applied. These rules relate to a case that was decided in 1978 involving an incident of alleged theft (*British Home Stores v Burchell* [1978] IRLR 379). The specific facts of the case are not particularly important, but it is significant because of the test of reasonableness that flowed from it. The Burchell test states that where an employee is suspected of a dismissable offence, an employer must show that:

- the dismissal was genuinely for that reason, and not using it as a pretext
- the belief that the employee committed the offence was based on reasonable grounds – that is, that on the evidence before it, the employer was entitled to say that it was more probable that the employee did, in fact, commit the offence than that they did not
- the belief was based on a reasonable investigation in the circumstances – that the employer's investigation took place before the employee was dismissed and included an opportunity for the employee to offer an explanation.

### The implications of the Burchell test

Let us look at this test in a little more detail and try to relate it to events as they might take place in the working environment. Take the example of a suspected fraudulent expense claim. The first part of Burchell says that the dismissal must be genuine and not on a pretext. This means not using the alleged offence as a convenient means of dismissing an employee whose face no longer fits, or who has a history of misconduct for which no previous action has been taken. The second and third parts of Burchell relate to the employer's belief in the employee's guilt and to the standard of the investigation carried out. As Lewis and Sargeant (2009; p.224) state:

> The question to be determined is not whether, by an objective standard, the employer's belief that the employee was guilty of the misconduct was well founded but whether the employer believed that the employee was guilty and was entitled so to believe having regard to the investigation conducted.

Using the Burchell test in the case of a suspected fraudulent expense claim, the employer would have to be very diligent in assembling the evidence. What guidelines were laid down for the benefit of those allowed to claim expenses? What expenses had been accepted in the past? Were the same standards applied consistently to all staff? Had any other employee made a similar claim in the past without challenge? Assembling such an array of evidence is only likely to happen if there is a thorough investigation – but this is only the first part of the process: the employee is also entitled to offer an explanation. What do you do if the explanation is linked to the lack of guidelines about what is and is not claimable?

While the findings in the *Parsons* case (see above) – that some things are so obvious that they do not need a rule – is relevant, the seniority of the employee concerned might also be relevant. A 'reasonable' belief that a senior employee, who regularly claimed expenses, was acting dishonestly might be easier to demonstrate than a situation in which a junior employee was claiming expenses for the first time. We acknowledged above the uncertainties that sometimes can be encountered when the possibility of criminal proceedings is on the agenda. A question we are often asked is, can we dismiss somebody if we have asked the police to investigate with a view to prosecution? The short answer is 'yes – provided that the Burchell test is followed'. Quite properly, the burden of proof placed on an employer in such circumstances is totally different from the burden of proof imposed by the criminal justice system. In a criminal trial the prosecution must prove 'beyond all reasonable doubt' that an offence was committed. This is entirely reasonable when an individual's liberty is at risk, and it is why, under the Burchell test, you can dismiss somebody *fairly* for dishonesty who might be found 'not guilty' in a criminal trial.

### LACK OF CAPABILITY

This is the second of the fair reasons for dismissing an employee, and we must consider it under two subcategories – firstly, lack of capability that is linked to an employee's inability to do their job because of poor performance; and secondly, lack of capability that relates to an individual's inability to do their job because of poor health or sickness.

## POOR PERFORMANCE

Advising a line manager who has a member of his or her team delivering less than adequate performance is very common for the employment relations specialist. Very often the initial step in this advisory role is to persuade the line manager not to take precipitate action. It is not unusual for the personnel professional to be told by a manager that a particular employee is 'useless' and that they need help to 'get rid of them'. Persuading a line manager not to launch into a formal disciplinary process without considering what other options are open to him or her is very important. Earlier, we looked at the question of counselling, and noted that in the event of an ultimate dismissal an employment tribunal would want to satisfy itself that an employee knew what standards were expected of them, and that they had been given an opportunity to achieve them – and that all this had happened before any formal disciplinary procedures had begun. Another option might be the provision of alternative work for the employee concerned if they had demonstrated incapability at the present tasks.

Whatever options are taken, the employee is entitled on grounds of fairness to be told exactly what is required of them – what standards are being set, and the time-scale in which they are expected to achieve them. During the period of time that an individual is being given to reach the desired standards, a good manager ensures that they are kept informed of their progress. This again is the operation of the principle of 'best practice' or good management habits.

One important point to remember in looking at capability is the obligations placed on employers by the Disability Discrimination Act (1995), the principal purpose of which is to protect disabled people from discrimination in the field of employment, and this issue is dealt with below.

## MANAGING ABSENCE

This can be one of the most emotive issues that any manager has to face, and must at all times be handled with sensitivity by managers. There is always scope for disputes to arise in this difficult area, and it is important that the employment relations professional makes himself or herself aware of all the circumstances in which absences can occur and, where these involve legal rights, ensures that he or she understands the scope of such rights. Time off work for domestic emergencies is one example.

Absence from work can occur for a number of reasons. Some – such as holiday, bereavement or paternity leave – are normally arranged in advance and cause minimum disruption to the employing organisation. The absences that cause disruption within any organisation are those that are unplanned, either because the employee concerned is sick, has simply failed to turn up for work, or a domestic emergency has intervened. In so far as the second reason is concerned, it would be normal to treat this as a breach of the rules on unauthorised absence and deal with it as a case of misconduct.

One reason for unauthorised absence could be that an employee has failed to return from a authorised absence – say, a holiday – at the due time. Individuals returning late from holiday has become a much more widespread problem in recent years due to the increase in overseas travel. For most individuals who return to work late in such circumstances the fault lies with delayed air flights or other travel problems. For some employers the disruption caused by a late return from holiday is minimal, and they may treat it as no more than an irritation. But for others, particularly at a time of the year when large numbers of people are on holiday, the disruption caused can be very serious. Notwithstanding the fact that the cause of the problem (a late flight) was outside the employee's control, the employer might take the view that steps could have been taken to minimise the disruption – for example, an explanatory telephone call. Whether disciplinary action is taken in such circumstances will clearly rest on the facts of each individual case, but in any event action should follow the guidance given above for preparing and conducting a disciplinary interview, particularly in respect of mitigating circumstances and other explanations.

However, in most establishments the most widespread cause of absence from work is sickness or alleged sickness, and while it would be wholly unreasonable to treat a case of genuine sickness as a disciplinary matter, incapacity for work on health grounds can be a fair reason for dismissing an employee. For this reason the way in which an employer deals with health-related absences is very important.

**Sickness absence**

Dealing with sickness absence can be a minefield for any manager, but for the employment relations specialist who is expected to give clear and timely advice it is even more so. Estimates of the cost to the UK economy of sickness absence run into several billions, and absence must therefore be managed effectively. Unauthorised absence is usually a disciplinary matter, but most absences do not fall into this category. They are recorded as sickness. Without wishing to suggest that any employee deliberately seeks to be untruthful, notifying the employer of 'sickness' remains the most common reason for absence from work, and although the overwhelming majority of employees have minimal periods of sickness absence, most organisations have staff whose sickness record is poor. Such people can consistently accumulate as many as 25 to 30 sick days per annum through a mix of 'flu', 'migraine' and 'stomach upsets'. As an indication of how sickness absence is perceived to be a cost that can be contained and reduced, see the budget of the outgoing Westminster Labour administration. One of the declared aims of the public expenditure cuts outlined in that budget is a determination to reduce sickness absence among public sector workers.

Each year the CIPD produces a survey of absence management policy and practice (see the CIPD website www.cipd.co.uk), and the tenth such survey –

published in July 2009 – showed that the average level of employee absence was 7.4 days per employee. This was down from 8 days per employee in 2008, and was the lowest level of absence recorded since the first survey in 2000. Whether this fall is connected with the 2008/9 recession and people's fears about job security will not become clear until the next survey report is published in 2010.

However, anecdotal evidence has it that there is a connection between the two events. Absence remains highest in the public sector at 9.7 days, which perhaps explains why reducing absence is a key element in public sector cost savings. Whatever the level of absence in different sectors, the cost continues to rise. The average cost of absence per employee per year is £692, which represents a very significant burden on business and does not take account of some of the hidden costs such as lost business opportunities. Minor illnesses continue to be the main cause of short-term absence. Stress is the number one cause of long-term absence among non-manual workers.

In order to formulate absence management policies in your organisation, or to benchmark those that you have, it is recommended that you study the survey in some detail on the CIPD website.

For managing absence effectively, the starting point has to be adequate record-keeping. ACAS advises that 'records showing lateness and the duration of and reason for all spells of absence should be kept to help monitor absence levels.' Such records enable a manager to substantiate whether a problem of persistent absence is real or imagined. All too often the employment relations specialist who is asked for advice is expected to work with insufficient data. Managing absence is not just about applying rules or following procedure – it is about addressing problems of persistent absence quickly and acting consistently. This sends out a clear and unambiguous message to all employees that absence is regarded as a serious matter.

But how do you act rigorously and at the same time retain fairness and consistency? The most effective way is through the return-to-work interview. The CIPD survey shows this to be the 'most commonly used approach to managing short-term absence', 83% of organisations using them. The return-to-work interview sends a clear message to employees that absence matters, that the employer has noticed their absence, and that they care.

In its booklet *Discipline and Grievance at Work*, ACAS provides some comprehensive guidance on 'dealing with absence' and handling frequent and persistent short-term absences, which supports the principle of the return-to-work interview and helps to ensure a consistency of approach. Among the factors that must be taken into account are:

- Absences should be investigated promptly and the employee asked to give an explanation.
- Where there is no medical advice to support frequent self-certified absences, the employee should be asked to consult a doctor to establish whether medical treatment is necessary and whether the underlying reason for absence is work-related.

- If after investigation it appears that there were no good reasons for the absences, the matter should be dealt with under the disciplinary procedure.

- Where absences arise from temporary domestic problems, the employer in deciding appropriate action should consider whether an improvement in attendance is likely. It is also important to consider whether any of the absences should, or could, have been covered by the Maternity and Parental Leave (time off for dependents in an emergency) Regulations (1999). These Regulations are discussed in more detail below.

- In all cases the employee should be told what improvement is expected and warned of the likely consequences if it does not happen.

- If there is no improvement, the employee's age, length of service, performance, the likelihood of a change in attendance, the availability of suitable alternative work and the effect of past and future absences on the business should all be taken into account on deciding appropriate action.

**Persistent absence**

Frequent short-term absences can be very difficult to manage and can be the cause of serious conflict between employees. Where one individual within a work group is constantly absent, it is usually their colleagues who suffer. This is because they have to take on additional duties or alter their hours at short notice. It is they, not the management, who are inconvenienced, and they are entitled to expect that their employer will do something to manage the problem. If doubt still remains about the nature of the illness, injury or disability, therefore, the employee can be asked if they are prepared to be examined by an independent doctor to be appointed by the company. Normally, unless there is some form of contractual provision which allows for this, an employee cannot normally be compelled to attend. However, with the growth of occupational sick pay schemes, many organisations have overcome this problem by building compulsion into their scheme rules. Very often, advising an employee that such an examination will be required if attendance does not improve is sufficient to resolve the problem. Complications can arise when the injury or illness which necessitates the persistent short-term absences is genuine. It could never be reasonable to discipline individuals in such circumstances – but it can be fair to dismiss the employee concerned. Where such a situation does arise, it is absolutely imperative that a careful process of assessment and examination is carried out. This would include obtaining a comprehensive medical report setting out full details of the individual's capacity to work, and the consideration of other options – part-time work, reduced hours, alternative work, etc.

All of the above makes good sense and is consistent with the principle of managing absence with a 'good practice' ethos. However, employment relations professionals must consider what other methods they can use for managing absence. This might include the introduction of flexitime and annual hours schemes so that employees can manage domestic commitments without resorting to 'taking a day off sick'. In short, employers might have to consider how they can become more family-friendly.

**Long-term absence**

The section above dealt with the persistent short-term absentee and noted that although some absences might not be genuine, many were. A similar problem arises in respect of employees whose absence is long term. It is reasonable to assume that the majority of long-term absences are also genuine and would certainly be covered by some form of medical certification. Nevertheless, they still have to be managed – and again, ACAS provides guidance. In its view it is important that:

- The employee should be contacted periodically, and they [the employee] should maintain regular contact with the employer.

- The employee should be advised if employment is at risk.

- The employee should be asked if they will consent to their own doctor being contacted, and should be clearly informed of the employee's right to refuse consent, to see the report and to request amendments to it.

- The employee's doctor should be asked if the employee will be able to return to work, and the nature of the work they will be capable of carrying out.

- On the basis of the report received, the employer should consider whether alternative work is available.

- Employers are not expected to create special jobs, nor are they expected to be medical experts. They should simply take action on the basis of the medical evidence.

- As with other absences, the possibility of an independent medical examination should be considered.

- Where an employee refuses to co-operate in providing medical evidence, they should be told, in writing, that a decision will have to be taken on the basis of what information is available – and that the decision may result in dismissal.

- Where the employee's job can no longer be kept open and no suitable alternative is available, the employee should be informed of the likelihood of dismissal.

This last point can be very emotive. Where you are dealing with an employee who has long service, an exemplary work record, and is genuinely suffering from a serious illness or a serious illness has left them unable to work, telling them that they are likely to lose their job can be very difficult – not only because the employer is genuinely concerned about the impact of such a decision but because the employer is concerned about the possibility of legal action for unfair dismissal being taken against him or her.

In cases where illness or injury is obvious and the medical prognosis reasonably clear, following the ACAS guidelines will help to ensure that the decisions that are made will stand up to external scrutiny. But what happens when the injury or illness is not so obvious? Bad backs and stress are two examples that spring to mind. Because the words 'stress' and 'backache' are used so loosely – even by doctors on medical certificates – an employer must deal with these cases both carefully and critically. The way forward may only emerge over time. Often both employer and employee will have to wait for many weeks, if not months, for further medical investigations to be carried out before the appropriate form of action can be decided. For employment relations professionals this can be a difficult time. They are often under pressure from line manager colleagues to support a premature decision to dismiss so that a replacement can be recruited. The effective employment relations professional who has developed his or her influencing skills will be able to persuade colleagues that acting precipitately is not in the best interests of the organisation.

### Disabilities and absence

It is possible that individuals who have contracted a serious illness, have suffered a serious injury or are suffering from 'stress' will be deemed to be suffering from a disability. So, whereas the above sections may contain useful advice in dealing with many types of absence, what happens if the reason for the absence amounts to a disability covered by the Disability Discrimination Act (DDA)?

As part of the protection provided by the DDA, employers may have to make 'reasonable adjustments' to employment arrangements – and in the context of managing absence, section 4(2)(d) of the Act states that 'it is unlawful for an employer to discriminate against a disabled person by dismissing them or subjecting them to any other detriment'. Because the Act applies equally to existing employees as well as to new recruits, employers should be careful of initiating action in respect of employees with a permanent health problem without paying due regard to the legislation. Section 6(1) of the Act states that an employer has a duty to make 'reasonable adjustments' if any employee is disadvantaged either by the physical features of the workplace or by the arrangements for the work itself. The Code of Practice which accompanies the Act lists a number of 'reasonable adjustments' that an employer might have to consider. These could include:

- making adjustments to premises
- allocating some of the disabled person's duties to another person
- transferring the person to fill an existing vacancy
- altering the person's working hours
- assigning the person to a different place of work
- allowing the person to be absent during working hours for rehabilitation, assessment or treatment
- giving the person – or arranging for them to be given – training
- acquiring or modifying equipment
- modifying instructions or reference manuals
- modifying procedures for testing or assessment
- providing a reader or interpreter
- providing supervision.

Clearly, employers will not have to make 'reasonable adjustments' in respect of all 'sick' employees – only those who fit the Act's definition of disability. A disabled person is a person with 'a physical or mental impairment which has a substantial and long-term adverse effect on [their] ability to carry out normal day-to-day activities' (section 1). This chapter is about discipline and not disability, but employment relations specialists must be aware that the disability legislation imposes challenges that must be taken into account when managing absence. Most importantly, it must be remembered that dismissal of a disabled employee is automatically unfair and on that basis will almost certainly be impossible to defend.

## Absence and domestic emergencies

The Employment Relations Act (1999) amended the Employment Rights Act (1996) to provide employees with a right to take a reasonable amount of time off work to deal with unexpected or sudden emergencies – for example:

- if a dependant falls ill or has been injured or assaulted
- when a dependant is having a baby (this does not include taking time off after the birth of a child)
- to make longer-term care arrangements for a dependant who is ill or injured
- to deal with the death of a dependant
- to deal with the disruption of care arrangements for a dependant
- to deal with an incident involving a dependant child during school hours.

The details of the time off right are contained in the Maternity and Parental Leave (time off for dependants in an emergency) Regulations (1999), and set out the circumstances in which an employee can use the provisions, and how they can, if necessary, enforce their rights. Essentially, the emergency for which an employee is claiming time off must involve a dependant of theirs. A dependant is the husband, wife, child or parent of the employee. It can also include someone who lives in the same household as the employee – for example, a partner or elderly relative. It does not include tenants or boarders.

Neither the number of times an employee can be absent from work nor the length of the time off that can be taken is specified in the Regulations, but in most cases one or two days should be sufficient to deal with the problem. The fact that the right is to *unpaid* time off is, in most circumstances, going to limit the length of the absence anyway.

However, like any right, it is open to abuse by both unscrupulous employers and by employees acting in bad faith. Where an employee believes that they have suffered a detriment, or in extreme cases been dismissed for seeking to take time off, they have the right to apply to an employment tribunal. If an employer believes that the right is being abused, the employer should deal with the situation according to the normal disciplinary procedures.

In the context of employee relations, however, this right could offer an opportunity to the employer. In Chapter 3 we said that it was important for the employment relations professional to see the law as more than an object of compliance – that some rights might be seen as a minimum standard that could be enhanced by a progressive employer, and that the proactive employment relations professional can provide the evidence to support such an enhancement. And we said above that in order to reduce some absences, employers might have to develop more family-friendly policies. The right to time off for domestic emergencies could be the springboard for the development of such a policy.

## SOME OTHER SUBSTANTIAL REASON

One other fair reason for dismissal set out in the 1996 Employment Rights Act, and that we need to consider, is 'some other substantial reason'. This concept was introduced into the legislation 'so as to give tribunals the discretion to accept as a fair reason for dismissal something that would not conveniently fit into any of the other categories' (Lewis and Sargeant, 2009; p.226). Dismissals for 'some other substantial reason' have, as those authors point out, been upheld in respect of employees who have been sentenced to a term of imprisonment, employees who cannot get on with each other, or where there are problems between an individual and one of the organisation's customers. Interestingly, the cases that Lewis and Sargeant quote all relate to the 1970s and 1980s – which might indicate that businesses are now less reliant on this rather vague concept. It is certainly the case that the more professional employment relations specialists, recognising that such issues and conflicts do arise, have amended their disciplinary procedures accordingly, and many organisations now have a rule relating to general conduct which may be worded in the following way:

> Any conduct detrimental to the interests of the company, its relations with the public, its customers and suppliers, damaging to its public image or offensive to other employees in the company, shall be a disciplinary offence.

It is easy to see how such a rule could be used to deal with any of the examples cited by Lewis and Sargeant. In the context of managing discipline, it is a much more systematic route. Some other substantial reason can, to the non-lawyer, be a rather vague concept, and by being able to proceed against an individual for a breach of a specific rule is much clearer to everybody involved.

## APPEALS

Every disciplinary procedure must contain an appeals process – otherwise, it is almost impossible to demonstrate that the organisation has acted reasonably within the law. In common with every other aspect of the disciplinary process, it is important to ensure fairness and consistency within an appeals procedure, which should provide for appeals to be dealt with as quickly as possible. An employee should be able to appeal at every stage of the disciplinary process, and common sense dictates that any appeal should be heard by someone who is senior to the person imposing the disciplinary sanction. This will not always be possible, particularly in smaller organisations, but if the person hearing the appeal is the same as the person who imposed the original sanction, ACAS advises that the person should hear the appeal and act as impartially as possible. In essence, an appeal in these circumstances is going to be no more than a review of the original decision, but perhaps in a calmer and more objective manner.

The appeals procedure generally falls into two parts: action prior to the appeal and the actual hearing itself. Before any appeal hearing the employee should be told what the arrangements are and what their rights under the procedure are. It is also important then to obtain, and read, any relevant documentation. At the appeal hearing the appellant should be told its purpose, how it will be conducted, and what decisions the person or persons hearing the appeal are able to make. Any new evidence must be considered and all relevant issues properly examined. Although appeals are not regarded as an opportunity to seek a more sympathetic assessment of the issue in question, it is equally true that appeals are not routinely dismissed. Overturning a bad or unjust decision is just as important as confirming a fair decision. It is an effective way of signalling to employees that all disciplinary issues will be dealt with consistently and objectively.

Many organisations fall into the trap of using their grievance procedure in place of a proper appeals process. This is to be avoided wherever possible. The grievance procedure should be reserved for resolving problems arising from employment – and is covered in the next chapter. Finally, not only should appeals be dealt with in a timely fashion but the procedure should specify time-limits within which appeals should be lodged.

## SUMMARY

In this chapter we have explained why managing employee performance and behaviour is such a key area. We have looked at the origins of disciplinary procedures and how they have developed over time. We have also provided an outline of the current legal position, but it is important a) to remember that this is not a legal text, and b) to check legal facts each time a performance or behaviour problem arises because the law is constantly evolving.

Poor management of performance and behaviour can create employment relations problems, and we therefore make no apology for the emphasis placed on the importance of best practice and the need to act professionally. We have tried to reflect the realities of managing these issues within an organisational context because discussions that we have had with managers from a whole range of organisations have shown that they can cause major employment relations problems – because breaches of rules are either ignored or treated with differing degrees of seriousness by different managers.

There is also an overwhelming business case for the effective management of employee performance and behaviour. More and more organisations are recognising the value that can be added by involving employees in the business and gaining their commitment to organisational objectives. Assuming that this is a trend that most organisations would wish to see continue, an employment relations climate that recognises the rights and responsibilities of both parties to the employment relationship is absolutely vital.

## KEY LEARNING POINTS

- Managing discipline is about acting with just cause, using procedures correctly, acting consistently, following the rules of natural justice. It is about developing these good management habits which ensure that you do follow procedure – you do act consistently and you do take account of the rules of natural justice when taking disciplinary action.

- A fair and effective disciplinary procedure is one that concentrates on improving or changing behaviour, and not one that relies on the principle of punishment.

- The purpose and scope of a disciplinary procedure is very clear. It should allow all employees to understand what is expected of them in respect of conduct, attendance and job performance, and set out rules by which such matters will be governed. The aim is to ensure consistent and fair treatment for all.

- It is important to discuss performance and behavioural patterns with the employee (counselling) before using the disciplinary procedure.

- Employees are entitled to know the cause of complaints against them, entitled to representation, entitled to challenge evidence, and entitled to a right of appeal.

- Managing absence should be a priority for any organisation and appropriate policies established for that purpose. It is important that employment relations professionals make themselves aware of the circumstances in which absence from work can occur, and where these involve legal rights ensure that they understand the scope of such rights.

## REVIEW QUESTIONS

1 Using research into the contemporary policy and practice of organisations, identify *at least three* factors that can affect the way discipline is handled in the workplace.

2 A senior manager wants you to brief supervisors about the different purposes of a disciplinary policy. The manager would like you to emphasise that discipline is not simply a matter of punishment. Using examples from your own organisation, outline what you would say, and add why.

3 An employee is regularly late back from lunch – as often as three or four times a week. His line manager has several times mentioned to him that this is unacceptable, usually in passing or during a conversation about something else. Provide the line manager with advice on how to progress the matter.

4 A number of employees have cited stress as the cause of absenteeism in recent months. The managing director has asked you, as the HR manager, to organise a briefing session for all members of the management on 'stress in the workplace'. Outline, and justify, the areas/issues you will cover in your briefing session.

5 A salesman in your organisation has submitted expenses for travelling and entertaining over a four-week period which do not tally with his record of customer visits. His line manager says he is 'on the fiddle' and should be dismissed. You are responsible for advising line managers on how to deal with difficulties like this. Explain how you would handle this situation.

**EXPLORE FURTHER**

Advisory Conciliation and Arbitration Service, *Discipline and grievances at Work: The ACAS Advisory Handbook.* London, ACAS, November 2009.

Advisory, Conciliation and Arbitration Service (2009) *Disciplinary and Grievance Procedures: The ACAS Code of Practice*. London: ACAS.

CIPD Employment Law Service.

CIPD (2009) *Employee Absence: A survey of management policy and practice*. London: CIPD.

Edwards, P. (1994) 'Discipline and the creation of order', in Sisson, K. (ed.) *Personnel Management: A comprehensive guide to theory and practice in Britain*. Oxford: Blackwell.

Employment Rights Act (1996).

Employment Rights (Dispute Resolution) Act (1998).

Employment Relations Act (1999).

Employment Act (2008).

Lewis, D. and Sargeant, M. (2009) *Essentials of Employment Law*, 10th edition. London: CIPD.

**Web links**

www.acas.org.uk/publications gives access to the Code of Practice on Discipline and Grievance Procedures

www.bis.gov.uk is the website of the Department for Business, Innovation and Skills and gives access to the main pieces of legislation relevant to discipline

www.cipd.co.uk gives access to the CIPD Employment Law Service

www.employmenttribunal.gov.uk gives access to the publications, press releases, etc, of the Office of Employment Tribunals

## CHAPTER 13

# Managing Employee Grievances

## OVERVIEW

The chapter begins by outlining the business case for resolving grievances, and then explains why employees may be reluctant to formally take up their complaint about management behaviour. Next, the chapter looks at grievance procedures in terms of their purpose, underlying principles, stages, time-limits, employee representation, their operation – and the role of HR in all this. The chapter then examines the law surrounding the managing of employee grievances and the ACAS Code of Practice, which provides guidance on minimum standards for dealing with grievance matters. We then move on to the chapter's main sections – on how to manage employee grievances, including how they may be dealt with informally as well as formally. Not all grievances are of a simple nature that can be resolved quickly. Management deal with all grievances in a competent and systematic manner, which involves a number of stages: the grievance interview, at the end of which a decision must be made on whether the grievance is genuine or not; the meeting with the employee and his or her representatives; preparing for that meeting; confirming the common ground between the employee and the management; resolving the grievance (or not); the possible appeal; and reporting the outcome of the appeal meeting. Dos and don'ts and good employment practice are addressed under each of these headings.

## LEARNING OUTCOMES

When you have completed this chapter, you should be aware of and able to describe:

- the business case for resolving grievances
- how to explain the term 'grievance' and outline its main subject matter
- why grievances are or are not taken up by employees
- the principles that underpin a grievance procedure

- how to justify the contents of a grievance procedure

- the importance of reviewing and of monitoring the operation of grievance procedures

- the law relating to grievance-handling management

- the significance of the skills required to manage employee grievances effectively

- why some grievances are dealt with by a specific procedure separate from a standard grievance procedure.

## INTRODUCTION

A grievance is a complaint by an employee that the behaviour of management, or that of another employee, has been unfair and unjust in its application to him or her. Employee complaints may be genuine or they may be the result of a misconception or misunderstanding. In either case, settling them quickly and effectively is vital. To the individual concerned, his or her grievance is of immediate importance. In addition, an organisation cannot ignore employee grievances since the mishandling of an individual's grievance can escalate into a collective dispute. The objective of grievance management is to rectify matters that have gone wrong by:

- thoroughly investigating the situation

- identifying the cause of the employee's complaint

- taking appropriate action to resolve the complaint to the mutual satisfaction of the employee and the management

- resolving the grievance as quickly as possible.

A key aspect of fairness at work is the opportunity for the individual employee to complain about, and receive redress for, unfair treatment. In this chapter, the fundamentals of managing employee grievances, as an important element in the work of the employment relations professional, are examined. The 2004 *Workplace Employment Relations Survey* reported that in 95% of workplaces the responsibilities of employment relations professionals included providing line managers with advice in managing employee grievances.

In managing employee grievances, line managers require help, advice, support and expertise from the employment relations professional. Such assistance includes devising effective grievance procedures and then training line managers to operate these procedures in a fair, reasonable and consistent manner. In addition, it is good practice on the part of the employment relations professional to take responsibility for monitoring and reviewing the effectiveness – especially in terms of outcomes – of the operation of the grievance procedure.

## THE BUSINESS CASE FOR RESOLVING GRIEVANCES

Employee grievances on a wide variety of issues (including discrimination, harassment and bullying) arise even in the best-managed organisations. If grievances are not dealt with or handled quickly, they are likely to fester and harm the employment relationship. A grievance may also be felt by a group as well as an individual, and if left unresolved, may develop into a major collective dispute that is likely to bring in the involvement of a trade union. However, whether individual or collective, all employee grievances have the potential to damage the quality of an organisation's employment relations and thereby its competitive position and labour market image. The golden rule for management to remember in managing employee grievances is that they are important to those who express them, and must therefore be treated very seriously.

Employee grievances are an outward expression of employee dissatisfaction which, if not resolved, can result in unsatisfactory work behaviour and performance which, in turn, will have adverse consequences for the organisation's competitive position. Unresolved employee dissatisfaction gives rise to:

- employee frustration
- deteriorating interpersonal relationships
- low morale
- poor performance, resulting in lower productivity and/or a poorer quality of output or service
- disciplinary problems, including poor performance by employees
- resignation and loss of good staff (increased labour turnover)
- increased employee absenteeism
- the withdrawal of employee goodwill
- resistance to change – if employees feel they have been treated badly, they are likely to oppose the introduction of change.

In addition, unresolved grievances can lead to employees' feeling so strongly that their 'employment rights' have not been respected that they resign from their employment and claim to an employment tribunal a fundamental breach of contract amounting to constructive dismissal.

If an organisation has a reputation for a high level of employee dissatisfaction, it will be a disincentive for individuals or organisations to purchase goods and/ or services from that organisation, believing that the goods and services are likely to be of poor quality. A reputation for employee dissatisfaction also gives an organisation a 'poor employer' image in the labour market. This image will accentuate the organisation's problems of recruiting and retaining the appropriate quantity and quality of labour services necessary to achieve its organisational objectives.

Organisations in which a significant number of employees experience feelings of unfairness will have relatively higher cost structures than a competitor organisation that has absolute and relatively lower levels of employee dissatisfaction. The former organisation has a competitive disadvantage relative to the latter which will be expressed in sales, revenue and profitability.

If an organisation does not address its employees' grievances, the quality of the organisation's working environment and conditions are likely to be affected adversely. It is essential to the continued prosperity and well-being of the organisation that its employee complaints about management behaviour are addressed as quickly as possible and as near to their source as possible.

If the clear business case outlined above for the effective and professional management of employee grievances is recognised as reality, then training for team leaders and supervisors to manage employee grievances effectively must be a high business priority. It is also important, if the business/organisational benefits of effective grievance management are to be delivered, that employees (both old and new) know to whom they can take their grievance. The main source of information by which employees are usually made aware of the existence, and content, of a grievance procedure are in their letter of appointment, in the staff handbook or on a noticeboard.

## WHAT IS A GRIEVANCE?                                            THEORY

A grievance usually arises because an aggrieved individual regards some management decision (or act of indecision) or behaviour on the part of another employee as unfair and unjust in its application to him or her. However, not all employee complaints are justified in that the action complained of may be legitimate behaviour within the terms and spirit of a collective agreement between the employees and the management, within a company rule contained in the staff handbook, or within the necessities of the business. If employee grievances are to be managed effectively, management must acquire and develop an ability to distinguish genuine from unfounded grievances, and in the case of the latter, explain clearly to the individuals concerned why their complaint merits no action by management.

However, every grievance, whether genuine or unfounded, is important to the individual concerned and has to be treated on its merits. When management receives a complaint which appears frivolous, it is not good practice to reject it without at least an investigation into how it has arisen. If this reveals the employee's complaint to be ill-founded, this must be explained to the individual. By acting on the basis of just cause after investigation and then behaving in a fair, reasonable and consistent manner, management demonstrate to their employees that both unfounded and genuine complaints are treated seriously and in a businesslike manner.

### NON-TRADING OF GRIEVANCES

In resolving employee grievances, management treat each one on its merits, thereby accepting that the complaint is a serious issue for the individual concerned. An employee's grievance has to be dealt with independently of the complaint of another employee(s). In managing employee grievances, management proceed on the basis of one at a time. They resolve the individual's grievance on a particular issue (for example, a denial of a training opportunity) and then move on to settle another employee's grievance over a different issue. The employment relations professional should avoid falling into the trap of having to deal simultaneously with a whole list of different grievances over different issues from a number of different employees.

The effective negotiation of grievances, unlike in bargaining, excludes a trade-off between employee complaints about the employer's or another employee's behaviour. It is not good employment practice for management to settle one person's grievance in exchange for another employee's agreeing to drop his or her grievance. In grievance-handling, management should resist the temptation to trade off one employee's grievance against another. In short, management do not say, 'If you drop your grievance over the lack of clean toilet facilities, we shall concede your colleague's grievance over the lack of parking facilities.'

Complaints from individual employees can centre on many aspects of management behaviour. An employee complaint may be to the effect that the employer has acted in breach of a collective agreement (ie management are not applying it as the parties intended), that tools and/or machinery have not been properly maintained, that the canteen facilities are poor and inadequate, that the workplace is too dark, too cold (or hot) and/or unhealthy, or that the imposed disciplinary penalty is too harsh. Other areas of likely individual employee complaint against management include that they have been passed over for promotion, they have been denied access to a training and development opportunity, their holiday dates allocation does not meet their family circumstances, a bonus has been paid late, a new working practice has been introduced without prior consultation, or their job is graded at an inappropriate level. Complaints by an individual employee against the behaviour of another employee are likely to centre around alleged bullying/ harassment issues.

Although the 2004 *Workplace Employment Relations Survey* did not ask a question about the actual number of grievances raised at the workplace, it did ask whether any grievances had been raised in the past year, whether formally or otherwise. Grievances had been raised in just under half of all workplaces (47%). This represented a marked decrease since 1998, when grievances had been raised in just under three-fifths (56%) of workplaces.

The probability that at least one employee will raise a grievance can be expected to rise with the number of employees at the workplace. The survey results confirmed this: 36% of workplaces with 10 to 24 employees reported that a grievance had been raised in the previous year, compared with 93% of workplaces with 500 or more employees. Grievances were also more commonly raised where unions were recognised – but this association no longer held after the weighting for workplace size. There was also some variation by industry (see Table 13.1). Grievances were most likely to be raised in the electricity, gas and water sector and in the construction sector (61% and 58% respectively) and least likely in the financial services sector (34%).

Table 13.1  Grievances, by industrial distribution, 2005

| Sector | Percentage of workplaces with any grievance |
| --- | --- |
| *All workplaces* | 47 |
| Manufacturing | 57 |
| Electricity, gas and water | 61 |
| Construction | 58 |
| Wholesale and retail | 42 |
| Hotels and restaurants | 40 |
| Transport and communications | 57 |
| Financial services | 34 |
| Other business services | 47 |
| Public administration | 57 |
| Education | 38 |
| Health and social work | 52 |
| Other community services | 42 |

Note: all workplaces have at least 10 employees

Turning to consider the role of formal procedures in resolving grievances, the 2004 *Workplace Employment Relations Survey* showed that almost 92% of those workplaces in which a grievance had been raised had a formal grievance procedure. However, less than half of these workplaces (45%) stated that their procedures had been used in the past year. It followed that a formal grievance procedure had been involved on at least one occasion in only 41% of workplaces where a grievance had been raised. In keeping with the proposition noted above, workplaces that had formal grievance procedures were more likely to have seen a grievance raised in the year preceding the survey than workplaces without a formal procedure. Grievances had been raised in 49% of workplaces with a formal procedure and in 34% of those without. However, no statistically significant differences remained after weighting for workplace size.

In workplaces where grievances had been raised but in which the grievance procedure had not been called upon during the year, managers were asked for their opinions on why the procedure had not been invoked. The vast majority cited good management/employee relations (73%), while many also noted that disputes had been resolved informally without recourse to the procedure (46%). Small proportions of management considered that employees might not have used the procedure because of fears about the consequences (2%) or because the procedure was ineffective (also 2%).

Managers were asked what types of grievance had been raised in the 12 months prior to the survey. The responses are shown in Table 13.2. It was most common for grievances to have been raised in respect of pay and conditions (18% of all workplaces). This was followed by relations with supervisors and line managers (16%) and working practices (12%). In one-tenth of all workplaces, employees had raised issues relating to working time, annual leave or time off. In the same proportion, employees had raised grievances relating to physical working conditions. The proportion of workplaces that cited grievances in respect of pay and conditions, promotion, job grading and appraisals were each lower in 2004 than in 1998. In contrast, there had been an increase in grievances relating to bullying. Changes across other items were not statistically significant.

Table 13.2  Types of grievance raised, 1998 and 2004

| Type of grievance | Percentage of workplaces | |
|---|---|---|
| | 1998 | 2004 |
| Pay and conditions | 25 | 18 |
| Relations with supervisors/line managers (ie unfair treatment) | 16 | 16 |
| Work practices, work allocation or the pace of work | 14 | 12 |
| Working time, annual leave or time off work | 13 | 10 |
| Physical working conditions or health and safety | 12 | 10 |
| Promotion, career development or internal transfers | 14 | 8 |
| Bullying at work | 3 | 7 |
| Job grading or classification | 13 | 6 |
| Disciplinary sanctions, including dismissal | 0 | 5 |
| Performance appraisal | 7 | 4 |
| Sexual harassment | 3 | 2 |
| Selection for redundancy | 0 | 2 |
| Relations with other employees | 0 | 2 |
| Sex or race discrimination | 3 | 1 |
| Racial harassment | 1 | 1 |
| Other grievances | 0 | 0 |
| Grievances raised in the past 12 months | 44 | 53 |

There was some variation between the private and public sectors in the types of grievances raised in 2004. Workplaces in the private sector were likely to have reported issues relating to pay and conditions (20%) compared with 8% in the public sector. Public sector workplaces were more likely to have reported issues relating to working practices (17%) compared with 11% in the private sector, bullying (11% compared with 6%) and job grading (10% compared with 5%).

Employee grievances can be collective in that a group of employees have a common complaint relating to their employment or an individual has a grievance which has collective implications. For example, all employees in an office may complain that the temperature is too high or too low, and employees collectively in the workplace may complain that their level of pay or bonuses seems unfair compared with other groups of employees in other sections of the organisation.

Research indicates that the main causes of grievances raised by a group of employees centre on:

- the interpretation and application of an existing agreement
- pay and bonus arrangements
- organisational change
- new working practices
- grading issues.

These issues should be handled in accordance with the organisation's collective (disputes) grievance process. Collective grievance procedures are not as universal as individual grievance procedures and tend to be associated with unionised workplaces. Most organisations had experienced few collective disputes in recent years.

## REFLECTIVE ACTIVITY

What are the main focuses of employee grievances in your organisation? How would you explain this pattern?

## THE TAKE UP OF GRIEVANCES

Employees who are unable to get their grievances resolved informally, enter their complaint into the formal grievance procedure. This procedure aims to encourage employees who believe they have been treated unfairly to raise their complaint without fear of reprisal and have it resolved as quickly as possible, in order to prevent minor disagreements developing into serious disputes and to help build an open and trusting organisational climate. A written procedure can help clarify the process and help ensure that employees are aware of their rights – for example, to be accompanied at grievance meetings (see below). Managers need a knowledge and understanding of how to operate these procedures, and most organisations provide training in managing employee grievances for team leaders and other front-line managers. In short, managers should be familiar with the content of the grievance procedure and know how to conduct or represent at grievance hearings. All organisations require effective formal complaints procedures in place to ensure that employee dissatisfaction is dealt with, to mutual satisfaction – but they should avoid using them if it is at all possible for the grievance to be resolved informally. Activating the grievance procedure is costly in terms of management time.

Most employees' complaints against management behaviour do not reach the formal grievance procedure. There are many reasons why employee complaints do not enter into formal procedure. First, something happens to make it unnecessary. As Torrington and Hall (2002) point out, the employee's dissatisfaction can disappear after a good night's sleep and/or after a cup of tea with a colleague. Second, the employees merely want to get their dissatisfaction off their chests. The grievance is resolved simply by an appropriate manager's listening to the employee. 'A shoulder to cry on' provides sufficient satisfaction for the employee to withdraw his or her disapproval of management's behaviour.

Third, in times of high levels of unemployment, individuals are reluctant to raise their grievance formally, fearing that management may hold it against them and react by denying them promotion or access to training and development programmes and merit award payments. Fourth, employees may, in some cases, see little point in raising their grievance since they perceive the procedure not to be a particularly effective mechanism for resolving problems. Fifth, some individuals are unwilling to express their dissatisfaction with management for fear of offending their immediate superior, who may see the complaint as a criticism of their competency. Finally, it may be that employees have nothing to complain about. In short, in organisations where managers have an open policy for communication and consultation, problems and concerns are often raised and settled as a matter of course. It is good employment practice on the part of line managers to try to settle grievances informally. Many problems can be raised and settled in the course of everyday working relationships. It also allows for problems to be settled quickly.

The grievance procedure is in addition a dangerous tool to be used by an employee where a strong union is not recognised in the workplace. The employee usually has a grievance against the boss – and the employee may win the battle, but not the war, because the manager will then hold a grudge. The grievance procedure is therefore more effective in local government, health service, education, etc, as opposed to a small engineering firm that does not recognise a union.

The lack of individual grievances being put formally into the grievance procedure does not mean that the quality (climate) of employment relations in the organisation is in good shape. However, employee dissatisfaction identified at an early stage can be resolved quickly through informal discussions. Behaving in this way considerably reduces the probability of the employees' level of dissatisfaction reaching a point at which they are prepared to make a formal complaint against management behaviour.

A situation in which employees' complaints are being suppressed because they feel that senior management will not act against a team leader/supervisor whose style of management is the cause of the grievance cannot be allowed to continue. Senior management might, for example, counsel the team leader/front-line manager as to why his or her management style has to change or provide him or her with formal training after which his or her style should change for the better. If such action fails to produce a more constructive management style, management must either redeploy the team leader/front-line manager elsewhere or consider dispensing with their services. If employee complaints are shown, following thorough investigation, to be the result of a personality clash between the team leader/front-line manager and an individual employee, redeploying the individual to another area of employment may be the best option.

## GRIEVANCE PROCEDURES

The grievance procedure provides the means by which individual employees process their complaint against management behaviour or the behaviour of another employee. In the former case, it informs the individual of the action he or she must take to raise a grievance and the steps management will take in giving it consideration.

A grievance procedure benefits employees because they know where they stand and know what to expect. The purpose of the procedure is to:

- ensure the fair and consistent treatment of employees
- reduce the risk of 'unpredictable' action
- clarify the manner in which grievances will be dealt
- maintain a good employment relations environment
- help the employer to avoid disputes or costly legal action.

It can therefore be useful to define, in advance, the purpose of the policy. For example, the grievance procedure for Tyco Fire and Security and ADT Fire and Security starts with the following explanation of purpose:

The purposes of this procedure are to ensure that you have an opportunity to raise formally with management any grievances relating to your job or complaints regarding the company or any member of the company. The company's aim is to ensure that your grievance or complaint is dealt with promptly and fairly by the appropriate level of the company's management.

Meanwhile, at Motherwell College the grievance policy and procedure states:

1.0 *Introduction*

This policy provides a mechanism whereby any grievance relating to employment within Motherwell College is settled fairly, consistently, quickly and as near to the point of origin as possible. This procedure is non-contractual.

The following procedure is written to take account of individual grievances. It is not intended to form part of any collective grievance procedure.

2.0 *Purpose*

The purpose of this policy and procedure is to ensure that a common approach will be followed in respect of individual grievances within Motherwell College.

The staff grievance procedure at the Scottish Prison Service states in its introduction:

> 1.2 From time to time, staff may have individual grievances related to employment matters. This procedure is designed to enable managers and staff to resolve such issues quickly, effectively and fairly.

> All grievances raised by employees will be dealt with confidentially and in private. This does not preclude discussions with other levels of management or trade union representatives to obtain or confirm information and to resolve the grievance.

## UNDERLYING PRINCIPLES

In managing employee complaints, management are guided by a number of principles – fairness, transparency, consistency, representation and promptness. Fairness is guaranteed, in that the procedure:

- prevents management from dismissing the employee's complaint out of hand on the grounds that it is trivial, too time-consuming and/or too costly
- ensures that there is a full investigation by an unbiased individual to establish the facts of the case
- provides the employee with adequate time to prepare their case and to question management witnesses
- allows for the case to be heard by individuals not directly involved in the complaint
- provides for the right of appeal to a higher level of management and, in some cases, to an independent external body.

A grievance procedure with a clearly demarcated number of stages and standards of behaviour at each stage provides consistency of treatment and reduces the influence of subjectivity.

When a complaint is raised, the procedure provides the individual with the right to be represented by another individual who is independent of the employer. Such a representative is usually internal to the organisation (for example, an employee representative, a shop steward, a work colleague) rather than external (for example, a full-time trade union official, a solicitor). The staff grievance procedure for the Scottish Prison Service, for instance, states that:

> The individual raising the employment-related grievance is entitled to be accompanied/represented by a trade union representative or a fellow staff member of his/her choice at all formal stages of the procedure.

The promptness principle is achieved by the procedure's having a small number of stages, each of which has time-limits for their completion. This enables the grievance to be resolved as quickly and as simply as possible.

To summarise, then: the grievance procedure ensures the right of an employee to complain if he or she experiences unfair treatment, and if he or she exercises this right, to be treated in a fair and reasonable manner consistent with the principles of natural justice. It provides that the individual employee is treated with dignity and respect. By establishing standards of behaviour and due processes to resolve employee grievances in a peaceful and constructive manner the grievance procedure thus provides 'order and stability' in the workplace.

## FORMS OF PROCEDURE

The form of grievance procedures varies immensely. In a small non-union establishment, the procedure is likely to be written into the employee's contract of employment – of which the following language would be typical:

> If you have a grievance relating to your employment, you should raise it with you immediate supervisor.

In larger organisations, a grievance procedure is likely to be a clause in a collective agreement. However, in large and medium-sized unionised and non-unionised organisations, the grievance procedure is likely to be reproduced in the company handbook, or be available as a separate document, and a typical wording would be:

> If you have any grievance relating to your employment, you should raise it with your immediate supervisor. If the matter is not settled at this level, you may pursue it through the grievance procedure agreed between the company and the trade union representatives. Further details of such procedural agreements are maintained separately in writing and may be consulted on request to management.

The Employment Act (2002), however, imposed upon employers statutory dispute resolution procedures, incorporated into every contract of employment, for employee grievances. This was, however, repealed by the Employment Act (2008), which made the ACAS Code of Practice on *Discipline and Grievance* the cornerstone of disciplinary and grievance procedures. The Code is not legally binding but provides guidance on minimum standards for dealing with grievance matters.

## A TYPICAL PROCEDURE

A typical grievance procedure has a standard format of:

- a policy statement of the purpose of the procedure (see above)
- a statement of the scope of the procedure
- a statement of the general principles to be applied in its application
- a number of stages – At each stage the aim is to identify action that stops the problem recurring or continuing. The number of stages in a procedure can range from two to five, but three stages are the most popular arrangement in practice

- a list of time-limits by which each stage should be completed, so that a speedy resolution of the grievance can be secured

- a list of the individuals who are to be involved at each stage

- notification of the right to representation, for the employee laying the complaint against management, by an individual independent of the employer

- notification of the monitoring and review arrangements: these are usually encapsulated in something like the following statement:

> Organisation X will continue to examine and review existing grievance procedures to reflect the organisation's needs on the basis of experience and statutory obligations ...

In most organisations, procedures for managing employee complaints relating to health and safety provision, job grading (job evaluation scheme), sexual harassment and discrimination, and 'whistle-blowing' are normally separate from the general grievance/disputes procedure. Grievances about job grading, harassment, bullying, etc, are instead normally dealt with by means of a purpose-built procedure. Their degree of differentiation from the general grievance procedure depends on the volume of business and on the speed, efficacy and acceptability required by the parties. These specific procedures are discussed in greater detail later in the chapter.

### STAGES

There are a number of stages in a typical grievance procedure. Factors common to all the stages are:

- They spell out the details of who hears the case (eg the departmental manager, the managing director) and the individuals to be present (eg the personnel manager, the line manger and the employee concerned), including who may represent the employee (eg a colleague, a friend or a shop steward).

- They explain the appeal mechanisms available to employees.

- They define the time-limits by which the stage must be complete.

- They explain what will happen if the grievance is not resolved or remains unsettled.

This is illustrated in the typical three-stage grievance procedure presented below.

#### A TYPICAL THREE-STAGE GRIEVANCE PROCEDURE

*Stage 1*

If you wish to raise a formal grievance you should, in the first instance, raise it orally or in writing with your immediate supervisor or manager. The supervisor/manager will normally respond within five working days.

*Stage 2*

If the matter is not resolved at Stage 1 or within five working days, you may refer it in writing within three working days to the next level of management, who may also involve a representative of the Personnel Department. You should set out the grounds for the complaint and the reasons for your dissatisfaction with the Stage 1 response. A meeting will normally take place to consider the matter within seven working days of the request being made.

*Stage 3*

It the matter is not resolved at Stage 2 or within seven working days, you may refer it in writing within three working days to the next level of management, who may involve a representative of the Personnel Department. You should set out the grounds for the complaint and the reasons for your dissatisfaction with the Stage 2 response. A meeting will normally take place to consider the matter within 10 working days of the request being made. The decision of the Divisional Executive is the final stage of the procedure and will be given in writing.

Although the aim of grievance procedures is to reach a resolution of the employee's complaint as quickly as possible, it cannot, however, be done with undue haste. As we have seen, a grievance procedure usually specifies how, and to whom, employees can raise a grievance and spells out the stages through which the complaint will be processed. To ensure a speedy settlement, time-limits are specified by which each stage of the procedure must be completed.

So in managing grievances management's objective is to settle the complaint as near as possible to the point of its source. If employee complaints are permitted unnecessarily to progress to a higher level, this principle is undermined. A professional employment relations manager ensures that his or her managerial colleagues – but particularly line managers – understand the limits of their authority when operating within the parameters of the grievance procedure. The procedure is a problem-solving mechanism and the significance of each of the different procedural stages is reinforced when grievances are settled as near as possible to the point of origin.

Although defined stages through which a grievance can be processed are essential, there is no ideal number of stages. The number is a function of many factors, including the size of the organisation. However, natural justice principles would point to a minimum of two stages because this at least ensures one level of appeal from the first immediate decision. Nor should the procedure contain too many stages, since this makes the process unduly long and is in conflict with the principle of resolving grievances as quickly as possible and as close as possible to their origin.

### ? REFLECTIVE ACTIVITY

Do you have a grievance procedure in your organisation? If not, why not? If you do, how many stages does it have? Why does it have that number?

### TIME-LIMITS

An employee with a complaint wants his or her grievance settled as soon as possible, and is likely to regard it as the highest priority for the manager to whom the complaint is made. That manager, on the other hand, needs time to gather the facts, consult with other managers and consider what action to take – all of which has to be fitted around the many other tasks for which that manager is responsible. The idea behind a time-limit is that it provides a manager with an opportunity to consider the problem seriously while at the same time also committing him or her to provide an answer within a fixed period of time. This relaxes the pressures on the employee, or his or her representative, both of whom now know that if a satisfactory answer has not been provided at the end of the time-limit, the complaint will proceed to the next stage.

The usual practice is to allow longer time-limits for the completion for each successive stage. Internal stages' time-limits can vary from a low of 24 hours to a maximum of five days, but such limits are longer for external stages. Time-limits alone do not ensure the expeditious handling of grievances but they are useful in establishing standards of reasonable behaviour by the parties. When the external stages of a grievance procedure are triggered, time-limits for their completion again provide reassurance for the employee that inordinately lengthy delays in dealing with the complaint is not possible. Most of the criticisms against time-limits (for example, loss of flexibility, undermining mutual trust, the issue is not dealt with properly at the lower levels) are avoided if there is a proviso in the procedure to permit, by mutual agreement, an extension of the time-limits by which each stage of the process must be completed. The guiding principle is that the employee's complaint progresses quickly to the level needed to find a solution to the problem, and that managers do not 'sit on' grievances.

### EMPLOYEE REPRESENTATION

Fair and reasonable behaviour by an employer in managing employee grievances requires the employee to have the right to representation by an individual who can advocate their case. Representation assists the individual employee, who may lack confidence and the experience to deal with his or her line manager or senior manager, especially those operating at the executive level (for example, the managing director). The individual's representative is independent of the interests of the employer and is not there merely to witness what management say to the individual. The employee's representative is, however, likely to be internal to the organisation. A wide range of practice applies to the role of the independent representative. They vary from a silent witness to a full-blown representative. In one organisation described by 2002 IRS research documentation, the role was to address the hearing, ask questions of the manager involved and the panel, and generally support the worker. At another organisation, the employee representative could address the meeting on points of procedure, could advise and generally represent the interests of the individual.

The former Department for Trade and Industry publication *Employee Representation in Grievance and Disciplinary Matters – Making a Difference,* published in 2006, revealed that among the workplaces surveyed, 83% allowed employees to confer privately with their representative. However, just under one in five workplaces did not allow companions to ask questions on behalf of the employee – something they are clearly permitted to do under the Employment Act (1999). Almost half of those workplaces where grievance hearings were held allowed companions to answer questions on behalf of the employee – a practice that the employer is not required to permit under the legislation. Eighty-one percent of the workplaces allowed companions to ask questions on behalf of the employee.

The Employment Relations Act (1999) gives workers a statutory right to be accompanied by a fellow-worker or trade union official where they are required or invited by their employer to attend certain categories of grievance hearings and when they make a reasonable request to be so accompanied. The introduction of a defined statutory right to accompaniment in grievance meetings was designed to ensure consistency in existing practice, afford individual employees increased protection and, most important of all, facilitate the resolution of workplace disputes. The chosen companion has a statutory right to address the hearing and to confer with the worker – but no statutory right to answer questions on the worker's behalf or to attend hearings in his or her place. Workers are free to choose an official from any trade union to accompany them at a grievance hearing regardless of whether or not a trade union is recognised by the employer. The former DTI research referred to above (2006) found that compliance with this right was patchy and uneven. Employees in more than one-third of workplaces did not have access to either a colleague or a trade union representative when asked to attend a formal grievance hearing. Unionised workplaces and to a lesser extent those with specialist HR managers were more likely to meet statutory requirements regarding being accompanied. The 2004 *Workplace Employment Relations Survey* found that in 67% of grievances employees were accompanied by either a trade union representative or work colleague. We must assume that in the other 33% of cases employees either chose not to exercise their right or were not aware of it.

### Representation at which stage?

In many procedures, representation starts at the second stage after the individual has raised their complaint with their immediate manager. Representation then only becomes necessary if the employee is dissatisfied with the response from their immediate manager and wishes to take the matter to a higher level of management. The assumption behind this is that a grievance is not a grievance if the individual employee's immediate manager resolves the problem.

However, there are employment relations managers who consider that the employee should have representation from the very start of their complaint. In these circumstances the employee's first step is to take the grievance to his or her workplace representative (where there is one) rather than to his or her immediate superior, and persuade the representative that he or she has a genuine grievance and ask for representation in processing the complaint. The employee's representative then has an important responsibility to act as a useful filter and sift the genuine grievances from the unfounded.

## The equality of representatives

In the internal stages of the procedure, the individual employee's representative is also an employee of the organisation. As an employee they are in a subordinate position to management who can give them instructions, empower them, verify the quality of their work, monitor their timekeeping and initiate disciplinary action against them. In short, they are contracted to supply work to the employer.

However, when they are in the role of an employee representative, they interact with management as partners of equal status. The acceptance of this equality of relationship is recognised by management in that they have committed themselves to a grievance procedure which sets out the 'players' to be involved in each stage of the procedure. When processing the grievance, the management and the employee's representative meet at the different stages on the basis of equality. So if, for example, as the third stage of the procedure stipulates, the employee's representative and the chief executive/managing director ultimately meet to try to resolve the grievance and the meeting is held in the managing director's office, they interact with each other as employment relations players and therefore of equal status. A professional managing director will always treat the employee's representative as such and ensure that he or she has the proper facilities (seating, appropriate space for their documents, etc) to represent his or her 'client' in a businesslike manner.

The grievance procedure also protects the employee representative from a refusal by the representative's front-line manager/team leader to allow him or her to leave his or her job to represent his or her 'client's' interests. The procedure is management's acceptance that in certain circumstances the individual employee's role as an employment relations player takes preference over his or her role as an employee. And because in managing grievances management and employee representatives are equal partners, they have a joint responsibility for settling grievances.

This equality relationship in grievance-handling is difficult for some line managers to understand. Many find it hard to recognise employee representatives other than as employees of the company and therefore subject to their control and direction. Some managers will never come to terms with the status distinction, relative to management, between the individual as an employee representative and the individual as an employee under their supervision and direction. They feel that their authority is undermined by more senior managers treating employees, when wearing their representative hats, as equals. They find it difficult to understand why their senior managers show so much consideration and grant such facilities towards individuals who they perceive as merely employees of the organisation. It is therefore an important responsibility for the employment relations professional to ensure that the management involved in grievance-handling understand, and accept, this equality of status in employment relations roles.

## THE OPERATION OF THE PROCEDURE

### The role of the employment relations professional

Grievance procedures are an integral part of the whole way in which an organisation is managed. They directly affect line management at all levels. Line managers have always had the main responsibility for operating the grievance procedure, assisted and advised by the employment relations professional. It is important that the employment relations professional does not take on board line managers' problems and take responsibility for them. It has become standard practice in modern organisations for team leaders/front-line managers to manage people in partnership with human resource managers (Kelly and Gennard, 1997; Whittaker and Marchington, 2003; Renwick, 2003). The role of the employment relations professional in managing grievances is therefore to:

- identify line management training and development needs with regard to managing grievances. It is important to train line managers both to listen to grievances properly and to deal with them in a consistent manner. This is where HR is important to arrange such training and act as the moderator to ensure fair and consistent action

- devise and implement a training and development programme so that line managers can acquire and develop the skills necessary to become effective managers of employee grievances

- ensure that line managers have a clear understanding of the way in which grievance procedures are intended to operate

- devise a grievance procedure which conforms with 'good practice' and spells out what has to happen at each stage, and why

- promote awareness among line managers of 'good practice' in managing grievances

- ensure that employees are aware of their rights under the procedure

- promote a constructive grievance policy at board level.

The employment relations professional also has an important role to play in monitoring and reviewing the operation of the grievance procedure, and in recommending revisions to its design or operation. This involves reviewing the outcomes of the grievance decisions taken following the procedure and assessing whether these outcomes have been those intended and desired by the management – and if not, why not. (For example, is it because line managers are not undertaking a thorough investigation of the complaint?) This review and monitor function also requires the employment relations professional to analyse the subject matter of individual employee grievances, to consider why the outcomes have been what they have, and to check that the procedure has been applied in all cases fairly and consistently (ie that management have behaved reasonably in processing employee grievances). It is thought that only a quarter (25%) of organisations monitor the outcome of resolving employee grievances on a regular basis.

### The role of the line manager

The front-line manager remains a key player in the operation of a grievance procedure. The filing of a grievance by an employee may be seen by front-line managers as reflecting badly on their managerial competence. If grievance procedures are to operate effectively, senior management must reassure front-line managers that their managerial competence may have nothing at all to do with the matter. On the contrary, front-line managers should be encouraged by their own line managers to hear and listen properly to grievances. It is important that front-line managers become aware of employee dissatisfaction as early as possible and deal with them in a consistent manner. It is usually easier to resolve grievances informally in a manner satisfactory to individuals and their managers if they are handled as quickly and as close to the source of the complaint as possible.

The front-line manager has the least executive authority, and this limits his or her ability (as well as confidence) to make decisions without reference to a more senior manager. If a front-line manager/team leader frequently refers a grievance up to a superior, the employee will realise that a possibly quicker way of having their problem resolved is to short-circuit the first-line manager and go directly to their superior. If this happens, the legitimate authority of the front-line manager becomes undermined. This then threatens the credibility of the procedure, since what has happened in reality is a reduction in the number of stages in the procedure. The ultimate impact is to remove the grievance from its source of origin, to slow down the process by having to refer the complaint back through its correct stages, to cause confusion and to create bad feeling. To avoid this happening, the employment relations professional must ensure three things – that:

- everyone knows, within the procedure, the limits of their own and others' authority
- the procedures are operated consistently by line managers
- front-line managers have the authority to settle grievances.

In situations where union workplace representatives believe that front-line managers are unable to take a decision at the appropriate level, good practice requires management to insist that the procedure be followed. Management thereby demonstrate that they will apply the procedure consistently, and that its operation is understood by those managers who have a part to play in its operation. It is essential that front-line managers have the authority to deal with as many types of grievances as possible. The front-line manager/team leader has to be able to say 'yes' as well as 'no'.

It is equally important that front-line management continues to be involved in the settling of grievances even if the complaint proceeds beyond the stage at which they are formally involved. This can be achieved by their attendance at subsequent meetings or at the very least by being kept informed of the outcome as the grievance proceeds through subsequent stages of the procedure. It is bad management practice for a front-line manager to hear the outcome of an employee's complaint first from the employee himself or herself and/or his or her representative.

## GRIEVANCE RECORDS

When a grievance progresses to a higher stage in the procedure, documentation of what happened at the previous stage is needed by those managers who now become involved for the first time and are not familiar with the issues involved. In practice, the extent to which records of grievances are kept varies widely. In some organisations the completion of grievance records is a required activity for front-line management. In others, only the personnel/HRM department keeps records. In yet others no documentation of any kind is kept except when an employee complaint progresses to the external stage of the procedure. The ACAS Code of Practice on *Disciplinary and Grievance Procedures* advises employers to keep a written record of any grievance cases with which they deal. Records should include the nature of the grievance, what was decided, the action taken, the reason for the action, whether an appeal was lodged, the outcome of the appeal, and any subsequent developments. Records have to be treated as confidential. Summaries or transcriptions of meetings should be given to the employee, including copies of any formal minutes that may have been taken.

Grievance records serve useful purposes for management. If there is a failure to agree at any stage, a written record clarifies the complaint and the arguments put forward about it by the individual employee and/or his or her representative. Such a record is also helpful to those managers involved in the next stage of the procedure. If the record is agreed by both parties – as commonly completed by the manager concerned and countersigned by the employee and/or his or her representative – it is even more valuable. Grievance record forms assist the personnel/HRM function to keep in touch with the progress of unresolved grievances and to analyse trends in the use and outcomes of the grievance procedure. Analysis of the record will show where, and why, delays in the procedure occur more frequently. When a resolution to the individual's grievance has been reached, a written and agreed statement helps ensure that there are no misunderstandings over what has been agreed. In the absence of an agreed statement, the parties may find they have different versions of what they thought they had actually agreed. A written statement is also useful for communicating the outcome of the employee's complaint.

However, systems which require line management to keep records of grievances are not easy to maintain unless management keep a watchful eye on matters. Some front-line managers who handle grievances complain that having to keep grievance records is an extra, irksome administrative chore. Grievance record systems at the front-line level will not operate effectively without the careful observation of more senior management.

---

### ? REFLECTIVE ACTIVITY

Does your organisation keep grievance records? If not, why not? If it does, what information does the record contain, and why?

---

## THE LAW

### THE EMPLOYMENT RELATIONS ACT (1999)

The Employment Relations Act (1999) introduced the right for workers to be accompanied at grievance hearings. Where the worker is required or invited by his or her employer to attend certain categories of grievance hearings and the worker reasonably requests to be accompanied, the employer must permit the worker to bring along a companion of his or her choice. The companion must be either a trade union official or a fellow-worker. This right was based on the widespread practice of allowing a chosen companion to attend these key meetings. Unsurprisingly, empirical evidence – for example, the Department for Trade and Industry study mentioned above – shows that this right has been applied unevenly. Very large workplaces (with 250 or more employees) all meet statutory requirements regarding being accompanied. The smaller the workplace, the less likely it is that employees will have access to being accompanied. The former DTI research (Saundry and Antcliff, 2006) shows that those workplaces that offered 'proper' accompaniment at grievance hearings were likely to have lower rates of employment tribunal applications. It also showed that large multi-site establishments dealt with grievance issues in a highly formalised manner. There are a number of reasons for this. As plant size increases, a procedural approach is vital if issues are to be handled consistently and effectively. Larger workplaces are also likely to be unionised and have a high degree of expertise in the shape of a specialist HR/personnel function. Smaller family-owned independent workplaces tend to handle matters in a more informal and personalised way. In many cases the way in which they deal with employee grievances does not meet minimum statutory requirements. Such workplaces are less likely to be highly unionised or to have a high level of HR knowledge or management expertise.

### THE EMPLOYMENT ACT (2002)

This Act set out statutory disputes resolution procedures and the consequences of failure to comply with them. Its statutory grievance procedure complemented the legal right to be accompanied in workplace hearings by a trade union official or fellow-worker of the employee's choice. The 'model' statutory internal grievance procedure formed part of the implied terms of all employment contracts and was binding on employees and employers irrespective of workforce size. The 2002 Act for the first time provided that employers were required to have procedures for dealing with employee grievances. These provisions were designed to encourage parties to avoid litigation by resolving their differences through proper internal procedures. The standard statutory grievance procedure had three steps: the employee sets out the basis of his or her grievance, the grievance meeting, and the appeal meeting.

## THE EMPLOYMENT ACT (2008)

The Government set up an independent review of the three stages of the statutory grievance procedure, led by Michael Gibbons. The Gibbons Review of the Employment Disputes Resolution process was published on 21 March 2007. Thereafter, the Government published a consultation paper setting out measures for taking the Gibbons Review forward. It sought views on a package of measures to help solve employment disputes successfully in the workplace, with the expressed intention that:

- productivity would be raised through improved workplace relations
- there would be access to justice for employees and employers
- the cost of resolving disputes would be reduced for all parties
- disputes would be resolved swiftly before they escalated.

Following the completion of the consultation period, the Government on 7 December 2007 presented the Employment Bill to Parliament. This subsequently became the Employment Act (2008), which became effective on 6 April 2009. From this date, the mandatory three-step process for grievances raised by an employee was replaced. Employment tribunals were now to decide cases on the basis of what was fair and reasonable, with the assistance of a revised ACAS Code of Practice – a non-statutory guide to disciplinary and grievance procedures establishing the principles of what an employer and an employee should do. In addition, the Government invested up to £37 million in additional resources for ACAS both to provide an enhanced helpline with extended opening hours and to offer employers and employees early consultation for problems that represent potential employment tribunal claims. As a result of the Act, employees and employers have greater flexibility to deal with workplace discipline and grievance issues in a way that suits each of them best.

## THE ACAS REVISED CODE OF PRACTICE

The ACAS revised Code of Practice on *Disciplinary and Grievance Procedures* became operative on 6 April 2009. Although a failure to follow the Code does not render an employer liable to any proceedings, the Code is admissible in evidence and can be taken into account by employment tribunals. The Code provides guidance on minimum standards for dealing with grievance matters. It advises that employees should let their employer know the nature of their grievance, and that the employer should arrange a meeting to allow the employee to explain the matter. Once the employer has decided on an appropriate course of action, the employer should give the employee an opportunity to appeal. The revised Code also sets out key principles to be followed in managing employee grievances:

- grievance issues must be dealt with promptly and consistently
- an appropriate investigation must be carried out
- meetings should be held by managers with no previous involvement in the case
- employees must be allowed to put their case
- employees may be accompanied in meetings
- employees must have the right of appeal.

The revised Code on *Disciplinary and Grievance Procedures* (2009) is the fifth version of the Code produced by ACAS since it was first published in 1977. The fourth version came into force on 1 October 2004 at the same time as the statutory three-step dispute resolution procedures. The revised Code of 2009 represents a broad return to the pre-2004 position, albeit in a new form.

## ❓ REFLECTIVE ACTIVITY

How has your organisation responded to the right of employees to be accompanied in grievance hearings? If it has not responded, why hasn't it? If it has responded, in what way, and why, did it react in this way?

## MANAGING GRIEVANCES

Much of an employment relations professional's time can be taken up in dealing with individual employees' problems or complaints. Most employee grievances are, however, dealt with satisfactorily before they reach the formal grievance procedure.

For example, take the case of an employee who claims that she has received an incorrect amount of pay. There are a number of possible ways this might be resolved.

- On checking, management accept that the amount of pay due has been miscalculated and rectifies the matter immediately. The grievance is resolved to everyone's satisfaction –

or

- The payment is correct, although the employee believes that she has been underpaid. There is no genuine grievance, and either of two things might happen now:

    – the situation is discussed and explained adequately and the matter is resolved

    – the employer fails to explain the details to the satisfaction of the employee, who still believes that she has been treated unfairly (even though that is not the case). Now there is a possibility that a collective complaint might develop, and if this happens, a simple problem is taken up to an inappropriate level –

or

- The details of the complaint are accepted by the employer who nevertheless fails to take corrective action quickly. Another grievance arises which takes the place of the original. The employee was relying on a correct payment to meet commitments but now cannot do so because the company is 'holding on' to her money.

The first possibility is obviously the preferred one because it puts right a genuine error promptly and efficiently. The second part of the second possibility and also the third possibility carry the risk of generating feelings of mistrust and suspicion.

However, not all grievances are of so simple a nature and can be resolved quickly. Management deal with all grievances in a competent and systematic manner, which involves a number of stages:

1  hearing the grievance

2  preparing for the meeting with the employee and/or his or her representative

3  meeting with the employee and/or his or her representative

4  confirming the common ground between the employee and the management

5  resolving the grievance

6  reporting the outcome.

## THE GRIEVANCE INTERVIEW

The grievance interview enables an individual to state his or her complaint, and management to discover and remove the cause of the employee's dissatisfaction. When explaining their grievance, employees should stick to the facts and avoid language that may be considered insulting or abusive. If the grievance is against the line manager, the employee may approach another manager or raise the issue with his or her HR department (if there is one). It is helpful if the grievance procedure sets out who the individual should approach in these circumstances. From the interview, management collect the facts of the situation, analyse the problem and, if appropriate, decide the action to resolve the grievance. Good management practice in preparation for a grievance interview is to check on the employee's employment record with the organisation. Although circumstances and time pressures may make this impossible, it is worth remembering that an employee with a grievance against management may be angry and possibly adopt an aggressive attitude. If this turns out to be the case, management must calm down the individual. When an individual loses his or her temper, management have to guard against responding in a similar way or being provoked into such a reaction. This can easily happen when faced with an aggressive employee critical of management's behaviour. Few people think rationally when they are angry.

Gathering information about an employee's grievance is extremely important. If incorrect, or insufficient, information is collected, it is likely to lead to a wrong analysis and an incorrect decision. Competent interviewing, watching and listening skills are crucial in this regard.

By the end of the interview, the manager will have an understanding of the employee's grievance and how he or she would like to see it resolved. If the employee's grievance is, for example, that he or she has been denied access to a training opportunity, the manager will explain to the employee why he or she was denied the opportunity. The employee, in turn, will also have the opportunity to explain to management how he or she wishes to see the complaint dealt with – perhaps, for example, enrolling him or her on the next available appropriate training opportunity. The 'why' question is always the most difficult to which to get an answer, since an individual always presents a favourable view of his or her case, withholding information that weakens it. The golden rule is, however, that the manager must gather all the facts, including those that might make the individual's case against management less clear-cut.

Management require all the facts. They have to make a decision on whether the employee's grievance is genuine and well-founded, and if it is, what action to take. If the grievance interview fails to bring out vital information, the manager may conclude – wrongly – that the employee does not have a genuine complaint. On the basis of the information collected from the grievance interview the manager makes an assessment of the complaint/problem. He or she decides upon an appropriate course of action, explaining to the individual employee, to the employee's representative and to managerial colleagues why he or she has decided upon that action.

### Unfounded grievances

At the end of the interview, management may conclude that the grievance is unfounded because:

- the real problem is a clash of personality between the individual employee and his or her immediate manager, or
- the employee has misunderstood something crucial (for example, a company rule).

Grievances can be actual or unfounded, and distinguishing between them is an important responsibility of both employer and employee representatives. They have a common interest to avoid wasting time, resources, effort and emotion in putting inappropriate issues through formal procedures. However, as we have stressed throughout this chapter, all grievances are important to the individual concerned – so if management receive a complaint which they judge to be ill-founded, it is not good practice to dismiss it in an arbitrary manner. They should:

- find out why, and how, it happened

- explain clearly and openly why it is a complaint which merits no action.

This not only sets the record straight but also allows everyone to see that even an imagined rather than a real complaint is being handled seriously. For instance, some organisations have accepted employment conditions which include the option of changing the location at which individuals work. Local authorities, for example, with offices in towns across their areas sometimes need to move their officers around to cover short- or long-term absences, and this is usually set out in employment contracts and/or collective agreements. In this case, an employee required to move location but who did not wish to do so would not have a legitimate grievance. However, if the employee did raise a complaint, it would have to be discussed and resolved as early as possible. This would provide the opportunity to clarify the facts of the situation and to forestall the individual from building up long-term resentment and thus damaging long-term relationships.

Since in the above case the grievance is imagined rather than real, management's action (ie relocation) is within the bounds of accepted behaviour. Nobody is acting contrary to the accepted way of behaving – even though the employee does not like the action that is taking place – there is no real grievance to be settled. Nonetheless, the employee's case has to be heard and the issue dealt with, if only to clarify the situation. It is important that the issue is handled in a way which avoids the individual's feeling ignored or snubbed.

### Genuine grievance

On the other hand, the manager may conclude – after interviewing the employee laying the complaint – that further information is required about the grievance before management's attitude to the issue can be established. (For example, what does the agreement say? What is company policy on the issue? Are there any witnesses or other people with relevant information who should also be interviewed?) In such circumstances management will make arrangements with the employee and his or her representative for a further meeting. Alternatively, following the grievance interview management may decide that the employee's grievance is genuine, be prepared to seek a resolution to the matter, but require time to prepare a considered response. In this situation management will also try to make arrangements on when and where next to meet with the employee and/ or his or her representative to resolve the issue.

## Explain how you would deal with the following situation.

You are the owner of a small firm. An employee has been complaining that she is being given too much work and cannot complete it on time. You have told the employee that her predecessor had no problem completing the same amount of work and that things got easier with experience. The employee is not happy and has put her grievance to you in writing.

One possible course of action would be, first, to invite the employee to a meeting to discuss the grievance, at the same time informing her of her right to be accompanied to that meeting.

The meeting reveals that:

- the employee has been working on a computer that is different from the one used by her predecessor

- the computer she has been using is slower, and uses an older version of the software required to carry out the work.

You decide to upgrade the computer, to provide the employee with training in how to use it, and to review the situation in a month's time.

You put this in writing, and you inform the employee of her right to an appeal meeting if she feels that her grievance has not been satisfactorily resolved.

## PLANNING TO MEET WITH THE EMPLOYEE AND HIS OR HER REPRESENTATIVE

More complex grievances which could potentially develop into a collective grievance require a more sophisticated approach. In such circumstances, there are normally three main stages to preparing to meet with the individual employee and his or her representative to negotiate a settlement to the individual's grievance. These are:

- analysis (or the research stage)
- establishment of the aims as to how the grievance can be resolved while at the same time protecting management's interests
- planning the strategy and tactics to achieve the established aims.

### Analysis

The analysis stage involves management's collecting and analysing relevant information to substantiate their proposals for resolving the individual employee's grievance. It also includes developing the argument(s) to be put to the employee and his or her representative to support management's case. In managing grievances the main sources of relevant information are the management colleagues and employees who are regarded as likely to have factually useful information (for example, they witnessed the incident about which the employee is complaining) relevant to the issue that is the subject of the complaint.

The analysis stage also involves management's checking whether the subject matter of the grievance has been complained of previously by employees, and if so, what the outcome was. Knowledge of such outcomes enables management to know whether any precedent exists for dealing with the employee's grievance. Other important management activities in the analysis stage include asking:

- Are any company rules relevant?
- Is custom and practice relevant?
- Are any collective agreements or personal contracts relevant?

The most important activity for management in the preparation stage is the identification of the exact details of the employee's complaint. Some of these details are more important to the complainant's argument than others, and some of them are more significant to the management's view of the matters than others. Any agreement on a resolution may be reached by the parties 'trading off' the importance of these details surrounding the issue but retaining certain principles. In making a decision about which 'details' to trade, management assess their significance to the complaint and try to anticipate which 'details' they believe the employee will be prepared to trade in return.

- For the purposes of illustration, let us assume that management have encountered a young male employee swearing in the presence of a front-line manager and suspended him from work for three working days without pay. The employee considers the penalty too harsh, and with his representative approaches management to register this fact.

Management might take the view that, in the light of the offence, for the employee to escape any disciplinary penalty would be unacceptable. However, before finally reaching this decision it is important to assess how strongly the individual's work colleagues feel about the harshness of the disciplinary penalty. Would they be prepared, for example, to impose industrial sanctions against the company? If they would, how successful might such action be? If the conclusion is that the employees would not take the issue to a collective dispute, then management can be confident that the initial penalty can be upheld. However, if the conclusion is the opposite, management are likely to take the view that although the principle of the imposition of a disciplinary penalty cannot be compromised, the severity of the penalty might be reduced.

### The establishment of aims

In situations such as that described above, it is important to recognise that some form of meeting will then take place between an aggrieved employee and their representative in order to resolve the perceived injustice. In order to achieve a satisfactory conclusion it is important that clear management objectives are set prior to any meeting taking place. For example:

How would they ideally like the grievance to be resolved?

- How do they think the grievance can realistically be resolved?
- What is the least for which management will settle (the fall-back position)?

As part of the objective-setting process it might be appropriate to construct an aspiration grid (see Chapter 11). A possible aspiration grid for management is shown in Table 13.3. It shows that management would ideally like the original penalty to stand. However, management have assessed this as an unrealistic position, and have established a 'realistic' position of a compromise resolution centring on a penalty of two days' suspension (rather than three) and no recovery of pay. Their fall-back position is to reduce the suspension to one day but with no recovery of lost pay

Table 13.3  Aspiration grid: grid centring on three days' suspension without pay

| Possible resolution to grievance | MANAGEMENT | | | EMPLOYEE | | |
|---|---|---|---|---|---|---|
| | Ideal | Real | Fall-back | Fall-back | Real | Ideal |
| 3 days' suspension – pay restored | X | X | X | O | O | X |
| 2 days' suspension – pay restored | X | X | X | O | O | X |
| 1 day's suspension – pay restored | X | X | X | O | X | X |
| 2 days' suspension – no pay | X | X | O | O | O | X |
| 1 day's suspension – no pay | X | O | O | O | O | X |

Remember: **O** means prepared to trade; **X** means not prepared to trade

Using an aspiration grid can help identify if there is a basis for a resolution to the employee's complaint and can help when meeting with the individual employee and their representative. At this point you would expect to present a broad picture of your proposals for resolving the grievance subject to discussion and negotiation between the parties.

## RESOLVING THE GRIEVANCE

If a manager is unable to find a resolution to the grievance, the matter can be referred to the next stage in the procedure at which a higher-level manager will prepare, present and try to find a mutually acceptable solution. When a grievance remains unresolved, the manager in passing the matter to the next stage must check that the complaint is taken up at that level, and not just lost sight of.

However, when a resolution to a grievance is found – but before finally accepting that the resolution has been agreed – management must:

- be convinced that the employee understands what has been agreed
- 'play back' to the employee what management understand the resolution of the grievance actually means, to prevent any misunderstanding from arising.

If this process reveals that the employee has indeed misunderstood what has been agreed, and that the misunderstanding cannot be cleared up in further discussion, the negotiations will have to restart.

Once management have an oral agreement for the resolution of the employee's grievance, it should be written up. In many grievances this will take the form of an internal memo/letter to another manager and to the employee recording what has been agreed. For example, if the complaint was one of denial of or access to a training opportunity, and it is upheld via the grievance-handling process, a manager will write to the personnel or the appropriate department reporting it has been agreed that the individual concerned should attend the next available appropriate training course. On the other hand, 'writing up' can – depending on the issue – take the form of a signed agreement by the manager concerned, the individual employee and his or her representative. The outcome is then reported to the appropriate interested parties. Clarity is important, and the manner in which what has been agreed is recorded should leave no room for doubt.

## REFLECTIVE ACTIVITY

Outline the skills required of managers in successfully handling grievances. Which do you consider to be the most important – and why?

## THE APPEAL MEETING

Where an employee feels that his or her grievance has not been satisfactorily resolved (ie he or she is unhappy with the decision) at the grievance meeting, he or she has the right of appeal. The employee should inform the employer of the grounds for his or her appeal without unreasonable delay and in writing. Appeals should likewise be heard without unreasonable delay, and at a time and place that should be notified to the employee well in advance. The appeal has to be handled with impartiality and by a more senior manager than the one who dealt with the original grievance. This senior manager must not previously have been involved in the case. Employees have a statutory right to be accompanied at any such appeal hearing. The outcome of the appeal must be communicated without unreasonable delay.

In small organisations, even when there is no senior manager available, another manager should, if possible, hear the appeal. If this is not possible, consider whether the owner or, in the case of a charity, the Board of Trustees, should hear the appeal. Whoever hears the appeal should consider it as impartially as possible. As with the first meeting, the employer should write to the employee with a decision on his or her grievance as soon as possible. The employer should also tell the employee if the appeal meeting is the final stage of the grievance procedure. Some larger organisations do permit a further appeal to a higher level of management, such as a director.

## SPECIFIC ISSUES/SPECIFIC PROCEDURES

The grievance procedure deals with the broad range of complaints and problems. However, some areas of organisational life have their own specific list of potentially thorny issues. These include:

- job grading and evaluation
- complaints by one employee about the behaviour of another
- sexual harassment
- discrimination in promotion and advancement.

So while some employee complaints remain general grievances, others are best dealt with by specific procedures designed to deal with the type of difficulties inherent in certain issues.

### REFLECTIVE ACTIVITY

Does your organisation have special issues/grievance procedures? If it does, what issues do they cover? Why do these specific procedures exist?

### JOB GRADING APPEAL PROCEDURES

Job evaluation helps determine the appropriate level of a job as measured against criteria such as decision-making, working conditions (for example, exposure to hazards, working in the open air as against in an office, etc), contacts within and outside the organisation, the degree of supervision received, the complexity of the work (for example, gathering and inputting data as opposed to gathering and then manipulating data to produce a report with recommendations) within the organisation's structure. The appropriate level in the structure influences the pay level and seniority associated with the job.

A grievance that centres on such an issue arises mostly when an individual claims that his or her job has changed relative to when it was last evaluated because it now carries greater responsibility for:

- people (in terms of supervising and training them)
- financial resources (increased budget, financial control)
- physical resources (modern high-tech expensive equipment)

– and therefore warrants a higher grading and level of remuneration.

On the other hand, management may argue that the post has not changed in responsibility and that what has changed is an increase in the volume of tasks, at the same level of responsibility. It therefore makes sense in resolving such a dispute to have a procedure tailored to cover the specific circumstances of job grading, including access to specialist and expert individuals.

In a typical job evaluation appeals procedure, the first stage normally requires the individual employee to discuss the basis of his or her appeal with his or her immediate line manager/team leader. The second stage normally requires the individual to complete a 'formal appeal form', which then goes before a meeting of a job evaluation appeals panel. The complainant, accompanied by his or her representative, presents the case to the appeals panel, as does the employer. The appeals panel will decide either to upgrade the job or to reject the appeal. The decision is usually communicated to the individual through his or her line manager. If the appeal is upheld, the decision will be implemented from the date of the panel's decision.

If the job-holder is dissatisfied with the decision of the appeals panel, he or she may request that the case goes to a third stage and be heard by an independent appeal body. At this stage the job-holder (assisted by his or her representative) will present the basis of the appeal, a member of the appeals panel will present justification for its decision and the independent appeal body – which is usually chaired by an independent chairperson acceptable to both parties – will make a decision that is final and binding. In some organisations with job-evaluated grading structures, this means that individual grievances over job gradings are, at the end of the day, decided by arbitration.

A job evaluation procedure is relatively clear-cut and straightforward. It has the advantage over the standard grievance procedure of building in access to experts at each appeal stage and providing more specialist panels to hear the appeals.

### DIGNITY AT WORK

Harassment based on gender, race and disability, and bullying at work have received increasing attention in recent years as organisations and worker representative bodies have become more concerned about the dignity of individuals in the workplace. Many organisations have policies and procedures which link the complaints procedure on harassment and bullying with the existing grievance procedure rather than establishing separate arrangements for such complaints. Others have treated it as a specific issue. Both approaches work.

Harassment, in general terms, is:

Unwanted conduct affecting the dignity of men and women in the workplace. It may be related to age, race, disability religion, nationality or any personal characteristics of the individual, and may be persistent or an isolated incident. The key is that the actions or comments are viewed as demeaning and unacceptable to the recipient ...

Bullying may be characterised as:

Offensive, intimidating, malicious or insulting behaviour, an abuse or misuse of power through means intended to undermine, humiliate, denigrate or injure the recipient ...

Bullying or harassment may be what one individual does to another individual (perhaps by someone in a position of authority, such as a manager or front-line manager) or involve groups of people. It may be obvious or it may be insidious. Whatever form it takes, it is unwarranted and unwelcome to the recipient individual. Bullying and/or harassing includes:

- spreading malicious rumours or insulting someone by word or behaviour

- copying memos that are critical about someone to others who do not need to know

- ridiculing or demeaning someone – picking on him or her or setting him or her up to fail

- unwelcome sexual advances – touching, standing too close, a display of offensive materials

- deliberately undermining a competent worker by overloading and constant criticism.

Bullying and/or harassment make someone feel anxious and humiliated. Feelings of anger and frustration at being unable to cope may be triggered. Some employees may try to retaliate in some way. Others may become frightened and demotivated. Stress, loss of self-confidence and self-esteem caused by bullying and/or harassment can lead to job insecurity, illness, absence from work and even resignation. Almost always job performance is affected and relations in the workplace suffer.

Employers are responsible for preventing bullying and harassing behaviour. It is in their interests to make it clear to everyone that such behaviour will not be tolerated. The costs to the organisation may include poor employment relations, low morale, lower productivity and efficiency, and potentially the resignation of staff. An organisational statement to all staff about the standards expected can make it easier for all individuals to be fully aware of their responsibilities to others.

In organisations where a harassment policy exists, it is normal for a dual system to operate. The initial action is usually confined to the specifics of the complaint within the procedure laid down for managing harassment and/or bullying. If the problem cannot be resolved within the limits of the policy and is proved to be an issue that merits disciplinary proceedings, the disciplinary procedure is triggered.

When an employee complains that he or she has suffered harassment and/or bullying from another employee, whether a manager or not, he or she has a grievance. He or she is, in fact, making a complaint to management. In dealing with allegations of harassment and/or bullying, the manager first conducts a thorough investigation to establish whether there is a *prima facie* case of harassment and/or bullying for the accused employee to answer. If the manager decides, on the basis of the investigation, that there is a case to answer, disciplinary proceedings are likely to be instigated against the accused employee.

However, this is conditional on the 'victim' agreeing to allow the issue to be taken to this stage. If the victim refuses to proceed any further with the matter – that is the end of it. If the disciplinary proceedings are started against the accused individual and the charge of harassment and/or bullying is upheld, an appropriate penalty will be imposed – up to and including, often as a last resort, dismissal of the employee. If, on the other hand, the manager decides that the harassment and/or bullying allegation has no foundation, the manager will explain fully to the 'victim' and his or her representative why this is the case.

So if a manager is sitting in his or her office and a woman employee comes in claiming that she has been sexually harassed and she has witnesses and wants action taken against the individual concerned, it is clear what the manager must do:

- investigate the claim thoroughly
- decide whether there is a case to answer
- if there is a case to answer and it cannot be settled amicably, and the 'victim' insists on pressing the complaint, initiate the disciplinary procedure
- if there is no case to answer, explain this carefully and sensitively to the 'victim'.

Different organisations define their acceptable standards of behaviour differently, particularly with respect to gross misconduct. In some organisations harassment and/or bullying is regarded as gross misconduct, carrying instant dismissal if proved. That this is the case will be spelled out to employees in the organisation's policy statement on sexual harassment and/or dignity at work. It is not the case in all organisations, however, for in some lesser penalties can, and are, imposed on the harasser.

There are therefore good reasons for dealing with harassment and/or bullying complaints outside of the general grievance procedure. First, there is a reasonable chance that the person who is the subject of the complaint is the line manager of the employee making the complaint. This can make it difficult to resolve the grievance as near to the point of its origin as possible. Second, there is a link between grievance, discipline and harassment. The role of the employment relations professional in harassment/bullying complaints is to act as a back-up for line managers in managing the issue, by providing them with general expertise and support, including access to training programmes to handle dignity at work issues.

## REFLECTIVE ACTIVITY

Briefly explain the process you would adopt when dealing with a case of alleged sexual harassment or bullying by one employee against another.

## OTHER AREAS

Other complex areas of employee complaint which justify having separate grievance procedures include discrimination in promotion and alleged unequal treatment in terms of pay, overtime, travel, etc. Each case is unique and requires thorough investigation before deciding whether the grievance is real or imagined, whether the offence is proven, and whether informal or formal action through procedures is appropriate. All cases of grievance have to be handled with equal care. Procedures offer the means for management to behave in a fair, reasonable and consistent manner in managing grievances.

## SUMMARY

This chapter began by examining the business case for resolving employee grievances, defining a grievance and identifying the issues that are most frequently the cause of employee grievances. It then went on to explain that the effective resolution of grievances, unlike bargaining, excludes a trade-off on the part of management between different employee complaints about management behaviour. The chapter also explained the extent to which employees take up (or do not take up) grievances, analysed the underlying principles of a grievance procedure, and described the main features of a typical procedure (ie the number of stages, time-limits, the representation of employees, etc).

The chapter further examined the operation of grievance procedures and the role of employment relations professionals in managing employee grievances (for example, the promotion of 'good practice' in managing grievances among line managers). In addition, it outlined the legal framework surrounding grievance management. The chapter then went on to point out that many grievances are of a simple nature and are resolved quickly – but that this is by no means always the case. The managing of complex employee grievances involves a number of stages – hearing the grievance (the grievance interview), preparing to meet the employee (analysis, establish aims, plan strategy and tactics), meeting with the employee and/or his or her representative, confirming as the basis for a successful resolution of the grievances the common ground between the employee and management, resolving the grievance, and reporting the outcome. The chapter also explained how crucial in managing employee grievances effectively it is that a manager is able to distinguish the genuine employee complaint from an unfounded one.

It was also pointed out in the chapter that the grievance procedure deals with the broad range of employee complaints and problems but that there are issues best dealt with by procedures designed to deal with specific difficulties that can arise from handling such issues. These include job grading and evaluation, complaints by one employee about the behaviour of another, sexual harassment, bullying and discrimination in promotion and advancement.

KEY LEARNING POINTS

- In resolving employee grievances, management must treat each complaint on its merits, accepting that each is a serious issue for the individual concerned. An employee's grievance has to be dealt with independently of the grievance of another employee. Management must proceed on the basis of one at a time. In managing employee grievances management should resolve one individual's complaint over a particular issue (for example, the denial of a training opportunity) and then move on to settle another employee's grievance over a different issue.

- Most employee complaints against management behaviour do not reach the formal grievance procedure.

- The grievance procedure ensures that employees are treated in a fair and consistent manner and they know where they stand and know what to expect. In managing employee complaints, management are guided by a number of principles – fairness, transparency, consistency and promptness. The grievance procedure ensures this.

- In managing grievances, management's objective is to settle the employee's complaint as near as possible to the point of its source.

- Although a failure to follow the ACAS Code of Practice on *Disciplinary and Grievance Procedures* does not render an employer liable to any proceedings, the Code is admissible in evidence and can be taken into account by employment tribunals.

- On the basis of a grievance interview, a manager can conclude whether the employee grievance is genuine or not. If the manager considers the grievance is unfounded, he or she must explain clearly to the individual why this is the case.

- If the manager decides that the grievance is genuine, he or she will consider how the grievance might be resolved and plan a strategy and tactics to achieve this aim. At the grievance meeting the manager will seek confirmation of the anticipated common ground for a resolution to the grievance. If the employee is not happy with the proposed resolution, he or she has the right to appeal.

## REVIEW QUESTIONS

1  Frank has been given the most unpopular job in this department for three weeks in a row. He thinks this is unfair and that the supervisor should be sharing it among all the employees in his department. You are the HR representative, and Frank has approached you and voiced his discontent. How do you deal with the situation, and why do you take this approach?

2  You are responsible for conducting workshops for new line managers on employment relations techniques. One of the topics you have been asked to deal with is managing employee complaints in the workplace. Explain, and justify, the key areas of knowledge and skills that you would cover in your workshop.

3  Explain, and justify, the criteria you would use to evaluate whether a grievance procedure was operating effectively.

4  An employee has approached you as her HR adviser. She feels that she is being bullied by her line manager and asks for your advice. She reports that the line manager constantly shouts at her in front of colleagues. She also alleges that he has made sexual innuendoes to her. What advice do you give the employee, and how will you deal with the situation?

5  Explain the principles that underpin a grievance procedure.

EXPLORE FURTHER

Advisory, Conciliation and Arbitration Service (2009) *Code of Practice on Disciplinary and Grievance Procedures.* London: ACAS.

Advisory, Conciliation and Arbitration Service (April 2009) *Bullying and Harassment: A guide for employers.* London: ACAS.

Advisory, Conciliation and Arbitration Service (1997) *Guide for Small Firms: Dealing with grievances.* London: ACAS.

Gaymer, J. (2004) 'Making a molehill out of a mountain', *People Management*, 26 February.

Industrial Relations Services (2002) 'Don't nurse a grievance: resolving disputes at work', *Employment Trends*, No 759, September.

Jackson, T. (2000) *Handling Grievances.* London: Chartered Institute of Personnel and Development.

Kelly, J. and Gennard, J. (1997) 'The unimportance of labels: the diffusion of the personnel/HRM function', *Industrial Relations Journal*, Vol.28, No.1.

Kersley, B., Alpin, C., Forth, J., Bryson, A., Bewley, H., Dix, G. and Oxenbridge, S. (2006) *Inside the Workplace: Findings from the 2004 Workplace Employment Relations Survey.* London: Routledge.

Renwick, D. (2000) 'HR line work relations: a review, pilot case and research agenda', *Employee Relations*, Vol.22, No.2.

Renwick, D. and Gennard, J. (2001) 'Grievance and discipline: a new set of concerns', in Redman, T. and Wilkinson, A. (eds) *Contemporary Human Resource Management*. Harlow: Pearson Education.

Renwick, D. (2003) 'Line manager involvement in HRM: an inside view', *Employee Relations*, Vol.25, No.3.

Rollinson, D., Hook, C., Foot, M. and Handley, J. (1996) 'Supervisor and management styles in handling discipline and grievance: Part 2 – Approaches to handling discipline and grievance', *Personnel Review*, Vol.25, No.4.

Saundry, R. and Antcliff, H. (2006) *Employee Representation in Grievance and Disciplinary Matters – Making a Difference?*, Department for Trade and Industry, Employment Relations Research Series No.69.

Torrington, D., Hall, L. and Taylor, S. (2002) *Human Resource Management*, 5th edition. Harlow: Financial times/Prentice Hall.

Whittaker, S. and Marchington, M. (2003) Devolving HR responsibility to the line: threat, opportunity or partnership?, *Employee Relations*, Volume 25, No. 3.

Web links

www.acas.org.uk is the website of ACAS and will give you access to the ACAS Code on *Grievance and Disciplinary Procedures* and other guidance for employers on employee grievance management.

## CHAPTER 14

# Managing Redundancies

## OVERVIEW

This chapter starts by examining the law surrounding the management of redundancies – for example, the Redundancy Payment Act (1965). It points out that the basic law in relation to redundancy compensation has not changed much since 1965 but there have been significant developments in respect of consultation, selection and the transfer of undertakings. Next, the chapter looks at redundancy policies and procedures, arguing that good employment relations practice dictates the need for clear policies and procedures which allow redundancy situations to be dealt with in a professional and equitable manner. The purpose of consultation is to establish whether any reduction in job numbers can be achieved by means other than compulsory redundancy – eg a ban on recruitment, retraining, voluntary redundancy and early retirement, etc. The chapter then discusses how compulsory redundancy can be managed, with particular reference to having objective criteria for the selection of the employees to be made redundant – for example, a points-scoring system based on factors such as skills, attendance and flexibility – and the basis on which employees would be compensated for the loss of their employment. Next, the chapter picks up the important question of consultation with the employees in a redundancy situation and points out that this should begin at the earliest opportunity, that the employer should provide all of the information required, that relying on 'what happened last time' may be worse than useless and be actually damaging, and that the consultation must be genuinely undertaken with 'a view to reaching an agreement' with employee representatives. The chapter concludes by examining 'good employment practice' in maintaining the well-being of the employees who remain in employment after the redundancy, covering issues such as counselling, outplacement and the problems of 'survivor syndrome' – pessimism, stress and disenchantment.

## LEARNING OUTCOMES

When you have completed this chapter, you should understand and be able to describe:

- the connection between redundancy and the management of change
- how to produce a redundancy policy and associated procedures
- the legal framework in respect of redundancy, in particular the requirements on consultation
- the need to have clear policies for managing the 'survivors' of a redundancy exercise.

## INTRODUCTION

Increasingly, since the end of World War II, but particularly since the end of the 1960s, British business has been exposed to ever-increasing competition in its own and world markets. In the 1960s, 1970s and early 1980s this tended to impact more heavily on manufacturing industry, which therefore experienced the greatest job losses. However, in the last 15 years this increase in competition has spread to the public and service sectors.

Notwithstanding the significant improvements in competitiveness of many UK businesses in the last decade, Britain has not always been successful in competing in overseas markets nor in defending home markets. In the 1970s and 1980s this supposed weakness of the British economy was variously blamed on trade union resistance to change, poor and badly trained management, too much or too little UK government spending, and a whole range of other economic and social factors. Since the mid-1990s, and notwithstanding the 2008/9 recession, the view of Britain's economy has changed and it is perceived as reasonably strong and stable, relative to those of our competitors. Yet despite this, we still see many organisations having to reduce their labour forces. As always, there are a number of factors which are blamed, depending on the circumstances at the time the labour-force reductions are taking place. At various points in time different factors have thus been blamed – an exchange rate that was too high, non-membership of the euro, a financial system geared to shareholder reward rather than capital investment, failure to invest in research and development – the list is endless.

Whatever the factor that is blamed, it highlights the point we made in Chapter 3 – namely, that the economic environment in which an organisation operates will have an influence on employment relations.

## INCREASES IN REDUNDANCY                                    THEORY

Every few years, the fluctuating nature of our economic life-cycles means that we become used to hearing the words 'downturn', 'slowdown', and 'downsize'. At different times in the economic cycle different sectors of the economy are affected. The impact of economic factors on the jobs market was reinforced during 2008/9 because of what was, by common consent, the worst recession to hit the UK for over 50 years. From the first quarter of 2008 organisations began to feel the pressure that was being generated by a downturn in financial markets. As John Philpott, Chief Economist of the CIPD, explained (*Impact*, Issue 28, August, 2009), 'by spring 2009 there were 0.4 million fewer people in employment than a year before.' Data from the Office for National Statistics (ONS) suggested that unemployment rates increased most for traditional blue-collar occupations. This was contrary to some suggestions that because of the crisis that hit the financial sector, the effects of the recession would be felt more drastically by white-collar and professional staff. In Chapter 3 we talked about the effects of globalisation, and there is no doubt that problems in the global market, increases in oil prices and instability in the Middle East can raise the spectre of large-scale redundancies. This is because global events of this kind can have an impact on a diverse number of sectors – such as travel, in which airlines have been particularly hard hit by the increase in fuel prices and increased security alerts. The CIPD *Labour Market Outlook* survey in February 2010 found that just under a fifth of employees (19%) thought that it was likely or very likely that they could lose their job as a result of the recession. The survey also identified increased worries by public sector workers over their future job security. These worries are probably justified given the sharp decreases in public expenditure that will have to take place over the next five years. For the employment relations specialist these external issues and their impact on the labour force mean that redundancy, or the possibility of redundancy, is always a factor that has to be considered – and is the reason that we are devoting a whole chapter to redundancy issues.

## THE LEGAL REGULATION OF REDUNDANCY

Prior to 1965 employees had no statutory protection in respect of redundancy. The 'right' of organisations to hire and fire at will was seen as one of those inalienable 'management rights' that were necessary if organisations were to compete successfully in a commercial world. However, by the beginning of the 1960s there was a widespread belief that economic growth was being held back because of a lack of labour mobility. The Redundancy Payments Act (1965) was part of the answer to this problem, and enjoyed the support of both major political parties as well as both sides of industry – a classic example of the post-war consensus that we discussed in Chapter 3. The Act set out for the first time that a worker with a minimum period of service was entitled to compensation for the loss of his or her job through redundancy. Compensation was decided on the basis of age and length of service, and was subject to both a maximum and a minimum amount. The basic law in relation to redundancy compensation has not changed much in the intervening years, but there have been significant developments in respect of consultation, selection and the transfer of undertakings.

## THE DEFINITION OF REDUNDANCY

In order to properly understand the way in which the law seeks to offer protection to those facing the loss of their employment there are a number of factors that have to be considered. The first of these concerns the definition of redundancy, which is set out in section 139 of the Employment Rights Act (1996). Principally, there are two ways in which a redundancy can occur, and these are set out in section 139(1) as follows:

(a) The fact that [the] employer has ceased or intends to cease –
   i)   to carry on the business for the purposes of which the employee was employed by him, or
   ii)  to carry on that business in the place where the employee was so employed, or

(b) The fact that the requirements of that business –
   i)   for employees to carry out work of a particular kind, or
   ii)  for employees to carry out work of a particular kind in the place where the employee was employed by the employer, have ceased or diminished or are expected to cease or diminish.

To put that in everyday language: redundancy occurs when the employer closes down completely, moves premises, requires fewer people for particular jobs or requires no people for particular jobs. Redundancy can also occur when an individual has been laid off or kept on short-time for a period that is defined in sections 147 to 152 of the 1996 Act. Assuming that the reason that an individual's employment comes to an end is within one of the statutory definitions, or that they have been laid off or kept on short-time, and assuming that they have a minimum period of qualifying employment, then they are entitled to a statutory redundancy payment.

Redundancy 'can mean different things to different people. Even as a specific legal concept, it has been the subject of differences and errors of interpretation' (Fowler, 1993). For that reason it is an area in which the employment relations professional must develop his or her skills.

## THE NEED FOR REDUNDANCY POLICY AND PROCEDURES

For personnel professionals, job security policies and the avoidance of redundancy are an increasingly important part of the employment relations framework. In Chapter 3, when discussing the management of change, we said that organisations have a continuing need to evolve, to constantly search for their distinctive capabilities. This in turn means a continuing process of change and leads to the inevitable weakening of employees' confidence in their employer's ability to maintain job security. Where redundancy is unavoidable, 'good practice' dictates that organisations have in place policies and procedures that enable them to deal with a difficult situation with sensitivity and equity. The employment relations specialist has a key role to play in this process in advising managerial colleagues on the scope and extent of any policies and in advising them how to manage the redundancy process.

Policies and procedures are important not only because the law dictates certain minimum requirements but also because, like most activities connected with employment relations, there is a good business case for doing so. An important element in the management of redundancy situations is the need to provide effective counselling and support for the redundant employee – support in terms of job-seeking, outplacement, etc. Of equal importance is the need to ensure that those who are to remain in employment and who may be fearful for their future are not ignored. Ignoring the 'survivors' is likely to produce a demotivated workforce that is prone to conflict with management.

## REDUNDANCY AND THE MANAGEMENT OF CHANGE — THEORY

In the context of redundancy we need to look at what it is that causes firms to have to change and ask whether job losses have to be the inevitable result. In many cases, organisations have had no option but to declare redundancies – for example, for an urgent need to cut costs, or because of a failure to win an important contract. These are just two examples of where immediate action must be taken. But redundancies could sometimes have been avoided if organisations had invested more time in human resource planning, training or skills development.

'In the struggle for survival, the fittest win out at the expense of their rivals because they succeed in adapting themselves best to their environment' (Charles Darwin). Zara Seager of ER Consultants – a business consultancy specialising in organisational behaviour – wrote in their quarterly management journal that:

> rushing to cut employee numbers without much thought for the future, or what 'fitter' actually means, can and does result in disaster.

Such an approach, she says, can:

> leave an organisation unfit to recover along with the economy, but if it recovers at all, it's usually at a much higher cost. It's something that many firms in the last downturn regretted doing, especially when they had to rehire many of the employees they let go at much higher consultancy rates when the economy picked up.

In a complex business world we have to recognise that business change will continue to lead to reduced workforces because organisations are under continuous pressure to:

- improve their effectiveness
- increase profitability
- reduce costs and remain innovative.

But businesses can be changed without wholesale job losses. Changes in markets have created a need for organisations to be much more responsive to their customers' requirements. In manufacturing, for example, consumers demand higher and higher standards combined with better value for money, but better long-term planning might indicate that costs, other than people ones, could be reduced – items such as uncontrolled purchasing, wasted information technology spending and bloated administration. But even here care must be taken. Sometimes there can be a knee-jerk reaction to perceived overspending or bloated administration. All the major political parties are committed to finding 'efficiency savings' as a means of making the necessary cuts in public expenditure that they feel are required. Unfortunately, such statements are easy to make but less easy to deliver – not because jobs have to be saved *per se*, but because there is generally insufficient evidence to identify the actual 'efficiency savings'.

One example of how a business can take a measured approach to the management of change is the experience of Transport for London (*People Management*, 12 August 2004). As Andy Cook, their Head of Corporate HR and Group Employee Relations, put it:

> We've got a potential funding gap of £1 billion if we don't meet all our aspirations … and we need to ensure that we are running as efficiently as we can.

Transport for London therefore had to embark on a change programme that involved job losses and staff redeployment, but – and this is the crucial part – it was not

> just about reducing costs and staff numbers: we have to make sure we've got the right skills mix to move forward.

## REFLECTIVE ACTIVITY

Has your organisation had cause to declare any redundancies in the past two years? If it has, could the redundancies have been avoided?

In Chapter 7 we looked in detail at the need for organisations to develop clear business strategies that would, in turn, help to identify what their people strategies ought to be and how they should manage change. For many, the answer has been to downsize the organisation or to introduce flexible working practices. According to Sparrow and Marchington (1998), these responses:

> raise questions about the most appropriate organisational form … Under the burden of economic and competitive pressure, a range of organisational strategies is aimed at competing not just on cost but on quality and speed of response.

Evidence suggests that had alternatives to redundancy been at the top of everybody's agenda, some of the large numbers of jobs that have disappeared over the past three decades might have been saved. For many senior managers the need to deliver very large productivity increases and cost savings made redundancy the only option (Lewis, 1993). While this lack of choice has to be acknowledged, there are two reasons why employers ought to be considering the alternatives to redundancy. One is that every organisation needs to maintain some form of competitive advantage. The other is that it is a reasonable presumption to say that competitive advantage is unlikely to be achieved and maintained without a committed and motivated workforce.

Remarkably, despite the forecast of huge job losses resulting from the 2008/9 recession, the outcome has been less draconian than feared. This is due to many organisations having learned the lessons from past downturns and seeking ways to mitigate the impact of lost business and reduced revenues. Throughout 2009 there were many examples of innovative alternatives to redundancy implemented by firms that understood the need to hold on to their best people. These ranged from reducing working hours, reducing pay, and wage freezes to sabbaticals. Such alternatives, if they are to have any meaning and value, cannot simply be imposed if employers want staff to 'buy in to' and be supportive of their organisation. Organisations cannot expect staff to submissively accept a pay freeze or cut – there has to be consultation.

At JCB – known the world over for its large earth-moving equipment and other construction industry machinery – thousands of people kept working and 350 jobs were saved as a consequence of consultation with staff, including the GMB union. Chief Executive Officer Matthew Taylor said that it showed:

> the tremendous unity amongst the JCB workforce and a great team spirit, which I applaud. They have looked after the needs of one another rather than the needs of the individual – and that is to be commended.

Decisions on redundancy, because they are often made to address an immediate and short-term problem, can create the wrong and entirely opposite effect. They can engender a mood of disillusionment and cynicism that if allowed to fester, can destroy any of the short-term financial gains of a redundancy exercise, together with any hope of gaining employee commitment to the future. Marchington and Sparrow (1998) make the point that in relation to downsizing and de-layering:

> immediate financial and performance measurements made today cannot assess the implications of correct or incorrect decision-making, as such decisions now tend to operate and be proved effective over a longer time-span.

## EMPLOYEE COMMITMENT

If employee commitment is to be obtained, together with high levels of motivation, employees have to feel secure in their employment, not afraid for their future. In 1983, when unemployment was running at over 3 million, Ron Todd – then General Secretary of the Transport & General Workers Union (TGWU) – commented that there were 3 million people on the dole, and another

23 million who were scared to death (Blyton and Turnbull, 1994). As noted above, the CIPD *Labour Market Outlook* survey would suggest that the fear factor has not gone away. In a 1996 report the IPD stated that 'Insecurity has damaged people's commitment, a state of affairs that if not remedied has the potential to damage competitive performance.' This is just as true today as it was in 1996, and there is continuing evidence that redundancy remains a spectre that can affect an individual's perception of his or her job security. While we can acknowledge that all businesses have to worry about competition, about retaining their competitive edge, about growth and even survival, these worries can be eased if they know they have a committed and loyal workforce. The challenge is how to overcome the fear factor and to achieve the necessary commitment that is so important.

Fear is often generated by a failure on the part of senior management to recognise the need for prompt and accurate communication when people's livelihoods are at risk. Linked to this need for timely communication is the need to ensure that when messages have to be communicated, they are done so in a way that will not cause distress to those affected. In today's technological age, the potential for poor communication is exacerbated by the use, or misuse, of media such as email or text-messaging. Sadly, there are a number of examples of organisations who have advised employees about impending redundancies by email or text message – not always with bad intentions, simply through lack of foresight. One of the most common ways in which poor communication impacts on redundancy situations is during the course of a merger or acquisition. Company A will often signal an intention to bid for, or merge with, company B, and as part of its strategy to win shareholder approval for its plans, will announce what savings may be expected if it is successful. These savings can often include a declared intention to downsize the workforce. The first the affected employees hear about it is through press announcements or email messages. A recent example is the successful bid by Kraft for Cadbury's. Initially, Kraft signalled an intention to reverse a previously announced factory closure made by Cadbury's – a promise Kraft subsequently reneged on. While the staff at the affected factory were no worse off than before the takeover, other staff are left wondering how much job security they have, going forward.

THEORY    There is no magic formula for achieving commitment, but a 1995 survey by the IPD and Templeton College, Oxford, identified some important elements that can help management to achieve this objective. One of these is trust, on which, says the survey, the psychological contract that the employer has with employees must rest. The employees will have trust if they are confident that the employer will continue to search for new customers and new markets, thus making it possible for their talents to be employed. Clearly, as the survey points out, 'trust is vulnerable to the incidence of redundancy in an organisation', and serious questions are now being raised about some of the cost reduction, redundancy and downsizing policies that have been prevalent in recent years. This, said the survey, had caused some employers to declare that they would offer continual employment except in the most unprecedented circumstances. Where businesses find it impossible to underwrite job security, they should commit to consulting employees on those strategic issues that can affect security of employment.

THEORY

Pfeffer, writing in 1998, noted that an employee's apprehension about his or her employment prospects will undermine the organisation's investment in innovative work practices, productivity improvements, and labour-management co-operative efforts. He wrote that:

> laying employees off too readily constitutes a cost for firms that have done a good job selecting, training and developing their workforce ... Layoffs put important strategic assets on the street for the competition to employ.

## REFLECTIVE ACTIVITY

Whether or not there have been redundancies in your own organisation, what do you think is the current position in respect of employee security? Do you and your colleagues feel secure, or is there some concern about the future?

Much depends on the interaction that can be created between managers and the workforce as a means of fostering the levels of commitment and loyalty that are being sought. These sorts of imperatives are the major reason that there has been such a concerted push by human resource specialists to integrate people management issues into strategic management. As Pettigrew and Whipp (1995) argue, one of the central contributors to competitive performance is the way in which people within a firm are managed. In employment relations terms this means creating a partnership between workers and their managers that is collaborative, not adversarial. There are a number of examples where employers and employees are prepared to negotiate and make agreements over job security, although these tend to be in unionised environments.

## REFLECTIVE ACTIVITY

Are you aware of any other arrangements of this kind? Is it something your organisation has considered?

## POLICIES AND PROCEDURES

No matter what sort of strategic vision an organisation employs, there will sometimes be no alternative to reducing the numbers employed. The possibility that this will occur is much higher now than it was 20 years ago. Good employment relations practice dictates a need for clear policies and procedures which allow redundancy situations to be dealt with in a professional and equitable manner. Not only are there legal regulations to be taken into account but the psychological contract has to be maintained, and if there is no policy, the wrong decisions can be made – as Virgin Airlines discovered in the aftermath of the 11 September 2001 terrorist attacks.

Speaking at the 2004 European HR Forum, Virgin's Director of Organisational Development, Moira Nagle, explained how, less than a week after the attack, the airline decided to lose 25% of its staff. But – and this is the key point – Virgin did not have any redundancy procedures. As a consequence, and as Nagle freely admitted, it lost some very skilled employees, many of whom have since been rehired:

> We thought getting people out of the door was the thing we needed to do [and] we probably lost some very skilled people we would have preferred not to lose.

## POLICY

A statement of policy on redundancy might in some ways be better classified as an organisation's statement of intent in respect of their commitment to maintaining employment. For example, a policy statement on redundancy might begin as follows:

> The company intends to develop and expand its business activities in order to maintain its competitive advantage within our existing marketplace. It is also our intention to seek new products and markets provided they have a strategic fit with the rest of the business. To achieve these objectives we need the active co-operation and commitment of the whole workforce. In return, our aim is to provide a stable work environment and a high level of job security. However, we also need to ensure the economic viability of the business in the competitive world in which we now have to operate. In such a world changes in markets, technology or the corporate environment may cause us to consider the need for reductions in staffing levels. In order to mitigate the impact of any reductions in staff the following procedure will be adopted.

Such a policy statement does not make any commitment to no compulsory redundancies, but it is an important first step in recognising people as an important asset. There is a reasonable amount of evidence that suggests that the downsizing, re-engineering culture of the late 1980s/early 1990s had a detrimental affect on businesses that needed to grow. A study by International Survey Research cites responses from a number of senior HR managers which found that downsizing went too far and the overall effect was negative (*People Management*, No.22, November, 1996; p.15). We have already quoted the Sparrow and Marchington view that decision-making should be evaluated over a longer time-scale and many organisations are now beginning to recognise, as Virgin did, that they have lost valuable experience and skills. Although Virgin appear to have rehired many of their key staff, this will not always prove possible, and valued employees once lost can prove difficult to replace.

Hendricks and Mumford in charting the rapid rise and fall of the re-engineering concept (*People Management*, May, 1996) argued that it failed as a technique because many of its followers did not understand people and change management techniques. They pointed to evidence that re-engineering always took longer than expected, involved more resources than were available and presented unforeseen problems. Developing a redundancy policy, or a statement of intent as described above, should be driven by an organisation's overall business strategy and can be an important first step in building that important management–workforce partnership. But even in the most strategically aware organisations, not everything (eg 11 September 2001, the war in Iraq) is predictable, and there may be situations in which job losses cannot be avoided. This is where the procedure, mentioned in our example of a policy statement, comes into play.

## REFLECTIVE ACTIVITY

Does your organisation have a redundancy policy? If it does, what does it say about job security?

## PROCEDURE

The first thing to say about a redundancy procedure, as with any other procedure, is that it must fit the business. That is, it must be written and designed to cater for the individuality of each organisation. Draft procedures can be obtained from professional bodies such as the CIPD or from commercial organisations such as Croner, but they should always be treated as guidelines or templates and be amended to meet individual organisations' requirements. However, below are some extracts from an actual redundancy policy that indicate some of the steps which have to be taken when redundancies do arise.

### REDUNDANCY POLICY

#### Philosophy

It is the aim of the Company to provide continuity of employment for staff consistent with the need for continuing efficiency and effectiveness in a changing business environment. The Company will constantly attempt to plan so that any required reductions in staffing levels can be accommodated through natural turnover or redeployment of employees. The Company recognises, however, that on occasions it may be necessary to undertake redundancies. If redundancies cannot be avoided (eg through redeployment), the Company will aim to treat all staff fairly and consistently.

#### Consultation

*Justification*

Justification for the redundancies must be thorough, robust and detailed.

*Communication*

1  Individual consultation/counselling to take place with affected people, who will be given the option to be accompanied by a work colleague or union representative.

2   The timing and method of communication of redundancies to be handled 'sensitively' wherever possible.

There may be occasional situations where the interests of the business do not allow for consultation prior to the selection of individuals for redundancy (eg for commercial reasons). Such situations should be exceptional.

**Voluntary redundancy**

A voluntary scheme to allow for volunteers to be identified from the affected area, before compulsory redundancy is applied (other than in the situation where a 'unique' role is identified as redundant).

To apply the rationale that volunteers will be allowed to leave on redundancy (subject to the numbers volunteering matching the numbers required), unless there is an overriding business reason (ie in respect of voluntary redundancy, the Company to reserve the right to be selective in sanctioning the redundancy, subject to an overriding business reason).

The judgement about whether an individual is business-critical (and therefore cannot be released) will be made by the line manager, who will provide a supporting justification to the appropriate Director/HR Director.

- Any employee affected in this way will have the right to appeal against this decision.

- He/she must do so in writing, within seven calendar days of being advised that he/she cannot be released for voluntary redundancy.

- This appeal will be made to the appropriate Director and the HR Director, who will conduct an appeal hearing. If the decision of this hearing is still disputed by the individual, he/she must register a further appeal in writing to the MD without delay. The MD will conduct an appeal hearing with the individual. The MD's decision will be final.

- All appeal hearings will be completed within 14 calendar days of the employee's first registering his/her appeal.

- This appeal process will take precedence over the Company's grievance procedure.

*Where the number of volunteers matches the number of redundancies*, the business-critical reasoning outlined above will apply.

*Where the number of volunteers exceeds the number of redundancies*, the business-critical reasoning outlined above will apply, but otherwise, preference will be given to those employees with the longest continuous service.

*Where the number of volunteers is less than the number of redundancies*, any volunteers will be included, subject to the business-critical reasoning outlined above. The method for making up the shortfall will be determined by the use of Compulsory Redundancy Selection Criteria.

**Compulsory Redundancy Selection**

To adopt the Compulsory Redundancy Selection Criteria form discussed in 2001, but with the following modifications:

- To remove the section that refers to Attendance/Absence Record altogether (in order to avoid potential disability discrimination issues and potential penalisation of the genuinely sick – it is accepted that the disciplinary measure would identify sickness-related capability issues).

- To increase the weighting for the Length of Service section from x 2 to x 3.

To apply a process of selection whereby:

- The immediate supervisor completes the selection criteria, with a detailed explanatory note. Wherever possible, the scores to be supported by objective measurements/justifications.

- This information to be passed to the Departmental Director and HR Department in order for the scores/reasoning to be verified.

- The employee(s) selected for redundancy will then be advised of the outcome by the Departmental Director and HR Department and will be given the option to be accompanied by a work colleague or union representative.

*Appeal process*

Any employee affected in this way will have the right to appeal against this decision. He/she must do so in writing, within seven calendar days of being advised of being selected for compulsory redundancy. This appeal will be made to the appropriate Director and the HR Director, who will conduct an appeal hearing.

If this decision is still disputed by the individual, he/she must register a further appeal in writing to the MD without delay. The MD will conduct an appeal hearing with the individual. The MD's decision will be final.

All appeal hearings will be completed within 14 calendar days of the employee's first registering his/her appeal.

This appeal process will take precedence over the Company's grievance procedure.

**Redundancy payment terms**

To apply a minimum payment of three months' basic (gross) pay, including all monies owing at the termination date except holiday pay and expenses. (In the case of staff whose earnings include a regular bonus/commission in addition to a basic salary, a monthly average of the previous 12 calendar months' bonus/commission will be calculated and added to the basic salary.)

Otherwise, to apply:

- Two weeks' basic (gross) pay for every completed year of continuous service. (Where adding the contractual or statutory notice period would increase the number of completed years of continuous service, this will be taken into account.)

- In the case of staff whose earnings are reliant on bonus/commission in addition to a basic salary – in these circumstances a weekly average of the previous 12 calendar months' bonus/commission will be calculated and added to the basic salary.

- If the amount is less than that equivalent to SRP (statutory redundancy pay), then this figure will apply.

The redundancy payment will be capped at an amount equivalent to the individual's annual salary at the effective redundancy date. (For those whose earnings are reliant on bonus/commission, in addition to the basic salary an average of the previous 12 calendar months' bonus/commission will be calculated and added to the basic salary.)

Redundancy payment calculations will be based on an individual's salary as at the effective date of the redundancy. Part-time workers will receive payment calculated on their salary pro-rata to the hours they work. (The Company will communicate this aspect to staff who move from full- to part-time work.)

## Termination agreements

All Company redundancies will be confirmed through a written termination (or compromise) agreement, the cost of legal advice for this to be borne by the Company up to a maximum value of £250 including VAT.

## Outplacement support

The Company will where necessary provide an outplacement service for all redundant staff (ie a facility to assist those people leaving the business in pursuing their careers elsewhere in the job market or in considering their next steps).

This outplacement service will include, as a minimum, advice and support in the areas of:

- CV preparation
- interview skills/techniques
- benefits agency advice
- information.

The outplacement provider will be selected by the Company. (In the case of single redundancies, the individual may choose the provider of his/her choice. In such instances the Company will be directly invoiced by the provider up to the value of an agreed sum for this service.)

Once an individual has been confirmed as an acceptable volunteer or has been selected for redundancy, the Company will allow him/her appropriate time off to attend job interviews. In addition, the person with the prior approval of the HR Director will be allowed reasonable use of Company photocopying/PC facilities to generate and produce CVs and job application material.

### Review of redundancies

Between three and six months after the effective redundancy date, the Company to review the outcome of the redundancies in order to determine any learning points and appropriate action to be taken.

### Re-engagement

Any individual made redundant should ideally not be re-employed by the Company for a period of at least 12 months after his/her release date.

The reasons for this are as follows:

- If redundant staff are re-employed in a similar role, it brings into question the original rationale for making that person's role redundant. The company would expect to have fully explored all suitable alternative positions *before* a redundancy becomes effective.

- The message that the speedy return of a redundant employee sends to staff in general would be highly negative. For an employee to see someone who has recently left the business (possibly with a significant payment) return quickly would be detrimental to morale.

- The Inland Revenue would also be likely to investigate the tax-free element of the severance payment made to a redundant employee, should that person return to the company's employment shortly after.

However, a person made redundant may be considered for re-engagement should a suitable position become available at a later date. In such circumstances, the company reserves the right to require repayment of part or all of the redundancy benefits paid to that person. The principle should be that the person should not be financially better off than if he/she had continued in employment.

Where the full excess is reclaimed, continuity of employment would be re-established, together with associated benefits and employment rights.

Where employment is discontinued for a period of 12 months or more, no reimbursement would be sought and continuity of employment would not apply.

The individual would be responsible for declaring the tax benefit received as a result of reimbursement based on net pay as against severance paid gross.

As the policy above shows, there are a number of things that a redundancy procedure should cover, starting with alternative courses of action. Where the possibility of a reduction in employee numbers arises, management should begin a process of consultation. There are a number of legal rules relating to the consultation that must take place with either trade unions, elected workplace representatives or individuals. The purpose of this consultation is to establish whether any potential job losses can be achieved by means other than compulsory redundancies. Factors that would normally be considered at this juncture include:

- a ban on recruitment (unless unavoidable)
- the retraining of staff
- the redeployment of staff
- the restricted use of subcontracted labour, temporary and casual staff
- a reduced amount of overtime working
- voluntary redundancy
- early retirement.

Depending on the nature of the business, other considerations – as we have seen above – might include temporary lay-offs, short-time working, pay cuts/freezes or even job-sharing.

## EARLY RETIREMENT

If there are any employees who are over normal retirement age, it may be possible – subject to whatever rules are in force in respect of default retirement ages – to insist on their immediate retirement, and at the same time it may be appropriate to ask for volunteers for early retirement. This is only an option if the business has its own regulated pension scheme – a state of affairs that is rapidly disappearing and does require careful consideration. As an absolute minimum the pension scheme must allow for the payment of pensions early on grounds of redundancy. Most certainly allow for some form of early retirement, but there is usually a penalty in the form of a reduced pension. So for any individual to consider such an option seriously, early retirement has to carry some form of financial inducement. In effect, the potential retirer is credited with more years of pensionable service than he or she has actually worked. The question of how many extra years to credit will depend on how near to normal retirement age a particular employee is, and the ability of the employer to make the necessary payments into the fund. It is possible that the employer might have to make a substantial payment into the pension fund – more than a redundancy payment, in many cases – to ensure that there is no detriment to the early-retired employee. Alternatively, the employer might have to provide a one-off lump sum that will take the employee up to an agreed date for receiving his or her pension.

It is important that these financial considerations are taken into account by employment relations professionals when they are asked, as they often are, to cost the available options for reducing the workforce. A further point to remember in considering early retirement is the position of pension trustees. Following the 'Maxwell' scandal, trustees now have much more responsibility for the management of individual schemes. To allow early retirement on redundancy grounds or to enhance the value of an individual's pension are not management decisions. They are trustee decisions. For the employment relations professional all of this means that the question of whether early retirement as an alternative to compulsory redundancy is an option must be carefully costed and researched.

When management have given very careful consideration to the alternatives discussed above but conclude that the need for redundancies still remains, the next step in the procedure would be for them to give employees, or their representatives, written details of their proposals. This would include details of the criteria that management propose to use for selecting individuals for redundancy.

## VOLUNTARY REDUNDANCY

Management may indicate at this stage that they are prepared to accept volunteers, but this must be subject to the company's need to retain a balanced workforce with the appropriate mix of skills and knowledge. As Lewis (1993) and others have pointed out, the concept of voluntary redundancy has become the most widely acceptable method of dealing with redundancy, and there are obviously a number of advantages in adopting the voluntary approach. Firstly, it can help to avoid some of the demotivating effects that redundancy inevitably has on an organisation.

Secondly, it can be cost-effective. While persuading people to go, rather than forcing them to leave, will probably require higher individual payments (possibly in pension costs), the financial benefits of a redundancy exercise can begin to impact much earlier if a costly and time-consuming consultation exercise can be avoided. There is a danger that if a voluntary approach is adopted, more people will want to opt out of work than was originally envisaged, and this can have unbudgeted cost implications. For this reason it is important, before paying extra costs in this way, that a comprehensive human resource planning exercise has been carried out in order to assess future labour requirements.

Another factor that must be considered before making any announcements about voluntary redundancy is an assessment of who might volunteer. It is the author's experience that individuals who have volunteered *and then been refused* display a serious lack of commitment to any reorganisation precipitated by the redundancy situation. Avoiding this requires a careful evaluation of which individuals would be allowed to go, if they volunteered – and again, it is the author's experience that too many managers make assumptions about individuals within their teams. This is where the employment relations professional, in his or her role as objective adviser, can make a valuable contribution.

## COMPULSORY REDUNDANCY

If the voluntary option is not feasible because the wrong people are volunteering or insufficient numbers are coming forward, the next step would have to be compulsory redundancies. At this point in the procedure there should be an acknowledgement that the organisation would, as far in advance of any proposed termination date as possible, notify all employees that compulsory redundancies are proposed and that a provisional selection has been made. This part of the procedure fulfils a statutory requirement. The easiest and most non-contentious method of selection is 'last in, first out' (LIFO), but the Employment Appeals Tribunal has now challenged even this. In the case of *Blatchfords v Berger and Others* (2001) the EAT observed that 'It could not be said with certainty that either selection on the basis of LIFO would always be reasonable or that no reasonable employer today would adopt LIFO as the sole criterion.' This view has been further strengthened by the age discrimination legislation, which could leave an employer facing a possible discrimination claim in that LIFO might impact disproportionately on younger workers. To use LIFO, an employer would now generally have to provide some objective justification for so doing.

For example, the Court of Appeal has ruled that taking service into account as a redundancy selection criterion is not unlawfully indirectly age discriminatory against young workers. In *Rolls-Royce plc v Unite The Union* (2009) the employers sought to circumvent a collective agreement which included service in the redundancy selection matrix giving one point per year of continuous service. They argued that taking into account length of service was no longer necessary in order to meet the reasonable needs of the business and therefore was not objectively justifiable. Giving the leading judgment, however, Lord Justice Wall held that:

> Viewed objectively, the inclusion of the length of service criterion is a proportionate means of achieving a legitimate aim. The legitimate aim is the reward of loyalty, and the overall desirability of achieving a stable workforce in the context of a fair process of redundancy selection. The proportionate means is ... amply demonstrated by the fact that the length of service criterion is only one of a substantial number of criteria for measuring employee stability for redundancy, and that it is by no means determinative. Equally, it seems to me, the length of service criterion is entirely consistent with the overarching concept of fairness ...

Lady Justice Arden, concurring, pointed out that the legitimate aim could be seen as adhering to the agreed redundancy selection scheme:

> thus removing the scope for disagreement and dissension among the vast majority of its workforce.

The Court of Appeal's judgment represents an authority that service can be a lawful redundancy selection criterion, notwithstanding that it is indirectly age discriminatory. Note, however, that in this case length of service was neither 'plainly dominant in, nor necessarily determinative of, the redundancy selection process'. It is doubtful whether a similar view would be taken if service was the *only* criterion for redundancy selection, as in last in, first out. Moreover, according to the Court of Appeal, the redundancy selection criterion also fell within the exception in regulation 32, which applies 'in relation to the award of the benefit' to a worker on the basis of length of service. Lord Justice Wall again:

To count a point for every year of service in a redundancy selection process is plainly capable of constituting a benefit, without any violence to the word's meaning.

Even if LIFO is deemed to be a reasonable selection process, it can nevertheless have significant downside effects. Using LIFO may, for many organisations, mean that they are losing their youngest employees or those with the most up-to-date skills. For this reason many organisations have adopted a selection system that is based on a number of criteria such as attendance records, range of work experience, disciplinary records, etc. Such criteria, which need to be as objective as possible and be based on a system of points scores, tend to be looked on very favourably by tribunals. It would be important to stress that any selection was provisional and subject to change following consultation with the employees affected.

## Creating a points score

Once management has determined what criteria should be used, it is suggested that each employee should be scored by an appropriate number of points for each criterion (usually on a scale of 10). There should be clear guidance given to the managers who are asked to make the decision on the number of points each individual receives, and some thought should be given to weighting each criterion by a factor that would take into account the importance of that factor to the employer.

For example:

You should decide which particular attribute or criterion is the most important and then multiply that score by a factor of, for example, 5. The criterion that has the lowest importance might be multiplied by a factor of, for example, 1.

It is important that great care is taken in setting scoring guidelines. When all the scores have been calculated, those employees with the lowest scores will be the ones who should be selected for redundancy, but it is often the case that companies produce scores in this way but still feel unhappy about the results. In other words, they feel unhappy about dismissing certain employees even though those employees have scored badly. In such cases the employers should consider very carefully *why* they would be unhappy about selecting those employees. There may be an objective reason why they should be retained, and had the selection criteria been drafted to take that reason into account, those employees would have scored more highly. An employee may be engaged in a particular project (eg to introduce information technology into the workplace), and because of this the employer may be loath to choose that employee for redundancy. For this reason, the selection criteria should include whether or not someone is engaged on a particular project, and that particular criterion should be assigned an appropriate weighting factor. Alternatively, employees who have some unique or special skill that it is essential for the employer to retain could be taken out of the pool for selection completely. The important point is that such considerations must be made when deciding on the type of system to be used. It is our experience that tampering with the results when they do not deliver the desired outcomes is more likely to lead to a legal challenge from those who are selected. Judge, in an interview for *People Management* (22 November, 2001), made it clear that:

> The key to devising a selection process that is seen to be fair and can withstand scrutiny by trade unions and employment tribunals is to be clear about the skills and experience the company will need in the future. This is only possible if business objectives are clear to all employees.

In summary, therefore, an employer should make a note of those objective criteria which it considers appropriate, decide upon a scoring system, and then decide upon the weighting factor for each criterion. A specimen matrix and score sheet is set out below.

| Matrix and score sheet | | | |
|---|---|---|---|
| **Name:** | | **Age:** | |
| **Date of birth:** | | **Years of service:** | |
| **Department:** | | **Job role:** | |

| Employee assessment | | | |
|---|---|---|---|
| **Criteria** | **Score out of 10** | **Weighting (maximum × 5)** | **Total** |
| | | X | |
| Skills | | X | |
| Attendance | | X | |
| Flexibility | | X | |
| | | X | |
| | | X | |
| | | X | |
| | | **Grand total** | |

**Assessed by:** ..............................................    **Checked by:** ...........................................

**REFLECTIVE ACTIVITY**

Do you think that in your organisation line managers have sufficient information about the skills of the workforce and the future skill requirements of the business?

## ASSISTANCE FOR REDUNDANT EMPLOYEES

Once the selection of individuals has been confirmed, it is important – particularly if the procedure is to be consistent with the policy – that an acknowledgement is made in respect of alternative employment. Of course, alternative employment is not always possible, nor is it always desired by those to be made redundant. Nevertheless, it is incumbent on the employer to make every effort to look for alternatives, and where they exist, to consider redundant employees for suitable vacancies. Where the organisation, or the number of jobs to be reduced, is very small, options in respect of alternatives are rare.

Nevertheless, the procedure needs to set out the basis on which employees will be interviewed for any vacancies and the terms and conditions on which alternative jobs will be offered. Terms and conditions may be the standard terms for the job in question. They may be the terms previously enjoyed by the individual concerned or there may be some form of transition. These are all issues that the employee relations specialist needs to consider. Naturally, the procedure needs to say something about trial periods.

It would be normal practice for a redundancy procedure to set out what steps the organisation proposed to take in assisting the redundant employee who could not be found alternative employment within the business. Such steps should include provisions for paid time off to attend interviews, to seek retraining opportunities or to attend counselling sessions. This latter point will be dealt with in more detail later in the chapter.

## COMPENSATION FOR REDUNDANCY

Finally the procedure might set out the basis on which employees will be compensated for the loss of their employment. There is a statutory entitlement to a minimum amount of redundancy pay, which is set out in section 162(2) of the 1996 Act as follows:

- one and a half week's pay for each year of employment in which the employee was not below the age of 41
- one week's pay for each year of employment that the employee was between the ages of 22 and 40
- half a week's pay for each year of employment under the age of 22.

No more than 20 years' service can be taken into account in calculating an individual's redundancy payment, and there is also a maximum weekly amount that an individual can receive irrespective of how much they earn. This maximum amount is now reviewed by the UK Government on an annual basis and uprated on an annual basis. However, some organisations are prepared to make enhanced payments in order to ease the trauma that redundancy can cause or to encourage volunteers to come forward. They can also pay for more than 20 years' service if they so wish, but it is important to remember that any enhancements, to either amounts or length of service, are entirely at the employer's discretion unless there is a specific contractual arrangement. Employment relations professionals who are charged with drawing up a procedure should be aware of the pitfalls of setting out too much detail on compensation. It is important to ensure that the organisation retains some flexibility on the issue of enhanced payments. Whatever motives lie behind paying more than the statutory amount, no organisation can predict the future or the circumstances in which redundancies may occur. It is important therefore to ensure that any payments set out in a procedure document are not considered to be contractual.

## ENTITLEMENT TO COMPENSATION

In the context of redundancy payments, the definitions of redundancy can be of particular importance. Before 1990 an employer had certain rights to reclaim part of any redundancy payment made to an individual employee, and although this rebate only applied to the statutory part of a redundancy payment, it was an important factor for an employer to take into consideration when considering an enhanced payment. With the ending of the rebate, employers now have to meet the total cost of all redundancy payments, and as a consequence have become much more concerned with ensuring that any loss or diminution of work does actually justify a payment.

## BUSINESS REORGANISATION

There are three sets of circumstances which an employer might argue create no entitlement to a redundancy payment. In the context of so much change management an employer might say that the events which led to an individual's leaving employment had nothing to do with redundancy but were simply the consequences of a legitimate and lawful business reorganisation that turned out to be unacceptable to the employee concerned. The likely scenario is that employees in such circumstances would resign and claim that they had been constructively dismissed. It is also likely that the employee would argue that the 'work of a particular kind' that he or she had been carrying out had 'ceased or diminished', and that he or she was entitled to the statutory rights. In the case of *Lesney Products v Nolan* (1977) IRLR 77, Nolan and some of his colleagues argued that the change from a long day shift with overtime to a double day shift was a diminution in the employer's requirements for work of a particular kind, and that they should have received a redundancy payment. The Court of Appeal held that such a change was a legitimate reorganisation, based on efficiency, and that therefore no payment was due.

## THE EMPLOYEE'S WORKPLACE

The second set of circumstances in which an employer might refuse to make a redundancy payment centre on the words 'in the place where the employee was so employed'. This raises the whole question of mobility clauses in the contract of employment, and how much the employer can rely on them. For example, if the contract states that an employee is required to work anywhere, a refusal to do so could lead to a dismissal for misconduct, but not for redundancy. For the employer to rely on the terms of a mobility clause to rebut a claim for a redundancy payment there must be an express clause in the contract that allows an employer to ask an employee to work at a different location or locations. Even then it is by no means certain that the employer will win the argument.

In 1995 the Court of Appeal held that a clause contained in a contract of employment requiring an employee to work in such parts of the UK as her employers might dictate constituted unlawful sex discrimination within the Sex Discrimination Act (1975). The case in question, *Meade-Hill and Another v British Council*, revolved around the British Council's decision to require Ms Meade-Hill to accept the incorporation of a mobility clause into her contract as a consequence of a promotion. Although this particular case, which was decided in Ms Meade-Hill's favour, was more concerned with sex discrimination than redundancy payments, it is important because of statements made by the Court of Appeal in respect of mobility clauses generally. It commented that even if [this particular mobility clause] could not be justified in its present form, the objectionable aspects would disappear if it were modified in a relatively minor respect. In the Court's view there was no great cause for celebration by employees as a result of this particular decision.

For most employment relations professionals the question of mobility is more likely to arise when the whole, or part, of a business is moving, either to a new geographical location some distance from the present workplace or to new premises broadly within the existing geographical location. In order that an organisation can retain a degree of flexibility in terms of its location it is important to be clear about an employee's place of work. For this reason it is important, when drawing up the employee's Statement of Terms and Particulars of Employment as required by the Employment Rights Act (1996), to identify whether 'the employee is required or permitted to work at various places' (section 1(4)(h)).

The case of *Blatchfords v Berger & Others* (2001) to which we referred above is a classic example of how important it is not only to issue a statement of terms but to be clear about where an individual can be expected to work. In the *Blatchfords* case the Employment Appeals Tribunal examined whether a mobility clause could be implied into the employees' contracts of employment.

There were seven applicants to the employment tribunal, six of them secretaries and one a cashier. They were all employed by the respondent (a firm of solicitors) at the same office in Holborn. They did not have written contracts of employment or section 1 statements.

Blatchfords had two other offices in the Greater London area – one at South Harrow, the other at Croxley Green. Largely due to the loss of an important client, the firm decided to amalgamate the Holborn and South Harrow offices and to close the Holborn office on 27 November 1998.

The six secretaries were offered the opportunity of relocating to the South Harrow office. Two initially said they were prepared to do so but then changed their minds. In the end, all six refused. However, Blatchfords required them all to relocate and argued that there was an implied term in their contract requiring them to do so.

None of the seven applicants took up employment at South Harrow and left the company's employment. They claimed unfair dismissal, but the tribunal found that the employer's requirement for them to relocate to South Harrow was, on the facts, a fundamental breach of their contracts – ie they were constructively dismissed. The employer's appeal to the EAT was also unsuccessful.

### REFLECTIVE ACTIVITY

What does your contract say about mobility? Are there any circumstances in which the current wording could bring you into conflict with an employee?

## ALTERNATIVE EMPLOYMENT

The third set of circumstances that might lead to a refusal to make a redundancy payment is when the employee refuses an offer of 'suitable alternative employment'. In circumstances when the employee is offered a new contract of employment, to begin immediately or within four weeks of the termination of the old contract, and the offer is unreasonably refused, there is no entitlement to a redundancy payment. However, the burden of proving that an offer is suitable lies with the employer. If the employee were to express the view that the proposed new job was inferior to the old one, it would be for the employer to demonstrate that it was not. How an employer might be able to do this has been the subject of many industrial tribunal cases. In *Hindes v Supersine Ltd* (1979) IRLR 343 it was argued that whether the proposed employment was 'substantially equivalent' to the former job was as objective assessment as any. In *Cambridge and District Co-op v Ruse* (1993) IRLR 156 the Employment Appeals Tribunal held that 'It is possible for an employee reasonably to refuse an objectively suitable offer of alternative employment on the ground of his personal perception of the job offered.' In this case Mr Ruse had refused an alternative job because he considered it represented a demotion and a loss of status.

It is very difficult to give absolute advice on such matters as alternative employment. The sensible employment relations specialist will deal with each case individually and on its merits. It may be that what is suitable for one employee may be totally unsuitable for another. One alternative is the provision within section 138(3) of the legislation that allows for a 'trial period'. This gives the redundant employee an opportunity to try a new job for a period of four weeks, or such longer (specified) period as may be agreed to allow for retraining. If, having opted for a trial period, the employee decides at the end of it that the job is not suitable, a redundancy payment is still payable.

## THE LAW AND CONSULTATION

Since the mid-1970s all member states of the European Union have been required to enact legislation which obliges employers to consult with workers' representatives about redundancy. This was generally assumed to mean consultation with recognised trade unions, and was first implemented into the UK legal framework by sections 99 to 107 of the Employment Protection Act (1975). The relevant provisions are now contained in sections 188 to 198 of the Trade Union and Labour Relations (Consolidation) Act (1992).

During 1992 the European Commission claimed that there were imperfections within the UK legislation because:

- There was no provision for consulting with employees in the absence of a recognised trade union.

- The scope of the UK legislation was more limited than was envisaged by the original European Directive (75/129/EEC).

- There was no requirement that an employer considering collective redundancies had to consult workers' representatives with a view to reaching agreement in relation to the matters specified in the Directive.

The Commission's complaints were considered to be well-founded, and amendments made by the Trade Union Reform and Employment Rights Act (1993) made it a requirement that consultations about proposed redundancies must include discussion and consultation about ways of avoiding dismissals altogether. This change to the legislation was considered to be insufficient and in 1994 the European Court of Justice ruled that the UK could not limit the right to be consulted to representatives of recognised trade unions. As a response to this, additional regulations, the Collective Redundancies and Transfer of Undertakings (Protection of Employment) (Amendment) Regulations 1995 were introduced and took effect from March 1996.

*Additional* requirements as a consequence of the European Directive on Information and Consultation of Workers at National Level, which we discussed in Chapter 3, *have also to be taken into account*. The main purpose of legislation arising from the Directive *has been to*:

- recognise at EU level the fundamental rights of employees to be informed and consulted on any decisions likely to affect them significantly

- *provide* arrangements for anticipating and forestalling the social consequences that may arise from changes in the organisation and running of a company

- strengthen the link between information and consultation on strategic and economic issues and consultation on how to address the social consequences arising therefrom.

What does this plethora of Directives, legislation and Regulations mean in practical terms for the employment relations specialist? What is an employer required to do if there is a possibility that employees will be made redundant? The question must be considered from two angles: collective redundancies and individual redundancies.

## COLLECTIVE REDUNDANCIES

The Trade Union and Labour Relations (Consolidation) Act (1992) together with the 1995 Regulations oblige any employer wishing to make 20 or more redundancies to consult with 'appropriate representatives'. These appropriate representatives should be union representatives where there is a recognised union in the workplace, but where this is not the case there is provision for employees to elect representatives. Where employees do decide that they want some form of collective representation in such circumstances, the intention is that:

- Employers will have to make suitable arrangements for the election of employee representatives which ensure that an election is carried out sufficiently early to allow for information to be given and consultation to take place in good time.

- The number of representatives to be elected and the terms for which they are to be elected will be matters for the employer to determine, so long as the number of employee representatives is sufficient to represent all employees properly and the period of office is long enough to complete the consultation.

- The candidates for election must be members of the affected workforce at the date of election.

- No one who is a member of the workforce may be unreasonably excluded from standing for election.

- Everyone who is a member of the affected workforce at the date of election must be entitled to vote, and each person may cast as many votes as there are representatives to be elected.

- The election should be conducted in such a way that those voting do so in secret and that the votes given at the election are fairly and accurately counted.

- In the event of any dispute as to the validity of the election, any of the affected employees may complain to a tribunal and the burden shall be on the employer to show that the election conditions were complied with.

### The timetable for consultation

Section 188(2) of TULR(C)A (1992) requires consultation about proposed redundancies to begin at the earliest opportunity, but in cases involving 20 or more people minimum time periods are a necessity. If the employer is proposing to dismiss over 100 employees, the consultation process must begin at least 90 days before the first dismissal takes effect. If the proposal is to dismiss fewer than 100 but 20 or more, the consultation process must begin no later than 30 days before the first dismissal. Some commentators have expressed doubt about how the phrase 'proposing redundancies' should be interpreted, particularly as the

Collective Redundancies Directive uses the phrase 'contemplating redundancies'. This is slightly different from the wording in TULR(C)A, which states that consultation must be 'with a view to reaching agreement'. Until two noteworthy Employment Appeals Tribunal (EAT) cases, many commentators had argued that consultation must start before decisions over redundancies are made. Employers took a different line, arguing that it was not practical to consult over something that had not been decided. The EAT declared, in *Securicor v GMB* (2003) All ER (D) 181 and *Dewhirst v GMB* (2003) All ER (D) 175, that employers do not have to consult about the business reasons for the job losses before a decision is made. In both the above cases the decision to implement redundancies had been made before consultation started. That for the moment is where the law stands, but both cases could be challenged in a higher court, or the European Court of Justice may consider the UK's implementation of the Directive unlawful. However, notwithstanding these legal arguments, it is still good employee relations practice to begin consultation as soon as possible if a satisfactory outcome is desired.

**Information required by employee representatives**

The timetable described above can only start to run once employees or their representatives have been provided with certain information:

- the reasons for the employer's proposals
- the numbers and descriptions of the employees to be dismissed
- the method of selection the employer proposes for dismissal
- the method of carrying out the dismissals the employer proposes, having due regard to any procedure agreement that might be in existence
- the period of time over which the programme of redundancies is to be carried out
- what method the employer intends to use in calculating redundancy payments, unless the statutory formula is being applied.

Should an employer fail to provide any or all of the information required, or the information that is provided is insufficient, the consultation period will be deemed not to have started. In such circumstances the employer faces the risk of a penalty being imposed (see below) for failing to consult at the earliest opportunity. It is difficult to give precise guidance on what, and how much, detail must be provided, but vague and open-ended statements will not be acceptable. For the employment relations specialist there has to be an acceptance that every case must be decided on its merits and will have to be researched.

It is no good relying on 'what happened last time'. That may not be good enough. In *MSF v GEC Ferranti (Defence Systems) Ltd* (1994) IRLR 113, the Employment Appeals Tribunal held that:

> whether a union has been provided with information which is adequate to permit meaningful consultation to commence is a question of facts and circumstances. There is no rule that full and specific information under each of the heads [of the legislation] must be provided before the consultation period can begin.

The EAT went on to confirm an earlier judgment, which held that a failure to give information on one of the heads may be a serious default, but that there is nothing to say that it must be treated as a serious default.

### Consultation must be genuine

For consultation to be deemed genuine it has to be undertaken 'with a view to reaching agreement' with employee representatives. Three things have to happen. An examination has to take place on ways to avoid dismissals. If avoidance is impossible, ways to reduce the numbers to be dismissed should be looked at. Finally, ways should be found of mitigating the consequences of any dismissals. How tribunals can measure whether these obligations have been fulfilled is open to question. It would be strange if the legislation, as amended, meant that the employer and the representatives have to reach an agreement. What is more likely is that employers must approach the discussions with an open mind and where possible take account of any proposals put to them by the representatives. This in itself can cause problems, insofar as the distinction between consultation and negotiation is concerned. Very often union representatives will see employer proposals as a matter for negotiation, and this can sometimes be a cause of conflict, particularly if an employer perceives that it has little room for manoeuvre.

### Penalties for failing to consult

If there has been a failure to follow the proper consultation process, an application can be made to an employment tribunal for a declaration to this effect, and for a 'protective award' to be paid. This is an award requiring the employer to pay the employee remuneration for a protected period. The legislation relating to protective awards is quite complex, but some of the important elements are:

- The affected employee receives payment at the rate of one week's gross pay for each week of the 'protected period'.

- Unlike some compensatory awards there are no statutory limits on a week's pay.

- Subject to certain maximums, the length of a protected period is at the employment tribunal's discretion; the test is 'what is just and equitable having regard to the seriousness of the employer's default'.

- The maximum periods are 90 days when 90 days should have been the consultation period, and 30 days when 30 days should have been the consultation period; in any other case the maximum is 28 days.

As Lewis (1993) points out, the financial implications of protective awards can be quite significant because there are often substantial numbers of employees involved.

It is unlikely that employers with well-established redundancy procedures will come into conflict with the law over a failure to consult. Notwithstanding this, the prudent employment relations specialist will keep the procedure under review in the light of any relevant tribunal decisions. The real problems arise for those organisations that do not have a procedure or that try to put together a procedure in a hurried and casual manner when redundancies are imminent. Such organisations might find that the price they pay for a lack of preparedness is extremely high. Tribunals have shown an increasing tendency to take a very narrow view of any special pleading by employers that there was no time to consult – and the guidelines set out by the Employment Appeals Tribunal in 1982 are still of very great relevance.

The EAT stressed (in *Williams v Compair Maxam* [1982] ICR 156 EAT) that:

- The employer should consult the union as the best means by which the management result can be achieved fairly and with as little hardship to employees as possible.

- The employer should try to agree with the union the criteria to be applied in selecting the employees to be made redundant.

- When a selection has been made, the employer should consider with the union whether the selection has been made in accordance with these criteria.

To be acceptable, non-consultation would have to be the result of some event that was quite out of the ordinary, but it would be very unwise to feel confident that circumstances which you believe to be 'out of the ordinary' would be accepted as such by a tribunal.

### INDIVIDUAL CONSULTATION

Consultation with trade unions and with the wider constituency of employee representatives has tended to attract most of the attention in studies of redundancy, and there is certainly a good deal of case law on the subject, but the necessity for individual consultation must not be overlooked. Many managers have fallen into the trap of assuming that when only one or two individuals are to be made redundant there is no obligation to consult or that consultation can be cursory. This is an incorrect assumption, and although there is no statutory framework for individual consultation as there is when collective redundancies are on the agenda, tribunals can still intervene. The Employment Rights Act (1996) identifies redundancy as a fair reason for dismissal (section 98(2)(c)), provided that the employer has acted 'reasonably'. This requirement opens the door for an employee to claim unfair dismissal on grounds that the employer, by failing to consult, had not acted reasonably. Although not giving rise to an employment tribunal claim, an article in *People Management* (22 November 2001) provided a classic case study on 'How not to shed staff" (see the case study below).

### Nicky H and redundancy

Nicky H has been made redundant three times in her working life, but the first occasion was the worst.

She worked for a publishing company as head of the central marketing team, which acted as an internal agency. The first inkling that anything was wrong came from a colleague who heard via an email that the team was to be disbanded in a reorganisation.

Nicky immediately tried to see her boss, but was told he was tied up in meetings all day. When they did meet, he was accompanied by a woman she had never seen before.

'He told me I was out of a job,' she says. 'Then he said: "But that's not the point. The point is that you are completely incompetent. The team can't stand you, you have no management skills, and I don't know why we hired you – you can't even photocopy anything."'

'I was then told I would be escorted straight to the HR department and would not be allowed to speak to my team. When I got to HR, the manager said she had no idea what was going on and offered me a box of tissues.'

The incident came a few weeks after Nicky's three-month review, at which, she says, no criticisms were made of her competence. 'I have never felt like such a piece of trash in my life,' she says. 'I had bad dreams about that day for a year afterwards, and it killed my confidence. To be treated like that in front of a complete stranger was absolutely horrendous.'

She did manage to get a message to her team, however. They met her in the pub later and were sympathetic. But she could do nothing more, having been at the company for less than six months.

Shortly afterwards, she took a low-level job at a friend's firm to help rebuild her confidence, until that suffered cash-flow problems and had to shed some staff. She then joined a major management consultancy, but again found herself a victim of cutbacks.

This latest redundancy was a complete contrast to Nicky's earlier experience. She got three months' salary, outplacement support and backing from the company, which allowed her to send emails to contacts, kept in touch, and invited her back for social events.

With the help of the consultancy, she has now decided to start her own business giving style advice to executives. She could also offer a few tips on redundancy.

Most claims for unfair dismissal in respect of redundancy are in either of two areas: unfair selection, and lack of consultation. If the scenario reported at the beginning of the case study had concerned an employee with the required length of service to register a claim for unfair dismissal, it is inconceivable that the employer's actions would have been judged anything other than unreasonable. But, as stated in Chapter 12, 'good practice' demands that you operate reasonably and with just cause on every occasion, not just when you think an employee can make a claim against you. Too often we hear managers say, 'They [a member of staff] have only been here a few months – do I really have to go through all that procedure?'

Many employers have argued that because the redundancy only affected one or two individuals, consultation would not have made any difference. This defence has been virtually closed to employers since the decision of the House of Lords in *Polkey v A E Dayton Services Ltd* (1987) IRLR 503, but unwise and unprofessional employers still try to use it. In *Polkey* the House of Lords did not say that consultation was an absolute requirement, but that the onus is on the employer to demonstrate that consultation would have been 'utterly useless'. In the majority of cases it would be difficult to demonstrate the uselessness of something that had not been tried.

By far the best option for employers is to recognise that good employee relations would be best served by adopting a systematic approach to consultation whether the proposed redundancies are going to affect five people or 50 people. This means that you should always allow enough time for a proper consultation exercise even when it is only one or two people that are to be made redundant. You should give very careful consideration to the possibilities of alternative employment, even lower-paid alternative employment. You must allow people time to:

- consider their options
- challenge the need for redundancy
- propose their own alternatives.

The employer does not have to go along with any alternatives proposed, but must be able to demonstrate that they have been given careful and objective consideration. It is sometimes too easy to be dismissive about suggestions made by a potentially redundant employee, but the way in which you approach the question of alternative employment will very often determine a tribunal's view of your reasonableness. In one case in which we were involved, the employer was found to have unfairly dismissed an employee because the employer had made assumptions instead of properly consulting. In the particular case, the employer had assumed that the employee, who was a long-serving manager, would not be interested in a lower-ranked and lower-paid job, and so had not discussed it with him. At the tribunal hearing the employee was asked by the Chairman whether he would have taken such a job – and he answered in the affirmative. As the Chairman explained to the employer:

> It was not about whether he should have been given the lower-paid job – that may not have been appropriate in the circumstances – but that it should have been discussed with him.

That would have been 'reasonable consultation'. Good practice dictates that you should always allow for the possibility of error in the judgements that you make. We have seen too many managers make the arrogant assumption that they must be right. As Judge (*People Management*, 22 November 2001) put it:

> It is important not to assume someone is dead wood unless you can be sure that they have no potential to develop new skills. I have known people take on a second lease of life because of the challenge posed by a redundancy.

Are you confident, having read the sections on consultation, that you fully understand the legal requirements? Do you need to advise any of your colleagues of their obligations?

## TRANSFERS OF UNDERTAKINGS

When the ownership of a business transfers, there is always the possibility that redundancies will be one of the results that flow from such a transfer. Under the Acquired Rights Directive of the European Union (Directive 77/187/EEC), member states are required to ensure, in broad terms, that all employees who are covered by employment protection legislation receive additional protection in respect of job security if the identity of their employer changes. This does not mean that an employer who acquires a new business is obliged to retain all the inherited employees irrespective of the commercial realities, but equally, the new employer cannot just dispense with those employees without just cause. Should employers find that, on the transfer of a business, there are sound commercial reasons for reducing the headcount, then subject to the normal rules on consultation and the operation of a fair selection procedure, the law does not stand in their way. What the law does insist on, however, is that the transferred employees' rights are retained. This means if they had the requisite period of service with their old employer to qualify for a redundancy payment, the new employer cannot avoid making a redundancy payment to them. In the context of consultation, all the issues of representation and the right to information that we have discussed above in respect of collective redundancies apply equally to transfers of undertakings.

## POST-REDUNDANCY

The rise in unemployment in recent years has meant that more attention is now paid to the needs of redundant employees. In this section we look at the growth in both counselling and outplacement services, and in addition, the position of those employees who remain in employment, and who may consequently suffer the so-called 'survivor syndrome'.

### COUNSELLING

We have decided to examine counselling and outplacement separately, notwithstanding that they overlap in many ways. In this section we analyse counselling in the sense of helping employees come to terms with the fact that they have lost their jobs. Counselling in respect of personal skills, job search and financial planning is dealt with under *Outplacement*.

Although redundancy has become part of everyday life, the loss of one's job usually comes as a tremendous personal blow. Even when 'the writing is on the wall' and the prospect of job losses in the organisation is inevitable, individuals still hope that they will be unaffected. To parody an advertising slogan made famous by the national lottery, they hope 'it will not be them'.

There can be a tendency for employers to want a redundancy exercise to be forgotten as quickly as possible, and this can manifest itself as an apparently very uncaring attitude. The employment relations specialist should be reminding managerial colleagues that they have a continuing responsibility for their redundant employees and, as the IPD guide on redundancy says, be providing displaced employees with a counselling service. Redundant employees can feel anger, resentment and even guilt – emotions which, if not carefully managed, can inhibit an employee from moving forward to the next phase of their career – and this is where effective counselling becomes crucial. However, it is important to proceed cautiously: earlier in this book, in another reference to counselling, we stressed the need for proper training. As Fowler (1993) says:

> Handling the first stage of redundancy counselling requires considerable skill, and should not be attempted by anyone who does not, as a minimum, understand the general principles of all forms of counselling.

Not every redundant employee will agree to or want counselling, but nevertheless it is important to understand its key purpose. If you talk to redundant employees, as we have done, you are struck by the violent mood swings that can occur during the initial post-redundancy phase. Depending on the personality of the individual concerned, the mood can swing from pessimism about the future to unfounded optimism, from anger at the former employer to a feeling that they have been given an opportunity to do something different. The objective of counselling is to bring all these emotions out into the open and to help individuals to make decisions about their future. It is not a panacea – it will not stop people being angry or feeling betrayed – but it might help them to view their future constructively.

For the employment relations specialist there is a further dimension to the provision of counselling. Not only is there a moral imperative but there are sound business reasons. Unless the organisation is closing down completely, there will be other employees left who you will want to build the organisation around. Richard Baker, Director of Human Resources at Hoechst Roussel, made a very valid point when he said (*People Management*, No.2, January 1996; p.31):

> People ... never forget the way they are treated when they are made redundant, and neither do the friends and colleagues who remain behind.

## OUTPLACEMENT

Outplacement is a process in which individuals who have been made redundant by their employer are given support and counselling to assist them in achieving the next stage of their career. There are a large number of organisations that offer outplacement services, but the range and quality of their services varies greatly and the employment relations specialist must carefully research prospective suppliers if a decision to use outplacement is taken.

Broadly, outplacement consultancies offer services on a group or individual basis which fall into the following general categories:

- CV preparation
- researching the job market
- communication techniques
- interview presentation
- managing the job search.

Each organisation operates differently, but in the best organisations the process would probably start with a personal counselling session with a trained counsellor. Once this has been carried out, the next step would be the preparation of the CV. This involves identifying key skills and past achievements so that the job-hunter can market himself or herself from a position of strength. Step three would be to make decisions about job search methods (cold-contact, advertisement, recruitment consultants, etc) and contact development – for example, networking. Step four would be to ensure that the key communication skills of letter-writing, telephone techniques and interview presentation were of a sufficiently high standard to enhance the job search. Where skills have to be improved, the better consultancies provide the necessary training at no extra cost.

---

### CASE STUDY

### Rolls-Royce

When aero engine company Rolls-Royce had to axe 4,800 jobs worldwide in the wake of the 11 September attacks on targets in the USA, it was well placed to deal with the crisis.

Here in Britain, the company had set up six resource centres in early 2000 to handle an anticipated downturn in the market.

The centres, one at each of the company's main UK sites, provide a three-day career transition training programme and continuing, open-ended support and advice.

The centres take CIPD good practice as a model. Each is staffed with a manager, a counsellor, several other dedicated Rolls-Royce personnel, and a flexible team from the company's two external outplacement providers, Capita Grosvenor and Winchester Consulting. The providers give access to national jobs databases with online search facilities.

Since the centres opened, hundreds of employees affected by cutbacks have used them for careers guidance, advice on writing CVs, training and so on. Eighty-five per cent have found new employment, typically after some weeks.

'One of the challenges was the reputation that resource centres have in other organisations,' says John McKell, Rolls-Royce head of employment policy. 'They are renowned for providing minimal provision to lower-paid workers in pokey surroundings, while managers get executive packages. But at Rolls-Royce, the service is gold-plated for everyone.'

The company has involved employees and unions from the start. In response to a proposal from union officers, it set up a resourcing committee by means of which employee and union representatives could review redundancy support. Several improvements, such as better communications, have resulted.

The final step is managing the actual job search, setting personal targets, keeping records of letters and phonecalls, maintaining notes of interviews, and carrying out a regular job search evaluation.

Running alongside these basic services are a range of support services, such as secretarial help, free telephone and office space, and financial planning advice. What an individual gets will depend on the particular package that the former employer purchases on his or her behalf.

Of course, not every employer will be able to afford the cost of outplacement, particularly if large numbers of employees are affected by the redundancies. In such circumstances, organisations must consider what they can do to help from within their own resources, or by using a mixture of internal and external resources. A classic example of a company taking its responsibilities seriously is evidenced by the case study overleaf.

Even the TUC has recognised the value of good advice being made available to workers facing redundancy and has produced a guide on how they can make the best use of the Government's Rapid Response Service (RRS). RRS was established in 2003 and aims to help workers affected by major redundancies. Operated through local JobCentre Plus centres, it aims to help people into new jobs before they lose their current ones by providing specialist advice services.

## ? REFLECTIVE ACTIVITY

Does your organisation have any sort of policy on counselling and outplacement? If not, who would make the decisions about what level of support to offer?

### SURVIVOR SYNDROME

THEORY

When people are forced to leave employment because of redundancy, those that are left behind can be affected just as much as those that have left. Anecdotal evidence we have gathered from the finance sector and local UK Government indicates that disenchantment, pessimism and stress are the likely result of even a small-scale redundancy exercise. Survivor syndrome, as it is called, can be minimised if, as we pointed out above, those who are to be made redundant are treated fairly and equitably and there is a decision made to invest in an effective post-redundancy programme. This usually means a time commitment from senior managers and a good communications process.

The feelings referred to above are the result of two factors. The first is that the remaining employees are often asked to 'pick up' the work of their former colleagues, either directly or indirectly, as the consequence of a reorganisation. In one local authority, individuals had to re-apply for their own jobs three times in three years, following a series of redundancies and reorganisations. The second factor concerns communication. Anecdotal evidence suggests that in many organisations the remaining employees are not always communicated with effectively, thus providing the opportunity for rumour and disenchantment to thrive. Getting the message across about why redundancies were necessary and what happens next is vitally important, and yet most people we have spoken to identify poor communication as one of the principal causes of their dissatisfaction.

THEORY    Blakstad and Cooper (1995) identify three sets of stimuli which can interfere with communications, one of which is internal stress. Internal stress can be caused by a number of variables, but one of the causes identified is 'group concerns'. The aftermath of a redundancy exercise is a classic example of 'group concerns', and yet many managers do not take this into account when communicating with the survivors. For the professional manager who wishes to minimise the effect of survivor syndrome, communication and communications methodology must be carefully worked out. As Blakstad and Cooper (1995) say:

> While it is usually impossible to understand the individual concerns of each member of the [group], structuring the communication around an awareness of group tensions can be used to strengthen retention of messages.

Although communication with those left behind is vital, there is another

---

### 👁 The Royal Mail

CASE STUDY

Having made a loss after tax of £940 million in 2001/2, the Royal Mail announced one of the biggest restructures in British corporate history. In 2002 around 30,000 redundancies were announced, and more have been made since then.

Andrew Kinder was formerly principal welfare co-ordinator and chartered occupational psychologist for the Royal Mail, and now provides the same services for the agency SchlumbergerSema. Describing the impact of such large-scale change on Royal Mail staff, he says: 'Many individuals find it hard to cope – some feeling that they have to work harder to secure their futures, others feeling deep concerns about why they kept their jobs. Royal Mail is committed to addressing these issues not only because they could have a negative effect on productivity but also because the organisation takes its legal duty of care to individuals very seriously. Reorganisations like this happen, and we as humans can't control change,

but we can control how we respond to it. Counselling is one of the key aspects of the firm's efforts to empower employees to cope with change.'

Pauline Leech, head of information services in the Royal Mail's property division, has taken advantage of Kinder's counselling services. 'The team in which I work has been going through so much change that we felt it would be useful to bring in a counsellor,' she says. 'Andrew ran a session helping us develop a number of coping strategies. We talked about our feelings and behaviour, completed a questionnaire and discussed responses to situations. A drama triangle – involving three people playing the role of victim, persecutor and rescuer – was very interesting and gave an insight into different approaches to the same situation. It gave us a good insight into the pressure felt by colleagues. For me it helped to know that the firm cared enough to offer this support.'

option that is worthy of consideration – and that is counselling. Because redundancies are often cost-cutting exercises, many organisations are reluctant to hire counsellors to help with the aftermath. But a study in 2003 by Professor John McLeod of the School of Social and Health Sciences at the University of Aberdeen suggests that it might be an investment worth making (as reported by Blyth in *People Management*, 1 May 2003).

> The findings of more than 80 studies on workplace counselling show that 90% of employees are highly satisfied with the process and outcome. Evidence suggests that counselling helps to relieve work-related stress and reduces sickness absence rates by up to half.

The case study above indicates the effectiveness of such an approach.

## SUMMARY

Redundancy is one of the most emotive issues that any manager can be called upon to deal with. Calling an individual into your office and informing them that they no longer have a job is never easy. For the employment relations specialist who is at the beginning of his or her career, managing a redundancy exercise can be just as traumatic for him or her as for the redundant employee.

No matter how experienced you become, managing redundancy is never straightforward, but in this chapter we have attempted to set the process into some sort of organised framework. Most redundancies occur because organisations need to change, and although we have recognised this, we nevertheless felt it important that employment relations specialists recognise that there should be alternatives to reducing an organisation's headcount. In particular, we stressed that in an era of constant change businesses need to retain their competitive advantage. This is unlikely to happen if their employees are constantly looking over their shoulders, fearing for their jobs. One of the challenges that all managers, whether or not they are personnel practitioners, face in the twenty-first century is how to reconcile the need for organisational change with the individual's need for contentment and security at work..

Not only does the employment relations specialist have to understand the need for organisations to change, but he or she must understand that this has to be accommodated within a well-developed legal framework that directs and constrains his or her actions.

Finally, as we saw in the last part of the chapter, redundancy leaves 'survivors' in its wake, and these individuals have to receive the highest levels of communication and consideration. They often experience a psychological state that is not unlike bereavement, and they inevitably suffer a loss of trust in their organisation or even in their immediate manager.

**KEY LEARNING POINTS**

- The definition of when redundancy occurs is important because it determines an individual's right to consultation, compensation, etc.

- Redundancy should always be a 'last resort', and it is therefore important to have effective policies and procedures for dealing with a redundancy situation.

- Selection in redundancy situations must be objective and capable of standing up to external scrutiny.

- If employers do not wish to pay out large sums in compensation, they must ensure that they fulfil their statutory obligations. Evidence from numerous employment tribunal cases demonstrates that not consulting is the most expensive form of failure.

- People do not forget how a redundancy exercise was handled, and the professional HR practitioner will take care to ensure that any redundancy exercise considers the needs of all individuals as well as those of the organisation.

- The 'survivors' of a redundancy are just as likely to be affected by its consequences as those who are actually made redundant, so it is important that they understand why the redundancy was necessary.

- When redundancy is unavoidable, 'good practice' dictates that the organisation has in place policies and procedures that enable it to deal with a difficult situation with sensitivity and equity. The employment relations professional has a key role to play in this process in advising management colleagues on the scope and extent of any policy, and in advising them on how to manage the redundancy process.

- An important element in the management of a redundancy situation is the need to provide effective counselling and support for the redundant employee, as well as giving support in terms of job security and outplacement. Of equal importance is the need to ensure that those who come to remain in employment and may be fearful for their future are not ignored. Ignoring the 'survivors' is likely to produce a demotivated workforce that is prone to conflict with management.

**REVIEW QUESTIONS**

1 Your organisation needs to reduce the workforce by 20%. Your Chief Executive Officer, who is fully aware of the statutory need to consult with the workforce, wants, in achieving this, to act in a fair, reasonable and consistent way. You have been asked to advise her on how the required redundancies can be achieved with the minimum of disruption to the organisation's business. Drawing on evidence-based research and policy and practice, justify what you would give as your advice.

2 You are employed as head of human resources (HR) at an organisation employing some 750 staff who will now have to be cut back drastically. It will mean a 50% reduction in the size of the

present workforce. You have been asked to produce a position paper for the senior management team explaining how the workforce reduction might be achieved while minimising any adverse impact on morale. Drawing on contemporary research and policy and practice, justify what you would include in your position paper.

3 You are the human resource (HR) adviser for a retail chain of 34 shops. The area manager has asked your advice on a possible redundancy situation. He has identified one shop that will probably have to close sometime in the next few months. The shop in question has 27 people. The organisation is non-unionised but there is an employee consultation forum. He does not know how to initiate the process and has asked your advice about what he should do, and why. How would you respond?

4 Your human resource director is concerned

that with a sudden downturn in the economy, the company needs to review its redundancy policy. She would like you to brief her on the things that a redundancy policy should include as a minimum, and what else could be considered good employment practice. Prepare an outline of the briefing you will give her, justifying what you will include.

5 The marketing director has asked for your advice. She has to make a presentation to the company board which will detail some substantial organisational changes in the marketing function, and possibly in related areas of sales and customer support. She is convinced of the business case for the change, but her expertise is minimal about possible employee resistance and how any concerns may be alleviated. What advice could you provide about change management, bearing in mind the need to overcome possible resistance?

**EXPLORE FURTHER**

Blakstad, M. and Cooper, A. (1995) *The Communicating Organisation*. London: Institute of Personnel and Development.

Blyth, A. (2003) 'The art of survival', *People Management*, Vol.9, No.9: 39–40.

Blyton, P. and Turnbull, P. (1994) *The Dynamics of Employee Relations*. Basingstoke: Macmillan.

Brown, D. (2001) 'Lopsided view', *People Management*, Vol.7, No.23, November: 36–7.

Fowler, A. (1993) *Redundancy*. London: Institute of Personnel and Development.

Griffiths, J. (2004) 'Q & A: all change', *People Management*, Vol.10, No.16, August: 14–15.

Hendricks, R. and Mumford, E. (1996) 'Business process re-engineering RIP', *People Management*, Vol.2, No.9, May: 22–9.

Judge, G. (2001) 'The judge who has to sit in judgement', *People Management*, Vol.7, No.23, November: 32.

Kay, J. (1993) *Foundations of Corporate Success*. Oxford: OUP.

Lewis, D. and Sargeant, M. (2009) *Essentials of Employment Law*, 10th edition. London: Chartered Institute of Personnel and Development.

Lewis, P. (1993) *The Successful Management of Redundancy*. Oxford: Blackwell.

Pettigrew, A. and Whipp, R. (1995) *Managing Change for Competitive Success*. Oxford: Blackwell.

Pfeffer, J. (1998) *The human equation: building profits by putting people first*. Boston: Harvard Business School Press.

Pickard, J. (2001) 'When push comes to shove', *People Management*, Vol.7, No.23, November: 30–5.

Sparrow, P. (1998) 'New organisational forms, processes, jobs and psychological contracts', in Sparrow, P. and Marchington, M. (eds) *Human Resource Management: The new agenda*. London: Pitman/*Financial Times*.

Sparrow, P. and Marchington, M. (1998) *Human Resource Management: The new agenda*. London: Pitman/*Financial Times*.

Summerfield, J. (1996) 'Lean firms cannot afford to be mean', *People Management*, Vol.2, No.2, January: 30–2.

Summerfield, J. and Van Oudtshoorn, L. (2003) *Counselling in the Workplace*. London: Chartered Institute of Personnel and Development.

Watkins, J. (2003) 'Direct line', *People Management*, Vol.9, No.10, May: 42–3.

**Web links**

www.bis.gov.uk is the website of the Department for Business, Innovation and Skills, and gives access to the law on redundancy

www.acas.org.uk is the website of ACAS, and gives access to ACAS publications, including guides and information on redundancy management

www.cipd.co.uk is the website of the CIPD, and gives access to the CIPD's wide range of publications and information on redundancy, and its *Labour Market Outlook* survey.

# Index

Absence 129–130, 443–450
  disabilities, and 448–449
  domestic emergencies, and 449–450
  long-term 447–448
  managing 443–450
  persistent 446
  sickness 444–446
Adjournment
  negotiation, of 405–406
Advisory, Conciliation and Arbitration
    Service (ACAS) 22–23, 200–209
  aims 200
    collective disputes 205
    conciliating disputes 202–205
    promoting good practice 201
    providing information and advice
      201–202
  arbitration process 207
    central features 124
    hearing 124–125
    issues for 207
    scheme 124–125
    use of 207–209
  conciliation 122–123
    pre-claim 122
    process 205–206
  disciplinary and grievance procedure Code
    of Practice 421–422, 475–476
  gross misconduct, on 426
  independence 200
  mediation 30
    process 206
  third-party intervention, and 29
Age discrimination 128–129
Agency workers
  EU law, and 163
  increasing use of, 83, *see also* Labour
    market; Part-time employment
Agreements 36–42
  collective 39–40
  dimensions of agreement rules 40–41
  non-union companies 41
  types of 36–39
    procedural 38–39
    substantive 36–37

  workforce agreements 41–42
Alternative employment
  redundancy, and 514–515
Appeals
  disciplinary procedures, and 450–451
  grievances, and 483
  job grading, and 484–485
Arbitration 29, 361–366
  ACAS scheme *see* Advisory, Conciliation
    and Arbitration Service
  award 365–366
  Central Arbitration Committee
    210–211
  choice of arbitrator 363
  hearing 364–365
  terms of reference 361–362
  written submission 363–364
Aspiration grid
  grievances, and 482
  negotiation, and 394–396
Attitudinal structures
  negotiation, and 383

Bargaining *see* Negotiation
Bargaining agreements, 345–346, *see also*
    Collective bargaining
Bargaining power
  balance of 5–6, 10–11, 93–94
    economic policy, and 93
    impacts on 69
    micro level 94
    new technology, and 93–94
  management behaviour, and 95–96
    employee commitment, and 95
Briefing groups 269–270
  employee involvement, and 269–270
Bullying 485–487
Burchell rules 441–442
  gross misconduct, and 441–442
Burden of proof
  discrimination 114
  EU law, and 161
Business Europe 149

Caulkin, Simon 217–218

Central Arbitration Committee (CAC) 23,
      210–211
   arbitration 211
   establishment 210
   functions 210
   membership 210
   powers 211
   trade union recognition 211
Certification Office 23–24, 199
   powers 199
   responsibilities 199
Chamberlain, Neil
   collective bargaining, on 339–340
Chartered Institute of Personnel and
      Development (CIPD)
   improvement in performance, on 63
   What is Employee Relations 17
CIPD HR Professional Map 2–3
   professional specialisms 3
      bands of competence 3
      behaviours 4
Collective agreements 39–40
   differences of interest, and 53
   legal status of 39–40
Collective bargaining 15–16, 27–28, 336–346
   bargaining agreements 345–346
      number of unions 345
      single union arrangements 345–346
      single-table arrangements 346
   conditions for 341–342
   decrease in 64
   dimensions of 342–345
      level of bargaining 342–343
      scope of bargaining 344–345
   employers' associations, and 183
   meaning 27
   pay determination methods, table 66
   removal from public sector 89
   theoretical approaches 336–341
      Chamberlain, Neil, on 339–340
      Flanders, Alan, on 338
      neo-classical economic theory 340–341
      Webb, Sidney & Beatrice, on 337
   UK government, and 89
Commission for Equality and Human Rights
      (CEHR) 110
Commitment strategy
   employee involvement, and 260, 261
Communications
   direct communication arrangements, table
      283

direct-employer-employee communication,
      table 281
   employee involvement, and 266–271
      briefing groups 269–270
      communication systems 266–267
      employee attitude surveys 270–271
      employee communications strategy
         267–269
      monitoring 269
   management-led changes in 16
   negotiating team, with 397
   people strategy, and 230–231
   redundancy, and 498
Compensation
   redundancy, for 511–512
Complaints
   employees' see Grievances
Compulsory redundancy, 507–510, see also
      Redundancy
Conciliation 29, 361
Confederation of British Industry (CBI) 19,
      182
Confidentiality
   employee engagement survey, and 319
Constructive dismissal 106, 456
   employee grievances, and 456
Consultation
   employee involvement, and 26
   joint 26, see also Joint consultation
      increase in 69
   meaning 26
   redundancy, and see Redundancy
Contract of employment 103–107
   categories of workers 103
   employee, definition 104
      disputing 105
      tests for 104
   EU law, and 164
   variations to 106
      constructive dismissal, and 106
      'reasonable' consultations 107
   'worker', concept of 105
Council of the European Union 144
Counselling
   employee performance, and 434–435
   redundancy, and 522–523

Dignity at work 485–487
Disability
   absence from work, and 448–449
Disciplinary procedures 415–453

ACAS Code of Practice 421–422
appeals 450–451
current legal position 417–421
   fair dismissals 418–421
   modified procedure 420
   standard procedure 419–420
discipline, meaning 415–416
good practice 416
gross misconduct 426–427
handling issues 433–436
   counselling 434–435
   duty to act reasonably 434
   formal approach 435–436
lack of capability 442–450
   absence *see* Absence
   poor performance 443
live warnings, expiry of 425–426
management problems with 416
misconduct during employment 440–442
   gross misconduct, 441, *see also* Gross
     misconduct
   types of 440
origins of 416–417
procedure 422–423
   formal stage 423
   informal stage 423
   purpose and scope 423
rules 427–433
   clarity, importance of 429–430
   example of 428–429
   IT policy, example 430–431
   scope 427
   theft policy, example 432
'some other substantial reason' 450
underlying principles 424–425
   ACAS guidance on 424
   right to be accompanied 424–425
using 436–440
   disciplinary interview 439–440
   hearing, preparing for 437–439
   investigation 436–437
Discrimination 109–114
  age 128–129
  burden of proof 114
  Commission for Equality and Human
    Rights (CEHR) 110
  complaints procedure 112–114
  costs of defending claims 110–111
  direct 109
  employers and managers, risk to 111
  equal opportunities policies 112

  grievances, and 487–488
  indirect 109
  law 109
  prominence of cases on 110
  scope of requirement 109
  warning signs for 111
Disguised messages
  negotiation, and 404–405
Dismissal 114–117
  absence, 443–450, *see also* Absence
  constructive 106, 456
  fair 418–421
  lack of capability 442–450
  misconduct 440–442
    gross 441–442
  modified procedure 420
  poor performance 443
  some other substantial reason 450
  standard procedure 419–420
  unfair *see* Unfair dismissal
Dispute resolution 360–366
  arbitration, 29, 361–366, *see also*
    Arbitration
  conciliation 29, 361
  employers' associations, and 184
  mediation 29
  typical procedure for avoidance of disputes
    360
Distributive bargaining 381–382
Domestic emergencies
  absence from work, and 449–450
Dunlop, John 42–43
  systems theory, and 42–43

Early retirement 506–507
Economic policies
  capabilities to restore growth 73
  factors influencing implementation 70
  globalisation, and *see* Globalisation
  impact on employment relations 34, 70–74
  interest rates, and 71
  job creation *see* Job creation
  objectives of 71
  party political differences 71–72
  principal economic theories 75–81
    Keynesian model 75–77
    monetarism, rise of 79–81
  public expenditure 89–90
    level of 72
  public sector pay, and 74
  recession, and 70–71

slow-burn policies 73–74
Employee attitude surveys 270–271
Employee engagement 26–27, 308–333
  attitude, and 315
  barriers to engagement 325–327
    lack of awareness 325
    managers and organisational culture 326
    resistance to change 327
    uncertainty about starting 326
    under-estimating engagement 326–327
  case for 321–325
    private sector 321–324
    public sector 324–325
  disengagement 317
  employee engagement survey 317–321
    alignment with business strategy 318
    analysis of results 320
    arrangements for 319
    benchmarking 320
    confidentiality 319
    employee involvement 319
    participation 319
    reports and action 320
    selection of questions 319–320
    support from management 318
    ten steps to running 318–321
  employment relations, and 309
  enablers of 327–331
    employee voice 329–330
    engaging managers 328–329
    integrity 330–331
    leadership 327–328
  engagement index 315
  extent of 313–315
    public sector 314
    reasons for low 315
    variation in levels of 313–314
  high-performance work practices, and 309
  HR, role 309
  justifying 313
  meaning 310–312
    definitions 311
    theoretical approaches 312
  nature of 316
  occupational groups, and 316–317
  types of 316
Employee involvement and participation
    (EIP) 25–26, 258–308
  communications, and, 266–271, *see also*
    Communications
  decision-making machinery, and 259

extent of practices 280–283
  Workplace Industrial Relations Survey
    series 280–283
financial participation 275–276
  profit-related pay 275–276
  profit-sharing 275
  share ownership 276
forms 259
high-performance workplaces 300–303
impact of 283–284
  research 283–284
  study of 283
implementation 290–300
  commitment by top management
    295–298
  context 292–293
  general principles 290–291
  good employee relations 294–295
  integration 294
  joint agreement 291
  legal requirements 294
  monitoring and review 300
  multiple arrangements 293
  organisation's needs 291
  resources 298–300
  selecting practices 292–298
  success elsewhere, and 294
  training and development 292
Information and Consultation of
    Employees Regulations, 285–290, *see*
    *also* Information and Consultation of
    Employees Regulations
management, role of 260
meaning of term 259
practices 265–266
  depth of 266
  four categories 265
  initiation of 259
representative participation 277–280
  free exchange of ideas 277
  joint consultation 277
  joint consultative committees 278–279
  laws and regulations 277–278
task and work groups 271–274
  quality circles 272–273
  teamworking 271–272
  total quality management (TQM)
    273–274
theory of 260–264
  commitment strategy, and 261
  economic efficiency gains 261

employee influence/ownership 263
employee voice 262
financial forms of 262
improved economic performance 262
loyalty and commitment 264
management objectives in introducing,
    table 263–264
management philosophy, and 261
outcomes of, table 262
passive, active and personal impacts 264
untapped resource, employees as 261
Employees
  collective organisations 20
  communications strategy 267–269
  discipline *see* Disciplinary procedures
  employee, definition 104
  employee engagement, 26–27, *see also*
      Employee engagement
  employee involvement 25–26, *see*
      *also* Employee involvement and
      participation
  employment relations, role in 20–22
  industrial sanctions 30
  interests in labour market 50–51
  managing grievances *see* Grievances
  organisations 20
  professional associations 20
  staff associations, 20–21, *see also* Staff
      associations
  trade unions, 21–22, *see also* Trade unions
Employers
  employment relations, role in 18–20
  industrial sanctions 30
  interests in labour market 48–51
    employers' employment package 48–50
  structures 68
  types of 18
    employers' associations 19
    large private sector businesses 18
    private businesses 18
    public sector organisations 18–19
    voluntary bodies 19
  unilateral action, and 25
Employers' associations 19
Employers' organisations 178–187
  activities of 183–186
    advisory and information services
        184–185
    case study 185–186
    collective bargaining 183
    dispute resolution 184

representation of members' interests 186
declining influence of 181
EU social dialogue procedure, and
    181–182
importance of 180–182
influence 179
main, table 179
meaning 178
national bodies 182
non-membership of 187
public sector 179–180
size of companies 181
types of 180–181
Employment law 100
  absence from work 129–130
  age discrimination 128–129
  contract of employment *see* Contract of
      employment
  dates for enacting changes to 101
  developments in 128–130
  discrimination *see* Discrimination
  dismissal *see* Dismissal
  employment relationship, impact on 100
  function of 107–109
    auxiliary 108
    regulatory 108–109
  Human Rights Act, impact 126–128
  redundancy *see* Redundancy
  rights of union members, 117–120, *see also*
      Trade unions
  sources of law 101
Employment relations 5–7
  1960s and 70s, during 78
    power of trade unions, and 78
  activities 9–11
    agreements, content of 10
    balance of bargaining power 10–11
    price on supply of labour 10
    'rules' governing employment
        relationship 9–10
  actors 17–18
    employees, 20–22, *see also* Employees
    employers, 18–20, *see also* Employers
    government agencies, 22–24, *see also*
        Government agencies
  agreements, rules and regulations 36–42
    types of agreements *see* Agreements
  bargaining power, balance of 5–6
  basic purpose 16–17
  business environment 64
  changing behaviours in 6

collective relationships, and 15
communications, and 16
conventional approach to 15
de-regulated labour market, and 81
employee engagement, and 309
environmental context 33–36
   economic policies 34
   impact of 33
   internal environment 35
   macro level 33–35
   micro level 35–36
   technology 34–35
EU law, and *see* European Union
future challenges 236
globalisation, and *see* Globalisation
government, role of 69
implementation of initiatives 218–219
   business case 219
innovations in policies in 6–7
institutions 177–178
IPD model of 17
law and 102–103
management practices 7
managers, behaviour of 6
meaning 14
non-union environments 5
processes 24–33
   collective bargaining 27–28
   employee engagement 26–27
   employee involvement 25–26
   industrial sanctions 30–32
   legal intervention 32–33
   state intervention 24
   third-party intervention 28–30
   types of 24
   unilateral action 25
reasonableness, and 6
recent changes in 16
relationships, basis of 16
relevance to all sectors 5–7
state, role of 68
strategies and policies 216–257, *see also*
    Strategy
   'good practice' 240
   selecting policies 240–242
   strategy, meaning 220–221
theories of 42–48
   frames of reference 46–48
   Marxist approaches 43–45
   systems theory 42–43
Employment relationship 51–58

alternative interest resolution mechanisms
   58
common interests 54–57
   employees, costs to 55
   employers, costs to 54–55
   recognition of 55–57
different interests within management
   51–52
employees, interests among 53
recognition of different interests 53–54
Employment tribunals 103, 120–123
   ACAS conciliation 122–123
   application process 121–122
   claims accepted by, table 117
   decision 123
   hearing 123
   number of applications 103
   powers of chair 121
   representation of claimants, table 118
   status of 120–121
Engagement
   employee engagement 26–27 *see also*
     Employee engagement
   growing influence of 69
Equal opportunities 160–161
   burden of proof 161
   equal pay 160
   equal treatment 161
   parental leave 160–161
Equal pay 160
Equal treatment 161
European Central Bank (ECB) 71
European Commission 144
European Court of Justice 145–146
European Parliament 145
European Trade Union Confederation
   148–149
European Union 133–176
   Council of 144
   Declarations 171–172
     Social Charter 171–172
   development of 135–143
     aims 136–137
     Maastricht Treaty (1993) 139–140
     origins 135
     Single European Act (1987) 138–139
     Treaty of Amsterdam (1999) 140–141
     Treaty of Lisbon (2009) 142–143
     Treaty of Nice (2003) 141–142
     Treaty of Rome (1957) 137–138
   Directives 33

joint consultations, and 69
employment protection/working
    conditions 162–165
  agency workers 163
  contracts of employment 164
  fixed-term contracts 162–163
  insolvency 164
  part-time workers 162
  posting of workers 164–165
  redundancy 163
  transfer of undertakings 164
employment relations 165–168
  European Company Statute 166–167
  European Works Council Directive 165
  industrial action and posted workers
    167–168
  information and consultation 165–166
equal opportunities see Equal opportunities
European Commission 144
European Court of Justice (ECJ) 145–146
European Parliament 145
health and safety 169–170
influence on employment 134
Information and Consultation of
    Employees Regulations 285–290
legislative instruments 146–148
  forms 146
  implementation 147–148
  softer instruments 147
legislative process 151–156
  co-decision procedure 152, 153
  co-operation procedure 151, 152
  legislative procedures 151–152
  social dialogue procedure 154–156
Single Currency, consequences of joining
    135
Social Chapter 157–160
  excluded issues 158–159
  impact on employment relations
    159–160
  meaning 157
  mechanism, as 157
  in practice 159
  qualified majority items 158
  unanimous vote issues 158
social partners 148–150
  Business Europe 149
  European Association of Craft, Small
    and Medium-Sized Enterprises
    (UEAPME) 150
  European Centre of Enterprises

    with Public Participation and of
    Enterprises of General Economic
    Interest (CEEP) 150
  European Trade Union Confederation
    (ETUC) 148–149
sources of employment law 101
workings of 143–144

Financial participation
  employee involvement, and see Employee
    involvement and participation
Fit notes 129
Fixed-term contracts
  EU law, and 162–163
Flanders, Alan 192–193
  collective bargaining, on 338
Flexible working 84, 86–87
  competitive advantage, and 86
Frames of reference
  pluralist 46
  radical 47
  theories of employment relations, and
    46–48
  unitary 46

Globalisation 74–75
  competition, and 75
  definition 74
  driver of change, as 74
Government
  implementation of economic policies 70
  role in employment relations 69
  state as employer before 1979 87–88
Government agencies 22–24
  statutory role in employment relations,
    with 22–24
    ACAS 22–23
    CAC 23
    Certification Officer 23–24
Grievances 455–489
  appeals 483
  bullying and harassment, and 485–487
  business case for resolving 456–457
    constructive dismissal, and 456
    employer reputation 456
    training, need for 457
    unsatisfactory performance, and 456
    working environment 457
  dignity at work 485–487
  discrimination 487–488
  fairness at work, and 455

formal grievance procedure 461–474
  employee representation 468–470
  employment relations professional, role of 471–472
  equality of representatives 470
  examples of 463–464
  forms of 465
  grievance records 473–474
  line manager, role of 472–473
  operation of 471–473
  purpose of 463
  stage for representation 469
  stages 466–467
  statutory right to be accompanied 469
  three-stage procedure, example 466–467
  time limits 468
  trade unions, and 462
  typical, example of 465–466
  underlying principles 464–465
  undue haste 467
governing law 474–476
  ACAS Revised Code of Practice 475–476
  Employment Act 2002 474–475
  Employment Act 2008 475
  Employment Relations Act 1999 474
group complaints 460–461
handling, 378–379, *see also* Negotiation
industrial distribution of 459
informal resolution 461–462
job grading 484–485
managing 476–482
  analysis 480–481
  aspiration grid 482
  establishment of aims 481–482
  genuine grievance 479
  grievance interview 477–479
  planning to meet employee 480–482
  unfounded grievances 478–479
meaning 455, 457
non-trading of 457–461
  management behaviour, and 458
  merits of grievance 457–458
  negotiation of 458
number of employees, and 458–459
objectives of managing 455
resolving 482–483
statistics on 458
  formal procedure, use of 459
  private and public sector 460
  types of grievances 459–460

  support for line managers 455
  suppression of complaints 462
  take-up of 461–462
Gross misconduct 426–427, 441–442
  Burchell rules 441
    implications of test 442
Group problem solving 384–385

Harassment 485–487
Health and safety 169–170
  European Union, and 169–170
High-performance workplaces
  definition 309
  employee engagement, and 309
  employee involvement, and 300–303
Human resources
  CIPD HR Professional Map 2–3
  effective HR manager, diagram 7
  shift in focus in 1–2
    survey of 2
Human Rights Act (HRA) 125–128
  courts and tribunals, impact on 125–126
  employers, impact on 125
  implications for employment 126–128

Industrial action 366–369
  coping with 367–369
Industrial sanctions 30–32
  ballots for 253–254
  employees' 30
  employers' 30
  extent of industrial action 31–32
  posted workers, and 167–168
  success of 31
  threat of 31
Information and Consultation of Employees Regulations 285–290
  impact 288–290
  negotiated agreements 285–288
    enforcement 287–288
    negotiations 287
    procedure for establishing agreements 286
    requests in case of existing agreements 285–286
    requests for information and consultation arrangements 285
    three-year moratorium 286–287
    voluntary agreements 288
Insolvency
  EU law, and 164

Institute of Personnel and Development
(IPD)
employment relations system, on 17
Integrative bargaining 380–381
International Monetary Fund (IMF)
public expenditure, and 72
Intra-organisational bargaining 382–383
Investigation
disciplinary procedures, and 436–437

Job creation 85–86
categories of 85
technology, and 91
Job grading
grievances, and 484–485
Joint consultation 26
EU Directive on 69
increase in 69
representative participation, and, 277–278,
see also Employee involvement and
participation
Joint Consultative Committees (JCCs)
278–279
Joint problem solving 384–385

Kahn-Freund, Otto 107
Keynes, John Maynard 75–76

Labour market 82–85
de-regulation, and 81, 88
employees' interests in 50–51
employers' interests in 48–50
flexible working 84, 86–87
influence on employment relations 82
legislative changes, and 82
McJobs 82
non-standard employment, and 83
numerical flexibility 84
removal of welfare, and 90
Lack of capability, 442–450, see also
Disciplinary procedures
Legal intervention 32–33
European Union Directives 33
UK Parliament regulation 32–33
Legislation 32–33
disciplinary procedures 417–418
employment law see Employment law
European see European Union
grievances, and, 474–476, see also
Grievances
Human Rights Act see Human Rights Act

impact on employment relations 34
legislative process 101–103
non-union companies, and 64
process for enacting 101
Green Papers 101
White Papers 101
redundancy, and 493–495
consultation, on 515–521
sources of law 101
unionised companies, and 64
Long-term absence 447–448

McJobs 82
Managers
behaviour in employment relations 6
disciplinary process, and 416
effective HR manager, diagram 7
employee engagement, and 328–329
employee involvement, commitment to
295–298
grievance procedures, role in 472–473
influential 7–9
interests of business 8
lacking professional competence 9
nature of business 8
network of contacts 8
objectives of HR function 8
record of competence 7–8
relationships with superiors 8
understanding of personnel function 8
management style 237–240
authoritarian 238
collectivism 239
constitutional 238
consultative 238
five styles of 238
individualism 239
internal constraints 237–238
leadership process, and 240
opportunist 238
paternalistic 238
pluralist approach 237
unitary approach 237
managing change 242–245
employee consultation, and 243
leadership themes, and 244
reasons for failure 242
negotiations between, 376–378, see also
Negotiation
trade unions, and see Trade unions
Marxism 43–45

political economy of industrial relations 44–45
    labour process debate 45
Mediation 29
  ACAS, by 30
  rise in use of 30
Minford, Patrick 88
Monetarism 79–81
  basic propositions 80
  reducing inflation, and 88
  'supply-side' economics 80
  UK economy, and 80–81
Motivation theory
  employee engagement, and 312

Negotiation 374–413
  adjournment 405–406
  analysis stage 389–392
    New Earnings Survey 391–392
  aspiration grid 394–396
  bargaining 380–383
    attitudinal structures 383
    bargaining team, selection 386–387
    distributive 381–382
    establishing aims 393–394
    integrative 380–381
    intra-organisational 382–383
    preparing for 386–388
    team discipline 388
  concluding agreement 406–408
    factors to consider 407–408
  grievance handling 378–379
    grievance issues 379
    grievance, meaning 378
    grievance procedure, and 379
  grievances, of, 458, *see also* Grievances
  group/joint problem solving 384–385
  identifying common ground 402–405
    disguised messages 404–405
    momentum, and 405
  individual managers, between 376–378
    courses of action 377
    gaining commitment 377–378
    obtaining resources 377
  outcome of 410
  planning strategy and tactics 396–397
    arguments and counter-arguments 396–397
    communicating with team 397
  presentation stage 398–402
    example of 399–402

    management begin meeting 398–399
    management receives proposal(s) 399
  purpose of 374–375
    common elements 374
    definition 375
  reconciliation of differences over time 409
  stages in process of 386
  tradable items, identification of 392–393
  types of situations 375–376
  writing up agreement 408–409
Neo-classical economic theory
  collective bargaining, and 340–341
New Earnings Survey 391–392

Organisational psychology theory
  employee engagement, and 312
Organisational structure 68–69
  private sector 68
  public sector 68
Outplacement
  redundancy, and 523–525

Parental leave 160–161
Part-time employment
  EU law, and 162
  impact on labour market 83
  increase in 81
  use of temporary agency workers, table 83, 85
Partnership agreements 347–360
  examples of 349–358
    fire and rescue service 353–354
    general print sector 355–358
    papermaking partnership 349–352
    Scottish Prison Service 354–355
  extent 348–349
  outcome of 358–360
  principles 347–348
Pension funds 67–68
  deficits 67
Persistent absence 446
Pluralism
  employee engagement, and 312
Poor performance
  dismissal, and 443
Posting of workers 164–165
  industrial action, and 167–168
Private businesses 18
  organisational structure 68
Procedural agreements 38–39
  example of 38–39

Productivity
  UK deficit in 92
Professional associations 20
Profit-related pay 275–276
Profit-sharing 275
Public sector organisations 18–19
  organisational structure 68
  quasi-private-sector employers, and 68

Quality circles 272–273
  employee involvement, and 272
  management's commitment to 273
  meaning 272

Reasonableness
  employment relations, in 6
Recruitment
  employment package, and 48–50
Redundancy 114–117, 491–530
  alternative employment 514–515
  assistance for redundant employees 511
  compensation for 511–513
    business re-organisation, and 512
    employees' workplace, and 513–514
    entitlement to 512
  compulsory 507–510
    'last in first out' (LIFO) 508
    matrix and score sheet, example 510
    notification 508
    points score 509–510
  consultation 515–521
    collective redundancies 516–519
    consultation must be genuine 518
    individual 519–521
    information for employee representatives 517–518
    law on 515–516
    penalties for failure to consult 518–519
    timetable for 516–517
  definition 494
  early retirement 506–507
  EU law, and 163
  fair dismissal, and 421
  increased competition, and 492
  increases in 493
  legal regulation of 493–495
  management of change, and 495–499
    alternatives to redundancy 496–497
    communication, and 498
    employee commitment, and 497–499
    examples of approaches to 496

    immediate action 495
    reducing costs, and 496
  policy 500–501
    example statement 500
    need for 494–495
  post-redundancy 522–527
    counselling 522–523
    outplacement 523–525
    survivor syndrome 525–527
  procedure 501–506
    compulsory selection 503
    consultation 501–502
    need for 494–495
    outplacement support 504–505
    payment terms 503–504
    philosophy 501
    re-engagement 505
    review 505
    termination agreements 504
    voluntary redundancy 502
  transfer of undertakings 522
  voluntary 507
Representative participation, 277–279, see also Employee involvement and participation
Retirement
  early 506–507
Rules and regulations
  employment conditions, governing, 40, see also Agreements

September 11th (9/11)
  economic policy, and 70
Share ownership
  employee involvement, and 276
Sickness absence
  lack of capability, and 444–446
Social Charter 171–172
Staff associations 20–21, 197–198
  ability to represent members' interests 198
  causes of formation 197
  effectiveness 198
  meaning 197
  membership density 198
  professional associations 198
Strategy 216–257
  characteristics 220–221
  definition of 221
  employment policies, and 234–236
    company philosophy 235
    maximising competitive advantage 234

levels of 225–234
  business-unit-level 226–227
  corporate-level 225–226
  functional-level 227–228
  strategic employment relations
    management 227
meaning 220
people strategy 228–234
  'business partner' model 228
  communication 230–231
  employees as individuals 231–232
  five-year human resource plan, example
    232–234
  job design 230
  management of performance 231
  understanding company culture 229–230
strategic formulation 221–225
  eight elements of 223–224
  environment 224–225
  leadership 223
  managing people 222
  steps for 221–222
  SWOT analysis 222
Substantive agreements 36–37
  example of 37
Supply-side economics 80
  increasing supply-side 88–89
Surveys
  employee attitudes 270–271
  employee engagement survey, 317–321, *see
    also* Employee engagement
  New Earnings Survey 391–392
  Workplace Industrial Relations Survey
    series 280–283
Survivor syndrome
  redundancy, and 525–527
Systems theory 42–43

Teamworking
  employee involvement, and 271–272
  forms of 272
  team size 272
Technology
  balance of bargaining power, and 93–94
  creator of unemployment, as 90
  defining term 90
  elimination of unpleasant tasks 90
  impact on employment relations 34–35,
    90–92
  job creation, and 91
  positive force, as 90

  productivity deficit, and 92
  skills development, and 91
  training opportunities, and 91
  workforce development 91
Theft
  disciplinary procedures, and 432
Third-party intervention 28–30
  ACAS, role 29
  arbitration 29
  conciliation 29
  mediation 29
  use of 30
Time limits
  grievance procedures, and 468
Total quality management (TQM) 273–274
  employees' responsibility, and 274
  meaning 273
  organisational structures, and 274
Tradable items
  negotiation, and 392–393
Trade unions 21–22, 187–196
  behaviour of, explaining 192–196
    economic policy, attitudes to 195
    industrial methods 195–196
    inter-union conflict 195
    'job-centred', as 193
    mergers 194
    political action 196
    recruitment 193
    solidarity 195
    structure of 193–194
    traditional characterisation of 192
    transnational unions 194
  characteristics of 21–22
  collective bargaining, and 15, 345–346
  conventional employment relations, and 15
  decline in membership 65
  employers use of law, and 252–253
  employment relations, and 5
  European Trade Union Confederation
    148–149
  future of 191–192
  grievance procedures, and 462
  Human Rights Act, and 127
  increased militancy 66–67
  industrial action ballots 253–254
  lobbying 188
  management, and 245–254
    non-union organisations 246–248
    non-unionism, meaning 245
  meaning 187

membership levels 188–191
  decline in 189–190
  new workplace/young worker thesis
    190–191
  overall 188–189
  study of 67
participation in political process, and 188
pension funds, and 67–68
postal dispute 2008/9, and 67
power in 1960s 77–78
presence in workplace, table 65
purpose and objectives 187–188
recognition 248–252
  CAC, and 211
  employer concerns 251–252
  obtaining 249–251
  right to request, impact 64
recruitment strategies 21
restrictions on 88–89
rights of members 117–120
  immunities 119–120
  restrictive function of law 119
small unions 21
Trades Union Congress *see* Trades Union
    Congress
young people, and 65
Trades Union Congress (TUC) 19, 196–197
  role 196–197
Training
  employee grievances, and 457
  technological development, and 91
Transfer of undertakings 522

EU law, and 164

Unemployment
  insecurity of employees, and 81
Unfair dismissal 114–116
  automatically unfair 115–116
  determining 418–419
  failure to consult on redundancy, and
    519
  fair reasons 115
  Human Rights Act, and 126–127
  jurisdictions disposed of at hearing, table
    118
Unilateral action 25
  meaning 25

Voluntary bodies 19
Voluntary redundancy 507

Warnings
  disciplinary procedures, and 425–426
Webb, Sidney and Beatrice
  collective bargaining, on 337
Winter of discontent 79
Work-life balance
  flexible working, and 84
Workforce agreements 41–42
Workplace Industrial Relations Survey
    280–283
  employee involvement practices, and
    280–283
Workplace rules 41